REGRESSION AND LINEAR MODELS

REGRESSION AND LINEAR MODELS

Richard B. Darlington
Cornell University

McGraw-Hill Publishing Company

New York St. Louis San Francisco Auckland Bogotá Caracas
Hamburg Lisbon London Madrid Mexico Milan Montreal
New Delhi Oklahoma City Paris San Juan São Paulo
Singapore Sydney Tokyo Toronto

This book was set in Times Roman by Better Graphics, Inc.
The editors were James D. Anker and Bernadette Boylan;
the production supervisor was Denise L. Puryear.
The cover was designed by Pencils Portfolio.
R. R. Donnelley & Sons Company was printer and binder.

REGRESSION AND LINEAR MODELS

1 2 3 4 5 6 7 8 9 0 DOC DOC 9 5 4 3 2 1 0

ISBN 0-07-015372-8

Library of Congress Cataloging-in-Publication Data

Darlington, Richard B.
    Regression and linear models / Richard B. Darlington.
        p.   cm.
    Includes bibliographical references.
    ISBN 0-07-015372-8
    1. Regression analysis.   2. Linear models (Statistics)
3. Psychology—Statistical methods.   4. Social sciences—Statistical
methods.   I. Title.
BF39.2.R44D37   1990
150′.1′51936—dc20   89–12956

ABOUT THE AUTHOR

Richard B. Darlington is Professor of Psychology at Cornell University. He holds joint appointments in the fields of Education, Public Affairs, and Human Development and Family Studies. He has been at Cornell since he received his Ph.D. in 1963 from the University of Minnesota.

Professor Darlington is a Fellow of the American Association for the Advancement of Science. He has published most extensively on regression and related methods, on the cultural bias of mental tests, and on the long-term effects of preschool programs. An elementary statistics text, *Behavioral Statistics: Logic and Methods*, by Darlington and Patricia M. Carlson, was published by the Free Press in 1987.

TO MY WIFE, BETSY,
an environmentalist for the world, for our city, and for me

CONTENTS IN BRIEF

CONTENTS

19   Log-Linear Models   462

Appendixes   503

PREFACE

PEDAGOGICAL APPROACH

This book's pedagogical approach has three distinctive features:

- Avoidance of matrix algebra except in tangential remarks.
- Pedagogical aids including chapter summaries, homework problems and answers, a glossary of symbols and abbreviations, and chapter-by-chapter lists of symbols, abbreviations, and technical terms.
- Detailed directions for using the MYSTAT computer package, with some directions also for SYSTAT and SAS.

MYSTAT

This book is accompanied by a disk containing MYSTAT. The time invested learning this package will be quickly repaid by the teaching time saved through the book's detailed directions to MYSTAT. I find it simply amazing that such a powerful package is available free; in my own opinion it is vastly superior, for linear models, to many of the best-known packages that cost hundreds or even thousands of dollars. When used as this book explains, MYSTAT's major features include:

- Available for both Macintosh and IBM-type microcomputers.
- Fits on a single floppy disk; works without a hard disk and without changing disks; not copy protected.
- Outstanding freedom from rounding error, far surpassing mainframe SAS.
- Automatic reporting of the tolerance and exact significance level p for each independent variable, along with its slope, standard error of slope, standardized slope, and t.

• The CATEGORY command, which works like the CLASS command in SAS. For instance, if *religion* is represented by categories numbered 1–8, the commands

>category religion = 8
>model attitude = constant + age + religion
>estimate

are all that is necessary to produce an analysis of covariance testing the differences in attitude among the 8 religious groups with age controlled statistically.

• The * operator to represent interaction and power terms. For instance, the commands

>category religion = 8
>model attitude = constant + age + religion + age*age + age*religion
>estimate

add to the previous model a square term for age, and a term for the interaction between age and religion.

• A full-screen data editor that includes the ability to make logarithmic and many other data transformations and combinations, search for specific values, and generate uniform or normal random numbers.

• Ability to find the exact significance level p for any F, including F's calculated by hand or by other packages; see Appendix 2.

• Ability to find slopes and their standard errors for numerical variables even when some variables are categorical; see Section 10.1.6.

• Tests on sets of variables; see Section 5.3.1.

• A full range of regression diagnostics, including leverage, Cook's measure of influence, and studentized residuals. Unlike similar options in SAS, these can be used with both categorical and numerical variables.

• Ability to detect cases with unusual leverage or influence on a particular regression slope. Such cases may not be detected by overall measures of leverage and influence. See Section 14.1.7.

• A structure that discourages the inappropriate use of what SAS calls "Type I" sums of squares and also what Cohen and Cohen (1983) call "Model II" error terms. This structure has been considered a disadvantage by some writers who don't understand the dangers in these methods; see Section 7.5.3.

OTHER DISTINCTIVE FEATURES

The following topics and features should be especially attractive to those seeking a book strong on basic principles:

• Immediate integration of discussions of numerical, dichotomous, and multicategorical variables (Section 1.1).

• The meaning of partial regression slopes (Sections 2.1, 2.2).

• An alternative to Venn diagrams, whose overlapping circles cannot represent negative simple or partial relationships, and which focus on contributions to variance rather than on the more important regression slopes (Section 2.2.5).

• Regression to the mean (Section 3.3).

• The relative advantages of statistical and experimental control for causal analysis (Chapter 4).

• The difference between the "adjusted" and "shrunken" multiple correlation (Section 6.4).

• Why "proportion of variance explained" is misleadingly conservative (Section 9.1).

• A short BASIC program for calculating exact values of p from F (Appendix 3.1), and a method for using MYSTAT for the same purpose (Appendix 2).

Users seeking more thorough treatment of specialized topics should note the following discussions:

• The advantage of reaching vague conclusions before specific conclusions (Section 5.1.5).

• The robustness advantage of partial regression slopes over partial correlations (Section 5.5.2).

• Dangers in the "Model II" error term (Section 7.5.3).

• Identifying collinear sets of variables (Section 8.1.2).

• Finding the variables producing singularities and identifying the conclusions possible when those variables are removed (Section 8.1.3.).

• Overcontrol (Section 8.1.4).

• Missing data (Section 8.1.7).

• The relative advantages of semipartial correlations, partial correlations, and standardized slopes (betas) for comparing the importance of regressors (Section 9.3).

• Complex contrasts (Sections 10.2.7–10.2.9).

• Nesting (Section 10.3).

• The Bonferroni method (Section 11.1).

• Philosophical issues in multiple tests: why not correct for all the tests performed in your lifetime, or in all of science? (Sections 11.4 and 11.5).

• The relative advantages of eight different types of scatterplot for detecting curvilinearity in partial relationships (Section 12.1.6).

• Spline (segmented) regression (Section 12.4).

• The difference between average effects and main effects (Section 13.6).

• Diagnostic statistics (Section 14.1).

• The jackknife, bootstrap, permutation, and normal scores tests for robust inference (Section 14.2).

    • Conclusions possible when assumptions of normality, homoscedasticity, and random sampling are violated (Section 14.3).

    • Choosing sample sizes (Chapter 15).

    • Power analysis versus precision analysis (Chapter 15).

    • The need to distinguish random from fixed scores in power and precision analysis (Chapter 15).

    • The multivariate approach to repeated measures (Section 17.5).

    • Nonlinear transformations *of the dependent variable* that increase linearity of regression (Section 17.6).

    • Logistic regression emphasized over discriminant analysis (Chapter 18).

    • Log-linear models (Chapter 19).

USING THIS BOOK AS A TEXT

A course with limited time can start with Chapter 1 and stop after almost any chapter. And the following material can be skipped or abbreviated more easily than most:

    • Section 5.5, on miscellaneous inferential methods
    • Chapter 6, on prediction
    • Section 9.2, on the value of tests in prediction
    • Sections 10.2.8, 10.2.9 and 10.3, on nesting
    • Section 12.4, on spline regression
    • Sections 13.6.4 and 13.6.5, on average effects
    • Chapters 17–19, on various advanced topics

    Answers to all homework problems appear in the book. Instructors can always ask students to prove they did the work by reporting answers to more decimal places than appear in the book, or by otherwise showing more detail than appears in the book.

    The most nonstandard aspect of the book's notation is that it uses the "pre-subscript" T to denote the true or population value of the statistic following it. Thus $_Tb$ and $_TR$ denote respectively population values of a regression slope and a multiple correlation. This is easy to remember, allows us to avoid Greek, and applies equally well to strings of letters such as MSE.

SOURCES

Much of my own introduction to linear models and related topics came from Anderson (1984), Graybill (1961), Searle (1971) and Morrison (1976), or from earlier editions of those works. Unreferenced assertions in this book are usually documented in two or more of these sources. Readers wanting more references should see Draper and Smith (1981), whose 567-item bibliography on linear models I have made no attempt to match. The SYSTAT manual (Wilkinson, 1988) provides the most important more recent references.

ACKNOWLEDGMENTS

I owe much to the Cornell students whose probing questions led to many of the discussions in this book. T. A. Ryan and Jason Millman have been especially valued colleagues. I have been working on this book for over ten years, so I am indebted to a whole series of deans, department chairs, and colleagues who have implemented the Cornell policy of demanding good work without measuring quality by volume of annual output. Jonathan Plotkin and Fred Horan have kept my computers and word processors operating smoothly. Leland Wilkinson and others at SYSTAT, Inc. have responded to questions with amazing speed and thoroughness. Bernadette Boylan, my editing supervisor at McGraw-Hill, has been consistently tactful and efficient in what I know is a trying job. James D. Anker, my executive editor, has been helpful when I needed it, and tolerant of my idiosyncracies. The reviewers he selected to read drafts have made many useful suggestions; they include Bettina L. Beard, Western Kentucky University; N. John Castellan Jr., Indiana University; Norman Cliff, University of Southern California; Albert D. Farrell, Virginia Commonwealth University; Silas Halperin, Syracuse University; Richard A. Lehman, Franklin & Marshall College; Jack McArdle, University of Virginia; Thomas Nygren, Ohio State University; and James P. Stevens, University of Cincinnati. Of course, I didn't adopt all their suggestions, and any remaining shortcomings are my own responsibility.

Richard B. Darlington

INDEX TO SYMBOLS
AND ABBREVIATIONS

SYMBOL	MEANING	SECTION
a	Y intercept	1.2.2, 2.2.2
alpha	chosen significance level (e.g., .05 or .01)	11.0
ANOVA	analysis of variance	5.2.4
augmented h_i	value of h_i relative to Y and the regressors	14.1.5
B	number of tests corrected for (= Bonferroni correction factor)	11.1
b	simple regression slope	1.2.2
b_j	partial regression slope	2.1.3
$b(hi.jk)$	slope measuring effect of X_i on X_h with X_j and X_k controlled	7.4.1*
beta$_j$	standardized partial regression slope	2.3.6
bg	between groups	10.1.5*
C_p	statistic proposed by Mallows for selecting the best of several regression equations	6.5.2*
c_j	coefficient in contrast	10.2.1*
CNH	composite null hypothesis	11.4.1
Cov	covariance	1.3.2
CR_j	crosswise multiple correlation for X_j	5.4.4
CV	conditional value	13.4.3*
D	dummy variable	10.1.2*
d_{ij}	change in $\hat{Y}_j$ when case i is removed from sample in which regression is derived	14.1.1*
df	degrees of freedom	5.2.1
df_r	residual df	5.2.1

* Denotes notation used primarily within the section noted.

SYMBOL	MEANING	SECTION
E	expected value	5.1.3
E	coefficient of forecasting efficiency	9.2.1*
e	expected frequency in a contingency table	19.1.1
e_i	residual	1.2.3, 1.5.1
EWR	experimentwise error rate	11.3.3
ex_i	residual from regression excluding case i	14.1.4*
F	statistic for testing R and related measures	5.2.4
Fit_i	model's probability of observed outcome	18.1.1
Fix_j	variable created by filling in missing data on X_j	8.1.7*
GLM	general linear model	10.1.2
h_i	leverage of case i	14.1.1
hb_j	hierarchical b_j	7.3.1
hpr_j	hierarchical pr_j	7.3.1
HR_i	R between I_i and regressor set	14.1.4*
HSD	"honestly significant difference"	11.3.4*
HSR	hierarchical semipartial multiple correlation	7.3.1
hsr_j	hierarchical sr_j	7.3.1
HSS_j	hierarchical SS_j	7.3.1
I_i	identifying variable for case i	14.1.4
$J0, J1, J2$	artificial variables created in spline regression	12.4.1*
k	number of categories in a multicategorical variable	10.1.3
Lackofit	measure of fit for log-linear models	19.2.2
LCL	lower confidence limit	15.3.5*
ln	natural logarithm	12.2.1
log	logarithm	12.2.1
LRFI	logistic regression fit index	18.1.5
M	mean	1.3.2
MD_i	Mahalanobis distance	14.1.4*
MDX_i	MD_i measured in sample with case i excluded	14.1.4*
$Miss_j$	dummy variable scored 1 when scores on X_j are missing	8.1.7*
MSE	estimated mean squared error of true regression	5.2.6
N	sample size	1.3.2
NLL	negative log likelihood	18.1.1
NLLC	NLL for a "constant" logistic model	18.1.5
o	observed frequency in a contingency table	19.1.1
P	number of regressors	2.2.3

SYMBOL	MEANING	SECTION
p	observed significance level	2.2.3
PC	p corrected for multiple tests	11.1
pm	most significant p in a set of B tests	11.1
PR	partial multiple correlation	3.4.1
pr_j	partial correlation	2.3.4
PS_i	model's probability of success	18.1.1
R	multiple correlation	2.3.2
$R(A)$	R with regressors in set A	3.4.1
$R(AB)$	R with regressors in sets A and B	3.4.1
r_{XY}	Pearson correlation coefficient	1.3.2
rel	reliability	17.7*
RS	shrunken multiple correlation	6.4.1
S_X	standard deviation	1.3.2
SE	estimated standard error	5.4.1
$SR(B.A)$	semipartial correlation for a set	3.4.1
sr_j	semipartial correlation	2.3.3
SS	sum of squares	5.2.3
str_i	standardized residual	14.1.5
T	true or population value of the quantity to follow, used as a subscript before the quantity	5.1.1
t	statistic for testing slopes and other values	5.4.1
Tol_j	tolerance	5.4.4
Totalfit	measure of fit for log-linear models	19.2.2
tr_i	t residual (Studentized residual)	14.1.5
UCL	upper confidence limit	15.3.5*
Var	variance	1.3.2
$Var(Y.X)$	proportion of variance in Y not explained by X	1.5.2
$Var(Y.C)$	Y variance independent of covariates	9.3.1
VIF	variance inflation factor	5.4.4*
VR	variance ratio	5.5.1*
wg	within groups	10.1.5*
X	regressor	1.2.1
x	deviation score	1.3.2
$Xi.j$	portion of X_i independent of X_j	2.2.1
X_j	one of several regressors	2.1.2
Y	dependent variable	1.2.1
z	Fisher z	5.5.4, 15.2

SYMBOL	MEANING	SECTION
^	estimated value	1.2.2
Σ	summation	1.3.1
.	"controlling for"; for example, $Y.X$ is Y with X controlled, and $r_{XY.C}$ is r_{XY} with c controlled	

REGRESSION AND LINEAR MODELS

CHAPTER

1

BASIC CONCEPTS

1.1 STATISTICAL CONTROL

1.1.1 The Need for Control

If you have ever described a piece of research to a friend, it was probably not very long before you were asked a question like, "But did the researchers control for this?" If the research found a difference between the average salaries of men and women, did it control for differences in years of employment? If the research found differences among several ethnic groups in attitudes toward social welfare spending, did it control for income differences among the groups? If the research found that high-status female wolves have more pups on the average than low-status wolves, did it control for age differences among the wolves?

All these studies concern the relationship between an *independent variable* and a *dependent variable*. The study on salary differences concerns the relationship between the independent variable of gender and the dependent variable of salary. The study on welfare spending concerns the relationship between the independent variable of ethnicity and the dependent variable of attitude. The study on wolves concerns the relationship between the independent variable of status and the dependent variable of fertility. In each case there is a need to control a third variable; this third variable is called a *covariate*. The covariates for the three studies are, respectively, years of employment, income, and age.

Suppose you wanted to study these three relationships without worrying about covariates. You may be familiar with three very different statistical methods for analyzing these three problems. You may have studied the *t* test for testing questions like the sex difference in salaries, analysis of variance for questions like difference in average attitude among several ethnic groups, and the Pearson or rank-order correlation for questions like the relationship between status and number of pups. But in this book we will regard the differences among these three problems as minor in comparison with their similarities. The problems differ primarily in the type of independent variable. Gender is *dichotomous;* that is, there are two categories—male and female. Ethnicity is *multicategorical,* since there are several categories—the various ethnic groups in the study. Status is *numerical,* since there is a more or less continuous dimension from high status to low status. For our purposes, the differences among these three variable types are relatively minor. You should begin thinking of problems like these as basically similar, since all concern the relationship between an independent and a dependent variable. We shall return to this point in Secs. 3.2 and 10.1.

1.1.2 Five Methods of Control

You may already be somewhat familiar with four ways of controlling covariates: by *random assignment on the independent variable,* by *exclusion of cases,* by *manipulation of covariates,* and by *other types of randomization.* For instance, suppose you want to know whether driver training courses help students pass driving tests. One problem is that the students who take driver training courses may differ in various ways from those who do not. A second problem is that in a particular town, some testers may be easier than others. The driving schools may know which testers are easiest and encourage their students to take their tests when they know those testers are on duty.

   You might control the first problem by using a list of applicants for driving courses, randomly choosing which of the applicants are allowed to take the course, and using the rejected applicants as the control group. This is *random assignment on the independent variable.* Or, if you find that more women take the courses than men, you might use a sample which is half female and half male for both the trained and the untrained groups. This would require discarding some available data, and is control by *exclusion of cases.* You might control the second problem by training testers to make them apply more uniform standards; that would be *manipulation of covariates.* Or you might control that problem by randomly altering the schedule different testers work, so that nobody would know which testers are on duty at a particular moment. That would not be random assignment on the independent variable, since you have not determined which applicants take the course; rather, it would be *other types of randomization.* This includes randomly assigning forms of the dependent variable (as in this example), choosing stimuli from a population of stimuli (for example, all common English adjectives), and manipulating the order of presentation of stimuli.

   All these methods except exclusion of cases are types of *experimental control,* since they all require you to manipulate the situation in some way rather than merely observe it. These methods are often impractical or even impossible. For instance, you might not be allowed to decide which students take the driving course, or to train testers or alter their schedules. Or, if a covariate is worker seniority, as in one of our earlier examples, you cannot manipulate the covariate by telling workers how long to keep their jobs. In the same example, the independent variable is sex, and you cannot randomly decide that a particular worker will be male or female the way you can decide whether the worker will be in the experimental or control condition of an experiment. Even when experimental control is possible, the very exertion of control often intrudes the investigator into the situation in a way that disturbs subjects and alters results; ethologists and anthropologists are especially sensitive to such issues. Experimental control may be difficult even in laboratory studies on animals. Researchers may not be able to control how long a rat looks at a stimulus, but they are able to measure looking time.

Control by exclusion of cases avoids these difficulties, because you are manipulating data rather than subjects. But this method lowers sample size, and thus lowers the precision of estimates and the power of hypothesis tests.

A fifth method of controlling covariates—*statistical control*—is the topic of this book. It avoids the disadvantages of the previous four methods. No manipulation of subjects or conditions is required, and no data are excluded. Several terms mean the same thing: to *control* a covariate statistically means the same as to *adjust for* it or to *correct for* it, or to *hold constant* or to *partial out* the covariate.

Statistical control has limitations. Scientists may disagree on what variables need to be controlled—an investigator who has controlled age, income, and ethnicity may be criticized for failing to control education and family size. And because covariates must be measured to be controlled, they will be controlled inaccurately if they are measured inaccurately. We shall return to these and other problems in Chaps. 4 and 8. But because control of some covariates is almost always needed, and because the other four methods of control are so limited, statistical control is widely recognized as one of the most important statistical tools.

1.1.3 Examples of Statistical Control

The nature of statistical control can be illustrated by a simple fictitious example, though the precise methods used in this example are not those we shall emphasize later. In Holly City, 130 children attended a city-subsidized preschool program and 130 others did not. Later, all 260 children took a "school readiness test" on entering first grade. Of the 130 preschool children, only 60 scored above the median on the test; of the other 130 children, 70 scored above the median. In other words, the preschool children scored worse on the test than the others. These results are shown in the "Total" section of Table 1.1; A and B refer to scoring above and below the test median.

But when the children were divided into "middle class" and "working class," the results were as shown on the left and center of Table 1.1. We see that of the 40 middle-class children attending preschool, 30, or 75%, scored

TABLE 1.1
Holly City

	Middle			Working			Total		
	A	**B**	**Tot.**	**A**	**B**	**Tot.**	**A**	**B**	**Tot.**
Preschool	30	10	40	30	60	90	60	70	130
Other	60	30	90	10	30	40	70	60	130

Raw frequencies

above the median. There were 90 middle-class children not attending pre-school, and 60, or 67%, of them scored above the median. These values of 75% and 67% are shown on the left in Table 1.2. Similar calculations based on the working-class and total tables yield the other figures in Table 1.2. This table shows clearly that within each level of socioeconomic status (SES), the preschool children outperform the other children, even though they appear to do worse than the other children in the "total" table. We have *held constant* or *controlled* or *partialed out* the covariate of SES.

When we perform a similar analysis for nearby Ivy City, we find the results in Table 1.3. When we inspect the total percentages, preschool appears to have a positive effect. But when we look within each SES group, no effect is found. Thus the "total" tables overstate the effect of preschool in Ivy City and understate it in Holly City. In these examples the independent variable is preschool attendance and the dependent variable is test score. In Holly City, we found a negative simple relationship between these two variables (those attending preschool scored lower on the test) but a positive partial relationship when SES was controlled. In Ivy City, we found a positive simple relationship but no partial relationship.

By examining the data more carefully, we can see what caused these paradoxical results. In Holly City, the 130 children attending preschool included 90 working-class children and 40 middle-class children, so 69% of the preschool attenders were working-class. But the 130 nonpreschool children included 90 middle-class children and 40 working-class children, so this group was only 31% working-class. Thus the test scores of the preschool group were lowered by the disproportionate number of working-class children in that group. This might have occurred if city-subsidized preschool programs had

TABLE 1.2
Holly City

	Middle	Working	Total
Preschool	75	33	46
Other	67	25	54

Percentage scoring above the median

TABLE 1.3
Ivy City

	Middle			Working			Total		
	Raw frequencies								
	A	**B**	**Tot.**	**A**	**B**	**Tot.**	**A**	**B**	**Tot.**
Preschool	90	30	120	10	30	40	100	60	160
Other	30	10	40	30	90	120	60	100	160

	Middle	Working	Total
	Percentage scoring above the median		
Preschool	75	25	62
Other	75	25	38

been established primarily in poorer neighborhoods. But in Ivy City this difference was in the opposite direction: the preschool group was 75% middle-class, while the nonpreschool group was only 25% middle-class; thus the test scores of the preschool group were raised by the disproportionate number of middle-class children. This might have occurred if parents had to pay for their children to attend preschool. In both cities the effects of preschool were seen more clearly by controlling for SES.

All three variables in this example were dichotomous—they had just two levels each. The independent variable of preschool attendance had two levels we called "preschool" and "other." The dependent variable of test score was dichotomized into those above and below the median. The covariate of socioeconomic status was also dichotomized. But any or all of the variables in this problem might have been numerical variables. Test scores might have ranged from 0 to 100, and SES might have been measured on a scale with many points. Even preschool attendance might have been numerical, if we scored the exact number of days each child had attended preschool. Changing some or all variables from dichotomous to numerical would change the details of analysis, but in its underlying logic the problem would remain the same. The use of numerical variables may be more complex, but it usually raises statistical power. Thus by dichotomizing SES and test scores in our examples above, we sacrificed power for simplicity.

Consider now a problem in which the dependent variable is numerical. At Swamp College, the dean calculated that among professors and instructors under 30 years of age, the average salary among males was $27,000 and the average salary among females was only $23,000. To see whether this difference might be attributed to different proportions of men and women who had completed the Ph.D., the dean made up the table given as Table 1.4.

If the dean had hoped that different rates of completion of the Ph.D. would explain the $4000 difference between men and women in average salary,

TABLE 1.4
Average salaries at Swamp College, by sex and completion of Ph.D.

	Ph.D. completed		
	Yes	No	Total
Men	$30,000	$26,000	$27,000
	$n = 10$	$n = 30$	$n = 40$
Women	$25,000	$21,000	$23,000
	$n = 15$	$n = 15$	$n = 30$

that hope was frustrated. We see that men had completed the Ph.D. *less* often than women: 10 of 40 men, versus 15 of 30 women. The first column of the table shows that among instructors with a Ph.D., the difference in mean salaries between men and women is $5000. The second column shows the same difference of $5000 among instructors with no Ph.D. Therefore, in this artificial example, controlling for completion of the Ph.D. does not lower the difference between the mean salaries of men and women, but rather raises it from $4000 to $5000.

This example differs from the preschool example in its mechanical details; we are dealing with means rather than frequencies and proportions. But the underlying logic is the same. In the present case the independent variable is sex, the dependent variable is salary, and the covariate is educational level. Again, the partial relationship differs from the simple relationship, though this time both relationships have the same sign, since men always have higher salaries than women.

These examples are so simple that you may be wondering why a whole book is needed to discuss statistical control. But when the covariate is numerical, it may be that no two subjects have the same score on the covariate and so we cannot construct tables like those in the examples above. And we may want to control many covariates at once; the college dean might want to simultaneously control teaching ratings and other covariates as well as completion of the Ph.D. Also, we need methods for testing the significance of partial relationships. Other complexities are introduced later.

1.1.4 What You Should Know Already

This book assumes a working familiarity with the concepts of means and standard deviations, score distributions, samples and populations, random sampling, sampling distributions, null hypotheses, standard errors, statistical significance, power, confidence bands, one-tailed and two-tailed tests, summation, subscripts, and similar basic statistical terms and concepts. It refers occasionally to basic statistical methods including t tests, 2×2 tests, binomial and sign tests, the Fisher z, and one-way and two-way analysis of variance. It is not assumed that you remember the mechanics of these methods in detail, but some sections of this book will be easier if you understand the uses of these methods.

1.1.5   Computer Programs for Statistical Control

Computer programs for statistical control are found in most statistical packages. These packages differ on two major dimensions: on the size of the computer they require—mainframe, minicomputer, or microcomputer—and on the amount of expertise needed to use the package correctly. For mainframes, the dominant packages are BMDP, SPSS-X, and SAS, with SAS at the top both in frequency of use and in expertise needed. MINITAB has been a widely used package at the minicomputer level. The "expert" end of the microcomputer market has for several years been dominated by SYSTAT, which has consistently been rated at the top by comparative reviews of statistical packages for microcomputers. Its program for regression and linear models is regarded as especially strong. The package costs several hundred dollars, and is available for both Macintosh and IBM-family microcomputers.

Systat, Inc., has issued a free one-disk package named MYSTAT, which contains a surprisingly large fraction of SYSTAT's power. Surprisingly, MYSTAT's program for regression and linear models outperforms every competing program I know of priced under $1000 except SYSTAT itself, and even some over that price. As of this writing, MYSTAT outclasses even SAS in minimizing rounding error and in offering diagnostics (see Chap. 14) in conjunction with the general linear model. A copy of MYSTAT is included in this book. Single additional copies are available free from Systat, Inc., 1800 Sherman Avenue, Evanston, IL 60201. Telephone support is not available on using MYSTAT, except to registered SYSTAT owners.

This book uses MYSTAT, SYSTAT, and SAS for illustrations. For each illustration, we generally use the cheapest of these packages that does the job. MYSTAT is used almost exclusively through Chap. 12, except for tests on sets of variables in Chap. 5 and on complex contrasts in Chap. 10. SYSTAT and SAS are used most heavily in Chaps. 13, 17, 18, and 19.

If you have SYSTAT available but have not yet learned to use it, I recommend starting with MYSTAT, which contains SYSTAT's most important features in a format easier to learn and use—for one thing, you avoid SYSTAT's 3-inch thick manual. Starting in Sec. 5.1.4, this book explains MYSTAT's regression program in detail. To learn to use its other features, read Appendix 1 in this book and use the DEMO and HELP commands in MYSTAT's menu. These will also review for you many features of basic statistics.

1.2 SCATTERPLOTS AND CONDITIONAL DISTRIBUTIONS

1.2.1 Scatterplots

Suppose you are in a group of 19 people who play miniature golf one Saturday night. Upon questioning your friends, you find that all 19 have played at least once before, and some have played as many as five times before. In this establishment the management awards each player points which can be used toward a discount next time. This evening all members of your group win from 2 to 6 points.

You decide to study the relationship between the number of points won and the number of times a player has played before. You start by numbering the people in your group from 1 to 19, and recording for each player the number of previous plays and the number of points won. In Table 1.5, identification numbers you assign from 1 to 19 are shown in the first column, labeled ID. The number of previous plays is shown in the column labeled X, and each player's point score is shown in the column labeled Y.

Figure 1.1 is a *scatterplot* showing the scores of the 19 people on X and Y. The three dots on the far right of the figure represent the people with ID numbers 17, 18, 19; they all score 5 on X, and they score 4, 5, and 6 on Y. The figure contains 19 dots—one for each person in Table 1.5.

TABLE 1.5
An artificial data set

ID	X	Y
1	1	2
2	1	3
3	1	4
4	2	2
5	2	3
6	2	4
7	2	5
8	3	2
9	3	3
10	3	4
11	3	5
12	3	6
13	4	3
14	4	4
15	4	5
16	4	6
17	5	4
18	5	5
19	5	6

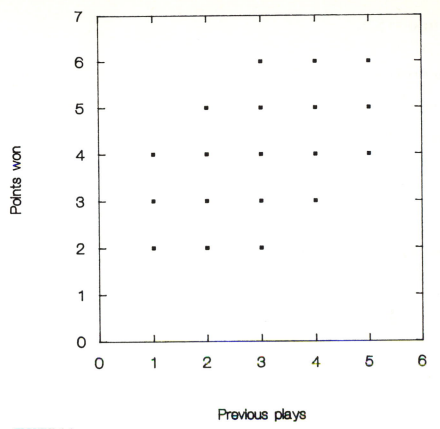

FIGURE 1.1
A simple scatterplot.

1.2.2   A Line through Conditional Means

The three people who score 1 on X score 2, 3, and 4 on Y. These three numbers (2, 3, 4) report the *distribution* on Y of the three people who meet the condition of scoring 1 on X, so the distribution is called a *conditional distribution*. The mean of these three Y values is 3. We say that 3 is the *conditional mean* of Y when $X = 1$. This conditional mean is represented by the open circle on the far left of Fig. 1.2. The four people who score 2 on X have Y scores of 2, 3, 4, and 5. The mean of these values is 3.5, so that is the conditional mean of Y when $X = 2$. This conditional mean is represented in the figure by the second open circle from the left. The conditional means at $X = 3$, $X = 4$, and $X = 5$ are also shown as open circles. The overall mean of all 19 Y scores is called the *marginal mean* of Y; in the current example the marginal mean is 4.

In this example, all five conditional means fall in a straight line. This line appears in the figure. This situation is called *linearity*. The number of units the

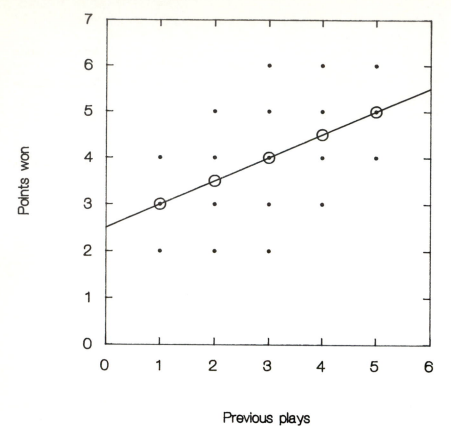

FIGURE 1.2
A line through conditional means.

line rises for each unit of X is called the *slope* of the line. In this example, the line rises $\frac{1}{2}$ unit for each unit of X: the line is at $Y = 3$ when X is 1, is at $Y = 3.5$ when X is 2, is at $Y = 4$ when X is 3, and so on. Therefore the slope of this line is .5. The slope of the line equals the gain in Y associated with each 1-unit gain in X. In the current example, we can say that each extra previous play is associated with a half-point average rise in points won. This answers our question about the relationship between points won and number of plays: each extra previous play is associated with an extra $\frac{1}{2}$ point won.

If a line fell toward the right, we would say that its slope was negative; if a line fell 2 units for each unit of X, we would say that its slope was -2. We might find a line with a negative slope if we plotted points won not against previous plays, but against number of alcoholic drinks before playing.

The Y value at which the line touches the vertical Y axis is called its Y *intercept*. In this figure, the line's Y intercept is 2.5.

Like any straight line, this line can be represented by an algebraic equation. In elementary algebra, a straight line is usually represented by the equation $Y = mX + b$. Here we use X and Y in the same way, but instead of m and b we use b and a, so the equation is written $Y = bX + a$. b is the slope and a the Y intercept. In the present example, $b = .5$ and $a = 2.5$, so the line's equation is $Y = .5X + 2.5$.

We can use the line or its equation to estimate new conditional means. For instance, if we extended the line to the right we would see that when $X = 6$, the line has a Y value of 5.5. This means that 5.5 is the estimated conditional mean of Y when $X = 6$. You can find the same value from the line's equation by substituting $X = 6$ into the equation $Y = .5X + 2.5$. We then have $Y = .5 \times 6 + 2.5 = 3 + 2.5 = 5.5$. Or, when $X = 7$, the estimated conditional mean is $Y = .5 \times 7 + 2.5 = 3.5 + 2.5 = 6$. The conditional mean found this way is also the Y value we estimate for any new player with a particular score on X. For instance, if someone has played 7 times before, we estimate that this player will win 6 points. An estimated value of Y is denoted by $\hat{Y}$, pronounced "hat Y." A "hat" over any value means an estimate of that value, so $\hat{Y}$ is an estimate of Y.

1.2.3 Errors of Estimate

How accurately can we estimate the Y values (points won) from X (number of previous plays)? Table 1.6 shows Y for each of the 19 people, as found from the

TABLE 1.6
Estimates and residuals

ID	X	Y	$\hat{Y}$	e	e^2
1	1	2	3	−1	1
2	1	3	3	0	0
3	1	4	3	1	1
4	2	2	3.5	−1.5	2.25
5	2	3	3.5	−.5	.25
6	2	4	3.5	.5	.25
7	2	5	3.5	1.5	2.25
8	3	2	4	−2	4
9	3	3	4	−1	1
10	3	4	4	0	0
11	3	5	4	1	1
12	3	6	4	2	4
13	4	3	4.5	−1.5	2.25
14	4	4	4.5	−.5	.25
15	4	5	4.5	.5	.25
16	4	6	4.5	1.5	2.25
17	5	4	5	−1	1
18	5	5	5	0	0
19	5	6	5	1	1
Sum	57	76	76	0	24
Mean	3	4	4	0	1.263

regression equation or the regression line. The column labeled e shows $Y - \hat{Y}$, the *residual* or *error of estimate* for each person. These errors average 0, so the average error is not a good estimate of our accuracy. But the *sum of squared errors* is a measure of accuracy. The column labeled e^2 shows the squared errors; its sum is 24.

If linearity holds, as it does in this example, it can be shown that the line through the conditional means has a smaller sum of squared errors than any other possible line that can be drawn in the scatterplot. For instance, Fig. 1.3 shows an alternative line through the scatterplot. The squared errors and their sum are:

$$0 + 1 + 4 + 1 + 0 + 1 + 4 + 4 + 1 + 0$$
$$+ 1 + 4 + 4 + 1 + 0 + 1 + 4 + 1 + 0 = 32$$

This is considerably larger than the previous sum of 24.

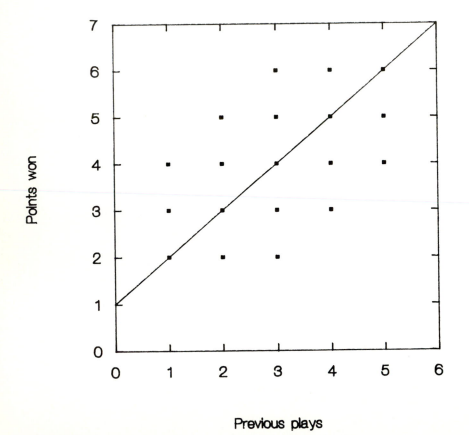

FIGURE 1.3
An alternative line with higher sum of squared errors.

1.3   SIMPLE REGRESSION

1.3.1   The Regression Line

Ordinarily, the data set we work with is a *sample* from a larger *population*. Linearity (conditional means falling in a straight line) hardly ever holds for a sample, though we usually assume that it holds for the larger population. In fact, in our sample there may not even be any two people with exactly the same scores on X, so the very concept of conditional means may have little or no meaning for the sample. Therefore we need a way to derive a line and its equation that does not rely on sample values of conditional means.

The solution to this problem relies on the fact that $\Sigma\, e_i^2$, the sum of squared errors, is defined even when there are no conditional means. There is always one straight line that has a smaller sum of squared errors than any other straight line. That line is called the *regression line*, and its equation is called the *regression equation*.

1.3.2   Variance, Covariance, and Correlation

Regression lines can be computed from *covariances*. Covariances have little scientific meaning by themselves, but they are useful for computing both regression slopes and correlations. We define

$$x_i = X_i - M_X$$

That is, x_i is the deviation of person i's X score from the mean of X. Also, y_i equals $Y_i - M_Y$, the deviation of person i's Y score from the mean of Y. The product $x_i y_i$ is the *cross product* for person i. The cross product is positive if person i is above the means on both X and Y, or below on both. The cross product is negative if person i is above the mean on one variable and below the mean on the other.

The *covariance* between X and Y is the mean of the cross products. It is denoted by Cov(XY). Thus

$$\text{Cov}(XY) = \frac{\Sigma x_i y_i}{N}$$

where N is the sample size. Unlike a mean or a standard deviation, a covariance is not a scientifically meaningful statistic in its own right. Its usefulness lies in our ability to compute more meaningful statistics from it.

The covariance of any variable with itself is the variable's *variance*. The variance of X is denoted by Var(X). We have

$$\text{Var}(X) = \Sigma \frac{x_i x_i}{N} = \Sigma \frac{x_i^2}{N}$$

Some textbooks define the variance by the formula $\text{Var}(X) = \Sigma x^2/(N-1)$, while others use the simpler formula

$$\text{Var}(X) = \frac{\Sigma x^2}{N}$$

The latter usage is more common in discussions of correlation and regression, and we shall use that definition. As explained more fully in Sec. 5.2.6, the former definition actually makes $\text{Var}(X)$ an unbiased estimator of the population variance, but this advantage is unimportant in regression analysis because the most important variance in regression is the residual variance, and a separate formula yields an unbiased estimator of it.

The variance is also the square of the variable's *standard deviation:*

$$\text{Var}(X) = S_x^2$$

The *Pearson correlation coefficient,* or simply the *correlation,* between X and Y is defined as

$$r = \frac{\text{Cov}(XY)}{S_X S_Y}$$

The correlation measures the size of the association between X and Y; there is perfect association between X and Y if $r_{XY} = 1$, whereas $r_{XY} = 0$ if X and Y are independent.

Since a variance is a type of covariance and a standard deviation is the square root of a variance, this formula shows that a correlation is determined entirely by covariances.

1.3.3   Finding the Regression Line

Covariances also define the regression slope, which is usually denoted by b. The formula is

$$b = \frac{\text{Cov}(XY)}{\text{Var}(X)}$$

An alternative formula is

$$b = r_{XY}\frac{S_Y}{S_X}$$

We can call the first formula the *computing formula* and the second the *definitional formula.* The second shows more clearly how b relates to the familiar concepts of correlations and standard deviations, while the first formula allows us to compute b without taking any square roots.

If we multiply the numerator and denominator of the computing formula each by N, they become respectively Σxy and Σx^2. Thus an alternative computing formula is

$$b = \frac{\Sigma xy}{\Sigma x^2}$$

Once b has been found, we can find the Y intercept a by the formula

$$a = M_Y - bM_X$$

Then the equation for the regression line is

$$Y = bX + a$$

The estimated conditional mean for any value of X is found by substituting that value of X in this equation. This also gives us the estimated Y score for any person with that value of X. Since the symbol ^ denotes "estimate of," the equation

$$\hat{Y} = bX + a$$

means that $bX + a$ yields an estimate of Y. This equation is the *regression equation*. It is also called the *model* of Y, since its purpose is to simulate or model Y as accurately as possible.

Readers familiar with regression analysis may notice that we have omitted familiar formulas for easy hand computation of variances, covariances, r_{XY}, and b from raw scores rather than deviation scores. This is primarily because we assume that readers interested primarily in simple regression will use other sources, and that the methods of this book will be applied by computer. The example in Sec. 1.3.4 uses the definitional formulas presented here.

The regression line found this way always passes through the center of the scatterplot—the point with coordinates M_X and M_Y. For the data set used, the regression line has a smaller sum of squared errors than any other straight line. If the sample was a random sample from a population in which linearity holds, then the slope of the regression line is an unbiased estimate of the slope of the population regression line, and any value of $\hat{Y} = bX + a$ is an unbiased estimate of the conditional mean for the value of X employed.

1.3.4 An Example

The formulas introduced in Secs. 1.3.2 and 1.3.3 are illustrated for the data set of 10 cases in Table 1.7.

TABLE 1.7
An artificial data set

ID	X	Y
1	2	6
2	4	2
3	6	4
4	2	8
5	4	9
6	6	8
7	8	5
8	4	11
9	6	13
10	8	9
Mean	5.0	7.5

The means of X and Y are $M_X = 5.0$ and $M_Y = 7.5$. Thus, for person 1, the deviation scores are

$$x_1 = 2 - 5 = -3$$

$$y_1 = 6 - 7.5 = -1.5$$

For person 1, we calculate

$$x_1^2 = (-3)^2 = 9$$

$$y_1^2 = (-1.5)^2 = 2.25$$

$$x_1 y_1 = (-3) \times (-1.5) = 4.5$$

The entire set of raw scores, deviation scores, squares, and cross products is shown in Table 1.8.

Thus, $\text{Var}(X) = 4.2$, $\text{Var}(Y) = 9.85$, $\text{Cov}(XY) = .3$, and $r_{XY} = .3/\sqrt{4.2 \times 9.85} = .047$. Also, $b = .3/4.2 = .0714$ and $a = 7.5 - (.3/4.2) \times 5 = 7.1429$. Figure 1.4 shows the scatterplot and the line with these values of a and b. A cross marks the center of the scatterplot at $X = 5$, $Y = 7.5$; notice that the regression line passes through it.

Using the formulas above to estimate the population conditional mean at $X = 2$, we have $.0714 \times 2 + 7.1429 = 7.2857$. This is also the estimated Y score for any new person scoring 2 on X. Person 4 has this value of X; for person 4, $X = 2$ and $Y = 8$. Thus person 4's residual is $e_4 = 8 - 7.2857 = .7143$, which equals the length of the short vertical line in Fig. 1.4.

1.4 b VERSUS r

Both r and b are measures of the relationship between X and Y; they are related by the formula $b = r_{XY}(S_Y/S_X)$. Since S_X and S_Y are always positive, b and r

TABLE 1.8
Regression computations

Person	X	Y	x	y	x^2	y^2	xy
1	2	6	-3	-1.5	9	2.25	4.5
2	4	2	-1	-5.5	1	30.25	5.5
3	6	4	1	-3.5	1	12.25	-3.5
4	2	8	-3	.5	9	.25	-1.5
5	4	9	-1	1.5	1	2.25	-1.5
6	6	8	1	.5	1	.25	.5
7	8	5	3	-2.5	9	6.25	-7.5
8	4	11	-1	3.5	1	12.25	-3.5
9	6	13	1	5.5	1	30.25	5.5
10	8	9	3	1.5	9	2.25	4.5
Sum	50	75	0	0	42	98.5	3.0
Mean	5	7.5	0	0	4.2	9.85	.30

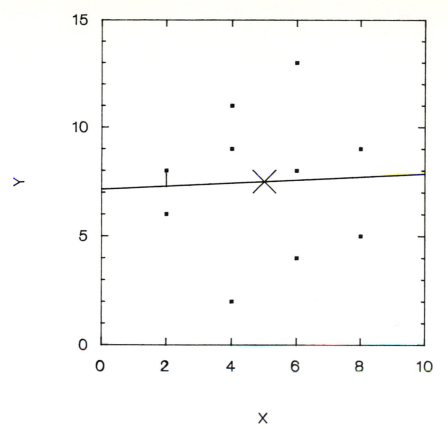

FIGURE 1.4
A regression line, residual, and scatterplot center.

always have the same sign. Therefore the two measures always agree on whether the relationship between X and Y is positive, negative, or zero.

The last statement applies to both samples and populations. Therefore, the hypothesis that a correlation is zero in the population is equivalent to the hypothesis that the corresponding regression slope is zero in the population. We will see later that there is a t test for testing the significance of r, and a very different-appearing t test for testing the significance of b. But in fact the two tests are equivalent, because in any one sample both tests always give exactly the same value of t. Thus both the null hypotheses and the tests are equivalent.

But b and r measure very different properties of a relationship. It has been estimated that every cigarette smoked lowers one's expected life span by about 5 minutes. If this were derived from a regression analysis (with life span measured in minutes!), we would have $b = -5$. Or suppose we studied the relation between hours of study for a test and number of points scored on the test, controlling for important covariates. If we found $b = 6$, it would mean that each extra hour of study is associated with a 6-point increase in test score. Statements like these convey information wholly lacking from statements like

"The correlation between study time and test score was $+.4$," or "The correlation between smoking and life span is $-.2$." The value of b is the increase in $\hat{Y}$ associated with each 1-point increase in X.

How, then, do b and r differ? In terms of their *formulas*, they differ primarily in just one way; in terms of their *properties*, they differ in three major ways; and in terms of their *uses*, they differ in four major ways. We shall examine all these differences.

In terms of their *formulas*, r is a standardized b. That is, if we replaced X and Y by their standard scores, which have means of 0 and standard deviations of 1, then r would not change but b would change to equal r.

1.4.1 Properties of r and b

The first difference in the *properties* of r and b is that b but not r is influenced by the *units* used to measure X and Y, so that b is *scale-bound* but r is *scale-free*. For instance, suppose we have a regression line predicting a child's weight from his or her age and we switch from measuring weight in pounds to measuring it in ounces. This switch will not change r_{XY}, but it will multiply S_Y by 16, since there are 16 ounces in a pound. The formula $b = r_{XY}(S_Y/S_X)$ shows us that b is then also multiplied by 16. Also, if we switch from measuring ages in months to measuring them in years, S_X will be divided by 12, which will result in multiplying b by 12. It is mathematically equivalent to say that children gain weight at an average rate of .2 pounds per month, or 2.4 pounds per year, or 38.4 ounces per year, or 3.2 ounces per month, even though four different numbers are used to express the fact. Any of these four numbers could be the b computed for the same set of children. But only one value of r_{XY} would be found.

The second difference in the properties of r and b is that r but not b increases with the *range* of the variables studied. For instance, suppose X is income, Y is amount saved annually for retirement, and there is a linear relation between X and Y. If investigators A and B each study the relation between X and Y but A studies the entire nation while B studies only one wealthy suburb, then it may well be that both will find the same value of b but A will find a much higher value of r because X ranges more widely in A's study.

Figure 1.5 illustrates the point. Figure 1.5b consists of the central three columns from Fig. 1.5a. In both parts, the diagonal lines pass through all conditional means, so we know without calculation that they are the regression lines. They have the same slope in both parts. The mean of squared residuals is also about the same in Figure 1.5a (5.94, where dots are 1 unit apart) as in Fig. 1.5b (5.76). But the correlation is clearly visible in part a, and hardly noticeable in part b; the values of r_{XY} are .54 and .16, respectively.

These figures relate to the formula $b = r_{XY}(S_Y/S_X)$, but we can see the relation most easily by rewriting the formula as $r_{XY} = b(S_X/S_Y)$. The values of b are equal in both parts of Fig. 1.5. The value of S_Y is slightly larger in part a than in part b (2.90 versus 2.43), which would tend to make r_{XY} smaller in part a. But S_X is much larger in part a (3.15 versus .80), which makes r_{XY} larger.

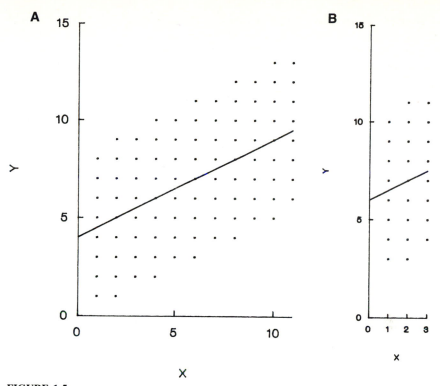

FIGURE 1.5
How range restriction affects r without affecting b.

The third difference in the properties of r and b is that when Y is affected by *other variables* uncorrelated with X, r_{XY} is lowered but b is not affected. r_{XY} is really a measure of the importance of the XY relationship, relative to other factors affecting Y; while b in a sense measures the absolute size of the relationship, ignoring other factors. For instance, if a nation had a safety campaign which greatly lowered the rate of accidental death, that would presumably not affect the regression slope mentioned above of -5 minutes of life span per cigarette. But the drop in accidental deaths would *raise* the correlation between smoking and life span (that is, make the correlation more negative), because it would raise the importance of smoking relative to other factors affecting life span.

In terms of the formula $r_{XY} = b(S_X/S_Y)$, where X is smoking and Y is life span, lowering the importance of accidental deaths would leave b and S_X unchanged but would lower S_Y, thereby raising r_{XY}.

1.4.2 Uses of r and b

We can summarize the difference in the *uses* of r and b by saying that b is a better measure of X's *effect* on Y, especially in *experiments*, while r is a better measure of *predictive power*, *relative importance*, and *statistical significance*.

The phrase "better measure" is chosen carefully to avoid the implication that *b* and *r* are always *good* measures of these qualities. But when we find statistically that every extra cigarette smoked is associated with a 5-minute decrease in life span, that is a useful way of describing a relationship that *may* be causal. The assumptions needed to infer causation from statistical relationships are spelled out later, especially in Sec. 4.1.1.

When *X* is manipulated in an experiment, then its range is a property of the experiment rather than a property of the natural world. For instance, suppose we correlate hours of exercise (*X*) with later physical fitness (*Y*). If an experimenter decides that subjects in an experiment will exercise for 1, 3, and 5 hours, the range of 5 − 1, or 4 hours, has nothing to do with the range of hours of exercise that people would choose for themselves. Since r_{XY} is affected by range, the value we find from experimental data tells us nothing about the correlation we would find in nonexperimental data or in data from an experiment with a different range. But we would expect to find approximately the same value of *b* in all these cases, since *b* is unaffected by range restriction.

But if we want to predict a student's grades in college from his or her grades in high school, or predict a worker's productivity from his or her score on an employment test, then *r* measures the *predictive power* of *X*. If we wished to select the test with the greatest predictive power, we would select the test with the highest value of *r*. A test which happens to have a low standard deviation S_X might have a very high value of *b*, because of the formula $b = r_{XY}(S_Y/S_X)$, but that would not matter.

And r_{XY} is more closely related to statistical significance than *b* is. In particular, with the proper assumptions, once you know r_{XY}, to test its statistical significance the only other information you need is the sample size *N*. Thus, with sample size fixed, the larger of two correlations is always more significant. The same is not true of *b*.

1.5   RESIDUALS

1.5.1   The Three Components of *Y*

After we have regressed *Y* on *X* (that is, predicted *Y* from *X*), we can partition each person's *Y* score Y_i into three components. Consider the equation

$$Y_i = M_Y + (\hat{Y}_i - M_Y) + (Y_i - \hat{Y}_i)$$

This is a simple algebraic identity; if you remove the parentheses and cancel values on the right, you find that the equation reduces to $Y_i = Y_i$.

The first of the three components, M_Y, is constant for all people in the sample. Because $\hat{Y}_i$ is computed from X_i, the second component $(\hat{Y}_i - M_Y)$, correlates perfectly with *X* and is called the portion or component of *Y* *explained* by *X*. The remaining component, $(Y_i - \hat{Y}_i)$, is the *unexplained* or *independent* or *residual* portion of *Y*. Thus, if John's grade-point average (GPA) in school is .8 units above the mean and we predict from his SES that it would be .3 units above the mean, then John's SES explains .3 of his .8 units of deviation, and the other .5 is unexplained by SES.

The unexplained portion is the residual e_i in the regression of Y on X; in Sec. 1.2.3 we defined $e_i = Y_i - \hat{Y}_i$. The explained and unexplained components are sometimes called the *model* and *error* components of Y. Thus the equation above can be written as:

$$Y = M_Y + \text{explained component} + \text{unexplained component}$$

or as

$$Y = M_Y + \text{model component} + \text{error component}$$

For instance, in the example of Sec. 1.3.4, the regression equation was $Y = .0714X + 7.1429$. We also had $M_Y = 7.5$, $Y_5 = 9$, and $\hat{Y}_5 = 7.4285$. Thus, for person 5 the residual or error component is $9 - 7.4285 = 1.5715$, the model component is $7.4285 - 7.5 = -.0715$, and the last equation becomes $9 = 7.5 - .0715 + 1.5715$.

The properties and uses of these three components will become clear gradually. The rest of Sec. 1.5 considers one of the three components—the residuals.

1.5.2 Algebraic Properties of Residuals

Residuals have three important algebraic properties that are always true in any sample or population:

1. The mean of the residuals is exactly zero.
2. The residuals have exactly zero correlation with X. There is no tendency for the residuals to be more positive or more negative as X increases. The model component of Y is completely determined by X and correlates perfectly with X, so the residuals also have zero correlation with the model component.
3. The variance of the residuals, denoted $\text{Var}(Y.X)$, is given by

$$\text{Var}(Y.X) = \text{Var}(Y) \cdot (1 - r_{XY}^2)$$

which can be written as

$$\frac{\text{Var}(Y.X)}{\text{Var}(Y)} = 1 - r_{XY}^2$$

The left side of this equation is the variance of the residuals expressed as a proportion of the total variance of Y. We can call this the proportion of variance in Y not explained by X. The proportion explained is then 1 minus this unexplained proportion, or r_{XY}^2. Therefore we often speak of r_{XY}^2 as the proportion of Y variance explained by X. Because the mean of the residuals is 0, $\text{Var}(Y.X)$ equals $\Sigma\, e_i^2/N$, the mean of the squared residuals.

In the example of Sec. 1.3.4, we had $\text{Var}(Y) = 9.85$, $\text{Var}(Y.X) = 9.8286$, and $r_{XY} = .04664$. Thus the last equation is

$$\frac{9.8286}{9.85} = 1 - .04664^2$$

As mentioned earlier, we often assume that linearity holds in the population from which our sample is drawn. Other assumptions about the population, notably homoscedasticity and conditional normality, are discussed in Sec. 5.1.2. However, the above three properties of residuals are strictly algebraic, and do not depend at all on these or other assumptions.

1.5.3   Residuals as Y Scores Adjusted for Differences in X

When we predict Y from X, we can think of the residuals in the regression as scores on a new variable which we can call Y *adjusted for X* or Y *corrected for X*. For instance, if Sally's residual is 3 and Nick's is 2, then Sally is 3 units higher on Y than we would have expected from her score on X, while Nick is only 2 units higher. Sally is then higher than Nick on Y in relation to what we would have predicted from their scores on X. In other words, Sally is higher than Nick on Y after adjusting or correcting for differences in their scores on X.

This use of regression residuals capitalizes on the fact that residuals have zero correlation with X. Thus there is no tendency for a person's residual to be high just because that person scores high or low on X.

Residuals are important for understanding partial relationship, but they have uses in their own right. For instance, consider the problem that organizers have when planning a footrace for amateurs. If all entrants compete against each other, then the older runners have little chance of winning. But if a separate division is made for runners over 40, then runners in their late thirties, and runners over 50, are still discriminated against. This problem could be solved by fitting a regression line predicting the running times from the runners' ages. The runner with the most *negative* residual (the lowest time adjusted for age differences) could be declared the winner. The disadvantage of this procedure is that no winner could be declared until all runners had completed the race, but it should help you understand the uses and meaning of residuals. When yachts of different sizes race against each other, a procedure like this is sometimes used, since larger boats go faster. The winning boat is the one that does best relative to its own predicted speed. Regression can be used to derive the necessary formula for predicted speed.

1.5.4   Residual Analysis

More serious examples abound. We can define *residual analysis* as the process of selecting the cases with highest and/or lowest residuals for scrutiny, in the hope that these will suggest insights into the factors affecting Y. For instance, investigators have selected the schools whose average student achievement is highest relative to the socioeconomic level of the school's neighborhood. Studying those schools has then led to important insights about the factors producing successful schools—notably, the fact that the personality and determination of the principal make a surprising difference (Edmonds, 1986).

Figure 1.6 shows another example of residual analysis. This figure shows the percentage growth in the population of the United States for each decade of American history since the first population census in 1790. If we number the decades 1 to 19 and regress Y on X (that is, predict Y from X), we get the line shown. The negative regression slope indicates that the rate of population growth has slowed considerably since 1790. The line slopes down because we have plotted percentage increases in population; if we had plotted absolute increases, the line would slope up.

An examination of this plot shows the five largest residuals to be for the decades following 1840, 1850, 1910, 1930 and 1950. Each of these is associated

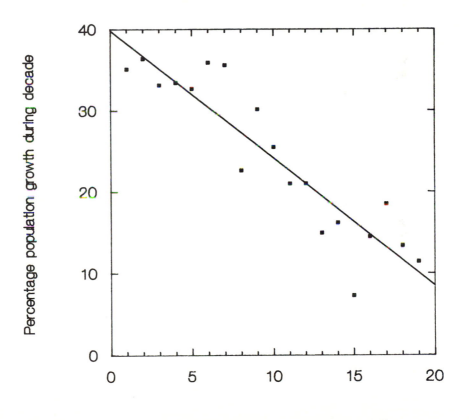

FIGURE 1.6
Percentage population growth in the United States for each decade of its history, with the regression line.

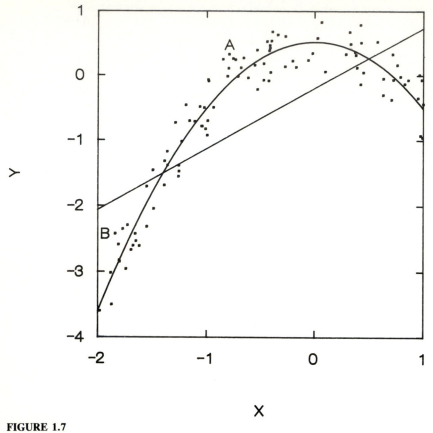

FIGURE 1.7
A violation of linearity.

with an important historical event. The decade of the 1840s witnessed the great potato famine, which drove millions to America. The 1850s were a decade of political repression in Europe, which also drove large numbers to the United States. In the second decade of the twentieth century, immigration was slowed by World War I, producing a negative residual. The 1930s saw the great depression, which lowered birthrates. And the 1950s saw the baby boom.

The largest of all these residuals was for the 1930s. This indicates that after correcting for the gradual slowing of the rate of population growth, the single most important event to affect population growth in the United States was the great depression.

Residual analysis is most meaningful if we can assume linearity and also assume that conditional distributions are identical except for means. Figure 1.7 illustrates a violation of linearity. In it, person A has the highest positive residual relative to the straight regression line, but person B is farther above the true curved line than A is.

Figure 1.8 was generated by a computer program which made the conditional standard deviation of Y proportional to X. In it, person A is over twice as

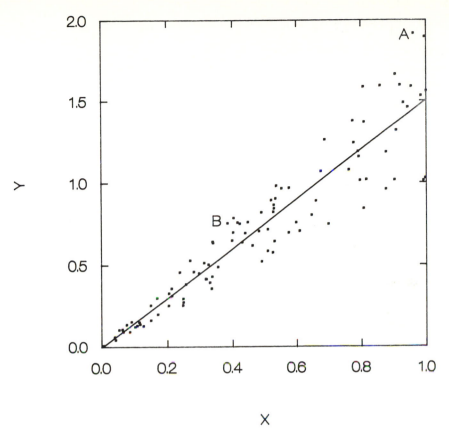

FIGURE 1.8
A violation of homoscedasticity (equality of conditional variances).

far above the regression line as person B. But when we correct properly for the differing conditional standard deviations, B is farther above the regression line than A. Thus residual analysis is of limited value if we cannot assume linearity and equality of conditional variances.

But these assumptions are often met, so residual analysis is an important tool in its own right. It is also the basis for understanding the concept of partial relationship, which is the fundamental tool of statistical control.

SUMMARY

1.1 Statistical Control

Our analyses include independent variables, dependent variables, and covariates. Any of these may have any of three scale types: numerical, dichotomous, or multicategorical. The distinction among these scale types merely determines details of statistical methods, not the methods themselves.

Four ways of controlling covariates are:

Random assignment on the independent variable
Exclusion of cases
Manipulation of covariates
Other types of randomization

The three experimental methods are difficult, while exclusion of cases loses power and precision.

control = adjust for = correct for = hold constant = partial out

Two limitations of statistical control are disagreement on what to control and the requirement that covariates be measured accurately.

1.2 Scatterplots and Conditional Distributions

$$\hat{Y} = bX + a$$

b is the slope and a the Y intercept. We can use the line or its equation to estimate new conditional means. An estimated value of Y is denoted by $\hat{Y}$.

1.3 Simple Regression

There is always one straight line that has a smaller sum of squared errors than any other straight line. That line is called the *regression line*, and its equation is called the *regression equation*.

$$x_i = X_i - M_X$$
$$y_i = Y_i - M_Y$$

$x_i y_i$ is the *cross product* for person i. The *covariance* between X and Y is the mean of the cross products. Unlike a mean or standard deviation, a covariance is not a scientifically meaningful statistic in its own right. The covariance of any variable with itself is the variable's *variance*. The *Pearson correlation coefficient*, or simply the *correlation*, between X and Y measures the size of the association between X and Y.

The regression line always passes through the center of the scatterplot—the point with coordinates M_X and M_Y. If the sample was a random sample from a population in which linearity holds, then the slope of the regression line is an unbiased estimate of the slope of the population regression line, and any value of $\hat{Y} = bX + a$ is an unbiased estimate of the conditional mean for a particular value of X.

1.4   *b* versus *r*

r is a standardized *b*. *b* is *scale-bound*, but *r* is *scale-free*. *r* but not *b* increases with the *range* of the variables studied. r_{XY} is really a measure of the importance of the *XY* relationship, relative to other factors affecting *Y*; while *b*, in a sense, measures the absolute size of the relationship, ignoring other factors. *b* is a better measure of *X*'s *effect* on *Y*, especially in *experiments*, while *r* is a better measure of *predictive power*, *relative importance*, and *statistical significance*.

1.5   Residuals

$$Y = M_Y + \text{model component} + \text{error component}$$

Algebraic properties that are always true in any sample or population:

1. The mean of the residuals is exactly zero.
2. The residuals have exactly zero correlation with *X*.
3. The variance of the residuals equals $\text{Var}(Y) \cdot (1 - r_{XY}^2)$.

These three properties of residuals are strictly algebraic and do not depend at all on assumptions about the population.

Residuals are *Y* scores adjusted for differences in *X*. We can define *residual analysis* as the process of selecting the cases with highest and/or lowest residuals for scrutiny, in the hope that these will suggest insights into the factors affecting *Y*.

KEY TERMS

independent variable	partial out
dependent variable	scatterplot
covariate	distribution
dichotomous	conditional distribution
multicategorical	conditional mean
numerical	marginal mean
random assignment	linearity
exclusion of cases	slope
manipulation of covariates	*Y* intercept
other types of randomization	residual
experimental control	error of estimate
statistical control	sum of squared errors
control	regression line
adjust for	regression equation
correct for	variance
hold constant	covariance

cross product	scale-free
Pearson correlation coefficient	explained and unexplained
computing formula	components of Y
definitional formula	model and error components of Y
model	residual analysis
scale-bound	

SYMBOLS AND ABBREVIATIONS

X Y b a $\hat{}$ e_i Σ x M Cov N Var S_X r Var($Y.X$)

A NOTE ABOUT PROBLEMS

In many problems at the end of this and other chapters, you will frequently be able to think of complicating factors not mentioned or even hinted at in the particular question. A question may ask about controlling for one variable of socioeconomic status when it seems clear to you that it would be better to control separately for education, income, and occupational prestige. Or a question about residuals may seem to be assuming equality of variances of conditional Y distributions when that assumption is implausible to you. These issues are certainly appropriate when considering real-life research problems. But our purpose at the moment is to acquaint you with the basic concepts; complications are examined at length in later chapters. We suggest that you ignore complicating factors that occur to you, unless the question itself seems to be asking about them.

PROBLEMS

1. Of 225 automobiles purchased by single men, 80 were expensive and sporty, 35 were inexpensive and sporty, 60 were expensive and nonsporty, and 50 were inexpensive and nonsporty. Of 254 automobiles purchased by single women, 48 were expensive and sporty, 70 were inexpensive and sporty, 36 were expensive and nonsporty, and 100 were inexpensive and nonsporty. Do men seem to prefer sporty cars more than women do? Answer both before and after controlling for price.
2. A straight line passes through the two points ($X = 3$, $Y = 18$) and ($X = 7$, $Y = 6$).
    (a) What is its slope?
    (b) If the two points just mentioned are the only two data points in a sample, find Var(X), Var(Y), Cov(XY), and r_{XY}.
    (c) What Y score would you estimate for someone scoring 2 on X?
3. In a copy of Fig. 1.9:
    (a) Mark the conditional means with small X's.
    (b) Draw the regression line.
    (c) Find the slope b.
    (d) Find the Y intercept a.
    (e) Write the regression equation.
    (f) Find Var(X), Var(Y), and Cov(XY). Use two different formulas to find b from these values. Check against the value found graphically.

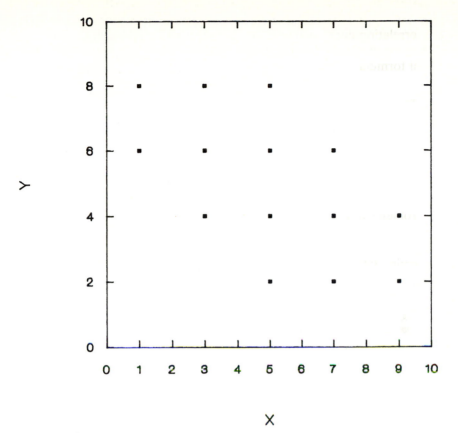

FIGURE 1.9
A sample scatterplot.

(g) What is the value of $\hat{Y}$ for someone for whom $X = 4$?
(h) What is the residual for the person at $X = 3$ and $Y = 4$?
(i) What are the deviation scores x and y for this same person?
(j) Find Var($Y.X$) from some of the statistics calculated above, and show that you get the same value from direct calculation.
(k) Find the mean of the e_i values as simply as possible.
(l) Find as simply as possible the correlation between e and X.
(m) Which is higher on Y after adjusting for differences in X:
   (1) The person at $X = 9$, $Y = 4$
   (2) The person at $X = 3$, $Y = 6$
(n) Notice the person in the upper left corner of the figure. Express this subject's Y score of 8 as the sum of model, error, and mean components.
4. Tell whether a correlation r or a regression slope b is suggested by each of the following phrases:
   (a) A measure of the effect of asbestos inhalation on life expectancy
   (b) A measure of a test's ability to predict grade-point average in college

(c) A measure that will give the same answer in part *b* whether the college assigns grades on a 4-point scale (A = 4, F = 0) or on a 100-point scale

(d) If *X* is age, the measure that might reasonably be the same in the age group 20 to 40 as in the population of all adults

(e) A measure of the effect of hours of practice on proficiency which has scientific meaning in an experiment in which each person is told how many hours to practice

(f) A measure of the importance of the *XY* relationship *relative to* other factors affecting *Y*

(g) A measure which, if higher (farther from 0) among 100 women than among 100 men, results in a more statistically significant *XY* relationship among women

5. Use Fig. 1.6 in Sec. 1.5.4 to answer this question: Population growth in the United States was increased by the Irish potato famine of the 1840s and by political repression in Europe in the 1850s, and was lowered by World War I in the years 1914 to 1918. In percentage terms, which of these three effects was smallest?

6. Suppose older runners were more variable in their running times than younger runners. Would an older runner in the 90th percentile of his or her age group (that is, faster than 90% of runners the same age) look better or worse by residual analysis than a younger runner in the 90th percentile of his or her age group? Can you use either Fig. 1.7 or Fig. 1.8 to illustrate the point? Let the *Y* axis be running time. Your answer need not pertain to the two people already labeled A and B in the figure. Is the sign of the slope correct for this example?

7. Consider a scatterplot in which the SAT scores (*Y*) of high school seniors are plotted against the income of their parents. Suppose it were found that each $1000 increase in parents' income was associated with a 2-point increase in SAT score. From that statement calculate as many of the following statistics as you can: M_X, M_Y, r_{XY}, X_X, S_Y, b, a. Consider *X* to be parents' income in dollars.

8. In Prob. 7, suppose Harriet's family income is $20,000 and she scores 530. Will's family income is $45,000 and he scores 590. Which of them has done better relative to family income?

9. Each of the seven rows in Table 1.9 refers to one of the seven statements *a* to *g*. On a copy of the table, fill in the boxes as follows.

In the first column, write R or S to tell whether the statement is a statement about the relationship between two variables (R) or a statement about the distribution of a single variable (S).

All the R statements here involve a dependent variable (DV), an independent variable (IV), and a covariate (C). Each of these three variables is either dichotomous (D), numerical (N), or multicategorical (M). For R statements, enter D, N, or M in each of the appropriate cells to show the types of variables being used. For S statements, think of the single variable as the dependent variable and enter D, N, or M in its cell.

In the final column, tell what statistical method would be appropriate for testing hypotheses about the statement if there were no covariates to be controlled. Answer by entering the number of the appropriate method from the list of methods below. A single method may apply to more than one hypothesis. *Do not* transform numerical variables into categorical variables by, for instance, dividing at the median, or by creating categories of low, medium, and high.

TABLE 1.9

	R/S	DV	IV	C	Method
(a)					
(b)					
(c)					
(d)					
(e)					
(f)					
(g)					

1. Chi-square test for association
2. Two-sample t test
3. t test for matched pairs
4. Binomial test
5. One-sample t test
6. One-way analysis of variance
7. Pearson r
8. $1 \times k$ chi-square
   - (a) Voters in five different districts distribute their votes very differently among eight school board candidates, even when the district's average income is controlled.
   - (b) The more years of foreign language a student takes in high school and college, the longer sentences he or she uses as an adult, even when a measure of general intelligence is controlled.
   - (c) The average income of felons convicted but now released is below \$15,000.
   - (d) Students who must ride school buses perform worse in school than other students, with SES controlled.
   - (e) More people favor increased welfare spending than oppose it.
   - (f) More boys than girls have absolute pitch, with years of music study controlled.
   - (g) There is a relationship between height and scores on math aptitude tests, even when sex is controlled.

CHAPTER 2

PARTIAL RELATIONSHIP

2.1 MODELS WITH TWO OR MORE FACTORS

2.1.1 An Example

In the example of Sec. 1.3.4, we avoided giving any names to the variables X and Y. But now let Y in that example denote the number of pounds lost during one week of a study on weight loss, and let X be a measure of the amount eaten during that week. In that example we found a small positive correlation between X and Y. This means that on the average, the people who ate the most during the study period also lost the most weight.

This surprising fact can be explained by considering differences among the people in amount of exercise. Table 2.1 repeats the data from the example, with the variables that were X and Y now named food intake and weight loss. The numbers in the column of the table headed "exercise" are daily hours of exercise.

As shown in the table, persons 1, 2, and 3 had no exercise, persons 4, 5, 6, and 7 exercised 2 hours daily, and persons 8, 9, and 10 exercised 4 hours daily. Figure 2.1 shows weight loss plotted against food intake. The three people with no exercise are represented by squares, those with 2 hours of exercise by circles, and those with 4 hours by triangles. In this figure, if we look just at the squares (people with no exercise), there is a substantial negative correlation between food intake and weight loss. If we look just at the circles (people with 2 hours of exercise), there is again a negative correlation. And if we look just at the triangles (people with 4 hours of exercise), we see once again a negative correlation. Thus, whenever we hold exercise constant, we find the expected

TABLE 2.1
Artificial data on exercise, food intake, and weight loss

ID	Exercise X_1	Food intake X_2	Weight loss Y
1	0	2	6
2	0	4	2
3	0	6	4
4	2	2	8
5	2	4	9
6	2	6	8
7	2	8	5
8	4	4	11
9	4	6	13
10	4	8	9
Means	2	5	7.5

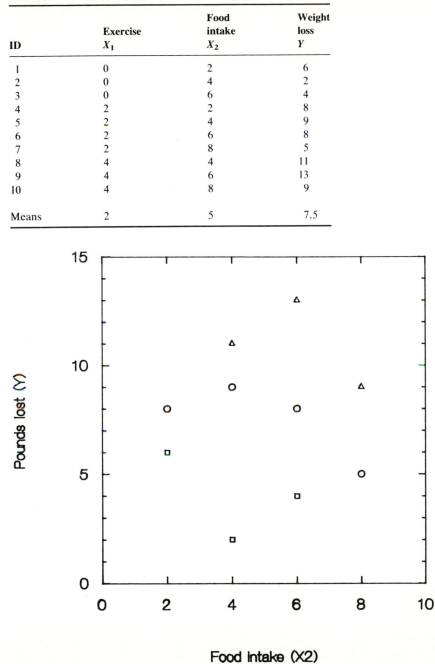

FIGURE 2.1
An example with positive simple association and negative partial association.

negative relationship between food intake and weight loss. The surprising positive relationship between food intake and weight loss occurred because those who ate the most in this sample also exercised the most, and those who exercised the most lost the most weight. The relationship between food intake and weight loss turns negative when exercise is held constant.

How can we state more precisely the relationship between food intake and weight loss when exercise is held constant? In the present example, the negative relationship between these two variables was clearly visible when we looked at subgroups of people equal on exercise. But we could imagine a sample in which no two people had exactly the same amount of exercise. How could we hold exercise constant in such a sample? Further, exactly how do we measure the size of a relationship between two variables with a third variable held constant? The rest of Sec. 2.1 describes methods for answering such questions.

2.1.2 Regressors

We have asked about the relationship between food intake and weight loss with exercise held constant. We might also ask about the relationship between exercise and weight loss with food intake held constant. In the first problem, food intake is the independent variable and exercise is the covariate, while these roles are reversed in the second problem.

We will see that in finding the answer to the first question, we almost automatically find the answer to the second. Because of this, we use the single term *regressor* to include both independent variables and covariates. In a typical regression problem, we tell the computer the names of one dependent variable and two or more regressors, making no distinction between independent variables and covariates. The computer then prints a measure of the partial relationship between the dependent variable and each regressor, controlling for all other regressors.

For instance, in MYSTAT, SYSTAT, and SAS, the desired analysis is controlled by a computer command called a *model* statement. The dependent variable is listed after the word *model*, and then all the regressors are listed after an equal sign. In MYSTAT and SYSTAT, the regressors are separated by plus signs and preceded by the word *constant* to refer to the additive constant a, while plus signs and the word *constant* are omitted in SAS. If the variables in the current problem are named WTLOSS, EXERCISE, and FOODIN, the SYSTAT or MYSTAT model statement will read

>model wtloss = constant + exercise + foodin

or

>model wtloss = constant + foodin + exercise

while the SAS model statement will read

>model wtloss = exercise foodin;

or

$$>model\ wtloss\ =\ foodin\ exercise;$$

The symbol $>$ is used in this book to denote computer commands. As shown here, SAS commands must end with a semicolon.

When the model statement is activated by the proper command, the computer will compute and print a measure of the relationship between the dependent variable and each regressor with all the other regressors held constant. Unless the user chooses to complicate the problem with optional SAS commands introduced in Sec. 7.3 (requesting what SAS calls "type I" sums of squares), the order of the regressors in the model statement has no effect on the statistics printed—though it will determine the order in which they are printed.

If there were a third regressor *metabolism*, denoted *metabol*, then the SYSTAT or MYSTAT model statement

$$model\ wtloss\ =\ constant\ +\ exercise\ +\ foodin\ +\ metabol$$

would produce measures of partial relationship between *wtloss* and:

  exercise with *foodin* and *metabol* controlled
  foodin with *exercise* and *metabol* controlled
  metabol with *exercise* and *foodin* controlled

Again, the order of the three regressors in the model statement will not change the statistics printed out.

The distinction between independent variables and covariates affects the analysis only when we examine the computer output, and then it merely affects what parts of the computer output we examine most carefully. If we are not interested in the relationship between the dependent variable and a covariate with other regressors held constant, we simply give that part of the computer output only a passing glance and concentrate on other parts of the output.

Because independent variables and covariates are both regressors, we usually do not even bother to distinguish between them in our notation. That is why we have named exercise and food intake X_1 and X_2, respectively, rather than, for instance, using X for the independent variable and C for the covariate.

Some authors use the term *independent variables* to refer to all regressors, but we will normally use it in the more restrictive sense explained here—as the variables whose relationship to Y interests us most.

2.1.3 Models

Suppose a survey of the literature on diet, exercise, and weight loss led you to the following conclusions:

1. If food intake is held constant, then each 1-hour increase in daily exercise leads to an average weight loss of 2 pounds per week.

2. If you regard 1000 calories per day as the minimum amount of food intake consistent with good health, and think of food intake above this minimum in units of 100 calories each, then someone who eats 2000 calories per day is consuming 10 units above the minimum. You conclude that each 1-unit reduction in daily food intake increases expected weight loss by .5 pounds per week.

3. You also conclude that if people ate the 1000-calorie minimum for a week and did not exercise, they would lose 6 pounds on the average in the week.

If you were asked to use these conclusions to estimate the weight loss of someone who ate 6 units of food and exercised 2 hours daily for a week, you would calculate as follows:

6 pounds for someone at the minimum on both food and exercise;

plus 4 pounds for exercising 2 hours daily (since $4 = 2 \times 2$);

minus 3 pounds for eating 6 units (since $3 = .5 \times 6$);

gives $6 + 4 - 3 = 7$ pounds expected weight loss for the week.

If you let:

$$Y = \text{weight loss}$$

$$X_1 = \text{hours of exercise}$$

$$X_2 = \text{units of food intake}$$

then this calculation in fact uses the following formula:

$$\hat{Y} = 2X_1 - .5X_2 + 6$$

This equation is a *model* of weight loss as a function of exercise and food intake; you can use it to estimate weight loss for any combination of exercise and food intake. It is a *linear model*, because the coefficients of X_1 and X_2 are simple numbers; *nonlinear models* are described in Chap. 12.

Notice that the coefficient of $+2$ for exercise is a statement about the effect of exercise with food intake held constant. That is, if two people ate the same amount but differed by 1 hour in their daily exercise, you would expect the one who exercised more to lose 2 pounds more per week. Similarly, the coefficient of $-.5$ for food intake is a statement about the effect of food intake with exercise held constant.

If you had decided that exercise and food intake were the important factors determining weight loss but had not yet selected the values of 2, $-.5$, and 6 in the model above, you could write the model in the general form

$$\hat{Y} = b_1X_1 + b_2X_2 + a$$

In this form, b_1 and b_2 are the coefficients of X_1 and X_2, respectively, and a is an additive constant as it is in simple regression.

The statistics b_1 and b_2 have several different names. They are called *coefficients*, since they are multiplied by scores on X_1 and X_2. They are also called the *weights* of X_1 and X_2. We shall see shortly that they are also the *slopes* in a geometric representation of the model. They are also often called *beta weights*, though we shall see later that the term *beta* is used differently by different authors.

Because the coefficients in a model are scale-bound, they cannot meaningfully be compared with each other. For instance, the coefficients of 2 and $- .5$ for exercise and food intake might lead you to believe that exercise is more highly associated with weight loss in this sample than food intake is, since 2 is larger in absolute value than $- .5$. But if you had expressed exercise time in minutes rather than hours, you would have found $b_1 = 2/60 = .033$, which would have made exercise look less important than food intake. The problem of comparing the importance of regressors is examined at length in Chap. 9.

2.1.4 Representing a Model Geometrically

We know that a simple regression model, of the form $\hat{Y} = bX + a$, can be represented geometrically by a straight line. A model of the form $\hat{Y} = b_1X_1 + b_2X_2 + a$ can be represented by a tilted plane in three-dimensional space, as in Fig. 2.2. In fact, this figure represents the very model $\hat{Y} = 2X_1 - .5X_2 + 6$ that we have already considered. The left-hand horizontal axis represents exercise

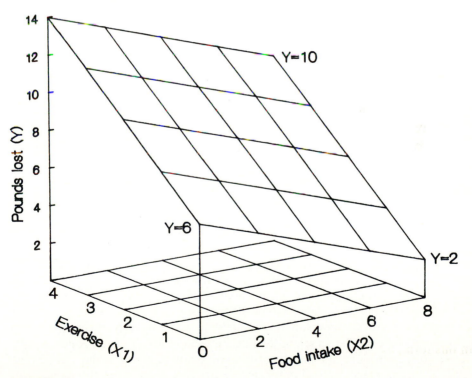

FIGURE 2.2
Plane representing the model $\hat{Y} = 2X_1 - .5X_2 + 6$.

(X_1), the right-hand axis represents food intake (X_2) and the vertical axis represents weight loss (Y).

To see how this plane represents the model, consider first someone scoring 0 on both X_1 and X_2. The model estimates that this subject will lose 6 pounds, since for that person $\hat{Y} = 2 \times 0 - .5 \times 0 + 6 = 6$. At the near corner of the figure, you see that the tilted plane has a Y value of 6.

Now consider someone for whom $X_1 = 4$ and $X_2 = 0$. Inserting these values into the model, we find $\hat{Y} = 2 \times 4 - .5 \times 0 + 6 = 14$. At the upper left corner of the tilted plane, you see that $\hat{Y} = 14$ when $X_1 = 4$ and $X_2 = 0$. Since the plane rises 8 units from 6 to 14 as X_1 rises 4 units from 0 to 4, its slope relative to X_1 is $8/4 = 2$. This is the coefficient of X_1 in the model.

Now consider someone for whom $X_1 = 0$ and $X_2 = 8$. Inserting these values into the model, we find that $\hat{Y} = 2 \times 0 - .5 \times 8 + 6 = 2$. At the far right corner of the tilted plane, you see that $\hat{Y} = 2$ at these values of X_1 and X_2. Since the plane falls 4 units from 6 to 2 as X_2 rises 8 units from 0 to 8, its slope relative to X_2 is $-4/8 = -.5$. This is the coefficient of X_2 in the model.

In summary, a model that represents $\hat{Y}$ as a linear function of two variables X_1 and X_2 can be represented as a tilted plane in three-dimensional space. The plane's Y value at $X_1 = X_2 = 0$ represents the additive constant a in the model, and the plane's slopes relative to X_1 and X_2 represent the coefficients of X_1 and X_2 in the model.

2.1.5   Model Errors

We have imagined that you made up the model above from reading the literature on weight loss. How could you measure the consistency between the model and data in a sample of people, like the 10-person sample in Table 2.1? Might a different model fit the data better—perhaps a model with coefficients of 2.1 and $-.6$ instead of 2.0 and $-.5$? As in simple regression analysis, we can measure the fit of the model for person i by $e_i = Y_i - \hat{Y}_i$, the difference between the subject's actual and estimated Y values. As before, e_i denotes the *error of estimate* for person i.

Table 2.2 repeats the 10 scores on exercise, food intake, and weight loss from above. It also gives values of $\hat{Y}$, calculated from the formula $\hat{Y} = 2X_1 - .5X_2 + 6$, and values of $e_i = Y_i - \hat{Y}_i$.

We can give these results a geometric interpretation. Figure 2.3 shows the scores for our 10-person sample plotted in three-dimensional space. For instance, for person 1 we have $X_1 = 0, X_2 = 2, Y = 6$. Person 1 appears in this figure atop a "lollipop stick" 6 units long, whose base is at $X_1 = 0, X_2 = 2$. Other people in the figure are represented similarly.

If we put the tilted plane and the 10 cases into the same figure, we get Fig. 2.4. In this figure, each person's vertical distance from the plane is shown by a short vertical line. The length of the line for person i is e_i, which is positive for those above the plane and negative for those below. Persons 2 and 9 are each 2 units from the plane, and all other people are just 1 unit from the plane.

TABLE 2.2
Residuals in the weight-loss data set

ID	Exercise X_1	Food intake X_2	Weight loss Y	Estimate $\hat{Y}$	Residual e
1	0	2	6	5	1
2	0	4	2	4	−2
3	0	6	4	3	1
4	2	2	8	9	−1
5	2	4	9	8	1
6	2	6	8	7	1
7	2	8	5	6	−1
8	4	4	11	12	−1
9	4	6	13	11	2
10	4	8	9	10	−1
Means	2	5	7.5	7.5	0

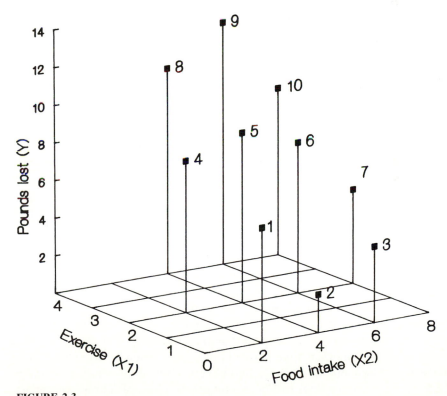

FIGURE 2.3
Ten data points plotted in three-dimensional space.

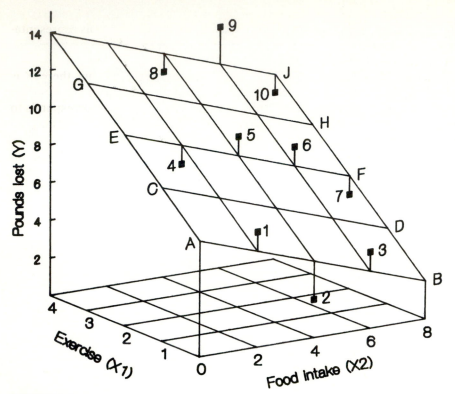

FIGURE 2.4
The data and the best-fitting plane.

2.1.6   An Alternative View of the Model

Three-dimensional figures are difficult to draw; therefore, someone who wants to represent a regression plane geometrically usually employs a two-dimensional figure like Fig. 2.5 that conveys all the same information. Line AB in Fig. 2.4 falls from 6 to 2 as X_2 rises from 0 to 8. Line IJ in Fig. 2.4 falls from 14 to 10 over the same range of X_2. Lines CD, EF, and GH are evenly spaced between them. Figure 2.5 shows the same five lines drawn in a diagram of Y against X_2. Like their counterparts in Fig. 2.4, line AB in Fig. 2.5 falls from 6 to 2, IJ falls from 14 to 10, and lines CD, EF, and GH are evenly spaced between them. Thus Fig. 2.5 conveys all the same information as Fig. 2.4; it represents the model in two-dimensional rather than three-dimensional space.

As you can see in Fig. 2.4, line AB applies when $X_1 = 0$, line IJ applies when $X_1 = 4$, and the other three parallel lines apply when X_1 equals 1, 2, and 3. The appropriate value of X_1 is written next to each sloping line in Fig. 2.5. Because the five sloping lines in Fig. 2.5 apply to values of X_1 one unit apart, the vertical distance between them is the amount the plane rises as X_1 increases 1 unit. But this is the slope of the plane relative to X_1. Thus, in this representation of the model, the vertical distance between parallel lines represents the slope or apparent effect of X_1.

Figure 2.6 also conveys all the information in Fig. 2.4, but there Y is plotted against X_1 instead of X_2. Like line AI in Fig. 2.4, line AI in Fig. 2.6 rises from 6 to 14 as X_1 rises from 0 to 4. Similarly, line BJ in Fig. 2.6 corresponds to line BJ in Fig. 2.4. But there the lines are for values of X_2 two units apart, so the vertical distance between them is twice b_2.

In summary, a linear model involving two X variables can also be represented by a series of parallel lines whose slope equals one slope of the tilted plane. If lines represent values 1 unit apart on the other X variable, then the vertical distance between adjacent lines represents the plane's other slope.

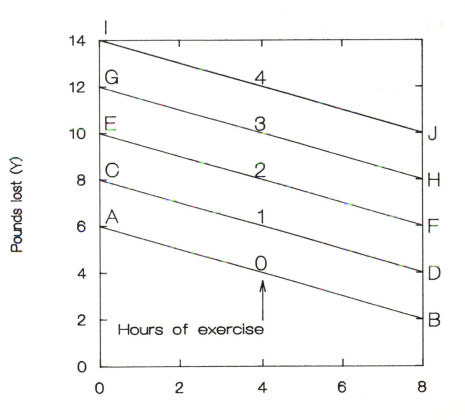

FIGURE 2.5
Another representation of the tilted plane.

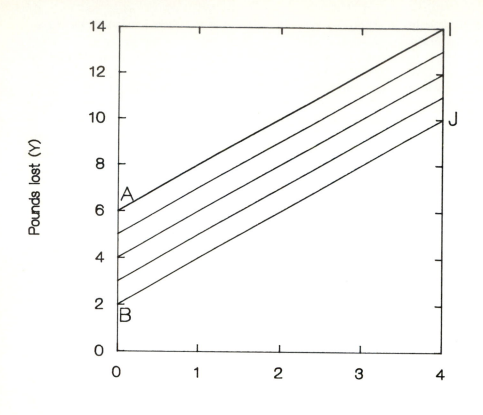

Exercise (X1)

FIGURE 2.6
Still another representation of the tilted plane.

2.2 THE BEST-FITTING MODEL

2.2.1 Partial Regression Slopes

Now suppose you have no prior literature to estimate the effects of diet and exercise on weight loss and need to base your model entirely on the new sample of data. With the model written as

$$\hat{Y} = b_1 X_1 + b_2 X_2 + a$$

the problem is to find the values of b_1, b_2, and a that make the model best fit the data. To measure goodness of fit, we will use Σe^2, the sum of squared errors. For the model in Fig. 2.4, the sum of squared errors is $\Sigma e^2 = 1 + 4 + 1 + 1 + 1 + 1 + 1 + 1 + 4 + 1 = 16$. We will define the *best-fitting model* for a data set as the model with the smallest value of Σe^2.

When starting from raw data, lengthy computations are usually required to find the best-fitting plane. These are almost always done by computer, so the steps described below are not steps you would actually follow in normal practice. Their purpose is to show you what the computer does.

If two variables X_1 and X_2 are uncorrelated, then the computations *are* simple. The slopes of the best-fitting plane can then be found by simple regression analysis. The plane's slope relative to X_1 equals the slope of the simple regression line predicting Y from X_1, and the plane's slope relative to X_2 equals the slope of the simple regression line predicting Y from X_2.

When X_1 and X_2 are correlated, we can still use the principles in the preceding paragraph, by employing the *components* of X_1 and X_2 independent of the other X variable. Consider a regression equation which ignores Y, predicting X_2 from X_1. The residuals in this regression equation can be called the *component* or *portion* or *part of X_2 independent of X_1*, denoted as $X2.1$; even though X_2 itself is not independent of X_1, we can find a part of X_2 which is. We will call it the *unique* part of X_2. If we now regress Y on the unique part of X_2, the regression slope is called the *partial regression slope* of X_2, because it is

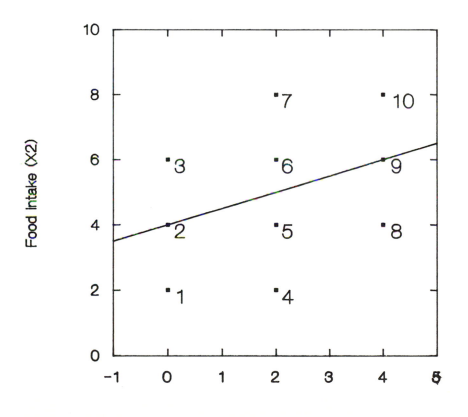

FIGURE 2.7
The meaning of $X2.1$.

TABLE 2.3
Values of $X2.1$ and Y

ID	$X2.1$	Y
1	−2	6
2	0	2
3	2	4
4	−3	8
5	−1	9
6	1	8
7	3	5
8	−2	11
9	0	13
10	2	9
Means	0	7.5

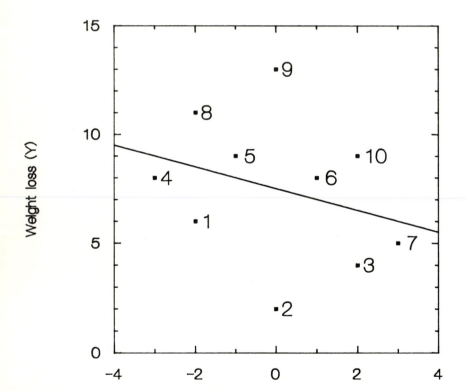

FIGURE 2.8
The meaning of b_2.

literally the slope for part of X_2. *This partial regression slope is the slope relative to X_2 of the best-fitting plane modeling Y as a function of X_1 and X_2.* As we have seen, this slope estimates the change in Y associated with each unit of change in X_2 with X_1 held constant.

Similarly, the plane's slope relative to X_1 equals the partial regression slope for X_1. This is the simple regression slope of Y on the unique part of X_1— the part independent of X_2.

This process is illustrated for the present data set. Figure 2.7 shows X_2 regressed on (predicted from) X_1. Table 2.3 shows $X2.1$, the residuals in this regression, along with the Y scores from above. Figure 2.8 shows Y regressed onto $X2.1$. The slope in this figure is $-.5$, so that is the slope relative to X_2 of the best-fitting tilted plane which models Y as a function of X_1 and X_2.

To find the plane's slope relative to X_1, we repeat the process with the roles of X_1 and X_2 reversed. That is, first we regress X_1 on X_2 as in Fig. 2.9. Figure 2.10 shows Y plotted against $X1.2$, the residuals from Fig. 2.9. It also

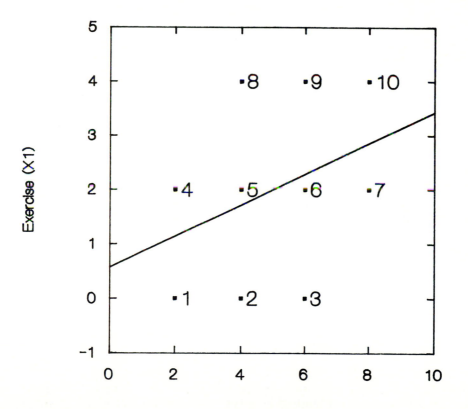

FIGURE 2.9
The meaning of $X1.2$.

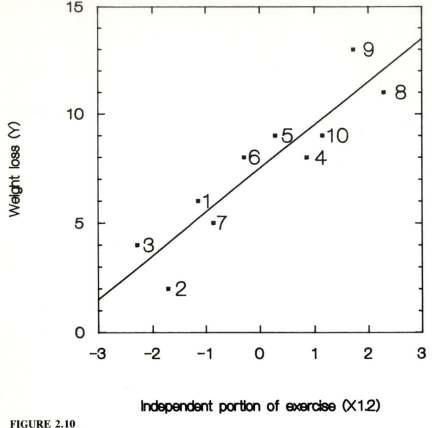

FIGURE 2.10
The meaning of b_1.

shows the regression line fitted to the scatterplot in Fig. 2.9. The line's slope is $+2$, so that is the slope relative to X_1 of the best-fitting plane which models Y as a function of X_1 and X_2.

The simple regression slopes of X_1 and X_2 are $1/14 = .0714$ and 1.75, respectively; and we have just found the partial slopes to be $-.5$ and 2. Thus the partialing process has changed both.

2.2.2   The Additive Constant

After b_1 and b_2 have been found as above, the additive constant a is chosen to make $M_{\hat{Y}} = M_Y$. This prevents the estimated values of Y from either consistently exceeding or consistently falling below the actual values of Y. This is done by choosing

$$a = M_Y - (b_1 M_1 + b_2 M_2)$$

In the current example, $M_Y = 7.5$, $b_1 = 2$, $M_1 = 2$, $b_2 = -.5$, $M_2 = 5$, so $a = 7.5 - (2 \times 2 - .5 \times 5) = 7.5 - 1.5 = 6$.

This formula for a makes $M_{\hat{Y}} = M_Y$, because the mean of $b_1 X_1$ is $b_1 M_1$ and the mean of $b_2 X_2$ is $b_2 M_2$, so the mean of $(b_1 X_1 + b_2 X_2)$ is $(b_1 M_1 + b_2 M_2)$. Thus, the mean of $\hat{Y} = b_1 X_1 + b_2 X_2 + a$ is $b_1 M_1 + b_2 M_2 + a$. Setting this equal to M_Y and solving for a gives the formula above.

The values $b_1 = +2$, $b_2 = -.5$, and $a = 6$ we have calculated are in fact the values already used in the tilted plane of Fig. 2.2.

2.2.3 Problems with Three or More Regressors

We often want to study the relation between an independent variable and a dependent variable when controlling or holding constant several covariates. For instance, we might want to study the relation between the school success of adopted children and aptitude scores of their biological mothers while holding constant several measures of the adoptive environment—school quality, education of the adoptive parents, number of books in the home, and similar factors. This section describes measures of partial relationship for problems like these. As before, these are not actual computing directions; their purpose is to help you see the meaning of the statistics computed.

Let P denote the number of regressors (independent variables plus covariates) in a problem. This must not be confused with a significance level p. The two should be easy to distinguish, since significance levels are less than 1 while the number of regressors is always an integer. Thus both the context and the value of p should eliminate confusion.

In previous sections, weight loss (Y) was regressed onto (modeled as a function of) weekly hours of exercise (X_1) and food intake (X_2). We shall now add to this example a new regressor X_3 of metabolic rate. Therefore, now $P = 3$. When scores on X_3 are added to the scores already used with this example, the complete data matrix is as shown in Table 2.4.

Consider the partial relationship between Y and X_3 with X_1 and X_2 held constant. This involves the unique portion of X_3, which we define as the residuals when X_3 is regressed on (predicted from) *both* X_1 and X_2, in the same way we have already regressed Y on X_1 and X_2. The unique portion of X_3 is denoted $X3.12$. A regression predicting one regressor from the other $P - 1$ regressors will be called a *crosswise regression*. Simple crosswise regressions were actually used in Sec. 2.2.1 to derive $X1.2$ and $X2.1$, though the term was not introduced there. We rarely perform crosswise regressions, but we can use the concept to define the partial regression slope. If you wish to take the time, you can verify that when X_3 is regressed onto X_1 and X_2, one finds $b_1 = 1.5$, $b_2 = 1$, and $a = 12$. The residuals in this crosswise regression are

ID	1	2	3	4	5	6	7	8	9	10
$X3.12$	1	-2	1	-2	2	2	-2	0	0	0

TABLE 2.4
Data matrix including metabolism

ID	Exercise X_1	Food intake X_2	Metabolism X_3	Weight loss Y
1	0	2	15	6
2	0	4	14	2
3	0	6	19	4
4	2	2	15	8
5	2	4	21	9
6	2	6	23	8
7	2	8	21	5
8	4	4	22	11
9	4	6	24	13
10	4	8	26	9
Means	2	5	20	7.5

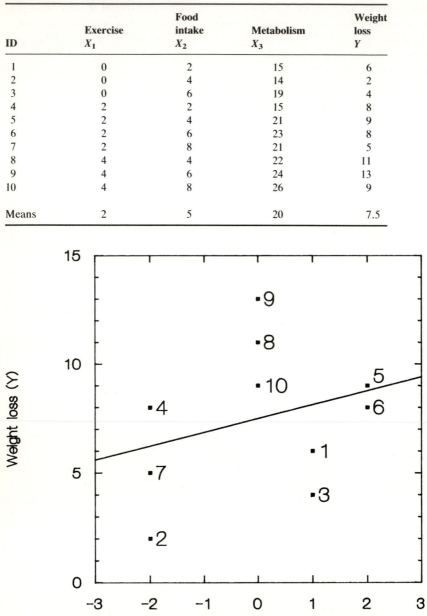

Portion of X3 independent of X1 and X2 (X3.12)

FIGURE 2.11
The meaning of b_3.

Plotting Y against $X3.12$ gives the scatterplot in Fig. 2.11. The slope in this scatterplot is 7/11, so $b_3 = 7/11 = .6364$. The unique portion of X_1 is $X1.23$, the portion of X_1 independent of X_2 and X_3. If we plot it against Y, we find the partial slope $b_1 = 23/22 = 1.0455$. Similarly, plotting $X2.13$ against Y gives $b_2 = -25/22 = -1.1364$. Notice that adding X_3 to the regression has changed b_1 and b_2 from their previous values of $+2$ and $-.5$. Adding a regressor usually changes the weights of all other regressors, sometimes even changing their signs.

Once the b's have been found, a can be found by the formula

$$a = M_Y - (b_1 M_1 + b_2 M_2 + \cdots + b_P M_P) = M_Y - \Sigma b_j M_j$$

This is a direct extension of the formulas for a when $P = 1$ or $P = 2$. As before, it ensures that $M_{\hat{Y}} = M_Y$, which in turn makes the mean of the residuals equal zero. In the present example, we have $b_1 = 23/22$, $b_2 = -25/22$, and $b_3 = 7/11 = 14/22 = .6364$. We also have $M_Y = 7.5$, $M_1 = 2$, $M_2 = 5$, and $M_3 = 20$. Inserting these values into the formula for a gives $a = -36/22 = -1.6364$.

The regression equation with P regressors is written as

$$Y = b_1 X_1 + b_2 X_2 + \cdots + b_P X_P + a = \Sigma b_j X_j + a$$

where the summation on the right is over the P values of j. In the present example, the regression equation is

$$Y = \frac{23}{22} X_1 - \frac{25}{22} X_2 + \frac{14}{22} X_3 - \frac{36}{22}$$

$$= 1.0455 X_1 - 1.1364 X_2 + .6364 X_3 - 1.6364$$

The values of $b_1, b_2, \ldots, b_P$, and a, when calculated as described here, minimize the sum of squared residuals Σe_i^2. Though we cannot visualize a plane in space when $P > 2$, mathematically we can say we have fitted a "hyperplane" (a plane in a space of more than three dimensions) to minimize the sum of squared residuals Σe_i^2. In the present example, addition of X_3 to the regression has lowered Σe_i^2 from 16 to $78/11 = 7.0909$.

2.2.4 The Normal Equations

It can be shown that the method we have described for deriving partial regression slopes b_j is equivalent to solving a set of P simultaneous linear equations in P unknowns. These are called the *normal equations*. The P unknown values are the partial slopes $b_1, b_2, \ldots, b_P$, while the known values in the equations are variances and covariances among the variables. The normal equations are shown in Table 2.5. The values on the right side are the covariances of the regressors with Y. The covariances among regressors appear as a matrix on the left side of the equations.

TABLE 2.5
Normal equations

$$\text{Var}(X_1)b_1 \quad + \text{Cov}(X_1X_2)b_2 + \ldots + \text{Cov}(X_1X_P)b_P = \text{Cov}(YX_1)$$
$$\text{Cov}(X_2X_1)b_1 + \text{Var}(X_2)b_2 \quad + \ldots + \text{Cov}(X_2X_P)b_P = \text{Cov}(YX_2)$$
$$\ldots \ldots \ldots \ldots \ldots \ldots \ldots \ldots \ldots \ldots \ldots \ldots \ldots \ldots \ldots \ldots \ldots$$
$$\text{Cov}(X_PX_1)b_1 + \text{Cov}(X_PX_2)b_2 + \ldots + \text{Var}(X_P)b_P \quad = \text{Cov}(YX_P)$$

For simplicity, we illustrate ignoring X_3, regressing Y onto just X_1 and X_2. We have $\text{Cov}(YX_1) = 4.2$, $\text{Cov}(YX_2) = .3$, $\text{Cov}(X_1X_2) = 1.2$, $\text{Var}(X_1) = 2.4$, and $\text{Var}(X_2) = 4.2$. Thus the normal equations for X_1 and X_2 are

$$2.4b_1 + 1.2b_2 = 4.2$$

$$1.2b_1 + 4.2b_2 = 0.3$$

You can see that these equations are solved by the values $b_1 = 2$, $b_2 = -.5$, which are the values we found before considering X_3.

2.2.5   How Covariates Affect b_j

To understand the effects of covariates on regression slopes, consider first the case of two regressors which both correlate positively with Y. Arbitrarily define X_1 as the variable correlating higher with Y, as in the two-regressor version of the weight-loss example.

When $r_{12} = 0$, b_1 and b_2 both equal the values they would have in simple regressions. Deviations from these values are determined by r_{12}. Figure 2.12 shows b_1 and b_2 as a function of r_{12}, assuming that all three variables have standard deviations of 1.0 and $r_{Y1} = .5$ while $r_{Y2} = .3$. The points in the next paragraph are illustrated by this figure, but they apply to any positive values of these correlations and standard deviations.

As r_{12} increases from 0, both b_1 and b_2 first drop. As r_{12} increases still further, b_2 continues to drop, eventually reaching 0 when r_{12} is high enough that the relationship between Y and X_2 can be explained entirely by their correlations with X_1. Meanwhile, b_1 has already begun to rise, returning to exactly equal X_1's simple regression slope when X_2 has effectively been removed from the equation because $b_2 = 0$. As r_{12} continues to rise still further, b_1 continues to rise while b_2 turns negative; at the limit, they approach positive and negative infinity, respectively. On the left side of the figure, as r_{12} moves from zero in the negative direction, both slopes rise, also becoming more equal when all standard deviations are 1.0, but do not approach infinity.

If r_{Y1} does not equal r_{Y2}, then r_{12} cannot reach either $+1$ or -1, since variables correlating differently with a third variable cannot correlate perfectly with each other; the figure reflects this fact.

The major point made here that generalizes to any number of regressors is that each partial regression slope b_j may fall either above or below the corres-

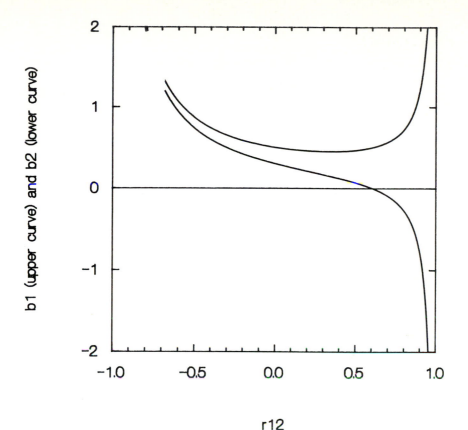

FIGURE 2.12

b_1 and b_2 as a function of r_{12} when $r_{Y1} = .5$, $r_{Y2} = .3$, and all standard deviations equal 1.0.

ponding simple regression slope, depending on X_j's pattern of correlations with other regressors. The two slopes will be equal if X_j is uncorrelated with all other regressors, or if all those other regressors have slopes of 0.

Perhaps most analyses with two regressors fall in the intermediate range of a figure like Fig. 2.12, where both b_1 and b_2 are positive but below the simple regression slopes of the same variables. But our weight-loss example falls to the right of this range. Adding X_2 (food intake) to the regression increased the slope of X_1 (exercise) from 1.75 to 2.00, whereas b_2 remained less than 0. And the last example of Sec. 1.1.3, on salaries of males and females with and without Ph.D.'s, fell to the left of this range. In that example, "maleness" correlated positively with salary but negatively with completion of the Ph.D., so the adjusted effect of gender on salary exceeded its unadjusted effect. The adjusted and unadjusted male-female salary differences in that example can be interpreted as adjusted and unadjusted regression slopes, as we will see more fully in Sec. 3.2.

2.3 SCALE-FREE MEASURES
OF RELATIONSHIP

2.3.1 Some Limitations of Scale-Free Measures

Section 2.3 introduces four scale-free measures of relationship: the multiple correlation R, the partial correlation pr_j, the semipartial correlation sr_j, and the standardized slope beta$_j$. R measures a model's overall fit to a set of data, while the other three statistics all measure the partial relationship between Y and one regressor X_j with other regressors held constant.

None of these four measures is routinely computed and printed by all standard regression programs, though virtually all print R^2. This neglect is intentional, and there are at least four good reasons for it. These reasons are developed more fully in other chapters, but are mentioned briefly here.

First, like simple correlations, all four of these measures are affected by a regressor's range. Thus, if a regressor like hours of practice has a range that has been determined by the investigator, then none of these measures assesses a property of the natural world. Second, R is often a seriously biased estimator of the population value of the multiple correlation, as we shall see in Sec. 5.2.6. Third, pr_j gives the best estimate of the correlation between Y and X_j when other regressors are held constant, but we shall see in Sec. 5.5.2 that the estimate is a reasonable one only under rather restrictive circumstances. Fourth, the three scale-free measures of partial relationship all have slightly different properties and values, and many investigators are confused about which one to emphasize. In Chap. 9, I attempt to eliminate this confusion, thus removing this particular reservation about these measures.

Despite all these reservations, these measures do have valid uses. And they are widely employed, correctly or incorrectly, by behavioral scientists in particular. Therefore a student should definitely become familiar with them.

2.3.2 The Multiple Correlation R

The multiple correlation R is defined as the correlation between the values of Y and $\hat{Y}$. Like Σe^2, R measures the overall fit between the model and the data used to construct the model.

R is never negative. To see why, consider a simple scatterplot showing a negative correlation between X and Y, like Fig. 2.13. In this sample there is perfect linearity, so the regression line goes through the three conditional means. Thus $\hat{Y}$ is 4 for the two subjects on the left, 3 for the three subjects in the middle, and 2 for the two subjects on the right; these values of $\hat{Y}$ are shown at the top of the figure. The dot on the upper left is above average on both Y and $\hat{Y}$, and the dot on the lower right is below average on both. Every other subject is average on Y or $\hat{Y}$ or both. Thus there is a positive correlation between Y and $\hat{Y}$ despite the negative correlation between X and Y.

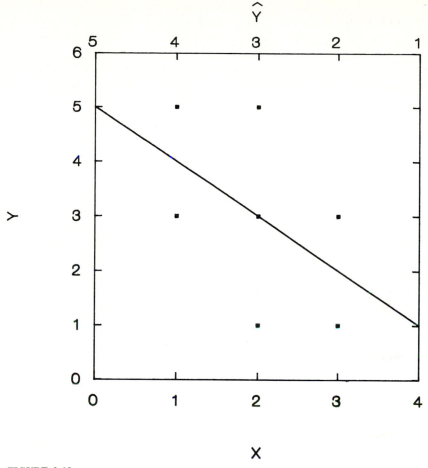

FIGURE 2.13
Why $R > 0$ even when $r_{XY} < 0$.

    R also never falls below the absolute value of any regressor's simple correlation with Y. In symbols, $R \geq |r_{Yj}|$ for all j. This occurs because R is the correlation between Y and the best possible weighted average of regressors. But if all regressors are weighted zero except X_j, then X_j is one possible weighted average, so its correlation with Y cannot exceed R.

    Like a simple correlation, R has an upper limit of 1. In the weight-loss example, R is .9152 when just X_1 and X_2 are in the model, and .9633 when all three regressors are in. These values are exceptionally high for the behavioral sciences, but are reasonable for this example. After all, we would expect that a person's weight loss during a given period could be estimated very well from exercise and food intake during the period, and that measuring metabolism would improve the estimation still more.

If a regressor X_j makes absolutely no independent contribution to the prediction of Y, then we will find $b_j = 0$, and R will be the same whether X_j is in the model or not. But since the regression formulas can always set $b_j = 0$ if X_j makes no independent contribution, adding a variable can never lower R.

R^2 is the proportion of Y variance explained by the model. Many researchers prefer it to R. This issue is examined in Chap. 9. R^2, like R, has a lower limit of 0 and an upper limit of 1.

2.3.3 Semipartial Scatterplots and sr_j

For simplicity, the rest of this chapter will emphasize the model in which Y is regressed on X_1 and X_2, ignoring X_3. We said earlier that the slopes of regression lines in Figs. 2.10 and 2.8 are the *partial slopes* of X_1 and X_2, respectively, because they are the regression slopes of Y on parts of X_1 and X_2. For reasons that will soon become clear, the scatterplots themselves are called *semipartial*

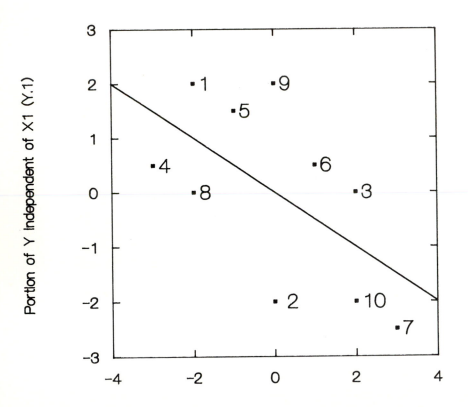

FIGURE 2.14
The partial scatterplot for X_2.

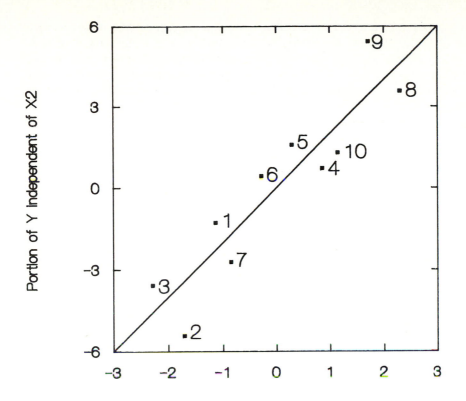

FIGURE 2.15
The partial scatterplot for X_1.

scatterplots, and the correlations in them (between Y and $X1.2$, and between Y and $X2.1$) are called *semipartial correlations*. These correlations are denoted sr_1 and sr_2. In the present example, $sr_1 = .9140$ and $sr_2 = -.3023$.

2.3.4 Partial Scatterplots and pr_j

Figure 2.8 plots Y against $X2.1$, the part of X_2 independent of X_1. Figure 2.14 shows a plot of $Y.1$ against $X2.1$. $Y.1$ is the set of residuals when Y is regressed on (predicted from) X_1. In other words, if we regress Y on X_1 and separately regress X_2 on X_1, then Fig. 2.14 is a plot of the two sets of residuals against each other. In words, Fig. 2.14 is a scatterplot of the portions of Y and X_2 independent of X_1. Figure 2.15 is the same thing with the roles of X_1 and X_2 reversed; that is, it shows $Y.2$ plotted against $X1.2$. In words, it is the scatterplot of the portions of Y and X_1 independent of X_2.

Figures 2.14 and 2.15 are called *partial scatterplots*. We now see why Figs. 2.8 and 2.10 are "semipartial" scatterplots: the partial scatterplot of Y against X_2 plots part of Y against part of X_2, while the semipartial scatterplot plots all of Y against part of X_2. In other words, the partial scatterplot uses parts of both variables, while the semipartial scatterplot uses part of one and all of the other.

The correlation in a partial scatterplot is a *partial correlation*. The partial correlation of X_j is denoted pr_j. In the present example, $pr_1 = .9150$ and $pr_2 = -.6$. The partial slope b_j, partial correlation pr_j, and semipartial correlation sr_j always have the same sign. sr_j can never exceed pr_j in absolute value, and equals it only if all other regressors have exactly zero correlation with Y—so pr_j usually exceeds sr_j in absolute value.

It can be shown that the regression slope in a partial scatterplot always exactly equals the slope in the corresponding semipartial scatterplot. Thus we do not have to distinguish between "partial slopes" and "semipartial slopes"; rather, the slope in either scatterplot is called a *partial regression slope*. As we have seen, the partial regression slopes equal the slopes in the best-fitting plane, so they employ the same notation: b_1 and b_2.

Values of sr_j and pr_j are always defined in terms of all the variables in the model. For instance, if X_3 is in the model, then sr_1 is defined as the correlation between Y and $X1.23$, the portion of X_1 independent of both X_2 and X_3—and pr_1 is the correlation between $Y.23$ and $X1.23$, the portions of Y and X_1 independent of X_2 and X_3.

2.3.5 Relations among Simple, Multiple, Partial, and Semipartial Correlations

In Chap. 1 we said that r_{XY}^2 is the proportion of Y variance explained by X and $1 - r_{XY}^2$ is the proportion unexplained. In similar terms, R^2 is the proportion of Y variance explained by the model as a whole. The amount R^2 drops when X_j is removed from the model is X_j's *unique contribution* to the standardized variance of Y. It is often called X_j's *incremental contribution*. But we will see in Chap. 7 that there are *hierarchical* and *unique* types of incremental contribution, so confusion between them is minimized by using different terms from the beginning.

It can be shown that the unique contribution of any variable X_j always equals sr_j^2. In the present example, with just X_1 and X_2, $R^2 = .83756$. If X_2 were dropped from the model, then only X_1 would remain, so R^2 would drop to r_{Y1}^2, which is .74619. Thus, for the two-factor model, $sr_2^2 = .83756 - .74619 = .09137$. Similarly, $sr_1^2 = R^2 - r_{Y2}^2 = .83756 - .00217 = .83539$.

While each value of sr_j^2 equals an increment in proportion of variance explained, each value of pr_j^2 equals that same increment expressed as a percentage of previously unexplained variance. For instance, a model containing only X_1 explains about 75% of the Y variance, since $r_{Y1}^2 = .74619$. Thus the proportion unexplained is $1 - .74619 = .25381$. We saw above that in the two-factor model the unique contribution of X_2 is .09137. When expressed as a proportion of the variance unexplained by X_1, it is $.09137/.25381 = .3600$, which equals pr_2^2. Similarly, the proportion of variance unexplained by X_2 is $.99782$, and the unique contribution of X_1 is $.83539$, so $pr_1^2 = .83539/.99782 = .83721$.

When two regressors are uncorrelated, $X2.1 = X_2$, so X_2's unique contribution is simply r_{Y2}^2. Thus R^2 equals the sum of the squared simple correlations with Y:

$$R^2 = r_{Y1}^2 + r_{Y2}^2 \quad \text{if} \quad r_{12} = 0$$

Regardless of whether $r_{12} = 0$, we can write:

$$R^2 = r_{Y1}^2 + sr_2^2$$
$$= r_{Y2}^2 + sr_1^2$$

These formulas are intuitively derived from the previous formula as follows. The two variables X_1 and $X2.1$ are mutually uncorrelated by definition of $X2.1$, so the previous formula tells us that if Y is predicted from those two variables, the resulting R^2 will equal the sum of their squared correlations with Y. These two squared correlations are respectively r_{Y1}^2 and sr_2^2. But these two variables together contain the same information as X_1 and X_2, since $X2.1$ was simply calculated from X_1 and X_2. Therefore R for X_1 and X_2 should equal that for X_1 and $X2.1$. That gives the first formula shown. The other formula follows from reversing the roles of X_1 and X_2 in this argument.

When two or more regressors correlate highly, R^2 may fall well below the sum of the individual values of r_{Yj}^2, perhaps being little higher than any single value of r_{Yj}^2. Thus each regressor's unique contribution is small even though the regressors, treated as a set, explain substantial variance in Y. Such regressors are said to be *collinear*.

Although the individual values of r_{Yj} set a lower limit on R, they set no upper limit. Artificial data sets can be created in which all values of r_{Yj} are near zero, but R approaches 1.0 or even equals it. To see how this can happen, imagine that in a sample of schoolchildren, skill at softball correlates highly with skill at basketball, so no child is much better at one than the other, though some children are much better than others at both. But suppose a child's answer to the question, "How much do you prefer softball to basketball?" (9 = much prefer softball, 1 = much prefer basketball) is determined primarily by the difference between his or her skills in the two sports, with every child preferring the sport in which he or she excels slightly. This difference is one possible linear function of the two skill measures. So when sport preference is regressed onto (predicted from) the two skill measures, R is very high even though each skill measure alone correlates quite low with preference.

We shall call a set of regressors *complementary* if R^2 for the set exceeds the sum of the individual values of r_{Yj}^2. So complementarity and collinearity are opposites, though either can occur only when regressors in a set are intercorrelated. As we shall see in Sec. 3.4.3, either collinearity or complementarity can exist within a subset of the whole set of regressors. For instance, in a problem with several regressors, two of them could be colinear or complementary with each other, but independent or nearly independent of all other regressors.

2.3.6 Beta$_j$, a Fourth Measure of Partial Relationship

We have mentioned three measures of partial relationship: b_j, pr_j, and sr_j. There is a fourth that we will call beta$_j$. This is the value we would have found for b_j if we had standardized all variables to standard deviations of 1 before performing the regression. We can actually find beta$_j$ without repeating the analysis, from the formula

$$\text{beta}_j = b_j \frac{S_j}{S_Y}$$

For reasons explained in Sec. 9.3.3, I do not recommend the use of beta$_j$ except in rare circumstances. But you may see it mentioned in the literature.

Confusingly, the word *beta* or its Greek-letter form β is sometimes used in no less than three different ways. Especially in oral conversation, the phrase *beta weight* is often used to refer to the *unstandardized* regression slope b_j. And the Greek letter β is often used to refer to the unknown population value estimated by b_j, following the convention that ordinary Roman letters are used to denote sample values while Greek letters are used for population values. But we shall employ only the third usage, in which beta$_j$ denotes the standardized regression slope of X_j. We shall not use the Greek letter, instead always writing the word out, as in beta$_j$.

2.3.7 Formulas for b_j, pr_j, sr, and R

We have defined b_j, pr_j, sr_j, and R in terms of residuals. But in fact they can all be calculated from simple correlations and standard deviations, without computing a single residual. The formulas for three or more regressors are too complex to include here. But for two regressors X_1 and X_2 the formulas are

$$b_1 = \frac{r_{Y1} - r_{Y2} \, r_{12}}{1 - r_{12}^2} \cdot \frac{S_Y}{S_1}$$

$$b_2 = \frac{r_{Y2} - r_{Y1} \, r_{12}}{1 - r_{12}^2} \cdot \frac{S_Y}{S_2}$$

$$pr_1 = \frac{r_{Y1} - r_{Y2} r_{12}}{\sqrt{1 - r_{Y2}^2} \, \sqrt{1 - r_{12}^2}}$$

$$pr_2 = \frac{r_{Y2} - r_{Y1} r_{12}}{\sqrt{1 - r_{Y1}^2} \, \sqrt{1 - r_{12}^2}}$$

$$sr_1 = \frac{r_{Y1} - r_{Y2} r_{12}}{\sqrt{1 - r_{12}^2}}$$

$$sr_2 = \frac{r_{Y2} - r_{Y1}r_{12}}{\sqrt{1 - r_{12}^2}}$$

$$R^2 = r_{Y1}^2 + sr_2^2 = r_{Y2}^2 + sr_1^2$$

$$a = M_Y - (b_1 M_1 + b_2 M_2)$$

In the weight-loss example, $r_{Y1} = .8638246$, $r_{Y2} = .0466421$, $r_{12} = .3779645$, $S_Y = 3.138471$, $S_1 = 1.549193$, $S_2 = 2.049390$, $M_Y = 7.5$, $M_1 = 2$, and $M_2 = 5$. Entering these values into the formulas above, we find the values already given: $b_1 = 2$, $b_2 = -.5$, $pr_1 = .9150$, $pr_2 = -.6$, $sr_1 = .9140$, $sr_2 = -.3023$, $R^2 = .8376$, $R = .9152$, and $a = 6$. If you happen to have values of standard deviations defined by the formula $\text{Var}(X) = \Sigma x^2/(N - 1)$ instead of $\text{Var}(X) = \Sigma x^2/N$ as was done here, you can just as well use the alternative values in these formulas. This is because these formulas use only ratios of two standard deviations, and the ratio of two standard deviations in the same sample will be exactly the same whichever definition is used.

SUMMARY

2.1 Models with Two or More Factors

We use the single term *regressor* to include both independent variables and covariates. The computer prints a measure of the partial relationship between the dependent variable and each regressor, controlling for all other regressors. In most computer programs the order of the regressors in the model has no effect on the statistics printed—though it will determine the order in which they are printed.

A model with two regressors can be written in the general form

$$\hat{Y} = b_1 X_1 + b_2 X_2 + a$$

In this form, b_1 and b_2 are the coefficients of X_1 and X_2, respectively, and a is an additive constant as it is in simple regression. The statistics b_1 and b_2 are called *coefficients* or *weights* or *slopes* or *beta weights* or simply *betas* by some authors. Raw coefficients in a model cannot meaningfully be compared with each other; see Chap. 9. Each slope of a plane represents a regression coefficient, and the Y intercept still represents a. Errors or residuals are vertical distances of points from the plane.

A linear model involving two X variables can also be represented by a series of parallel lines whose slope equals one slope of the tilted plane. If lines represent values 1 unit apart on the other X variable, then the vertical distance between adjacent lines represents the plane's other slope.

2.2 The Best-Fitting Model

We define the *best-fitting model* for a data set as the model with the smallest value of Σe^2. If two variables X_1 and X_2 are uncorrelated, then the slopes of the best-fitting plane can be found by simple regression.

When X_1 and X_2 are correlated, we can regress Y on the unique part of X_2, denoted $X2.1$. The slope in this regression is called the *partial regression slope* of X_2, because it is literally the slope for part of X_2. This partial regression slope is the slope relative to X_2 of the best-fitting plane modeling Y as a function of X_1 and X_2. This slope estimates the change in Y associated with each unit of change in X_2 with X_1 held constant. Similarly, the plane's slope relative to X_1 equals the partial regression slope for X_1. This is the simple regression slope of Y on the unique part of X_1—the part independent of X_2. After b_1 and b_2 have been found as above, the additive constant a is chosen to make $M_{\hat{Y}} = M_Y$.

Similar principles apply for any number of regressors. A regression predicting one regressor from the other $P - 1$ regressors here is called a *crosswise regression*. The residuals in this regression form the unique portion of the variable in question. When there are three regressors X_1, X_2, and X_3, the unique portion of X_3 is denoted $X3.12$. Regressing Y onto $X3.12$ gives the partial regression slope b_3. b_1 and b_2 can be found analogously. Once the b's have been found, a is chosen to make $M_{\hat{Y}} = M_Y$. These are not actual computing directions for you to follow; they are an explanation of what the computer is doing. The regression equation with P regressors is written as

$$\hat{Y} = b_1 X_1 + b_2 X_2 + \cdots + b_P X_P + a = \Sigma b_j X_j + a$$

where the summation on the right is over the P values of j. The values of b_1, $b_2, \ldots, b_P$ and a, when calculated as described here, minimize the sum of squared residuals Σe_i^2.

The method we have described for finding partial regression slopes b_j is equivalent to solving a set of P simultaneous linear equation in P unknowns. These are called the *normal equations*.

To visualize the effect of a single covariate on the slope of another variable when both correlate positively with Y, use a plot like Fig. 2.12, which plots the partial regression slopes of two regressors against the correlation r_{12} between regressors. Define X_2 as the regressor correlating lower with Y. The plot has three regions:

- When $r_{12} < 0$, both partial slopes exceed the simple slopes.
- When $0 < r_{12} < r_{Y2}/r_{Y1}$, both slopes fall below the corresponding simple slopes.
- When $r_{12} > r_{Y2}/r_{Y1}$, one slope is negative and the other exceeds the corresponding simple slope.

2.3   Scale-Free Measures of Relationship

Four scale-free measures of relationship have four limitations. First, like simple correlations, all four of these measures are affected by a regressor's range. Thus if a regressor has a range that has been determined by the investigator, then none of these measures assesses a property of the natural world. Second, R is often a seriously biased estimator of the population value of the multiple correlation. Third, pr_j gives the best estimate of the correlation between Y and X_j when other regressors are held constant, but we shall see in Sec. 5.5.2 that the estimate is a reasonable one only under rather restrictive circumstances. Fourth, the three scale-free measures of partial relationship all have slightly different properties and values, and many investigators are confused about which one to emphasize.

The multiple correlation R is defined as the correlation between the values of Y and $\hat{Y}$. R is never negative. R also never falls below the absolute value of any regressor's simple correlation with Y. Like a simple correlation, R has an upper limit of 1. R^2 is the proportion of Y variance explained by the model. R^2, like R, has a lower limit of 0 and an upper limit of 1.

If a regressor X_j makes absolutely no independent contribution to the prediction of Y, then we will find $b_j = 0$, and R will be the same whether X_j is in the model or not. But adding a variable can never lower R.

A semipartial correlation sr_j is the correlation between Y and the unique portion of X_j. The scatterplot of these two variables is a semipartial scatterplot.

The partial scatterplot of Y against X_j plots part of Y against part of X_j, while the semipartial scatterplot plots all of Y against part of X_j. The correlation in a partial scatterplot is a *partial correlation*, denoted pr_j. The partial slope b_j, partial correlation pr_j, and semipartial correlation sr_j always have the same sign. sr_j can never exceed pr_j in absolute value, and equals it only in the rare case in which all other regressors have exactly zero correlation with Y.

The regression slope in a partial scatterplot always exactly equals the slope in the corresponding semipartial scatterplot. Therefore the slope in either scatterplot is called a *partial regression slope*. Partial regression slopes equal the slopes in the best-fitting plane, so they use the same notation: b_1 and b_2. Values of sr_j and pr_j are always defined in terms of all the variables in the model.

The amount R^2 drops when X_j is removed from the model is X_j's *unique contribution* to the standardized variance of X_j. The unique contribution of any variable X_j always equals sr_j^2. While each value of sr_j^2 equals an increment in proportion of variance explained, each value of pr_j^2 equals that same increment expressed as a percentage of previously unexplained variance.

Let $beta_j$ denote the standardized regression slope of X_j. Then

$$beta_j = b_j \frac{S_j}{S_Y}$$

KEY TERMS

regressor
linear model
best-fitting plane
weight
coefficient
beta weight
unique component
crosswise regression

normal equations
multiple correlation
partial correlation
partial regression slope
partial scatterplot
semipartial correlation
semipartial scatterplot
unique contribution
collinear

SYMBOLS AND ABBREVIATIONS

b_j $X1.2$ $X2.1$ a P R sr_j $Y.2$ pr_j $beta_j$

PROBLEMS

1. If we looked at birds of many different species, we might find paradoxically that the heavier the bird, the greater its ability to fly long distances. The paradox would disappear if we measured wingspan. We might find that for birds with the same wingspan, the lighter the bird, the greater the flying ability; and we might conclude that the paradox was caused by the fact that in general, birds with larger wingspans are heavier.

   The three variables in this discussion are flying ability (F), weight (W), and wingspan (S). What has the discussion suggested about the signs (positive, negative, or zero) of the following simple and partial correlations? (The variable after the dot is the variable controlled.) Not all correlations have been mentioned explicitly, but you should be able to deduce the signs of all.

$$r_{FW}, \ r_{FS}, \ r_{SW}, \ r_{FW.S}, \ r_{FS.W}$$

2. The most prestigious universities have the highest average faculty salaries, but professors who get offers from two universities at once almost always find that the more prestigious university offers them the lower salary. ("Surely, salary is not the only compensation. You'll have wonderful facilities and colleagues.") Suppose prestigious universities find that this argument works and they can generally pay less than other universities for the same person, or for someone with the same qualifications. We can consider three variables:

   P prestige of university
   Q quality of individual professor
   S individual's salary

   What have we said about simple and partial relationships among these variables?
3. Why is there no "semipartial regression slope" in the list of terms?
4. If *larger* means larger in absolute value, then a semipartial correlation is (never larger than, never smaller than, never equal to) the corresponding partial correlation.
5. What relation holds between the means of Y and $\hat{Y}$?
6. Can a Y intercept a be negative? If not, why not? If so, what does it mean?
7. If r_{Y1} and r_{Y2} are both negative, then R is (positive, negative, zero).
8. In Fig. 2.16, X is years of schooling, Y is income at age 50, and triangles represent high values, circles, medium values, and squares, low values of the person's score I on interest in school. Can you tell by inspection the sign of $r_{XY.I}$?

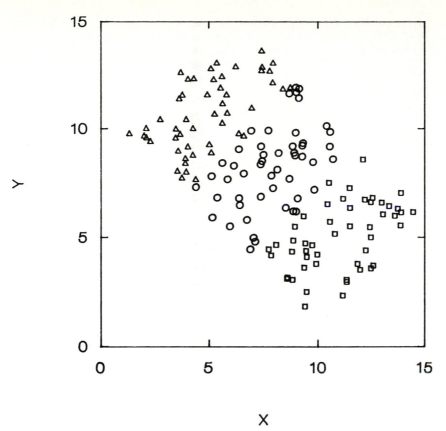

FIGURE 2.16
Partial versus simple association.

9. A data set is shown in Table 2.6. Define $X.C$ and $Y.C$ as the components of X and Y independent of C. Make up four scatterplots (the variable listed first should go on the vertical axis): Y against X, Y against C, X against C, and $Y.C$ against $X.C$. Tell by inspection of these plots whether the relationship between X and Y is positive, negative, or zero when C is controlled.

TABLE 2.6
Scores on three variables

ID	X	Y	C
1	1	1	1
2	3	3	1
3	4	1	2
4	2	5	2
5	5	3	3
6	3	5	3

Several hints will make this easier. Virtually no calculation is required; if you find yourself doing much calculation, then your answer is probably wrong. Scores on $X.C$ range from -1 to 1, and scores on $Y.C$ range from -2 to 2. The problem is much easier if you write each person's ID number next to his or her dot in each figure—especially X against C and Y against C. Keep a copy of at least the last figure; Prob. 5 at the end of Chap. 3 requires it.

10. Note the list of 18 values below. For each of the descriptions a to t, give the number of the value it describes. Two or more descriptions may fit the same value, but there is only one value for each description.

1. pr_j
2. $1 - r^2_{XY}$
3. Conditional mean
4. $\hat{Y}_i$
5. a
6. $\mathrm{Var}(Y.X)$
7. sr^2_2
8. R
9. b_1
10. b_2
11. e_i
12. (M_X, M_Y)
13. $\mathrm{Cov}(XY)$
14. R^2
15. 1
16. .5
17. .25
18. 0

    (a) Y_i as estimated by regression
    (b) Slope of the regression plane relative to X_1
    (c) Error of prediction for person i
    (d) Vertical distance of person i above a tilted plane
    (e) $\hat{Y}$ for a person who scores 0 on all regressors
    (f) Basic scale-free measure of partial relationship
    (g) Amount Y is expected to increase with each unit of increase in X_2
    (h) $r_{Y\hat{Y}}$ when Y is regressed on two other variables
    (i) Increase in proportion of Y variance explained when X_2 is added to a regression containing X_1
    (j) Y intercept of a regression line or plane
    (k) Vertical distance of a tilted plane above the base plane at the X values of person i
    (l) Mean of the xy cross products, where x and y are deviations from means
    (m) Proportion of Y variance unexplained by X
    (n) Scale-bound measure of partial relationship between Y and X_2
    (o) Residual
    (p) Mean of squared residuals
    (q) A point in the XY scatterplot through which the regression line always passes
    (r) Quantities assumed to fall in a straight line in most regression analyses
    (s) Correlation between X and $Y.X$ in simple regression
    (t) Proportion of Y variance explained by X_1 and X_2 together

CHAPTER
3

EXTENDING THE CONCEPT OF PARTIAL RELATIONSHIP

Someone who needs a temporary doorstop might not think of using a screw-driver for the purpose, but the idea *would* be likely to occur to a carpenter who uses screwdrivers daily. This chapter describes a variety of uses and exten-sions of the concept of partial relationship. Each is important in its own right, but in addition we hope that all the examples together will make the idea of partial relationship so familiar to you that you will think of it when it might not otherwise be obvious.

3.1 TYPES OF CASE

In almost all the examples of Chap. 1 and 2, the *cases* in the analysis were people or animals. Cases may also be called *units*, or *observations*, or *units of observation*, or *units of analysis*. Cases need not be people or animals; they might be almost anything. This section illustrates some of the more common types of case.

3.1.1 Stimuli

Suppose we monitor the blood pressure of a subject who is viewing a series of slides on different topics. Suppose judges have previously rated each slide on the degree to which it emphasizes each of several themes: sex, violence, and love, for example. We might use the methods of this book to study whether the subject's blood pressure varies with the emphasis on love in the slides when the emphasis on sex is held constant.

To determine what cases are being used in an analysis, think of the raw data as a rectangular matrix of cases × variables. We have mentioned four variables: blood pressure, sex rating, violence rating, and love rating. If these were all the variables, and if there were 30 slides, then the raw data matrix would be a 30 × 4 matrix showing the score of each slide on each variable. Since the matrix is of slides × variables, we know that the cases are slides. The cases in this example are not people; all the data in the entire analysis came from one person.

3.1.2   Groups of People or Animals

Suppose 30 baboon troops are rated on their degree of hierarchical structure and we correlate the rating with troop size, to see whether larger troops are more hierarchical than smaller ones. Then the units in our analysis are troops rather than individual animals. At the human level, the unit of analysis might be high school cliques, or towns, or nations, or many other kinds of group.

Units may also be whole animal species. If we have a measure of intelligence or behavioral complexity for many animal species and we also measure the average brain size and body size for each species, then we can correlate intelligence with brain size while controlling for body size, with species as the unit of analysis. We shall return to this example in Sec. 3.3.6.

3.1.3   Neurons

In a single animal, we might measure the response of each of 50 neurons to three smells: a sexual pheromone, chocolate, and grain. This gives a 50 × 3 data matrix in which neurons are the cases and the stimuli are the variables. Are the patterns of response to chocolate and the pheromone similar in a way not shared by the responses to the smell of grain? If so, it would suggest that general pleasure is one of the determinants of neuronal response. To answer this, we might study the partial relationship between the responses to chocolate and the pheromone with the response to grain controlled.

3.1.4   Occasions

Phillips (1983) reported that in the United States, the daily murder rate is higher for several days around well-publicized prizefights. The observational units in this analysis were *days*; the sample was all the days of 1973–1978, a period which included 18 major prizefights. The dependent variable was the day's nationwide murder rate. Covariates controlled were year, day of the week, month of the year, and six major holidays. In the 12 days around each prizefight, the total number of murders averaged 26 above other 12-day periods, so apparently 26 additional lives were the toll for each prizefight. Phillips suggests that prizefights affect people's behavior more than fictional violence because people know that both the violence of the fight and the rewards to the winner are real. The June 1985 issue of *American Sociological Review* contains two attacks on this hypothesis, and Phillips's defense.

Many other kinds of units might be imagined, but these examples should give some sense of the possibilities.

3.2   DICHOTOMOUS REGRESSORS

3.2.1   Indicator or Dummy Variables

The methods already described can easily be adapted to include dichotomous regressors like gender. The use of categorical independent variables together with numerical covariates used to be called *analysis of covariance*, but today we think of it as merely one of the many types of linear model.

To illustrate the procedure, we shall add gender to the model on weight loss. Suppose our sample of 10 people includes 4 women and 6 men. The sexes are distributed as shown in Table 3.1, where F and M denote female and male respectively. The procedure consists of making the dichotomous variable numerical by scoring one group 0 and the other group 1. A variable created this way is called an *indicator variable* or *dummy variable*. If we score males 0 and females 1, the data matrix appears as shown in Table 3.2.

For simplicity, we shall first consider the simple regression of weight loss on gender. Using the scores above, the scatterplot of Y against X_4 is shown in Fig. 3.1. We know from Sec. 1.2 that if conditional Y means fall in a straight line, the regression line will pass through them. But in this figure there are only two conditional Y means. The straight line connecting those two conditional means is therefore the regression line.

TABLE 3.1
Weight-loss data set including gender

ID	Exercise X_1	Food intake X_2	Metabolism X_3	Gender X_4	Weight loss Y
1	0	2	15	M	6
2	0	4	14	M	2
3	0	6	19	M	4
4	2	2	15	F	8
5	2	4	21	F	9
6	2	6	23	M	8
7	2	8	21	F	5
8	4	4	22	F	11
9	4	6	24	M	13
10	4	8	26	M	9
Means	2	5	20		7.5

TABLE 3.2
Data set with gender coded numerically

ID	Exercise X_1	Food intake X_2	Metabolism X_3	Gender X_4	Weight loss Y
1	0	2	15	0	6
2	0	4	14	0	2
3	0	6	19	0	4
4	2	2	15	1	8
5	2	4	21	1	9
6	2	6	23	0	8
7	2	8	21	1	5
8	4	4	22	1	11
9	4	6	24	0	13
10	4	8	26	0	9
Means	2	5	20	.4	7.5

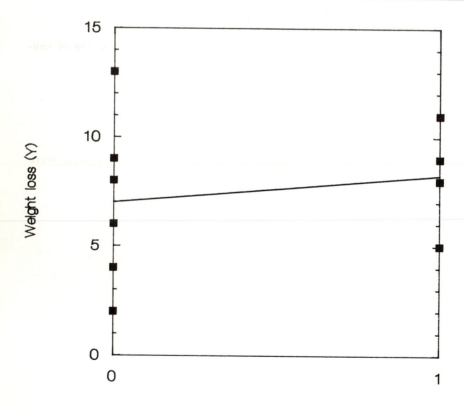

FIGURE 3.1
Plot of Y against dummy variable X_4, for the weight-loss data set.

3.2.2   The Slope of an Indicator Variable Is a Difference

We have defined the slope of a line as the amount it rises for a 1-unit increase in X. But in Fig. 3.1, there is only one such increase in X—the increase from 0 to 1. Thus the slope equals the difference between the two conditional means. The two means are 7.00 and 8.25, so their difference of 1.25 is the regression slope. Put the other way, the value that a computer calculates as the regression slope is really a difference.

In Sec. 5.4.1, we shall see a significance test for the null hypothesis that a true simple or partial regression slope is zero. When there is only one regressor and it is dichotomous, that test is equivalent to the familiar two-group t test for the null hypothesis that two means are equal. In the present example, the difference between the two means is 1.25. Using the ordinary formula for the standard error of a difference between means and assuming equal population variances, we estimate the standard error of the difference to be 2.221. By the t test, the significance of the difference is tested by computing $t = 1.25/2.221 = .5627$, $df = N - 2 = 8$, $p = .59$ (two-tailed). The regression test in Sec. 5.4.1 would give exactly the same values of t and p.

Similar principles apply when the dichotomous regressor is one of several. In multiple regression analysis, the slope of a dichotomous regressor coded 0, 1 can be interpreted as the Y difference between the two groups, adjusted for differences between the groups on other regressors. For instance, when all four regressors are used in the current example, we find $b_4 = -.4037$. This means that after adjusting or correcting for differences between the four women and six men on exercise, food intake, and metabolism, the women lost on the average about .4 pounds *less* than the men—less because women were coded as 1 and the regression slope was negative. By the test introduced in Sec. 5.4.1, this partial slope is not statistically significant.

3.2.3   A Graphic Representation

In Fig. 2.5 in Sec. 2.1.6, we saw an example in which the regression slope of X_1 equaled the vertical distance between parallel lines of best fit for X_2 where the lines apply to X_1 values 1 unit apart. If there is a dichotomous regressor scored 0, 1, then the adjusted slope or adjusted difference for the dichotomous regressor can be interpreted as the vertical distance between two parallel lines or planes of best fit for the other regressors. For instance, if we regress Y on the numerical regressors of exercise (X_1) and food intake (X_2) and the dichotomous regressor of gender (X_4), we find $b_1 = 2.126$, $b_2 = -.584$, $b_4 = -1.008$, and $a = 6.571$, so the model is

$$\hat{Y} = 2.126X_1 - .584X_2 - 1.008X_4 + 6.571$$

When $X_4 = 0$, this equation reduces to

$$\hat{Y} = 2.126X_1 - .584X_2 + 6.571$$

whereas when $X_4 = 1$, it reduces to

$$\hat{Y} = 2.126X_1 - .584X_2 - 1.008 + 6.571 = 2.126X_1 - .584X_2 + 5.563$$

Each of these models of Y can be represented by a tilted plane. Putting both planes in the same figure gives Fig. 3.2, in which the upper tilted plane represents the model for men and the parallel plane just below it represents the model for women. The vertical distance between the two planes is 1.008, which is b_4. This is the difference between the average weight losses of the four women and six men in the sample, adjusted for differences between the groups on exercise and food intake. When hypothesis tests are introduced in Chap. 5, we will see that the difference between these two planes is not statistically significant.

3.2.4   The Disadvantage of Artificial Categorization

Scientists using analysis of variance often artificially transform numerical variables into categorical variables—for instance, dividing numerical variables like exercise and food intake into two levels (low and high) or three levels (low,

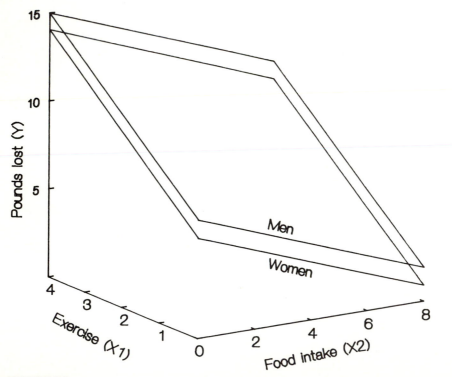

FIGURE 3.2
A model of weight loss which fits separate but parallel planes for men and women.

medium, high). This is done primarily to simplify computation. But this computational simplification is not necessary when using regression analysis, and it has three disadvantages: it lowers statistical power, it increases computation time if three or more categories are used, and it changes the meaning of the hypothesis tested. If a 5-point scale is treated as a multicategorical variable, then the conclusion that the five groups differ from each other on Y is not at all the same as the conclusion that Y increases or decreases with higher scores on the scale.

But there are at least two occasions when dichotomous variables *are* recommended. First, suppose you can include only a limited number of subjects in a study but you can scan many subjects to select a few for your study. If you want one of the regressors to be a natural numerical variable like age or wealth and you are confident that the effect of this natural variable on Y is linear, then power is maximized by using two extreme groups—for example, very old and very young, or very poor and very rich. Second, when a regressor is manipulated and is assumed to have a linear effect on Y, then power is maximized by having just two groups—very high and very low.

3.3   REGRESSION TO THE MEAN

3.3.1   How Regression Got Its Name

In its most general form, regression to the mean applies whenever two variables X and Y are correlated less than perfectly in a sample of cases. The principle asserts that if we select a subsample of cases with extreme scores on X, then the subsample's mean on Y will almost always be less extreme than its mean on X—that is, it will *regress* toward the mean of the total sample. Sec. 3.3 explains why, and shows how the phenomenon can lead the unwary researcher into a variety of errors which are avoided by the proper use of linear models. When Sir Francis Galton first noticed the phenomenon in the late nineteenth century, he considered it so important that the linear models he used came to be known as *regression* models.

3.3.2   The Basic Phenomenon

Galton noticed the phenomenon when he studied the heights of a large sample of middle-aged men and their grown sons. He observed that most of the older men who were above average in height had sons shorter than they, while most of the older men who were shorter than average had sons taller than they. In other words, the heights of the sons were regressing toward the mean height. This regression seemed to imply that the younger generation was more homogeneous in height than the older generation. But this conclusion was not supported; the standard deviation of the sons' heights was found to be almost exactly equal to the standard deviation of the fathers' heights. This equality of standard deviations seemed to contradict the regression; how could both be true?

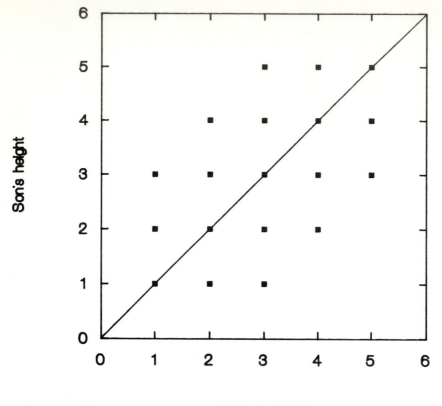

FIGURE 3.3
Simple data set illustrating regression to the mean.

We now know that this paradox was caused not by any peculiar proper-ties of the English or father-son pairs or height, but by the very general statistical phenomenon of regression to the mean. For simplicity, suppose we measure height on a 5-point scale: 1 is far below average, 2 is slightly below average, 3 is average, 4 is slightly above average, and 5 is far above average. Also for simplicity, imagine a sample of 19 fathers and their grown sons. Let the height of the fathers be denoted by X and the height of the sons by Y. Then Fig. 3.3 shows an imaginary data set that illustrates our paradox. The dot in the upper right corner represents a family in which both the father and the son score 5, the dot below it represents a family in which the father scores 5 and the son scores 4, and so on.

In the figure, the distributions of X and Y are identical; each variable has three scores of 1, four scores of 2, five scores of 3, four scores of 4, and three scores of 5. In this artificial example, then, the heights of the sons are distributed just like the heights of the fathers. Therefore the mean and standard deviation of the sons' heights equal the mean and standard deviation of the fathers' heights.

Now note the diagonal line:

- For the five cases along the line, $X = Y$. In these five families, the son's height equals the father's.
- For the seven cases above the line, $Y > X$. In these seven families, the son's height exceeds the father's.
- For the seven cases below the line, $Y < X$. In these seven families, the father's height exceeds the son's.

The seven families with fathers below average in height are represented by the seven leftmost dots in the figure. Four of these seven dots are above the diagonal line, meaning that the sons are taller than their fathers. Therefore most of the shorter-than-average fathers have sons taller than they.

The seven families with fathers above average in height are represented by the seven rightmost dots in the figure. Four of these seven dots are below the diagonal line, meaning that the sons are shorter than their fathers. Therefore most of the taller-than-average fathers have sons shorter than they.

We see that this example has all the features of the paradox: most taller-than-average fathers have sons shorter than they, and most shorter-than-average fathers have sons taller than they, but the standard deviation of sons' heights equals that of the fathers'.

Notice that the effect is symmetric; most of the tallest *sons* have fathers shorter than they, and most of the shortest sons have fathers taller than they. That would lead you to think that the standard deviation of the sons' heights exceeds that of the fathers' heights, while the original paradox led you to believe that the opposite was true, although in fact the two standard deviations are equal.

One way of resolving the paradox is to note that if we select a subsample of fathers at or near the mean height, such as the five cases scoring 3 in the present example, the sons' heights in that subsample are *less* close to the mean than the fathers' heights. This balances out the other subsamples in which sons' heights are generally closer to the mean than fathers' heights.

We can also describe regression to the mean in terms of *gain* or difference scores, defined as $Y - X$. Then regression to the mean implies that gains correlate negatively with X. In the current example, each father-son pair is a case; each case's gain or loss (a loss is a negative gain) equals its distance above or below the diagonal line in Fig. 3.3. The three cases at $X = 1$ have gains of 0, 1, 2; the four at $X = 2$ have gains of $-1, 0, 1, 2$; the five cases at $X = 3$ have gains of $-2, -1, 0, 1, 2$; the four at $X = 4$ have gains of $-2, -1, 0, 1$; and the three at $X = 5$ have gains of $-2, -1, 0$. All these gains are plotted in Fig. 3.4. We see a clear negative correlation of gain with X; the correlation in this figure is $-.5$.

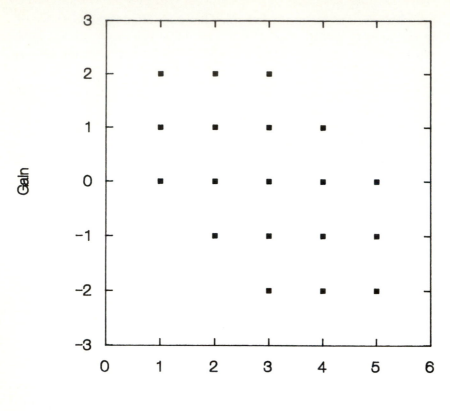

FIGURE 3.4
The negative correlation between gain and X.

3.3.3 Four Versions of the Phenomenon

The phenomenon of regression to the mean can be stated in several different ways, depending on the conditions. For simplicity, let us think in terms of a subsample selected for high scores on X. Parallel rules apply for subsamples selected for low scores on X and for those selected for high or low scores on Y.

The father-son example has included four conditions:

1. Two variables X and Y correlate imperfectly.
2. X and Y are measured in equal units.
3. X and Y have equal standard deviations.
4. X and Y have equal means.

When all four conditions hold, as in the father-son example, we can say that in a subsample selected for high scores on X, scores on Y will tend to be *below* those on X.

If we discard the last of the four conditions, so that X and Y no longer have equal means, then we can say that the subsample's scores will tend to be *closer to the overall mean* on Y than on X. The three remaining conditions are also the minimum conditions for asserting confidently that gain correlates negatively with X. For instance, if "the rich get richer and the poor get poorer," then gain in wealth correlates *positively* with initial wealth—but then inequality of wealth is increasing, so the two standard deviations are not equal.

If we further discard the second and third conditions, then the subsample's scores are no longer necessarily closer to the overall mean on Y than on X. But even given only the first of the four conditions (imperfect correlation between X and Y), we can still use the most general form of the regression principle—that the subsample's scores will be *less extreme* on Y than on X. For instance, let X and Y be height and weight. These variables are not measured in equal units, so it is not even meaningful to ask whether their means and standard deviations are equal. But it is still meaningful to ask whether Fred is more extreme on height than on weight, by referring to ranks or standard scores on height and weight. That is the sense in which regression to the mean still applies.

3.3.4   Four Errors Fostered by Regression to the Mean

Regression to the mean is often overlooked even by those who have studied it. This oversight produces four common errors:

1. *Incorrectly estimating a person's score on one measure from the person's score on a parallel measure.* If a person scores 1 standard deviation above the mean on one measure X, it is all too easy to estimate that the same person will score about 1 standard deviation above the mean on Y because Y is correlated with X. The correct estimate is in fact shown by formulas from Chap. 1. If X and Y are both expressed in standard scores, then $S_X = S_Y = 1$, so

$$b = r_{XY}\frac{S_Y}{S_X} = r_{XY}$$

Since standard scores have means of 0, we also have

$$a = M_Y - bM_X = 0 - b \times 0 = 0$$

Therefore

$$\hat{Y} = bX + a = r_{XY} X$$

We thus see that the best estimate of someone's standard score on Y is not the person's standard score on X, but r_{XY} times that score. Thus, for instance, if $r_{XY} = .6$, then someone who scores 2 standard deviations above the mean on X would be estimated to score $.6 \times 2 = 1.2$ standard deviations above the mean on Y. The regression method was named for its ability to estimate accurately the amount of regression to the mean in problems like this.

2. *Incorrectly assuming that S_Y must be below S_X because regression to the mean has been observed.* As we saw earlier, if most taller-than-average fathers have sons shorter than they while most shorter-than-average fathers have sons taller than they, it seems inevitable that the heights of the sons will be less variable than the heights of the fathers. But we have seen the fallacy in this conclusion.

3. *Inventing some causal mechanism to explain the phenomenon when it is adequately explained by chance variation.* For instance, suppose 19 students in a course take one exam X and then take a second exam Y a few weeks later. If the two sets of exam scores do not correlate perfectly with each other, then the people with the highest or lowest scores on the first exam will attain less extreme scores on the second. If you noticed this in a set of real data, you might think that those who scored highest on the first exam had not studied so hard for the second while those who scored lowest on the first had worked especially hard before the second. But in fact there is no evidence for this conclusion; regression to the mean will occur whenever two measures correlate less than perfectly.

4. *Using gain as a dependent variable in experiments lacking random assignment.* In Sec. 3.3.5 we examine this error in more detail, and show how it can be avoided through a linear model that includes pretest score as a covariate.

3.3.5 How Linear Models Correct for Regression to the Mean

The last error in the list above can be illustrated with a simple example. To evaluate a course in driver safety, we might count the number of traffic accidents involving students of the course in the years before and after taking the course and call the difference in accident rates a gain in safety. We might compare the mean gain among these students with the mean gain in another group of drivers. But it may be that students in the course have had far more room for improvement, especially if many of them were required to take the course because of accidents they had caused. Thus we would expect a far greater gain in measured safety (drop in accident rate) in the student group than in the comparison group, even if the course has had no effect.

We really want to know whether there is a difference between the student and comparison groups in safety gain, when the previous accident rate is controlled. We can do this simply by including that rate as a covariate. Thus in the current example we might define the dependent variable Y as drop in accident rate and include two regressors: previous accident rate, and a dummy variable measuring attendance in the course.

The general point is that when we define a dependent variable as gain or change from a pretest to a posttest, we are almost always most interested in measuring that gain with the pretest level controlled. We can do this simply by including pretest score as a covariate in the analysis.

An alternative design is actually equivalent, and slightly simpler. If a dependent variable is gain or change and one of the regressors is pretest score, then the slopes b_j for all *other* regressors will be exactly the same as if the dependent variable were simply posttest score rather than gain. And b_j for pretest will simply increase by exactly 1. To see why, imagine we derived the regression

$$\text{Gain} = .4 \times \text{pretest} + .7 \times \text{age} + 8$$

But gain = posttest − pretest so posttest = pretest + gain. Replacing gain in this equation by the right side of the first equation gives

$$\text{Posttest} = 1.4 \times \text{pretest} + .7 \times \text{age} + 8$$

Thus the same data set will yield either regression, depending on whether the dependent variable is entered as gain or posttest. But the coefficient of age is the same in both equations.

Thus the measured effect of each independent variable is exactly the same, regardless of whether gain or posttest score is used as the dependent variable. Therefore, there is no need to use actual change scores, though they may make the research results easier for others to understand.

3.3.6 Ratios versus Residuals

Scientists sometimes try to correct for a variable X by taking the ratio between X and the dependent variable Y. But our criticisms of gain scores apply to ratios as well. For instance, scientists often express the weight of an animal's organ— its brain or ovary, say—as a proportion of the animal's total body weight, in order to correct or adjust the organ's weight for the animal's body weight. But ratios, like differences, may correlate either positively or negatively with the variable corrected for—body weight, in this example. For instance, within almost every broad class of animals, such as mammals, fish, birds, amphibians, or reptiles, the largest species have the smallest ratios of brain weight to body weight—scientists disagree why. The only species whose average brain weight/body weight ratios substantially exceed the human ratio are very small mammals like shrews.

Since the same phenomenon occurs in fish, birds, and other types of animals, it seems misleading to say that shrews have larger brains than humans after adjustment for the difference in body weight. Rather, it seems more appropriate to fit a regression line predicting brain weight from body weight

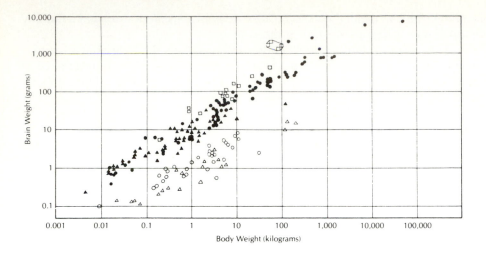

FIGURE 3.5
Brain size of 200 species of living vertebrates plotted against body size on logarithmic scales. Open squares are primates, with humans included in the circled box of four squares. Mammals are solid dots, birds solid triangles, bony fishes open circles, and reptiles open triangles. (*From Bonner, 1980, p. 46*)

and to use residuals as measures of brain weight corrected for body weight. This is exactly what specialists in this area do. By this measure humans have the largest brains of all land animals, after correcting for differences in body size. You can see this by imagining a regression line such as the one in Fig. 3.5.

Like most work done by specialists in this area, this figure uses logarithms of both brain size and body size. The difference between the logarithms of two numbers is the logarithm of the ratio of the numbers, so on a logarithmic scale two creatures weighing 10 and 20 grams are as far apart as two creatures weighing 1000 and 2000 kilograms. The use of logarithms ensures that the difference between shrews and squirrels will not be totally submerged by the inclusion of whales and elephants. If you have never studied logarithms, be assured that they are more accessible than they were a generation ago; the logarithm of a number is the value you get when you enter the number in your calculator and press the button labeled LOG. Logarithms are discussed more fully in Chap. 12.

Figure 3.6 illustrates similar points for humans and great apes. The figure shows average brain volumes and body weights for the four species of great ape. Average weights for pygmy chimpanzees and gorillas are about 35 kilograms, and 105 kilograms, while brain volumes are about 340 and 500 cubic centimeters. Thus the gorilla weighs about 3 times the weight of the pygmy chimpanzee, but its brain volume is less than 1.5 times that of the pygmy chimp. The use of ratios suggests that the gorilla's brain is much smaller than the pygmy chimp's after correction for body weight. But in the figure, the four species fall almost exactly in a straight line. If we use the line to suggest the "normal" relation between brain size and body weight, then the four species are about equal in corrected brain size. But the figure also shows that the human brain is about 3 times the size of 400 cubic centimeters we would expect for a great ape of our size.

We do not mean to say that ratios are never useful. They are certainly understood by more readers than are residuals of logarithms. However, if you use ratios, you should normally check to see whether they correlate with X, and then consider whether that affects the analysis. If the correlation is negligible, that fact can be stated; you can then avoid the complexities of logarithms while reassuring readers who prefer residuals.

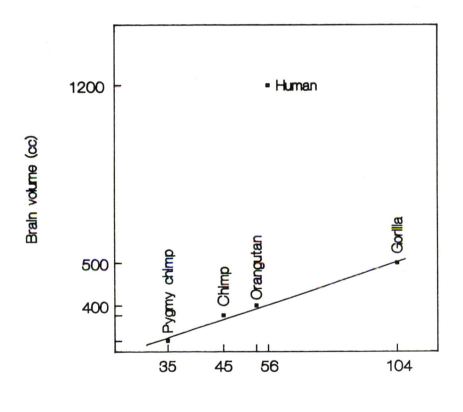

FIGURE 3.6
Brain size versus body weight for humans and the four species of great ape. (*From Bonner, 1980, p. 50*)

3.4 MULTIDIMENSIONAL SETS

Many measures of interest can be thought of as multidimensional. For instance, we could probably construct an attitude measure that most people would agree measures at least roughly what they mean by the word *liberalism*. But if we wished to assess liberalism in a more comprehensive manner, we might create several different scales—for instance, measures of liberalism in foreign policy, liberalism in economic policy, and liberalism on social issues such as abortion and school prayer. We would then be representing liberalism as a *multidimensional set* of variables. Or we might think of socioeconomic status (SES) as being composed of three variables: income, occupational prestige, and years and quality of education.

To say that some external variable is unrelated to a set is to say that it is uncorrelated with all the variables in the set. For instance, to say that a measure of political preference is unrelated to SES is to say that it is uncorrelated with all three variables in the SES set—which is also to say there is a multiple correlation R of 0 between preference and the SES set.

A single analysis may contain two or more sets of variables. For instance, we might have a *demographic set* including age, race, and gender, and a *socioeconomic set* including income, education, and occupational prestige. Or one set might simply be a "miscellaneous" set including all regressors in an analysis that do not measure, for instance, SES.

3.4.1 The Partial and Semipartial
Multiple Correlation

In Sec. 2.3.5 we said that a regressor's *unique contribution* to a regression can be defined as the amount R^2 would drop if the regressor were removed from the analysis. We saw that this unique contribution equals 0 if and only if $sr_j = 0$, which implies that the other measures of partial relationship (b_j, beta$_j$, and pr_j) also equal 0. These ideas can be extended to sets.

Let A and B denote two *sets* of variables. For example, let set A include several demographic measures while set B includes several SES measures. We shall define the partial multiple correlation $PR(B.A)$ as the multiple correlation between Y and set B with all the variables in set A held constant. To be precise, if P_B is the number of variables in set B, imagine P_B separate regressions in which each of these B variables is regressed on (predicted from) all the variables in set A. The residuals in all these regressions give us P_B variables which we can call the *portions* or *components* of B independent of A. Imagine also regressing Y onto the set of A variables; the residuals there are the portion of Y independent of A. Finally, imagine regressing this portion of Y onto the portions of set B independent of A; the multiple correlation in this regression is $PR(B.A)$. If set B has only one variable, the value of $PR(B.A)$ equals the absolute value of the ordinary partial correlation.

We can similarly define a semipartial multiple correlation $SR(B.A)$ as the correlation between *all* of Y and the portions of set B independent of set A. Again, if set B has only one variable, $SR(B.A)$ reduces to the absolute value of the ordinary semipartial correlation.

We do not have to actually compute all these residuals to find $SR(B.A)$ and $PR(B.A)$; they are easily calculated from other statistics. Define $R(A)$ as the multiple correlation between Y and set A, and define $R(AB)$ as the overall multiple correlation when both A and B variables are in the regression. Then

$$SR(B.A)^2 = R(AB)^2 - R(A)^2$$

while

$$PR(B.A)^2 = \frac{SR(B.A)^2}{1 - R(A)^2}$$

$$= \frac{R(AB)^2 - R(A)^2}{1 - R(A)^2}$$

These formulas are consistent with previous interpretations of partial correlations. $SR(B.A)^2$ is the *unique contribution of set B* to the regression. If we think of Y as standardized to unit variance, then $SR(B.A)^2$ is the amount of Y variance explained by set B independent of A. And the denominator $1 - R(A)^2$ of the last ratio is the amount of Y variance unexplained by A, so $PR(B.A)^2$ is the proportion of previously unexplained variance explained by set B. A similar interpretation of pr_j^2 was given in Sec. 2.3.5.

The formulas also show clearly another useful fact about a partial or semipartial multiple correlation: to say that $PR(B.A) = 0$ or $SR(B.A) = 0$ is to say that the multiple correlation between Y and set A equals that between Y and sets A and B together. Adding set B to set A does not increase the regression's ability to explain variance in Y.

3.4.2   What It Means If $PR = 0$

In the SES example, the word *correlation* strongly suggested positive simple correlations, but that is not a necessary property of multiple and partial multiple correlations. For instance, suppose we want to study the relation between a city's rate of homelessness and the two variables of poverty rate and availability of public housing. One social scientist might guess that the homelessness rate is related primarily to the poverty rate, while a second guesses it is related primarily to the availability of public housing. A third might guess that homelessness is related to the *difference* between the poverty rate and the availability of public housing (expressed as a proportion of the city's population). A fourth scientist might guess that only two-thirds of poor people want to live in public housing, so that homelessness might be related to the difference between the availability of public housing and two-thirds of the poverty rate. A fifth scientist might guess that public housing is more a symptom of a problem than an effective cure and thus suggest a positive correlation between homelessness and public housing.

These five views are all quite different, but all imply that there is a correlation between homelessness rate and *some* linear function of poverty rate and public housing availability—so all imply a nonzero multiple correlation between the homelessness rate and the other two variables. If the multiple correlation were found to be zero, it would contradict all five of these views plus many others involving other specific combinations of the two variables. Thus, a hypothesis test on a single multiple correlation, of the type introduced in Chap. 5, can test an entire array of specific hypotheses. This is true even if some of the hypotheses involve negative correlations.

A related set of questions might be answered by a partial multiple correlation. Homelessness might be higher in larger cities or in cities with warmer climates—Miami currently has the nation's highest rate of homelessness. Suppose we want to see whether homelessness relates to poverty and public housing while controlling these variables. We could then include a city's population and average winter temperature in set A, include poverty rate and public housing availability in set B, and examine the relation of homelessness to set B with set A held constant.

3.4.3 Collinear Sets

As mentioned in Sec. 2.3.5, collinearity between two regressors occurs when they correlate highly, and this correlation diminishes the unique contribution of each to the regression. In larger problems, collinearity may pervade an entire set of regressors. In fact, the examples we have used, involving liberalism and SES, might have this property. Three measures of liberalism might correlate so highly with each other that when they are used together in a regression, any one might contribute nearly as much to the regression as the entire set of three. They then form a *collinear set*—a set whose members all correlate highly and thereby lower each other's unique contribution. (Collinearity is frequently defined in terms of the standard errors of regression slopes. We shall show in Chap. 5 that this definition is essentially equivalent to the one given here.) Occasionally, collinearity may pervade all the regressors in an analysis, but the usual situation is for it to pervade merely one set of regressors, not affecting others in the same analysis.

3.5 A GLANCE AT THE BIG PICTURE

This section explains how regression analysis relates to several other statistical methods; it also lists a number of difficulties and complications that can arise. This discussion has a dual role. First, as the section title implies, it conveys a rough impression of the role regression plays in a larger context. Second,

Sec. 3.5.3, in particular, is intended for later use, as a checklist of the problems that you should think about in planning a regression analysis.

3.5.1 Further Extensions of Regression

The previous sections of this chapter have described several extensions of the basic type of linear model introduced in Chap. 2. More are still to come. Chapter 4 examines the use of linear models in *causal analysis*, and Chap. 6 in *prediction*. Chapter 5 introduces *inferential methods*—estimation, hypothesis tests, and confidence bands. Chapter 7 introduces the concept of *indirect effects*, in which one variable affects another through a third. In Chap. 10 we shall see that a *multicategorical regressor* can be treated as a set of dichotomous variables. For instance, the multicategorical variable of religion can be thought of as a set of yes-no questions: for example, "Are you Protestant?" or "Are you Catholic?" A variable treated this way is called a *factor*. By *nesting* factors, we can analyze category systems with multiple levels. For instance, we might categorize religion at the level of major religion (Christian or Jewish, for example), at the level of denomination (Baptist, Catholic), and at the level of subdenomination (such as Southern Baptist).

In Chap. 12, we will see ways of fitting *curves and curved surfaces* rather than straight lines and planes to a data set. A great many curvilinear relations can be fitted by the techniques of Chap. 12. Still more can be fitted by more complex techniques not covered in this book, such as the NONLIN program in SYSTAT or PROC NLIN in SAS.

Extensions of the analysis-of-variance concept of *interaction* (differences between differences) are treated in Chap. 13. Interaction allows you to fit models in which one variable's relationship to Y is higher for some subjects than for others—for instance, the relationship or partial relationship between wealth and political conservatism might be higher among men than among women, or might decrease with years of education.

Regression models can also be fitted *without the constant*, to force the regression plane to pass through the origin; see Sec. 17.1. This might be useful, for instance, if you know that proficiency on a particular skill, such as knowledge of the Eskimo language, is zero for people who have zero hours of instruction and you want to fit a regression line predicting proficiency from hours of instruction and you also want to force that line to pass through the origin.

The *weighted least-squares* method is a variation of regression analysis in which some cases are given more weight than others in fitting the regression plane; see Sec. 17.2. This is especially useful if the units of analysis are aggregates—say, cities or nations—and you want to give larger aggregates more weight than smaller ones.

All the extensions and variations above are available even in the free program MYSTAT. Others, described below, are available in SYSTAT and SAS but not in MYSTAT.

MANOVA (multivariate analysis of variance) is an extension of regression analysis that allows you to test whether the variables in a regression have the same relative weight in affecting one dependent variable as another; see Secs. 17.3 and 17.4. For instance, SES might be less important, relative to other variables, in affecting mathematics achievement than in affecting vocabulary, or gender might have a more important effect on attitudes about foreign affairs than it has on attitudes about domestic affairs.

Repeated-measures models can be used if the same dependent variable is measured two or more times, or if several dependent variables have scales with the same units; see Sec. 17.5. For instance, the same attitude might be measured several times for the same subjects, or attitudes toward several different ethnic groups might be measured on comparable scales. In MANOVA there is no requirement that the dependent variables have similar scales. For instance, in an example just cited, proficiency in mathematics might be measured on a 100-point scale while vocabulary is measured on a 50-point scale.

3.5.2   How Regression Relates to Other Methods

Some problems require computer programs other than regression programs, even though the problems are quite similar conceptually to regression and the user familiar with regression can often use these other methods with a minimum of additional study. In most cases, regression can be used to approximate the more accurate results obtained from the more specialized methods.

Four methods differ from regression primarily in being designed for categorical dependent variables while regression is restricted to numerical dependent variables. The differences among these four techniques also involve types of variables. *Discriminant analysis* requires that all regressors be numerical and normally distributed. *Log-linear analysis* requires that all regressors be categorical. *Probit analysis* and *logit analysis*, or *logistic regression*, are more general, allowing any mix of numerical and categorical regressors. Chapters 18 and 19 are devoted to these methods, especially to logistic regression and log-linear analysis. SYSTAT has different modules or sections; discriminant analysis is performed with the regression module, and log-linear analysis is performed with the module for contingency tables. Simple logistic models can be fitted with SYSTAT's general nonlinear program NONLIN, though there is also an extra-cost module named LOGIT.

Survival analysis applies when the dependent variable is the time or date at which an event occurs and by definition the event can occur only once for each person, such as death or first marriage.

Censored regression can be used when scores above a certain level cannot be recorded. For instance, a meter may go only so high, or subjects who take longer than an hour at a task may not be allowed to finish, so that no exact measure is available of the time they would take.

Time-series analysis is superior to regression analysis for some inferential purposes when the units of analysis are sequential time periods, such as months or years. The example on changes in the population of the United States, in Sec. 1.5.4, illustrates this kind of data.

Other methods use regression and cannot be understood or used effectively without a knowledge of regression, but deal with problems substantially more complicated. The *two-stage least-squares* method is a method widely used in economics and sociology for studying variables that affect each other—for instance, national income affects consumer spending, but spending also affects national income. *Factor analysis* is a method for studying patterns among a large number of dependent variables—for instance, many measures of attitudes, aptitudes, or skills—to discover patterns of relationship among them when no independent variables are measured at all. *LISREL* is a very general computer program that applies to many of the same problems as two-stage least squares and factor analysis, as well as to problems which seemingly lend themselves to regression analysis but in which variables are measured imperfectly. LISREL is so general and so complex that we cannot begin to describe all its uses here.

All these methods, including regression, start with a *rectangular score matrix* which contains the scores of *N* subjects or units on several variables. An individual investigator may start instead with a correlation or covariance matrix, but typically that matrix itself is derived from a rectangular score matrix. *Multidimensional scaling* and *cluster analysis* differ from all these methods in starting from a triangular matrix of similarities, such as subjects' judgments of the level of similarities between kinds of automobiles, or the frequency with which laboratory rats confuse two stimuli. They search for patterns of similarity among the objects rated, in a manner somewhat similar to the way factor analysis searches for patterns of similarity among variables.

All these methods except LISREL are available in SYSTAT itself or in extra-cost additions to SYSTAT, and all except LISREL and multidimensional scaling are available in SAS.

In summary, regression analysis requires the following conditions:

1. There must be a set of *cases* or *units*. If this condition is violated, then virtually all statistical methods are inapplicable.
2. Each of those cases must have known scores on several *variables*, each of which is numerical, dichotomous, or multicategorical. A set of 100 biographies from the library satisfies condition 1 but not this one.
3. Scores on the variables must form a *rectangular score matrix*. If this condition is violated and the question is how cases relate to each other, then consider cluster analysis or multidimensional scaling.
4. One variable must be identifiable as the *dependent variable*. If there are several, consider two-stage least squares, LISREL, factor analysis, MANOVA, or repeated-measures analysis. The last two of these are actually extensions of regression analysis and use regression programs in both SYSTAT and SAS. But this book discusses them only briefly, in Chap. 17.

5. The dependent variable must be numerical. If it is not, consider logit, probit, log-linear, or discriminant analysis.

6. If the special conditions for time-series analysis, survival analysis, censored regression, or weighted least squares apply, then use those methods. Again, the last is a special type of regression analysis.

3.5.3   Some Difficulties and Limitations

This section lists the major problems that can arise in regression analysis. It is included here to assure you early in the book that statisticians have thought about these problems. You may also find it convenient to use this section as a checklist when planning an analysis. Of course, no list can cover all conceivable problems, and this list is not meant as a substitute for careful thought or common sense.

1. *Undercontrol* is the basic problem we have considered from the very beginning of the book—failure to control all relevant variables.

2. *Overcontrol* means destroying an otherwise valid design by including as covariates variables affected by Y; see Sec. 8.1.4.

3. *Collinearity* is the loss of power of hypothesis tests and precision of estimation that results from highly correlated regressors. As emphasized in Sec. 5.4.5, collinearity does not destroy the validity of regression analyses. See also Secs. 5.3.2, 5.4.4, and 8.1.2.

4. *Singularity* is the inability to compute regression slopes at all because at least one regressor is perfectly predictable from other regressors; see Sec. 8.1.3.

5. *Nonlinearity* occurs when a curved line or surface fits the data better than a straight line or plane; see Chap. 12.

6. *Interaction* occurs when one regressor's relationship to Y depends on the score on another regressor; see Chap. 13.

7. *Heteroscedasticity* means that the conditional Y distributions do not all have equal standard deviations. This destroys the validity of ordinary methods of statistical inference in regression. See Chap. 14, especially Sec. 14.1.8.

8. *Nonnormality* means that conditional Y distributions are not normal; see Chap. 14.

9. *Outliers* are cases with Y scores that are extreme for their pattern of regressor scores; see Chap. 14.

10. *Leverage points* are cases with very unusual patterns of X scores. They do not destroy the validity of regression by themselves, but they make it more difficult to detect outliers. See Sec. 14.1.4.

11. *Influential outliers* are cases that heavily affect one or more partial regression slopes, even if they are not leverage points or ordinary outliers. See Sec. 14.1.6.

12. *Noninterval scaling* arises when units along a scale do not have comparable meanings; see Secs. 8.1.5 and 17.6.

13. *Range restriction* occurs when cases with high or low scores on some regressors are disproportionately omitted from the sample; see Sec. 8.1.6.

14. Some computer programs for regression are susceptible to *rounding error* in calculations; see Sec. 8.1.8 and Sec. 17.8.

15. *Missing data* occur when a case has known scores on some variables and unknown scores on others, as when some people omit their income from questionnaires. See Sec. 8.1.7.

16. *Measurement error* is perhaps the most common and important problem of all. It occurs when variables are simply not measured accurately. See Secs. 8.2 and 17.7.

3.5.4   An Example on Deterring War

Despite all these potential problems, it is amazing how often linear models are at least somewhat useful. For instance, virtually every citizen is concerned about the causes of war. Debates on the topic are usually frustrating because they often focus on a few incidents that may be atypical. For instance, in the 1930s it was widely believed that World War I had occurred primarily because of secret treaties and the willingness of the great powers to mobilize and attack in response to small provocations. Whether right or wrong, that belief may have led to World War II, which may have been caused by just the opposite situation—the unwillingness of the great powers to act decisively and promptly to contain an obviously expansionist state. Then, a generation later, our desire to avoid repeating the error of the 1930s may have led to our ill-advised intervention in Vietnam. In each instance, momentous national decisions were made with most of the historical references focusing on just one case each.

Several recent works have collected dozens of instances of successful and unsuccessful attempts to avoid war, and subjected them to statistical analysis (Buena de Mesquita, 1981; Carsten, Howell, and Allen, 1984; Huth and Russett, 1984; Vasquez, 1987). We shall describe briefly the paper by Huth and Russett, which concerns attempts to avoid war by third-party deterrence—in which a defender seeks to prevent an attacker from invading a smaller nation by threatening retaliation. For instance, World War II began in Europe in 1939 when Britain and France failed in their attempt to deter Nazi Germany and the U.S.S.R. from invading Poland. Controlling covariates such as the relative strength of the defender and the attacker and the distance between the defender and the threatened nation, Huth and Russett used regression analysis to study the effect of several variables on success in preventing war. They found that hastily arranged mutual-defense treaties apparently had no effect or were actually counterproductive; the treaties were apparently interpreted as bluffs by attackers. But obvious mutual interests between the defender and the threatened nation, such as high trade volumes between them, made deterrence more effective by increasing the credibility of the defender's threats. World

War II fits this model well; Britain and France had little trade with Poland, and arranged a treaty with it at the last minute.

This analysis used *occasions* as the unit of analysis, and used logistic regression (see Chap. 18) because the dependent variable (success or failure in preventing war) was dichotomous. But familiarity with even ordinary regression analysis should enable anyone to read all of these important works on the prevention of war.

3.1   SUMMARY

3.1   Types of Case

Cases may also be called *units, observations, units of observation,* or *units of analysis*. Some common types of case are stimuli, groups of people or animals, neurons, and occasions.

3.2   Dichotomous Regressors

The use of categorical independent variables together with numerical covariates used to be called *analysis of covariance*. Dichotomized regressors scored 0, 1 are called *dummy* or *indicator* variables. An indicator variable's slope is a difference. If there are just one or two other regressors, then this slope can be represented as the vertical distance between two regression lines or planes. You can always use an indicator variable to transform a numerical variable into a dichotomy, but this loses power and is not advised.

3.3   Regression to the Mean

If X and Y are imperfectly correlated and you select from a sample or population all the most extreme cases on X, then those cases will not be as extreme on Y as they are on X. Similarly, if you select the cases most extreme on Y, they will not be as extreme on X as they are on Y.

Ignoring regression to the mean produces four common errors:

1. *Incorrectly estimating a score on one measure from a person's score on a parallel measure.* The best estimate of someone's standard score on Y is not the same person's standard score on X, but r_{XY} times that score. The regression method was named for its ability to estimate accurately the amount of regression to the mean in problems like this.

2. *Incorrectly assuming that S_Y must be below S_X because regression to the mean has been observed.*

3. *Inventing some mechanism to explain the phenomenon when it is adequately explained by chance variation.*

4. *Using gain as a dependent variable in experiments lacking random assignment.* When we define a dependent variable as gain or change from a pretest to a posttest, we are almost always most interested in measuring that gain

with the pretest level controlled. We can do this simply by including pretest score as a covariate in the analysis. But if we do that, we do not need to define the dependent variable as gain at all.

When you are considering using a ratio of two variables, consider instead using the "denominator" variable as a covariate. Also consider transforming both scales to logarithms.

3.4 Multidimensional Sets

Define the partial multiple correlation $PR(B.A)$ as the multiple correlation between Y and set B with all the variables in set A held constant. $PR(B.A)^2$ is the proportion of previously unexplained variance explained by set B. $PR(B.A) = 0$ if and only if the multiple correlation between Y and set A equals that between Y and sets A and B together.

We can also define $SR(B.A)$ as the semipartial multiple correlation between Y and set B with set A controlled.

$$SR(B.A)^2 = R(AB)^2 - R(A)^2$$

$PR(B.A) = 0$ or $SR(B.A) = 0$ if and only if no linear function of variables in set B correlates with Y when variables in set A are held constant.

3.5 A Glance at the Big Picture

Regression analysis is related to discriminant analysis, log-linear analysis, probit analysis, logit analysis or logistic regression, survival analysis, censored regression, time-series analysis, the two-stage least-squares method, factor analysis, and LISREL. All these methods, including regression analysis, start with a rectangular score matrix which contains the scores of N subjects or units on several variables. Multidimensional scaling and cluster analysis differ from all these methods in starting from a triangular matrix of similarities. They search for patterns of similarity among the objects rated.

Regression requires the following conditions:

1. There must be a set of *cases* or *units*.
2. Each of those cases must have known scores on several *variables*, each of which is numerical, dichotomous, or multicategorical.
3. Scores on the variables must form a *rectangular score matrix*.
4. One variable must be identifiable as the *dependent variable*.
5. The dependent variable must be numerical.
6. If the special conditions for time-series analysis, survival analysis, censored regression, or weighted least squares apply, then use those methods instead.

Sixteen difficulties and limitations in regression analysis are listed in this chapter and discussed more fully later.

KEY TERMS

case	analysis of covariance
unit	gain score
unit of observation	regression to the mean
unit of analysis	partial multiple correlation
indicator variable	semipartial multiple correlation
dummy variable	collinear set

SYMBOLS AND ABBREVIATIONS

PR   SR   R(A)   R(AB)

PROBLEMS

1. We have explicitly mentioned five types of case:
   (1) Individual people or animals
   (2) Stimuli
   (3) Groups of people or animals
   (4) Neurons
   (5) Events or occasions
   Identify the type of case implied by each of the following questions.
   (*a*) Do small nations tend to spend more or less per capita for arms than large nations when per capita income is controlled?
   (*b*) Are more babies born per day on weekdays or weekends?
   (*c*) Has Judge A in an art contest consistently chosen paintings with bright colors over more subdued paintings in previous contests?
   (*d*) Are most married women more liberal politically than their husbands?

2. Students took a pretest of gymnastic ability (*X*), were trained in gymnastics by either method P or method Q, and then were tested on a posttest (*Y*). Parts 1 through 6 of Fig. 3.7 represent six possible situations. In each part, the two small squares represent the means of the scatterplots of scores of students taught by methods P and Q. The within-group regression lines are also shown.

   Six of the descriptions *a* to *j* below match a diagram in Fig. 3.7, while the other four descriptions match no diagram. In each diagram one of the two small squares is clearly closer to the origin—the lower left corner of the diagram. For each description give the number (if any) of the diagram fitting the description, and the appropriate letter (P or Q) of the square closer to the origin.
   (a) The P and Q groups did not offer in mean pretest ability, but the P group outperformed the Q group on posttest.
   (b) The two groups did not differ on average posttest score. However, group Q was better on pretest, so method P appears to be more effective.
   (c) The Q students outperformed the P students on both pretest and posttest. However, it appears that method Q is superior because (surprisingly) there is no relation between pretest and posttest scores within groups. Thus the Q students gained no unfair advantage over the P students by virtue of being more able at pretest.

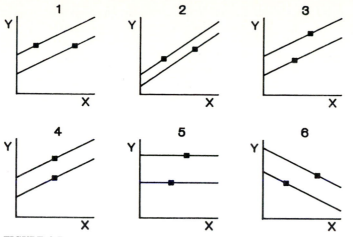

FIGURE 3.7
Six possible relations between treatment and control groups.

(d) Within groups there was no relation between pretest and posttest scores. However, we conclude that method P was superior to method Q because it started with poorer students and the difference between groups was smaller at posttest than at pretest.

(e) Both methods P and Q were so different from what these students had seen before that in both groups the students who did best on pretest actually did worse on posttest. The P students did worse than the Q students on pretest, but this was actually an advantage for the P students because of the negative relationship. Therefore we conclude that Q is a better method even though the P's outperformed the Q's on the posttest.

(f) Both methods P and Q were so different from what these students had seen before that in both groups the students who did best on pretest actually did worse on posttest. The Q students were superior on pretest and posttest, as well as on posttest after correcting for the difference on pretest.

(g) Group Q was above group P on posttest. However, Q was so much higher than P on pretest, and the relation within groups between pretest and posttest was so strong, that after correcting for the difference in pretest scores, P appears to be the better method.

(h) Groups P and Q did not differ on either the pretest or the posttest.

(i) Group P was above group Q on both pretest and posttest, and also after correcting for the pretest difference. The posttest difference exceeded the pretest difference.

(j) Group P was above group Q on both pretest and posttest, and also after correcting for the pretest difference. The pretest difference exceeded the posttest difference.

3. One of the 10 descriptions in Prob. 2 (a description which matched no diagram) reflected the error of using gain scores rather than partial relationship. Which description was that?

4. It is known that the pupils of the eyes dilate (become larger) when people see pictures they consider attractive. Pupil size can be measured from a photograph of the eyeball. Advertisers sometimes use pupil dilation as a measure of public acceptance of their products. The eyes are photographed just before subjects see a picture of the product, and again while they are viewing the product.

To test the effect of an advertising campaign, this was done both in a district that had been exposed to the campaign and in another district that had not. The following results were obtained:

   District with campaign
   Mean pupil size before seeing product: 8 mm; standard deviation, 3 mm
   Mean pupil size while seeing product: 12 mm; standard deviation, 4 mm
   Correlation between "before" and "after" measurements: .6; $N = 40$

   District without campaign
   Mean pupil size before seeing product: 9 mm; standard deviation, 4 mm
   Mean pupil size while seeing product: 10 mm; standard deviation, 8 mm
   Correlation between before and after measurements: .4; $N = 60$
   (a) What is the estimated effect of the advertising campaign, measured in millimeters of pupil dilation? Be sure to adjust for differences between districts in mean pupil size before subjects have seen the product.
   (b) If someone incorrectly used gain scores to answer part a, would the effect of the campaign be overestimated or underestimated? Show your work.

5. Examine the plot of $Y.C$ against $X.C$ that you made for Prob. 9 in Chap. 2. With what you know now, you should be able to use this plot to find, with almost no calculation, the partial regression slope of Y on X controlling for C. Verify your answer by using a definition given in Chap. 2 and a formula in Chap. 1. In the same way (using a definition in Chap. 2 and a formula in Chap. 1), find the partial correlation $r_{XY.C}$.

6. A researcher knew the scores of 100 college freshmen on two tests of academic aptitude and the answers the freshmen gave to three questions about their attitudes toward studying and academic success. The researcher also knew the students' grade-point averages (GPA) at the end of the freshman year. When GPA was predicted from aptitude scores alone, the multiple correlation was .5. When GPA was predicted from aptitude scores and attitudes, the multiple correlation was .7. Find the partial multiple correlation and the semipartial multiple correlation between attitude and GPA, controlling for aptitude.

CHAPTER
4

CAUSATION AND EXPERIMENTAL CONTROL

Now that you have a general idea of the applications of statistical control, it is time to consider its advantages and disadvantages relative to its principal competitor—experimental control, especially random assignment. The two can actually be used together, so they are not necessarily competitors, but we shall start by supposing that they are.

This is a chapter of lists. First, we have five limitations of statistical control that are overcome by random assignment. Then we describe five things often confused with random assignment, and five nonstandard forms of random assignment that are sometimes not correctly recognized as random assignment. We next describe seven limitations common to statistical control and random assignment, and then three problems often produced by or associated with random assignment in particular. A philosophical discussion of the concept of causation follows, and finally we present three reasons for combining statistical control with random assignment when both are practical.

4.1 WHY RANDOM ASSIGNMENT?

4.1.1 Limitations of Statistical Control

Statistical control has five major limitations:

1. The list of potential covariates is often endless. If we control statistically for age, race, sex, and income, then a critic may ask why we have not con-

trolled for education, IQ, and political preference. No matter how many variables are controlled, we always know that treatment and control groups must differ in some nonrandom way we do not fully understand, simply because the cases in the treatment group are in that group and others are not.

2. This problem cannot be avoided by indiscriminately controlling all variables that occur to us. A phenomenon called *overcontrol*, described in Sec. 8.1.4, means that a single covariate *added* improperly can invalidate an otherwise sound design.

3. Even if we could control all the right variables and no others, statistical control still does not tell us whether X affects Y or Y affects X.

4. Statistical control requires not only that we measure covariates, but that we measure them accurately. Covariates like SES and IQ, which are never measured with full accuracy, can never be fully controlled.

5. Statistical control cannot distinguish causation from correlation produced by excluding certain cases from the population. For instance, if we found a correlation between age and wealth in a society, we might at first say that age must have caused the wealth, because wealth cannot influence the date one was born. But if poor people die younger on the average, then there is a different sense in which wealth produces age. We will call this *correlation by selective exclusion*.

These five limitations imply the five assumptions necessary to infer causation from statistical control: that we have controlled all necessary variables, that we have controlled no variables that would distort the relationship, that Y does not affect X, that covariates are measured accurately, and that correlation is not produced by selective exclusion.

4.1.2   The Advantage of Random Assignment

Random assignment can provide an elegant way around these limitations. The essential feature of random assignment is that all covariates that are properties of cases, such as a person's age or education, are validly controlled without even being measured. If a study's validity depends upon the control of such covariates, then random assignment guarantees this validity more surely than statistical control.

Random assignment can give valid control of covariates even for very small samples. Validity means that significance at, say, the 5% level will be found only 5% of the time if the null hypothesis is correct; and designs with random assignment can have this property even if N is very small. Of course, if we use parametric methods that assume normal distributions, that assumption is especially important when N is small—but that is a separate issue.

We might imagine an argument against random assignment that goes like this. Even with random assignment to treatment and control groups, there is a

5% chance that the two groups will differ on average age at the 5% level of significance. There is also a 5% chance that the two groups will differ on average educational level. Likewise for income, race, sex, IQ scores, and other covariates. When we consider that the number of potential covariates is infinite, the two groups certainly differ significantly on at least one. Then what have we gained by random assignment?

This argument is answered by recalling that while there may be many covariates, there is typically only one dependent variable. If assignment is random, then the probability is only 5% that the two groups will differ significantly (at the .05 level) *on the dependent variable* by chance alone.

Therefore random assignment, even with no attention at all paid to covariates, can produce valid hypothesis tests more surely than the most exhaustive and careful statistical control. If this argument seems incomplete to you, there is good cause; wait until we consider the limitations of random assignment in Sec. 4.2.

4.1.3 The Meaning of Random Assignment

Random assignment is often confused with five other things, so that random assignment is often claimed to exist when it does not. On the other hand, there are five unusual forms of random assignment which may not be correctly recognized as random assignment. The five things often confused with random assignment are:

1. *Mere manipulation.* Random assignment requires us to manipulate subjects (except in unusual cases like lotteries); but manipulation, though a necessary condition, is not a sufficient condition for random assignment. We are manipulating subjects even when we just require them to sit still and listen to our directions, but that does not mean that we have random assignment.

2. *Other types of randomization.* As mentioned in Sec. 1.1.2, random assignment must not be confused with other types of randomization. A researcher may randomize the order of presentation of stimuli, or randomize which form of a test each subject takes; but that does not constitute random assignment unless these are the effects under study.

3. *Forced equality of cell frequencies.* Some analysis-of-variance designs require forced equality of cell frequencies, but that requirement actually makes random assignment more difficult unless the experimenter uses the proper procedure. Suppose an experimenter has a 2×2 design and flips a coin twice for each subject, using the first flip to place the subject in a row and the second flip to place that subject in a column. Then assignment is random, but the four cells will probably end up with unequal cell frequencies.

One way to ensure n cases in each cell, while retaining random assignment, is to assign each subject a number several digits long from a random-number table. The experimenter can then rank the subjects by the random numbers (breaking any ties randomly) and place the first n subjects in cell 1, the next n in cell 2, and so on.

4. *Random but nonindependent assignment.* The phrase *random assignment* is really shorthand for *random and independent assignment*. If we choose two schools for an experiment involving a new curriculum and flip a coin to see which school gets the new curriculum, then, speaking literally, we have assigned all students in each school randomly to the experimental or the control group. But the students will not be assigned independently to the two groups, so we do not have random assignment as that phrase is used here. Unlike true random assignment, this design does not allow us to assume that the two groups have been equated on covariates.

5. *Random sampling. Sampling* refers to the process by which cases are selected from a larger population for inclusion in an analysis, while *assignment* refers to the process by which the selected cases are allocated to positions on the independent variable(s). For instance, if there are 40 people in a class and 20 are randomly placed in the treatment group of a class experiment while the other 20 are placed in the control group, then some people might say we have randomly selected the groups. But in our terminology this is an example of *random assignment without random sampling*. We have used the entire population (the class) in the analysis rather than selecting part of it. But there is random assignment, because after the sampling (or, in this case, nonsampling) is made, subjects are randomly assigned to conditions.

Despite the uniformity with which introductory statistics textbooks assume random sampling, it is well known among statisticians that valid statistical inferences may sometimes be drawn without random sampling— and in fact without either random sampling or random assignment. For instance, suppose a college hired 100 new professors in the 1960s and another 100 in the 1970s. If women made up 10 of the first group and 30 of the second, a 2×2 test could usefully be performed to test the null hypothesis that the difference was due to chance. But there is no hint of either random sampling or random assignment. Section 14.3.2 explores in more detail the kinds of statistical inferences that can be made in the absence of random sampling.

As mentioned above, there are also five forms of random assignment which are sometimes not recognized as such:

1. Random assignment is usually employed with categorical independent variables, but may also be employed with numerical independent variables. For instance, subjects may be randomly assigned to various hours of practice on a task.

2. If a process is truly random, it need not be under our control. If we study the differences between winners and losers in a fair lottery, we can assume that

assignment has been random. But if we study the differences between lottery players and others, there has been no random assignment.

3. Although random assignment is usually easier in laboratory experiments than in field studies, it may be present in field studies or absent from laboratory experiments. For instance, if we are studying the differences in responses to male and female pollsters and a random process determines whether any given respondent is approached by a male or female pollster, then assignment is still random. On the other hand, if subjects who can participate in a laboratory experiment in the morning are placed in the experimental group while subjects who can participate in the afternoon are placed in a control group, then assignment is nonrandom.

4. If a study has two or more independent variables, assignment might be random on some and not others. For instance, if there are women and men in treatment and control conditions, then assignment may be random on condition though it can never be random on sex.

5. If a study has three or more treatment conditions, assignment might be random among some of the conditions and not others. For instance, in a stressful experiment, all subjects in poor health might be placed in an extra control condition while others are randomly assigned to the remaining groups. Then the advantage of random assignment applies to some comparisons and not to others.

4.2   LIMITATIONS OF RANDOM ASSIGNMENT

4.2.1   Limitations Common to Statistical Control and Random Assignment

Despite the advantages of random assignment, there are several problems it fails to solve.

First, we never know for certain what *facet* of an independent variable has produced an observed effect. For instance, was the effect of a new school curriculum due to the curriculum itself or to the particular teachers who implemented it?

Second, even when we have both random assignment and random selection from some population, we always have nonrandom selection from the population to which the results will be applied. If we establish an effect on human populations through an experiment run in April, then by October all the people in the population are 6 months older, some have died, and others have been born. And everyone has changed; the attack on Pearl Harbor in 1941 changed in one day the way Americans perceived the world, affecting every aspect of their lives. A beautifully randomized experiment on the most effective advertisement for coffee performed in November 1941 might have no relevance a month later.

But even if we cannot automatically generalize an experiment's results to the future, doesn't an experiment at least establish a causal conclusion for the precise population and moment of the experiment? This brings us to the third insoluble problem: we never know whether a conclusion applies to everyone in a population or only to some subpopulation. Thus, even if we were to show, via a randomized experiment on human subjects, that smoking causes cancer, we should qualify the result with the phrase "in at least part of the population." For all we would know even after this experiment, there may be some unidentified subpopulation in which smoking *prevents* cancer. Another way to state this point is that we never know whether we have identified all important moderator variables (a *moderator variable* is a variable that affects the relation between independent and dependent variables, so that, for instance, this relation is positive for cases high on the moderator and negative for cases low on the moderator).

The fourth limitation is that we can never study all possible *side effects* of the treatment. To make the point in an extreme form, we may show conclusively that a motivational program lowers the number of teenagers who drop out of high school, but we merely assume rather than know for sure that the program does not cause cancer. More realistically, it is possible that the program has positive short-term effects but deleterious long-term motivational effects that we have never studied; perhaps people exposed to such programs adapt so that they never do anything positive without special incentives rarely available in the real world.

The fifth limitation is that with numerical dependent variables, neither ordinary nor "distribution-free" statistical methods allow us to draw truly firm conclusions about the difference between treatment and control *means* without making some assumption about the shapes of the population distributions of scores. For instance, suppose there is a 1000-point scale and the population distribution of scores in the control group is positively skewed, with most of the scores bunched between 490 and 500 but with a long tail extending up to 1000. Suppose the population distribution of the treatment group is the mirror image of this, with most of the scores bunched between 500 and 510 but with a long tail extending down to 0. Examples of this sort can be constructed in which the treatment population has a lower *mean* than the control population, but even "distribution-free" tests with large samples typically find the treatment group significantly above the control group. For maximum relevance to policy and practical conclusions, we usually want our conclusions to concern means. But distribution-free tests either reach conclusions about medians or other statistics or, more commonly, reach "nonparametric" conclusions, which are vague conclusions that are not even phrased in terms of specific parameters such as means or medians. Thus a conclusion about the difference between two means cannot actually be reached without some assumption about the shapes of distributions, contrary to the pretense that random assignment allows us to avoid all assumptions that are even slightly questionable.

An example involving only one skewed distribution illustrates the same point less abstractly. Suppose a randomized experiment on a new headache medicine uses 5000 subjects in a treatment group and another 5000 in a control group and finds an enormously significant effect of the medicine in curing headaches. It seems indisputable that "this medicine cures headaches on the average—or at least it did the month the study was performed." But suppose the medicine leaves 1 subject in 10,000 with a paralyzing headache for the rest of his or her life, and by chance no such subjects appeared among the 5000 in our treatment group. The experimental results give us absolutely no grounds for rejecting this hypothesis, which in ordinary language means that we cannot say that the medicine cures headaches "on the average." Rather, we must say that "average" is defined not as a mean but in terms of proportions or medians, or some other statistic that cannot be affected by rare extreme cases. But this limits the relevance of our conclusions to policy recommendations or to everyday life: would you take a headache medicine that had 1 chance in 10,000 of leaving you with a paralyzing headache for the rest of your life?

Sixth, whether or not random assignment is used, we never find ultimate causation. Rather, we must always assume that causation operates indirectly through intermediate variables. For instance, the independent variable of parents' opinion of the importance of school does not magically and directly increase the dependent variable of school grades. Rather, it presumably works its effect by causing the child to study harder, by causing the parents to provide a quiet place for homework, and so on. The situation is the same in even the simplest physics problems. When a block is dragged across a surface, physicists say that the resulting friction is determined or caused by the block's weight. But this weight works its effect through intermediate mechanisms, such as molecules on the block hooking with those on the surface. Even the simplest cause-effect relationships work through intermediate mechanisms.

Seventh, in the behavioral and social sciences, almost any study that takes more than an hour or two of a subject's time will suffer from nonrandom attrition. Subjects fail to return for the final session in which the dependent variable is measured; or they misunderstand experimental directions so that no measure of the dependent variable is possible; or they fail to finish a task or questionnaire within the required time period. Thus random assignment is effectively destroyed because the experimenter is forced to nonrandomly delete subjects from both the treatment and control groups. Even if by chance equal *numbers* were deleted from the two groups, there is often little assurance that subjects removed from the two groups are comparable. Subjects may drop out of the treatment group because they find it too time-consuming, and subjects in the control group may drop out because they are disappointed at not being in the treatment group. Any assurance that the two groups of dropouts are equivalent must be based on statistical association or its lack, and the whole purpose of random assignment is to avoid the limitations of statistical control.

One way to minimize the problems of attrition under random assignment is to establish a particular moment in the experimental procedure we shall call the *differential treatment point*. Treat all subjects exactly alike before that point. Also before that point, make every effort to find out who will be able to complete the experiment—ask subjects whether they understand the directions, whether they will be able to come back the following week, whether they have any plans to move out of town, and so forth. Before the experiment, establish firm rules about the kinds of responses before the differential treatment point that will cause retention versus removal of a subject's data. All subjects may well be allowed to continue to the end of the experiment, but in the analysis use data only from those subjects whose responses before the differential treatment point have satisfied the rule. If you are successful in capturing all attrition this way, then you still have true random assignment, though the results can only be generalized to the population of subjects who meet the rules for retention in the experiment. Under this procedure you may well end up deleting from the analysis data from subjects who said that they planned to move out of town but changed their plans, or who said that they might not understand the directions but whose later responses indicated that they did. But the advantages of keeping attrition equivalent in the two groups are so great that they usually outweigh this loss of data.

In summary, random assignment does in principle allow us to make firmer statements than statistical control about the effect of an independent variable on a dependent variable. But even if there is no attrition, we are still unsure about the operative facets of the independent variable, the population to which the results apply, moderators, side effects, means, and ultimate causation.

4.2.2   Limitations Special to Random Assignment

The title of this section is not meant to imply that the problems discussed here are unique to random assignment. But these problems differ from those in Sec. 4.2.1 in that these are more likely to be serious under random assignment.

The most obvious problem with random assignment is that it is often illegal, immoral, impractical, or simply impossible. It is simply impossible to manipulate a subject's age, race, or genetic sex. Or if we wanted to study the effect of college attendance on income at age 40, random manipulation of college attendance would require us to decide randomly who attends college. This would be impractical, immoral, and probably illegal. Often, the more important the independent and dependent variables in our study, the less practical it is to use random assignment. But as mentioned in Sec. 1.1.2, random assignment may be impractical even in laboratory experiments with animals. You may have no control over the length of time a rat looks at a stimulus, but you may be able to measure that time accurately.

A second problem is that subjects in a randomized experiment often know they are being manipulated. This may change their responses. If they resent the manipulation or their placement in a control group, and if that resentment makes them more likely to drop out of the study, then random assignment can actually make groups *less* comparable after nonrandom attrition has occurred.

The third major problem associated with random assignment is not so much a problem of using it yourself, as of evaluating research in which others have used it. The words *random assignment* have such blinding effects on journal editors and granting agencies that there is enormous temptation for an author to use the phrase when it is not completely accurate. A research assistant in an educational experiment may feel a special sympathy for a particular handicapped child and stretch the rules by making sure that the child ends up in the treatment group rather than the control group. When the chief scientists learn of this by accident a year later, they are reluctant to drop the magic words from the research report. My own experience is that when experimenters *and their assistants* are questioned in detail about every single case, the words *random assignment* are often found to cover a wide range of methodological sins.

4.2.3 Correlation and Causation

The limitations of statistical control, described in Sec. 4.1.1, are the basis for the familiar saying "correlation does not imply causation." In this saying, the word *correlation* refers not specifically to the correlation coefficient, but to any type of statistical analysis based entirely on observation rather than experimental manipulation. Another version of the saying was suggested by Holland (1986): "No causation without manipulation." These sayings are intended to apply not to just the two words *cause* and *effect*, but to the very concept of causation, thereby affecting our usage of dozens or hundreds of words implying causation, such as *produce*, *increase*, *harm*, and *prevent*. We shall use the term *manipulationism* to denote the viewpoint expressed by these sayings.

A few manipulationists have argued that causation should be inferred only after random assignment, not after other kinds of experimental manipulation. This seems to be distinctly a minority position even among manipulationists; almost everyone accepts causal conclusions when a nonrandomized manipulation precedes a result predicted by the experimenters but never before observed, such as the explosion of an atomic bomb or the transmission of information over telegraph wires. But this has little relevance to the social and behavioral sciences, where manipulationism effectively equates causation with random assignment.

The manipulationist position helps us remember the difficulties of Sec. 4.1.1, but in my opinion it should not be taken too literally. Most of us work to keep our jobs or professional status, drive carefully to avoid accidents, dress before going outside to avoid embarrassment or arrest, and lock doors to prevent robbery. But none of the causal relationships implied by these phrases has ever been established experimentally. We speak with conviction about which political candidates or government policies will best promote peace and prosperity, despite the almost complete lack of experimental verification for such claims. Scientists have never established experimentally on human subjects the lifesaving effects of seat belts and the toxic effects of leaded gasoline exhaust, but seat belts are required and leaded gasoline is banned for new cars, and few informed people question the wisdom of these policies.

Like most people, I think of the concept of causation as providing the fundamental distinction between science and mere history or description of events. Thus manipulationism would reduce fields like biology, geology, meteorology, astronomy, and even astrophysics to pseudosciences or quasi sciences, because these fields are based almost entirely on observation rather than manipulation of the phenomena under study. An investigator building a weather satellite or slicing tissues for microscopic examination is manipulating the immediate objects at hand, but in a broader sense the process is one of observation.

And we all find it convenient to use phrases that are not merely uncertain but known to be false. We talk about the sun rising in the east rather than the earth rotating toward the east. In the same way, it is convenient to talk and think in terms of causal relations even though we know that they have not been established experimentally.

One answer sometimes given to these points is that there is a difference between our words or actions as scientists and our words or actions in everyday life, and there is also a difference between causal relationships that are truly known or proven to exist and those we are merely quite sure of. When speaking as scientists we should use words implying causation only when we are absolutely sure. And much as we might be awed by astrophysicists, the fact is that nobody is really sure what is going on in outer space.

This answer has two difficulties. The minor difficulty involves the distinction between science and everyday life. When a chemist says, "That brand of beaker breaks if it's heated too quickly," is he or she speaking as a scientist? If the quoted conclusion is nonscientific because it is not based on a randomized experiment, are we saying that scientists cannot in fact do science without constantly making and using nonscientific conclusions? Physicists use Newtonian principles in their work and everyday professional language as regularly as the rest of us talk about the sun rising in the east, even though they know the Newtonian principles to be false in terms of a more sophisticated Einsteinian framework.

But the major difficulty with the attempted distinction between science and everyday life is its reliance on the concept of absolute certainty. Sections 4.2.1 and 4.2.2 have already mentioned a variety of limitations that apply even to studies with random assignment. The philosopher Karl Popper (1961) has emphasized that we are never absolutely sure of any general scientific law. To take a simple example, few laws are more firmly established than the law that when an object is dragged across a surface, the friction between the two increases with the weight of other objects placed on top. Presumably simple randomized experiments could establish this conclusion about as firmly as any general scientific conclusion has ever been established. But we can always imagine inventing a new substance X such that when a block of X is placed on the dragged object, friction decreases as the weight of the block increases. If we ever observed this, we would no doubt devise a new set of scientific laws that explained both why the previous law had been accepted for centuries and why it is actually incorrect. This is exactly what happened early in this century when relativity theory replaced Newtonian physics, after a single well-documented observation—the Michelson-Morley experiment—contradicted Newtonian principles that had fitted countless observations for centuries. Thus any attempt to equate causation with absolute certainty reduces it to a kind of scientific holy grail that is endlessly sought and never found.

If manipulationism has any point, it is to suggest that the problems of statistical control are always far more serious than the problems that random assignment either produces or fails to avoid—and that is simply not the case. The concentration of fluoride in drinking water varies widely around the world, with towns just a few miles apart sometimes differing drastically in fluoride concentration. Detailed statistical analyses of these differences can show the preventive effect of fluoride on tooth cavities. In my opinion it would be at least as accurate to summarize such studies with the sentence "Fluoride has been shown to prevent cavities in children" as it would be to summarize a typical randomized study on the effects of two algebra curricula with the sentence "Curriculum A has been shown to be more effective than curriculum B."

I agree that it is useful to have a simple word or phrase that distinguishes causal relations established experimentally on the population of interest from conclusions like those on seat belts and leaded gasoline that are established merely by observation and by experiments on animals and dummies. But there is such a phrase: *experimentally verified causal relationship*. Anyone is free to invent a shorter phrase, but no one should try to monopolize the entire concept of causation for this purpose unless they are genuinely uncertain that careless driving causes accidents.

Popper's view, which has been applied by Suppes (1970) to the concept of causality, is that we should never think of general scientific laws as being "proven" or "known." The highest status such a law can ever attain is that of being the simplest and most plausible hypothesis consistent with the data we have observed to date. For instance, you cannot really prove that this book exists. Perhaps you and your friends just think you see it and feel it. But the hypothesis that the book exists is certainly the simplest and most plausible hypothesis consistent with your observations. This is the kind of conclusion we always draw, regardless of whether random assignment is used.

4.2.4 Combining Random Assignment and Statistical Control

We have been speaking as if statistical control and random assignment were simply competitors. But there are at least three good reasons for combining statistical control with random assignment.

First, random assignment is not always perfect, as we have seen—especially after attrition. A combination of statistical control and random assignment can often equate treatment and control groups better than either one alone.

Second, a combination of random assignment and statistical control can make the standard error of a regression slope lower than either method used alone, so that hypothesis tests are more powerful and effects are estimated more precisely. Section 5.4 analyzes in detail the factors affecting the precision of b_j. The precision of any statistic is defined as the reciprocal of the statistic's squared standard error. But all you need to remember is that the higher the standard error, the lower the precision. We will see in Sec. 5.4 that covariates have both a positive effect and a negative effect on the precision of b_j. The positive effect is produced by the covariates' correlation with Y, and the negative effect is produced by their correlation with X_j. Either the positive or the negative effect can predominate, or conceivably the two effects can exactly cancel each other out. But the covariates will always have a zero or low correlation with X_j when X_j is determined by random assignment. Thus, by combining statistical control with random assignment, we can have the positive effect of covariates on precision without their negative effect. This point will become clearer in Sec. 5.4.

The third reason for combining statistical control with random assignment is that even if random assignment establishes *that* an effect exists, statistical control may be needed to show *how* the effect works. For instance, suppose some subjects are told that their test scores indicate they are good at a certain type of mental problem, and those subjects thereafter take longer trying to solve problems of that type which are in fact impossible. Is the effect caused by the subjects' increased confidence in their abilities, or by an attempt to "re-pay" the experimenter who has complimented them? We can study this question by examining the relationship between the experimental manipulation and later working time, controlling alternately for a measure of confidence in one's abilities taken just before beginning the solution, and for a measure of liking of the experimenter. If the effect is produced by confidence, then controlling for confidence should eliminate the effect but controlling for liking should not. If the effect is produced by liking, the opposite result should be found. These are actually examples of what are called *indirect effects*, which are introduced more fully in Sec. 7.2.

SUMMARY

The lists in this chapter are summarized below.

Five limitations of statistical control
The need to control all necessary covariates
The need to avoid overcontrol
The impossibility of ruling out that Y affects X
The possibility of disruption by measurement error
Correlation by selective exclusion

(f) Working from a list of the 2000+ members of a veterans' organization in a city, investigators call 100 veterans and ask if they are satisfied with government services for veterans. One caller is male, the other female. They work side by side from the same list, crossing off each name as it is called, and randomly selecting another name from the list just before each call. They then test whether veterans called by the woman answer questions differently, on the average, from those called by the man.

2. The six lists in this chapter are named below, as items 1 to 6. Parts *a* to *p* of the problem include 12 items from these lists and 4 other items not appearing on any list. Identify the list associated with each item. Use an X to denote items from no list.
   1. Five limitations of statistical control
   2. Five things often confused with random assignment
   3. Five nonstandard forms of random assignment
   4. Seven limitations common to statistical control and random assignment
   5. Three limitations special to random assignment
   6. Three reasons for supplementing random assignment with statistical control
       (a) Gaining power and precision
       (b) Rounding error
       (c) Stretching truth for political gain
       (d) Numerical independent variables
       (e) Measurement error in covariates
       (f) Categorical dependent variables
       (g) Unidentified atypical subgroups
       (h) Random sampling
       (i) Lotteries
       (j) Missing data
       (k) Correlation through selective exclusion
       (l) Identifying how effects operate
       (m) Extreme cases
       (n) Noninterval scaling
       (o) Forced equality of cell frequencies
       (p) Resentment of being manipulated

3. In Sec. 4.2.3, we imagined a chemist saying, "That brand of beaker breaks if it's heated too quickly." A detailed examination of this statement and its implications would require a study with two independent variables—a categorical variable that is not possible to assign randomly, and a numerical variable that could be assigned randomly. What are the variables?

4. Perhaps you have flown on a magic carpet to an enchanted isle, and are merely dreaming that you are doing statistics homework. What logical argument suggests that you should not rely too heavily on that pleasant thought?

CHAPTER
5

STATISTICAL
INFERENCE
IN REGRESSION

5.1 BASIC CONCEPTS

5.1.1 Introduction

This chapter deals with inferential methods—estimation, confidence bands, and hypothesis tests—for most of the statistics we have discussed in previous chapters. A *statistic* is a value computed in a sample, while a *parameter* is a population or true value. For instance, an unknown population mean and standard deviation are both parameters.

We deal with many different kinds of statistics and parameters: multiple and partial correlations, partial multiple correlations, simple and partial regression slopes, ordinary and residual variances, marginal and conditional means, additive constants, and others. If we used the familiar convention of letting Roman letters denote statistics and Greek letters denote parameters, the reader would have to remember the names and meanings of most of the letters of the Greek alphabet. Therefore we use a nonstandard approach, in which the presubscript T before a symbol or abbreviation denotes the true or population value of the corresponding statistic. Thus, $_TM_Y$, $_Tb_j$, $_TR$, and $_Tpr_j$ denote, respectively, a population mean, partial regression slope, multiple correlation, and partial correlation. As applied, for instance, to b_j, this can be pronounced either "sub-T-b-sub-j" or "true b-sub-j."

This chapter considers inferences concerning five types of parameter:

- The multiple correlation $_TR$
- The residual variance $_T\text{Var}(Y.X)$
- The partial regression slopes $_Tb_j$
- The partial correlations $_Tpr_j$
- Any partial multiple correlations $_TPR$

For each parameter type there are four inferential problems:

- Estimating the parameter
- Testing the null hypothesis that the parameter equals 0
- Testing other null hypotheses about the parameter
- Finding confidence bands for the parameter

Thus we have altogether 5×4, or 20, inferential problems. This chapter covers all 20, but 12 of the 20 are considered less important than the other 8 and are lumped together at the end in Sec. 5.5. Most of the chapter concerns general topics on inference in linear models, plus the following eight problems:

- Estimating the multiple correlation $_TR$ (Sec. 5.2.6) and testing the hypothesis $_TR = 0$ (Sec. 5.2.7).
- Estimating the residual variance $_T\text{Var}(Y.X)$ (Sec. 5.2.6).
- Testing the null hypothesis that a set B of variables makes no unique contribution to $_TR$ (Sec. 5.3.1). This is equivalent to the null hypothesis $_TPR(B.A) = 0$.
- All four inferential problems involving $_Tb_j$ (Sec. 5.4).

Two of these eight problems concern the null hypothesis that a multiple or partial multiple correlation is zero. It might at first seem that these tests are of limited use because of the limitations on correlations mentioned in Sec. 2.3.1. In particular, when the investigator controls the distributions of regressors, then all correlations are merely properties of the particular experiment rather than properties of the natural world. But this limitation does not apply to the test of the hypothesis that a correlation equals zero. Such hypotheses can always be stated without reference to correlations, as the hypothesis that a *relationship* is zero. But since we have no specific symbol for a "relationship," we shall state these hypotheses and tests in terms of correlations, even though their usefulness is wider than that.

5.1.2 Assumptions Used for Inference

There are four assumptions that we will call the *standard assumptions* of regression theory. The first is *random sampling* of cases from a population, which requires that all the cases be sampled independently. For instance, randomly selecting a county in New York State and then randomly selecting 100 residents of that county does not give a random sample of the entire state.

The other three standard assumptions all concern the nature of conditional Y distributions in the population:

Linearity: Their means fall in a straight line or plane.
Homoscedasticity: They have equal variances.
Normality: They are normal distributions.

The terminology is not standard, but we shall distinguish between *primary* and *secondary* assumptions. A primary assumption is one whose violation jeopardizes the very meaning of the parameters under study, while violation of a secondary assumption merely threatens the accuracy of our inferences about those parameters. Thus linearity is a primary assumption, because without linearity it is not meaningful even to call the parameter $_Tb_j$ the change in $_TM_Y$ associated with each 1-unit change in X_j. Rather, under nonlinearity a change in X_j from 1 to 2 may be associated with an increase in Y while a change from 2 to 3 is associated with a decrease in Y.

But random sampling, homoscedasticity, and normality are all secondary assumptions. The damage done by violation of these assumptions can always be lessened by collecting a larger or more representative sample, whereas the damage done by nonlinearity can be undone only by reconceptualizing the entire model. This may not be very difficult, as we shall see in Chap. 12, but failure to do so invalidates the entire analysis, no matter how large and representative the sample.

Even with small samples, none of the four standard assumptions is absolutely essential for useful inference. Chapter 12 describes methods for transforming nonlinear relations into linear ones. In Chap. 14, we shall see some very general methods for drawing inferences in the absence of normality and homoscedasticity. And in Sec. 14.3.2 we will see that even in the absence of random sampling, we may be able to draw conclusions which are more modest but still of some value.

There are a few inferential methods in regression that require assumptions more restrictive than the standard assumptions. When there are just two variables X and Y, we can specify an assumption of *bivariate normality*. This requires that the standard assumptions of linearity, homoscedasticity, and normality hold *both* for the regression of Y on X and for the regression of X on Y. Thus, the conditional distributions of X must be normal, as well as those of Y. Figure 5.1 shows a bivariate normal distribution; you can see that both types of conditional distribution are normal. Figure 5.2 shows a distribution that satisfies the standard assumptions but not the assumption of bivariate normality; you can see that the conditional distributions of Y are normal while those of X are not.

We will say that *conditional bivariate normality* holds for a particular regressor X_j if the distribution of Y and X_j has bivariate normality when the other $P - 1$ regressors are held constant. Thus conditional bivariate normality may hold for some regressors in an analysis and not for others. As we shall see

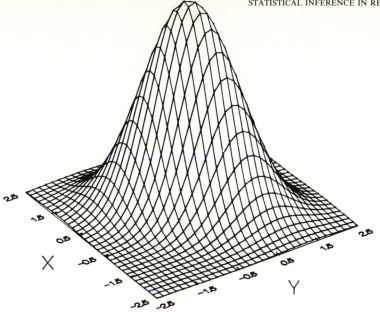

FIGURE 5.1
A bivariate normal distribution.

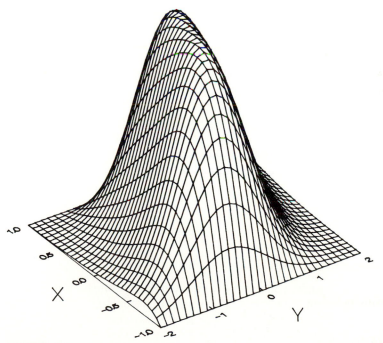

FIGURE 5.2
Distribution satisfying standard assumptions without bivariate normality.

in Sec. 5.5.2, some inferences concerning partial correlations $_T pr_j$ require conditional bivariate normality of X_j with Y. This is perhaps the major reason partial correlations are not reported more often.

There are a few specialized formulas and methods that require the even more restrictive assumption of *multivariate normality*. This holds if and only if the standard assumptions of linearity, homoscedasticity, and normality apply in every possible crosswise regression plus the main regression. This assumption is automatically violated if any variables are categorical. Methods using this assumption include the Gurland test on nonzero values of $_T R$ (Sec. 5.5.1), the Browne and Stein formulas for estimating validity shrinkage (Secs. 6.4.2 and 6.4.4), an F test on leverage values (Sec. 14.1.4), a computer program for power analysis (Sec. 15.3.2) and a table based on that program (Sec. 15.3.3), and discriminant analysis (Sec. 18.2.2). Several of these methods are not particularly robust in the absence of multivariate normality—a fact that restricts their use substantially.

This chapter merely introduces statistical inference in regression; the topic also arises in many later chapters. In particular, Chap. 11 considers the problem of multiple tests, and Chap. 15 considers the sample sizes needed for powerful and precise inferential methods.

5.1.3 Expected Values and Unbiased Estimation

The symbol E before any statistic denotes the *expected value* of that statistic. For instance, the expected value of a sample mean M is denoted by $E(M)$. To understand expected values, imagine drawing infinitely many independent, equal-sized random samples from a population, computing some statistic (such as M) in each sample, and finding the mean of all those values; that mean is defined as the expected value of the statistic.

If a statistics's expected value equals some population parameter, the statistic is said to be an *unbiased estimator* of that parameter. It can be shown that M is an unbiased estimator of the true mean $_T M$, even if the population distribution of scores is nonnormal and skewed. We shall see that each sample regression slope b_j is an unbiased estimator of its parameter $_T b_j$ but R is not an unbiased estimator of $_T R$.

5.1.4 Sample Computer Input and Output

This chapter explains most computations in detail. But most are done by computer programs, so that your first task is merely to understand the output. For instance, in MYSTAT and SYSTAT, if the variables of weight loss, exercise, food intake, metabolism, and gender have been given the names *wtloss, exercise, foodin, metabol*, and *gender* in a data set titled *diet*, then typing the simple commands

>use diet
>model wtloss = constant + exercise + foodin + metabol + gender
>estimate

puts onto the computer screen the display shown in Table 5.1.

So far we have discussed only a few of the entries in this printout. The top line gives the dependent variable, sample size, R, and R^2. The column headed "Variable" lists the regressors. The next column, headed "Coefficient," gives the regression slopes b_j. The "Constant" in that column is the additive constant a. The column headed "Std Coef," for "standardized coefficient," gives values of $beta_j$. This chapter explains all other entries in the printout.

5.1.5 Which Tests Should Come First?

In a problem with 10 or 20 regressors, there may be many hypotheses to test. There are P simple correlations with Y, P values of b_j or pr_j, a multiple correlation R, and perhaps several partial multiple correlations concerning specific sets of variables. Which hypotheses should be tested first? The details of the answer will depend upon the particular problem, but the general answer is that the most powerful tests—the tests most likely to yield significant results—should be performed first. Then, if later tests are nonsignificant, you will still be left with some conclusions.

In general, statistical power can be increased by sacrificing two desirable qualities that will be defined shortly: *specificity* and *relevance*. These are not being sacrificed in the long run, because if hypothesis tests with low specificity and relevance turn out significant, they can be followed by other tests with more of these qualities.

Consider first specificity. A multiple correlation is nonzero if and only if one or more of the regressors has a nonzero correlation with Y. Thus, a significant R yields only the vague conclusion that at least one regressor correlates with Y, without necessarily telling us which one or ones. The investigator with this result can be compared to a detective who knows a murder has been committed by at least one of five people, without knowing which one or ones. Both conclusions are vague.

But it is an inescapable fact of life that vague conclusions are reached more easily than more specific conclusions. Just as it is easier for the detective to arrive at a vague conclusion than to identify the actual murderer, so tests on R are usually more powerful than tests on simple or partial correlations. For instance, if 10 independent regressors each have a correlation of .3 with Y in a sample of 25 cases, then each correlation is nonsignificant ($p = .15$, two-tailed) but R is highly significant ($R = .949$, $p = .000023$). Just as the detective typically develops a short list of suspects before trying to identify the actual murderer, the wise researcher will attempt to reach vague but easily established conclusions before testing more specific hypotheses. Then, if the latter tests fail to attain significance, the investigator has at least come to some conclusions rather than none at all.

TABLE 5.1
A sample SYSTAT/MYSTAT display of regression results

DEP VAR: WTLOSS   N: 10   MULTIPLE R: .965   SQUARED MULTIPLE R: .931
ADJUSTED SQUARED MULTIPLE R: .876   STANDARD ERROR OF ESTIMATE: 1.166

VARIABLE	COEFFICIENT	STD ERROR	STD COEF	TOLERANCE	T	P(2 TAIL)
CONSTANT	-0.967	3.455	0.000	1.0000000	-0.280	0.791
EXERCISE	1.151	0.507	0.568	.2206892	2.272	0.072
FOODIN	-1.133	0.316	-0.740	.3249818	-3.591	0.016
METABOL	0.600	0.261	0.750	.1297610	2.299	0.070
GENDER	-0.404	0.869	-0.063	.7506313	-0.465	0.662

ANALYSIS OF VARIANCE

SOURCE	SUM-OF-SQUARES	DF	MEAN-SQUARE	F-RATIO	P
REGRESSION	91.703	4	22.926	16.864	0.004
RESIDUAL	6.797	5	1.359		

Tests on R can also be much more powerful than other tests under patterns of complementarity. In Section 2.3.5 we gave an example in which skills at softball and basketball are highly correlated, and in which measures of these skills can accurately predict preference for softball over basketball, even though each measure individually correlates very low with this preference. In situations like this the test on R may be vastly more powerful than tests on simple relationships.

Conclusions about sets of variables (see Sec. 3.4) are intermediate in vagueness between conclusions about simple and multiple correlations. Therefore tests on sets can follow tests on R and precede tests on more specific relations.

The power advantage of vague conclusions over specific ones does not necessarily apply to *anticipated* conclusions. If only one regressor out of five relates to Y and the other four do not, then a test on that one regressor's simple or partial relationship to Y will be more powerful than a test on R. Thus, if you believe that some regressors are especially important, they should be tested first despite the general power advantage of vague conclusions.

Some conclusions are more *relevant* than others. Often an investigator is more interested in partial relationships than in simple correlations. But we will see in Secs. 5.3.2 and 5.4.4 that the phenomenon of collinearity usually causes tests on partial relationships to be less powerful than tests on simple relationships. In fact, the more covariates are controlled, and the more highly they correlate with the independent variable of interest, the less powerful are the tests. Therefore an investigator may sometimes choose to test simple correlations before the partial relationships of most interest, so that nonsignificant results in the final tests will leave him or her with results of some interest.

5.2 ANALYSIS OF VARIANCE FOR REGRESSION

5.2.1 Model and Residual Degrees of Freedom

A straight line is determined by two constants—the Y intercept a and the slope b. By choosing those constants we can make the line fall anywhere we choose. We know that if a sample contained only two cases, so that its scatterplot contained only two dots, then we could choose a and b to make the line pass exactly through those two dots. We are free to choose any values of the two constants a and b, and so we have 2 *degrees of freedom*. A tilted plane, like the plane we saw in Sec. 2.1.4, has three constants—b_1, b_2, and a. By freely choosing appropriate values for these constants, we can make the plane pass exactly through any three points in three-dimensional space. Therefore the plane has 3 degrees of freedom. In a regression model with any number of regressors P, we have 1 degree of freedom for each regressor, and an extra degree of freedom for the additive constant a, making $P + 1$. When a sample size N equals $P + 1$, we know before inspecting the data that we can make the model fit the data perfectly—except in the rare case in which two or more cases are tied on all regressors but have different Y values.

We are rarely interested in testing hypotheses about a, so we usually think of the model as containing just P degrees of freedom—one for each regression slope b_j in the model. We often let df denote "degrees of freedom," so P is the model degrees of freedom, or "model df."

The larger our sample, the better we can estimate a model's fit to the population. We have seen that when a sample size N equals only $P + 1$, we know before inspecting the data that the model will fit the sample data perfectly, so the model's fit to the sample will tell us nothing at all about its fit to the population. Thus $N - (P + 1)$, or $N - P - 1$, is the number of cases in the sample actually available to estimate the model's fit to the population. For instance, if $P = 3$, we know beforehand that the model will perfectly fit a sample of four cases. Thus, if $N = 10$, only the last six cases are actually useful for estimating the model's fit to the population, since $N - P - 1 = 10 - 3 - 1 = 6$. Therefore $N - P - 1$ is called the *residual degrees of freedom*, or *residual df*, or df_r.

We can also view $N - P - 1$ as the number of regressors or degrees of freedom we could add to the model before completely exhausting the sample's ability to tell us how well the model fits the population. For instance, if again $N = 10$ and $P = 3$, we know that if we added 6 regressors (and thus 6 degrees of freedom) to the model, making $P = 9$, then the model would necessarily fit the sample data perfectly, so that its fit would tell us nothing about its fit to the population. Thus $N - P - 1$ is the number of variables or df we could add to the model before we could no longer tell anything at all about the new model's fit to the population.

In Sec. 17.1, we will see problems in which the regression plane's Y intercept is assumed to be zero. It will turn out that in such problems, df_r is $N - P$ instead of $N - P - 1$. But such problems are relatively rare, so the formula $df_r = N - P - 1$ is one of the few we suggest you memorize.

5.2.2 The Components of Y

In Sec. 1.5.1, we introduced the idea that each person's Y score could be broken into three portions or parts or components by the mathematical identity

$$Y_i = M_Y + (\hat{Y}_i - M_Y) + (Y_i - \hat{Y}_i)$$

We called the three parts of Y on the right respectively the *mean, model,* and *error* components of Y.

The same identity holds when $\hat{Y}_i$ is derived by multiple regression rather than simple regression. Heretofore we have emphasized primarily the last, or residual, component of Y. But useful formulas for statistical inference involve all three components, so we shall explore them further now.

A useful fact is that the three parts of Y are uncorrelated. M_Y is a constant, and by definition a constant cannot correlate with a variable. But the model and error components are also uncorrelated. Thus we have broken Y not just into three components, but into three independent components.

The model and error components sum to $Y_i - M_Y$, which we will call the *corrected total*. The corrected total and M_Y sum to Y_i, the *raw total*. The model component and M_Y sum to $\hat{Y}_i$, which we shall call the *augmented model*— augmented to include the mean. These quantities can be combined in various ways to give five simple summations:

$$\text{Raw total} = \text{mean} + \text{model} + \text{error}$$

$$\text{Corrected total} = \text{model} + \text{error}$$

$$\text{Augmented model} = \text{model} + \text{mean}$$

$$\text{Raw total} = \text{mean} + \text{corrected total}$$

$$\text{Raw total} = \text{augmented model} + \text{error}$$

But by far the most important of these is the second:

$$\text{Corrected total} = \text{model} + \text{error}$$

5.2.3 Sums of Squares

The equations above contain six terms: mean, model, error, augmented model, corrected total, and raw total. Any of these six values can be computed for each of the N subjects in the analysis. For any of the six, we can then square all N values and sum the squares. If we do this for the error values, the sum is called the *error sum of squares,* or $SS(\text{error})$. The comparable sum for the model values is the *model sum of squares,* or $SS(\text{model})$. The sum of squares of the "corrected total" values is denoted simply $SS(\text{total})$, while that for "raw total" values is denoted $SS(\text{raw total})$. The corrected total is usually of more interest than the raw total, since the raw total is affected by adding a constant to all Y scores and we usually are most interested in statistics that are unaffected by such additions.

Since the mean M_Y is constant for all subjects, the sum of the N squared means is $SS(\text{means}) = N \times M_Y^2$. Finally, we have $SS(\text{augmented model})$.

Analysis of variance is based on the fact that *sums of squares of independent components add up in the same manner as the components themselves.* Thus, from the five equations at the end of Sec. 5.2.2, we can write:

$$SS(\text{raw total}) = SS(\text{mean}) + SS(\text{model}) + SS(\text{error})$$

$$SS(\text{total}) = SS(\text{model}) + SS(\text{error})$$

$$SS(\text{augmented model}) = SS(\text{model}) + SS(\text{mean})$$

$$SS(\text{raw total}) = SS(\text{mean}) + SS(\text{total})$$

$$SS(\text{raw total}) = SS(\text{augmented model}) + SS(\text{error})$$

But the one we shall emphasize is the second:

$$SS(\text{total}) = SS(\text{model}) + SS(\text{error})$$

Dividing each term in any equation by N gives a related equation. For instance, in the last equation, dividing $SS(\text{total})$ by N gives $\text{Var}(Y)$, while dividing $SS(\text{model})$ and $SS(\text{error})$ by N gives the variances of the model and error components of Y. Thus this equation becomes

$$\text{Total variance of } Y = \text{model variance} + \text{error variance}$$

So these equations, which describe the additive properties of sums of squares, also specify the additive properties of variances.

We shall illustrate these points by the regression of Y onto X_1, X_2, X_3, and X_4 in the weight-loss example of Chap. 2. The relevant data are repeated in Table 5.2. The *raw total sum of squares* ΣY^2 is

$$\Sigma Y^2 = 6^2 + 2^2 + 4^2 + 8^2 + 9^2 + 8^2 + 5^2 + 11^2 + 13^2 + 9^2 = 661$$

The *corrected total sum of squares* is the sum of squared deviations from the mean of Y. It is often called simply the *total sum of squares*, or $SS(\text{total})$. By definition,

$$SS(\text{total}) = \Sigma(Y - M_Y)^2$$

Also,

$$SS(\text{total}) = SS(\text{raw total}) - \frac{(\Sigma Y)^2}{N}$$

$$= SS(\text{raw total}) - N \times M_y^2$$

In our example,

$$SS(\text{total}) = 661 - 10 \times 7.5^2 = 661 - 562.5 = 98.5$$

TABLE 5.2
The weight-loss data set repeated

ID	Exercise X_1	Food intake X_2	Metabolism X_3	Gender X_4	Weight loss Y
1	0	2	15	0	6
2	0	4	14	0	2
3	0	6	19	0	4
4	2	2	15	1	8
5	2	4	21	1	9
6	2	6	23	0	8
7	2	8	21	1	5
8	4	4	22	1	11
9	4	6	24	0	13
10	4	8	26	0	9
Means	2	5	20	.4	7.5

Further,

$$\text{Var}(Y) = \frac{SS(\text{total})}{N}$$

In the example,

$$\text{Var}(Y) = \frac{98.5}{10} = 9.85$$

The model and error sums of squares are $SS(\text{model}) = 91.703$ and $SS(\text{error}) = 6.797$, which sum to $SS(\text{total}) = 98.5$.

5.2.4 The Analysis-of-Variance (ANOVA) Table

Table 5.3 shows the entries appearing in an analysis-of-variance table for regression. Table 5.4 shows the specific values for the present example. The first two columns of the table show how model and error (residual) SS add up to total SS, and how model and residual df add up in the same way. Each entry in the *mean square*, or *MS*, column is the ratio of the corresponding SS value to the corresponding df. Finally, F is the ratio of the two mean square (MS) values. This F can be used to test the null hypothesis of no relation between Y and the model.

5.2.5 The F Distribution

A significance level p is found from F. Tables for this purpose appear in many textbooks, including this one (see Appendix 4). You must know the model and residual df, often called df_1 and df_2. In the present case, $df_1 = P$ and $df_2 = df_r$. But where, for instance, a z table is entered with one argument (entry value), an F table is entered with three. Thus, moderate-sized tables are often inadequate, and other methods must be used to find p.

TABLE 5.3
ANOVA table for regression

Source	SS	df	Mean Square	F
Model	$\Sigma(\hat{Y} - M_Y)^2$	P	$\dfrac{SS(\text{Model})}{P}$	$\dfrac{MS(\text{Model})}{MS(\text{Error})}$
Error	$\Sigma(Y - \hat{Y})^2$	$N - P - 1$	$\dfrac{SS(\text{Error})}{N - P - 1}$	
Total	$\Sigma(Y - M_Y)^2$	$N - 1$		

TABLE 5.4
ANOVA table for the weight-loss data set

Source	SS	df	Mean Square	F	
Model	91.703	4	22.926	16.864	$p = .0042$
Error	6.797	5	1.359		
Total	98.5	9			

When MYSTAT, SYSTAT, and SAS print an ANOVA table, they all print p next to the F. In SYSTAT and SAS, it is almost always possible to make the program print the ANOVA table, and thus the p, for the F of interest. And the FCF function in SYSTAT calculates the p for any combination of df_1, df_2, and F. But when performing more advanced tests with MYSTAT, such as the three-way decomposition in Sec. 5.3.1, you will sometimes calculate an F by hand from SS values found with two different "model" statements. If a sufficiently accurate p cannot be found from tables, you can find an exact p by "tricking" MYSTAT into printing an ANOVA table with the desired values of df_1, df_2, and F. Appendix 2 provides the details of this process. You should be able to use it immediately if necessary, but the reasoning behind the method will be somewhat clearer after you have read Chap. 10.

For those familiar with the BASIC computer language, Appendix 3.1 includes a program which computes an exact p from F when df_2 is even and exceeds 2. Once running, it is much easier to use than Appendix 2. Acceptably accurate values for odd df_2 can be found by averaging the two even values on either side. For instance, suppose $F = 3$, $df_1 = 6$, and $df_2 = 19$. The program yields $p = .03271$ for $df_2 = 18$, and $p = .02948$ for $df_2 = 20$. Averaging them yields $p = .03110$. The exact p is .03100.

5.2.6 Unbiased Estimation of R^2 and Residual Variance

In an ANOVA table, the mean square for error (MSE) is often called the *mean squared error*. This term is misleading, because MSE is *not* the mean of the squared errors. Since the sum of the 10 squared errors in Table 5.4 is 6.797, the mean of squared errors is actually $6.797/10 = .6797$. MSE is rather an unbiased estimator of the true residual variance $_T\text{Var}(Y.X)$. The residual standard deviation, the square root of the residual variance, is estimated by the square root of MSE; this statistic is called the *standard error of estimate*.

The actual mean of squared errors is denoted $\text{Var}(Y.X)$. To see why this is a biased estimator of true residual variance, consider a scatterplot containing only two points. Since a straight line can always be drawn connecting any two points, we know before examining the data that a regression line can be fitted exactly to two points, leaving residuals of zero.

Similarly, imagine a three-dimensional scatterplot containing only three points. A plane can always be drawn that passes exactly through any three points, again leaving residuals of zero. More generally, whenever the number of regressors equals $N - 1$ and no two cases are tied on all regressors, we will always be able to fit a regression equation that passes exactly through all N points. Since all residuals are 0, the mean of squared residuals is also 0. But if we know in advance that the mean of squared residuals is 0, then that mean cannot possibly be an unbiased estimator of the true residual variance. When sample sizes are larger than $P + 1$, the mean of squared residuals does not underestimate the true residual variance so extremely, but it always tends to underestimate somewhat. The mean of squared residuals, of course, equals $SS(\text{error})/N$. It can be shown that multiplying this mean by $N/(N - P - 1)$, resulting in $MSE = SS(\text{error})/(N - P - 1)$, gives an unbiased estimator of the true residual variance.

A similar point applies to R and R^2. In keeping with Sec. 1.3,

$$R^2 = \frac{SS(\text{model})}{SS(\text{total})}$$

Since

$$SS(\text{model}) = SS(\text{total}) - SS(\text{error})$$

this equation can be written

$$R^2 = \frac{SS(\text{total}) - SS(\text{error})}{SS(\text{total})} = 1 - \frac{SS(\text{error})}{SS(\text{total})}$$

Dividing the numerator and denominator of the last fraction by N, we have

$$R^2 = 1 - \frac{\text{Var}(Y.X)}{\text{Var}(Y)}$$

But just as we saw a moment ago that $\text{Var}(Y.X)$ underestimates the true residual variance $_T\text{Var}(Y.X)$, the same argument suggests that R^2 overestimates $_TR^2$. When a regression equation exactly fits a set of data points with all residuals equal to 0, then $R = 1$. Thus, whenever $P = N - 1$, we know in advance that R will equal 1.0. We thus see that R and R^2 generally tend to overestimate $_TR$ and $_TR^2$.

To correct for this, we can use MSE as an unbiased estimator of $_T\text{Var}(Y.X)$. And imagine a "regression" with no regressors, using only an additive constant a to predict Y. In that regression, $P = 0$. But if an unbiased estimate of true residual variance is obained from $SS(\text{error})/(N - P - 1)$, then, when $P = 0$, this becomes $SS(\text{error})/(N - 1)$. But $SS(\text{error})$ in this case is $SS(\text{total})$. Thus, an unbiased estimator of the true variance $_T\text{Var}(Y)$ is $SS(\text{total})/(N - 1)$. Just as we used MSE to denote the unbiased estimator of residual variance, we can use $MS(\text{total})$ to denote the unbiased estimator of total variance.

Using these two unbiased estimators gives a more nearly unbiased estimator of $_TR^2$, called adjusted R^2. That is,

$$\text{Adjusted } R^2 = 1 - \frac{MSE}{MS(\text{total})}$$

This or equivalent formulas for adjusted R^2 were suggested independently by Ronald Fisher and R. J. Wherry, and the statistic is sometimes known by the name of one or the other of these authors—but today it is most often called simply adjusted R^2. It is printed by most standard computer programs for regression, including MYSTAT, SYSTAT, and SAS.

It can be shown algebraically that the last formula can be written as

$$\text{Adjusted } R^2 = R^2 - \frac{P(1 - R^2)}{N - P - 1}$$

This version shows clearly that the larger P and the smaller N, the more adjusted R^2 falls below R^2. Adjusted R^2 can fall below 0, though $_TR^2$ cannot. Thus any negative value of adjusted R^2 should be "rounded up" to 0. The square root of adjusted R^2 is adjusted R.

For all hypothesis tests on $_TR$, use ordinary R, not adjusted R. The test formulas could be written to require entry of adjusted R, but the formulas would be more complex, and no standard texts do it that way.

It can be shown that MSE and MS(total) give exactly unbiased estimates of their respective parameters, even without normality and homoscedasticity. Even with those assumptions, adjusted R^2 is not an exactly unbiased estimator of R^2, but the difference is small enough to ignore. Exactly unbiased estimators of R and R^2 do exist (Olkin and Pratt, 1958), but they are rarely used, because their standard errors are larger than those of adjusted R and adjusted R^2, so that the expected squared difference between true and estimated values is actually larger than for adjusted R and R^2. This book does not give these standard errors, since they are not used in finding confidence bands on $_TR$ and $_TR^2$; see Sec. 5.5.1.

Many otherwise respectable authors confuse adjusted R with a related quantity we shall call *shrunken R*, which is more useful in studies involving prediction. The distinction between the two is explained in Chap. 6.

5.2.7   Testing the Null Hypothesis $_TR = 0$

The F test in an ANOVA table actually tests the null hypothesis $_TR = 0$ and can be expressed in terms of R. In this form, the test is

$$F = \frac{R^2}{1 - R^2} \times \frac{df_r}{P} \qquad df = P, df_r$$

The higher F, the more significant the result, and you see from the formula that for fixed values of df, F increases with R^2. Also, the larger N, the larger df_r and the larger F. But F falls as P increases. The larger P, the larger we would expect R^2 to be by chance, since adding each new regressor never lowers R and usually raises it. Thus, the larger P, the less impressive is a given value of R^2.

5.3   INFERENCES CONCERNING SETS OF VARIABLES

5.3.1   Testing the Unique Contribution of a Set

In Sec. 3.4 we saw that many questions of interest concern the contribution of a *set* of variables to a model's ability to explain variance in Y. To show that set B

can make a unique contribution above and beyond the contribution of set A, we can test whether the two sets together explain more variance than set A alone. When stated in terms of residual variances, the null hypothesis is $_T\mathrm{Var}(Y.AB) = {}_T\mathrm{Var}(Y.A)$. When stated in terms of multiple correlations, the same null hypothesis is $_TR(AB) = {}_TR(A)$. As we saw in Sec. 3.4.2, this is equivalent to the hypothesis $_TPR(B.A) = 0$, where the correlation on the left is a partial multiple correlation.

In this test, SS(total) is decomposed into three components: the portion explained by set A, the portion explained by set B independent of A (also called the *unique* contribution of set B), and a residual or error portion. Then values of df, mean square, and F are computed much as in Sec. 5.2.4.

For instance, consider the example of Sec. 5.1.4, in which weight loss was regressed onto exercise, food intake, metabolism, and gender. We might divide these four regressors into two sets: those a person can control directly (exercise and food intake) and those not under direct control (gender and metabolism). Suppose we want to test the null hypothesis that when exercise and food intake are controlled, the variables not under direct control have no effect on weight loss. Then we define exercise and food intake as set A, while gender and metabolism form set B.

In the weight-loss data set, SS(total) $= 98.5$. When weight loss is regressed onto set A (exercise and food intake), this total is decomposed into SS(model) and SS(error) components of 82.5 and 16.0, respectively. When set B (gender and metabolism) is added to the regression, SS(model) rises 9.2027 to 91.7027, while SS(error) drops the same amount to 6.7973. These two regressions decompose SS(total) into the three components shown in the SS column of Table 5.5: the contribution of set A, the unique contribution of set B, and the final residual component. We shall call this analysis a *three-way decomposition*.

As before, the total df is $N - 1$, the df associated with each set is the number of variables in that set, and the residual df is the difference. Also as before, dividing values of SS by df gives values of MS (mean square), whose expected values are equal if the null hypothesis is correct. Their ratio is F, with $df = 2, 5$; and the associated p is .118. Thus there is no evidence in this artificial data set that gender and metabolism make a unique contribution to weight loss above that made by exercise and food intake.

TABLE 5.5
A three-way decomposition for the weight-loss data set

Source	SS	df	MS	F	p
A	82.5	2			
$B.A$	9.2027	2	4.6013	3.3847	.118
Error	6.7973	5	1.3595		
Total	98.5	9			

In MYSTAT, a three-way decomposition must be performed by running two regressions—one with and one without the set being tested. The smaller of the two values of SS(model) is SS(A), the smaller value of SS(error) is SS(error), and the difference between the two values of SS(model) is SS(B.A). The same rules apply to df. If an exact p is desired, use one of the methods of Sec. 5.2.5 to find it. In the present example, the commands

>model wtloss = constant + exercise + foodin + gender + metabol
>estimate

yield SS(model) = 91.7027, SS(error) = 6.7973; and the commands

>model wtloss = constant + exercise + foodin
>estimate

yield SS(model) = 82.5, SS(error) = 16. The values of 6.7973 and 82.5 appear in Table 5.5, and the value of 9.2027 in that table equals 91.7027 − 82.5.

A more direct test is available in SYSTAT: after estimating the larger model, type a set of three commands like

>hypothesis
>effect = gender & metabol
>test

The output from these commands includes a table that contains all the values on the $B.A$ and "error" lines of Table 5.5, including the crucial F and p values. The same test is performed in SAS with the single command

>test gender, metabol;

This test can also be expressed in terms of $R(B.A)$ and $R(A)$. Let Q denote the number of variables in set B, the set being tested. Then the test is

$$F = \frac{R(AB)^2 - R(A)^2}{1 - R(AB)^2} \times \frac{df_r}{Q}$$

or, in terms of the partial multiple correlation $PR(B.A)$,

$$F = \frac{PR(B.A)^2}{1 - PR(B.A)^2} \times \frac{df_r}{Q}$$

In the present example, for instance, we have $R(AB)^2 = .9310$, $R(A)^2 = .8376$, $PR(B.A)^2 = .5752$, $Q = 2$, and $df_r = 5$. Thus the first formula gives

$$F = \frac{.9310 - .8376}{1 - .9310} \times \frac{5}{2} = 3.3847$$

and the second gives

$$F = \frac{.5752}{1 - .5752} \times \frac{5}{2} = 3.3847$$

5.3.2   Collinearity

We could imagine performing a three-way decomposition in which set B includes only one variable X_j. This analysis would test whether X_j makes a unique contribution over the other variables in the regression. This same hypothesis is more often performed as described in Sec. 5.4.1—as a t test on b_j. But the two tests are equivalent; the two-tailed p from the t test will always exactly equal the p calculated by the three-way decomposition. Further, the value of F found in the three-way decomposition will exactly equal the square of the t found for b_j.

In Sec. 3.4.3, we defined a *collinear set* of regressors as one whose member variables are highly correlated and largely interchangeable, so that deleting any one member from the analysis would lower R^2 very little, even though deleting the entire set might lower R^2 substantially. We suggested there that three measures of liberalism might form a collinear set for some dependent variables—or three measures of SES such as income, education, and occupational prestige. But now, in the preceding paragraph and in Sec. 5.3.1, we have seen that the unique contributions of a set or its individual members are used directly in testing for partial relationships of the set or its members to Y. Thus we can well have a situation where no individual member of a set is statistically significant, even though the set as a whole is significant.

The proper conclusion in such cases is that one or more members of the set affect Y, even though we do not know which one. This is a vague conclusion of the sort discussed in Sec. 5.1.5; such conclusions are especially common in collinear sets.

5.4   THE DISTRIBUTION OF b_j

5.4.1   Tests on b_j

Unlike R, each regression weight b_j is an unbiased estimator of the corresponding true weight $_Tb_j$. That is, $E(b_j) = {}_Tb_j$, whether or not normality and homoscedasticity exist.

Next to each value of b_j, most computer printouts include $SE(b_j)$, the estimated standard error of b_j. This value *does* require normality and homoscedasticity. The formula for $SE(b_j)$ is examined at length in Secs. 5.4.3 and 5.4.4, but first we shall examine the uses of $SE(b_j)$.

The value $t = b_j/SE(b_j)$ is usually printed next to $SE(b_j)$. This t tests the null hypothesis $_Tb_j = 0$. The value of df for the t is $N - P - 1$, the error df for the analysis as a whole. Often the two-tailed significance level associated with the t is printed as well. For instance, in the data set of Sec. 2.1 we had $b_1 = 2$. In Sec. 5.4.7, we will see that for this data set, $SE(b_1) = .3333$. Thus $t = 2/.3333 = 6$. For this problem we had $N = 10$, $P = 2$, so $df = 10 - 2 - 1 = 7$ and $p = .00057$ (two-tailed).

Occasionally you may wish to test the null hypothesis that b_j equals some value other than 0. In the present example, for instance, $b_1 = 2$, which means that each daily hour of exercise is associated with 2 pounds of weekly weight loss. If someone hypothesized that $_Tb_1$ did not exceed 1, you could test that hypothesis with the formula

$$t = \frac{b_j - \text{null value of } b_j}{SE(b_j)}$$

In the present example, we have $t = (2 - 1)/.3333 = 3.0$, $df = 7$, $p = .010$ (one-tailed).

5.4.2   Confidence Limits on b_j

You can also use $SE(b_j)$, along with a t value from a t table, to place a confidence band around b_j. The formula is

$$\text{Confidence limits} = b_j \pm \text{tabled } t \times SE(b_j)$$

For instance, for a two-sided 95% confidence interval, a t table gives a t value of 2.365. Thus, in the present example, the 95% confidence limits for b_1 are $2 \pm 2.365 \times .3333 = 2.788, 1.212$.

If you are concerned about errors only in one direction—either over-estimation or underestimation of b_j—you may use a one-sided confidence interval. For instance, in the present example we may be little concerned with the error of concluding that exercise is *less* effective than it really is. We can then use a one-sided confidence band. To construct a one-sided 95% confidence band, we use the critical t for a one-tailed test at the .05 level. This value is found from a table to be 1.895. Thus the one-sided 95% confidence limit on the effect of exercise is $2 - 1.895 \times .3333 = 1.368$.

5.4.3   Factors Affecting $SE(b_j)$

The smaller the standard error of b_j, the less values of b_j will vary from sample to sample and the more accurately they will tend to estimate the true value $_Tb_j$. We shall denote the estimated standard error of b_j as $SE(b_j)$. Its square is $SE^2(b_j)$, defined by the formula

$$SE^2(b_j) = \frac{MSE}{N \times \text{Var}(X_j) \times \text{Tol}_j}$$

Since $SE(b_j)$ can be found from this formula, we shall speak of it as the formula for $SE(b_j)$, although to be precise it is the formula for $SE^2(b_j)$. As we shall see, all four entries in the formula make good intuitive sense. The last entry, Tol_j, is defined in Sec. 5.4.4. The other three entries have appeared before.

The simplest of all the entries is the sample size N. The formula shows that b_j is like all standard statistics: as N increases, its standard error decreases.

The appearance of $Var(X_j)$ in the denominator states that $SE(b_j)$ decreases as $Var(X_j)$ increases. The reason for this is seen most easily if we think of a simple regression in which X is dichotomous. If X is scored 0, 1, then, as we saw in Sec. 3.2.2, the regression slope b is actually the difference between the Y means of the two conditional distributions at $X = 0$ and $X = 1$. Since the slope and the difference are algebraically identical, they have identical standard errors, so $SE(b)$ equals the standard error of the difference between the two conditional Y means. But if we arbitrarily chose to use scores of 0 and 10 for X, instead of 0 and 1, the regression line would still pass through the two conditional Y means. Then the line would rise a distance equal to the difference between the two means as X increases from 0 to 10. Therefore b would equal one-tenth the difference between the two conditional Y means. Thus $SE(b)$ would equal the standard error of one-tenth that difference, which, of course, is one-tenth the standard error of the difference. Therefore, other things equal, $SE(b)$ is inversely proportional to the range of X. The same is true for multiple regression.

MSE is the unbiased estimator of $_TVar(Y.X)$. Its effect on $SE(b_j)$ is also intuitively reasonable, as Fig. 5.3 illustrates. The diagonal line is the regression line for the subsample comprising the four small circles, while the horizontal line is the regression line for the subsample comprising the four crosses. With no calculation, you can see that if any one of the circles were deleted, the former regression line would not move at all. But if any of the crosses were deleted, the latter regression line would move substantially. But values of S_X and S_Y are exactly the same for the four crosses as for the four circles. The only thing that differs between the two subsamples is r_{XY}, which is 1.0 for the four circles and 0 for the crosses. The higher r_{XY} in absolute value, the lower MSE. Thus we can also say that the two subsamples differ only in MSE. That diference makes one subsample far more sensitive than the other to random changes such as the deletion of a single case.

The extreme of this phenomenon occurs when $_TVar(Y.X) = 0$, which implies $_TR = 1$. To understand what happens in this case, think first about simple regression with $_Tr_{XY} = 1$. Since every case in the population falls on a straight line, every case in every sample will fall on the same straight line. Therefore, every sample will show $r_{XY} = 1$, and all samples will have the same value of b. Thus $SE(b) = 0$.

The effect is similar when there are two regressors. If $_TR = 1$, then every case in the population falls on the same tilted plane. Thus every case in every sample will fall on the same tilted plane. We will find $R = 1$ in every sample, and the same slopes will be found in every sample. Thus $SE(b_1) = SE(b_2) = 0$.

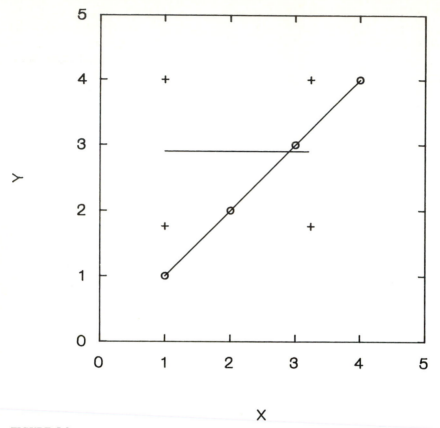

FIGURE 5.3
Two subsamples equal on S_X and S_Y but with very different values of r_{XY}, MSE, and $SE(b)$.

The general rule is that when $_TR = 1$, then $R = 1$ in every sample and $SE(b_j) = 0$ for every regressor.

5.4.4   Tolerance

Tol_j is the last entry in the formula for $SE(b_j)$. This is called the *tolerance* of X_j. Let CR_j be defined as the multiple correlation in the crosswise regression predicting X_j from the other $P - 1$ regressors; crosswise regressions were introduced in Sec. 2.2.3. Then

$$\text{Tol}_j = 1 - CR_j^2$$

Thus Tol_j is a measure of the *independence* of X_j from the other regressors. Tol_j can range from 0 to 1. If X_j is perfectly independent of the other regressors, then $\text{Tol}_j = 1$; if it is perfectly dependent, then $\text{Tol}_j = 0$. Tol_j also measures X_j's *collinearity* with other regressors, with low tolerance indicating high collinearity; see the discussion of collinearity in Sec. 5.3.2.

High correlation between X_j and other regressors increases $SE(b_j)$ by lowering Tol_j. In fact, the reciprocal of tolerance is sometimes called the *variance inflation factor*, or VIF, because it is the ratio between $SE^2(b_j)$ and the value $SE^2(b_j)$ would have if X_j were uncorrelated with all other regressors. Since N is simply multiplied by Tol_j in the formula for $SE(b_j)$, we can think of VIF as the factor by which we would have to increase N to compensate for the loss in precision of estimating $_Tb_j$ caused by collinearity.

Any first-rate regression package will print values of Tol_j if asked. In fact, absence of this capacity would by itself make a package second-rate. In SYSTAT and MYSTAT, tolerance values are printed even when not requested.

In the extreme case in which two regressors are perfectly correlated, it is completely impossible to separate their effects on Y. In terms of our formulas, the perfect correlation will make both values of tolerance equal 0, which will make both values of $SE(b_j)$ infinitely large, which in turn says that estimation of individual effects is impossible. A data set containing any tolerance values of 0 is said to be *singular*. Though collinearity is common in the behavioral sciences, singularity is rare, partly because random measurement error in variables prevents any multiple correlations from equaling 1.

We can also view the effect of collinearity as an extension of the principle that $SE(b_j)$ varies inversely with $Var(X_j)$. If we want to estimate the effect of X_j on Y while holding other regressors constant, then we are concerned not so much with the total variance of X_j as with the variance of that portion of X_j independent of the other regressors. The larger CR_j, the lower Tol_j and the lower the variance of that portion of X_j.

The formula for $SE(b_j)$ can be rewritten to clarify the point in the last paragraph. If we apply the formula $Var(Y.X) = Var(Y) \times (1 - R^2)$ to the crosswise regression predicting X_j from the other regressors, then $Var(Y)$ becomes $Var(X_j)$, $1 - R^2$ becomes Tol_j, and $Var(Y.X)$ becomes the variance of the unique portion of X_j, so the relation becomes

$$Var(\text{unique portion of } X_j) = Var(X_j) \times Tol_j$$

Substituting this in the formula for $SE(b_j)$ gives

$$SE^2(b_j) = \frac{MSE}{N \times Var(\text{unique portion of } X_j)}$$

This formula, too, is intuitively reasonable. For instance, suppose we want to study the degree to which assertiveness is influenced by upbringing— specifically, by encouragement of assertiveness in the child by the parents. We would probably decide to control for the child's sex. But if the study is performed in a society where assertiveness is strongly encouraged in all boys and strongly discouraged in all girls, then the encouragement variable will have little variance independent of sex, so its effect on later assertiveness cannot be measured accurately. In terms of the last formula, the unique portion of "encouragement" has little variance, even though that variable has large variance in a pooled sample of boys and girls. This small variance raises $SE(b_j)$, making accurate estimation of b_j difficult.

Another version of the same formula arises from the fact that a sum of squares (SS) equals N times a variance. Because of this, the last formula is sometimes written as

$$SE^2(b_j) = \frac{MSE}{SS(\text{unique portion of } X_j)}$$

5.4.5   How Great a Drawback Is Collinearity?

Collinearity is often a far less serious problem than researchers fear. There are four reasons for this.

First, collinearity affects only the power of tests on regression slopes—not their validity. The standard errors of the partial regression slopes are increased for collinear variables. This widens the confidence bands on those values of b_j, and makes it harder to find statistically significant values of b_j. But a significant value of b_j is just as conclusive when collinearity is present as when it is absent.

Second, collinearity often affects only a few of the regressors. If those affected are merely covariates, then values of $SE(b_j)$ are not raised for any of the independent variables. For instance, suppose you have several measures of socioeconomic status (SES) and cannot decide which to use as a covariate. If you decide to avoid the problem by using them all, little or no harm results from the fact that they may be highly collinear. $SE(b_j)$ will then be high for those covariates, but not for the independent variables. (The related problem of excessive numbers of covariates is examined in Secs. 5.4.6 and 15.2.4; it, too, is a less serious problem than is widely believed.)

Third, although you cannot perform powerful tests on the individual effects of collinear variables, collinearity does not reduce the power of a test on the effect of the set as a whole. For instance, if you want to test whether SES affects a dependent variable, you can do so efficiently even if SES is measured by several highly collinear variables. Such tests were described in Sec. 5.3. Methods for discovering collinear sets are discussed in Sec. 8.1.2.

The fourth point is addressed to those already familiar with the concept of validity shrinkage—the difference between a regression's apparent validity, as measured by R, and its actual validity in the population. Chapter 6 discusses validity shrinkage in detail. Intuitively, it seems that validity shrinkage should increase with collinearity. After all, collinearity increases the standard errors of regression slopes, and these slopes are used in predicting Y. But it turns out that under collinearity, errors in estimating individual slopes tend to cancel each other out. For instance, if r_{12} is high, then $SE(b_1)$ and $SE(b_2)$ may both be high. But it can be shown that when r_{12} is high, overestimates of b_1 will tend to occur in the same samples as *under*estimates of b_2, and vice versa. But since X_1

and X_2 are highly correlated, they can partially substitute for each other, and underestimation of one slope will partially compensate for overestimation of the other. If this were not true, the formula for estimating shrunken R in Sec. 6.4.2 would not be as simple as it is. Rather, the estimate of shrunken R would be lower when collinearity is high. But in fact this estimate is unaffected by collinearity.

Another common misconception about collinearity is that it is somehow a problem specific to regression, and that more advanced statistical methods might someday eliminate the problem. But the problem is essentially that when two variables are highly correlated, it is harder to disentangle their effects than when the variables are independent. This is simply an unalterable fact of life; the only solutions lie not in cleverer analytic methods, but in such straightforward devices as larger sample sizes or experimental manipulation of the variables.

5.4.6 Sample Size and Nonsignificant Covariates

To minimize standard errors and maximize the power of tests, should you limit the number of covariates or delete nonsignificant covariates? Generally not. If a covariate correlates with no other variables in the analysis, then its inclusion lowers the power of tests on independent variables by the same amount as the loss of one subject from the sample—both lower df_r by 1. Thus, when sample sizes are moderate or large, little power is lost by adding a few extra covariates which turn out to be independent of other variables. A covariate X_j which correlates highly with an independent variable X_k can substantially increase $SE(b_k)$ and thus lower power. But that very fact is usually evidence that it would be invalid to arbitrarily exclude X_j. The collinearity between X_j and X_k will also raise $SE(b_j)$, perhaps making b_j nonsignificant. Therefore, the nonsignificance of a covariate's regression slope is not a good reason for deleting it from the model.

A common but misleading rule of thumb is that a regression should not contain more variables than one-tenth the sample size. This and related rules are examined more closely in Chap. 15. But we will say now that the most important tests are usually on values of b_j, and the power of those tests is determined not by the ratio N/P suggested by this rule of thumb, but by df_r, which usually equals $N - P - 1$, which, of course, is determined by $N - P$. Thus the power of the most important tests is determined by the difference between N and P, not their ratio. When $N - P = 40$, a two-tailed test on b_j, at the .05 level, has power of .8 if $_Tpr_j = .43$, so one simple rule is that unless the effects of interest are believed to be quite large, the sample size should exceed P by 40 or more. But as we will see, especially in Chaps. 13 and 15, large samples allow a great variety of potentially useful analyses that are not practical in small samples, so the overriding rule is simply that more is better.

5.4.7   When $P = 2$

In Sec. 5.4.3, we saw that

$$SE^2(b_j) = \frac{MSE}{N \times \text{Var}(X_j) \times \text{Tol}_j}$$

When there are only two regressors, this formula reduces to a fairly simple function of correlations and standard deviations. We have seen that $MSE = \Sigma e_i^2/(N - P - 1)$, so that when $P = 2$, we have $MSE = \Sigma e_i^2/(N - 3)$. But $\Sigma e_i^2 = N \times S_{Y.X}^2 = N \times \text{Var}(Y) \times (1 - R^2)$, so

$$MSE = \frac{N}{N - 3} \text{Var}(Y) \times (1 - R^2)$$

Also, when $P = 2$, we have

$$\text{Tol}_j = 1 - r_{12}^2$$

Substituting these two expressions in the formula for $SE(b_j)$, the N's cancel and we have

$$SE^2(b_j) = \frac{\text{Var}(Y) \times (1 - R^2)}{(N - 3) \times \text{Var}(X_j) \times (1 - r_{12}^2)}$$

For instance, in the example of Sec. 2.1, where Y = weight loss, X_1 = exercise, and X_2 = food intake, we had $N = 10$, $\text{Var}(Y) = 9.85$, $\text{Var}(X_1) = 2.4$, $\text{Var}(X_2) = 4.2$, $r_{12} = .3780$, and $R = .9152$, so that

$$SE^2(b_1) = \frac{9.85 \times (1 - .9152^2)}{7 \times 2.4 \times (1 - .3780^2)} = .1111$$

$$SE^2(b_2) = \frac{9.85 \times (1 - .9152^2)}{7 \times 4.2 \times (1 - .3780^2)} = .0635$$

By taking square roots of the last two values, we find $SE(b_1) = .3333$, and $SE(b_2) = .2520$. Since $b_1 = 2$ and $b_2 = -.5$, we have $t_1 = 2/.3333 = 6.0$ and $t_2 = -.5/.2520 = 1.984$. With $df = N - P - 1 = 7$, the two-tailed p's are respectively .00054 and .088. Thus exercise (X_1) has a significant partial relationship with weight loss, while food intake (X_2) does not.

5.4.8   When $P = 1$

Simple regression is, of course, the special case of multiple regression in which $P = 1$. Thus the aforementioned test on b_j, and the test on R in Sec. 5.2.7, can also be applied to simple regression. The two tests then test the same null hypothesis: the hypothesis of no association between Y and the single regressor X. Further, the two tests are equivalent. The F found in testing R will always equal the square of the t found in testing b, and the two-tailed p of the t test will equal the p in the F test. Both tests are also equivalent to the following test on a simple correlation *r:*

$$t = r\sqrt{\frac{N-2}{1-r^2}} \qquad df = N - 2$$

Section 5.5.3 gives a *t* test for a partial correlation pr_j. Since a simple correlation can be thought of as a partial correlation with no covariates, the present test is the special case of that test in which $P = 1$. Thus the *t* test just above is actually a special case of three different tests: the *F* test on *R*, the *t* test on b_j, and the *t* test on pr_j.

5.5 OTHER INFERENTIAL METHODS

This section describes several inferential methods that are less widely used than those above, but which are useful for specific purposes.

5.5.1 Testing Hypotheses about $_TR$ Other Than $_TR = 0$

Occasionally we may want to test the null hypothesis that $_TR$ equals some specified value other than zero. Tests for the multivariate normal case have been suggested by Gurland (1968). Gurland describes three exact tests and one approximation. We shall present one of Gurland's exact tests and the approximation.

The approximate test is more easily expressed if we transform R^2 by the formula $VR = R^2/(1 - R^2)$. *VR* stands for "variance ratio," since *VR* equals the ratio of the variance in *Y* explained by the regressors to the variance not explained. Similarly, we transform the hypothesized true value $_TR^2$ to $_TVR = _TR^2/(1 - _TR^2)$. Then we compute

$$F = \frac{VR\dfrac{N-P-1}{P}}{1 + {_TVR}\dfrac{N-1}{P}}$$

df_2 has its usual value of $N - P - 1$, but we compute

$$df_1 = \frac{[(N-1)\,{_TVR} + P]^2}{(N-1)\,{_TVR} \times ({_TVR} + 2) + P}$$

and then round df_1 to the next lower integer. For the special case of $_TVR = 0$, this test reduces to the test in Sec. 5.2.7.

To illustrate, when regressing *Y* on exercise, food intake, and metabolism, we observed $R = .9633333$. Suppose we wish to test the null hypothesis that this observed *R* might reflect a true multiple correlation of .3 or less. We have $N = 10$, $P = 3$, and

$$VR = \frac{.9633333^2}{1 - .9633333^2} = 12.891$$

$$_TVR = \frac{.3^2}{1 - .3^2} = .0989$$

Then

$$F = \frac{12.891 \times (10 - 3 - 1)/3}{1 + .0989 \times (10 - 1)/3} = 19.88$$

$$df_1 = \frac{[(10 - 1) \times .0989 + 3]^2}{(10 - 1) \times .0989 \times (.0989 + 2) + 3} = 3$$

(rounded down from 3.108) and

$$df_2 = 10 - 3 - 1 = 6 \qquad p = .00162$$

Gurland's exact method is implemented by the BASIC computer program in Appendix 3.2. When applied to the same data set, it yields $p = .00157$.

You can use Gurland's methods repeatedly to find confidence limits for R, since a confidence limit is the null value that makes the observed result just significant. For instance, letting $N = 50$, $P = 5$, and $R = .6$, I tried $_TR$ values of 0, and then in succession .1, .2, .4, .3, .32, .34, and .33, to find that .33 is the lower 95% confidence limit for this R.

5.5.2 Inferences Concerning Partial Correlations

One type of inference concerning partial correlations is handled by methods already discussed. The null hypothesis that a partial correlation $_Tpr_j$ is zero is equivalent to the null hypothesis that $_Tb_j$ is zero, so the t test on b_j also tests the null hypothesis $_Tpr_j = 0$.

But other inferences concerning partial correlations are more problematic. Partial correlations are not available, even as an option, in the output of most major regression packages. The omission is deliberate, because partial correlations are considerably less *robust* than the more standard regression statistics. Robustness is the absence of reliance on restrictive assumptions.

In Sec. 5.1.2 we defined a primary assumption as one whose violation jeopardizes the very meaning of the parameter in question, while violations of secondary assumptions merely threaten the accuracy of our inferences about that parameter. The latter violations can be overcome merely by using larger or more representative samples, while the former cannot. As we saw, linearity is the only primary standard assumption. But the most obvious uses of partial correlations require *primary* assumptions that are not among even the *secondary* assumptions of most regression theory.

The most common inferential use of the partial correlation pr_j is to estimate the *conditional correlation* between Y and X_j—the correlation between those variables in a subpopulation in which all other regressors are held constant at some fixed value. There may be infinitely many such correlations—one for every possible combination of scores on the other regressors. To visualize a conditional correlation, consider Fig. 5.4. It shows the familiar tilted plane from Chap. 2, but also shows a vertical plane at the value $X_2 = 4$. In the example using the tilted plane, only 3 of the 10 sample cases fell in the plane $X_2 = 4$ (see Fig. 2.3). But we can imagine that in the total population the number of cases at $X_2 = 4$ is large—even infinite. The correlation between Y and X_j in the plane $X_2 = 4$ is a conditional correlation. When scientists say "the correlation between Y and X_j with other variables held constant," they ordinarily mean a conditional correlation of just this type. Thus the primary value of pr_j as an estimator lies in its ability to estimate such a correlation.

But this use of pr_j requires bivariate conditional normality as a primary assumption. Violation of this assumption is not trivial. In one artificial population satisfying all the standard assumptions but not bivariate conditional normality, each conditional correlation between Y and X_2 in a problem with two regressors was .3162, but the *population* value $_T pr_2$ was .8489. Thus pr_j can grossly overestimate all conditional correlations, even in a very large and

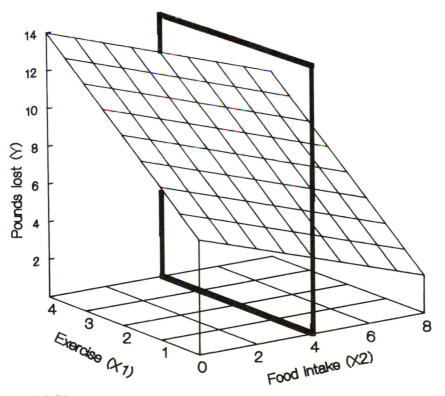

FIGURE 5.4
A slice defining a bivariate conditional distribution of Y and X_1 with X_2 constant.

representative sample. Even more extreme examples can be created. Bivariate conditional normality can never be satisfied if X_j is categorical, since then the crosswise regression predicting X_j can never attain linearity.

5.5.3 Finding pr_j from Computer Printouts

Because partial correlations are so easily misinterpreted, many standard regression programs do not compute them, even as an option. This "ban" seems excessive to me; the necessary assumptions are sometimes met, and in Chap. 9 we will suggest another use of pr_j. To find pr_j, we can take advantage of the fact that the t for testing the significance of pr_j equals the t for testing the corresponding value of b_j. Since printouts give values of t for b_j (or F, where $F = t^2$), we can use the formula

$$t = pr_j \sqrt{\frac{N - P - 1}{1 - pr_j^2}}$$

This formula actually tests the significance of both simple and partial correlations; simple correlations are merely the special case in which $P = 1$. With a little algebra we can rewrite this formula as

$$pr_j^2 = \frac{t^2}{t^2 + N - P - 1}$$

This formula allows us to find pr_j^2 from the t on the computer printout. Then we take the square root and use the sign of b_j for the sign of pr_j. If the computer has printed F instead of t, we can recall that $F = t^2$.

To illustrate, the printout in Table 5.1 shows that for testing b_1 for exercise, $t = 2.272$. Since $df_r = 5$, we have

$$pr_1^2 = \frac{2.272^2}{2.272^2 + 5} = .508$$

$$pr_1 = .713$$

5.5.4 Confidence Bands on pr_j

The Fisher z method is often used to place confidence bands around simple Pearson r's, but it can also be used to place a confidence band around a value of pr_j. Simply pretend that pr_j is a simple correlation measured in a sample of size $N - P + 1$, and apply the Fisher method to it. This means that where the ordinary Fisher method uses $N - 3$, you will use $N - P - 2$ instead. Thus the method involves the following steps:

1. Translate pr_j into a Fisher z by a Fisher z table (see Appendix 4), or by the formula

$$z = .5 \times \ln \frac{1 + r}{1 + r}$$

The symbol ln denotes a natural logarithm; logarithms are explained in Sec. 12.2.

2. Find the standard error of the z from the formula

$$SE(z) = \frac{1}{\sqrt{N - P - 2}}$$

3. From an ordinary normal or z table, select the value of z for the desired confidence level. For example, for a two-tailed confidence interval at the 95% level, set $z = 1.96$.

4. The confidence limits on the Fisher z are then found by the formula

Confidence limits on Fisher z = Fisher $z \pm$ tabled $z \times SE(z)$

5. To translate these limits into confidence limits for pr_j, either use the Fisher z table again, or translate from z to r with the formula

$$r = \frac{e^{2z} - 1}{e^{2z} + 1}$$

As explained more fully in Sec. 12.2, the letter e denotes a value that is approximately 2.718282.

For instance, in the last example we find that a correlation of .713 translates to a Fisher z of .893. Since $N = 10$ and $P = 4$, the standard error of the Fisher z is $1/\sqrt{10 - 4 - 2} = .5$. For a two-tailed 95% confidence interval, we find confidence limits of $.893 \pm 1.96 \times .5 = 1.873, -.087$. These values translate back into correlations of .954 and $-.087$. These are the 95% two-tailed confidence limits on pr_3. The confidence limits show that we know little about $_T pr_j$—it could be high positive, zero, or even negative. That is not surprising in an example with $N = 10$.

5.5.5 Partial Multiple Correlations

Inferences concerning a partial multiple correlation $_T PR$ suffer from the same lack of robustness discussed in Sec. 5.5.2. When the appropriate assumptions are met, however, you may wish to estimate a value of $_T PR$, or test the null hypothesis that it equals some value other than zero or find confidence limits for it. Methods for all these rely on the fact that the distribution of PR is the same as the distribution of R with the same residual df and the model df or number of variables equal to Q.

For instance, the formula for adjusted $PR(B.A)^2$ is much like that for adjusted R^2:

$$\text{Adjusted } PR(B.A)^2 = PR(B.A)^2 - \frac{Q[1 - PR(B.A)^2]}{df_r}$$

Using the figures of Sec. 5.3.1, namely, $PR(B.A)^2 = .5752$, $Q = 2$, and $df_r = 5$, we can calculate adjusted $PR(B.A)^2 = .4053$ and adjusted $PR(B.A) = .6366$.

In Sec. 5.5.1 we saw methods for testing the null hypothesis that a multiple correlation $_TR$ is some nonzero value such as .3, and for finding confidence limits on R. The rule in the first paragraph of Sec. 5.5.5 can be used to adapt these methods for drawing inferences concerning PR.

5.5.6   Testing Hypotheses about $_T\text{Var}(Y.X)$

The residual variance $_T\text{Var}(Y.X)$ is related to $_TR$ by the formula

$$\frac{_T\text{Var}(Y.X)}{_T\text{Var}(Y)} = 1 - {_T}R^2$$

$_T\text{Var}(Y.X)$ may be more useful than $_TR$ or $_TR^2$ when emphasis is on the remaining errors of predictions rather than on their ratio to existing predictive power. For instance, if we want to predict someone's future life span, there is little doubt that gender and present age are very useful predictors. If we expressed predictive power as R or R^2, it would therefore be very high. But we may be less interested in that than in the size of the typical errors of estimation.

No test is needed to test the null hypothesis $_T\text{Var}(Y.X) = 0$. This hypothesis implies that all cases in the population fall exactly in the same plane. If that is true, then all cases in every sample will fall in the same plane, and in every sample we will observe $R = 1.0$ and $\text{Var}(Y.X) = 0$. Thus, whenever we observe $R < 1.0$, we can reject the null hypothesis $_T\text{Var}(Y.X) = 0$ with no further test.

Given the standard assumptions, we can test hypotheses about nonzero values of $_T\text{Var}(Y.X)$ using

$$\frac{SS(\text{error})}{_T\text{Var}(Y.X)} = \text{chi-square} \qquad df = df_r$$

Notice that in this formula, the higher the value of $_T\text{Var}(Y.X)$ we test, the lower chi-square will be. We are usually concerned that prediction of Y might be much worse in reality than it appears in the sample, so we usually want to test null hypotheses about values of $_T\text{Var}(Y.X)$ *larger* than the unbiased estimate MSE. Thus we must find the probability that chi-square will be as *low* as the observed value. Finding this probability requires the left-hand tail from the chi-square table, not the right-hand tail used in most applications, so we must use a chi-square table that includes the left-hand tail.

In our weight-loss example, we have $N = 10$, $P = 3$, and $SS(\text{error}) = 78/11 = 7.0909$. Our unbiased estimate of $_T\text{Var}(Y.X)$ is $MSE = (78/11)/6 = 1.18$. Consider the arbitrarily chosen null hypothesis $_T\text{Var}(Y.X) = 2$. To test this hypothesis, we calculate chi-square $= 7.09/2 = 3.55$. We have $df = N - P - 1 = 10 - 3 - 1 = 6$. Table 5.6 shows a few entries from a chi-square table for $df = 6$.

The calculated chi-square of 3.55 is just above the tabled value of 3.45, so we know that the probability of finding a chi-square of 3.55 or higher is just under .75, while the probability of finding a chi-square of 3.55 or lower is just

TABLE 5.6
Sample chi-square table for *df* = 6

Area to right	.95	.75	.50	.25	.05
Area to left	.05	.25	.50	.75	.95
Chi-square	1.64	3.45	5.35	7.84	12.59

over .25. An exact formula shows these probabilities to be .74 and .26. The latter is the p in our hypothesis test; if the true residual variance $_T\text{Var}(Y.X)$ were 2, the probability would be .26 of finding *MSE* less than or equal to the value of 1.18 we observed. Since .26 > .05, we cannot reject that hypothesis.

5.5.7   Confidence Limits for $_T\text{Var}(Y.X)$

As already mentioned, we are usually concerned with the possibility that Y might be less related to the predictors than it appears in our sample. We are therefore usually interested in an *upper* confidence limit on $_T\text{Var}(Y.X)$, because a high value of $\text{Var}(Y.X)$ means low predictability of Y. This can be calculated from the formula

$$\begin{matrix} \text{Upper } X\% \\ \text{confidence limit} \\ \text{on } _T\text{Var}(Y.X) \end{matrix} = \frac{SS(\text{error})}{\begin{matrix}\text{tabled chi-square} \\ \text{value with } X\% \\ \text{to the right}\end{matrix}}$$

As in Sec. 5.5.6, we must use the lower end of the chi-square distribution to find an upper confidence limit for $_T\text{Var}(Y.X)$. For instance, to find the upper 95% confidence limit for $_T\text{Var}(Y.X)$, we use the value of chi-square with 5% to the left. In our previous example with $df = 6$, the table shows this value to be 1.64. Thus the upper one-sided confidence limit for $_T\text{Var}(Y.X)$ is 7.09/1.64 = 4.34.

Earlier, we found that an unbiased estimate of $_T\text{Var}(Y.X)$ is 1.18, and found that it could easily be as high as 2; now we see that its upper one-sided 95% confidence limit is 4.34.

We would rarely want a lower confidence limit, but in the present example the lower one-sided 95% confidence limit would be 7.09/12.59 = .563. If we used both the upper and lower limits just calculated, we would call the band a two-sided 90% confidence band, since the true residual variance will fall between the upper and lower limits in only 90% of all samples.

SUMMARY

5.1   Basic Concepts

We use nonstandard notation in which the presubscript T before a statistic denotes the true or population value. This chapter considers inferences concerning five types of parameter:

- The multiple correlation $_TR$
- The residual variance $_T\text{Var}(Y.X)$
- The partial regression slopes $_Tb_j$
- The partial correlations $_Tpr_j$
- Any partial multiple correlations $_TPR$

For each parameter type, there are four inferential problems:

- Estimating the parameter
- Testing the null hypothesis that the parameter equals 0
- Testing other null hypotheses about the parameter
- Finding confidence bands for the parameter

Thus we have altogether 5 × 4, or 20, inferential problems. We discuss all 20 but emphasize the following 8:

- Estimating the multiple correlation $_TR$ and testing the hypothesis $_TR = 0$.
- Estimating the residual value $_T\text{Var}(Y.X)$.
- Testing the null hypothesis that a set B of variables makes no unique contribution to $_TR$. This is equivalent to the null hypothesis $_TPR(B.A) = 0$.
- All four inferential problems involving $_Tb_j$.

The hypothesis that $_TR$ or $_TPR$ is 0 is important because it implies that a *relationship* is zero, even when we are generally reluctant to use R or PR to measure the size of that relationship.

There are four assumptions that we call the *standard assumptions* of regression theory. The first is *random sampling* of cases from a population, which requires that all the cases be sampled independently. The other three standard assumptions all concern the nature of conditional Y distributions in the population:

Linearity: Their means fall in a straight line or plane.

Homoscedasticity: They have equal variances.

Normality: They are normal distributions.

Even with small samples, none of the four standard assumptions is absolutely essential for useful inference.

The symbol E before any statistic denotes the *expected value* of that statistic. If a statistic's expected value equals some population parameter, the statistic is said to be an *unbiased estimator* of that parameter.

The most powerful tests should be performed first. In general, statistical power can be increased by sacrificing *specificity* and *relevance*. These are not being sacrificed in the long run, because if hypothesis tests with low specificity and relevance turn out significant, they can be followed by other tests with more of these qualities.

5.2   Analysis of Variance for Regression

The value of the degrees of freedom *df* in a model is the number of parameters estimated by the model. The difference between N and model *df* is the *residual degrees of freedom*, or *residual df*, or df_r. In regression, $df_r = N - P - 1$. But in counting model *df* we often ignore a, so we say that model *df* is P.

We can also regard df_r as the number of regressors we could add to the model before we have completely exhausted the sample's ability to estimate the model's fit to the data.

We can divide Y into three components:

$$Y_i = M_Y + (\hat{Y}_i - M_Y) + (Y_i - \hat{Y}_i)$$

We call the three parts of Y on the right respectively the *mean, model*, and *error* components of Y. The three parts of Y are uncorrelated. The model and error components sum to $Y_i - M_Y$, which we call the *corrected total*. The corrected total and M_Y sum to $\hat{Y}_i$, the *raw total*. The model component and M_y sum to Y_i, which we call the *augmented model*—augmented to include the mean. Thus we have five simple summations:

$$\text{Raw total} = \text{mean} + \text{model} + \text{error}$$

$$\text{Corrected total} = \text{model} + \text{error}$$

$$\text{Augmented model} = \text{model} + \text{mean}$$

$$\text{Raw total} = \text{mean} + \text{corrected total}$$

$$\text{Raw total} = \text{augmented model} + \text{error}$$

But the second of these is by far the most important. We use five sums of squares:

$$SS(\text{error}) = \text{sum of squared errors}$$

$$SS(\text{model}) = \text{sum of squared model values}$$

$$SS(\text{total}) = \text{sum of squared ''corrected total'' values}$$

$$SS(\text{raw total}) = \text{sum of squared ''raw total'' values}$$

$$SS(\text{mean}) = N \times M_y^2$$

Sums of squares of independent components add up in the same manner as the components themselves. Thus, from the second equation above, we can write:

$$SS(\text{total}) = SS(\text{model}) + SS(\text{error})$$

Dividing each term in this equation by N gives

$$\text{Var}(Y) = \text{explained variance} + \text{unexplained variance}$$

The first two columns of the regression ANOVA table (Table 5.1) show how model and error (residual) SS add up to total SS, and how model and residual *df* add up in the same way. Each entry in the *mean square*, or *MS*, column is the ratio of the corresponding *SS* value to the corresponding *df*. Finally, *F* is the ratio of the two mean square (*MS*) values. This *F* can be used to test the null hypothesis of no relation between *Y* and the model.

In the ANOVA table, the mean square for error (*MSE*) is often called the *mean squared error*. But *MSE* is *not* the mean of the squared errors. *MSE* is rather an unbiased estimator of the true residual variance $_T\text{Var}(Y.X)$. The residual standard deviation, the square root of the residual variance, is estimated by the square root of *MSE*; this statistic is called the *standard error of estimate*. The actual mean of squared errors is denoted $\text{Var}(Y.X)$.

An approximately unbiased estimate of $_TR^2$ is given by

$$\text{Adjusted } R^2 = R^2 - \frac{(1 - R^2) \times P}{N - P - 1}$$

The larger *P* and the smaller *N*, the more adjusted R^2 falls below R^2. Adjusted R^2 can fall below 0, though $_TR^2$ cannot. Therefore any negative value of adjusted R^2 should be "rounded up" to 0. The square root of adjusted R^2 is adjusted *R*. For all hypothesis tests on $_TR$, use the ordinary *R*, not adjusted *R*.

MSE and *MS*(total) give exactly unbiased estimates of their respective parameters, even without normality and homoscedasticity. Even with those assumptions, adjusted R^2 is not an exactly unbiased estimator of R^2, but the difference is small enough to ignore.

The *F* test in an ANOVA table actually tests the null hypothesis $_TR = 0$ and can be expressed in terms of *R*. In this form the test is

$$F = \frac{R^2}{1 - R^2} \times \frac{df_r}{P} \qquad df = P, df_r$$

5.3   Inferences Concerning Sets of Variables

The null hypothesis on the unique contribution of a set is $_T\text{Var}(Y.AB) = {}_T\text{Var}(Y.A)$ or $_TR(AB) = {}_TR(A)$ or $_TPR(B.A) = 0$. In this test, *SS*(total) is decomposed into three components: the portion explained by set *A*, the portion explained by set *B* independent of *A* (also called the *unique contribution* of set *B*), and a residual or error portion. Then values of *df*, mean square, and *F* are computed as in an ANOVA table. If set *B* includes only one variable X_j, this test is equivalent to the ordinary *t* test on b_j.

Collinearity arises when high correlations among regressors make it difficult to disentangle their individual effects on the dependent variable. Removing either variable from the regression would produce little drop in R^2 or in explained variance, because the high correlation between the two allows the other variable to fill the gap. But removing both would produce a large drop. Thus the *unique* contribution of each variable may be very small, although the two together make a large contribution.

Collinearity is usually confined to *collinear sets* of regressors. There is no precise definition of a collinear set, but generally we mean that each variable in the set, taken alone, would add nearly as much to SS(model) or to R^2 as the entire set does.

5.4   The Distribution of b_j

Unlike R, each regression weight b_j is an unbiased estimator of the corresponding true weight $_Tb_j$, regardless of whether the standard assumptions hold. But calculating $SE(b_j)$, the estimated standard error of b_j, *does* require the standard assumptions. This is used in the formulas

$$t = \frac{b_j - \text{null value of } b_j}{SE(b_j)}$$

Confidence limits $= b_j \pm$ tabled $t \times SE(b_j)$

One-sided confidence limits may be used if you are concerned about errors only in one direction. $SE(b_j)$ is a function of four quantities:

$$SE^2(b_j) = \frac{MSE}{N \times \text{Var}(X) \times \text{Tol}_j}$$

All four entries in the formula make good intuitive sense.

Tol$_j$ is the *tolerance* of X_j. Let CR_j be defined as the multiple correlation in the crosswise regression predicting X_j from the other $P - 1$ regressors. Then

$$\text{Tol}_j = 1 - CR_j^2$$

Thus Tol$_j$ is a measure of the *independence* of X_j from the other regressors. Tol$_j$ can range from 0 to 1. Tol$_j$ also measures the *collinearity* of X_j with other regressors, with low tolerance indicating high collinearity. The reciprocal of tolerance is sometimes called the *variance inflation factor*, or VIF, because it is the ratio between $SE^2(b_j)$ and the value $SE^2(b_j)$ would have if X_j were uncorrelated with all other regressors. We can think of VIF as the factor by which we would have to increase N to compensate for the loss in precision of estimating $_Tb_j$ caused by collinearity.

A data set containing any tolerance values of 0 is said to be *singular*. Though collinearity is common in the behavioral sciences, singularity is rare, partly because random measurement error in variables prevents any multiple correlations from equaling 1.

We can also view the effect of collinearity as an extension of the principle that $SE(b_j)$ varies inversely with Var(X_j). The larger CR_j, the lower Tol$_j$ and the lower the variance of the portion of X_j independent of the other regressors. Collinearity is often a far less serious problem than researchers fear.

To minimize standard errors and maximize the power of tests, you should generally *not* limit the number of covariates or delete nonsignificant covariates.

A common but misleading rule of thumb is that sample size should always be at least 10 times the number of regressors. A better simple rule is that unless the effects of interest are believed to be quite large, the sample size should exceed P by 40 or more. But large samples allow a great variety of potentially useful analyses that are not practical in small samples, so the overriding rule is simply that more is better.

5.5   Other Inferential Methods

Formulas are given for testing hypotheses about $_T R$ other than $_T R = 0$.

Partial correlations pr_j are not robust as estimators of conditional correlations, because the primary assumptions for this use of pr_j include linearity and homoscedasticity of *both* the main regression and the crosswise regression predicting X_j from the other regressors, plus the assumption that all conditional correlations between Y and X_j are equal. The extra assumptions can never be satisfied if X_j is categorical, since then the crosswise regression predicting X_j can never attain linearity.

To find a value of pr_j, we can use

$$pr_j^2 = \frac{t^2}{t^2 + N - P - 1}$$

We then take the square root and use the sign of b_j for the sign of pr_j. If the computer has printed F instead of t, then we recall that $F = t^2$.

The Fisher z method is often used to place confidence bands around simple Pearson r's, but it can also be used to place a confidence band around a value of pr_j. Simply pretend that pr_j is a simple correlation measured in a sample of size $N - P + 1$, and apply the Fisher method to it. This means that where the ordinary Fisher method uses $N - 3$, you will use $N - P - 2$ instead.

Several formulas exist for inferences concerning a partial multiple correlation $_T PR$, though estimates of $_T PR$ suffer from the same lack of robustness as estimates of $_T pr_j$. Chi-square methods can be used for inferences about $_T Var(Y.X)$.

KEY TERMS

parameter	multivariate normality
statistic	expected value
statistical inference	unbiased estimator
linearity	vague versus specific conclusions
homoscedasticity	relevance of conclusions
normality	model degrees of freedom
standard assumptions	residual degrees of freedom
primary and secondary assumptions	mean, model, and error components
bivariate normality	of Y
conditional bivariate normality	augmented model

model sum of squares
error sum of squares
residual sum of squares
corrected total sum of squares
raw total sum of squares
total sum of squares
mean square
mean squared error

standard error of estimate
adjusted R and R^2
three-way decomposition
tolerance
variance inflation factor
singular
robust
conditional correlation

SYMBOLS AND ABBREVIATIONS

presubscript T E df df_r SS ANOVA F MSE Q SE t Tol_j
CR_j VIF VR z

PROBLEMS

1. An artificial data set, created by Dr. Lisa Hudson, appears in Table 5.7. "Satisfy" means satisfaction with life. Use a regression computer program to regress "satisfaction" onto the other variables. Explain the meaning of each item on the computer printout. Interpret some of the coefficients as adjusted differences as well as partial regression slopes.

TABLE 5.7
Some artificial data on the determinants of life satisfaction

	Income	Education	Race	Sex	Age	Satisfy
1	16	12	0	1	35	85
2	22	14	0	0	30	82
3	9	10	1	0	28	77
4	15	12	0	1	26	65
5	30	16	1	0	34	80
6	35	16	0	1	27	92
7	17	16	0	1	31	76
8	26	12	1	0	42	86
9	25	16	0	1	33	88
10	20	14	0	1	30	82
11	9	10	0	0	35	66
12	30	16	0	0	28	83
13	15	16	0	1	33	82
14	25	12	1	1	25	90
15	16	12	1	0	40	80
16	18	12	0	0	29	77
17	10	12	0	0	22	75
18	20	12	1	0	27	84
19	19	13	1	1	31	93
20	35	18	0	1	39	85

2. In Prob. 1, put a 95% two-sided confidence band around the coefficient for sex. Find a 95% one-sided confidence limit on the coefficient for income. Explain the meaning of these bands.

3. Report the t and df for testing the null hypothesis that the true coefficient of race is -1.

4. We can think of the five regressors as falling into two categories. Race, sex, and age are demographic variables over which a person has no control, while income and education are sociological variables over which a person can exert some control. Test the null hypothesis that the sociological variables have no relation to satisfaction when the demographic variables are controlled.

5. Collinearity lowers the (power, validity, both, neither) of hypothesis tests in regression. Collinearity among covariates is (more, less, equally) important in relation to collinearity among independent variables. Collinearity (raises, lowers, does not affect) validity shrinkage. The importance of the collinearity problem (will, will not) diminish as computers increase in speed and can perform ever more complex analyses.

The problems below concern Sec. 5.5 and are based on the data set of Table 5.7. Do only those problems pertaining to the parts of that section you have studied.

6. Find the one-sided 95% lower confidence limit for R.

7. Find the partial correlation between age and satisfaction, controlling the other four variables. Put a 95% two-sided confidence band around that correlation.

8. Find the unadjusted and adjusted values of the partial multiple correlation tested in Prob. 4.

9. Is the upper or the lower 95% confidence limit for Var($Y.X$) usually of more interest? Find the confidence limit you name.

CHAPTER

6

REGRESSION FOR PREDICTION

6.1 MECHANICAL PREDICTION AND REGRESSION

6.1.1 The Advantages of Mechanical Prediction

The need to predict one variable Y from several others arises in many contexts. College admissions officers may want to predict the grade-point average a student would achieve in the college if he or she were admitted. A firm hiring new employees may want to predict employee performance from a variety of factors. An insurance company may want to predict the remaining life span of someone applying for an insurance policy. Or a parole board may want to predict whether a prison inmate will commit more crimes if released.

Most people assume that there is no substitute for human judgment in these matters. However, it has been found that even when human judges follow the right rules in making predictions, they often follow them carelessly, so that they might make one prediction one day and make a different prediction the next day from the very same information. For this and other reasons, dozens of studies comparing mechanical prediction methods and human judgment have found that the mechanical methods outperform human judges far more often than the opposite; see Wiggins (1973).

Multiplication of two large numbers was no doubt once considered a great mental feat, but today we do not consider computers a threat to human values because they can multiply more quickly, cheaply, and accurately than we can. Prediction of weather, human behavior, and other events appears to be going

147

the same way. Humans can usefully design prediction systems and collect the data entering those systems, but it appears that in most cases the predictions themselves are best made mechanically.

6.1.2 Regression as a Mechanical Prediction Method

Regression is the standard method for mechanical prediction when sample sizes are large. For small samples there are many alternatives that we cannot begin to explore here; see Wiggins (1973) and Darlington (1978).

Consider a very simple case in which a college admissions office is considering the relative importance of tests of verbal and mathematical ability, labeled X_1 and X_2, respectively, in predicting success in college. One admissions officer might suggest that verbal ability is more important than mathematical ability, so that if the office must choose between the two tests it should choose X_1 over X_2. A second officer might point out that there is no need to choose between the two: they can be weighted equally, and the office will then select the applicants with the highest scores on the simple sum $X_1 + X_2$. A third officer might suggest that if it is agreed that verbal ability is more important than mathematical ability for most applicants, then X_1 should be weighted twice as heavily as X_2, which amounts to selecting the students highest on $2X_1 + X_2$. All these different ideas amount to using different weighted sums of X_1 and X_2; our three hypothetical admissions officers have suggested weighted sums of $1X_1 + 0X_2$ (which is the same as X_1), $X_1 + X_2$, and $2X_1 + X_2$, respectively.

You can use regression to help resolve questions like this. To do so, take a sample of current students, look back at their test scores in their admissions folders, and use regression formulas to construct the weighted sum which best predicts the cumulative college grade-point averages of these current students. Then use that same weighted sum for the new applicants. When we use regression for prediction in this manner, the regressors are often called *predictors*.

In this example you may have assumed that X_1 and X_2 were measured on roughly equal scales—for instance, if X_1 ranged from 200 to 800, then X_2 had the same range rather than ranging from, say, 1 to 10. If such different ranges were used, then the simple unweighted sum $X_1 + X_2$ would not weight the two tests equally in any meaningful sense—the sum would be determined almost entirely by scores on X_1. If the tests had used different scales, this would have complicated the discussion among the admissions officers.

But regression requires absolutely no assumption that different predictors are measured on comparable scales. For instance, X_1 and X_2 might be tests of verbal and mathematical ability ranging from 200 to 800, but the regression might include as X_3 high school grade-point average, which might range only from 1 to 4. The regression formulas will still find the weighted sum which yields the best prediction of Y in the sample of cases studied. Regression compensates for a predictor's low range by giving it a larger b. For instance, if we changed the range of high school grades from 1–4 to 100–400 by multiplying all the grade-point averages by 100, it would not change the predictions at all but would simply make b_3 one-hundredth the size it would be otherwise.

There are a great many differences between regression's use in prediction and its use in causal analysis. In prediction we refer to *predictors* and the *criterion* instead of regressors and the dependent variable. There is no distinction between independent variables and covariates—the terms are not used. The word *validity* loses its former meaning, and refers instead to the accuracy with which Y can be predicted. Variables are included or excluded from the analysis primarily on the basis of availability and ease of measurement. Interest focuses on R and related statistics; much less attention is paid to individual variables than to causal analysis. And when individual variables are studied, each variable's contribution to predictive power is of more interest than its regression slope. A valid analysis need not test individual slopes or contributions for significance. Cross validation or a close substitute must be used—a step not necessary in causal analysis. Modified versions of regression such as ridge regression, stepwise regression and item analysis are appropriate for prediction but not for causal analysis. And the next section introduces a whole set of concepts that have little or no relevance to causal analysis.

6.2   SEVEN PREDICTOR CONFIGURATIONS

As we might guess, the most important determinants of R are the correlations of the predictors with Y, called the *validities* of the predictors. But relations among predictors can also affect R, as described in this section.

6.2.1   Overview of Seven Configurations

We shall explore four configurations that can arise in prediction, called *independence, redundancy, complementarity,* and *suppression.* Redundancy, complementarity, and suppression can all be either partial or complete, while the word *independence* implies complete independence. Thus altogether we have seven configurations: independence, partial and complete redundancy, partial and complete complementarity, and partial and complete suppression.

The four "complete" configurations all require certain exact equalities (for instance, a certain correlation may have to be exactly 0), while the three "partial" configurations merely require certain inequalities (for instance, a certain correlation may have to be negative). Thus the three "partial" configurations are the ones usually observed. But the four "complete" configurations can help you understand the others, and they do occur occasionally. Partial redundancy is by far the most common of all seven configurations, and we shall call it the *standard configuration*.

In describing the seven configurations, we shall first consider only problems with two predictors, and then show how the seven configurations occur with more predictors.

6.2.2   Independence

When predictors are all independent, a very simple relation holds:

$$R^2 = r_{Y1}^2 + r_{Y2}^2 + r_{Y3}^2 + \cdots + r_{YP}^2 = \Sigma R_{Yj}^2$$

That is, R^2 is the sum of the squared validities. This formula makes it useful to think of each squared validity as a "proportion of variance explained" when predictors are independent. In this special case, proportions of variance simply add up, so that two variables accounting for 20% and 30% of the Y variance will together account for 50%. In Chap. 9 we will see that it is misleading to say that a variable accounting for 20% of Y variance is only two-thirds as "important" as one accounting for 30%. But provided that they are not misinterpreted, the additive nature of proportions of variance provides a convenient way to talk about differences among variables.

6.2.3   Partial Redundancy (the Standard Configuration)

Ordinarily, predictors correlate with each other, and thus duplicate each other's functions to some extent. We can then increase predictive accuracy by minimizing this duplication or redundancy. For instance, suppose we are predicting future performance in college and we know that overall college performance is predicted better by tests of verbal ability than by tests of mathematical ability. But if we already have a test of verbal ability, a second test of verbal ability is likely to improve the accuracy of predictions less than some other test with less redundancy, such as a test of mathematical ability. In the standard configuration, the higher the correlation between two predictors, the greater their redundancy.

6.2.4   Complete Redundancy

To say that one predictor X_2 is completely redundant with another predictor X_1 is not to say that the two correlate perfectly. Rather, it implies that adding X_2 to a regression containing X_1 does not increase R at all. A predictor variable may occasionally be completely redundant in this sense even though it correlates fairly highly with Y. For instance, suppose we are trying to predict college grade-point average Y and our two predictors are high school GPA and a test of academic ability. Suppose the ability test correlates positively with Y but this correlation falls to 0 when high school GPA is controlled. In other words, in a group of people with the same high school GPA, there is no correlation between the ability test and college GPA. You can probably see intuitively that the ability test is then useless in supplementing high school GPA as a predictor of college GPA. This is a case of complete redundancy.

6.2.5   Venn Diagrams

For problems involving three variables Y, X_1, and X_2, diagrams called *Venn diagrams* can illustrate the configurations of independence and complete or partial redundancy. In a Venn diagram, each variable is represented by a circle. The squared correlation between any two variables is represented by the degree of overlap between their circles, as in Fig. 6.1*a*.

   With three circles, the total overlap between the Y circle and the other two circles represents R^2. Figure 6.1*b* represents the case of *independence,*

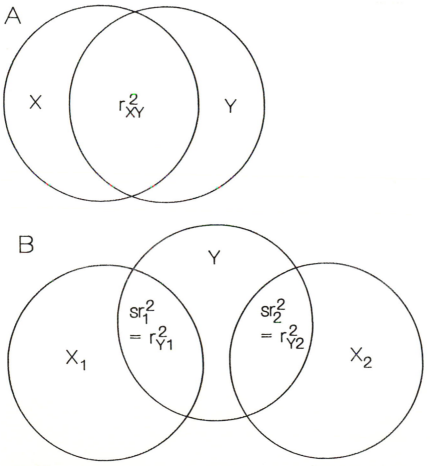

FIGURE 6.1
Four Venn diagrams illustrating (*a*) simple correlation, (*b*) independence of two regressors, (*c*) partial redundancy, and (*d*) complete redundancy.

C

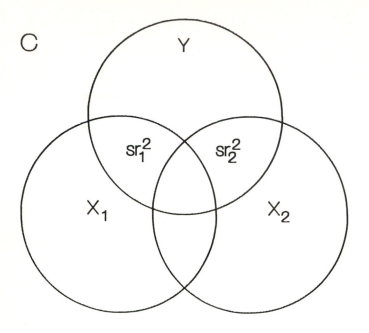

D

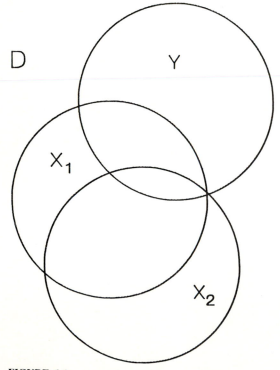

FIGURE 6.1
continued

since the X_1 and X_2 circles do not overlap. Because $R^2 = r_{Y1}^2 + r_{Y2}^2$ in this special case, the overlap of the X_1 and X_2 circles with the Y circle equals R^2.

In Fig. 6.1c, the values of r_{Y1}^2 and r_{Y2}^2 equal those in Fig. 6.1b. But the total overlap with Y is smaller than before, because of the overlap between X_1 and X_2. Each regressor's unique contribution, represented by the areas marked sr_1^2 and sr_2^2, is less than its squared correlation with Y, represented by its total overlap with circle Y. This illustrates the case of *partial redundancy*.

Figure 6.1d illustrates *complete redundancy*; X_2 adds nothing to the prediction of Y, even though it correlates somewhat with Y.

Venn diagrams are only approximate representations. They cannot represent negative simple or partial correlations, which arise in suppression and complementarity. And they cannot represent a case in which R^2 exceeds $r_{Y1}^2 + r_{Y2}^2$, which can arise under either suppression or complementarity. Figures 6.2 and 6.3 in Sec. 6.3.3 provide a more general way of visualizing the effect of r_{12} on the unique contributions of two predictors.

6.2.6 Complementarity

In Sec. 2.3.5 we defined complementarity as any situation in which the unique contribution of a set of regressors exceeds the sum of their individual unique contributions. In prediction we distinguish betwen ordinary complementarity and a type of complementarity we call suppression. In common usage in predictive contexts, only ordinary complementarity is even called complementarity, and we shall continue that usage here. So for predictive contexts with two predictors we shall define the predictors as complementary if they both have positive validities but correlate negatively with each other.

Under independence, R^2 equals the sum of the squared validities, but under complementarity R^2 may be far above this sum—a circumstance that Venn diagrams cannot represent. For instance, imagine that success as a trial lawyer is determined primarily by two traits—scholarly ability and acting ability. Imagine also that the correlation between these two abilities is highly

TABLE 6.1
An artificial data set illustrating perfect complementarity

X_1	X_2	Y
1	8	9
2	9	11
3	6	9
4	7	11
5	5	10
6	3	9
7	4	11
8	1	9
9	2	11

negative. Then either trait alone might be rather poor at predicting success as a trial lawyer, even though the two together could predict success excellently.

A numerical example can illustrate the point. In Table 6.1, scores on X_1 are simply the first nine integers, scores on X_2 are chosen to make r_{12} very negative but not -1 (here, $r_{12} = -14/15 = -.933$), and scores on Y are simply the sums of scores on X_1 and X_2. Because X_1 and X_2 correlate so negatively, their sum Y cannot correlate highly with either one; here, $r_{Y1} = r_{Y2} = \sqrt{1/30} = .183$. But we know that $R = 1$, since Y can be predicted perfectly from the other two variables. Thus the example actually illustrates *complete* or *perfect complementarity*. In this case, $r_{Y1}^2 + r_{Y2}^2 = 1/15 = .067$, so R^2 falls far above that sum.

6.2.7   Suppression

Imagine that we have a multiple-choice history test (X_1) which is an excellent measure of knowledge of history (Y), *except* that the test is highly speeded so that it favors people with high reading speed. Suppose we have a separate measure of reading speed X_2. Even though X_2 correlates positively with Y, we might find a surprising way to use it. If two people scored equally on the multiple-choice history test but person A scored higher than person B on reading speed, then we could argue as follows: low reading speed has lowered B's performance on the history rest relative to A, but B has still scored as high as A on that test, so B probably knows more history than A. In other words, for a given score on the multiple-choice history test, the lower a person's score on reading speed, the *more* history we guess that person knows.

But this is equivalent to giving reading speed a negative regression weight even though it correlates positively with Y. For instance, in the regression equation $\hat{Y} = 5X_1 - 2X_2 + 6$, the lower a person's score on X_2, the *higher* our estimate of the person's score on Y.

This illustrates a rule we can state more generally: if X_2 is a good measure of the sources of error (such as reading speed) in X_1, then, by giving X_2 a negative weight, we may be able to predict Y very accurately, even though neither X_1 nor X_2 alone is a very good predictor of Y. We are using X_2 to subtract out or correct for or *suppress* the sources of error in X_1. X_2 is then called a *suppressor variable*.

When we use regression, we do not have to guess whether suppression might work in a given data set. Regression automatically derives the weights b_j that yield best prediction in the current sample. If a variable having a positive or zero correlation with Y receives a significantly negative value of b_j, then by definition it is a suppressor.

In the extreme case, X_1 could have very large sources of error such as reading speed, but if X_2 measured those sources of error perfectly, we could completely correct for them and get perfect prediction, even though neither X_1 nor X_2 correlated highly with Y. Thus we would have *complete* or *perfect suppression*. For a simple fictitious example, imagine a sample of adults, each of whom was the older child in a two-child family. Suppose a personality trait Y is completely determined in such people by the subject's age when his or her younger sibling was born. Then Y will correlate little with the subject's age, and little with the age of the subject's younger sibling, but will correlate perfectly with the difference between the two.

Suppression rarely occurs in real data. But in one real case, school performance in the second grade was being predicted from the preschool version of the Stanford-Binet IQ test and another test called the Preschool Inventory. Best prediction of school performance in the second grade was actually obtained by weighting the Stanford-Binet negatively and the Preschool Inventory positively. This means that the Preschool Inventory was so much better a predictor than the Stanford-Binet that the latter test was actually most useful as a measure of the sources of error in the former.

As a matter of policy, most employment and admissions offices refuse to take advantage of any suppressors they may find in regression analyses. Few administrators in schools, government agencies, or corporations would survive publication of the fact that they actually select people with the lowest scores on certain tests. Rather, the insight gained by the discovery of suppressors is typically used to modify the other tests in the regression, to try to reduce the influence of reading speed or other forms of test-taking ability. The actual use of negative weights for tests is typically confined to analyses in research rather than actual selection of candidates.

6.3 RELATIONS AMONG THE SEVEN CONFIGURATIONS

6.3.1 The Centrality of r_{12}

The seven configurations of independence, partial and complete redundancy, partial and complete complementarity, and partial and complete suppression seem to represent a mind-boggling array of possibilities. But it turns out that if we have two predictors and think of the two validities r_{Y1} and r_{Y2} as fixed values, then the seven configurations simply represent different values or ranges of r_{12}. To explore this topic further, we must first consider the possible range of r_{12} for fixed values of r_{Y1} and r_{Y2}.

6.3.2 Possible and Impossible Combinations of Correlations

It should not surprise you to learn that if two variables have a correlation of .9 with each other, then it would be impossible for one to have a correlation of .9 with a third variable while the other has 0 correlation with the same variable. The material in Sec. 6.3.3 requires us to understand which combinations of correlations are possible and which are impossible. Therefore, for the case of two regressors, we now develop a formula showing the possible range of r_{12} as a function of r_{Y1} and r_{Y2}.

We know that $r_{12.Y}$, the partial correlation between X_1 and X_2 after partialing out Y, cannot fall above 1 or below -1. But we can use the formulas for partial correlation in Sec. 2.3.7 to write

$$r_{12.Y} = \frac{r_{12} - r_{Y1} r_{Y2}}{\sqrt{1 - r_{Y1}^2} \sqrt{1 - r_{Y2}^2}}$$

This formula shows that, for fixed values of r_{Y1} and r_{Y2}, $r_{12.Y}$ increases with r_{12}. Therefore we can find the range of possible values of r_{12} by setting $r_{12.Y}$ equal to $+1$ and -1 and solving for r_{12}. We find from this that the limits on r_{12} are

$$r_{Y1} r_{Y2} \pm \sqrt{(1 - r_{Y1}^2)(1 - r_{Y2}^2)}$$

For instance, if $r_{Y1} = .5$ and $r_{Y2} = .3$, then $-.676 < r_{12} < +.976$.

6.3.3 How the Seven Configurations Relate to r_{12}

As will be explained in Sec. 7.1.2, it is always possible to reflect a predictor variable (that is, reverse its scoring direction, making low scores high scores, and vice versa) so that it has a positive or zero correlation with Y. The following discussion assumes that this has been done for both X_1 and X_2. But this still allows r_{12} to be negative. Figure 6.2 shows how R relates to r_{12} when r_{Y1} and r_{Y2} are fixed at .5 and .3, respectively. In Sec. 2.3.7, we saw that

$$R^2 = r_{Y1}^2 + sr_2^2 = r_{Y1}^2 + \frac{(r_{Y2} - r_{Y1} r_{12})^2}{1 - r_{12}^2}$$

Figure 6.2 was constructed by using this formula to compute values of R for various values of r_{12} when $r_{Y1} = .5$ and $r_{Y2} = .3$. We shall use this figure to show how r_{12} relates to the seven configurations.

Two of the seven configurations have already been related to r_{12}; we said that *independence* implies $r_{12} = 0$ and *complementarity* implies $r_{12} < 0$. These configurations are marked in the figure.

We can define *suppression* as the case in which either b_1 or b_2 is negative even though r_{Y1} and r_{Y2} are both nonnegative. We shall consider the case in which b_2 is negative and then derive the result for b_1 by analogy. We have

$$b_2 = \frac{r_{Y2} - r_{Y1} r_{12}}{1 - r_{12}^2} \times \frac{S_Y}{S_2}$$

But S_Y, S_2, and $1 - r_{12}^2$ are all nonnegative, so b_2 is negative whenever $r_{Y2} - r_{Y1} r_{12}$ is. This, in turn, occurs if and only if $r_{12} > r_{Y2}/r_{Y1}$. A symmetrical argument shows that b_1 can be negative only if $r_{12} > r_{Y1}/r_{Y2}$. We have assumed

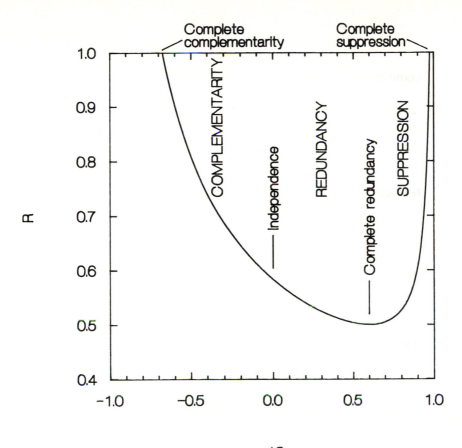

FIGURE 6.2

Complementarity, redundancy, and suppression as a function of r_{12} when $r_{Y1} = .5$ and $r_{Y2} = .3$.

that r_{Y1} and r_{Y2} are nonnegative, so we conclude that suppression occurs only if r_{12} is positive and above the lower of r_{Y1}/r_{Y2} and r_{Y2}/r_{Y1}. In the present example, these two values are $.5/.3$ and $.3/.5$, so suppression occurs if $r_{12} > .3/.5 = .6$. Figure 6.3 shows the values of sr_1 and sr_2 for each value of r_{12}; notice that sr_2 is negative in the suppression region. Note the overall similarity between Fig. 6.3 and Fig. 2.12 in Sec. 2.2.5, which plots b_1 and b_2 against r_{12} for the same values of r_{Y1} and r_{Y2}.

Complete redundancy occurs for X_2 if its optimum weight is 0. At the point of complete redundancy, R reaches its lowest possible value for fixed values of r_{Y1} and r_{Y2}; it equals the higher of these two validities. We see from the formula for b_2 that $b_2 = 0$ if $r_{Y2} - r_{Y1}r_{12} = 0$, which implies $r_{12} = r_{Y2}/r_{Y1}$. For the present example, we have $r_{12} = .3/.5 = .6$. This value is also shown in Fig. 6.2. Lower positive values of r_{12} yield the standard configuration of *partial redundancy*.

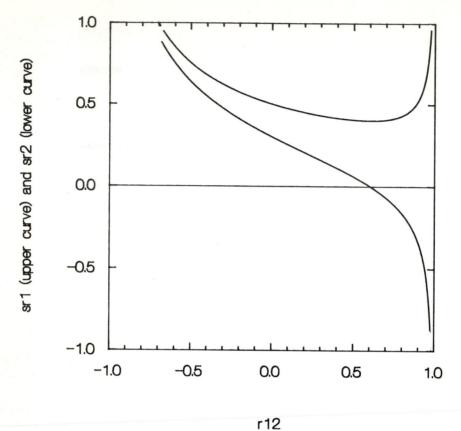

FIGURE 6.3
b_1 and b_2 as a function of r_{12} when $r_{Y1} = .5$ and $r_{Y2} = .3$.

As r_{12} becomes more negative with r_{Y1} and r_{Y2} fixed, the predictors become ever more complementary, until at the most negative possible value of r_{12} *complete complementarity* is achieved (at the far left in Fig. 6.2). At the right, as r_{12} increases, suppression becomes ever better, until at the maximum possible value of r_{12} we have *complete suppression*.

Thus, in summary, as r_{12} rises from its lowest to its highest possible value, we move through the seven configurations of complete and partial complementarity, independence, partial and complete redundancy, and partial and complete suppression.

6.3.4 Configurations of Three or More Predictors

When there are three or more predictors, we can define suppression as any case in which a variable receives a significant negative weight when it has a positive or zero correlation with Y. Complementarity can be defined as any significant negative correlation between regressors when both have a positive or zero correlation with Y. As before, complete complementarity or suppression occurs if $R = 1$ when no simple validity is 1, and complete redundancy occurs if some b_j is exactly zero. Independence occurs if all predictor correlations are zero. The standard configuration of partial redundancy can be defined as the absence of the other six configurations. We may be able to predict perfectly well without even knowing whether nonstandard configurations exist in the data. But understanding these configurations can help explain unexpected findings like negative b's or surprisingly high values of R.

6.4   ESTIMATING TRUE VALIDITY

6.4.1   Shrunken versus Adjusted R

Adjusted R was introduced in Sec. 5.2.6 as an estimate of the population multiple correlation $_TR$. This value is often confused with another value we shall denote $_TRS$.

There are actually two different senses in which $_TR$ is a population value: it itself is computed in the population, and it is computed from the population values $_Tb_j$. We could imagine correlating Y with $\hat{Y}$ in the *population* when $\hat{Y}$ has been computed from *sample* values of b_j. This correlation will be denoted $_TRS$. While the estimate of $_TR$ is called *adjusted R*, the estimate of $_TRS$ will be called *shrunken R* and will be denoted RS. The differences among R, $_TR$, and $_TRS$ can be represented as shown in Table 6.2.

When are we interested in $_TR$ and when in $_TRS$? Most questions concerning cause and effect concern $_TR$, while most questions concerning practical prediction concern $_TRS$. If we ask, "How well will the regression formula we have found predict Y in the total population or in a new random sample from the population?" we are asking about $_TRS$. If we ask, "How important are these variables in affecting Y?" we are asking about $_TR$. We might call $_TR$ the true predictive power of the *variables* in the regression analysis, while $_TRS$ measures the true predictive power of the *regression weights* b_j in the analysis.

A parameter can merely be estimated from sample data, and also it has a fixed though unknown value that is independent of the sample drawn. $_TRS$ has

TABLE 6.2
Shrunken R versus adjusted R

		Compute $r_{Y\hat{Y}}$ in:	
		Sample	**Population**
Compute b's in:	**Sample**	R	$_TRS$
	Population		$_TR$

the former property but lacks the latter; there is a different value of $_T RS$ for each sample drawn, though there is only one value of $_T R$. $_T R$ is a property of the population, while $_T RS$ is also a property of the sample's relationship to the population. We shall call $_T RS$ a *semiparameter* to reflect this fact.

Since $_T R$ is defined as $r_{Y\hat{Y}}$ when the true population weights $_T b_j$ are used to compute Y, no other set of weights can yield a higher value of $r_{Y\hat{Y}}$ in the population. Thus $_T RS$ cannot possibly exceed $_T R$ and will usually fall below it, often by a substantial margin. This is very important when we are interested in prediction; adjusted R is sometimes used as an estimate of the true validity, $_T RS$, but instead it estimates the completely different value $_T R$. $_T RS$ also almost always falls below R; this is known as *validity shrinkage*.

6.4.2   Estimating $_T RS$

Not counting adjusted R, $_T RS$ can be estimated in at least four different ways. By far the most common is *cross validation*. This method requires two samples of subjects with known scores on Y. The two samples may be randomly drawn subsets of one larger sample. Regression slopes b_j are calculated in one sample and then used to estimate the Y scores of all subjects in the other sample. These estimates are then correlated with the actual known Y scores of the subjects in the second sample.

Validity figures found by cross validation are often accepted as gospel (that is, as if they were $_T RS$ itself), when in fact they are merely approximately unbiased estimates of $_T RS$. They are subject to the same sampling errors as any simple correlation. When used to estimate $_T RS$, the uncorrected R suffers from both bias and random variability; cross validation removes the bias but not the random variability. To handle this problem, the Fisher z method of Sec. 5.5.4 can be used to find confidence limits for any correlation found by cross validation.

A little experimentation with the Fisher z method shows that if much faith is to be put in cross-validity figures, cross-validation samples must be moderately large. For instance, suppose we decide in advance that if our estimate of $_T RS$ turns out to be .4, we would like 95% confidence that $_T RS$ is at least .3. Formulas for the Fisher z, using a one-sided confidence band, show that the necessary cross-validation sample size is 211. If another 100 cases were used to derive regression weights, we would need over 300 cases altogether. Therefore cross validation with far smaller samples (a common practice) should be viewed as more a negative test than a positive one. That is, with smaller samples a low cross validity means we can have little faith in the predictions made from the regression, but a high cross validity may not mean we can have much faith in them.

Cross validation can be followed by deriving a second regression based on all cases in the two samples together. Even if there is no direct estimate of the validity of this regression, we can accept the cross-validity figure as a conservative estimate of the validity of this regression.

An extension of cross validation has the interesting name of *double cross validation*. In this method, the total available sample is divided in half, a regression or other prediction method is developed in each half and cross-validated in the other half. The average of these two cross-validity figures is taken as a conservative estimate of the validity of the final regression, which is developed in the total sample.

A third method called the *leave-one-out* method eliminates nearly all the conservatism of ordinary and double cross validation. In a sample of N cases, imagine developing a regression using cases 2 through N and using the regression to estimate Y for case 1. Then return case 1 to the sample and draw out case 2, develop the regression using the $N - 1$ cases left in the sample, and use the regression to predict case 2. Repeat this process N times, each time leaving out a different case. At the end you will have an estimate of Y for each case, made by a regression developed in a sample that has excluded that case. Any measure of the accuracy of the $\hat{Y}$ values is a true cross-validity estimate.

The leave-one-out method actually takes far less computer time than the previous paragraph implies. It can be shown that the error of prediction made by leaving out case i is $e_i/(1 - h_i)$, where h_i is a value defined in Sec. 14.1.4. We can use this knowledge to find fairly easily each case's estimated Y score as made from the sample of $N - 1$ omitting that one case.

If validity is expressed as a correlation, as it usually is, then the leave-one-out method has another problem. The higher the Y score of the omitted case, the lower the Y mean of the subsample omitting that case. This tends to increase the size of the errors as computed by the leave-one-out method, typically yielding negative values of $r_{Y\hat{Y}}$ when the method is applied to random numbers, which should typically yield correlations of 0. This can be corrected by computing the other $N - 1$ values of $\hat{Y}$ calculated from the regression based on $N - 1$ cases, computing the mean and standard deviation of those $N - 1$ values, and expressing $\hat{Y}_i$ as a standard score using that mean and standard deviation. This too can be done in far less computer time than one might imagine; formulas in Secs. 14.1.4 and 14.1.5 allow calculation of the mean and standard deviation of all the aforementioned leave-one-out values of $\hat{Y}$ without actually calculating the individual values. Details are available from the author; mention program LEAVOUT7.

A fourth estimate of $_TRS$, for the multivariate normal case, is due to Browne (1975). It uses the series of formulas shown below. In them, RSQ is R^2, ARS is adjusted R^2, RHO4 is an estimate of $_TR^4$, and RS is the estimate of $_TRS$.

$$\text{ARS} = R^2 - \frac{P \times (1 - R^2)}{N - P - 1}$$

If ARS < 0, then stop and take RS as 0.

$$\text{RHO4} = \text{ARS}^2 - \frac{2 \times P \times (1 - \text{ARS})^2}{(N - 1) \times (N - P + 1)}$$

If RHO4 $<$ 0, then set RHO4 $=$ 0.

$$RS = \sqrt{\frac{(N - P - 3) \times \text{RHO4} + \text{ARS}}{(N - 2 \times P + 2) \times \text{ARS} + P}}$$

My own unpublished studies have confirmed the accuracy of the Browne formula. Table 6.3 shows some values of RS calculated by it. Unless P is very small, the output of the Browne formula is determined primarily by the ratio N/P. For several combinations of adjusted R and N/P, shrunken R was calculated by the Browne formula for each of the 96 values of P from 5 to 100. Table 6.3 shows the maximum and minimum of these 96 values of RS for each combination of adjusted R and N/P.

All four of these methods—ordinary and double cross validation, leave-one-out, and the Browne method—yield approximately unbiased estimates of $_TRS$. But only ordinary cross validation gives a known fairly exact method—the Fisher z method—for finding confidence limits on $_TRS$. My own analyses indicate that when $_TRS$ is low, the standard error of the leave-one-out method is about $\sqrt{2/N}$; P has very little effect. When $_TRS$ is high, the standard error is

TABLE 6.3
Values of expected shrunken R

See text for detailed explanation.

				Adjusted R			
N/P	.2	.3	.4	.5	.6	.7	.8
2 Min	0.020	0.030	0.075	0.162	0.302	0.453	0.611
Max	0.090	0.137	0.185	0.241	0.355	0.487	0.638
3 Min	0.020	0.049	0.119	0.255	0.414	0.560	0.705
Max	0.088	0.131	0.202	0.313	0.435	0.567	0.707
4 Min	0.020	0.067	0.160	0.327	0.469	0.603	0.734
Max	0.087	0.133	0.237	0.352	0.475	0.604	0.737
5 Min	0.025	0.085	0.217	0.366	0.499	0.624	0.749
Max	0.085	0.153	0.261	0.377	0.499	0.627	0.753
6 Min	0.030	0.098	0.252	0.390	0.515	0.637	0.759
Max	0.084	0.168	0.278	0.395	0.518	0.642	0.763
8 Min	0.040	0.141	0.292	0.418	0.536	0.653	0.770
Max	0.086	0.190	0.302	0.420	0.541	0.658	0.774
10 Min	0.048	0.179	0.315	0.433	0.549	0.663	0.776
Max	0.099	0.205	0.318	0.437	0.554	0.667	0.780
12 Min	0.058	0.201	0.329	0.443	0.557	0.669	0.780
Max	0.108	0.216	0.329	0.448	0.562	0.673	0.783
15 Min	0.073	0.222	0.341	0.454	0.565	0.676	0.785
Max	0.119	0.228	0.344	0.459	0.570	0.679	0.787
20 Min	0.106	0.241	0.354	0.465	0.574	0.682	0.789
Max	0.132	0.242	0.358	0.469	0.578	0.685	0.790
25 Min	0.127	0.252	0.363	0.472	0.579	0.685	0.791
Max	0.141	0.253	0.366	0.476	0.582	0.688	0.792
30 Min	0.140	0.258	0.368	0.476	0.583	0.688	0.792
Max	0.148	0.261	0.372	0.480	0.585	0.690	0.794

below this value, so that $\sqrt{2/N}$ is always conservative. The leave-one-out and Browne methods give very similar estimates of $_TRS$ when distributions are approximately normal and both estimates are positive; the major difference betweeen the two is that the leave-one-out method can yield negative estimates of $_TRS$ while the Browne method cannot. Thus the figure of $\sqrt{2/N}$ can also be taken as a conservative estimate of the standard error of the Browne formula when distributions are approximately normal.

6.4.3 Fixed versus Random Regressor Scores

The methods of Sec. 6.4.2 all apply to random scores. The distinction between random and fixed scores is not needed for the inferential methods of Chap. 5, but it arises here and again in Chaps. 7 and 15. The distinction is essentially between planned (fixed) and observed (random) regressor scores. For instance, if an investigator decides in advance that a study will use five men and five women, then scores on the variable of gender are planned. But if the investigator merely draws a sample of ten people and then observes that five are men and five are women, the scores are random.

The distinction between random and fixed scores has nothing to do with the distinction between random and fixed effects in analysis of variance—a distinction that does not arise in this book. In fact, in ANOVA it is frequently assumed that cell frequencies are equal, which implies that they are planned or fixed.

The standard error of a regression slope is higher when scores are random than when they are fixed. This is easily seen in the present example, because even if the population is evenly split between men and women, there is a certain chance that a random sample of 10 cases will contain 0 men and 10 women, or 0 women and 10 men. In that case the regression slope of gender cannot be estimated at all, so its standard error is infinite. This is confirmed by the fact that an indicator variable's simple regression slope is a difference, and the sampling variance (the squared standard error) of a difference is $_TVar(Y.X) \times (1/n_1 + 1/n_2)$, which is infinite when either n_1 or n_2 is zero. But when N is 10, the overall sampling variance is a weighted average of the 11 possible conditional sampling variances that exist when there are 0, 1, 2, ... , 10 women in the sample. Since two of these 11 conditional sampling variances are infinite, the overall sampling variance is infinite. But if the distribution is fixed at 5 men and 5 women, the sampling variance is finite. The higher sampling variances under random scores translate into lower expected values of $_TRS$.

When regressor scores are normally distributed rather than dichotomous as in this example, sampling variances and standard errors are no longer infinite, but they are still higher than with fixed scores. This shows the need to assume normally distributed regressor scores for certain applications.

How could we have gotten through an entire chapter on statistical inference (Chap. 5) without mentioning the distinction between fixed and random scores? Why are dichotomous regressors like gender allowed if they produce infinite standard errors of regression slopes? The values of $SE(b_j)$ used in Chap. 5 are actually *conditional* standard errors—conditional on the particular pattern of regressor scores observed in the sample. Use of conditional standard errors is perfectly valid in hypothesis tests and confidence bands. For instance, if we happen to draw a sample of five men and five women, then we can justifiably have more confidence in the calculated value of b(gender) than if we happen to draw a sample of nine men and one woman. Thus, for hypothesis tests and confidence bands, it is reasonable to use the precise sample distribution of regressor scores to calculate standard errors, regardless of whether we would have exactly that same distribution in other samples—that is, regardless of whether regressor scores are random or fixed.

But the distinction between fixed and random scores arises in the discussion of power analysis in Chap. 15. For instance, when we have not yet collected any data and are estimating the power of a test on the difference between men and women, we can expect higher power if we know that the sample will contain five men and five women than if it might contain nine men and one woman, or even ten men and no women. The distinction between random and fixed scores also arises in Sec. 7.5.3, for reasons explained there.

6.4.4 Expected Squared Error of Estimate in New Samples

We can define a parameter which has the same relation to $_T\mathrm{Var}(Y.X)$ that $_T RS$ has to $_T R$. That is, if the *weights* derived in a sample are applied to the population as a whole, or to a new sample from the population, what is the expected mean squared error? Under random scores and multivariate normality, the unbiased estimator of this mean squared error is

$$MSE \times \frac{(N-2)(N+1)}{(N-P-2)N}$$

Under fixed scores, the unbiased estimator is

$$MSE \times \frac{N+P+1}{N}$$

(Darlington, 1968, pp. 173–174).

6.5   SELECTING PREDICTOR VARIABLES

We have seen that the true validity $_T RS$ is nearly always below $_T R$, which in turn is nearly always below R. Although regression analysis always finds the set of weights b_j that maximize validity in the immediate sample as measured by R, other methods may yield predictions which are more accurate for the population. This is especially true when N is small and P is large. These other methods are discussed in books on psychometric theory, and in Darlington (1978). Four journals that publish articles in the field are *Psychological Bulletin, Journal of Educational Measurement, Applied Psychological Measurement,* and the engineering statistics journal *Technometrics.*

Validity shrinkage can be minimized in ordinary regression by reducing the number of variables in an analysis. The rest of Sec. 6.5 discusses several methods used to accomplish this.

6.5.1 Stepwise Regression

The first method is stepwise regression. Standard computer programs for stepwise regression differ from each other more than do standard programs for ordinary regression, so we shall describe the method only in general terms. Both "forward" and "backward" versions exist. A simple "forward" stepwise regression starts by selecting, from a set of P predictors, the one predictor with the highest absolute validity $|r_{Yj}|$. We shall call the chosen variable Pre1, for "first predictor." The stepwise program then scans the remaining $P - 1$ predictors and selects the one which yields the highest value of R when combined with Pre1; we shall call this new predictor Pre2. The program then scans the remaining $P - 2$ predictors and selects the one yielding the highest R when combined with Pre1 and Pre2. It can proceed in this way until all P predictors have been added. This process yields P regressions: one with one predictor, one with two, one with three, and so on up to P.

The worker can then select, from these P different regressions, the one that seems to best combine small P with high R. One reasonable way to do this is to estimate $_rRS$ as in Sec. 6.4.2 for each of the P regressions and select the one regression with the highest estimate.

"Backward" stepwise regression starts with the full regression containing all P predictors and deletes predictors one at a time, each time deleting the one producing the smallest drop in R. Most modern statistical computer packages, including SYSTAT and SAS, have methods which can go either forward or backward. These programs add predictors one at a time, but if the addition of new predictors lowers the predictive contribution of some predictor added at an earlier step, that predictor may be dropped.

6.5.2 All-Subsets Regression

Because each of P predictors may be either included or excluded and these decisions are independent, there are actually no fewer than 2^P different regressions possible, counting the one containing no predictors. For large P, this number can be huge; when P is 5, 10, 15, or 20, 2^P is 32, 1024, 32,768 or 1,048,576, respectively. The various versions of stepwise regression each consider only a few possibilities. A method called *all-subsets regression* considers all possibilities. A statistic called the Mallows C_P is often used to choose the "best" of these regressions. In my opinion there is no clear rationale for C_P, and a superior strategy would be to use any of the estimates of $_TRS$ described in Sec. 6.4.2.

6.5.3 Which Variable-Selection Methods Are Best?

Once we have used stepwise regression or all-subsets regression to select a prediction formula, the estimates of $_TRS$ or mean squared error no longer apply to that one formula. The phenomenon is like regression to the mean; once we have selected the highest value of many values, we can no longer have confidence that its true value is as high as it appears.

When this factor is considered, some studies have found that forward stepwise regression is superior to backward, which in turn is superior to all-subsets regression. Thus the methods which appear most sophisticated may actually perform worst. This occurs because the major advantage of the backward and all-subsets methods is in discovering suppressor relationships that would be missed by the forward method. True suppressor relationships are fairly rare, but apparent ones are fairly common. Therefore methods that systematically look for them, especially without accompanying hypothesis tests, may be misleading more often than simpler methods that ignore them.

We repeat that stepwise regression and all-subsets regression are crude methods in comparison with other prediction methods available in the literature on psychometric theory. However, they may be reasonably satisfactory if N is large relative to P.

SUMMARY

6.1 Mechanical Prediction and Regression

Dozens of studies comparing mechanical prediction methods and human judgment have found that mechanical methods outperform human judges far more often than the opposite. Regression provides *one* method of mechanical prediction. When we use regression for prediction in this manner, the regressors are often called *predictors*. Regression requires absolutely no assumption that different predictors are measured on comparable scales. The most important determinants of R are the correlations of the predictors with Y, called the *validities* of the predictors. But relations among predictors can also affect R.

6.2 Seven Predictor Configurations

Four configurations that can arise in prediction are *independence, redundancy, complementarity,* and *suppression*. Redundancy, complementarity, and suppression can all be either partial or complete, while the word *independence* implies complete independence. Partial redundancy is by far the most common of all seven configurations, and we call it the *standard configuration*.

When predictors are all independent, R^2 is the sum of the squared validities. This fact makes it useful to think of each squared validity as a "proportion of variance explained" when predictors are independent.

To say that one predictor X_2 is completely redundant with another predictor X_1 is not to say that the two correlate perfectly. Rather, it implies that adding X_2 to a regression containing X_1 does not increase R at all. A predictor variable may occasionally be completely redundant in this sense even though it correlates fairly highly with Y.

For problems involving three variables Y, X_1, and X_2, diagrams called *Venn diagrams* can illustrate the configurations of independence and complete or partial redundancy. In a Venn diagram, each variable is represented by a circle. The squared correlation between any two variables is represented by the degree of overlap between their circles. Venn diagrams cannot represent negative simple or partial correlations, which arise in suppression and complementarity. And they cannot represent a case in which R^2 exceeds $r_{Y1}^2 + r_{Y2}^2$, which can arise under either suppression or complementarity.

If two predictors with positive validities correlate negatively with each other, they are said to be *complementary*. Under complementarity, R^2 may greatly exceed the sum of squared validities.

If X_2 is a good measure of the sources of error in X_1, then by giving X_2 a negative weight we may be able to predict Y very accurately even if neither X_1 and X_2 alone is a very good predictor of Y. We are using X_2 to subtract out or correct for or *suppress* the sources of error in X_1. X_2 is then called a *suppressor variable*. We do not have to guess whether suppression might work in a given data set. Even when suppression is present, regression automatically derives the weights b_j that yields best prediction in the current sample. If a variable having a positive or zero correlation with Y receives a significantly negative value of b_j, then by definition it is a suppressor. In the extreme case, X_1 could have very large sources of error, but if X_2 measured those sources of error perfectly, we could completely correct for them and get perfect prediction even if neither X_1 or X_2 correlated highly with Y. Thus we would have *complete* or *perfect suppression*.

6.3   Relations among the Seven Configurations

If we have two predictors and think of the two validities r_{Y1} and r_{Y2} as fixed values, then the seven configurations simply represent different values or ranges of r_{12}. As r_{12} rises from its lowest to its highest possible value, we move through the seven configurations of complete and partial complementarity, independence, partial and complete redundancy, and partial and complete suppression.

When there are three or more predictors, we can define suppression as any case in which a variable receives a significant negative weight when it has a positive or zero correlation with Y. Complementarity can be defined as any significant negative correlation between regressors when both have a positive or zero correlation with Y. Complete complementarity or suppression occurs if $R = 1$ when no single predictor correlates perfectly with Y, and complete redundancy occurs if some b_j is exactly zero. Independence occurs if all predictor correlations are zero. The standard configuration of partial redundancy can be defined as the absence of the other six configurations.

6.4   Estimating and Maximizing True Validity

We define *shrunken R* as an estimate of $_T RS$, the true predictive power of the *regression weights* b_j in the analysis. In contrast, $_T R$ is the true predictive power of the *variables* in the regression analysis when their weights are the true population weights. $_T RS$ cannot possibly exceed $_T R$ and will usually fall below it, often by a substantial margin. We call $_T RS$ a *semiparameter,* because on the one hand, like a parameter, it is an important value that can only be estimated from sample data, but on the other hand its value is determined by the sample, unlike a true parameter.

Four methods for estimating $_T RS$ are ordinary and double cross validation, the leave-one-out method, and a formula by Browne. Of these, only ordinary cross validation gives a known fairly exact method—the Fisher z method—for finding confidence limits on $_T RS$.

The standard error of a regression slope is lower when regressor scores are fixed (planned in advance) than when they are random (merely observed).

We can define and estimate a parameter which has the same relation to $_T \text{Var}(Y.X)$ that $_T RS$ has to $_T R$.

6.5   Selecting Predictor Variables

Stepwise regression and all-subsets regression are two variants of regression often used to select a few predictor variables from many. Stepwise regression may work forward (starting with no variables and adding one at a time) or backward (starting with all and deleting one at a time) or both. Forward stepwise regression is the simplest of these methods, but often works better than the more complex methods. All these methods are crude in comparison with other prediction methods available in the literature on psychometric theory. However, they may be reasonably satisfactory if N is large relative to P.

KEY TERMS

mechanical prediction
predictor
criterion
validity
independence
partial and complete redundancy

partial and complete
   complementarity
partial and complete suppression
standard configuration
Venn diagram
validity shrinkage

shrunken R

semiparameter

cross validation

double cross validation

leave-one-out method

Browne formula

fixed versus random regressor scores

conditional standard error

stepwise regression

forward and backward stepwise
 regression

all-subsets regression

SYMBOLS AND ABBREVIATIONS

C_P RS

PROBLEMS

1. To which of the seven basic configurations do Venn diagrams apply?
2. Under which configurations can R^2 exceed the sum of squared validities?
3. Find R when $r_{Y1} = .4$, $r_{Y2} = .2$, and $r_{12} = .1$.
4. How many different regressions are examined in forward stepwise regression when $P = 7$? In all-subsets regression? In both cases include the "null" regression that has no predictors except the constant.
5. Before collecting any data, you guess that $_TR = .4$ when $P = 7$. If you fit the regression in a sample of 70 cases, what is the lowest you would expect $_TRS$ to be, assuming multivariate normality?

The problems below are more difficult, and should be done only if specifically assigned.

6. Use the Browne formula to estimate $_TRS$ if the correlation in Prob. 3 were found in a sample of 50 cases.
7. If $r_{Y1} = .6$ and $r_{Y2} = .4$, find the values or ranges of r_{12} which yield each of the seven configurations.
8. How large a cross-validation sample would be needed to make the lower 95% one-sided confidence limit on $_TRS$ equal to .2 if the estimated value of $_TRS$ were .4?

PATH ANALYSIS AND HIERARCHICAL DESIGNS

7.1 PATH DIAGRAMS

7.1.1 Causal Arrows

Path diagrams are used to represent hypotheses or conclusions about causal relations between variables. To construct a path diagram, we simply write the names of the variables and draw an arrow from each variable to any other variable we believe it affects. *A* plus or a minus next to an arrow tells whether the effect is believed to be positive or negative.

For instance, recall the preschool example in Sec. 1.1.3. In Holly City we found three results: working-class children attended preschool more often than middle-class children, middle-class children outperformed working-class children on a test of school readiness, and preschool attendance related positively to school readiness when socioeconomic status (SES) was controlled. These findings are consistent with the hypothesis that in Holly City, SES affects school readiness positively but affects preschool attendance negatively while preschool attendance affects school readiness positively. The three parts of this hypothesis are represented by the three arrows in Fig. 7.1.

In Ivy City, on the other hand, we found middle-class children attending preschool more often than working-class children and found no association between preschool attendance and school readiness when SES was controlled. As in Holly City, we found a positive association between school readiness and SES. These findings are consistent with the causal hypotheses in Fig. 7.2.

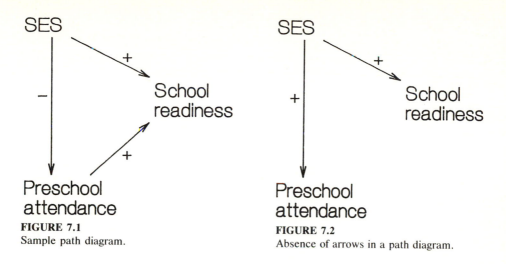

FIGURE 7.1
Sample path diagram.

FIGURE 7.2
Absence of arrows in a path diagram.

The terminology is not standard, but we shall distinguish between *input* and *output* path diagrams. An output path diagram is one like Fig. 7.1 or Fig. 7.2, representing the output or results of a statistical analysis. Methods for creating output path diagrams are described in Sec. 7.4.1. An input path diagram is one that is drawn before the analysis to help plan the analysis. Diagrams of this kind are particularly useful for planning the kinds of analyses described later in this chapter.

An input path diagram contains *primary* and *secondary* arrows. Primary arrows mark the effects of primary interest between independent and dependent variables; we can mark them with question marks to show that we hope to determine whether the effect in question exists. In the preschool example, for instance, the primary question is whether preschool attendance affects test scores, so we can mark the arrow representing this question as shown in Fig. 7.3.

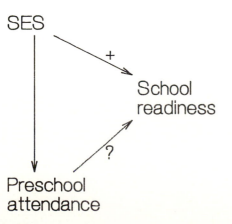

FIGURE 7.3
An input path diagram.

Secondary arrows point to or from covariates. They represent effects of only minor interest, which we may not even bother to test. In Fig. 7.3, the two arrows from SES are secondary arrows. We might say that we merely assume that secondary arrows exist, but this is misleading, since the word *assumption* suggests that the study may be invalid if the assumption is false, and that is not the case here. It is more accurate to say that we *allow* that the secondary arrows may exist. Our study would be simpler if we were confident that they did not exist. In Fig. 7.3, we would not have to control for SES if we were confident that the arrows from SES did not exist. But by studying the partial relationship instead of the simple relationship between preschool attendance and later school readiness, we are performing the analysis in a way that allows that the arrows from SES may exist.

Because secondary arrows merely *allow* causal connections to exist, assumptions are represented by their *absence* rather than their presence; we exclude a secondary arrow between two variables only when we are confident that neither affects the other. This is the opposite of what you might imagine.

Plus and minus signs are optional in input path diagrams; they merely aid thinking. They represent mere guesses, and an error in the guess does not invalidate the analysis. In Fig. 7.3, the plus sign on the arrow from SES to school readiness shows that we are fairly confident that this relationship is positive if it exists at all. The absence of signs on the other two arrows in Fig. 7.3 shows that we have little idea of the signs of those effects.

7.1.2   Reflecting Variables

If we wish, we can sometimes rewrite path diagrams to eliminate negative relationships by *reflecting* variables. For instance, Fig. 7.4 suggests that wealth increases with age while liberalism decreases. But the same idea is expressed with positive signs by Fig. 7.5. *Reflecting* a variable means replacing it by its opposite, such as replacing liberalism by conservatism or extroversion by introversion. All correlations involving the reflected variable are equal to the original correlations, but opposite in sign. For instance, if liberalism has a correlation of $-.3$ with age, then conservatism has a correlation of $+.3$. It is

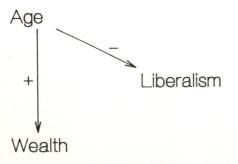

FIGURE 7.4
A negative arrow.

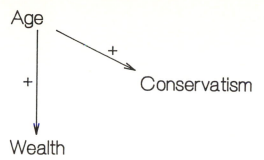

FIGURE 7.5
The result of reflection.

not always possible to eliminate all negative correlations by reflection, but the number of such correlations may be reduced.

7.1.3 Double-Headed and Headless Arrows

Figure 7.5 indicated that if we held age constant by taking a sample of people all about the same age, then in that sample we would observe no correlation between wealth and conservatism. On the other hand, if wealth caused greater conservatism, then the diagram would be as shown in Fig. 7.6. This diagram suggests a positive partial relationship between wealth and conservatism when age is controlled.

Sometimes we believe or allow that there is some causal relation between two variables X and Y but we have little idea whether X affects Y, or Y affects X, or each affects the other, or some unmeasured variable affects both. For instance, a positive relationship between wealth and conservatism might occur because wealth creates conservative attitudes, or because conservative ideology fosters a work ethic which produces wealth. Or some conservatives might argue that increased intelligence produces both wealth and conservatism. Often we cannot distinguish among these various hypotheses but still wish to show in a path diagram that there is some association between the two variables, independent of the other variables in the diagram. This can be done

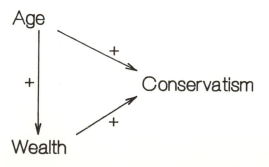

FIGURE 7.6
Another path diagram.

Wealth ⟵⟶ Conservatism

Wealth —————— Conservatism

either by a double-headed arrow or simply by a line between the two variables, as shown in Fig. 7.7.

7.2   DIRECT, INDIRECT, AND TOTAL EFFECTS

7.2.1   Basics

One variable may affect another either directly or indirectly, through other variables. Or it may have both direct and indirect effects. For instance, exercise may affect weight loss in three ways: directly, as calories are consumed during exercise; indirectly, by curbing or stimulating appetite; and also indirectly by "permanently" raising metabolic rate. Each variable's regression weight b_j measures only its *direct effect* on Y, ignoring any *indirect effects* that may work through other regressors. A variable's *total effect* is the sum of its direct and indirect effects. In Sec. 2.2.3 we regressed weight loss onto exercise, food intake, and metabolism and found a regression slope of 1.045 for exercise. This was only the direct effect of exercise, not the total effect, which includes any indirect effects operating through food intake and metabolism.

The fact that b_j measures only part of the effect on X_j on Y is another reason, besides that given in Sec. 2.2.1, for calling b_j a measure of the partial relationship between X_j and Y. But a variable's total effect is not necessarily larger than its direct effect; if a direct effect were positive and the indirect effects were negative, the total effect might even be zero.

We saw in Sec. 4.2.1 that all effects are indirect in a sense. Even something as simple as a hammer blow's effect on a nail is mediated by forces between individual molecules. We call an effect indirect only if it operates through another *measured* variable.

The simplest way to estimate a total effect rather than a direct effect is simply to leave the mediating variables out of the regression. Several examples of this appear in Sec. 7.2.2.

7.2.2   Examples of Direct and Indirect Effects

Suppose a school system raises the requirements for promotion from eighth grade to ninth grade. School officials hope that this will encourage students to study harder, and will thus increase their average performance as measured by a nationally standardized achievement test. If we wanted to study the effect of the new requirements on test performance by comparing average performance before and after the change in requirements, we certainly should not control for study time. Controlling for study time is much like selecting a group of students whose average study time after the change matches that before the change. Even if the new requirements improve test performance by making students study harder, we would still expect to find no difference between the two groups when average study time is controlled. Rather, the simple change in test performance would better measure the effect of the change in requirements. Controlling for study time is controlling out the very mechanism causing the effect of interest. In this case we are most interested in the new policy's total effect on achievement, not its direct effect. To estimate the total effect, we leave out of the regression the mediating variable of study time.

Both direct and total effects may provide useful information. If we controlled for study time, then the direct effect of requirements on achievement could tell us whether the change in requirements affects test performance by any mechanism *other* than by increasing study time. For instance, the change in requirements might send a message to teachers and principals that more effective teaching is expected. In terms of the path diagram in Fig. 7.8, controlling for study time is studying the presence of the upper right arrow. This diagram shows one direct arrow or path from requirements to test performance, and another, indirect path from requirements to performance through study time. Like the hammer's effect on the nail, the direct effect is considered to be direct only because we have not measured mediating variables such as teacher effort.

In this example we are more interested in the total effect of changed requirements than in their direct effect, but in other examples we might be most interested in the direct effect of an independent variable, and in still other examples we might be interested in both. For instance, suppose we assume or allow that SES affects grades in school, and that grades affect the school track that teachers recommend to a child's parents. Thus, we assume that SES affects track placement indirectly through grades, as shown in Fig. 7.9. The question of interest is whether SES also affects track placement directly. That

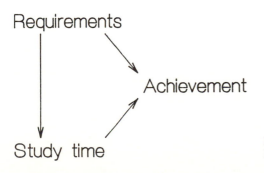

FIGURE 7.8
Direct and indirect effects.

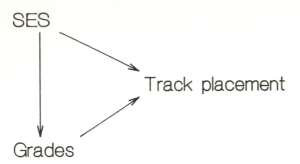

FIGURE 7.9
More direct and indirect effects.

is, is a child from a middle-class background more likely to be placed on a high track than children from a working-class background who have earned the same grades? In this case we might be most interested in the direct effect.

Or consider the effect of preschool attendance on school achievement as measured at the end of second grade. Suppose an experiment had been done in which some children were randomly assigned to a preschool program while others were assigned to a control group. There is then no need to control for factors like SES, because it can be assumed that those factors relate only randomly to the independent variable of preschool attendance. But some educators might argue that preschool attendance produced a temporary artifactual inflation of IQ test scores, that children with high IQ scores were given more attention by the first- and second-grade teachers, and that this mechanism produced the positive effect of preschool on achievement scores at the end of second grade. In Fig. 7.10, this hypothesis is represented by the indirect path from preschool to achievement through IQ scores. Other educators might consider this implausible, or argue that it does not matter how preschool affects achievement so long as the effect does exist. The former educators would be most interested in assessing the direct effect of preschool on achievement with IQ scores controlled; the latter group would be most interested in the total effect. This is a case, then, where both effects are of substantial interest.

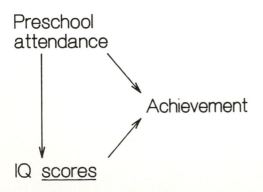

FIGURE 7.10
Still more direct and indirect effects.

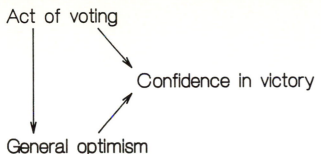

FIGURE 7.11
Direct and indirect effects in a randomized experiment.

7.2.3 Examples Involving Random Assignment

In Sec. 4.2.4 we considered an example in which people in one randomly chosen experimental group were told they were probably good at tasks of a certain type and were then found to persist longer than others in trying to solve impossible problems of that type. Given that the effect exists, we might want to know whether the effect is produced by self-confidence or by liking for the experimenter. We suggested seeing whether controlling measures of either characteristic eliminated the effect. This was actually an example of studying indirect effects in experiments.

A second example is given by an experiment that took place during the 1984 presidential election (Regan and Kilduff, 1988). Voters were asked to rate their confidence that their candidate would win. A randomly chosen half of the voters were asked just before entering the polling place, while the other half were asked just after leaving. Average confidence ratings were significantly higher for the second group; the act of voting seems to somehow increase a voter's confidence that his or her candidate will win. But how does voting produce this effect? Does it work merely because exerting power by voting will increase one's optimism about the world in general? To control for this, voters were asked a question designed to measure general optimism. The difference

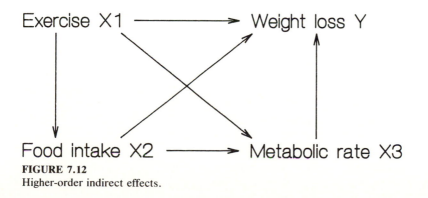

FIGURE 7.12
Higher-order indirect effects.

between the two groups was still significant when this covariate was controlled, and optimism did not have a significant partial relation to confidence, so the effect does not appear to work through general optimism. In this case, then, the effect appears to be direct rather than indirect. The two hypotheses are diagrammed in Fig. 7.11.

7.2.4   Larger Problems and Higher-Order Indirect Effects

When there are more variables, the situation can be more complex than in previous sections. Consider again the example of Sec. 2.2.3, with four variables:

$$X_1 = \text{exercise}$$

$$X_2 = \text{food intake}$$

$$X_3 = \text{metabolic rate}$$

$$Y = \text{weight loss}$$

It is reasonable to suppose that exercise might directly affect food intake, metabolic rate, and weight loss; that food intake might directly affect metabolic rate and weight loss; and that metabolic rate might directly affect weight loss. Thus there may be six direct effects altogether, each corresponding to an arrow in Fig. 7.12. This diagram shows that exercise might affect weight loss in four different ways: directly, indirectly through food intake, indirectly through metabolic rate, and via a *doubly indirect* path through both food intake and metabolic rate. In still larger problems there could be even higher-order indirect effects, such as triply or quadruply indirect effects.

7.3   HIERARCHICAL REGRESSION

7.3.1   Terminology and Notation

If we assume that two regressors X_1 and X_2 both affect each other, then we cannot estimate the total effect of either on Y—at least not without additional data or assumptions that are beyond the scope of this book. But if we assume that X_1 affects X_2 while X_2 does not affect X_1, then we have seen in Sec. 7.2 that we can estimate the total effect of each, by controlling X_1 while measuring the effect of X_2 but not controlling X_2 while measuring the effect of X_1. This assumption establishes a *causal hierarchy* between X_1 and X_2, so the analysis is *hierarchical*. The analysis is also called *sequential*, because we first predict Y from X_1 alone and then from X_1 and X_2 together, so that we add the variables to the regression sequentially. The analyses of previous chapters are now called *simultaneous* to distinguish them from hierarchical analyses. To indicate that a value of b_j, pr_j, sr_j, PR, SR, or SS is computed in a hierarchical analysis, we shall precede it by h or H, so that the statistic becomes hb_j, hpr_j, hsr_j, HPR, HSR, or HSS.

HSS values are sometimes called *incremental* sums of squares, but this is somewhat ambiguous, since a regressor's "incremental sum of squares" could also be taken to mean its *unique SS*—the amount SS(error) would increase if the regressor were deleted from an ordinary simultaneous regression. We shall not use this term.

7.3.2 Four Types of Hierarchical Analysis

An analysis like that just described, which measures effects by regression slopes, can be called an "ordinary" hierarchical analysis to distinguish it from a *hierarchical variance decomposition*, or *hierarchical decomposition*, for short. In this analysis, the contribution of each successive regressor or set of regressors is measured by the reduction in sum of squared errors when the regressor or set is added to those preceding it in the hierarchy. This reduction, of course, equals the increase in SS(model) when the regressor or set is added. The contribution of each regressor or set is also proportional to its value of hsr^2 (for a single regressor) or HSR^2 (for a set), and is sometimes reported in those terms; each value of HSS is SS(total) times the corresponding value of hsr^2 or HSR^2.

A hierarchical analysis may be either *complete* or *partial*, depending on whether the regressors are placed in a complete causal sequence. For the example on weight loss, in Sec. 7.2.4 we assumed that food intake (X_2) affects metabolism (X_3) but metabolism does not affect food intake. This latter assumption is questionable. It may be that exercise suppresses appetite *by* raising the blood sugar level and metabolic rate. But food intake also affects metabolism; people's metabolism drops if they have not eaten for a day but rises again as soon as they eat. This suggests that the proper path diagram is not Fig. 7.12 but Fig. 7.13. This figure contains all the arrows of the previous one, plus an arrow from metabolism to food intake.

If this is the correct diagram, then we should analyze this example in a partially hierarchical manner, first entering exercise, then entering food intake

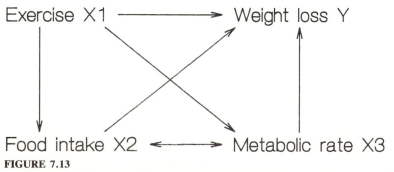

FIGURE 7.13
A double-headed arrow in the weight-loss model.

and metabolism. This change does not affect the measured importance of exercise, whether measured by a regression slope or by a contribution to variance.

Both an ordinary hierarchical analysis and a hierarchical variance decomposition can be either complete or partial, so we have 2×2 or 4 varieties of hierarchical analysis. The choice between complete and partial analyses is, of course, determined by the ability or inability to place regressors in a complete causal hierarchy. And ordinary analyses cannot be applied to sets of variables. My own opinion is that the ordinary approach is more informative and should be used whenever possible. I believe that decompositions are popular primarily because of their similarity to the classical ANOVA approach. Leland Wilkinson, the creator of SYSTAT and MYSTAT, appears to feel the same way, since those packages make decompositions considerably less convenient than SAS does. If in doubt, both ordinary analyses and decompositions can be reported. Both appear frequently in the literature. Complete and partial varieties of both approaches are illustrated in Sec. 7.3.3.

7.3.3 Examples of the Four Types

For the current example, a *complete ordinary hierarchical analysis* would report the following statistics:

> b(exercise) $= 1.75$ when neither exercise nor food intake is controlled.
> b(food intake) $= -.5$ when exercise is controlled.
> b(metabolism) $= .636$ when food intake and exercise are controlled.

The t and significance level p for each slope would, of course, normally also be reported; these values appear near each slope on the printout. In the present example we have the results shown in Table 7.1.

A *partial ordinary hierarchical analysis* would report only the value 1.75 for exercise and its significance level; the mutual causality between food intake and metabolism prevents us from estimating the total effect of either.

A *complete hierarchical decomposition* would report the results shown in Table 7.2. The *HSS* values are given directly by SAS as type I sums of squares, requested by adding the option SS1 to the MODEL statement. In SYSTAT and MYSTAT they would be calculated as follows. SS(total) can be found from any regression at all to be 98.5, so that is the value of SS(error) we would find in a

TABLE 7.1
Sample results of an ordinary hierarchical analysis

Effect	b	t	p (two-tailed)
Exercise	1.75	4.850	.0013
Food intake	$-.5$	-1.984	.0876
Metabolism	.636	2.746	.0335

TABLE 7.2
**Sample results of a complete
hierarchical decomposition**

Source	HSS	df
Exercise	73.5	1
Food intake	9.	1
Metabolism	8.9091	1
Residual	7.0909	6
Total	98.5	9

TABLE 7.3
**Sample results of a partial
hierarchical decomposition**

Source	HSS	df
Exercise	73.5	1
Food and metabolism	17.9091	2
Residual	7.0909	6
Total	98.5	9

"model" which included only a constant. When exercise is added to that model, SS(error) is lowered by 73.5, from 98.5 to 25.0. When food intake is added to exercise, SS(error) further drops 9.0, from 25.0 to 16.0. When metabolism is added to this model, SS(error) drops by 8.9091, from 16.0 to its final value of 7.0909. If we choose to report the three contributions in terms of sr^2, we divide the numbers in the table by 98.5 to get values of .7462, .0914, and .0904, respectively. We would then report that exercise, food intake, and metabolism explain, respectively, about 75%, 9%, and 9% of the variance in weight loss, for a total of about 93%. This total is the model R^2.

A *partial hierarchical decomposition* would be just like the complete decomposition, except that we would pool the contributions of food intake and metabolism, treating them as a set. This produces the results shown in Table 7.3. Or hierarchical contributions could be reported as percentages of total variance explained; we have hsr^2(exercise) $= 73.5/98.5 = 74.6\%$ and HSR^2(food and metabolism) $= 17.9091/98.5 = 18.2\%$.

7.3.4 Hypothesis Tests in Hierarchical Decompositions

If the figures for a completely hierarchical decomposition were found with SYSTAT, MYSTAT, or SAS, there would be no need to test values of HSS or hsr^2 for significance, since the same printouts that give the successive values of SS(error) also give the significance of each contribution. For instance, the p's of the hierarchical contributions of 73.5, 9.0, and 8.9091 are the same as the p's for the regression slopes of 1.75, $-.5$, and .636 mentioned earlier. Note that these slopes come from three separate regressions.

But this approach does not allow us to test the significance of the HSS value for a set in a partially hierarchical decomposition, such as the value 17.9091 for food intake and metabolism in Table 7.3. Therefore we need a more general approach. That approach is provided by the formula

$$F = \frac{\text{mean square of effect or source being tested}}{\text{mean square for all later sources, including the residual}}$$

A mean square is the ratio of a sum of squares to its associated df. The denominator mean square is the sum of all *later SS* values, including the residual, divided by the sum of all the associated df. When testing all effects, it is most efficient to start summing the SS column from the bottom.

When this approach is applied to a completely hierarchical decomposition, we find the same significance levels as by the previous method. In the present example, we start with the HSS and df values shown in Table 7.4. Starting at the bottom of the HSS column, the successive partial sums are 7.0909, 16, and 25, giving the F's shown at the bottom of the table. The p values for these tests are the same as given in Table 7.1; in the order the F's are listed here, the p's are .0335, .0876, and .0013.

For the partial hierarchical decomposition, we have

$$F(\text{food \& metabolism}) = \frac{17.9091/2}{7.0909/6}$$

$$= 7.5769 \quad df = 2, 6; p = .0228$$

It might seem reasonable to use the final residual mean square as the denominator for testing all HSS values, not just the final one. Such tests are

TABLE 7.4
Sample F tests in a hierarchical decomposition

Source	HSS	df
Exercise	73.5	1
Food intake	9.	1
Metabolism	8.9091	1
Residual	7.0909	6

$$\text{Metabolism } F = \frac{8.9091/1}{7.0909/6} = 7.5385 \qquad df = 1, 6$$

$$\text{Food intake } F = \frac{9/1}{16/7} = 3.9375 \qquad df = 1, 7$$

$$\text{Exercise } F = \frac{73.5/1}{25/8} = 23.52 \qquad df = 1, 8$$

called "model II" tests by Cohen and Cohen (1975, 1983). Section 7.5.3 describes the limitations of this approach.

7.4 PATH ANALYSIS

7.4.1 Basics

Path analysis provides a more complete description than hierarchical analysis of the pattern of relationships among a set of variables. In a path analysis, we simply regress each variable in turn onto the set of variables preceding it in the hierarchy. We test the significance of every slope in each regression. Then we create an *output path diagram* by drawing an arrow for each significant slope. We may sometimes define "significant" to imply practical as well as statistical significance, so that we draw arrows only for effects that are both statistically significant and large enough to be of interest.

Note that opposite "default options" are used for input and output path diagrams. In input diagrams, arrows are included by default, and their omission represents an active assumption. In output diagrams, arrows are not included unless there is actual evidence for them.

Path analysis computes so many different statistics that we need a whole new type of notation to describe them. Let the partial relationship between a dependent variable A and an independent variable B, controlling for covariates C, D, and E, be denoted by $AB.CDE$. That is, the dependent variable is listed first, then the independent variable; and then all covariates are listed after a dot. Thus the partial relationship between Y and X_1, controlling for X_2 and X_3, is denoted by $Y1.23$. To denote a particular measure of partial relationship such as a regression slope b or a correlation r, we will show the b or r followed by parentheses showing which relationship is meant. For instance, $b(Y1.23)$ is the regression slope of X_1 when Y is regressed onto X_1, X_2, and X_3. Statistics involving Y can also be described by the h notation of Sec. 7.3.1. Thus, in a completely hierarchical analysis with $P = 3$, we have $hb_1 = b(Y1)$, $hb_2 = b(Y2.1)$, and $hb_3 = b(Y3.12)$.

7.4.2 Path Analysis of the Weight-Loss Data

In the following example, we assume a complete causal hierarchy. We omit the hypothesis tests, so the diagrams will show every value, whether significant or nonsignificant. Where exercise is X_1, food intake is X_2, metabolic rate is X_3, and weight loss is Y, we first regress X_2 on X_1, then regress X_3 on X_1 and X_2, and then regress Y on X_1, X_2, and X_3. The first regression gives the value in the first row of Table 7.5, the second gives the two values in the second row, and the third gives the three values in the last row. All six of these values were actually calculated in Chap. 2. They are given here in exact fractional form to illustrate a point in Sec. 7.5.1. Each of these values corresponds to one of the arrows in Fig. 7.14.

TABLE 7.5
Some slopes computed in the weight-loss data set

$b(21) = .5$
$b(31.2) = 1.5$ $\quad\quad b(32.1) = 1$
$b(Y1.23) = \dfrac{23}{22}$ $\quad\quad b(Y2.13) = \dfrac{-25}{22}$ $\quad\quad b(Y3.12) = \dfrac{14}{22}$

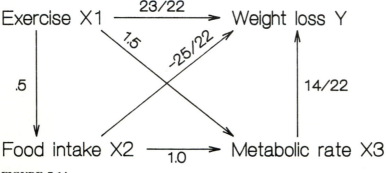

FIGURE 7.14
Estimated effect sizes in the weight-loss model.

7.4.3   An Example on Faculty Unions

Figure 7.15 was inspired by a study on the factors making university professors favor or oppose a faculty union. Besides age, academic rank, and salary, the three variables in the path diagram are three questionnaire items: how much the respondent trusts his or her department head, how much the respondent trusts the central administration of the university, and how strongly the respondent favors or opposes a faculty union. Only statistically significant relationships are

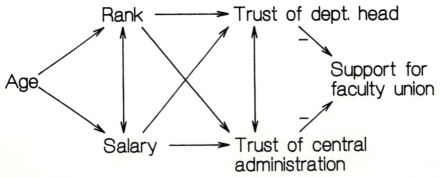

FIGURE 7.15
A path diagram on support for faculty unions.

represented by arrows. Many statements about partial relationships can be read from this diagram. A few of them are:

• Rank and salary correlate even when age is held constant, since a line connects them.
    • When rank and salary are held constant, age does not correlate with any of the opinion items, since no path connects them directly.
    • Age, rank, and salary correlate with opinions about a faculty union, but not when the two trust variables are held constant.

7.5 CONCLUDING REMARKS

Hierarchical analysis and path analysis require many difficult judgments. We have neglected the point because there is not much we can say about it, but a conscientious researcher may agonize for days over some of the choices that we may have implied are easily made.

7.5.1 Relations among Direct, Indirect, and Total Effects

We can define additive and multiplicative laws for hierarchical regression. These have nothing to do with the additive and multiplicative laws of basic probability. The additive law says that every total effect is the sum of its constituent direct and indirect effects. The multiplicative law says that every indirect effect is the product of its constituent direct effects.

    The multiplicative law makes good intuitive sense. For instance, if each baby born increased demand for disposable diapers by an average of 500 (if this figure seems low, remember that not all families use disposable diapers) and each such diaper sold, on the average, increased employment in that industry by .02 hours, then each baby born would increase employment in that industry by $500 \times .02$, or 10 hours.

    We can use our weight-loss example to show that the additive law is also intuitively reasonable, and to illustrate both laws. Consider the total effect of X_1 on Y. As mentioned earlier, this effect has four constituents: the direct effect, the indirect effect through X_2, the indirect effect through X_3, and the "doubly indirect" effect through both X_2 and X_3. First we can compute the values of the three indirect effects:

Indirect effect through X_2:

$$.5 \times \left(\frac{-25}{22}\right) = \frac{-12.5}{22}$$

Indirect effect through X_3:

$$1.5 \times \frac{14}{22} = \frac{21}{22}$$

Indirect effect through X_2 and X_3:

$$.5 \times 1 \times \frac{14}{22} = \frac{7}{22}$$

The direct effect was $\frac{23}{22}$. The total effect is the sum of all four direct and indirect effects:

$$\text{Total effect} = \frac{23}{22} - \frac{12.5}{22} + \frac{21}{22} + \frac{7}{22} = \frac{38.5}{22} = 1.75$$

By the same laws, the total effect of X_2 on Y is $1 \times \frac{14}{22} - \frac{25}{22} = -.5$. These values (1.75 and $-.5$) are the values for total effects we found by hierarchical analysis in Table 7.1.

The calculations just illustrated are not ones you would ordinarily perform. If you used the additive and multiplicative laws to calculate total effects from direct effects, you would not know the standard errors of the total effects and would thus be unable to apply inferential statistics. Sequential analysis gives total effects and their standard errors as well. The purpose of this section is merely to help you understand the relations among direct, indirect, and total effects.

7.5.2   Sequential and Path Analysis Using Standardized Slopes

As mentioned in Sec. 2.3.6, a standardized slope beta_j is defined as the slope b_j that would be found if Y and X_j were adjusted to standard deviations of 1 before the analysis. Standardized slopes can be found without actually performing these adjustments; they can be computed from ordinary slopes by the formula $\text{beta}_j = b_j \times (S_j/S_Y)$.

All the formulas we have presented using slopes apply to standardized slopes as well. In particular, the relations in Sec. 7.5.1 among direct, indirect, and total effects apply to standardized slopes. Many textbooks describe those relations primarily in terms of standardized slopes.

Standardized slopes are used primarily to enable workers to compare regressors with each other in a way that cannot be done with ordinary slopes. For instance, $b_1 > b_2$ does not imply at all that X_1 is "more important" than X_2, because the relative sizes of b_1 and b_2 are determined by arbitrary units of measurement. Thus the College Board could easily decide to score its tests on a scale from 0 to 4, like grades in most high schools and colleges, instead of the present scale from 200 to 800. That would lower each test's range and standard deviation by a factor of 600/4, or 150, and thus increase b_j by 150 times, without changing the real importance of the tests at all. Standardized slopes avoid this problem.

However, for reasons explained in Sec. 9.3, I prefer other scale-free measures—especially semipartial correlations—for comparing the importance of regressors. Therefore standardized slopes are de-emphasized throughout this book.

7.5.3 An Easily Misused Test Employing *HSS* Values

In a hierarchical analysis it might seem reasonable to use the residual mean square as the denominator of all F's, not just the F testing the last effect. This mean square is called a "model II" error term by Cohen and Cohen (1975, 1983). Such error terms are routinely used in analysis-of-variance (ANOVA) designs, where the final residual mean square is normally used to test all effects. But this is valid only under two circumstances: when scores are fixed (see Sec. 6.4.3), or when the regressor tested interacts with another variable whose population mean is known and has been set to zero. The latter condition is discussed in Sec. 13.4.3; the former is considered next.

The limitations of model II error terms are seen most clearly in testing the effect of X_1 on Y when another variable X_2 comes after X_1 in the hierarchy and in fact X_2 correlates perfectly with Y. If X_1 actually has no effect on Y, then in the population X_1 has zero correlation with Y—and also with X_2, because of the perfect correlation between Y and X_2. With fixed scores, we know the population correlations among regressors and we set sample values to equal the population values. We will thus set $r_{12} = 0$, forcing r_{Y1} to be zero as well. We thus find the correct answer: X_1 has no effect on Y. But with random scores, r_{Y1} will rarely be exactly zero. But since the denominator of F is zero (or can be made arbitrarily close to zero), the effect can be highly significant. This point is apparently little known to behavioral scientists but well known to mathematical statisticians; despite the obvious nature of model II error terms, I have been unable to find them recommended for random-score analyses in any text written by a mathematical statistician.

SUMMARY

7.1 Path Diagrams

Path diagrams are used to represent hypotheses or conclusions about causal relations between variables. To construct a path diagram, we write the names of the variables and draw an arrow from each variable to any other variable we believe it affects. A plus sign or a minus sign next to an arrow tells whether the effect is believed to be positive or negative.

An *input* path diagram is one based on little or no data, which we use to express our beliefs about the causal relations among the variables in a planned analysis. An *output* path diagram is one based on that analysis. In an input path diagram, we draw an arrow not only when we *assume* that the corresponding effect exists, but also whenever we *allow* that it may exist. In an input diagram, the *absence* of an arrow represents an assumption. In an output diagram, arrows are typically drawn only for effects confirmed by the data.

We can sometimes reduce the number of negative relationships in a path diagram by *reflecting* variables—replacing a variable by its opposite.

Sometimes we believe or allow that there is some causal relation between two variables X and Y but we have little idea whether X affects Y, Y affects X, each affects the other, or some unmeasured variable affects both. Such relations can be represented by either a line or a double-headed arrow between the two variables.

7.2   Direct, Indirect, and Total Effects

One variable may affect another either directly or indirectly, through other variables. Or it may have both direct and indirect effects. A variable's *total effect* is the sum of its direct and indirect effects. All effects are indirect in a sense; we call an effect indirect only if it operates through another *measured* variable. Indirect effects may operate in a variety of complex ways. The simplest way to estimate a total effect rather than a direct effect is simply to leave the mediating variables out of the regression.

7.3   Hierarchical Regression

If we assume that X_1 affects X_2 while X_2 does not affect X_1, this assumption establishes a *causal hierarchy* between X_1 and X_2, so the analysis is *hierarchical*. The analysis is also described as *sequential*, because we add the variables to the regression sequentially. The analyses of previous chapters are now described as *simultaneous*, to distinguish them from hierarchical analyses.

To indicate that a value of b_j, pr_j, sr_j, *PR*, *SR*, or *SS* is computed in a hierarchical analysis, we precede it by h or H, so that the statistic becomes hb_j, hpr_j, hsr_j, *HPR*, *HSR*, or *HSS*.

In an "ordinary" hierarchical analysis, the sizes of effects are measured by regression slopes. In a *hierarchical variance decomposition*, the contribution of each successive regressor or set of regressors is measured by the reduction in sum of squared errors when the regressor or set is added to those preceding it in the hierarchy. The contribution of each regressor or set is proportional to its value of hsr^2 (for a single regressor) or HSR^2 (for a set); each value of *HSS* is *SS*(total) times the corresponding value of hsr^2 or HSR^2. My own opinion is that the ordinary approach is more informative for single variables.

A hierarchical analysis may be either *complete* or *partial*, depending on whether the regressors are placed in a complete causal sequence.

In a hierarchical decomposition, the contribution of each regressor or set can be tested by the formula

$$F = \frac{\text{mean square of effect or source being tested}}{\text{mean square for all later sources, including the residual}}$$

7.4   Path Analysis

In a path analysis, we regress each variable in turn onto the set of variables preceding it in the hierarchy. We test the significance of every slope in each regression. Then in a path diagram we draw an arrow for each significant slope. We may sometimes define "significant" to imply practical as well as statistical significance.

7.5 Concluding Remarks

The additive law of hierarchical regression says that every total effect is the sum of its constituent direct and indirect effects. The multiplicative law says that every indirect effect is the product of its constituent direct effects. If you used the additive and multiplicative laws to calculate total effects from direct effects, you would not know the standard errors of the total effects and would thus be unable to apply inferential statistics. Sequential analysis gives total effects and their standard errors as well. But these laws help you understand the relations among direct, indirect, and total effects.

Sequential and path analysis are often performed using standardized slopes. This practice is not really incorrect, but standardized slopes are de-emphasized in this book for reasons explained in Sec. 9.3.

Tests using "model II" error terms are valid only under restricted circumstances.

KEY TERMS

path diagram	doubly indirect effect
causal arrow	hierarchical regression
input path diagram	simultaneous regression
output path diagram	sequential regression
primary arrows	completely hierarchical regression
secondary arrows	partially hierarchical regression
reflection of variables	hierarchical decomposition
double-headed arrow	type I SS
direct effect	path analysis
indirect effect	incremental SS (two meanings)
total effect	model II error term

SYMBOLS AND ABBREVIATIONS

hb_j hpr_j hsr_j HSR HSS $b(Yj.kh)$

PROBLEMS

1. Subjects in a learning experiment are given a short booklet to read on the behavior of apes. In condition A, the booklet's pictures are in color. In condition B, the same pictures appear but are in black and white. Booklets are distributed randomly. All

subjects are asked to study the booklets for 30 minutes, after which they will be tested on the material. No particular reward is offered for performing well. The experimenter then leaves the room. Without the subjects' knowing, the experimenter watches through a peephole and measures the amount of time each subject spends actually looking at the booklet. After 30 minutes, subjects are tested on the material.

The methods of this chapter suggest four causal hypotheses that might be tested from these data—three concerning direct effects and one concerning a total effect. Describe them, and describe the methods for testing each one.

2. In Prob. 1, suppose exactly half the subjects in each experimental condition are male and half are female. Suppose also that subjects in condition A (color pictures) score substantially higher on the test than those in condition B.
   (a) Where would sex fit in the causal hierarchy established in Prob. 1?
   (b) If you found HSS values using a computer program for completely hierarchical analysis, would HSS(sex) depend on whether "sex" appeared before or after "color" in the analysis?
   (c) If "color" has a large effect on test scores, then will placing sex first rather than second in this analysis raise, lower, or leave unchanged its F?
   (d) What about its t?

3. Use the data from three variables—income, education, sex—in the *problems* for Chap. 5 (see Table 5.7). Put the variables in what you consider to be a reasonable causal sequence.
   (a) Use path analysis to calculate the three direct effects. Draw the appropriate path diagram. Which of the three effects is (are) significant?
   (b) Find the one "total effect" that is not also a direct effect. Using all three direct effects, whether significant or not, show that the total effect is the sum of a direct and an indirect effect.
   (c) Use hierarchical sums of squares to test the two total effects on Y. Show that the F's you find are the squares of t's you found earlier.

4. If we draw a path diagram while planning a study, does each arrow in the diagram mean that we *assume* that an effect exists, or that we *allow* that it exists? What is the difference between the two?

CHAPTER
8

MAJOR
AND
MINOR
PROBLEMS:
AN
OVERVIEW

This chapter describes about a dozen problems that often arise in regression analyses. Some are less serious than you might imagine. Others are serious if unattended, but have solutions that are often simple and acceptable. Still others require supplementary analyses, such as checks for nonlinearity or outliers (extreme scores), that are described in later chapters. Still other problems are best handled by more advanced or more specialized statistical methods that are detailed in other works. The purpose of this chapter is to convey a general idea of the seriousness of various problems and the complexity of their solutions, without yet examining the more complex solutions in detail.

8.1   AN ASSORTMENT OF PROBLEMS

8.1.1   Violations of the Basic Sampling Assumptions

The central sampling assumptions of regression were mentioned in Chap. 5: linearity, normality, homoscedasticity, and random sampling. Chapter 12 shows methods for detecting nonlinearity and for transforming variables to make them satisfy the requirement of linearity. The assumptions of normality and homoscedasticity are relatively unimportant when sample sizes are large.

For smaller samples, Chap. 14 describes procedures for detecting and correcting for deviations from these two conditions. And Sec. 14.3.2 shows that useful conclusions can sometimes be drawn even in the absence of random sampling. Thus we are not completely lost even if all four of the standard sampling assumptions of regression are violated.

8.1.2   Collinearity

Collinearity was examined at length in Chap. 5, especially in Secs. 5.3.2, 5.4.4, and 5.4.5. But one major problem left unsolved is the problem of identifying collinear sets. When the number of regressors P is large, there will frequently be several regressors with nonsignificant partial relations to Y. But removing all these variables from the regression may lower R^2 significantly. This suggests strongly that the regressors contain one or more collinear sets. But which variables are in those sets, and which are not? Knowing the answer allows us to be far more specific in our conclusions. For instance, if the three variables of income, education, and occupational status form a collinear set that relates significantly to $Y,$ you may be able to conclude that Y is affected by socioeconomic status. But if you merely know that these three variables are among 10 heterogeneous variables whose removal significantly lowers R^2, you cannot draw such a specific conclusion.

We can often tentatively identify collinear sets merely by inspecting the names of the variables or the matrix of correlations among the regressors. But more elaborate methods are available for more difficult problems.

Factor analysis and cluster analysis of regressors are two methods capable of discovering sets of regressors highly correlated with each other. These methods are too complex to explain here, but many statisticians are familiar with them. Recently, much attention has been paid to a method by Belsley, Kuh, and Welsch (1980) for discovering patterns of collinearity. This method is essentially a crude form of factor analysis; it is my personal (minority) opinion that the interested worker would do better to read a standard source on factor analysis, or to consider the method in the next paragraph.

A better solution is offered by all-subsets regression. This method was described in Sec. 6.5.2, although we did not end up recommending it highly for the prediction problems considered there. As described in that section, all-subsets regression can efficiently find R^2 for every possible subset of regressors. It was invented for the purpose of finding subsets of *few* regressors yielding *high* values of R^2. But suppose we turn it around, using it to find subsets of *many* regressors yielding values of R^2 well *below* the R^2 found from the entire set. Such cases suggest that the *excluded* subset of variables is highly important. For instance, if a subset of seven regressors out of 10 yields an R^2 far below that found from the entire set of 10, it means that the excluded three regressors are highly important when considered as a set. By having the computer print out all possible values of R^2, we can scan the printout to find low values of R^2 associated with large numbers of regressors. Then the excluded variables are important as a set even though none may be significant individually. Because all-subsets regression examines every possible set of regressors, this method identifies without fail those sets of regressors whose deletion most lowers R^2.

This method, however, does have a weakness related to regression to the mean. When we scan many sets of regressors to identify the most important sets, the sets so identified may not actually be as important as they appear in the current sample. Methods for dealing with multiple hypothesis tests, discussed in Chap. 11, can deal with this problem.

8.1.3   Singularity

Singularity is the extreme case of collinearity, in which one or more regressors is predicted perfectly from other regressors, making $\text{Tol}_j = 0$ for those regressors. Singularity always occurs in sets of two or more variables. Two regressors that have a correlation of $+1$ or -1 with each other form a two-variable singular set; each is perfectly predictable from the other, so $\text{Tol}_j = 0$ for both. If it takes two or more variables to perfectly predict a regressor X_j, then each of the involved variables is itself perfectly predictable from others. For instance, if X_4 is predicted perfectly from X_2 and X_3 by the equation $X_4 = 2X_2 + 5X_3 + 8$, then simple algebra shows that $X_2 = .5X_4 - 2.5X_3 - 4$ and that $X_3 = .2X_4 - .4X_2 - 1.6$. This illustrates a three-variable *singular set*. In most cases of singularity, some of the regressors are included in a singular set and others are not. Any variable in a singular set contains no information not contained in other variables in the set, so its unique contribution to Y is zero and its value of $SE(b_j)$ is infinite.

There are at least four ways a computer program can handle singular sets. Worst of the four is to arbitrarily drop from the analysis as many variables as necessary to remove the singularity. This does correctly warn the worker that singularities exist and that no conclusions can be drawn concerning the omitted variables. But this procedure artificially lowers values of $SE(b_j)$ for the other variables in the singular sets, often without warning the worker that this has occurred.

Two better approaches are for the program to refuse to run, identifying the reason as singularity, or to run but to omit printing any values of $SE(b_j)$ or the t's calculated from them. MYSTAT, SYSTAT, and SAS all do one or the other of these. Better still would be to make these omissions only for regressors in singular sets, printing the full range of output for other regressors, since all these statistics are valid. If the singular sets include only covariates rather than any independent variables of primary interest, then this approach gives you all the output you need. Unfortunately, this approach is currently rare.

If there is only one singularity, you can use SYSTAT, MYSTAT, or SAS to find the variables in the singular set by starting to run all P crosswise regressions, one at a time. If the dependent variable in a particular crosswise regression is *not* in the singular set, then the computer will print for that regression the same singularity message it has printed for the overall regression. But if the dependent variable in a particular crosswise regression *is* in the singular set, the regression will run and will print a multiple correlation of 1.0. And in this regression, all other variables in the singular set will have nonzero values of b_j, while $b_j = 0$ for all variables not in the singular set. You need not run all P crosswise regressions; you may stop as soon as you have identified the variables in the singular set. You can then run the original regression with one of these variables omitted, paying no attention to results for any variables from the formerly singular set. Results for all other variables are meaningful, and will be the same regardless of which variable has been removed from the singular set. But note the difficulty in the next paragraph.

Occasionally, the crosswise regressions may themselves contain singular sets. This can occur if the original regression contains two or more singular sets, or if two or more variables must be dropped from a singular set to remove the singularity. To identify singular sets under these circumstances, apply the method of the previous paragraph to ever smaller sets of variables until the singularities are uniquely identified.

8.1.4   Specification Error and Overcontrol

Specification errors are errors in assumptions about which variables affect which others. These assumptions are essential for causal analysis but irrelevant for prediction. The basic specification errors are *undercontrol* and *overcontrol*.

Undercontrol is essentially the problem we have been considering since the beginning of this book: failure to control relevant variables. In any sort of causal analysis, we must assume that the regression includes all variables affecting Y, or that any excluded variables affecting Y are uncorrelated with those in the regression. This is simply saying we must control for all necessary covariates.

We must also assume that Y does not affect any of the regressors. Inclusion in the regression of a variable affected by Y will be called *overcontrol*. One part of this requirement is obvious and another part is not. It is obvious that if we want to interpret an association between X_j and Y as due to the effect of X_j on Y, then we must assume that the association is not produced by the effect of Y on X_j. Thus, when interpreting any given partial slope b_j, we must assume that Y does not affect that particular regressor.

But the problem of overcontrol has a second, less obvious aspect. Even when interpreting a single partial slope b_j, we must assume that Y does not affect any of the *other* regressors. Therefore unnecessary inclusion of extra covariates can raise the problem of overcontrol.

The problem of overcontrol can best be explained by an example. Suppose we are interested in the effect of academic aptitude on study time. It might be argued that naturally bright students foresee professional careers that require studious preparation, so those students study harder than others. Contrariwise, it might be argued that bright students find that they can obtain

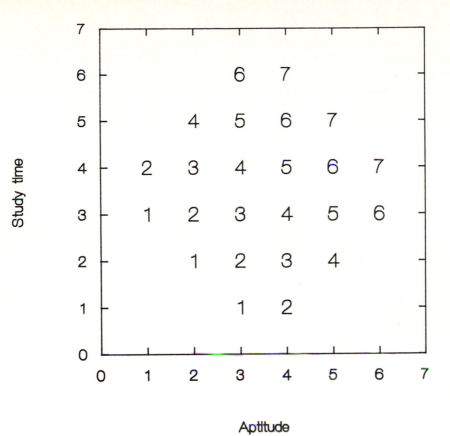

FIGURE 8.1
Illustration·of overcontrol.

satisfactory grades without much study, so that they study less than others. Both of these might be true, but it is still meaningful to ask which effect is stronger. We can examine this question by seeing whether the correlation between an aptitude measure (X_1) and study time (Y) is positive or negative.

Suppose that in fact aptitude has no effect on study time, so that $_Tr_{Y1} = 0$. In a sample of 24 people, we might observe a scatterplot somewhat like that in Fig. 8.1. For the moment, ignore the numbers in the body of the table; just interpret each number as a dot. The scatterplot clearly shows a correlation of 0.

Suppose this is just one of several related questions we are studying, and in the questionnaire measuring aptitude and study time we have also asked for each student's grade-point average. We enter this into the computer with our other variables. Then, since the grade-point average is in our data set anyway, we decide to control for it statistically; we add it to the regression as X_2.

The numbers in the body of the scatterplot are these grade-point averages, measured on a 7-point scale. We see that they are arranged much as we might expect; students high on both aptitude and study time have the highest grade-point averages, those low on both have the lowest, and the intermediate grade-point averages are obtained by the students high on aptitude but low on study time, or high on study time but low on aptitude, or intermediate on both.

The simplest way to see the effect of controlling for grade-point average is to consider a simpler method of control: select a subgroup of people who all have the same grade-point average and observe the conditional correlation (the correlation in that subgroup) between aptitude and study time. For instance, select all the people represented by scores of 4 in the body of the scatterplot. But a glance at the scatterplot shows this conditional correlation to be highly negative. This negative correlation is what we would expect; speaking loosely, it says that there are three kinds of students getting intermediate grade-point averages of 4: those low on aptitude but high on study time, those high on aptitude but low on study time, and those intermediate on both. All other students will have grade-point averages either above or below 4. Thus, within the group scoring 4, there will have to be a negative correlation between aptitude and study time, no matter what the overall correlation is. The same negative correlation would be observed if we computed partial regression slopes. Thus we find a negative partial relationship when the true effect is zero.

Figure 8.2 shows how we have violated the rule. Our dependent variable of study time affects grade-point average, so controlling that average is an error. One way to think about the problem of overcontrol is to say that if X_j affects Y and Y affects another regressor X_k, then by controlling X_k we are controlling or removing part of the effect of X_j, and we do not want to do that.

The major factor tempting us to make the error of overcontrol is that the very word *control* sounds so good that controlling more variables would always seem to be better. Students in introductory courses in experimental psychology are often encouraged to control as many variables as possible in their experiments. The existence of computers and statistical measures of partial relationship would appear to make that easy. If extra variables are in the data set anyway, why not control for them? But in fact, the decision to control or not control each variable should be based on careful thought.

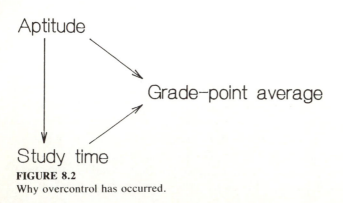

FIGURE 8.2
Why overcontrol has occurred.

Some authors use the term *overcontrol* to refer to the small loss of statistical power that results from the inclusion of each unnecessary covariate; see Secs. 5.4.6 and 15.2.4. I prefer the meaning given in this section. Since *under*control refers to a potentially drastic loss of validity that can result from failure to control even one covariate, it is reasonable to use *overcontrol* to refer to a potentially drastic loss of validity resulting from incorrectly controlling even one extra variable, rather than to refer to a *small* loss of *power* from such control.

8.1.5   Noninterval Scaling

Regression might seem to rely heavily on the assumption of equal-interval scaling. Yet many of the scales behavioral scientists use are merely ordinal: attitude scales, measures of success, and the like. How can we justify using such variables in regression analyses?

Unfortunately, the term *equal-interval scaling* is used to refer to three separate issues: linearity, normality, and equality of importance of a variable's units. A critic may say that a variable lacks equal-interval scaling because its scatterplot with other variables in the analysis exhibits nonlinearity. Or a nonnormal distribution may be cited. Or it may be argued that a variable's units are not equal to each other in importance. We can deal with all three of these issues, but the solutions have little to do with each other.

Chapter 12 describes tests for nonlinearity in a regression analysis and regressor transformations that can restore linearity. Section 17.6 describes linearity-restoring transformations of *Y*. Chapter 14 describes methods for detecting nonnormality, and significance tests and confidence bands that can be used in regression even when distributions are nonnormal. But differences in importance of units must be dealt with on a case-by-case basis. Suppose a high-jumper is considering a new training regimen which may raise the best jumps from 6.5 to 7 feet but which may just as well produce minor strains that will lower performance to 6 feet; the jumper simply has to make a subjective judgment about the relative importance of the two differences: between 6 and 6.5 feet, and between 6.5 and 7 feet. A gymnast rated on a 10-point subjective scale must make exactly the same kind of judgment. It is totally irrelevant that the units of the high-jumper's scale are equal-interval in a simple physical sense while the units of the gymnast's scale are not. Similarly, conclusions based on regression must often be supplemented by subjective judgments about the importance of the effects predicted by the regression, but the questions are the same whether or not the variables are equal-interval in some mechanical sense.

In summary, questions raised about equal-interval scaling actually concern three separate issues, and methods exist for dealing with all three.

8.1.6   Range Restriction

Range restriction on some variables probably occurs in most research. Samples of college students have restricted range on age, scholastic background, and many other variables. Regression requires us to assume that there is no range restriction on the dependent variable Y. But we saw in Sec. 1.4.1 that range restriction does not affect the simple regression slope b.

In fact, range restriction on the regressors distorts regression statisics only in certain specifiable ways. The statistics b_j, a, $\hat{Y}_i$, e_i, and MSE are not distorted by range restriction. That is, they estimate and test the same parameters whether range restriction exists or not. However, range restriction on some regressors will generally lower R, Var(Y), all values of r_{Yj}, and the values of pr_j for the restricted variables. Thus, use of the latter statistics as estimators assumes the absence of range restriction, while use of the former does not. In general, the statistics undistorted by range restriction are those used in causal analysis, while the distorted statistics are used in prediction. Therefore prediction studies are seriously distorted by range restriction more often than causal analyses.

Some or all regressors in a design may be artifically manipulated variables, such as treatment condition or hours of practice. The range of a manipulated variable like hours of practice is usually a property of the experiment rather than a property of the natural world. In such experiments, then, any of the statistics affected by range restriction cannot estimate a property of the natural world. This is a major reason why partial regression slopes are emphasized over partial correlations in most computer programs: in experiments, they estimate a property of the natural world rather than a value whose size is determined by the range of variables manipulated in the particular experiment.

8.1.7   Missing Data

The problem of missing data in regression is sometimes confused with the problem of unequal cell frequencies in analysis of variance, but the two problems are in fact completely separate. If an investigator designs an experiment with 10 subjects in each cell but at the last moment 2 subjects fail to report for the experiment so that one cell has only 8 observations, then the problem is one of unequal cell frequencies. Unequal cell frequencies may lower the power of regression analyses and complicate their interpretation. But as we shall see in Chap. 10, they pose absolutely no threat to the validity of the analysis, provided only that there is at least one observation in each cell. In regression, the term *missing data* refers rather to the situation in which there are cases with data available on some regressors but missing on others. For instance, a respondent may answer all the items in a questionnaire except those on income and marital status.

We shall consider four approaches to the problem of missing data: pairwise deletion, listwise deletion, imputation (filling in estimates of missing scores), and two-stage data collection. The first two of these are well known, while the last two are described in detail by Little and Rubin (1987), who provide the first book-length discussion of missing data.

Pairwise deletion and listwise deletion are the simplest and best-known approaches to the problem. In *pairwise deletion*, each covariance is calculated using those cases for which data are available for the two variables involved. Thus, in principle, every covariance in an analysis could be computed on a different subset of cases. When a regression analysis is done using covariances computed in this way, it can yield results that could never occur in a single sample, such as multiple correlations above 1. Pairwise deletion is rarely recommended for linear models. In fact, MYSTAT, SYSTAT, and SAS have all deliberately chosen not to offer pairwise deletion even as an option for linear models.

By far the most common approach to missing data is *listwise deletion:* deleting from the analysis any cases for which any data are missing on any variable in the analysis. Listwise deletion will distort the estimated mean of Y unless the data meet a rather strict assumption—that data are missing solely due to chance. But we are usually more interested in regression slopes than in means. For estimating regression slopes, the validity of listwise deletion depends upon a much less strict assumption we shall call the *noncontribution of missingness.* Little and Rubin call this the assumption of *random missingness,* but I feel that the name is not sufficiently informative. Whatever it is called, the assumption is that missingness makes no contribution to the prediction of Y, independent of the regressors. To understand the assumption more precisely, imagine for every regressor X_j a variable Fix_j, where Fix stands for "filled-in X." That is, Fix_j is what X_j would be if all the missing data were magically and accurately filled in. Imagine also a dummy variable $Miss_j$ which is 1 when a score on X_j is missing, and 0 otherwise. There are also variables Fix_Y and $Miss_Y$ for Y. Then the crucial assumption for listwise deletion is that the "Miss" variables make no contribution to the prediction of Fix_Y independent of the Fix_j variables.

Why is this assumption necessary? Recall from Chap. 2 that controlling any regressor amounts to estimating the effects of other regressors in a subpopulation of cases which all have the same scores on that regressor. One way of accomplishing that end would be an extreme form of exclusion of cases— restricting the sample to a subsample of cases with the same score on the regressor. Listwise deletion effectively controls the "Miss" variables by this method; it deletes from the sample any case scoring 1 on any such variable, leaving only the cases scoring 0 on all. But if a variable makes no independent contribution to Y, then controlling it does not change the slopes of other variables in the regression. Therefore controlling the "Miss" variables by listwise deletion does not affect the slopes of the other regressors.

Listwise deletion also leaves the analysis undistorted if the "Miss" variables are all uncorrelated with the "Fix" variables, but this condition is too rare to be of interest. On the other hand, it is often reasonable to assume the noncontribution of missingness. For instance, in a questionnaire study, suppose that the "Miss" variables are determined primarily by secretiveness. Then there may be a great many regression problems in which it is reasonable to assume that secretiveness has no relation to Y independent of the regressors. Often secretiveness or missingness will be determined largely by the regressors themselves. For instance, people with exceptionally high or low incomes might be especially reluctant to report them. If income is one of the regressors in the analysis, then it may be quite plausible to assume the noncontribution of missingness.

Two-stage data collection is often the best of the four methods, but it is rarely practical and we shall describe it only briefly. From the set of cases with incomplete data, the investigator selects a subsample to be studied more diligently. For instance, if the initial data have been collected by a mailed questionnaire, this subsample is telephoned or visited personally. Analysis of this subsample can shed light on the nature of the rest of the missing data. If 5000 people are contacted originally and 2000 have some missing data, then a follow-up on 300 of the 2000 can provide estimates of the missing data for all 2000 cases. But as this example implies, two-stage data collection is practical only if the subsample contacted in the second stage is itself fairly large. Little and Rubin (1987, especially pp. 262–264) provide a more complete discussion.

Imputation—estimation of missing scores from the available data—is more complex than pairwise or listwise deletion but less complex than two-stage data collection. Simple imputation methods, such as replacing each missing score by the mean of the known scores on the same variable, are rarely satisfactory. A better method, described in detail by Rubin and Little, is the EM algorithm of Orchard and Woodbury. Missing scores for case i are estimated using the pattern of correlations among variables and the known scores of case i on other variables. If data are missing on only one variable (a rare but simple case), the algorithm reduces to using regression to predict that variable from the others, using cases with known data, and then finding regression estimates of the missing scores.

The standard errors $SE(b_j)$ cannot simply be calculated in the usual way after scores have been imputed; a method described by Little and Rubin must be used. The method is complex and is not included in standard packages, but we can give three general rules about the bias and precision of regression slopes after EM imputation.

First, no power or precision in estimating slopes is gained by imputing scores on independent or dependent variables. This is particularly obvious in a simple correlation or regression problem when r_{XY} is high. If r_{XY} is high and you know someone's score on one variable but not the other, then you can estimate the missing score with substantial accuracy from the person's score on the other variable, but clearly the imputed score adds no information about the size of the relationship between the two variables. The same thing is true in more complex cases. Thus imputation is useful only for missing scores on covariates.

Second, the usefulness of imputing covariate scores increases with the degree of collinearity or even singularity among them. In the extreme case of singularity among covariates, missing scores can be filled in with perfect accuracy, thus potentially salvaging many cases that would be discarded by listwise deletion.

Third, values of b_j calculated after imputation are typically biased estimators of true regression slopes. But if there are just one independent variable and one dependent variable and they are included in the data set used to impute missing scores on covariates, then the bias is conservative, tending to underestimate the partial relationship between independent and dependent variables. This is because the imputed scores are being estimated partly from scores on the independent and dependent variables, so that imputation tends to raise the computed correlations between those variables and the covariates, thus introducing a conservative bias into the estimation of the partial relationship with covariates controlled.

In summary, imputation of covariate scores is especially useful when covariates are collinear or even singular, and should be done using only one independent variable and one dependent variable at a time. Different imputations may be made for different partial relationships.

8.1.8   Rounding Error

Many modern statistical programs carry most or all computations to about 14 digits of accuracy. Surprisingly, rounding error can still occasionally creep into such computations. To see how, consider subtracting 10,000,000,000,000.4 from 10,000,000,000,000.5. The correct answer is .1. But if the two values are rounded to 14 total places before calculating their difference, the result is 10,000,000,001 − 10,000,000,000,000 = 1. The difference is off by a factor of 10 despite use of 14 digits of accuracy. Unfortunately, statistical calculations frequently face problems like this, in which one must find the difference between two extremely similar numbers. This occurs especially under conditions of near-singularity, when tolerances are .001 or below.

Although no computer program can give accurate answers to all problems, it is reasonable to expect a program to issue warnings when rounding error is likely. Unfortunately, this expectation is not always justified. Among well-known commercial statistical programs, MYSTAT and SYSTAT are widely accepted as the ones most resistant to rounding error; their publisher offers a free booklet pointing out rounding-error problems in their competitors. SAS is not as free of rounding error as its price would suggest, but it is not so bad as to be a serious problem in typical applications. Section 17.8 discusses the problem of rounding error more fully, and presents a simple test for rounding error in regression.

8.2   MEASUREMENT ERROR

8.2.1   What Is Measurement Error?

Each variable in a regression may be measured with some error. Even height and weight are not measured perfectly, and variables like attitudes, skills, and socioeconomic variables are measured far less accurately.

Measurement error must not be confused with sampling error. *Sampling error* refers to the error in estimating means or other characteristics of the entire population, while *measurement error* refers to the error in estimating individual scores. If height and weight are measured in small samples, we may have little measurement error but much sampling error. If attitudes are measured in large samples, we may have little sampling error but much measurement error. Parameters such as $_Tb_j$ are by definition unaffected by sampling error, but may be distorted by measurement error. We could imagine using a symbol like $_{TT}b_j$ to denote a "true true" parameter from which both measurement and sampling error have been eliminated. We shall not in fact use this notation, but merely mention it to emphasize the point that ordinary parameters eliminate one source of error but not the other.

Measurement error may be either random or nonrandom. If men tend to overreport their incomes on a questionnaire while women underreport, the nonrandom measurement error can obviously distort conclusions about the relative earnings of men and women. There is little we can say about nonrandom measurement error except to note its seriousness, so our discussion will use the term *measurement error* to mean *random* measurement error.

A variable's *reliability* is defined as the proportion of its variance explained by true scores. The estimation of reliability is a complex matter. The corrections for unreliability presented in Sec. 17.7 assume that the worker understands these complexities but has nevertheless been able to find reasonable estimates of reliabilities.

8.2.2   Measurement Error in Y

We have seen that in causal analysis, b_j estimates the direct effect of X_j on Y. Thus it is both important and fortunate that $_Tb_j$, the parameter estimated by b_j, is not affected at all by random measurement error in Y. To see why this is so, think first about a single mean. Even though measurement error changes the scores of individual subjects, it will not change the mean of a population of subjects, since it will randomly raise half the scores and lower half. Therefore measurement error will not change a marginal (overall) mean, and by the same argument it will not change conditional means. But the population regression plane passes through those conditional means, so it too is unchanged. And the position of this plane is determined by $_Ta$ and the values of $_Tb_j$, so they must not change. On the other hand, adding more and more measurement error to Y would eventually lower $_TR$ and all values of $_Tpr_j$ to zero, so these values are clearly affected by measurement error.

With these conclusions concerning population values, we are now ready to consider the effects of measurement error on samples. We know that $E(b_j) = {}_Tb_j$; that is, b_j is an unbiased estimator of the true regression slope. Since measurement error does not change the true slope, b_j is still an unbiased estimator of the "true true" slope that would exist with no measurement or sampling error. By the same argument, a is still an unbiased estimator of $_Ta$. But R and values of pr_j, which are somewhat biased to begin with, are biased more by measurement error in Y.

Random measurement error in Y does increase the standard error of b's, and therefore lowers the statistical power of tests on b's. But the tests are still valid.

8.2.3 Measurement Error in Independent Variables

When regression is used for prediction, random measurement error in regressors lowers R but does not invalidate whatever predictive power is found. Thus, when we are using regression for prediction we need not assume absence of measurement error.

In causal analysis, measurement error in an independent variable X_j tends to lower b_j toward zero, and also to raise its standard error. Both these effects produce a conservative bias, lowering the power of the test on b_j. This means that a significant value of b_j is not invalidated by measurement error in X_j, since the effect of that error is to make it harder to find such significance.

8.2.4 The Biggest Weakness of Regression: Measurement Error in Covariates

Measurement error in covariates has much more serious effects than measurement error in independent or dependent variables. Random measurement error in any regressor X_j changes the values of b and pr for all other regressors in the direction they would be moved if X_j were omitted from the regression. One cannot usually tell this direction by inspection, so the investigator often does not know whether measurement error in covariates has raised or lowered the values of b_j or pr_j for the independent variables.

To see how this can work, consider the formula for b_1 with two regressors. Suppose that without measurement error the three correlations among the variables are $r_{Y1} = .3$, $r_{Y2} = .4$, and $r_{12} = .5$ and all standard deviations are 1. Then

$$b_1 = \frac{r_{Y1} - r_{Y2}\, r_{12}}{1 - r_{12}^2} \times \frac{S_Y}{S_1}$$

$$= \frac{.3 - .4 \times .5}{1 - .5^2} \times \frac{1}{1} = .1333$$

Now suppose that measurement error in X_2 lowers both correlations involving X_2 to half their correct value, so that we observe $r_{Y2} = .2$ and $r_{12} = .25$. Measurement error in X_2, of course, will not affect S_Y, S_1, or r_{Y1}. Therefore we calculate

$$b_1 = \frac{.3 - .2 \times .25}{1 - .25^2} \times \frac{1}{1} = .2667$$

Measurement error in X_2 has in this case doubled b_1. In more complex situations, we cannot easily predict either the size or the direction of the change in any b_j produced by measurement error in the other regressors.

8.2.5 Summary: The Effects of Measurement Error

We can list three possible effects of measurement error, in order of seriousness:

1. Least serious is to leave values of b_j as unbiased estimates of $_Tb_j$ but to raise their standard errors $SE(b_j)$. This widens confidence bands and lowers the power of tests, but does not destroy the validity of the tests.
2. More serious is to introduce conservative bias into estimates of $_Tb_j$ while still leaving tests on $_Tb_j$ as valid tests.
3. Most serious is to introduce unknown bias into estimates of b_j; this simply invalidates tests on $_Tb_j$.

Measurement error in Y has the first of these three effects, error in an independent variable has the second, and error in covariates has the third. These points were all developed in the preceding sections.

The effect of measurement error in covariates may be the most important single weakness in regression analysis. This should come as no surprise: the whole purpose of the method is to control covariates, and it cannot control them accurately if they are not measured accurately. If a covariate were measured with total inaccuracy, so that the scores were determined entirely by random error, then the true covariate would not be controlled at all. Thus the result of measurement error is that we have less control than we wish. Section 17.7 describes some partial solutions for the problems created by random measurement error.

SUMMARY

8.1 An Assortment of Problems

Methods exist for managing violations of all four sampling assumptions of regression: linearity, normality, homoscedasticity, and random sampling.

Collinear sets may be identified merely by inspecting names of variables or correlations among regressors, or by factor analysis or related methods, or by all-subsets regression.

A method is given for identifying singular sets. Once you have identified all variables in the singular set, run the original regression with one of these variables omitted, paying no attention to results for any variables from the formerly singular set. Results for all other variables are meaningful, and will be the same regardless of which variable has been removed from the singular set. An extension of this method applies if the crosswise regressions themselves contain singular sets.

The basic specification errors are *undercontrol* and *overcontrol*. Overcontrol consists of including in a regression one or more variables affected by Y; this can distort all values of b_j.

The term *equal-interval scaling* is used to refer to three separate issues: linearity, normality, and equality of importance of a variable's units. Methods exist for dealing with all three.

The statistics b_j, a, $\hat{Y}_i$, e_i, and MSE are not distorted by range restriction. However, range restriction on some regressors will generally lower R, $\text{Var}(Y)$, all values of r_{Yj}, and the values of pr_j for the restricted variables. In general, the statistics undistorted by range restriction are those used in causal analysis, while the distorted statistics are used in prediction. When some or all regressors in a design are artificially manipulated variables, any of the statistics affected by range restriction cannot estimate a property of the natural world.

To handle missing data, pairwise deletion is rarely recommended for linear models. For estimating regression slopes, the validity of listwise deletion depends upon an assumption we call the *noncontribution of missingness*. A more complex method for dealing with missing data involves estimating or "imputing" values for missing scores. This is useful only for missing data in covariates; its usefulness increases with the degree of collinearity or even singularity among covariates. Estimates of b_j are then biased, but there is a way to ensure that the bias is in a conservative direction. Values of $SE(b_j)$ must be calculated by special formulas after imputation. A method involving two stages of data collection is good but rarely practical.

Rounding error is a more serious problem in linear models than one might expect from the fact that most calculations are carried to 14 significant digits. Among packages that are easy to use and widely distributed, SYSTAT and MYSTAT are widely accepted as the ones most resistant to rounding error.

8.2 Measurement Error

We can list three possible effects of measurement error, in order of seriousness:

1. Least serious is to leave values of b_j as unbiased estimates of $_Tb_j$ but to raise their standard errors $SE(b_j)$. This widens confidence bands and lowers the power of tests, but does not destroy the validity of the tests.
2. More serious is to introduce conservative bias into estimates of $_Tb_j$ while still leaving tests on $_Tb_j$ as valid tests.
3. Most serious is to introduce unknown bias into estimates of b_j; this simply invalidates tests on $_Tb_j$.

Measurement error in Y has the first of these three effects, error in an independent variable has the second, and error in covariates has the third. The effect of measurement error in covariates may be the most important single weakness in regression analysis.

KEY TERMS

collinearity   missing data
singularity   pairwise deletion
singular set   listwise deletion
specification error   noncontribution of missingness
undercontrol   rounding error
overcontrol   measurement error
noninterval scaling   random measurement error
ordinal scale   reliability
range restriction

SYMBOLS AND ABBREVIATIONS

Fix_j $Miss_j$

PROBLEMS

1. The basic sampling assumptions of regression are linearity, homoscedasticity, normality, and random sampling. This chapter suggests that something can be done about violations of
   (a) None
   (b) Some
   (c) All
   of these assumptions.
2. Name the method the author suggests for identifying collinear sets.
3. Find the variables involved in the singularity in the data set of Table 8.1, and report the values of b_j and $SE(b_j)$ for the other variables.
4. The term *overcontrol* is used in two different ways. Explain. Which does the author prefer, and why?
5. What sort of variable produces overcontrol?

TABLE 8.1
Some data containing a singularity

Y	X_1	X_2	X_3	X_4	X_5
7	3	2	5	8	1
9	6	3	4	6	6
1	3	6	2	8	5
7	4	9	7	8	8
6	2	4	7	5	9
4	6	4	6	1	17
3	7	4	5	2	15
1	7	5	8	7	6
5	6	3	4	1	16
4	7	9	2	8	8

6. IQ scores are approximately normally distributed in large random samples of people. It has been claimed that this is a strong argument that IQ forms an equal-interval scale which relates linearly to other variables and whose units are equal in importance. This chapter suggests that the current author:
   (*a*) Feels that this is a very sound argument
   (*b*) Feels the position is reasonable but not proven
   (*c*) Rejects the argument
   (*d*) Has not said anything relevant to this question in this chapter

7. Later chapters of this book discuss transformations of (regressors, *Y*, both, neither) that may create linearity when nonlinearity has been found in the original data.

8. Which regression statistics are affected, and which are unaffected, by range restriction?

9. Name and briefly describe the minimal assumption necessary to make listwise deletion a valid approach to the problem of missing data.

10. Five hundred people have answered a 30-item questionnaire, but nearly everyone has omitted at least one answer. Different people have omitted different answers. You want to perform a regression involving all 30 variables. There is no practical way to recontact the respondents to fill in the missing data.
    (*a*) Would listwise deletion allow you to use most of the data collected, or would most have to be discarded?
    (*b*) Answer the same question for pairwise deletion.
    (*c*) Is pairwise deletion recommended for such situations?
    (*d*) Imputation is recommended especially for estimating missing scores on (independent variables, dependent variables, covariates). Choose as many as are correct.
    (*e*) Imputation is especially (useful, useless) when there is collinearity (but not singularity, or even singularity) among (independent variables, dependent variables, covariates).

11. If a computer program uses "double precision," in which all computations are carried to about 14 significant digits, then you can have good confidence that rounding error is little or no problem in regression computations. True or false?

12. A military psychologist who wants to study the relationship between self-sacrifice and patriotism in the army, with IQ held constant, has devised some short paper-and-pencil tests and administers them to a random sample of 10,000 soldiers. In this example, sampling error is probably (large, small) and measurement error is probably (large, small).

13. In Prob. 12, tell whether random measurement error in each of the three variables would:
    (*a*) Raise the absolute value of the correlation studied
    (*b*) Lower it
    (*c*) Leave it unchanged
    (*d*) Have an unpredictable effect.

14. Suppose the psychologist thinks of self-sacrifice as the dependent variable *Y* and patriotism as the independent variable *X* and computes the appropriate partial regression slope. Remembering the sample size, what can you say about the effect on this slope of random measurement error in self-sacrifice? In patriotism?

CHAPTER 9

ASSESSING THE IMPORTANCE OF REGRESSORS

We have seen that there is little ambiguity concerning the interpretation of the partial regression slope b_j. Given the single assumption of linearity, $_Tb_j$ is the change in average Y associated with each 1-unit change in X_j when other regressors are held constant. The sample value b_j is an unbiased estimator of $_Tb_j$. But b_j cannot be used to compare the importance of regressors. For instance, if one regressor is measured in inches, then changing its units to feet will multiply its slope by a factor of 12 but will not change its importance at all. Therefore we must use scale-free measures to assess importance.

There are three basic scale-free measures: the standardized slope beta_j, the partial correlation pr_j, and the semipartial correlation sr_j. The latter two are often squared; as mentioned in Sec. 2.3.5, sr_j^2 is the proportion of Y variance uniquely explained by X_j, and pr_j^2 is the same value expressed as a proportion of the Y variance unexplained by the $P - 1$ regressors excluding X_j.

Thus, we have at least four questions: Which if any of the three basic scale-free statistics should be used? Should they be squared? Are there other measures of importance? And what *do* we mean by importance? Statisticians and scientists are not fully agreed on the answers to these questions—so this chapter more than most is an expression of my own opinions.

When measures of importance take negative values, we compare their absolute values. For instance, if we were using partial correlations to measure importance and we found $pr_1 = .2$ and $pr_2 = -.3$, we would say that X_2 was more important than X_1.

9.1 SHOULD CORRELATIONS BE SQUARED?

We have said that r_{XY}^2 represents the proportion of variance in Y explained by X. This proportion is only .09 for a correlation of .3, but is .36, or 4 times as great, for a correlation of .6. More generally, if one correlation is g times as large as a second, then the proportion of variance associated with the first will be g^2 times as great. In the present example, $g = 2$ and $g^2 = 4$.

Proportions of variance have two important properties illustrated by this example. First, if one r is somewhat larger than another, it often looks much larger when both are expressed as proportions of variance. Second, moderately small correlations, such as .2 or .3, account for very small proportions of variance and thus appear trivial. This second property is really a special case of the first, since when you say that a correlation accounts for $X\%$ of the variance, you are implicitly comparing it with a hypothetical correlation of 1.0, which accounts for 100%.

Thinking in terms of proportions of variance is extremely entrenched among both scientists and statisticians. But this approach can be very misleading. A more precise approach involves the use of decision theory.

9.1.1 Decision Theory

In decision theory, we define the importance of the relationship between two variables as proportional to the *expected gain* from taking advantage of the relationship. For instance, if we use a psychological test to decide which of two kinds of therapy to administer to patients in a mental hospital, then the expected gain from use of the test might be measured in the number of days by which the average patient's hospital stay is shortened. The importance of the relationship between the test and the choice of therapy is defined as proportional to the number of days by which the test can shorten the average hospital stay. In this way the importance of the relationship of test A to therapeutic choice can be said to be 2 or 3 times that of test B; in other words, we have a ratio scale for measuring the importance of a correlation.

In this example, gain is measured in days of hospitalization. Gain can be measured in almost any units, but the simplest and most widely used units are dollars. This is particularly easy to understand for personnel-selection tests used by businesses: how many dollars can the business expect to gain by using the test?

In Sec. 9.2, we shall see that a decision-theory approach yields no single relationship between r and importance. But if we had to pick the most common single relationship, it would be more accurate to say that the importance of a correlation r is proportional to r than to r^2. This point is widely accepted among psychometricians; see, for instance, Cronbach and Gleser (1965). But it is hardly known at all outside this small circle, so we shall develop it in some detail.

9.1.2   An Example on Prediction

Suppose 19 people apply for a very small training program, but only the 7 people scoring highest on a test are admitted and the other 12 are rejected. In real life, we would never learn the true ability of these latter 12 to succeed in the program. But let us imagine briefly that we do know these values. Let Fig. 9.1 represent the observed test scores (X) of all 19 people, plotted against their actual ability to succeed in the training program (Y).

We see that $M_Y = 3$. Therefore, if we had no test and had to select seven people randomly, 3 is the expected mean of the selected group. On the other hand, if we had a hypothetical perfect test, we would pick the seven people with Y scores of 4 or 5. The Y mean of these seven people is $(4 + 4 + 4 + 4 + 5 + 5 + 5)/7 = \frac{31}{7}$. The use of this hypothetical perfect test has raised the expected Y mean of those selected from 3, or $\frac{21}{7}$, to $\frac{31}{7}$, a gain of $\frac{10}{7}$.

But using the actual test X, we select instead the seven people with X scores of 4 or 5. Inspection of the figure shows that the Y mean of this group is $(2 + 3 + 4 + 5 + 3 + 4 + 5)/7 = \frac{26}{7}$, which represents a gain of $\frac{5}{7}$ over the mean of $\frac{21}{7}$ expected by random selection. This gain of $\frac{5}{7}$ is exactly half the expected gain of $\frac{10}{7}$ produced by a hypothetical perfect test. Thus test X is half as valuable as a hypothetical test correlating 1.0 with Y. But in this sample of 19 cases, $r_{XY} = .5$, so in this example the value of the test is proportional to r, not r^2.

Brogden (1946) and Cronbach and Gleser (1965) have shown that this result applies generally when there are only two "treatments" to choose for each subject, such as selection or rejection, and we assume a linear relation between X and Y. That is, suppose we define the value of a test as in this example, as the expected mean gain in ability of people selected by the test, divided by the expected mean gain from a hypothetical perfect test. These authors have shown that assuming linearity, this value always equals r, not r^2 or some other value. As they point out, this result actually applies only if we assume that the number of people receiving each treatment (for example, the number of people to be hired) is fixed in advance. Otherwise the result depends upon the precise characteristics of the two treatments.

9.1.3   An Example with Two Separate Regressions

Suppose you are taking two different courses, A and B. In each one a study has been done examining the relation between course grade (Y) and the hours of

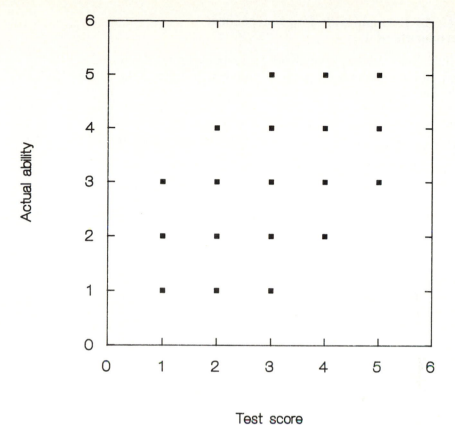

FIGURE 9.1
How gain from prediction is usually proportional to r_{XY}, not r_{XY}^2.

study on that course (X), as recorded in student diaries. Both studies have adequately controlled for contaminating factors such as a student's ability and previous knowledge of course material. Suppose the values of S_X are equal for the two courses, as are the values of S_Y. Now suppose these two studies have observed $r_{XY} = .3$ for course A and $r_{XY} = .6$ for course B. Since the standard deviations of X and Y are equal for the two courses, their ratio S_Y/S_X is also equal. Thus the formula $b = r_{XY}(S_Y/S_X)$ tells us that b is twice as high for course B as for course A. This means that, on the average, each extra hour of study produces twice the increase in grade in course B as in course A. If your objective is to maximize your average grade, you will presumably then study harder for course B than for course A. But the important point here is that the expected gain per study hour in course B is twice that in course A, not 4 times. Thus, as in the two-treatment case of prediction, a correlation twice as high implies twice the importance, not 4 times.

9.1.4 An Example with Two Independent Determinants of Y

Consider now an example involving coins. In each "trial" you flip a nickel and a dime. If the dime comes up heads, you win 10 cents. If the nickel comes up heads, you win 5 cents. Thus, on each trial you have a 25% chance of winning 15 cents (if both coins come up heads), another 25% chance of winning 10 cents (if the dime comes up heads and the nickel, tails), another 25% chance of winning 5 cents (if the dime comes up tails and the nickel, heads), and a 25% chance of winning nothing (if both come up tails).

In a long series of trials, results from the nickel will be independent of results from the dime. Since winnings are totally determined by the two coins, the proportions of variance attributable to the nickel and the dime will sum to 100%. It can be shown that the dime will account for 80% of the variance in total winnings, while the nickel accounts for only 20%. That is, if D is a dummy variable scored 1 whenever the dime lands heads and scored 0 when it lands tails, N is a similar dummy variable for the nickel, and W equals total winnings, then in a long series of trials we would find $r^2_{DW} = .8$ and $r^2_{NW} = .2$.

These numbers make the dime seem 4 times as important as the nickel. But in ordinary language we would say that the dime affects your winnings twice as much as the nickel, not 4 times. The simple (unsquared) correlations of the dime and the nickel with winnings are, respectively, $r_{DW} = .894$ and $r_{NW} = .447$, which are in the proper ratio of 2 to 1.

9.1.5 An Example on Heredity and Environment

This example concerns the relative importance of heredity and environment in determining IQ scores. We deliberately say "IQ scores" instead of "IQ" because it might be debated whether "IQ" even exists, but there is no doubt that IQ *scores* exist. Some scientists have suggested that as much as 80% of the variance in IQ scores is determined by heredity and as little as 20% by environment. Most specialists regard the 80% figure as too high, but for the moment let us just ask what it would imply if it were correct. The standard deviation of the Stanford-Binet IQ test is about 15 points, so the variance of scores on the test is 15^2, or 225. If 20% of that variance were due to environment, then the variance due to environment would equal $.2 \times 225 = 45$. Then the *standard deviation* of the environmental components is $\sqrt{45}$, or 6.71. That is, if there were a large number of people with identical genes whose environments varied as much as environments in America vary today, then we would expect their IQ scores to have a standard deviation of 6.71 points.

Now suppose we took a group of children whose environments were in the bottom 2% or 3% of all environments (though we still do not know what features of the environment we would measure to make that determination), so that their environments were 2 standard deviations below the mean on environmental quality. Suppose we somehow arranged to move those children into environments 2 standard deviations above the mean—in the top 2% or 3% of all environments. We would then raise the quality of their environments by 4 standard deviations. Each increase of 1 standard deviation would raise the expected mean IQ score of these children by 6.71 points, so the environmental change would be expected to raise the average IQ score by 4 × 6.71, or almost 27 points. And this is assuming that the figures of 80% and 20% are correct! Thus, the claim that some factor accounts for only a small percentage of the variance in some Y variable does not necessarily contradict the assertion that manipulating the factor can produce dramatic and important changes in Y.

9.1.6   Conclusion

We will see in Sec. 9.2 that there is no single relationship between r and importance that applies in all situations. But the four examples of Secs. 9.1.2 through 9.1.5 show that if there is one single rule that fits more situations than any other, that rule is that importance is proportional to r itself, not r^2. Thus small and moderate correlations are usually more important than is often realized. The four examples demonstrating this, in the order presented, covered predictive value, the comparison of two separate causally interpreted regressions, a comparison between two uncorrelated variables in the same regression, and an application that does not directly use regression at all. Squared correlations fit remarkably well into algebraically simple formulas— but algebraic simplicity does not imply substantive meaningfulness.

9.2   THE VALUE OF PREDICTIVE TESTS

This section gives a more detailed statement of the relationship between r and expected gain in prediction problems. There seem to be two especially important cases in prediction that we will call the *two-treatment* and *infinite-treatment* cases. If someone either does or does not receive a new drug, or is or is not hired for a job or admitted to college, we have the two-treatment case. The infinite-treatment case arises if a drug dosage can vary on a continuum from 0 to a large amount, or if an applicant can be placed in a college program or a job ranging anywhere from very easy to very difficult. This last example shows that the very same situation may be a two-treatment case from the perspective of a single institution—for example, a single college that may either select or reject an applicant—and an infinite-treatment case from the perspective of society as a whole.

9.2.1   The Infinite-Treatment Case

In the infinite-treatment case, a physician may estimate the optimum drug dosage for a patient, or a clinical psychologist may try to guess the optimum level of directiveness to use with a given patient, or a music teacher may guess how rapidly to teach a given topic. The infinite-treatment case also has many subcases. But the simplest assumption for this case is that the expected gain or loss for a given subject is linearly related to the error of prediction for that subject; if a subject's actual Y score is 5, it is twice as bad to estimate it as 1 or 9 as to estimate it as 3 or 7.

The standard error of estimate, defined in Sec. 5.2.6, is appropriate for such problems. It measures, in effect, the size of the typical error in estimating Y; it is the square root of *MSE,* the mean squared error. It is meaningful to say that the standard error of estimate is, say, half as large for one regression or variable as for another.

The standard error of estimate is linearly related to the *coefficient of forecasting efficiency,* denoted by E. It is defined by the equation

$$E = 1 - \sqrt{1 - r^2}$$

(The fact that we use E to denote expected value does not complicate notation, since the coefficient of forecasting efficiency is not mentioned again after this section.) The index is suggested by the fact that $E = (S_Y - S_{Y.X})/S_Y$, which is the proportion by which the unexplained standard deviation of Y is reduced by Y's correlation with X. Like r, E ranges from 0 to 1, equaling 1 when $r = 1$ and equaling 0 when $r = 0$. In large samples, $S_{Y.X}$ nearly equals the standard error of estimate; it is the square root of the actual mean of the squared errors or residuals.

E gives very conservative statements of the importance of a correlation; for instance, when $r = .5$ so that $r^2 = .25$, we have $E = .13$. E always falls below r^2, while r always falls above r^2. E is the simplest measure of importance for the infinite-treatment case, while r is the simplest measure of importance for the two-treatment case. Thus the proper measure of importance may fall either above or below r^2, depending on whether we are dealing with the two-treatment case or the infinite-treatment case.

9.2.2 Some Uncommon and Complex Cases

The two-treatment case itself has various subcases, depending among other things on whether the number of subjects receiving each treatment is fixed in advance. For instance, will a fixed number of people be hired, or will more people be hired if more qualified applicants are found? If the number to be hired varies, then the solution becomes messy, with further sub-subcases; see Cronbach and Gleser (1965). But when the number receiving each treatment is fixed, Cronbach and Gleser showed that if we assume only linearity, then the expected gain from a test is proportional to r, the test's correlation with the criterion variable it is supposed to predict.

The personnel psychologists Taylor and Russell (1939) present an analysis in which employees scoring above a certain Y value are considered "satisfactory" while other employees are "unsatisfactory." Taylor and Russell give tables for finding the percentage of employees who will be satisfactory if a firm selects all applicants whose scores on a test X exceed a certain level—expressed as a function of the correlation r between X and Y. This is a genuine decision-theory approach, which in principle might apply to a broad range of problems having nothing to do with personnel selection. But this approach applies only when, for instance, the difference between Y scores of 69 and 70 is of great consequence while the difference between scores of 70 and 100, or between 69 and 0, is of no consequence at all. Such cases seem to me rather rare. Further, in the Taylor-Russell approach, the relation between test value and r turns out to depend heavily on the proportion of applicants who are "satisfactory" and also on the proportion of applicants hired. Thus, no simple statement is possible for the cases considered by Taylor and Russell.

9.2.3   When the Standard Is Perfection

Sometimes we expect very accurate prediction and naturally focus not on our ability to predict better than chance but on whatever errors remain. For instance, if we are trying to predict temperature readings, which vary across both time and place, we assume that we can achieve a very high correlation using predictors of latitude, altitude, day of the year, and time of day. We would not be much impressed by a weather predictor who claimed to be superaccurate because the correlation between his or her predictions and actual temperature was .99 when calculated in this way.

This reflects a problem that is not unique to regression and correlation. If a certain training program raised the success rate of subjects on a difficult task from 10% to 20%, we would naturally tend to say that the training had doubled the success rate. But if training raises the success rate on an easy task from 98% to 99%, thus increasing the number of successes by only 1%, it seems more natural to point out that training cuts the failure rate in half. By the same token, there is a sense in which a correlation of .99 is much higher than one of .98, not just 1% higher. For either of the methods mentioned above—r or E—it is a matter of judgment whether the natural standard of comparison should be taken as 0 or 1.

9.3   CAUSAL ANALYSIS

This section considers causal analysis rather than prediction. Sections 9.3.2 through 9.3.5 consider the problem of comparing the importance of two or more regressors in the same regression. Section 9.3.1 examines the case in which a regression has a single variable that is thought of as the independent variable, with all other regressors thought of as covariates. In that case, the independent variable is not to be compared with any other variables; rather, its importance must be expressed in some other terms.

Nothing in this section deals with the issue of cost-effectiveness. A variable might be rather small in importance by the measures discussed in this section but still be the best way to increase or decrease Y because it is so cheap and easy to manipulate.

9.3.1   Assessing the Importance of a Single Independent Variable

Instead of comparing regressors with each other, you may want to compare a regressor's importance with its theoretical maximum importance. In one sense this is impossible. If each hour of foreign-language vocabulary training expands a student's working vocabulary by 10 words, we can at least imagine some superefficient training method that adds 1000 or even 10,000 words for each hour, so for all we know the actual training method might be only one-hundredth or one-thousandth as effective as some other method.

But it is possible to calculate the maximum possible association between two variables if we think of certain quantities as fixed. For instance, in a certain sample, suppose we have calculated that the standard deviation of annual incomes is \$20,000 and that the standard deviation of education is 4 years. We have not yet calculated either the correlation or the regression slope between the two variables. If the correlation between these two variables were perfect, the simple regression formula

$$b = r_{XY} \frac{S_Y}{S_X}$$

tells us that the regression slope predicting income from education would be $1 \times 20,000/4$, or 5000. Since r_{XY} cannot exceed 1, that is the highest the slope could be for the given standard deviations of income and education. If we think of those standard deviations as fixed, then $b = 5000 \times r_{XY}$, so b is proportional to r_{XY}. Therefore r_{XY} is the ratio of b to its maximum possible value; to say that $r_{XY} = .4$ is to say that b equals .4 times its maximum possible value given the two standard deviations. This is a possible interpretation of r_{xy}—as the ratio of b to its theoretical maximum given the two standard deviations.

A similar but more complex rule applies to multiple regression. Suppose we think of all statistics in the sample as fixed except statistics measuring the partial relationship between Y and a particular regressor X_j. These conditions fix a maximum possible value of b_j, and pr_j equals the ratio between the actual value of b_j and that theoretical maximum. This is a useful interpretation of pr_j which does not require the limiting conditions on pr_j mentioned in Sec. 5.5.2.

The point can be expressed in a formula. Let C (for "covariates") denote the set of $P - 1$ regressors that does not include a particular regressor X_j of interest. Then $\text{Var}(Y.C)$ is the mean of the squared residuals (which we saw in Chap. 5 is not the same as the residual mean square) when Y is regressed onto these variables. It can be shown that

$$pr_j = b_j S_j \sqrt{\frac{\text{Tol}_j}{\text{Var}(Y.C)}}$$

This formula shows that pr_j and b_j are proportional to each other if we think of the three statistics S_j, Tol_j, and $Var(Y.C)$ as fixed. Thus pr_j equals the ratio between b_j and the maximum possible b_j with the same values of those three statistics.

9.3.2   Some Equivalences among Measures

We now turn to the problem of comparing the importance of two or more regressors in the same regression. The measures in the list below appear repeatedly in the following discussion, so we shall mention now that in simultaneous designs, all these measures rank regressors in the same order; the regressor that is most important by any one measure will be most important by all of them. We shall thus think of these measures as a family. We shall call them measures of the *unique contribution* of X_j to the regression. The measures are:

1. pr_j and pr_j^2.
2. sr_j and sr_j^2.
3. t_j or F_j, the value of t or F used to test the significance of b_j. Since df is equal for all these tests, the regressors with the highest values of t or F also have the most significant values of b_j.
4. The change in R, R^2, adjusted R, or adjusted R^2 when X_j is deleted from the regression.
5. Unique SS: the rise in SS(error) and fall in SS(model) when X_j is deleted from the regression.

Most of these measures do not have similar proportionality or ratio properties: for instance, if pr_1 is twice pr_2, it does *not* mean that sr_1 is twice sr_2. But proportionality does hold for some of these measures: sr_j^2, F_j, unique SS, and change in R^2 are all proportional to each other; and sr_j and t_j are also proportional to each other.

9.3.3   The Limitations of Beta$_j$

The most widely used measure of a regressor's relative importance is beta$_j$, which is defined as the value of b_j we would find if we standardized all variables including Y to unit variance before performing the regression. I shall argue that beta$_j$ should rarely if ever be used, and that sr_j is a better measure of relative importance. I shall contend that sr_j has ratio properties, so that if $sr_2 = .2$ and $sr_1 = .1$, then it is meaningful to say that X_2 has twice the importance of X_1.

Beta$_j$ can be interpreted as the difference in expected standardized Y values between two people who are 1 standard deviation apart on X_j and are tied with each other on all other regressors. But it seems to have been overlooked that if X_j correlates highly with other regressors, it may be nearly impossible for two such people to even exist. For instance, if there are two standardized regressors X_1 and X_2, and if $r_{12} = .99$, then the unique variance of either variable is only $1 - .99^2 = .0199$. In a crosswise regression predicting either X_j from the other, the standard deviation of the conditional distribution of X_j is only $\sqrt{.0199} = .141$. Since $1/.141 = 7.09$, two people who are tied on X_1 but 1 standard deviation apart on X_2 are actually 7.09 standard deviations apart on the conditional distribution of X_2 in which they both fall. Even in a sample of over 1000 cases, we would not expect to find two people who fall 7.09 standard deviations apart.

But now suppose we add to that same regression a third variable X_3 uncorrelated with both X_1 and X_2. There will be no difficulty at all in finding two people who are 1 standard deviation apart on X_3 but tied on all other regressors. Therefore a comparison between beta$_3$ and beta$_1$ or beta$_2$ understates the relative importance of X_3, because beta$_3$ reflects only a small fraction of the total range of X_3, while beta$_1$ or beta$_2$ in effect reflects the total possible range of those variables—or even more than the possible range—given that other variables are held constant.

9.3.4 The Advantage of sr_j

The obvious solution to this problem is to use a measure of relative importance which takes into account the standard deviations of the *conditional* distributions of regressors. For X_j, the ratio of this conditional standard deviation to the unconditional or marginal standard deviation is $\sqrt{\text{Tol}_j}$. The importance of X_j is overstated by the reciprocal of this amount. For instance, in the example in Sec. 9.3.3 the importance of X_2 was overstated relative to X_3 by a factor of $1/\sqrt{\text{Tol}_2} = 7.09$. We correct the problem by multiplying each value of beta$_j$ by $\sqrt{\text{Tol}_j}$. Thus the corrected measure of a variable's importance is beta$_j \times \sqrt{\text{Tol}_j}$.

But it can be shown that this measure equals sr_j. We conclude that sr_j equals the expected difference in standardized Y scores between two people who are equal on all regressors except X_j and who differ on X_j by the standard deviation of the *conditional* distribution of X_j. For any two regressors X_j and X_k, the ratio sr_j/sr_k equals the ratio of these expected differences.

Although the ratio of two semipartial correlations is meaningful in principle, there is no simple way to put a confidence band around such a ratio. If one value sr_j is not statistically significant, then its true value could be zero, so the ratio between it and another value could be infinite. Thus ratios of semipartial correlations are useful primarily in large samples.

Values of sr_j are not printed routinely by any of the best-known regression programs. But sr_j can be computed from t_j and R^2 by the formula

$$sr_j = t_j \sqrt{\frac{1 - R^2}{N - P - 1}}$$

Since R, N, and P are constant for all variables in a regression, this formula shows that values of t_j also measure relative importance in a ratio sense. Thus computing sr_j may be unnecessary. If values of sr_j are desired, they can be computed either from the last formula or from the aforementioned formula

$$sr_j = \text{beta}_j \sqrt{\text{Tol}_j}$$

In Sec. 9.1.4 we concluded that with uncorrelated regressors, each regressor's causal importance is proportional to its simple validity. But when all regressors are uncorrelated, each variable's sr_j equals its simple validity. Thus the conclusions in this section are consistent with the earlier conclusions.

9.3.5 Hierarchical Designs

To compute relative importance in a hierarchical design, we must compute for each regressor a semipartial correlation that controls for variables preceding it in the hierarchy but not those following it. It can be shown that the absolute value of this semipartial correlation equals $\sqrt{HSS_j/SS(\text{total})}$. Since $SS(\text{total})$ is constant for all regressors, we see that importance is proportional to $\sqrt{HSS_j}$. For instance, in Sec. 7.3.3 we had

$$HSS(\text{exercise}) = 73.5$$

$$HSS(\text{food intake}) = 9$$

$$HSS(\text{metabolism}) = 8.9091$$

$$SS(\text{total}) = 98.5$$

Then importance for the three regressors is in the ratio $\sqrt{73.5} = 8.57$, $\sqrt{9} = 3$, $\sqrt{8.9091} = 2.98$.

SUMMARY

We must use scale-free measures to assess importance. The three basic scale-free measures are the standardized slope beta_j, the partial correlation pr_j, and the semipartial correlation sr_j. When any of these take negative values, we compare their absolute values. The last two measures are often squared.

9.1 Should Correlations Be Squared?

In decision theory, we define the importance of the relationship between two variables as proportional to the *expected gain* from taking advantage of the relationship. A decision-theory approach yields no single relationship between r and importance. But if we had to pick the most common single relationship, it would be more accurate to say that the importance of a correlation r is proportional to r than to r^2. Thus small and moderate correlations are usually more important than is often realized.

9.2 The Value of Predictive Tests

There seem to be two especially important cases in prediction that we call the *two-treatment* and *infinite-treatment* cases.

The standard error of estimate is appropriate for the infinite-treatment case. The standard error of estimate is linearly related to the *coefficient of forecasting efficiency*, denoted by E. It is defined by the equation

$$E = 1 - \sqrt{1 - r^2}$$

E gives very conservative statements of the importance of a correlation. E is the simplest measure of importance for the infinite-treatment case, while r is the simplest measure of importance for the two-treatment case. Thus the proper measure of importance may fall either above or below r^2, depending on whether we are dealing with the two-treatment case or the infinite-treatment case.

It is always ambiguous whether one should compare the accuracy of prediction with chance or with a standard of perfection.

9.3   Causal Anlaysis

Nothing in Sec. 9.3 deals with the issue of cost-effectiveness. A variable might be rather small in importance by the measures discussed in this section but still be the best way to increase or decrease Y because it is so cheap and easy to manipulate.

Suppose we think of all statistics in the sample as fixed except statistics measuring the partial relationship between Y and a particular regressor X_j. These conditions fix a maximum possible value of b_j. Then pr_j equals the ratio between the actual value of b_j and that theoretical maximum. This is a useful interpretation of pr_j which does not require the limiting conditions on pr_j mentioned in Sec. 5.5.2.

In simultaneous designs, all the measures in the list below rank regressors in the same order:

1. pr_j and pr_j^2.
2. sr_j and sr_j^2.
3. t_j or F_j, the value of t or F used to test the significance of b_j. Since df is equal for all these tests, the regressors with the highest values of t or F also have the most significant values of b_j.
4. The change in R, or R^2, adjusted R, or adjusted R^2 when X_j is deleted from the regression.
5. Unique SS: the rise in SS(error) and fall in SS(model) when X_j is deleted from the regression.

Most of these measures do not have similar proportionality or ratio properties: for instance, if pr_1 is twice pr_2, it does *not* mean that sr_1 is twice sr_2. But proportionality does hold for some of these measures: sr_j^2, F_j, unique SS, and change in R^2 are all proportional to each other; and sr_j and t_j are also proportional to each other.

I hold that sr_j is superior to $beta_j$ as a measure of relative importance in causal analysis. $Beta_j$ is used mainly because it equals the expected standard-score difference on Y between two hypothetical cases that are 1 standard deviation apart on X_j but tied on all other regressors. But it would be more reasonable to consider two hypothetical cases that are 1 standard deviation apart not on X_j itself, but on the component of X_j independent of other regressors. When we use this approach to develop a variant of $beta_j$, the variant turns out to equal sr_j. I argue that sr_j has ratio properties, so that if $sr_2 = .2$ and $sr_1 = .1$, then it is meaningful to say that X_2 has twice the importance of X_1.

Values of sr_j can be computed from t_j and R^2 by the formula

$$sr_j = t_j \sqrt{\frac{1 - R^2}{N - P - 1}}$$

Since R, N, and P are constant for all variables in a regression, this formula shows that values of t_j also measure relative importance in a ratio sense. Thus computing sr_j may be unnecessary. If values of sr_j are desired, they can be computed either from the last formula or from the formula

$$sr_j = beta_j \sqrt{\text{Tol}_j}$$

To compute relative importance in a hierarchical design, we must compute for each regressor a semipartial correlation that controls for variables preceding it in the hierarchy but not those following it. It can be shown that the absolute value of this semipartial correlation equals $\sqrt{HSS_j/SS(\text{total})}$.

KEY TERMS

decision theory
expected gain
two-treatment case
infinite-treatment case
coefficient of forecasting efficiency
unique contribution

SYMBOLS AND ABBREVIATIONS

E $\text{Var}(Y.C)$

PROBLEMS

1. Using the data set on life satisfaction in Table 5.7, consider satisfaction as a function of age, education, and income. Ignoring for the moment whether relationships are statistically significant, measure the relative importance of the three independent variables in determining satisfaction. Do it two ways: as a simultaneous analysis, and as a hierarchical analysis with regressors in the order listed. Using a crosswise regression to clarify the point, explain in ordinary English why education is so much more important, relative to income, in one of these analyses than in the other.

CHAPTER
10

MULTICATEGORICAL
VARIABLES

10.1 MULTICATEGORICAL VARIABLES AS SETS

Multicategorical variables are categorical variables with three or more categories, like religion, occupation, nationality, or ethnicity. Categorical variables are often called *factors*. Manipulated variables also are often multicategorical; in an analysis of variance, any factor with three or more categories is a multicategorical variable. For instance, a 3×4 analysis of variance involves one factor with three categories and one with four. (Interaction is ignored for the moment, but will be treated in Chap. 13.)

We have seen that a dichotomy like sex or like treatment versus control can be represented by an indicator or dummy variable scored 0 and 1, and that the indicator variable can be used as a regressor just like a numerical variable. The indicator variable is called a *coded* variable, because we use a code like "treatment = 1, control = 0" to translate between the original categorical variable and the indicator variable used in the regression. A multicategorical variable can be represented as a *set* of indicator variables. There are many ways of forming such sets, with different advantages. Section 10.1.1 presents the simplest one, and Secs. 10.2.5 and 10.2.6 present two others.

10.1.1   Simple Dummy Coding

Consider the following questionnaire item:

Religion:

Protestant   _____

Catholic   _____

Jewish   _____

Other or none _____

We could collect the same information in a second format:

Are you Protestant? Yes__ No__

Are you Catholic?   Yes__ No__

Are you Jewish?   Yes__ No__

No question is needed for "other or none," since anyone answering no to all three questions is presumed to answer yes to that question.

    The second format is less convenient for respondents, since they must check three spaces instead of one. But by using simple dummy codes (yes = 1, no = 0), the responses can be entered directly into a regression analysis, as three separate variables. Just as a dichotomy was entered into the computer as a single numerical variable, a multicategorical variable is entered as a *set* of numerical variables.

    But we can perform a regression analysis without inconveniencing our respondents with the awkward second format. We ask the question in the more convenient format, but recode the data and enter the answers into the computer as if the second format had been used. That is, anyone answering "Protestant" is given scores of 1, 0, 0 on three dummy variables; anyone answering "Catholic" is given scores of 0, 1, 0; anyone answering "Jewish" is given scores of 0, 0, 1; and anyone answering "other or none" is given scores of 0, 0, 0. The same procedure applies to any multicategorical variable. In an analysis of variance with four cells, we can use three coded variables to tell the computer which cell each case (for instance, each person or animal) is in; the first cell is represented by codes of 1, 0, 0; the second by 0, 1, 0; and so on as above. We may appear to be ignoring the last cell; but we shall see later that the computer output may actually tell us more about this cell than any other.

    For instance, consider the data set on life satisfaction, from Table 5.7 in the problems of Chap. 5. Suppose the 20 people in that data set fall into the four religious categories as in Table 10.1. To predict satisfaction from religion, we would express the data as shown in Table 10.2. Then the last column would be

TABLE 10.1
Membership in four religious categories

Case	1	2	3	4	5	6	7	8	9	10	11	12	13	14	15	16	17	18	19	20
Religion	3	2	4	4	1	3	2	2	3	1	3	4	1	1	2	1	3	2	4	1

TABLE 10.2
Indicator variables representing religion

Case	D1	D2	D3	Satisfy
1	0	0	1	85
2	0	1	0	82
3	0	0	0	77
4	0	0	0	65
5	1	0	0	80
6	0	0	1	92
7	0	1	0	76
8	0	1	0	86
9	0	0	1	88
10	1	0	0	82
11	0	0	1	66
12	0	0	0	83
13	1	0	0	82
14	1	0	0	90
15	0	1	0	80
16	1	0	0	77
17	0	0	1	75
18	0	1	0	84
19	0	0	0	93
20	1	0	0	85

regressed on (predicted from) $D1$, $D2$, and $D3$ by the formulas of previous chapters. A matrix using 1s and 0s to denote category membership, as in columns $D1$, $D2$, and $D3$ of this example, is often called a *design matrix* in analysis of variance, though we shall not need the term in this book.

10.1.2 Compound Variables and GLM Programs

Almost all regression packages allow you to create dummy variables with a few commands, so that you need not actually type in long columns of 1s and 0s. For instance, suppose our data set contains codes of 1, 2, 3, and 4, respectively, for the Protestant, Catholic, Jewish, and "other" categories of the variable "religion." A set of commands like

```
>if religion = 1 then d1 = 1 else d1 = 0
```

>if religion = 2 then d2 = 1 else d2 = 0
>if religion = 3 then d3 = 1 else d3 = 0

will create the three dummy variables $D1$, $D2$, and $D3$ shown above; $D1$ is 1 for Protestants and 0 for all others, while $D2$ and $D3$ are 1 for Catholics and Jews, respectively. Almost all regression packages have some provisions for commands like these, though the details of the commands vary from package to package. In MYSTAT, you can go to the command line of the data editor and issue the following commands:

>let d1 = 0
>let d2 = 0
>let d3 = 0
>if religion = 1 then let d1 = 1
>if religion = 2 then let d2 = 1
>if religion = 3 then let d3 = 1

In SYSTAT, you could enter commands like this in either the editor or the data module.

But it is even easier than this. In SYSTAT, MYSTAT, or SAS, you can simply label the variable as a multicategorical variable; the computer program automatically creates the necessary coded variables. For instance, in SYSTAT and MYSTAT the commands

>category religion = 4, occup = 3
>model satisfy = constant + age + religion + occup
>estimate

would first code religion as a multicategorical variable with four categories (three coded variables) and code "occup" (occupation) as a multicategorical variable with three categories (two coded variables), and then regress "satisfaction" on these variables plus age. The comparable command in SAS PROC GLM is

>class religion, occup;

In SAS you need not specify the number of categories; it counts them.

The ability to create a whole set of coded variables with a single command is the fundamental distinction between an ordinary regression program and a *general linear model* program. We will use the term GLM to refer to these programs as a class. Although we think of the multicategorical variable as a single variable, the GLM program treats it as a set of variables. We shall define a *compound variable* as any variable which we think of as one variable but which is represented by a set of variables in the analysis. We shall also use compound variables in Chap. 12, on nonlinear methods. The *df* for a compound variable equals the number of simple variables used to represent it in the computer, each of which has 1 *df*. In the present example, $df = 3$ for religion.

In SAS PROC GLM, the codes on a multicategorical variable may be entered in any alphanumeric form using eight characters or fewer; for instance, data on religion could be entered as Prot, Catholic, Jewish, Other. In SYSTAT and MYSTAT, the codes must be sequential integers starting with 1, such as 1, 2, 3, 4. SAS handles empty cells automatically, while in SYSTAT and MYSTAT you must recode to eliminate any empty cells. An easy way to check for empty cells is to plot the variable's distribution with the HISTOGRAM command.

Even if a GLM program is available, you should know the alternatives to GLM that are described in the rest of this chapter, since they are often used in the scientific literature. Also, MYSTAT lacks a CONTRAST command (see Sec. 10.2.1), and the 1985 GLM program in SAS lacks diagnostics (see Chap. 14), but the alternatives to GLM allow you to avoid these deficiencies.

10.1.3 The Base Category

In our example on religion, the "other or none" category was treated differently from all other categories; it had no dummy variable of its own. Most coding systems require that one category be treated differently from the others; this category is called the *base category* or *reference category*. If we perform the coding by hand, we have a number of options concerning the base category; the GLM programs also handle the base category in a number of ways.

What happens if we fail to select a base category in simple dummy coding, and instead enter a dummy variable for each category? This will produce a singularity; every dummy variable will have a tolerance of 0 and a crosswise multiple correlation (CR_j) of 1. To see why, consider our example on religion. Suppose we form four dummy variables, one for each of the four categories. Consider the sum of a person's scores on the first three dummy variables, the variables for the Protestant, Catholic, and Jewish categories. This sum can be only 0 or 1, because each person scores 1 on only one dummy variable and 0 on all others. Further, anyone with a sum of 0 must score 1 on the fourth ("other or none") category, and anyone with a sum of 1 must score 0 on the fourth category. Therefore the fourth dummy variable is perfectly predictable, with a crosswise multiple correlation of 1, from the other three. Similarly, the first dummy variable is perfectly predictable from variables 2, 3, and 4; the second is perfectly predictable from variables 1, 3, and 4; and the third is perfectly predictable from variables 1, 2, and 4. Thus every dummy variable has a tolerance of 0 and therefore an infinite value of $SE(b_j)$, producing a disruptive singularity, as described in Sec. 8.1.3. The simplest way to avoid the problem is to identify one category as a base category and omit its coded variable. If there are k categories, we thus create $k - 1$ coded variables.

We could actually use any one of the k categories as the base category, but some practices are more convenient than others. If there are several treatment groups and one control group in an experiment, then it is usually most convenient to use the control category as a base category, so that every treatment category has a dummy variable. Or if there is a catchall "other" category, that is often used. Or the largest group is sometimes used; the advantages of that procedure are described in Sec. 10.2.4. Many GLM programs simply use the last category as the base category.

10.1.4 Testing the Equality of Several Means

Although simple dummy coding can be used in complex analyses with many regressors, we shall consider first its simplest possible use: to test the equality of several means. For instance, suppose we want to test the differences among several religious groups on satisfaction, ignoring age, income, and all other variables. We can use the data set of Table 10.2 in Sec. 10.1.1. As above, let k denote the number of cells in the analysis. There is no requirement of equal cell frequencies, but we do assume that each cell contains at least one case. Let N denote the total number of cases, and let n_j denote the number of cases in cell j. Also let M_j denote the cell mean for cell j. Let the last cell, cell k, be the base cell, so that it has no dummy variable. Thus there are $k - 1$ dummy variables, labeled $D1$, $D2$, and so on. In our example, there are four religious categories, so $k = 4$. There are six cases in group 1, five in each of groups 2 and 3, and four cases in group 4, so $n_1 = 6$, $n_2 = n_3 = 5$, and $n_4 = 4$. In this example, the four cell means M_1, M_2, M_3, and M_4 are nearly equal; they are respectively 82.67, 81.60, 81.20, 79.5.

Consider the meaning of the simple correlation $r(Y, D1)$. This is the correlation between life satisfaction Y and the dichotomous variable scored 1 for Protestants and 0 for all three groups of non-Protestants. In our example, the mean Y for the 6 Protestants is 82.67, and the mean for the 14 non-Protestants is 80.86. Since the Protestant mean is slightly above the non-Protestant mean, $r(Y, D1)$ is slightly positive. Similarly, $r(Y, D2)$ is positive only if the mean of group 2 is above the mean of the 15 people from groups 1, 2, and 4; and $r(Y, D3)$ is positive only if the mean of group 3 is above the mean of the 15 people from groups 1, 2, and 4.

Now suppose that all four cell means were exactly equal—that is, the various religious groups all had exactly equal average scores on life satisfaction. Then $r(Y, D1)$, $r(Y, D2)$, and $r(Y, D3)$ would all be zero. But if the regressors all have 0 correlation with Y, then the multiple correlation R is also 0. Thus R is 0 if and only if all cell means are equal.

This argument applies to the population as well. The true multiple correlation $_TR$ equals 0 if and only if all k true cell means are equal. Therefore the F testing the null hypothesis $_TR = 0$ tests the null hypothesis of equal cell means.

In our example, when Y is regressed onto (predicted from) $D1$, $D2$, and $D3$, the ANOVA table (Sec. 5.2.4) for the regression is as shown in Table 10.3.

TABLE 10.3
ANOVA table for religion variables

Source	SS	DF	MS	F	p
Model	24.467	3	8.1557	.128	.94
Error	1016.333	16	63.521		
Total	1040.8	19			

The nonsignificant F means that there is no significant relation between Y and the regressor set, which tells us that the four cell means do not differ significantly. This confirms the earlier observation that the four means were nearly equal.

10.1.5   Parallels with Analysis of Variance

If you have studied one-way analysis of variance, you know that 10 principal calculated values are ordinarily given the names shown in Table 10.4, and arranged as shown in the table, where bg denotes "between groups" and wg denotes "within groups." All 10 of these values exactly equal the values calculated by regression. Table 10.3, for the religion example, with SS(total) = 1040.8 and $p = .94$, is the exact table you would find by performing a one-way analysis of variance. Only the names differ; regression uses the terms *model* and *error* instead of *bg* and *wg*.

The last paragraph must be qualified. There are two varieties of ANOVA: weighted-means and unweighted-means. The two methods are equivalent when all cell frequencies are equal. When cell frequencies are unequal, unweighted-means ANOVA is merely an approximate method. If cell frequencies are very unequal, it can give severely incorrect results; I have found cases in which there is a probability over .3 of rejecting a true null hypothesis at the .001 level. But weighted-means ANOVA is an exact method for any pattern of cell frequencies, so long as the usual assumptions of normality and equal within-cell variances are met. Regression is equivalent to the exact weighted-means method, not the approximate unweighted-means method. Henceforth we shall use the term ANOVA to mean the exact method of weighted-means ANOVA.

Other equivalences between regression and ANOVA parallel the equivalences that occur with simple indicator variables: each value of $\hat{Y}_i$ is the cell

TABLE 10.4
The 10 values in a simple ANOVA table

$SS(bg)$	$df(bg)$	$MS(bg)$	F	p
$SS(wg)$	$df(wg)$	$MS(wg)$		
SS(total)	df(total)			

mean of the cell containing person i, and each residual e_i is the deviation of person i from his or her cell mean. Again, if we had to estimate a person's Y score from his or her regressor scores, our best estimate would be that person's cell mean on Y, and R would be the correlation between these estimates and the actual Y scores. In analysis of variance, the size of the association between Y and the cell differences is sometimes expressed as eta-squared; in regression terms, eta-squared $= R^2$.

10.1.6 More Complex Designs

For a simple one-way analysis of variance, it is certainly easier to employ ordinary ANOVA formulas than a regression approach. But the regression approach allows us to develop models with two or more intercorrelated multicategorical variables, plus correlated dichotomous and numerical regressors. For instance, we could model life satisfaction as a function of sex, age, income, and religion, with religion entered as a multicategorical variable. As in previous chapters, we would find a measure of the unique contribution of each variable. The F for a categorical variable tests the null hypothesis that the cell means on that variable are equal after controlling for all other regressors.

There can be two or more multicategorical variables. For instance, if we have three types of occupation—manufacturing, service, and sales—then we might use the following commands in SYSTAT or MYSTAT:

>category occup = 3, religion = 4
>model satisfy = constant + educ + sex + occup + religion
>estimate

These commands were applied to a data set with the data given on satisfaction, education, sex, and religion in Tables 5.7 and 10.1, plus the scores on occupation shown in Table 10.5. These commands produced the output shown in Table 10.6.

In SAS, SYSTAT, and MYSTAT, the inclusion of even one variable in a CATEGORY command eliminates all output of regression slopes and standard errors, even for numerical and dichotomous variables. Each variable's unique contribution is expressed only as a sum of squares. To find slopes, standard errors, and so forth, in MYSTAT add a command of the form SAVE MYFILE after the MODEL statement. For instance, the commands

TABLE 10.5
Occupational categories for the satisfaction data set

Case	1	2	3	4	5	6	7	8	9	10	11	12	13	14	15	16	17	18	19	20
Occupation	3	2	3	1	2	1	2	1	3	2	1	2	2	3	1	1	2	2	3	1

TABLE 10.6
Sample SYSTAT/MYSTAT output when some variables are multicategorical

DEP VAR: SATISFY   N: 20   MULTIPLE R: .733   SQUARED MULTIPLE R: .537

ANALYSIS OF VARIANCE

SOURCE	SUM-OF-SQUARES	DF	MEAN-SQUARE	F-RATIO	P
EDUC	214.726	1	214.726	5.353	0.039
SEX	7.320	1	7.320	0.182	0.677
OCCUP	349.366	2	174.683	4.355	0.038
RELIGION	101.420	3	33.807	0.843	0.496
ERROR	481.376	12	40.115		

230

TABLE 10.7
Output showing slopes despite the presence of categorical regressors

```
DEP VAR:  SATISFY   N: 20    MULTIPLE R:  .733    SQUARED MULTIPLE R:  .537
ADJUSTED SQUARED MULTIPLE R:  .268   STANDARD ERROR OF ESTIMATE:  6.334
```

VARIABLE	COEFFICIENT	STD ERROR	STD COEF	TOLERANCE	T	P (2 TAIL)
CONSTANT	56.440	10.501	0.000	.	5.375	0.000
X(1)	1.968	0.851	0.613	0.5493211	2.314	0.039
X(2)	-1.636	3.829	-0.113	0.5470927	-0.427	0.677
X(3)	-3.358	2.053	-0.358	0.8064442	-1.636	0.128
X(4)	-4.992	2.477	-0.548	0.5209597	-2.015	0.067
X(5)	0.680	2.493	0.066	0.6587840	0.273	0.790
X(6)	3.851	2.736	0.357	0.5986401	1.407	0.185
X(7)	-1.232	2.550	-0.114	0.6894118	-0.483	0.638

ANALYSIS OF VARIANCE

SOURCE	SUM-OF-SQUARES	DF	MEAN-SQUARE	F-RATIO	P
REGRESSION	559.424	7	79.918	1.992	0.140
RESIDUAL	481.376	12	40.115		

>save dummies
>estimate

immediately after the MODEL statement would make MYSTAT create a data file named DUMMIES which contains scores on all the variables in the analysis, including the coded variables created by MYSTAT. The comparable commands in SYSTAT are

>save dummies/model
>estimate

In the file DUMMIES created by this command, the regressors are named X(1) through X(P), in the order they appear in the model statement. In the current example, X(1) is education, X(2) is sex, X(3) and X(4) are the two variables created to code the three categories of occupation, and X(5), X(6), and X(7) are the three variables created to code the four categories of religion.

You can then use this new file to run a regression without the CATEGORY command. This will give regression slopes, standard errors, and the other familiar statistics for all variables. In the current example, you can see from Table 10.6 that the effect of education is statistically significant, but only by running this additional analysis would you find that the effect is positive rather than negative, since the coefficient of X(1) is positive. The complete output from this analysis is shown in Table 10.7.

SYSTAT and MYSTAT use effect coding, discussed in Sec. 10.2.6, rather than simple dummy coding, so the lines of output for X(3) through X(7) are discussed in that section. If you happen to look in the data file created by your SAVE command, you will also find there six new variables named ESTIMATE, RESIDUAL, LEVERAGE, STUDENT, COOK, and SEPRED. ESTIMATE contains values of $\hat{Y}$, while RESIDUAL contains the residuals. The other four variables are described in Chap. 14.

10.2   COMPARISONS AND CONTRASTS

10.2.1   Contrast Commands in GLM Programs

Many questions about differences among ordinary or adjusted cell means can be phrased as questions about *contrasts*. The simplest type of contrast is a *pairwise comparison*, which is the difference between two cell means. Other contrasts involve three or more means. For instance, suppose the 10 cells in a one-way ANOVA compare 10 drugs for the treatment of an ailment. Suppose drugs 1 and 2 are in one chemical family, drugs 3, 4, and 5 are in a different chemical family, and drugs 6 through 10 are in other families. Let M_j denote the mean of cell j. Then $(M_1 + M_2)/2$ measures the average response to the first family, $(M_3 + M_4 + M_5)/3$ measures the average response to the second family, and the difference $(M_1 + M_2)/2 - (M_3 + M_4 + M_5)/3$ measures the difference in average responses to the two families. This difference is a more complex contrast or comparison among cell means than a simple pairwise comparison.

This contrast can be written as $M_1/2 + M_2/2 - M_3/3 - M_4/3 - M_5/3$, so the coefficients of the five cell means are respectively $\frac{1}{2}, \frac{1}{2}, -\frac{1}{3}, -\frac{1}{3}$, and $-\frac{1}{3}$. If we let c_j denote the coefficient of M_j, then a contrast can be written as

$$\text{Contrast} = c_1 M_1 + c_2 M_2 + c_3 M_3 + \cdots + c_k M_k$$

A contrast among k cell means is defined as any function of this form, where the M's are cell means, the values of c_j are chosen by the investigator, and $\Sigma\, c_j = 0$ but the values of c_j are not all 0. Notice that in this example, the five coefficients sum to 0.

In a pairwise comparison, one c_j is $+1$, one is -1, and the rest are 0. For instance, if we wish to compare cells 1 and 2, we can set $c_1 = 1$, $c_2 = -1$, and all other c's equal to 0, so that the contrast becomes $M_1 - M_2$.

Tests on contrasts are unaffected by multiplying all values of c_j by a constant. Above we considered the contrast with coefficients

$$\frac{1}{2} \quad \frac{1}{2} \quad -\frac{1}{3} \quad -\frac{1}{3} \quad -\frac{1}{3} \quad 0 \quad 0 \quad 0 \quad 0 \quad 0$$

Multiplying all values by 6 simplifies them to

$$3 \quad 3 \quad -2 \quad -2 \quad -2 \quad 0 \quad 0 \quad 0 \quad 0 \quad 0$$

Suppose we have already used a command like:

>class drug;

in SAS or

>category drug = 10

in SYSTAT to identify DRUG as a categorical variable with 10 levels, and have run a model using that effect. Then in SAS the command

>contrast "families" drug 3 3 −2 −2 −2 0 0 0 0 0;

or in SYSTAT's program MGLH the commands:

>hypothesis
>effect = drug
>contrast
>3 3 −2 −2 −2 0 0 0 0 0
>test

will yield an F or t testing the hypothesis specified by the contrast. The simplification to integers is not necessary; it simply enables you to avoid having to enter longer numbers like $-.3333$ in this example.

The CONTRAST commands in both SAS and SYSTAT are more flexible than we have described here; you may wish to read the manual of the package you use.

The concept of interaction will not be introduced until Chap. 13. But for those already familiar with it, we can say now that interactions can also be expressed as contrasts. For instance, in a 3 × 4 two-way design, the interaction involving the four cell means M_{22}, M_{24}, M_{32}, and M_{34} is $(M_{22} - M_{24}) - (M_{32} - M_{34})$, which can be written as $M_{22} - M_{24} - M_{32} + M_{34}$. This is a contrast with coefficients $+1$, -1, -1, and $+1$ for those four cells and 0 for the other eight cells.

10.2.2   Computing SE(contrast) in Simple Designs

When a linear model is used to simulate a one-way or orthogonal ANOVA design, the standard error of a contrast can be estimated by hand calculation. Assuming equal population cell variances, the estimated standard error of a contrast is

$$SE(\text{contrast}) = \sqrt{MSE \sum \frac{c_j^2}{n_j}}$$

For instance, if a five-cell contrast has coefficients of 3, 3, -2, -2, and -2, as above, and the five cell frequencies are 10, 14, 8, 16, and 5, then

$$\sum \frac{c_j^2}{n_j} = \frac{9}{10} + \frac{9}{14} + \frac{4}{8} + \frac{4}{16} + \frac{4}{5} = 3.0929$$

As before, MSE is the residual mean square for the analysis as a whole.

Then we can test the significance of any contrast using

$$t = \frac{\text{contrast}}{SE(\text{contrast})}$$

Or we can put a confidence band around a contrast using

Confidence limits = contrast ± tabled t × SE(contrast)

Or we can find the critical value of a contrast using

Critical value of contrast = tabled t × SE(contrast)

The df for t in all these formulas is the overall residual df for the analysis.

Kirk (1982) reports more robust formulas for SE(contrast) which do not assume equal within-cell variances. However, these formulas are not readily generalized to the general linear model as a whole. More general robust methods are discussed in Chap. 14.

10.2.3 Testing Comparisons without CONTRAST Commands

MYSTAT and many other statistical packages lack CONTRAST commands, but simple alternatives allow you to test two-cell comparisons. You should understand these alternative methods even if your package has a CONTRAST command, since they are often used in the scientific literature. They use various coding schemes; simple dummy coding is only one of three we shall consider. All these coding schemes have $k - 1$ coded variables for k cells, so the df for the coded variables is $k - 1$. Except for possible rounding error, all the schemes yield the same values for both hierarchical and unique SS, mean squares, and F's. But they differ in the individual contrasts or comparisons provided in the computer output. A coding scheme can be designed so that two-cell comparisons are tested by the t tests on values of b_j for coded variables. To see how this works, consider first the meaning of these values in simple dummy coding.

10.2.4 The Meaning of Slopes and t's in Simple Dummy Coding

To see what each b_j equals in simple dummy coding, consider again the example of Sec. 10.1.4, in which simple dummy coding was used to simulate a one-way ANOVA. The regression equation for that example is

$$\hat{Y} = b_1 D1 + b_2 D2 + b_3 D3 + a$$

where $D1$, $D2$, and $D3$ are three dummy variables representing the four-category variable of religion. This equation has three D's because our example on religion has three D's, but the general equation can include any number of D's.

We know that $\hat{Y}$ for each cell equals the cell mean. We also know that for every person except those in the base category, one X is 1 and all the others are 0. Now consider a Protestant, for whom $D1 = 1$ and $D2 = D3 = 0$. We know that $\hat{Y} = M_1$, $a = M_4$, $D1 = 1$, and $D2 = D3 = 0$. Substituting these values in the regression equation, we have $M_1 = b_1 + M_4$, which can be rewritten as $b_1 = M_1 - M_4$. In the same way, we can show that $b_2 = M_2 - M_4$ and $b_3 = M_3 - M_4$. The general rule is:

> When simple dummy coding is used to imitate a one-way ANOVA, each b_j equals the difference between the mean of the corresponding cell and the mean of the base cell.

Further, the t associated with each b_j tests the difference of that particular cell mean from the mean of the base cell. In the present example, the mean satisfaction scores of the four groups are $M_1 = 82.67$, $M_2 = 81.6$, $M_3 = 81.2$, and $M_4 = 79.5$, so

$$b_1 = 82.67 - 79.5 = 3.17 \qquad t = .62$$

$$b_2 = 81.6 \;\; - 79.5 = 2.1 \qquad t = .39$$

$$b_3 = 81.2 \;\; - 79.5 = 1.7 \qquad t = .32$$

We now see that even though the base cell lacks its own dummy variable, in simple dummy coding it is not ignored at all. Rather, the base cell mean provides a *standard of comparison* for all the other cells. The regression output shows and tests its difference from every other cell mean, while only one test is provided for each of the other cells. Of course, these tests are not yet corrected for multiple comparisons; that topic is considered in Chap. 11.

We see now why simple dummy coding is especially useful in designs with one control or comparison group. By making the control group the base cell, we obtain a comparison of each cell mean with the control mean. We also see the result of making the base category the largest category, such as Protestant in our example on religion. By making it the base category, we obtain a comparison of each group's mean with the "standard" or largest group.

10.2.5 Sequential Coding

In sequential coding, we assign cell 1 codes of 0 on all $k - 1$ dummy variables, cell 2 codes of 0 on all but the first, cell 3 codes of 0 on all but the first two, and so on. All other assignments are 1. The resulting pattern of scores is shown on the left of Table 10.8 for four cells.

To see the meaning of the b's in this coding scheme, recall that $\hat{Y}$ for the entries in each cell equals the cell mean, so $M_j = \hat{Y} = b_1 D1 + b_2 D2 + b_3 D3 + a$. When we replace $D1$, $D2$, and $D3$ in this equation by the values 0, 0, and 0 from the first row of the table, we obtain the equation $M_1 = a$, shown to its right. Substituting the values in each other row produces the equation shown to its right. Then subtracting adjacent pairs of equations from each other shows $b_1 = M_2 - M_1$, $b_2 = M_3 - M_2$, and $b_3 = M_4 - M_3$. We see that in sequential coding, each b_j equals the difference between the means of two adjacent cells. For instance, if four cell means are 3.2, 3.8, 4.1, and 4.9, respectively, sequential coding with no other regressors yields

$$b_1 = 3.8 - 3.2 = .6$$
$$b_2 = 4.1 - 3.8 = .3$$
$$b_3 = 4.9 - 4.1 = .8$$

Thus the t associated with each b_j tests the significance of the difference between two adjacent cells.

This pattern of coding is especially useful when k cells or categories can be ranked on some a priori basis, such as the cost or complexity of the treatment applied in the various cells. Then each b_j measures the increase in Y associated with a particular cost increase. Further, the t associated with each b

TABLE 10.8
Why sequential coding reveals successive mean differences

Cell	D_1	D_2	D_3	
1	0	0	0	$M_1 = a$
2	1	0	0	$M_2 = b_1 + a$
3	1	1	0	$M_3 = b_1 + b_2 + a$
4	1	1	1	$M_4 = b_1 + b_2 + b_3 + a$

tests the significance of the associated Y increase. If other regressors are included, such as age and sex, then the b's equal the increases in Y associated with successive increases in cost, corrected for differences in the other regressors.

10.2.6 Effect Coding

Effect coding is like simple dummy coding, in that one cell is chosen as the base cell and a coded variable is created for each cell except the base cell. However, the standard of comparison is the average of the k cell means, instead of the mean of the base cell. Thus the computer output includes no direct information on the base cell, where simple dummy coding provides a comparison with every other cell.

For instance, suppose as above that the means of cells 1, 2, 3, and 4 are 3.2, 3.8, 4.1, and 4.9. The mean of these four cells means is 4.0. If cell 4 is the base cell, then we will find

$$b_1 = 3.2 - 4.0 = -.8$$
$$b_2 = 3.8 - 4.0 = -.2$$
$$b_3 = 4.1 - 4.0 = +.1$$

The t associated with each b_j tests the null hypothesis that the mean of cell j equals the unweighted average of all k cell means, which is equivalent to the hypothesis that the mean of cell j equals the unweighted average of the $k - 1$ *other* cell means. For instance, if three cell means are 10, 20, and 30 and the fourth mean equals their average value of 20, then 20 is also the average of all four.

As before, by adding other regressors we can control for differences between cells on these other regressors.

The codes producing this result are like simple dummy codes, except that the base cell is coded -1 rather than 0 on all variables. Thus, for four cells with cell 4 as base cell, we have the codes shown in Table 10.9.

If a test is needed comparing the base cell with the average of the others, you can either run the analysis again with a different cell as base cell or use a GLM program with a CONTRAST command.

TABLE 10.9
Effect coding for four categories

	D_1	D_2	D_3
1	1	0	0
2	0	1	0
3	0	0	1
4	−1	−1	−1

To see why this works as it does, recall that $\hat{Y}$ for each cell equals the cell mean. We can combine this fact with the equation

$$\hat{Y} = b_1 D_1 + b_2 D_2 + b_3 D_3 + a$$

For cell 1, $D_1 = 1$, $D_2 = D_3 = 0$, so

$$M_1 = b_1 D_1 + b_2 D_2 + b_3 D_3 + a = b_1 + a$$

Doing this for each of the four cells, we find

$$M_1 = b_1 + a$$
$$M_2 = b_2 + a$$
$$M_3 = b_3 + a$$
$$M_4 = -b_1 - b_2 - b_3 + a$$

Adding the four equations, we find that the b's cancel out, so that $\Sigma M = 4a$, which implies that $a = \Sigma M/4$, which in turn says that the Y intercept a is the unweighted average of the four cell means. But $b_1 = M_1 - a$, so b_1 equals the deviation of M_1 from this average. Similarly, $b_2 = M_2 - a$ and $b_3 = M_3 - a$, so b_2 and b_3 equal the deviations of M_2 and M_3 from the same average.

10.2.7   Weighted Effect Coding

Weighted effect coding is a method for comparing the mean of every cell but the base cell with a *weighted* average of cell means. Section 10.2.9 shows how weighted effect coding can be extended to test any contrast with any regression program. To illustrate the method, we will use Table 10.10, which shows the proportion of the population of the United States living in eight regions of the nation in 1987.

Weighted effect coding works like ordinary effect coding, except that instead of coding the base or reference cell with scores of −1, the entry for each variable is

$$\frac{-\text{Weight of cell identified by the variable}}{\text{Weight of base cell}}$$

For instance, suppose we want to compare the cell mean for each region of the

TABLE 10.10
Proportion of the population living in eight regions in the United States in 1987

Region	Proportion	Ratio to last cell
New England	.0527	7.97
Mid-Atlantic	.1536	23.2
Midwest	.2371	35.9
Border and mid-south	.2667	40.3
Deep south	.0855	12.9
Rocky Mountain	.0541	8.18
West coast	.1435	21.7
Alaska and Hawaii	.00661	
	1.000	

United States to the national mean. Since there are eight regions, we would use seven coded variables: the first coded 1 only for New England, the second coded 1 only for mid-Atlantic, and so on. If the last cell is used as the base cell, the codes entered for this cell will be -1 times the values shown in the last column of Table 10.10: -7.97, -23.2, and so on. When these codes are used, the slope b printed for each dummy variable equals the difference between the appropriate cell mean and the weighted average—in this example, the national average. And the corresponding t tests the null hypothesis that this difference is zero. As with other coding methods, these differences are adjusted for all other regressors in the model. In the present example, if the dependent variable were satisfaction and race and age were included in the model, then except for the base region, the procedure would estimate and test the difference in satisfaction between each region and the national average, controlling for differences among regions in race and age.

10.2.8 Nested Coding

Often categories can be grouped. We might divide the eight categories of the present example into eastern and western groups, or into northeastern, southeastern, and western groups. This section shows how any of the previous coding methods can be applied *within each group*, while simultaneously using a separate set of coded variables to differentiate the groups from each other. For the current example, we will use the word *zone* to refer to these groups of *regions*.

If desired, each group can have its own coding method, and between-groups codes can be created by still another method. I can think of no reason for doing so, but in the present example one could apply simple dummy coding within the northeastern zone, sequential coding within the southeastern zone, effect coding within the western zone, and weighted effect coding to differentiate among the three zones.

In nested coding the worker first identifies a *standard of comparison* for each group of categories. The between-groups coded variables will compare these standard values with each other, and some or all of the within-group comparisons will also be made against these standards. In the present example, the obvious standard of comparison within each group is the within-group weighted average with weights proportional to the known population frequency in each cell. For instance, let the New England, mid-Atlantic, and midwest regions of the nation make up the northeastern zone, let the "border and mid-south" and deep south regions make up the southeastern zone, and let the Rocky Mountain, west coast, and Alaska and Hawaii regions constitute the western zone. Within the northeastern zone, Table 10.10 shows that the populations of the New England, mid-Atlantic, and midwestern regions are in the ratio .0527, .1536, .2371. Thus, if we had a cell mean on a dependent variable Y for each of these three regions, the best estimate of $_TM_Y$ for the zone would be found by weighting the three cell means in proportion to these values. That weighted average would be the standard of comparison for the zone.

We do not actually compute the weighted average or other standard of comparison, but we use an appropriate coding method to define it. Simple dummy coding defines the standard of comparison as the base cell, sequential coding defines it as the first cell in the sequence (the one coded with all zeros), and effect coding or weighted effect coding defines it as the unweighted or weighted average of all cells in the group. Cases outside the group are coded 0 on all these variables.

In the present example, we have decided to use a weighted average within each group, so we use weighted effect coding within each zone. Since there are three regions within the northeastern zone, for this zone we define two coded variables $D1$ and $D2$. If the last category is the base, then individual cases from the New England, mid-Atlantic, and midwestern regions can be coded respectively 1, 0, and $-.0527/.2371 = .222$ on $D1$, and 0, 1, and $-.1536/.2371 = -.648$ on $D2$. Cases from the five regions outside the northeast are coded 0 on both $D1$ and $D2$.

We do this for each group of categories. In the present example, there are two regions within the southeastern zone, so we use a single coded variable $D3$. Since the two regions within the zone have populations proportional to the values .2667 and .0855, $D3$ can be coded 1 and $-.2667/.0855 = -3.12$ for the two regions, respectively. The three regions of the western zone have populations proportional to .0541, .1435, .00661. Thus we can define $D4$ with codes of 1, 0, and $-.0541/.00661 = -8.18$, respectively, and $D5$ with codes of 0, 1, and $-.1435/.00661 = 21.7$, respectively.

We now use either the same coding system or a different coding system to define variables which differentiate among groups. In the present example, we might decide to compare the western zone with each of the other zones. If so, we use simple dummy coding with the western zone as the base zone. That is, we define two more coded variables $D6$ and $D7$. $D6$ is coded 1 for all cases in the northeastern zone and 0 for all others. $D7$ is coded 1 for all cases in the southeastern zone and 0 for all others. Whatever coding method we choose, the differences tested will be differences *among the within-group standards of comparison.* In the present example, these standards of comparison are the best estimates of the within-zone means, so these are the values compared with each other by $D6$ and $D7$.

Like other coding methods, nested coding can be used with covariates. In the present example, adding race and age as covariates would test all the regional and zonal differences just described, adjusted for differences among regions and among zones on race and age.

10.2.9 A General Test for Contrasts

Nested coding can be used to estimate and test any imaginable contrast with any regression program. Any contrast defines three groups of cells: those with positive weights, those with negative weights, and those with zero weights. (The last group may be empty.) Using the weights defining the contrast, use weighted effect coding to define weighted means within the positive and negative groups separately. Then use simple dummy coding to estimate and test the difference between those two weighted means. The regression slope for the coded variable equals the form of the contrast in which the positive and negative weights each sum to 1 in absolute value, and the associated t tests the contrast. This test is equivalent to the test for a contrast in SYSTAT or SAS.

10.3 NESTED FACTORS AND MULTILEVEL CATEGORY SYSTEMS

10.3.1 Nested Sets

Category systems can have two or more levels. For instance, the multicategorical variable of religion can be divided into major religions such as Christian, Jewish, and Islamic, and into a second level of denominational categories such as Catholic, Presbyterian, and Baptist or Orthodox, Conservative, and Reform Judaism. There may be several levels in the hierarchy, and some parts of the category system may have more levels than others: a recent *World Almanac* showed 15 Baptist subdenominations in the United States, but only one Roman Catholic church.

In this example, the category system has three levels: major religion, denomination, and subdenomination. Let us denote these as REL, DEN, and SUB, respectively. Each level can be represented as a separate factor or multicategorical variable. The categories at all levels together form a *nested set* of factors. One factor B is said to be nested within another factor A if knowing someone's category on B tells you without fail that person's category on A. Thus the factor SUB is nested within DEN, because, for instance, someone cannot be Southern Baptist without being Baptist. And DEN is nested within REL, because you cannot be Baptist without being Christian.

Factors not nested are said to be *crossed*. All factors in previous sections were crossed.

Nested factors are handled very simply in SAS by writing MODEL statements with the name of the nesting factor in parentheses at the end of the name of the nested factor. Thus, if factors are named REL, DEN, and SUB in the data set, in MODEL statements they are referred to as REL, DEN(REL), and SUB(DEN(REL)), respectively. The methods in SYSTAT and MYSTAT are more complex, as we shall see.

10.3.2   Coding Nested Sets

The SYSTAT manual describes a way for analyzing nested factors that cannot be done with MYSTAT. This section and Sec. 10.3.3 describe two other methods which, in my opinion, are more flexible and easier to understand, and which can be used with either SYSTAT or MYSTAT. The method in Sec. 10.3.3 is generally superior to the present one, but it is difficult to understand until the present method is studied. And the method of this section is quite adequate for problems with no interactions (see Chap. 13).

In the first method, the worker simply codes the nested factors with different numbers of categories. For instance, in our example, REL might be coded 1 to 5; DEN, 1 to 20; and SUB, 1 to 80. If a category in a nesting factor has no subcategories, then all members of the category are given the same code on the nested factor—a code unique to that category. For instance, Roman Catholic might be coded 15 on DEN and 36 on SUB.

In this method, nested sets are handled in one of two ways, depending on whether they are being used as independent variables or as covariates. When they are used as covariates, simply use in the model whichever level of factor you prefer, depending on the level at which you wish to control the variable. When the sets are used as an independent variable, run the regression two or more times with different factors from the nested set and test the difference between consecutive values of SS(model) using the three-way decomposition formulas of Sec. 5.3.1. Thus, differences among denominations within major religions are tested by the increase in SS(model) when REL is replaced in the model by DEN, and differences among subdenominations within denominations are tested by the increase when DEN is replaced by SUB. In each test, df_r is the smaller of the two values of df_r in the two models being compared. The numerator df is the difference between the two values of df_r, which is also the difference in number of categories in the two factors. In the religion example, there are 5 major religions, 20 denominations, and 80 subdenominations. Thus the numerator df is $20 - 5$, or 15, in testing the difference between DEN and REL, and $80 - 20$, or 60, in testing the difference between SUB and DEN.

10.3.3   A More Complex Method

The method of this section is more complex than the method of Sec. 10.3.2 but has advantages which will become clear when interactions are introduced in

TABLE 10.11
A classification of the apes (modified from Hrdy, 1981, p. 198)

	Family	Genus	Species
Family Hylobatidae (gibbons and siamangs)			
Gibbons			
White-handed	1	1	1
Silvery	1	1	2
Pileated	1	1	3
Mueller's	1	1	4
Dark-handed	1	1	5
Hoolock	1	1	6
Concolor	1	1	7
Kloss's	1	1	8
Siamang	1	2	1
Family Pongidae (great apes and humans)			
Orangutan	2	1	1
Chimpanzees			
Chimpanzee	2	3	1
Pygmy chimpanzee	2	3	9
Gorilla	2	4	1
Human	2	5	1

Chap. 13. This method is like the previous one, *except* that in each nested factor, a code of 1 is used for any subcategory that is the first subcategory within its category of the nesting factor. This rule is illustrated in Table 10.11. Notice that there are no codes for any category that itself has subcategories. For instance, there are no codes for chimpanzees, because there are two species of chimpanzee. But even though the words *gorilla* and *Human* appear at the same level of the category system as *chimpanzee* (the genus level), there are codes for these groups because in this classification each contains only one species.

The factor "family," the first factor in the nested set, is coded exactly as before, since it has no nesting factor to force modifications by the rule above. The effect of this rule first becomes visible in the genus code for orangutan. The orangutan is the first genus listed under the family Pongidae (great apes and humans), so it is coded 1. All species of gibbon are also coded 1, but they are differentiated from orangutans at the family level. The easiest way to create the codes is to first fill in all the 1s and then go back to the top and number all the remaining categories in order—in this case, from 2 for siamangs to 5 for humans.

Six different species—white-handed gibbons, siamangs, orangutans, ordinary chimpanzees, gorillas, and humans—are all coded 1 on "species," because each is the first or only species listed within its genus. After the 1s are filled in, the remaining species are coded—in this case, from 2 to 9.

Factors coded in this way are used differently from those created by the method of Sec. 10.3.2. In that method, two factors from the same nested set are never entered in the same model. In the present method, no nested factor is ever used without all its nesting factors. In the present example, the factors "family," "genus," and "species" have 2, 5, and 9 categories, respectively, so the CATEGORY command will create for them 1, 4, and 8 coded variables, respectively. Inclusion of just the "family" factor in a model divides the 14 species listed into just two families distinguished by just one coded variable. Inclusion of the "family" and "genus" factors together uses $1 + 4$, or 5 coded variables, which distinguish among the 6 genera (gibbons, siamangs, orangutans, chimpanzees, gorillas, and humans). Inclusion of all three factors uses $1 + 4 + 8$, or 13 coded variables, which distinguish among all 14 species.

The effect of each factor is measured or tested in the presence of its nesting factors but in the absence of the factors nested within it. Thus differences among families are tested while the "genus" and "species" factors are excluded, and differences among genera are tested while the "species" factor is excluded.

SUMMARY

10.1 Multicategorical Variables as Sets

A multicategorical variable or factor can be represented as a set of $k - 1$ indicator variables, where k is the number of categories.

In simple dummy coding, cases in category 1 are coded 1 on variable 1 and 0 on all other variables, those in category 2 are coded 1 on variable 2 and 0 on all others, and so on. No variable is used or needed for the last, or kth, category, since cases in that category are the only ones scoring 0 on all $k - 1$ variables.

Almost all regression packages allow you to create dummy variables with a few commands. The ability to create a whole set of coded variables with a single command is the fundamental distinction between an ordinary regression program and a *general linear model*, or GLM, program.

Most coding systems require that one category be treated differently from the others; this category is called the *base category* or *reference category*. Many GLM programs simply use the last category as the base category.

When Y is regressed onto a set of dummy variables, the true multiple correlation $_TR$ equals 0 if and only if all k true cell means are equal. Therefore, the F testing the null hypothesis $_TR = 0$ tests the null hypothesis of equal cell means. The ANOVA table produced by a regression program will contain the same entries as an ANOVA table computed to test the null hypothesis of equal cell means.

Other equivalences between regression and ANOVA parallel the equivalences that occur with simple indicator variables: each value of $\hat{Y}_i$ is the cell mean of the cell containing person i, and each residual e_i is the deviation of person i from his or her cell mean. If we have to estimate a person's Y score from his or her regressor scores, our best estimate is that person's mean cell on Y, and R is the correlation between these estimates and the actual Y scores. Eta-squared $= R^2$.

One or more sets of dummy variables can be included in a regression along with other regressors. In SAS, SYSTAT, and MYSTAT, the inclusion of even one variable in a CATEGORY command eliminates all output of regression slopes and standard errors, even for numerical and dichotomous variables. Each variable's unique contribution is expressed only as a sum of squares. To find slopes, standard errors, and so forth, in MYSTAT or SYSTAT, use the SAVE command and then run a second regression using the data file created by that command.

10.2   Comparisons and Contrasts

Many questions about differences among ordinary or adjusted cell means can be phrased as questions about *contrasts*. The simplest type of contrast is a *pairwise comparison*, which is the difference between two cell means. If we let c_j denote the coefficient of M_j, then a contrast can be written as

$$\text{Contrast} = c_1 M_1 + c_2 M_2 + c_3 M_3 + \cdots + c_k M_k$$

A comparison or contrast among k cell means is defined as any function of this form, where the M's are cell means, the values of c_j are chosen by the investigator, and $\Sigma\, c_j = 0$ but the values of c_j are not all 0. In a pairwise comparison, one c_j is $+1$, one is -1, and the rest are 0. Tests on contrasts are unaffected by multiplying all values of c_j by a constant.

When a linear model is used to simulate a one-way or orthogonal ANOVA design, the standard error of a contrast can be estimated by hand calculation. Assuming equal population cell variances, the estimated standard error of a contrast is

$$SE(\text{contrast}) = \sqrt{MSE \sum \frac{c_j^2}{n_j}}$$

As before, MSE is the residual mean square for the analysis as a whole. Then we can test the significance of any contrast using

$$t = \frac{\text{contrast}}{SE(\text{contrast})}$$

Or we can put a confidence band around a contrast using

$$\text{Confidence limits} = \text{contrast} \pm \text{tabled } t \times SE(\text{contrast})$$

Or we can find the critical value of a contrast using

$$\text{Critical value of contrast} = \text{tabled } t \times SE(\text{contrast})$$

The df for t in all these formulas is the overall residual df for the analysis.

MYSTAT and many other statistical packages lack CONTRAST commands, but simple alternatives allow you to test some contrasts, and more complex procedures allow you to test any contrast. All these coding schemes have $k - 1$ coded variables for k cells, so the df for the coded variables is

$k - 1$. Except for possible rounding error, all the schemes yield the same values for both hierarchical and unique *SS*, mean squares, and *F*'s. But they differ in the individual contrasts or comparisons provided in the computer output.

When simple dummy coding is used to imitate a one-way ANOVA, each b_j equals the difference between the mean of the corresponding cell and the mean of the base cell. Further, the *t* associated with each b_j tests the difference between that particular cell mean and the mean of the base cell. Although the base cell lacks its own dummy variable, it provides a *standard of comparison* for all the other cells. The regression output shows and tests the difference between it and every other cell mean.

In sequential coding, we assign cell 1 codes of 0 on all $k - 1$ dummy variables, cell 2 codes of 0 on all but the first, cell 3 codes of 0 on all but the first two, and so on. All other assignments are 1. Then each b_j equals the difference between the means of two adjacent cells, and the *t* associated with each b_j tests the significance of the difference between two adjacent cells. This pattern of coding is especially useful when *k* cells or categories can be ranked on some a priori basis, such as the cost or complexity of the treatment applied in the various cells.

Effect coding is like simple dummy coding, in that one cell is chosen as the base cell and a coded variable is created for each cell except the base cell. The *t* associated with each b_j tests the null hypothesis that the mean of cell *j* equals the unweighted average of all *k* cell means, which is equivalent to the hypothesis that the mean of cell *j* equals the unweighted average of the $k - 1$ *other* cell means. The codes producing this result are like simple dummy codes, except that the base cell is coded -1 rather than 0 on all variables.

Weighted effect coding is like effect coding, except that the base cell is coded

$$\frac{-\text{Weight of cell } j}{\text{Weight of base cell}}$$

on the variable scored 1 for cell *j*. For each cell except the base cell, it tests the null hypothesis that the cell mean equals a weighted average of all cell means.

In nested coding, the categories are formed into groups. Any of these coding schemes may be used to differentiate cells within each group, and some coding scheme is used to differentiate between groups. Nested coding can be combined with weighted effect coding to use any regression program to test any contrast.

10.3   Nested Factors and Multilevel Category Systems

Factor B is said to be *nested* within factor A if knowing someone's category on B tells you without fail that person's category on A. Nested sets can be handled very simply in SAS by writing MODEL statements with the name of the nesting factor in parentheses at the end of the name of the nested factor. In SYSTAT and MYSTAT, there are two ways to proceed. In the simpler method, factors are simply represented by different multicategorical variables with different numbers of categories. In this method, nested sets are handled in either of two ways, depending on whether they are being used as independent variables or as covariates. When they are used as covariates, simply use in the model which-ever level of factor you prefer, depending on the level at which you wish to control the variable. When you are using them as an independent variable, run the regression two or more times with different factors from the nested set, and test the difference between consecutive values of SS(model) using the three-way decomposition formulas of Sec. 5.3.1. In each test, df_r is the smaller of the two values of df_r in the two models being compared. The numerator df is the difference between the two values of df_r, which is also the difference in number of categories in the two factors.

The advantage of the more complex method applicable in SYSTAT and MYSTAT is that it is easier to test for interaction (see Chap. 13). In this method, each category is coded 1 if it is the first subcategory within its category of the next higher nesting factor. All remaining categories are then numbered in sequence, starting with 2. In this method, no nested factor is ever used without using all its nesting factors.

KEY TERMS

factor	pairwise comparison
code	sequential coding
coded variable	effect coding
compound variable	weighted effect coding
GLM program	nested coding
base category	standard of comparison
reference category	nested set of factors
contrast	

SYMBOLS AND ABBREVIATIONS

D GLM k bg wg c_j

PROBLEMS

Add the data on religion and occupation, from Tables 10.1 and 10.5, to the life-satisfaction data set in Table 5.7. Keep a copy of your answers to the problems below; you will need them in the problems for Chap. 11.

1. Fit a model regressing satisfaction on income, education, and occupational category. Test the null hypothesis that occupational category has no effect on life satisfaction when income and education are controlled. Do this in four ways: simple dummy

coding, sequential coding, effect coding, and using the CATEGORY command. For the first three methods, show the IF statements you use to create the codes. You should get the same F all four ways.

2. In Prob. 1, you generated all the computer output necessary to test all three pairwise comparisons between occupational categories. Show all three adjusted differences between categories, together with the values of t and p for each. In Chap. 11 we will correct the three p's for multiple tests.

CHAPTER 11

MULTIPLE TESTS

If a categorical regressor has 10 categories, then the number of comparisons we could make between pairs of category means is $(10 \times 9)/2 = 45$. If the 10 sample groups are large and equal in size, it can be shown that the probability is about .63 that at least one of those 45 comparisons will be significant at the .05 level, even if all 10 population means are equal. Thus, if there are only one or two significant results, they cannot simply be accepted at face value. This illustrates the problem of *multiple comparisons*, which generally refers to comparisons among the cells of a categorical regressor.

The problem of multiple comparisons is just part of the broader problem of multiple tests. Suppose 20 experimenters test an effect and the most significant result found by any of the 20 is $p = .01$. It can be shown that the probability is about .18 that such a significant result will occur by chance at least once in 20 studies, so again the apparently significant result cannot be accepted at face value. Or suppose we scan a correlation matrix for 15 variables and select the highest correlations and see that they are significant. If we note that the matrix contains 105 correlations, we must recognize that we would expect several to be significant just by chance.

In turn, the problem of multiple tests is closely related to the problem of multiple confidence bands. If we derive many 95% confidence bands, then our confidence may be far below 95% that all of the confidence bands include the true values of the parameters they estimate.

All these topics are included in the domain of *simultaneous statistical inference*. The topic of multiple comparisons is by far the most widely analyzed individual topic in this domain, so our review of available methods necessarily emphasizes that topic. We shall also consider the broader topic of multiple tests. We shall make little direct reference to confidence bands; but conclusions concerning confidence bands follow directly from the fact that a confidence band is the range of a parameter that would not be rejected by a hypothesis test, so any test can be converted into a confidence-band method. Thus our discussion covers, directly or indirectly, all areas of simultaneous inference.

Multiple-test methods are organized here in terms of the breadth of their applications, with the broadest methods first. Section 11.1 discusses the Bonferroni method, which applies to an enormous range of problems. Section 11.2 covers the Fisher method, which is less broad, and the Scheffé method, which is still narrower. Section 11.3 covers five methods: the Tukey HSD, or a, method, the Dunnett method, the Newman-Keuls method, the Tukey b method, and the Duncan "new multiple range test." All five are for quite specific problems. In fact, I argue in Sec. 11.3 that these methods are too narrow for most scientists to bother learning, since they can all be adequately simulated by the enormously flexible Bonferroni method. The Ryan layering method is also discussed, in Sec. 11.3.8, but is not counted as one of these five because it is really a Bonferroni-based alternative to the Tukey b method.

The topic of simultaneous statistical inference raises complex philosophical questions. For instance, if we correct for the fact that we perform 10 or 20 tests as part of a single experiment, it is valid to ask why each experimenter does not correct for all the tests in his or her lifetime, or for all the tests in that area of science, or indeed for all the tests in the entire history of science. Section 11.4 suggests answers to these questions. Section 11.5 then evaluates the aforementioned methods in terms of this philosophical perspective.

In most of our examples of tests we shall find t and an exact p for a contrast, rather than a critical value for a contrast based on some arbitrarily chosen significance level alpha. I regard this as preferable in general because reporting an exact p enables the reader of a research report to compare it with his or her own value of alpha, rather than be forced to accept the value used by the report's author.

11.1   THE BONFERRONI METHOD

Let PC denote a corrected significance level, and let pm denote the most significant of B values of p. The Bonferroni method is very simple; it simply approximates PC by the value $B \times pm$. Thus, if the most significant result from 10 tests is $p = .01$, the corrected significance level PC for that result is calculated to be $10 \times .01$, or $.10$. Or if the most significant of five results yields $p = .0042$, then its corrected significance level is $5 \times .0042 = .021$. The multiplier B is called the *Bonferroni correction factor*. Ryan (1960) has shown that $B \times pm$ never underestimates PC, so we can define the Bonferroni formula as

$$PC \leq B \times pm$$

This formula was recognized early in this century by Ronald Fisher and others as one possible approach to the problem of multiple tests. But contrary to majority opinion today, these early authors considered it an inferior method. The first authors to emphasize the method's advantages are Ryan (1959, 1960), who published in a psychological journal, and Dunn (1961), who published in a statistical journal. The name *Bonferroni* was first attached to the method by Miller (1966), who pointed out its similarity to the Bonferroni inequality, a formula used in other areas of mathematics. In some past works I have called the method the *Ryan* method—the name I still prefer—while others have called it the *Dunn* method. But in recent years, the name *Bonferroni* seems to have won out, and here we shall continue that usage.

11.1.1   Independent Tests

The reasonableness of the Bonferroni method is shown most easily for independent tests; the concept of independence is explained more fully in Sec. 11.1.3. If the same hypothesis is tested by 10 different investigators, what is the probability that just by chance, at least one of the 10 tests will be significant at the .01 level? We can calculate the answer as follows: the probability is .99 that any given test will *fail* to be significant at the .01 level. Because the tests are independent, the probability is $.99^{10}$, or .904, that all 10 tests will fail to be significant. Therefore the probability that at least one will be significant at the .01 level is $1 - .904 = .096$. As we have seen, the Bonferroni method estimates this figure quite accurately, giving a corrected significance level of .10 for this problem.

11.1.2   The Conservatism of the Bonferroni Method for Independent Tests

The formula we just used to find the exact probability is

$$PC = 1 - (1 - pm)^B$$

We calculated $PC = 1 - (1 - .01)^{10} = 1 - .904 = .096$. The Bonferroni inequality states that if we have two numbers a and B, and if $0 < a < 1$ and $B > 1$, then $1 - (1 - a)^B < Ba$. If we substitute pm for a, the left side of the Bonferroni inequality equals PC by the formula above, and the right side equals $B \times pm$. Thus, applied to the problem of multiple tests, the inequality states

$$PC < B \times pm$$

In this example, PC and $B \times pm$ are very similar: .096 and .1. It can be shown that if PC is small, then this is always true. We are particularly interested in corrected significance levels around .05, so it is useful to know that when tests are independent and $PC = .05$, $B \times pm$ never exceeds .052 for any value of B; and when $B \times pm$ equals .05, PC never falls below .048 for any value of B. We shall consider the difference between .05 and .052, or between .05 and .048, small enough to ignore. Most readers will find this reasonable already, but it will appear even more reasonable after we consider all the sources of error and subjectivity in analyses involving multiple tests. Therefore we shall consider $B \times pm$ a good approximation to PC, which for independent tests errs on the conservative side by slightly overestimating PC.

11.1.3 The Bonferroni Method for Nonindependent Tests

If a regression contains P regressors, then tests on the P values of b_j are not statistically independent, because the regressors are not independent. Or if a categorical regressor has k cells, then there are $k(k - 1)/2$ possible pairwise comparisons, and these tests are not mutually independent either. The comparison $M_1 - M_2$ is not independent of $M_1 - M_3$, because the chance selection of a very high score in cell 1 will increase both comparisons. The comparisons $M_1 - M_2$ and $M_3 - M_4$ are orthogonal or independent, but the *tests* on the comparisons are not fully independent. This is because both use the same *MSE* in the denominator of the t's; a random fluctuation downward in *MSE* will raise both t's. Because of this nonindependence, the Bonferroni method first seems irrelevant to this problem. But it turns out to be quite relevant.

Ryan (1960) was the first to publish a proof that if we replace the sign $<$ in the Bonferroni inequality by $\leq$, then the formula applies to nonindependent tests as well. Ryan's proof also showed that when $B \times pm$ is small (which is the only case of interest), the overestimation of PC is small for most nonindependent tests. Thus the Bonferroni formula gives an accurate but slightly conservative estimate of PC for most sets of nonindependent tests as well as all independent sets.

11.1.4 Some Basic Uses and Properties of the Bonferroni Formula

If we choose, we can regard symmetrical two-tailed tests as a special case of the Bonferroni formula in which $B = 2$. Suppose we use the same sample mean M to test two null hypotheses: $_TM \leq 0$ and $_TM \geq 0$. These tests illustrate one extreme of nonindependent tests; they have a correlation of -1, since we know in advance that the two t's will be equal but opposite in sign. The Bonferroni formula states that the probability of finding at least one of these results significant at the .025 level does not exceed $2 \times .025 = .05$. In this case, the exact equality holds: $PC = B \times pm$. What we have done is express the familiar argument for two-tailed tests in terms of the Bonferroni formula.

Dunn (1961) and Sidak (1967) have shown that for symmetric two-sided tests, the expression $1 - (1 - pm)^B$ rather than $B \times pm$ provides an upper limit for PC. Because the former expression is always smaller than the latter, this provides a less conservative estimate of PC. But we have just seen that the Bonferroni method is not always too conservative. Thus the Dunn-Sidak method is sometimes too liberal. Earlier, we saw that in cases of interest the difference between the two expressions is very small (for example, .05 as opposed to .052). Therefore we shall always use $B \times pm$ as our estimate of PC.

Our discussion of two-sided tests shows that when two tests have a correlation of -1, the Bonferroni formula does not overestimate PC at all. Other things equal, the overestimation of PC increases as the correlations among the tests increase from -1 toward $+1$. To see the other extreme, we can imagine a case in which several tests have a correlation of $+1$. This can arise if a one-way design has $k - 1$ treatment groups and one control group and we consider only the comparisons of the control group with various treatment groups. If the treatment groups all have equal true means and infinite sample sizes but the control group has a finite sample size, then all $k - 1$ values of t will be equal in every sample. Thus the probability of making one or more type 1 errors equals the probability of each error. That is, in this unusual case, the correct formula for PC is $PC = pm$. Thus, in extreme cases like this, the Bonferroni formula can substantially overestimate PC.

Extreme cases like this are rare, so the Bonferroni formula has many useful applications. We will soon see several of these. To illustrate just one such application, we can apply it to a one-way analysis of variance as follows. The number of possible pairwise comparisons between cell means is $k(k - 1)/2$, which equals 45 if $k = 10$. If we compare the highest cell mean and the lowest, then we are selecting the largest of the 45 differences. Suppose this largest t is 3.29 and residual df is 60. Then the two-tailed p for this comparison is .00168. Thus the Bonferroni formula $PC \le B \times pm$ yields $PC \le 45 \times .00168 = .0756$. It can be shown that the actual value of PC is .05, so that the overestimation of PC is noticeable but not severe.

Occasionally the Bonferroni formula may yield a value above 1. For instance, if the most significant p in 20 tests is .07, then $B \times pm = 20 \times .07 = 1.4$. In such cases, we must remember that the Bonferroni formula normally overestimates PC, and the overestimation is small only if PC itself is small. Thus, when you find $B \times pm > 1$, the proper conclusion is not that $PC > 1$, which is impossible, but rather that PC is not small.

Some other tests, notably the Fisher "protected t" test of Sec. 11.2.1, are used only after a significant overall F is found in an ANOVA. This notion is so widespread that we should mention that this restriction is *not* necessary for the Bonferroni test or for most of the methods of this chapter.

11.1.5   Finding an "Exact" p from t

Effective use of the Bonferroni formula with t and F tests requires us to find nearly exact p values, even when t or F is very high. This can be done fairly easily in SYSTAT; see the manual. But there are also several ways that do not require an expensive program.

Section 5.2.5 gave two ways of finding exact or nearly exact p values for F, one using MYSTAT and the other using a short BASIC program. These methods can be used to find the two-tailed p from a t test: write $t^2 = F$ and test the resulting F with $df_1 = 1$ and df_2 set to equal the df for the t test. By using the FORMAT 9 command with MYSTAT, even very small p values can be read accurately.

Several other methods are quicker and only slightly less accurate. One approach is to convert t to a normal deviate z and then use a normal table which includes high values of z. The conversion to z can be done simply as follows:

$$|z| = df \times \ln\left(\frac{t^2}{df + 1} + 1 \right)$$

I have found that errors in this formula are small and usually conservative; so long as $df \geq 7$ and $p \geq .000005$, the value of p found from this formula and a normal table is never more than 10% below the true p.

A more complex but noticeably more accurate formula is given by Peizer and Pratt (1968):

$$\left(df - \frac{2}{3} + \frac{.1}{df} \right) \sqrt{\frac{\ln(1 + t^2/df)}{df - \frac{5}{6}}}$$

The symbol $\ln$ denotes a natural logarithm; logarithms are explained in Sec. 12.2. If $t = 2$ and $df = 20$, the simpler formula gives $z = 1.867$ while the Peizer-Pratt formula gives $z = 1.886$. In my opinion, almost any behavioral scientist with a calculator capable of storing programs will find it worthwhile to store the Peizer-Pratt formula permanently in the calculator, while others may prefer the simpler formula. In both formulas, the sign of z is the sign of t.

Many z tables give no p values for $z > 3$, though a table in Appendix 4 covers z values at intervals of .05 up to $z = 9.95$ or $p = 1.26\text{E} - 23$.

Extreme values can also be found fairly accurately from the formula

$$p = .3989 \times \frac{\exp(-z^2/2)}{z}$$

The notation $\exp(a)$ denotes e^a; where $e = 2.7183$ approximately. For instance, if $z = 3$, we have $-z^2/2 = -4.5$, $\exp(-4.5) = .0111$, $p = .3989 \times .0111/3 = .00148$. The formula becomes more accurate, in both absolute and percentage terms, as z increases. It always overestimates p, which fortunately makes the formula conservative. When $z = 3$, the correct value of p is .00135, so the formula overestimates p by just under 10%.

For greater accuracy, use the table for large z in Appendix 4 to find the formula's percentage overestimation at the desired value of z. Use the next higher level of z to avoid overcorrection. We illustrate for $z = 3.01$, which is the "worst case" for this method. Applying the formula to the next higher z of 3.05, we calculate $p = .00125$. The table shows that this p should be .00114, so the formula overestimates by approximately 9.6%. Using the formula to calculate p for $z = 3.01$, we find $p = .00143$. Dividing this p by 1.096 to correct for overestimation gives $p = .00130$. The correct p is $.00131$. This method gives answers accurate to three significant digits, meaning, as in this example, that the third digit may be off by 1.

11.1.6 Layering

So far we have discussed the use of the Bonferroni formula for finding a corrected significance level PC for the most significant of B results. If this first PC is significant, we can use *layering* to find a corrected significance level for the second-most significant result, third-most significant result, and so on. Layering relies on the fact that the second-most significant result is the most significant result left after the first (that is, most significant) result is removed from the set, the third is the most significant result left after the first two are removed, and so on. In a set of 10 results ranked by significance, the first is the most significant of all 10, the second is the most significant of the remaining 9, the third is the most significant of the remaining 8, and so on. Therefore the first should be corrected by a Bonferroni factor of 10, the second by a factor of 9, the third by a factor of 8, and so on.

More generally, the jth-most significant result among B tests is the most significant result in a set of $B + 1 - j$ results, so to layer in the Bonferroni method, we multiply the jth-most significant p among B by a Bonferroni factor of $B + 1 - j$. For instance, if the most significant three results out of 10 yield p's of $.0012$, $.0038$, and $.0092$, then the corrected significance levels are $.0012 \times 10 = .012$, $.0038 \times 9 = .034$, and $.0092 \times 8 = .074$. Only the first two are significant at the $.05$ level. We normally stop the layering process after the first nonsignificant result is found.

As described in Sec. 11.3.8, Ryan (1960) has described a different Bonferroni-based layering method for analysis-of-variance designs. Its results usually do not differ dramatically from those of ordinary layering.

11.1.7 Planned Comparisons

We have emphasized "data snooping," in which an investigator selects post hoc the most significant of several results for emphasis. If an investigator plans several tests in advance, writers disagree on the proper approach. Several writers have argued that mutually orthogonal planned comparisons need not be corrected at all. On the other hand, Ryan (1959) argues that if more than one comparison is made, the investigator should correct for the number of comparisons, even if the comparisons are orthogonal. Section 11.5.2 considers this issue. But if corrections are to be made, the Bonferroni method provides a convenient method for doing so. The most significant of B planned comparisons is corrected by a Bonferroni factor of B, the next-most significant by $B - 1$, and so on. This avoids the one extreme of not correcting planned comparisons at all no matter how many there are, and the other extreme of treating planned comparisons as if they were unplanned comparisons selected post hoc as the most significant results.

11.1.8   Flexibility of the Bonferroni Method

The Bonferroni method is extremely flexible, especially in comparison with some of the competing methods we shall review in Sec. 11.3. As mentioned earlier, the original tests may be either independent or nonindependent. They may also be part of the same experiment or different experiments by the same or different investigators; they may be one-tailed or two-tailed tests; they may be parametric or nonparametric or a mixture of both; and they may be different in form, as when different investigators use chi-square, t tests, and Pearson correlations to test hypotheses which are similar in scientific content. Or we might use the Bonferroni method when we scan a correlation matrix and select the highest correlations in the matrix. If the matrix involves k variables, then p for the highest correlation is corrected by a Bonferroni factor of $k(k - 1)/2$, the next highest by $k(k - 1)/2 - 1$, and so on.

We will see soon that the Bonferonni method by itself applies to a much wider variety of multiple-test problems than a whole array of competing methods. The Bonferroni method is not merely more flexible than the competing methods; it surpasses them in flexibility by several orders of magnitude.

11.1.9   Power of the Bonferroni Method

Intuitively, the power of the Bonferroni method seems very poor. This is because most printed tables do not show p values below .01, and many computer packages do not show them below .0001. Therefore scientists frequently fail to realize just how small their p values really are. For instance, a correlation of .4 in a sample of size 100 seems like a modest and everyday result, but its two-tailed p is actually .0000374, and it would still be significant at the .05 level after a Bonferroni correction by a factor of 1337. A related example appears in Sec. 11.4.2.

In Sec. 11.3, we will see that in comparison with a variety of competing methods for multiple pairwise comparisons involving the cells of a categorical variable, the Bonferroni method is consistently less powerful than the competing method, but the difference is small for all competing methods whose validity is unchallenged. In my opinion, the small loss in power is more than balanced by the enormous flexibility of the Bonferroni method.

11.1.10   Robustness of the Bonferroni Method

It is known that the t test is less robust at high values of t than at low values. That is, the same degree of nonnormality that makes the t test yield $p = .04$ when the true p is .05 (a relative error of 20%) may make the t test yield $p = .0005$ when the true p is .001 (a relative error of 50%). Because the Bonferroni method applies primarily to very high values of t, it might appear to be less robust than other methods. However, all methods of correcting for multiple tests suffer from the same problem. As we shall see, many methods for correcting pairwise comparisons work in terms of a "critical Studentized range" instead of a t, thus inadvertently concealing the fact that the t's involved are very high. But in fact the "critical Studentized range" is merely $\sqrt{2}$ times a critical t, so methods employing this range have the same problem. As we shall see in Chap. 14, there are some practical and extremely general methods for increasing the robustness of tests. These methods apply not just to contrasts involving categorical variables, but to regression slopes in general. If these methods are incorporated soon into statistical packages, the problem of robustness will be partly solved. But in the meantime, this problem provides no reason for preferring some multiple-test methods over others.

11.2   THE FISHER AND SCHEFFÉ METHODS

The Fisher and Scheffé methods are intermediate in flexibility between the Bonferroni method and the narrower methods of Sec. 11.3.

11.2.1   The Fisher Protected t Method

One of the oldest of all multiple-test methods was suggested by Fisher. Fisher's precise suggestion was for one-way ANOVA problems (comparisons among cell means of a single categorical regressor), but, as he recognized, the general approach can be extended to a great variety of problems. In a one-way ANOVA problem, the investigator tests the overall F and performs no individual comparisons if the F is not significant. If the F is significant, then all desired contrasts and comparisons may be made. The t's in these contrasts are "protected" by the significance of the F. In a regression problem with P numerical regressors, we would test R^2, and if that test is significant, all tests on individual b's may be performed.

The Fisher approach is clearly less conservative than Bonferroni layering, which is an obvious alternative. The weakness of the Fisher approach is illustrated by a regression problem with a great many regressors, of which only one actually affects Y. R may then be found to be significant. This opens the door to a large number of tests on individual regressors of which all but one have no effect. Thus the investigator is very likely to make at least one type 1 error. But I argue in Sec. 11.5.4 that the Fisher method still has some valid uses.

11.2.2   The Scheffé Method for Testing All Possible Contrasts

The Scheffé method is substantially narrower than the Fisher method. Like the five methods of Sec. 11.3, it applies only to ANOVA problems—comparisons among the cells of a categorical regressor. But it is more flexible than those methods because it applies to any contrast, not just to pairwise comparisons.

In the Scheffé method, we use the methods of Sec. 10.2 to compute the t for any contrast of interest. Then we compute

$$F = \frac{t^2}{k - 1}$$

and compare F with an F table, using the same df we would use to test the null hypothesis that all k cell means are equal.

Scheffé showed that if an investigator chose the coefficients c_j in the contrast completely post hoc to produce the maximum possible t [which is done for one-way ANOVA by setting $c_j = n_j(M_j -$ grand mean) for each cell], the F found in the last formula would equal the overall F for the analysis. Given the usual assumptions of normality and homoscedasticity, we know that the F test is valid. Thus, no matter how many orthogonal or intercorrelated contrasts an investigator tests, and no matter how much he or she uses the actual data to choose values of c_j maximizing t, the probability of finding a significant result will not exceed the nominal alpha. In other words, the Scheffé method is always valid, given only the basic distributional assumptions.

The price paid for this validity and flexibility is loss of power. If the real-life investigator does not act like Scheffé's hypothetical "worst-case" investigator, who carefully uses the data to find the very highest t possible, then the Scheffé formula is more conservative than necessary. Therefore the Bonferroni method rather than the Scheffé should be used for pairwise comparisons. For instance, in a one-way ANOVA with nine cells containing nine cases each so that $df_r = 72$, a t of 3.5 for a pairwise comparison has an uncorrected two-tailed p of .00080. A Bonferroni correction factor of $k(k - 1)/2 = (9 \times 8)/2 = 36$ yields $PC = 36 \times .00080 = .029$, while the Scheffé method yields $F = 3.5^2/8 = 1.53$, $p = .162$.

11.3 METHODS FOR MULTIPLE PAIRWISE COMPARISONS

11.3.1 Inflexibility of the Methods

We have seen that the Bonferroni method's forte is flexibility, while its major weakness is a slight loss in power relative to the theoretically optimum methods. This section reviews five methods: the Tukey HSD, or a, method; the Dunnett method; the Newman-Keuls method; the Tukey b method; and the Duncan "new multiple range test." Except for the Tukey b method, all five are theoretically optimum if one accepts the philosophical assumptions of their creators.

The relative inflexibility of these methods is conveyed by the fact that all five methods apply only to *pairwise comparisons* among *means* in *ANOVA designs* with *equal cell frequencies*, *equal within-cell variances*, and *normal distributions*. They further require tables created specifically for them, and readily available tables cover a *maximum of 20 cells* and only *specific signifi-*

cance levels such as .05 and .01. Each of the eight emphasized phrases specifies a limitation shared by all five methods but not the Bonferroni method. Thus there are eight different ways in which the Bonferroni method is more flexible than all five methods together.

Variants of several of these methods have been developed which are approximately correct without equal cell frequencies, equal variances, or normality. But in my opinion, the other limitations in this list are too important to justify space for these variants. Further, even the basic forms of these methods require their own tables, and I regard these methods as too inflexible to justify inclusion of these tables. Therefore our examples of these methods are brief, and rely on tables not included in this book. Our examples emphasize not so much the method itself as the ease of simulating it with the Bonferroni method.

11.3.2 The Critical Studentized Range

All these methods provide tables of the *Critical Studentized Range*, which for the problems discussed equals $\sqrt{2}$ times the critical t. This relation stems from the expression $\Sigma(c_j^2/n_j)$, which appears in the formula for SE(contrast) in Sec. 10.2.2. If all cell frequencies equal the same value n, and if we consider only pairwise comparisons so that two values of c_j are 1 and -1 and the other values of c_j are 0, then $\Sigma(c_j^2/n_j) = 2/n$, and so

$$SE(\text{contrast}) = \sqrt{MSE \times \frac{2}{n}} \quad \text{and} \quad t = \frac{\text{contrast}}{\sqrt{MSE \times 2/n}}$$

The Studentized range is defined as $\text{contrast}/\sqrt{MSE/n} = \sqrt{2} \times t$. Thus the critical Studentized ranges given in tables for these methods are $\sqrt{2}$ times the critical values of t specified by the methods.

11.3.3 Validity and the Experimentwise Error Rate

Although four of the methods are theoretically optimum, given certain philosphical assumptions, these assumptions have remained free of serious attack for only three methods. Criticisms concern the degree to which the method successfully controls the *experimentwise error rate EWR*. This was defined by Ryan (1959) as the probability of making at least one type 1 error (rejecting a true null hypothesis) in the whole set of comparisons. The EWR criterion applies when tests are performed at a fixed significance level alpha, and defines a method as valid only if its EWR does not exceed alpha.

The two Tukey methods and the Dunnett method are *fully valid* by the EWR criterion, which means that it can be proved that for any pattern of true cell means, the probability of making a single type 1 error does not exceed the nominal level of alpha. The Newman-Keuls method is *partially valid* by the

EWR criterion, meaning that it meets that criterion when all k true cell means are equal but not in some other cases. Duncan simply rejected the validity of a fixed value of EWR on philosophical grounds, so his multiple range test is *invalid* by the EWR criterion. It meets the criterion only when $k = 2$, which does not allow *multiple* comparisons. This philosophical issue is considered in Sec. 11.5.3.

11.3.4   The Tukey HSD Method

The Tukey "honestly significant difference," or HSD, method is designed to test the difference between the highest and lowest of k cell means. As we have seen, the Bonferroni method applies to this problem if we set the Bonferroni factor B equal to $k(k - 1)/2$. When $k = 10$, residual $df = 60$, and we set alpha $= .05$, critical t's for the HSD method and the Bonferroni method are respectively 3.29 and 3.43. Given the assumptions above, both methods are *fully valid* by the EWR criterion.

11.3.5   The Dunnett Method

The Dunnett method applies when the k cells include one control cell and one-tailed comparisons are made between that cell mean and the $k - 1$ other cell means, with no other comparisons being made. The Bonferroni method applies to this problem by setting the Bonferroni factor B equal to $k - 1$ for the highest cell mean. Layering uses factors of $k - 2$, $k - 3$, . . . , down to 1. For instance, if there were one control group and seven treatment groups, the one-tailed p for the highest treatment group would be corrected by a Bonferroni factor of 7, the second highest by 6, and so on. Given the assumptions above, both the Dunnett method and its Bonferroni simulation are *fully valid* by the EWR criterion.

11.3.6   The Newman-Keuls Method

The Newman-Keuls method is a layering method formed by a simple extension of the Tukey HSD method. In the Newman-Keuls method, we rank the k cell means. Then we use the HSD method to test the difference between any two cell means, while ignoring the cells that fall above both or below both. For instance, when comparing the second and eighth of 10 cells, we ignore the cells ranked 1, 9, and 10 and perform the HSD analysis as if the experiment contained only seven cells.

We first compare the highest and lowest cells, then compare the highest with the second lowest and the lowest with the second highest, and continue in this way to compare cells increasingly close together. After any nonsignificant result declares a particular range to be nonsignificant, we perform no more tests within that range.

Since the Bonferroni method simulates the HSD method and the New-man-Keuls method consists of repeated applications of the HSD method, the Bonferroni method can simulate it as well.

The Newman-Keuls method is only *partially valid* by the EWR criterion. To see why, imagine that 10 true cell means equal 10, 10, 20, 20, 30, 30, 40, 40, 50, and 50. Imagine that the standard error of each sample mean is only about 1. Thus all unequal cell means are at least 10 standard errors apart. For most of the comparisons we make, the power of the comparison is near 1.0. Therefore, we will end up testing five true null hypotheses: the test on the two means whose true values are both 10, the test on the two whose true values are both 20, and so on. Since we are performing five independent tests on true null hypotheses, the probability of finding at least one result significant at the .05 level is $1 - .95^5 = .226$. Therefore the Newman-Keuls test fails the EWR criterion for this case. I argue in Sec. 11.5.1 that the Newman-Keuls method is often logically defensible despite this failure, but for now we will say merely that its validity is more questionable than the validity of the HSD or the Dunnett method.

11.3.7 The Tukey *b* Method

To overcome the questionable validity of the Newman-Keuls method, Tukey suggested finding a critical t for each comparison by averaging the critical t suggested for that comparison by the Newman-Keuls method with the critical t of the HSD method. For instance, we have seen that when $df = 60$ and $k = 10$, the HSD method uses a critical t of 3.29 for tests at the .05 level. For comparing the second cell mean with the eighth, the Newman-Keuls method ignores cells ranked 1, 9, and 10, so it acts as if k were 7, which requires a critical t of only 3.05. The average of this critical t and the HSD critical t is 3.17, so this is the critical t for the Tukey *b* method.

The Tukey *b* method was never formally published by Tukey, but it is well known because it was included in both editions of the enormously popular text by Winer (1971). (The *b* designation is Winer's; he referred to the Tukey HSD method as the Tukey *a* method.)

11.3.8 The Ryan Layering Method

One fully valid solution to this problem is provided by layering in the Bonfer-roni method, as described in Sec. 11.1.6. However, Ryan (1960) has proposed a Bonferroni-type layering method specifically for ANOVA designs, which for those designs may surpass simple layering in power, and which Ryan showed to be *fully valid*. Let m denote the number of steps two cells differ when a set of k cells is ranked. For instance, the second-highest and seventh-highest cells differ by five steps. Letting k denote the total number of cells in the analysis, Ryan suggests a Bonferroni correction factor of $k \times m/2$. Thus the correction factor equals the HSD value of $k(k - 1)/2$ when the two extreme cells are compared, but is smaller for all other comparisons.

11.3.9   The Duncan Multiple Range Test

The Duncan multiple range test is based on Duncan's view that the experiment-wise error rate (EWR) should not be forced to equal a fixed value alpha like .05 or .01, but should be allowed to increase with the number of cells in the analysis. All other methods in this chapter are at least partially valid by the criterion of a fixed EWR; they have been challenged primarily on the ground that they are not fully valid by that criterion. The Duncan method simply rejects the fixed-EWR criterion on philosophical grounds, and is therefore *invalid* by that criterion. Duncan's discussion is in terms of a "protection level," defined as $1 - $ EWR, but we shall describe the method in terms of EWR.

The Duncan method is based on the fact that it is always possible to form $k - 1$ orthogonal or statistically independent contrasts among k cells. One such way is to form the contrasts $M_1 - M_2$, $M_3 - (M_1 + M_2)/2$, $M_4 - (M_1 + M_2 + M_3)/3$, and so on. Many authors have argued that if an investigator planned $k - 1$ orthogonal contrasts before collecting the data, then he or she could test all these contrasts with no correction for multiple tests. It is argued that these tests are independent statistically (except for the shared denominator, which seems unimportant) and are also testing different hypotheses, so that they are just as independent as tests performed by different investigators on different topics. But an investigator who performs $k - 1$ independent tests at the alpha level has a probability of $1 - (1 - \text{alpha})^{k-1}$ of making at least one type 1 error. Therefore, Duncan argues, we should choose a value of alpha like .05 or .01 and then let EWR $= 1 - (1 - \text{alpha})^{k-1}$, rather than limit EWR itself to .05 or .01. The Duncan method is designed to allow this value of EWR.

The Duncan value of EWR equals alpha only when $k = 2$ (in which case *multiple* comparisons are not possible), and increases rapidly with k. For instance, if alpha $= .05$ and $k = 10$, Duncan allows EWR $= 1 - .95^9 = .37$. As a result, the Duncan method is considered *invalid* by writers who argue that EWR should be limited to the usual alpha values of .05 or .01.

The Duncan method can be imitated by the Bonferroni method only when the Duncan EWR is low; when k is large, this occurs only when alpha is very low. To simulate the Duncan method, we would set the Bonferroni correction factor at $k/2$. This is because Duncan sets EWR at approximately $(k - 1)$ times that of the HSD method, and we have seen that the Bonferroni factor for the HSD method is $k(k - 1)/2$; dividing this value by $k - 1$ gives $k/2$.

To illustrate, suppose $df = 60$, alpha $= .001$, and $k = 10$. The Duncan critical t is then 3.888. The uncorrected p for this value of t is .000256. Multiplying this by the Bonferroni correction factor of $\frac{10}{2}$ gives $PC = .00128$, which falls slightly above the Duncan value of .001. For this problem, EWR $=$

$1 - .999^9 = .00896$. Thus, in this case the Duncan method gives a corrected significance level about $\frac{1}{9}$ the value generally considered valid.

11.4   SOME BASIC ISSUES SURROUNDING MULTIPLE TESTS

It is almost impossible to perform or even evaluate scientific research without facing the problem of multiple tests, and one cannot consider multiple tests without facing difficult philosophical questions. Methods whose validity is rarely if ever questioned, like the Scheffé, HSD, Ryan, Dunnett, and Bonferroni methods, are almost always less powerful than methods like the Newman-Keuls, Fisher, and Duncan methods, whose validity is more often challenged. Therefore it seems essential to agree on some concept of validity. But this requires us to face two questions which are even more fundamental.

First, why correct for multiple tests at all? After all, regardless of the number of tests performed, won't it still be true that, in the long run, only 5% of all true null hypotheses will mistakenly be rejected at the .05 level?

At the other extreme, we can ask why we do not make more conservative corrections. If we correct for all the tests that might have been performed in a single experiment, then why not correct for all tests in the experimenter's lifetime, or for all tests in that area of science, or indeed for all tests in the entire history of science?

Until we can answer broad questions like these, it seems unlikely that we will agree on the answers to narrower philosophical questions concerning the validity of specific methods. This section attempts to answer these two broad questions. Section 11.5 applies these answers to a variety of more specific questions concerning the use of multiple tests.

11.4.1   Why Correct for Multiple Tests at All?

The argument for correcting for multiple tests relies heavily on the concept of a composite null hypothesis (CNH). A CNH is the hypothesis that two or more simple null hypotheses are all true. Familiar types of CNH include the one-way ANOVA hypothesis that three or more true means are equal, and the regression hypothesis $_T R = 0$, which implies $_T r_{Yj} = 0$ for every j.

Composite null hypotheses play a very important role in the scientific process, because tests on them can be far more powerful than tests on the specific hypotheses nested within them. This is because of the point first made in Sec. 5.1.5—that vague conclusions are reached much more easily than specific conclusions. Rejection of a CNH is a vague conclusion; it asserts that there is at least one real effect or difference nested within the CNH, without telling us which one or ones. As mentioned in Sec. 5.1.5, such tests can be far more powerful than tests of more specific hypotheses.

But rejection of any specific null hypothesis within a CNH implies rejection of the CNH itself. In a one-way ANOVA design with 10 cells, if we conclude that any two cells differ, then we have thereby rejected the CNH that all 10 cell means are equal. Thus if we perform a thousand experiments without correcting for the fact that there are, say, 10 cells in each experiment, far more than 5% of the thousand CNH's will falsely be rejected at the .05 level. Thus it is simply not true, as hinted above, that even with no corrections only 5% of all true null hypotheses will be rejected.

This is important; CNH's define whole areas of science. For instance, the assertion "No baldness lotions work" is a CNH. But folk medicine around the world mentions hundreds of lotions for baldness. We would not want to adopt rules that made rejection of a CNH almost certain if we simply tested enough simple hypotheses within the CNH. That is why we need corrections for multiple tests—a correction transforms the test of a simple hypothesis into a valid test of the CNH within which it is nested.

11.4.2   Why Not Correct for the Whole History of Science?

A CNH can be nested within a broader CNH. In a 4 × 6 ANOVA design, the CNH that all four row means are equal is nested within the broader CNH that all 24 cell means are equal. The CNH that humans lack mental telepathy is nested within the broader CNH that all species lack it. All null hypotheses in all areas of science are nested within the broadest CNH of all—the hypothesis that every significant result in the entire history of science was found only because of the very large number of tests scientists have performed in world history—"All science is bunk."

Section 11.4.1 implied that the broader the CNH, the vaguer is the conclusion and the easier it should be to reject the CNH. This is true; the CNH "All science is bunk" is easier to reject than you might imagine. Consider that the opinion polls sponsored regularly by newspapers and television networks usually have sample sizes around 1500. Suppose such a poll split 60–40 on some issue. If we tested the null hypothesis of a 50-50 split, what Bonferroni correction factor would change the two-tailed p of a 60-40 split to .05? Might it be 100, or 1000, or 10,000? The answer amazes most people: the two-tailed p in this example is 1 in 100 trillion, which would be raised to .05 only by a Bonferroni correction factor of 5 trillion. It is a reasonable guess that no more than 5 trillion hypothesis tests have been performed in the entire history of science. Thus we see that even very modest and everyday results in moderately large samples are more than capable of rejecting the CNH that "all science is bunk."

A similar argument applies to CNH's which are narrower than this one but still very broad—such as the CNH that "all social psychology is bunk" because all significant results in that area can be explained by the sheer number of hypothesis tests. Because the number of tests ever performed in this area is far less than the number performed in all of science, we need an even less impressive result to reject it—and results at the required significance level are common in social psychology. In this way we work down a hierarchy of nested CNH's. Except in a few areas such as mental telepathy, this line of reasoning usually allows the experimenter to conclude that the broadest CNH he or she need consider is the one spanning his or her particular experiment. That is why we do not need to correct for the whole history of science, or, usually, for any tests at all outside our present experiment.

11.4.3 Plausibility and Independence of Hypotheses

The concepts of the plausibility and independence of hypotheses can clarify the process just described, and also help us later when we apply these broad ideas to evaluation of the specific methods for multiple tests.

Suppose that the investigators in a given lab work in different areas of a well-established scientific discipline. Suppose that five studies by different investigators in the lab happen to be completed in a given month. One of the results is significant at the .02 level, and the other four do not even approach significance. If the one result were corrected for the other four by the Bonferroni method, it would no longer be significant. But most scientists would assert that such correction is unreasonable because the tests are "independent."

By *independence*, they clearly do not mean statistical independence. If five investigators in different cities tested the same null hypothesis and got the results just mentioned, most scientists would consider it quite reasonable to correct the one significant result for the other four. In other words, the crucial independence is not statistical independence of the tests, but logical independence of the hypotheses themselves.

But what does that mean? Consider the hypothesis that in New York State more women than men will vote for the Democratic candidate in the next presidential election. By changing the state, we can generate 49 other forms of that hypothesis. Those 50 hypotheses are certainly distinguishable; some may be true and others false. But are they logically independent in the sense intended here?

We shall define two or more hypotheses as logically independent if firm knowledge of the truth or falsehood of one hypothesis would not change our opinion of the plausibility of the other hypotheses. In this sense the 50 hypotheses in the last paragraph are not independent. Learning that more women than men had voted Democratic in New York State would, for most people, increase the plausibility of the hypothesis that the same result will be found in other states. By the same definition, the five hypotheses tested in the same lab *are* logically independent. As we define the term, the logical independence of hypotheses is a subjective matter.

The multiplicative law of probabilities states that when two or more events are independent, the probability that all the events will occur equals the product of the individual probabilities. If each of many independent events has a probability well below 1, then there is only a small probability that all will occur. When several hypotheses are independent, the probability that all are true is small. Thus the CNH spanning the hypotheses is implausible. Because the five experiments in the same lab have tested logically independent hypotheses, the CNH spanning all five hypotheses is too implausible to need testing.

On the other hand, if several hypotheses are not independent, then the CNH spanning them may be much more plausible. In the next presidential election, if we learned that women and men in New York State had voted for the Democratic candidate with about equal frequency, we might consider it quite plausible that the same thing had happened in all 50 states.

In summary, we define hypotheses as logically independent if firm knowledge concerning one hypothesis would not change our opinion concerning the plausibility of the others. If a CNH comprises many logically independent hypotheses, then the CNH is too implausible to need testing.

Some scientists object to using the word *probability* to refer to subjective probabilities like our confidence in a hypothesis. However, changing the terminology would not change our central conclusions. Almost anyone will agree that if five null hypotheses are selected at random from five different scientific areas, they all are less likely to be true than five hypotheses from the same area.

11.4.4 New Information and Logical Clustering

Suppose that shortly after an election, we learn that, in the nation as a whole, more women than men have voted for the Democratic candidate. If we then learn that the same thing has happened in New York State, the information about New York no longer changes noticeably our confidence that it has happened in California. The hypotheses about New York and California are logically nonindependent, but after we learn about the nation as a whole they are independent. But even after we learn about the nation as a whole, new information about New York may affect our guesses about Pennsylvania, which is both nearby and demographically similar.

Similarly, when a new area of scientific study appears, there may be a period when we should consider the hypothesis that all apparent phenomena reported in the area are caused by the multiplicity of hypothesis tests in the area. We do this by correcting each reported significant result for all reported results in the area. But after the area becomes accepted as legitimate, we no longer do this.

But we may make some corrections. The area develops subareas, and tests within one subarea are corrected for tests in that subarea but not for tests in other subareas. This is reasonable, because hypotheses within one subarea are considered independent of hypotheses in other subareas. That is why we specified, in our example of the five tests in the same lab, that the lab worked in a well-developed area of science.

Thus to work down any hierarchy of hypotheses, we actually use a repetitive cycle of hypothesis testing and logical analysis. At each stage we ask which untested hypotheses are logically nonindependent, and form them into clusters. We then test the CNH spanning each cluster. Each time a CNH is rejected, we form new, smaller clusters, by another logical analysis which includes the new information that the previous CNH is false. We will call this process *logical clustering*.

A number of sources, including the SYSTAT manual (Wilkinson, 1988, p. 505), mention that F tests on the different lines of an ANOVA table are almost never corrected for multiple tests, even though a single analysis may include a great many such tests. This practice is indeed inconsistent with an emphasis on experimentwise error rates. But in terms of the present analysis, this practice is reasonable if we regard these various tests as logically independent from the beginning. If not, then one overall test on the entire analysis may make them independent by logical clustering.

11.4.5   Summary

Because broad null hypotheses are rejected more easily than narrower ones, it is natural to test them first. Thus the natural sequence in any scientific area is to identify and test the broadest plausible CNH that has not yet been tested, use the result to reassess the plausibility of narrower hypotheses nested within the CNH, and repeat this process until all hypotheses of interest have been tested. Corrections for multiple tests are essentially methods for implementing this approach.

Scientists will necessarily disagree on the plausibility of hypotheses, so they will not always agree on the exact sequence of tests implied by these recommendations. But we have attempted to clarify the philosophical issues so that these inevitable disagreements are the only major source of disagreement that need exist concerning the proper use of corrections for multiple tests. This enables us to examine more closely the validity of the various methods for multiple tests.

11.5   CONCLUSIONS ON THE VALIDITY OF SPECIFIC METHODS

This section applies the philosophical perspective of Sec. 11.4 to the various methods introduced earlier in the chapter.

11.5.1   The Newman-Keuls Method

Our first conclusion is that the Newman-Keuls method seems acceptable more often than not, despite its failure to control the experimentwise error rate EWR in all cases. Thus, the more conservative Ryan method is rarely needed. This is because we have concluded that tests of logically independent hypotheses need not be corrected for each other. If we have four cells A, B, C, and D and we have shown convincingly that the means of cells A and B both differ from those of C and D, and if we then test the AB and CD differences, the Ryan method corrects these latter two tests for each other while the Newman-Keuls method does not. But in most situations it seems that the demonstration of the AD difference would make the question about an AB difference logically independent of the question about a CD difference, so these two tests need not be corrected for each other. This makes the Newman-Keuls method usually valid.

In Sec. 11.3.6 we saw that if 10 true cell means equal 10, 10, 20, 20, 30, 30, 40, 40, 50, and 50, then the Newman-Keuls method may allow the true experimentwise error rate (EWR) to far exceed the nominal value of .05 or .01. We now say that possibilities like this are too implausible to force us to design our whole sequence of tests around them, just as we rarely repeat an experiment 12 times to make sure the effect exists in each month of the year.

11.5.2 Mutually Orthogonal Planned Comparisons

It is often argued that when several comparisons in the same experiment are planned and orthogonal, we need not correct for the number of such comparisons. The arguments of Sec. 11.4 suggest that this procedure is valid only if the experimentwide CNH is implausible, which occurs primarily when the hypotheses tested are logically independent. But if the experiment pioneers a new area of study, then the CNH must be considered plausible enough to be tested. And if the experiment does not pioneer a new area, then we must ask why previous experimenters have left this particular set of hypotheses untested, if not because they considered other leads more promising. Thus the CNH normally seems sufficiently plausible to need testing. Recall that the power of the test on the CNH will typically exceed the power of any of the individual tests. We can further increase the power of the analysis by using layering.

To see more clearly the limitations of multiple orthogonal planned comparisons, imagine an experiment with 21 cells and 20 orthogonal planned comparisons. If only one of the 20 comparisons reached significance at the .05 level, we should surely be concerned about the possibility that the result had occurred by chance. But if we are concerned about 20 comparisons, why not be concerned about 10 or 5 or 2?

11.5.3 The Duncan Multiple Range Test

Our third conclusion is that the Duncan multiple range test is rarely if ever valid, because it contains no valid test of the experimentwide CNH that all k cell means are equal. Duncan recognized this, but argued that as k increases, there is a decreasing probability that all k true means are equal. Since the CNH is implausible to begin with, he argued that we need not include a specific test for it. But this view seems oversimplified at best. Folk medicine around the world mentions hundreds of cures for baldness. But if we included all these in one large experiment, surely we should consider seriously the possibility that none work, rather than merely assuming that some do work. If the Duncan method were applied to 100 cells using alpha $= .05$, it would allow an EWR of $1 - .95^{99} = .994$. That is, if 100 true cell means were all equal, the probability is .994 that we would mistakenly conclude they were not.

In Sec. 11.3.9 we made the Duncan method appear reasonable by referring to the independence of $k - 1$ mutually orthogonal contrasts. But now we have seen that the crucial form of independence is logical rather than statistical independence, and we have also seen that no contrasts are logically independent until the overall null hypothesis has been rejected. The Duncan method provides no valid test of that hypothesis.

11.5.4 Fisher-Type Methods versus Bonferroni Layering

The choice between Fisher-type methods and a more conservative Bonferroni layering approach arises in a great many contexts, as shown by the following examples:

- In a regression analysis with P regressors, we have P separate tests on values of b_j. If the overall R^2 were significant, a Fisher-type approach would not correct these P tests for multiple tests. But a Bonferroni layering approach would correct the most significant of the P tests by a Bonferroni factor of P, the next most significant by a Bonferroni factor of $P - 1$, and so on.
- In a one-way ANOVA design, the Fisher approach allows all pairwise comparisons to be performed with no further correction if the overall F is significant, while the Bonferroni approach does not.
- Suppose we have treatment and control conditions for k different types of subject and we find that when subjects from all k groups are pooled there is a significant difference between treatment and control means. If we test the treatment-control difference in each group separately, should we correct for the fact that we are performing k tests? We would in a Bonferroni approach, and we would not in a Fisher approach. (Readers familiar with two-way ANOVA will find the wording in this paragraph odd; remember that the concepts of interaction and main effect have not yet been introduced.)
- If we reject the null hypothesis that all the correlations in a correlation matrix are 0 (a test does exist of this hypothesis), should we then correct or not correct individual correlations?

The arguments of Sec. 11.4 suggest that in cases like these, the choice between Fisher and Bonferroni approaches centers on the concept of logical independence. Specifically, does the rejection of a CNH—for instance, a significant R^2 in the first example above—create logical independence among the hypotheses nested within the CNH? If it does, then tests on the individual hypotheses need no longer be corrected for each other, and the Fisher approach is valid. If not, then corrections should be made, and Bonferroni layering is usually the best approach.

Actually, most scientists can judge the need for Bonferroni corrections more easily than they can judge the presence of logical independence. Thus our argument suggests that the choice between Fisher and Bonferroni approaches is often a subjective one—do whichever seems more reasonable for the particular case. But it also suggests some other possibilities.

11.5.5   Approaches between the Fisher and Bonferroni Methods

There are also approaches intermediate between the Fisher and Bonferroni methods. We will illustrate with a one-way ANOVA and introduce the concept of a *comparison matrix*. This is a $k \times k$ triangular matrix whose cell in row i and column j represents the comparison between the ith-highest cell mean and the jth-highest, where $i < j$. For instance, the cell in row 3 and column 5 represents the comparison between the third- and fifth-highest cell means.

Suppose we compare the highest of the k cell means with the average of the other $k - 1$ means, compare the second-highest cell mean with the average of the remaining $k - 2$ means, compare the third-highest with the average of the remaining $k - 3$, and so on, stopping with the first nonsignificant result. A Bonferroni approach suggests that the first of these tests must be corrected by a Bonferroni factor of k because we have selected the highest of k cell means, the second must be corrected by $k - 1$, the third by $k - 2$, and so on. These conclusions are of some interest in their own right; each shows that a single cell mean is higher than some of the others tested. In our new terminology, each establishes the existence of at least one real effect in a given row of the comparison matrix.

But each such conclusion also makes the comparisons in a given row of the matrix logically independent of comparisons in other rows. For instance, if $k = 10$, then the third row of the comparison matrix contains seven cells. If the overall test for this row is significant, then the seven pairwise comparisons in this row become logically independent of the other 38 comparisons in the experiment. We can then layer within the row, correcting the largest difference by a Bonferroni factor of 7, the second largest by 6, and so on. This is considerably more powerful than simple Bonferroni layering.

This method is not fully valid by the EWR criterion, but neither is the widely used Newman-Keuls method; both simply use the concept of logical independence within experiments as well as between them. If we did not use the concept at all, then we would have to correct every test by all tests in the history of science.

Section 13.7.2 applies this general approach to tests for interaction. As explained in Chap. 13, a model with P regressors may have an interaction between each pair of regressors, making $P(P - 1)/2$ possible interactions. This number can be very large. In fact, there are even more possible interactions, as explained in Sec. 13.7.2. Ideas similar to those presented here provide a way of organizing tests for interaction into a manageable sequence.

SUMMARY

The problem of *multiple comparisons* generally refers to comparisons among the cells of a categorical regressor. This is just part of the broader problem of multiple tests, which is closely related to the problem of multiple confidence bands. All these topics are included in the domain of *simultaneous statistical inference*.

11.1 The Bonferroni Method

Let *PC* denote a corrected significance level, and let *pm* denote the most significant of *B* values of *p*, so that *pm* is actually numerically the *smallest* of the *p* values. The Bonferroni method approximates *PC* by the value $B \times pm$. The multiplier *B* is called the *Bonferroni correction factor*. $B \times pm$ never underestimates *PC*, so we can define the Bonferroni formula as

$$PC \le B \times pm$$

This formula gives an accurate but slightly conservative estimate of *PC* for most sets of nonindependent tests as well as all independent sets.

If we choose, we can regard symmetric two-tailed tests as a special case of the Bonferroni formula in which $B = 2$. Other things equal, the overestimation of *PC* increases as the correlations among the tests increase from -1 toward $+1$.

When you find $B \times pm > 1$, the proper conclusion is not that $PC > 1$, which is impossible, but rather that *PC* is not small.

Some other tests, notably the Fisher "protected *t*" test, are used only after a significant overall *F* is found in an ANOVA. This restriction is *not* necessary for the Bonferroni test or for most of the methods of this chapter.

Effective use of the Bonferroni formula with *t* and *F* tests requires us to find nearly exact *p* values, even when *t* or *F* is very high. Section 5.2.5 mentioned two ways of finding exact or nearly exact *p* values for *F*, one using MYSTAT and the other using a short BASIC program. These methods can be used to find the two-tailed *p* from a *t* test.

Several other methods are quicker and only slightly less accurate. Two formulas are given, one simpler and the other more accurate, for converting any *t* to a *z* whose significance level can be found in a *z* table.

Significance levels for extreme values of *z* can be found from the table of large *z* in Appendix 4 or from the formula

$$p = .3989 \times \frac{\exp(-z^2/2)}{z}$$

For greatest accuracy the two methods can be combined.

If the most significant of B results is significant after correction, we can use *layering* to find a corrected significance level for the second-most significant result, third-most significant result, and so on. We normally stop the layering process after the first nonsignificant result is found. Ryan (1960) has described a different Bonferroni-based layering method for analysis-of-variance designs. Its results usually do not differ dramatically from those of ordinary layering.

If planned comparisons are made, the Bonferroni method can correct for the number of such comparisons. The Bonferroni method by itself applies to a much wider variety of multiple-test problems than a whole array of competing methods. In comparison with a variety of competing methods for multiple pairwise comparisons involving the cells of a categorical variable, the Bonferroni method is consistently less powerful than the competing method, but the difference is small for all competing methods whose validity is unchallenged. All methods of correcting for multiple tests are less robust than single uncorrected tests; the Bonferroni method is no better or worse than other methods in this respect.

11.2   The Fisher and Scheffé Methods

The Fisher protected t method uses a general approach that can be extended to a great variety of problems. In a one-way ANOVA problem, the investigator tests the overall F and performs no individual comparisons if the F is not significant. If the F is significant, then all desired contrasts and comparisons may be made. In a regression problem with P numerical regressors, we would test R^2, and if that test is significant, all tests on individual b's may be performed. The Fisher approach is less conservative than Bonferroni layering. There are some cases in which the Fisher approach is clearly invalid, but I argue that the method still has some valid uses.

The Scheffé method applies only to ANOVA problems—comparisons among the cells of a categorical regressor. But it applies to any contrast, not just to pairwise comparisons. The method is always valid, given only the basic distributional assumptions. The price paid for this validity and flexibility is loss of power.

11.3   Methods for Multiple Pairwise Comparisons

We have seen that the Bonferroni method's forte is flexibility, while its major weakness is a slight loss in power relative to the theoretically optimum methods. This section reviews five methods, four of which are theoretically optimum if one accepts the philosophical assumptions of their creators.

The relative inflexibility of these methods is conveyed by the fact that all five methods apply only to *pairwise comparisons* among *means* in *ANOVA designs* with *equal cell frequencies*, *equal within-cell variances*, and *normal distributions*. They further require tables created specifically for them, and readily available tables cover a *maximum of 20 cells* and only *specific significance levels* such as .05 and .01. Each of the eight emphasized phrases specifies a limitation shared by all five methods but not the Bonferroni method. Thus there are eight different ways in which the Bonferroni method is more flexible than all five methods together. All these methods provide tables of the *critical Studentized range*, which for the problems discussed equals $\sqrt{2}$ times the critical *t*.

The *experimentwise error rate (EWR)* is the probability of making at least one type 1 error (rejecting a true null hypothesis) in the whole set of comparisons. The EWR criterion applies when tests are performed at a fixed significance level alpha, and defines a method as valid only if its EWR does not exceed alpha. By the EWR criterion, the Tukey HSD, Tukey *b*, and Dunnett methods are fully valid, the Newman-Keuls method is partially valid, and the Duncan method is invalid.

The Tukey "honestly significant difference," or HSD, method is designed to test the difference between the highest and lowest of *k* cell means.

The Dunnett method applies when the *k* cells include one control cell and one-tailed comparisons are made between that cell mean and the $k - 1$ other cell means, with no other comparisons being made.

In the Newman-Keuls method, we rank the *k* cell means. Then we use the HSD method to test the difference between any two cell means, while ignoring the cells that fall above both or below both. We first compare the highest and lowest cells, then compare the highest with the second lowest and the lowest with the second highest, and continue in this way to compare cells increasingly close together. After any nonsignificant result declares a particular range to be nonsignificant, we perform no more tests within that range.

The Tukey *b* method consists of finding a critical *t* for each comparison by averaging the critical *t* suggested for that comparison by the Newman-Keuls method, with the critical *t* of the HSD method.

Ryan has proposed a Bonferroni-type layering method specifically for ANOVA designs, which for those designs may surpass simple layering in power, and which Ryan showed to be fully valid.

The Duncan multiple range test is based on Duncan's view that the experimentwise error rate EWR should not be forced to equal a fixed value alpha like .05 or .01, but should be allowed to increase with the number of cells in the analysis. The Duncan method simply rejects the fixed-EWR criterion on philosophical grounds, and is therefore invalid by that criterion.

11.4 Some Basic Issues Surrounding Multiple Tests

A CNH is the hypothesis that two or more simple null hypotheses are all true. Rejection of a CNH is a vague conclusion; it asserts that there is at least one real effect or difference nested within the CNH, without telling us which one or ones. But rejection of any specific null hypothesis within a CNH implies rejection of the CNH itself. Thus, if we perform many tests of specific hypotheses within a given CNH, the probability of falsely rejecting the CNH can far exceed the nominal alpha. This is important, since CNH's define whole areas of science.

A CNH can be nested within a broader CNH. The most powerful sequence is to test first the broadest plausible CNH and then work down through a hierarchy of nested CNH's. Except in a few areas (such as mental telepathy), this line of reasoning usually allows the experimenter to conclude that the broadest CNH he or she need consider is the one spanning his or her particular experiment. That is why we do not need to correct for the whole history of science, or usually even for any tests at all outside our present experiment.

We define hypotheses as logically independent if firm knowledge concerning one hypothesis would not change our opinion concerning the plausibility of the others. If a CNH comprises many logically independent hypotheses, then the multiplicative law of probabilities makes the CNH too implausible to need testing.

When a new area of scientific study appears, there may be a period when we should consider the hypothesis that all apparent phenomena reported in the area are caused by the multiplicity of hypothesis tests in the area. We do this by correcting each reported significant result for all reported results in the area. But after the area becomes accepted as legitimate, we no longer do this.

But we may make some corrections. The area develops subareas, and tests within one subarea are corected for tests in that subarea but not for tests in other subareas. This is reasonable, because hypotheses within one subarea are considered independent of hypotheses in other subareas.

Thus to work down through any hierarchy of hypotheses, we actually use a repetitive cycle of hypothesis testing and logical analysis. At each stage we ask which untested hypotheses are logically nonindependent, and form them into clusters. We then test the CNH spanning each cluster. Each time a CNH is rejected, we form new, smaller clusters, by another logical analysis which includes the new information that the previous CNH is false. We call this process *logical clustering*.

11.5 Conclusions on the Validity of Specific Methods

This section applies the philosophical perspective of Sec. 11.4 to the various methods introduced earlier in the chapter.

Our first conclusion is that the Newman-Keuls method seems acceptable more often than not, despite its failure to control the experimentwise error rate EWR in all cases.

Second, it is often argued that when several comparisons in the same experiment are planned and orthogonal, we need not correct for the number of such comparisons. In my opinion this argument confuses the statistical independence of tests with the logical independence of hypotheses. I believe that planned comparisons should be corrected for the number of such comparisons.

Our third conclusion is that the Duncan multiple range test is rarely if ever valid, because it contains no valid test of the experimentwide CNH that all k cell means are equal. Duncan's argument confuses logical and statistical independence, or at best uses an oversimplified view of logical independence.

Fourth, the choice between Fisher and Bonferroni approaches centers on the concept of logical independence. Specifically, does the rejection of a CNH create logical independence among the hypotheses nested within the CNH? If it does, then tests on the individual hypotheses need no longer be corrected for each other, and the Fisher approach is valid. If not, then corrections should be made, and Bonferroni layering is usually the best approach.

Our argument also suggests another method that falls between the Fisher and Bonferroni methods in conservativeness. The worker arranges hypotheses into families and tests the families as sets, using Bonferroni layering across families. When any family is significant, one tests individual hypotheses within the family using Bonferroni corrections only for the number of tests within the family, not within the entire experiment.

KEY TERMS

multiple comparisons
multiple tests
multiple confidence bands
simultaneous statistical inference
Bonferroni method
Bonferroni correction factor
independent and nonindependent
  tests
layering
planned comparisons
post hoc tests
Fisher protected t method
Scheffé test
critical Studentized range

experimentwise error rate (EWR)
Tukey HSD method
Dunnett method
Newman-Keuls method
Tukey b method
Ryan layering method
Duncan multiple range test
composite null hypothesis (CNH)
broad and narrow CNH's
plausibility
independent and nonindependent
  hypotheses
logical clustering

SYMBOLS AND ABBREVIATIONS

alpha PC pm B EWR   HSD   CNH

PROBLEMS

1. Use Bonferroni layering on the three pairwise comparisons tested in Prob. 2 of Chap. 10.

2. The three comparisons tested in Prob. 1 are just a few of the infinitely many *contrasts* we could imagine among these three cells. If we had looked at all these contrasts, what is the largest t we would have found? *Hint:* Apply the Scheffé method to the output of Prob. 1.
3. Apply Bonferroni layering to the significance levels found in the Chap. 10 problems on the effects of income, education, and occupation on satisfaction. For occupation, use the F found when occupation is treated as a single multicategorical variable. Summarize the arguments for and against performing corrections like this in actual practice.

CHAPTER 12

NONLINEAR
RELATIONSHIPS

12.1 INTRODUCTION

12.1.1 How "Linear" Regression Can Fit Curves

Figure 12.1 contains three diagrams representing some nonlinear relationships. Such relationships are best represented by curved ("curvilinear") lines or surfaces, while linear relationships are represented by straight lines or by planes. One would think that methods with names like *linear regression* and *general linear model* would simply not apply to curvilinear relationships—but in fact they do.

We saw in Chaps. 1 and 2 that equations like $\hat{Y} = bX + a$ or $\hat{Y} = b_1X_1 + b_2X_2 + a$ can be represented by straight lines and planes. But other equations are represented by curves or curved surfaces. For instance, the curves representing the equations $\hat{Y} = X^2 - 2$ and $\hat{Y} = X^3 - 3X$ are shown in Fig. 12.2.

Just as $\hat{Y} = bX + a$ is the general equation for a straight line, so is $\hat{Y} = b_1X + b_2X^2 + a$ the general equation for a parabola. And just as the problem of linear regression is to find the equation of the *line* or *plane* that best fits a given data set, our problem now is to find the equation of the *curve* or *curved surface* that best fits a data set. For instance, consider the 25 data points in Fig. 12.3. Inspection of these points suggests that a parabola might fit the data well. It can

277

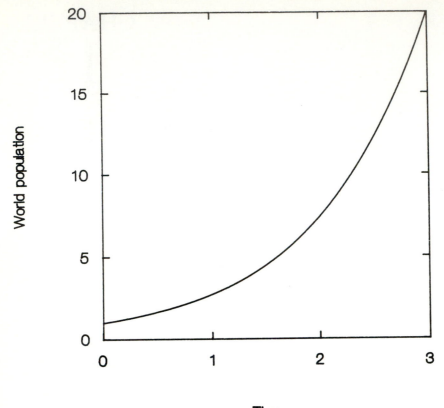

FIGURE 12.1
Three possible curvilinear relations.

be shown that of all possible parabolas, the one that best fits these 25 points has the equation $\hat{Y} = -2.168X + .1143X^2 + 15.580$. The curve representing that equation appears in the figure.

To find a curve like this, we treat the problem as a problem in *multiple regression*, even though there is only one independent variable X. We tell the computer that we have two independent variables, X and X^2. Cases for which $X = 2$ have scores of 4 on X^2, cases for which $X = 3$ have scores of 9 on X^2, and so on. We simply treat X^2 as a new regressor. The computer then uses the formulas of multiple regression to find the coefficients b_1 and b_2 for these two variables, plus the additive constant a. In this example it has found $b_1 = -2.168$, $b_2 = .1143$, and $a = 15.580$. As in linear regression, R provides a measure of the curve's fit to the data. In the present case, $R = .895$.

As with multicategorical variables (see Sec. 10.1), we use two or more regressors to represent a single variable. Thus the variable becomes *compound* as defined in Sec. 10.1.2.

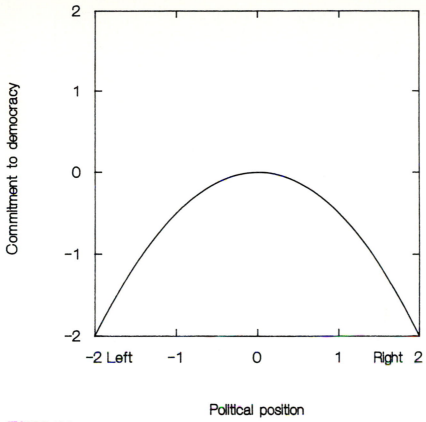

FIGURE 12.1
continued

In this example, we have supplemented the linear term X with the nonlinear term X^2, while retaining X itself. In other cases we may *replace* linear terms by nonlinear terms, or we may replace Y by a nonlinear function of Y; in these cases no variables are compound. Examples of all these possibilities appear later.

12.1.2   Two Types of Nonlinear Function

There are some very general methods for fitting curves or curved surfaces to data, as represented, for instance, in SAS PROC NLIN or the SYSTAT program NONLIN. These are sometimes called *nonlinear regression* methods. However, they are in fact not based on regression methods, so we might better call them *general curve-fitting methods*. These methods are more general and more complex than the methods discussed here. They would, for instance, enable you to find the unknowns b_1, b_2, b_3, and b_4 in a function like

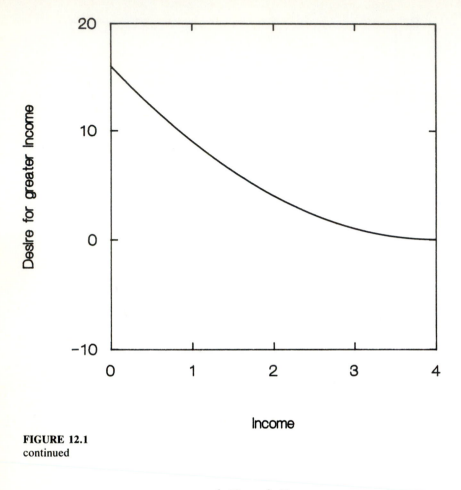

FIGURE 12.1
continued

$$\hat{Y} = \frac{b_1X_1 + b_2X_2}{b_3X_3 + b_4X_4}$$

The essential difference between the two classes of method is that in the methods of this book, $\hat{Y}$ for each case is a linear function of *known transformations* of the X's.

12.1.3 Local and Global Properties and Terms

We shall define a *global* property of a curve as a property of the entire curve, while a *local* property applies to only part of the curve. For instance, a straight line has the same slope at all points, so slope is a global property of a straight line. But a parabola has different slopes at different points, sloping downward in some sections and upward in others. Thus slope is a local property of a parabola. But a parabola is either concave (having a slope that becomes more

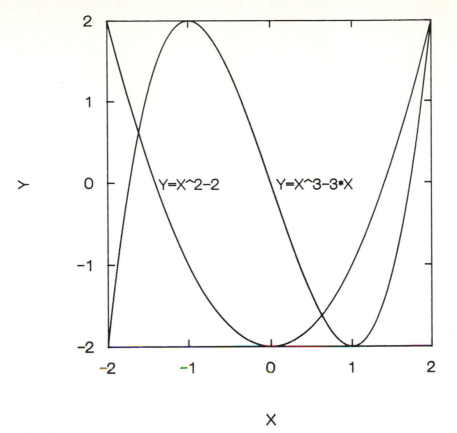

FIGURE 12.2
Some second- and third-order polynomials.

positive as X increases), as in Fig. 12.3, or convex (as when the parabola of Fig. 12.3 is turned upside down), so concavity and convexity are global properties of parabolas.

In a parabolic equation it can be shown that the parabola is concave if the coefficient of X^2 is positive, and convex if that coefficient is negative. It can be shown that this coefficient equals a measure of the parabola's curvature, defined as the difference between the $\hat{Y}$ value of any point and the average of the two $\hat{Y}$ values 1 unit to the left and right of that point. For instance, if $\hat{Y} = 2X^2$ and we arbitrarily use $X = 5$, then $\hat{Y}$ is 32, 50, and 72 when X is 4, 5, and 6, respectively. We then have $(32 + 72)/2 - 50 = 2$, which is the coefficient of X^2. We would find the same value of 2 if we chose any other X value besides 5. Thus the coefficient of X^2 measures a global property of the equation, and we shall call X^2 a *global term* in the regression.

On the other hand, it can be shown that the coefficient of X in a parabolic equation measures the slope of the parabola at the single point where $X = 0$.

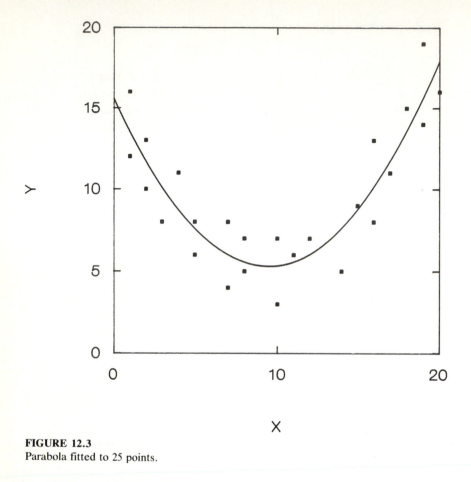

FIGURE 12.3
Parabola fitted to 25 points.

Readers who know calculus can see why this is so; if $\hat{Y} = b_1X + b_2X^2 + a$, then $d\hat{Y}/dX = b_1 + 2b_2X$, which equals b_1 when $X = 0$. In our example this slope is -2.168, and you can see by inspecting the figure that this is about the slope of the parabola where it meets the Y axis. Therefore we shall call X a *local term*, since its coefficient measures a local property of the regression.

12.1.4 When Must Curves Be Fitted?

Sometimes merely seeing a nonlinear relationship in a scatterplot tells you all you need to know about the relationship, and no curve needs to be drawn. Other times, a simple curve drawn freehand through an array of dots will suffice. But there are at least four occasions when you must use regression methods to fit curves to data:

1. When you must compute $\hat{Y}$ values.
2. When you must test the significance of the nonlinearity, against the hypothesis that the relationship is linear.
3. When you must estimate from a small sample the value of X at which Y is maximized or minimized—for instance, the amplifier volume at which speech is rated clearest, or the length of rest breaks that maximizes production. One way to do this is to fit a curve and then find the X value of the curve's maximum or minimum; see Sec. 12.3.4.
4. When you must correct for a nonlinear relation between Y and a covariate. This type of nonlinearity can distort the relations between Y and *other* variables. This is illustrated in Sec. 12.1.5.

12.1.5   Curvilinear Control of Covariates

Consider a sample of nine people with the scores shown in Table 12.1 on an independent variable X, a dependent variable Y, and a covariate C. Figure 12.4 shows X and Y plotted against C. In this artificial example there is no random error; both X and Y are perfectly predictable from C, by the equations $Y = (C - 4)^2 + 1$ and $X = (C - 6)^2 + 1$. The figure also shows the straight regression lines predicting X and Y from C.
    In Chap. 2, we saw that the $XY.C$ partial scatterplot is constructed by plotting the $Y.C$ residuals against the $X.C$ residuals—in this example, the residuals in the left-hand scatterplot against the residuals in the right-hand scatterplot. But the cases with C scores of 1, 2, 8, and 9 have positive residuals in both figures, while the other five cases all have negative residuals in both figures. Thus all the cases with positive scores on $X.C$ also have positive scores on $Y.C$, and all those with negative scores on $X.C$ also have negative scores on $Y.C$. This means that the $XY.C$ partial relationship is high. In fact, for this artificial example, $r_{XY.C} = 1$.

TABLE 12.1
A data set illustrating the need
for curvilinear control

C	X	Y
1	26	10
2	17	5
3	10	2
4	5	1
5	2	2
6	1	5
7	2	10
8	5	17
9	10	26

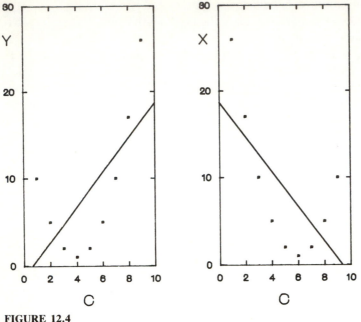

FIGURE 12.4
The need for curvilinear control.

But we know that, in this artificial example, Y can be predicted perfectly from C by the formula $Y = (C - 4)^2 + 1$. X does not affect Y at all, since it does not appear in this formula. But when we use linear rather than curvilinear regressions, we mistakenly find a high $XY.C$ partial relationship.

The general conclusion is that when a covariate has nonlinear relations with Y and with other regressors, failure to recognize the nonlinearity can distort the partial relations between Y and those other regressors. In this case, X has no partial relationship with Y at all, but failure to control C properly makes the partial relationship appear high. Thus we must be concerned about possible nonlinear relations involving covariates, not just independent variables.

12.1.6 Detecting Nonlinearity

There are two ways to detect nonlinearity. Both have flaws, so a combination of the two is best for most purposes.

The first way is to add nonlinear terms to the regression. Occasionally the user knows exactly what kind of term is needed—for instance, a logarithmic term. But usually this is unknown, and in such cases the usual practice is to add a square term. This can always be done by modifying the data set itself. For instance, in the SYSTAT or MYSTAT data editor, we could type a command like

>let incomesq = income^2

or

>let loginc = log(income)

on the command line. The symbol ^ is used to denote exponents in several computer languages and programs, including BASIC, MYSTAT, SYSTAT, and SAS, so that $X\hat{}2$ is what we ordinarily call X^2.

In MYSTAT, SYSTAT, and SAS PROC REG and PROC GLM, square terms can be added to a model without modifying the data set, by adding terms to the model statement using the * operator to represent multiplication. For instance, to add square terms to the command

>model attitude = constant + age + income

we could write

>model attitude = constant + age + income + age*age + income*income

The terms age*age and income*income will then be treated like any other term, and the *t* printed for each term tests the nonlinearity of that term.

The limitation of this method is that nonlinearity might not be well represented by a square term. This limitation is avoided by the other major way to detect nonlinearity. This is to examine a *residual scatterplot* of the relationship between *Y* and each regressor suspected of nonlinearity. The horizontal axis in this scatterplot is the regressor in question, and the vertical axis shows the residuals *e* from the regression containing all linear terms including the regressor in question.

To find residuals in MYSTAT, use the LET command on the command line of the MYSTAT editor. For instance, in Sec. 2.1 we regressed *wtloss* (weight loss) onto *exercise* and *foodin* (food intake) and found b(exercise) = 2, b(foodin) = $-.5$, a = 6. With that data set in the editor, you could go to the command line and type

>let resid = wtloss − (2*exercise − .5*foodin + 6)

This command would create a new variable, with the arbitrarily chosen name *resid*, whose scores were defined by the LET command to equal the residuals in the regression. Then outside the editor, the commands

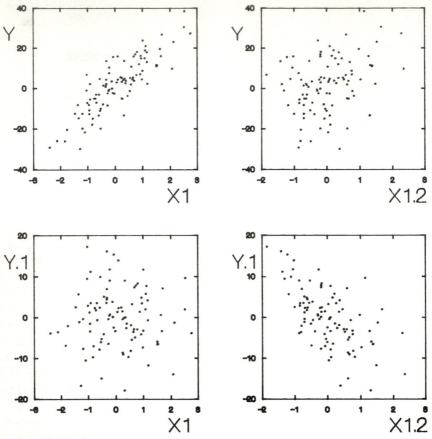

FIGURE 12.5
The eight scatterplots that one might think would reveal nonlinearity between X and Y in the presence of C.

>plot resid*exercise
>plot resid*foodin

would create the two residual scatterplots for this model. In SYSTAT you can also use the command line of the editor, but it is faster to use the LET command in the DATA module; see the SYSTAT manual.

When using residual scatterplots, you should keep four points in mind.

First, use the right kind of scatterplot. This point is not as obvious as it may seem. If *Y* is regressed onto an independent variable *X* and one or more covariates *C*, then there are no fewer than eight scatterplots that we might hope will reveal nonlinearity in the *XY* relationship. This is because there are four "forms" of *Y* we might consider: *Y* itself, plus *Y.X*, *Y.C*, and *Y.XC*, the

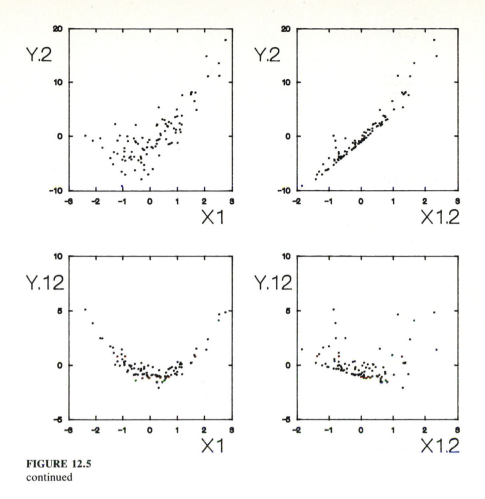

FIGURE 12.5
continued

portions of Y independent of X, C, and both. There are also two forms of X we might consider: X itself, and $X.C$, the portion of X independent of C. By combining the four forms of Y with the two forms of X, we can generate eight different scatterplots that display different aspects of the XY relationship. Only one of these is the residual scatterplot. But even when nonlinearity stands out with crystal clarity in this plot, it is often completely invisible in the other seven plots. Therefore it is important to use the right kind of plot. One of the "other seven" is the partial scatterplot described in Sec. 2.3.4. As we shall see in Sec. 14.1.7, partial scatterplots have other uses and can be obtained very easily in SAS. But they are unlikely to reveal even substantial nonlinearity.

This point is illustrated in Fig. 12.5, which shows the eight scatterplots just described. They are for a sample of 100 cases whose scores on X_1 and X_2 are shown in Fig. 12.6. In this artificial data set, Y was defined as an exact

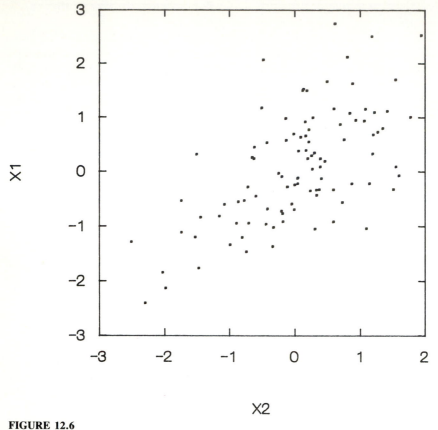

FIGURE 12.6
The XC scatterplot for the sample used in Figure 12.5.

nonlinear function of X_1 and X_2 (with $R = 1.0$) to make any nonlinearity especially visible. (The exact definition of Y used was $Y = 5X_1 + 10X_2 + X_1^2$.) But nonlinearity is clearly visible only in the residual scatterplot—the one on the lower left on page 287. Figure 12.6 shows that there is nothing very unusual about the pattern of scores on X_1 and X_2 in this sample, especially since homoscedasticity in crosswise regressions is not one of the standard assumptions of regression.

The second point is that you should display scatterplots with the highest resolution available, even if this means that graphs must be printed on paper rather than merely displayed on a computer screen. SYSTAT (but not MY-STAT) has a PAGE WIDE command designed for printing graphs on 17-inch-wide paper rather than the ordinary 8.5-inch paper. But it can also be used with 8.5-inch paper by setting the printer to print 15 or 17 characters per inch rather than the usual 10 or 12. This produces a more detailed graph than can be viewed on the screen. Often nonlinearity that would be undetected in the cruder scatterplot is visible in this more detailed plot.

Third, even substantial nonlinearity may be completely invisible in a residual scatterplot if there are also nonlinear relations *among* regressors. Artificial examples can be created in which $Y = X^2$ exactly, with $R = 1.0$, but in which the nonlinearity is completely invisible in a residual scatterplot because of the nonlinear relation between X and another regressor. To avoid this problem, supplement residual scatterplots with nonlinear terms in MODEL statements whenever nonlinearity among regressors is possible.

Fourth, the human eye and mind are not extremely efficient detectors of nonlinearity even when it is theoretically visible in a scatterplot. This point is illustrated in Fig. 12.7. Figure 12.7a shows a simple XY scatterplot uncomplicated by any covariates. Nonlinearity is only barely visible. But in this data set of 100 cases, linearity is both substantial and highly significant. Figure 12.7b

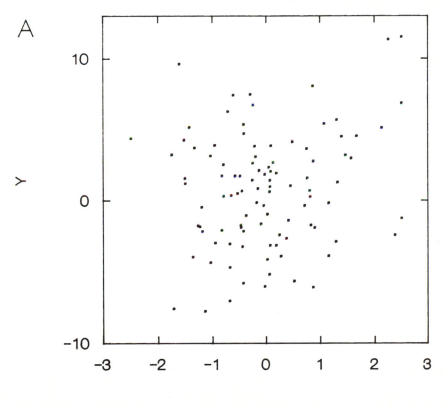

FIGURE 12.7
The difficulty of seeing nonlinearity.

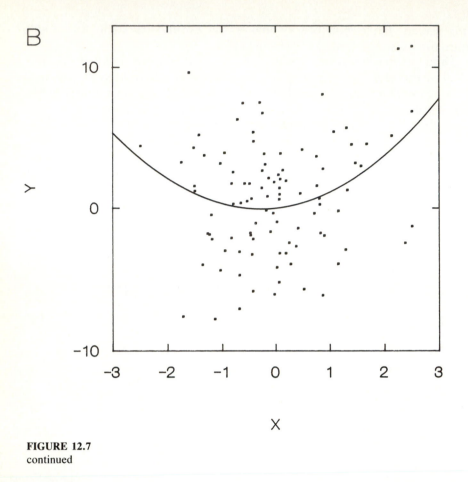

FIGURE 12.7
continued

shows the very same scatterplot with the best-fitting parabola added. The quadratic (nonlinear) term is both substantial and highly significant; $p = .0079$ (two-tailed).

12.2   LOGARITHMS

12.2.1   When Logarithms Are Useful

Logarithms (or "logs") are used primarily when the importance of the difference between two scores is judged to be proportional to their ratio rather than their absolute difference. For instance, if we are studying the effect of an animal's size on some feature of its behavior or structure, we might consider the difference between body weights of 100 and 200 kilograms to be no more important than the difference between 1 and 2 kilograms. In absolute terms, the former difference is 100 times as large, but both ratios are 2:1. If we transform weight to logarithms, then on the transformed scale the difference between 100 and 200 kilograms will equal the difference between 1 and 2 kilograms.

Or if the difference between incomes of \$50,000 and \$100,000 has the same average effect on attitudes toward wealth as the difference between \$10,000 and \$20,000, then income will have a nonlinear relation to attitude, but a logarithmic transformation can make the relation linear.

Use of logarithms in constructing graphs makes differences between small numbers visible even when much larger numbers appear on the same variable. For instance, the size difference between a mouse and a squirrel would still be visible in a graph even if whales and dinosaurs were included in the same graph. We saw such a graph in Sec. 3.3.6.

Only positive numbers have logarithms; it would be meaningless to talk about the proportional difference between incomes of \$10,000 and $-\$10,000$.

We need not discuss ways of finding logarithms. All you really need to know is what button to press on your calculator, or what command to use in a computer program.

Two types of logarithm are widely used: common logarithms and natural logarithms. The standard symbols for common and natural logarithms are log and ln, respectively. Other notation is widely used in computer languages; for instance, SAS denotes common and natural logarithms by LOG10 and LOG, respectively. SYSTAT and MYSTAT use LOG to denote natural logarithms; common logarithms can be found by dividing the natural logarithms by ln(10):

>let comlogx = log(x)/log(10)

where "comlogx" is an arbitrarily chosen variable name.

12.2.2 Common Logarithms

The common logarithm of any positive number X is the power of 10 which equals X. For instance, the common logarithms of 100 and 1000 are, respectively, 2 and 3. In algebraic form, the equation $X = 10^A$ implies that $A = \log(X)$.

12.2.3 Basic Rules Involving Logarithms

The logarithm of the product of two numbers equals the sum of their logarithms. For instance, $\log(100) = 2$, $\log(1000) = 3$, and $\log(100,000) = 5 = \log(100) + \log(1000)$.

A parallel rule applies to division: the logarithm of the ratio of two numbers equals the difference between their logarithms. Thus, $\log(10,000) = 4$, $\log(1000) = 3$, and $\log(10,000/1000) = \log(10,000) - \log(1000) = 4 - 3 = 1 = \log(10)$.

If $A^B = C$, then $\log(C) = B \times \log(A)$. Suppose $A = 1000$ and $B = 2$, so that $A^B = 1,000,000$. Then $\log(A) = 3$ and $\log(C) = 6$, so that $\log(C) = 2 \times \log(A) = B \times \log(A)$.

The logarithm of the kth root of A equals $(\log A)/k$. The kth root of A is the number which, when raised to the kth power, equals A. The cube root of $1,000,000$ is 100, since $100^3 = 1,000,000$. We then have $\log(1,000,000)/3 = 6/3 = 2 = \log(100)$. This rule is actually the special case of the previous one in which B is the reciprocal of a positive integer; in the present example, $B = \frac{1}{3}$.

Consider now a fractional power of 10, like $10^{7/4}$, which can be written as $(10^7)^{1/4}$. We can find this quantity by taking the seventh power of 10 (which equals $10,000,000$), and taking the fourth root of that (which equals 56.234). Thus $10^{7/4} = 56.234$, which implies that $\log(56.234) = \frac{7}{4} = 1.75$. We see that numbers like 56.234, which are not integral powers of 10, also have logarithms. Any positive number has a logarithm.

12.2.4   Natural Logarithms

Natural logarithms are denoted by *ln*. A common logarithm is a power of 10; a natural logarithm is a power of e, where $e \approx 2.71828$. Like pi, e cannot be written exactly. Natural logarithms have all the properties of common logarithms shown in the previous section. The major advantage of a natural logarithm is that when two numbers A and B are nearly equal, the difference between their natural logarithms approximately equals the proportional difference between them. For instance, 63 is 5% larger than 60, and their natural logarithms are 4.1431 and 4.0943. These two values differ by .0488, which approximately equals .05, or 5%. Thus, if the weights of two animals differed by .05 on a natural logarithmic scale, you would know without calculation that one was about 5% heavier than the other. As two numbers approach equality, this relationship approaches exactness. For instance, the natural logarithms of 1000 and 1001 differ by .000999500, which to four significant digits is .001000, or 1/1000.

Natural logarithms are proportional to common logarithms; for any number X, the natural logarithm of X equals approximately 2.302589 times the common logarithm of X. If the common logarithms are linearly related to another variable Y, then the natural logarithms will be also. Thus, if we say that a logarithmic transformation makes a relationship linear, we need not specify which type of logarithm.

12.2.5   Using Logarithms in Regression Analysis

Use of logarithms can make nonlinear relationships linear. The firing rates of optic neurons relate linearly to the logarithm of light intensity, when intensity is measured in lumens. When the population of the United States is plotted on the Y axis against year (1790 to the present) on the X axis, the curve rises exponentially, but when we transform the population scale to a logarithmic scale, the relation is approximately linear. Another example of this point appeared in Sec. 3.3.6; when brain weights and body weights of different animal species are both expressed as logarithms, the relationship between them is remarkably linear.

We might transform either an independent variable or a dependent variable or both. In the example just given on optic neurons, the independent variable of light intensity was transformed. In the population example, the dependent variable was transformed. In the brain-weight example, both were transformed. Inspection of a scatterplot can indicate whether a logarithmic transformation of only one variable will produce a better fit to the data. A logarithmic transformation of X is suggested when it appears that a curve like Fig. 12.8a might fit the data in a scatterplot; it is convex and has no negative values of X. A logarithmic transformation of Y is suggested when it appears that a curve like Fig. 12.8b might fit; it is concave and has no negative values of Y.

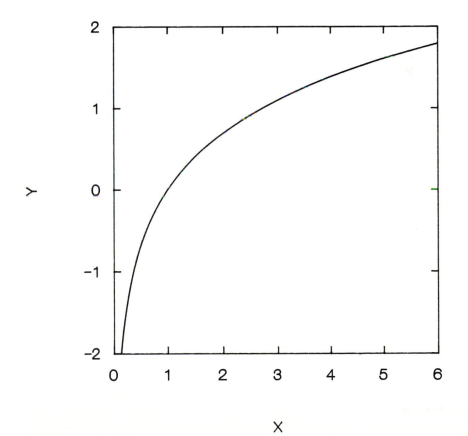

FIGURE 12.8
Logarithmic and exponential curves.

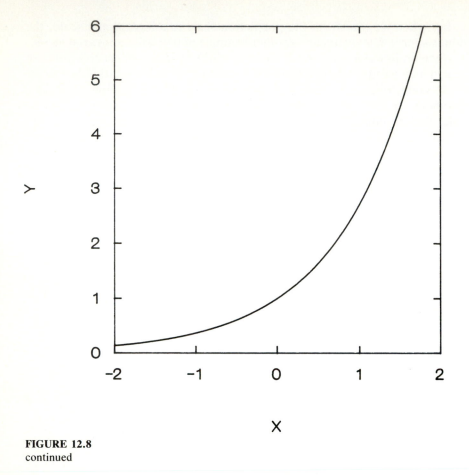

FIGURE 12.8
continued

12.3   POLYNOMIAL REGRESSION

12.3.1   Basics

Polynomial regression fits curves to data by creating new regressors which are successive powers of another variable: age, age^2, age^3, age^4, and so on. Figure 12.2 illustrates the kinds of curves that can be produced, and Fig. 12.3 shows how a parabola can be fitted to a set of data points. The number of successive powers of X we use is called the *order* of the set of terms.

Some authors criticize polynomial regression as being excessively mechanical, and suggest instead trying to choose a curve whose functional shape makes scientific sense. This is certainly good practice when possible. But polynomial regression is especially useful for controlling covariates with non-linear relations to Y, since little attention is then paid to the coefficients of the polynomial terms.

The most common form of polynomial regression is also the simplest: the second-order set includes just the two regressors X and X^2. This fits a parabola; more complex curves are rarely needed. The standard approach is to add successively higher powers until the highest-power term is nonsignificant. But if curvilinearity is expected, it is perhaps more common to add powers until two terms in a row are nonsignificant and then discard those two. Either way, in MYSTAT or SYSTAT this requires a series of regressions, with one additional term in each. In SAS, the tests can all be done in one regression, using type I SS; see Sec. 7.3.3.

In polynomial regression, we would rarely eliminate any term while retaining a higher-power term. To see why, consider the parabola $Y = bX^2$. It must have its maximum or minimum exactly at the origin, while the more general parabolic formula $Y = b_1X + b_2X^2 + a$ can represent a parabola located anywhere. Deleting lower-order terms from a polynomial regression eliminates an ability we ordinarily wish to retain—the ability of the curve to be located anywhere.

As mentioned in Sec. 12.1.6, polynomial terms can be added right in the MODEL statement of MYSTAT, SYSTAT, or SAS. For instance, a third-order polynomial for age might appear in MYSTAT or SYSTAT as

>model attitude = constant + age + age∗age + age∗age∗age

A linear variable, together with its higher-order terms, forms a *compound* variable as defined in Sec. 10.1.2—a variable thought of as a single variable even though it is represented in the model by several different regressors. But this type of compound variable appears as several terms in the MODEL statement, instead of one term as with multicategorical variables in Chap. 10. If desired, we can test the effect of the variable as a whole by testing the contribution of the whole set of terms—though a more common strategy is to test successive terms as described above.

Unlike regression using logarithms, polynomial regression is always mechanically possible to apply, since it works with negative X scores as well as positive. This makes it the favorite model for performing quick initial checks for curvilinearity, as mentioned in Sec. 12.1.6.

Perhaps the major disadvantage of polynomial regression is that for sufficiently high and low values of X, the curve is always very steep. Thus polynomial regression is not very suitable for fitting curves with long nearly horizontal sections, like those in Fig. 12.9. Spline regression, described in Sec. 12.4, is more suitable for such curves.

Adding a higher-power polynomial term, of course, leaves unchanged both the simple correlations of lower-order terms with other variables and the hierarchical contributions of those terms, since a variable's hierarchical contribution is defined as its contribution before the addition of later terms. But the higher-order term will change the meaning of the regression slopes of all lower-

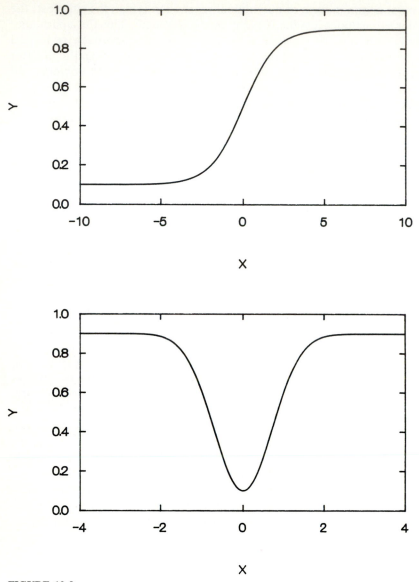

FIGURE 12.9
Some curves not suitable for polynomial regression.

order terms. In fact, only the highest-order term is a global term; all others are local. We saw an example of this in Sec. 12.1.3, in which addition of a quadratic (square) term changed the coefficient of X to the parabola's slope *at the Y intercept*. This is also one of the points illustrated in Sec. 12.3.2.

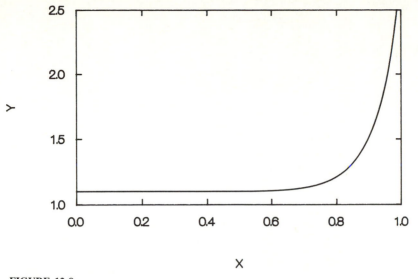

FIGURE 12.9
continued

12.3.2   An Example

Let *Y* be agreement with the statement, "The United States should provide military support to friendly nondemocratic regimes which are threatened by Soviet-supported guerrilla movements." The generation that came of age during the unpopular Vietnam war is generally more opposed to such views than either previous or later generations, so we might expect a curvilinear relation between age and *Y*. But since age correlates with income, failure to recognize this curvilinearity could distort the measured relation between *Y* and income. This situation is illustrated by the artificial data set in Table 12.2.

TABLE 12.2
Illustrating the need for curvilinear control

Age	Income	Attitude
23	12	46
27	19	41
31	22	35
35	30	37
40	28	33
43	35	41
47	37	47
52	40	59
60	45	90

TABLE 12.3
MYSTAT output with and without curvilinear control of age

DEP VAR: ATTITUDE   N: 9   MULTIPLE R: .814   SQUARED MULTIPLE R: .663
ADJUSTED SQUARED MULTIPLE R: .551   STANDARD ERROR OF ESTIMATE: 11.849

VARIABLE	COEFFICIENT	STD ERROR	STD COEF	TOLERANCE	T	P(2 TAIL)
CONSTANT	-6.938	16.386	0.000	.	-0.423	0.687
INCOME	-2.724	1.752	-1.644	0.0502008	-1.555	0.171
AGE	3.412	1.549	2.329	0.0502008	2.203	0.070

ANALYSIS OF VARIANCE

SOURCE	SUM-OF-SQUARES	DF	MEAN-SQUARE	F-RATIO	P
REGRESSION	1659.562	2	829.781	5.910	0.038
RESIDUAL	842.438	6	140.406		

DEP VAR: ATTITUDE   N: 9   MULTIPLE R: 1.000   SQUARED MULTIPLE R: 1.000
ADJUSTED SQUARED MULTIPLE R: 1.000   STANDARD ERROR OF ESTIMATE: 0.253

VARIABLE	COEFFICIENT	STD ERROR	STD COEF	TOLERANCE	T	P(2 TAIL)
CONSTANT	164.557	1.536	0.000	.	107.118	0.000
INCOME	0.950	0.049	0.573	0.0289558	19.285	0.000
AGE	-7.946	0.104	-5.423	0.0050386	-76.074	0.000
AGE*AGE	0.100	0.001	5.643	0.0105715	114.650	0.000

ANALYSIS OF VARIANCE

SOURCE	SUM-OF-SQUARES	DF	MEAN-SQUARE	F-RATIO	P
REGRESSION	2501.680	3	833.893	13016.205	0.000
RESIDUAL	0.320	5	0.064		

Table 12.3 shows the MYSTAT output for two different models: the linear model regressing attitude on age and income, and the same model with the term age × age, or age², added. Adding age² changes the coefficient of age itself from almost significantly positive to very significantly negative, and also changes the coefficient of income from nonsignificantly negative to significantly positive. Thus, failure to control for curvilinear effects of age could lead to completely erroneous conclusions about the effect of *income* on attitudes.

In the second model, the coefficient of −7.946 for age has only a local meaning; it means that when a parabola is fitted for age, that parabola's slope is highly negative when age = 0. Since it is meaningless even to talk about a newborn baby's attitudes on foreign policy, this coefficient has no scientific meaning. And in any example it would have at best a local meaning.

12.3.3 Centering Variables in Polynomial Regression

A variable is *centered* by subtracting its mean from all scores, creating an adjusted variable with a mean of zero. A variable may be centered relative to its sample mean, or relative to its population mean if that happens to be known. There are two reasons for sometimes centering variables in polynomial regression.

First, if the mean M_X is high relative to S_X, then the successive terms X, X^2, and so on, might correlate with each other so highly as to produce rounding error. For instance, in a five-person sample with X values of 1000, 1001, 1002, 1003, and 1004, the correlation between X and X^2 is .99999983, which is high enough to induce rounding error in some computer programs. This can be corrected by centering X, or at least subtracting some value near M_X, before computing the powers of X. If we subtract 1000 from all X scores in this example, they become 0, 1, 2, 3, and 4. These scores have a correlation of "only" .9589 with their squares, which is low enough to avoid serious rounding error. By subtracting 1002 (the exact value of M_X) instead of 1000, the scores become −2, −1, 0, 1, and 2, which have exactly 0 correlation with their squares.

The second reason for sometimes centering a variable X before computing powers of X is that the coefficient of X is then the slope or effect of X not just at some randomly chosen spot, but at the mean of X. A proof of this point for second-order polynomials was given in Sec. 12.1.3 for readers familiar with calculus. The proof is readily extended to polynomials of any order.

Centering variables, or changing scores on a variable by any constant at all, has no effect on regression slopes or correlations when only linear terms are used. But the situation with polynomial regression is more complex. Measures of simple relationship, such as correlations or simple regression slopes, are affected by such adjustments for all but the linear, or *first*-power, term. For instance, if five scores on X are 1, 2, 3, 4, and 5, then the five scores on X^2 are 1, 4, 9, 16, and 25. But if we subtract 5 points from X before computing X^2, the

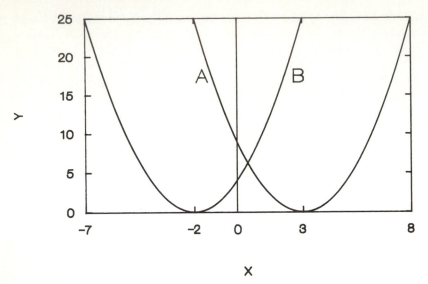

FIGURE 12.10
Effect on b_j of changing M_j when X_j^2 is in the regression.

new X scores are -4, -3, -2, -1, and 0, and the new scores on X^2 are 16, 9, 4, 1, 0. Thus the cases having the highest scores on X^2 now have the lowest. This will of course change the correlation of X^2 with other variables.

Measures of unique contribution, such as b_j, pr_j, sr_j, or the values of t or F that test their significance, are affected by centering for all but the *highest-power* term. This is illustrated in Fig. 12.10. Consider curve A; its slope is negative at $X = 0$. If we subtract 5 points from all scores on X, then scores of 3 become -2. But they still fall at the parabola's minimum, so the minimum shifts to $X = -2$ and the curve shifts to the position of curve B. This makes the parabola's slope positive at $X = 0$. But the parabola's slope at $X = 0$ is the coefficient of X, so changing that slope from negative to positive changes this coefficient.

Measures of hierarchical contribution, such as HSS_j, hpr_j, and hsr_j, are not affected by centering. We usually want statistics that are not affected by centering or similar adjustments, so measures of hierarchical contribution are normally the most useful measures in polynomial regression.

12.3.4 Finding a Parabola's Maximum or Minimum

Let $b(X_j)$ and $b(X_j^2)$ denote respectively the coefficients of the terms X_j and X_j^2 in a second-order polynomial regression. Curvilinear terms for other variables may also be included in the regression, but they may not interact with X_j.

(Interaction is introduced in Chap. 13.) Then the value of X_j that maximizes or minimizes Y relative to X_j is

$$X_j = \frac{-.5 \times b(X_j)}{b(X_j^2)}$$

For instance, in Sec. 12.1.1 we had the equation

$$Y = -2.168X + .1143X^2 + 15.580$$

in which $b(X) = -2.168$ and $b(X^2) = .1143$, so that the value of X minimizing Y is $.5 \times 2.168/.1143 = 9.40$. The parabola appears in Fig. 12.3 in Sec. 12.1.1; you can verify this value there.

12.4 SPLINE REGRESSION

12.4.1 Basics

In its simplest form, spline regression is a method for fitting to data a jagged line like that in Fig. 12.11. By increasing the number of line segments, even extremely complex shapes can be fitted. Or by replacing each line segment by a section of a parabola or higher-order polynomial, we can fit smooth curves to the data. In either case, the fitted variable becomes a compound variable, since it is represented by two or more regressors. More complete discussions are given by Ahlberg, Nilson, and Walsh (1967) and by Greville (1969). This section considers only straight line segments, while Sec. 12.4.2 explains the use of polynomials.

The user chooses the X values but not the Y values of the "joints" in the jagged spline curve. In Fig. 12.11, these are marked J1, J2, J3, and J4. Each joint uses up one residual degree of freedom. If there are many residual df, joints may simply be placed equidistant across the range of the variable in question. Or you can use a scatterplot to identify the best locations for joints.

Choosing joints by examining the sample data tends to increase the variance explained by the variable in question. When this variable is a covariate, it introduces a conservative bias into tests on the independent variables; but if the variable is an independent variable, the bias is toward exaggerating the importance of the variable.

Spline regression computes the slope of the first line segment, plus the change in slope at each joint. In the figure, the slopes of the five line segments are $-.75$, 2, .5, $-.5$, and 1.5, so the changes in slope at J1, J2, J3, and J4 are $+2.75$, -1.5, -1.0, and $+2.0$. In spline regression we create artificial variables whose b_j values equal these changes in slope. The slopes determine the Y values of the joints; the user has already chosen the X values.

To see how this is achieved, consider Fig. 12.12. Line segment A fits the first four points perfectly, but overestimates the next two points by 3 and 6 units, respectively. Suppose we create the variable J1 by a command like

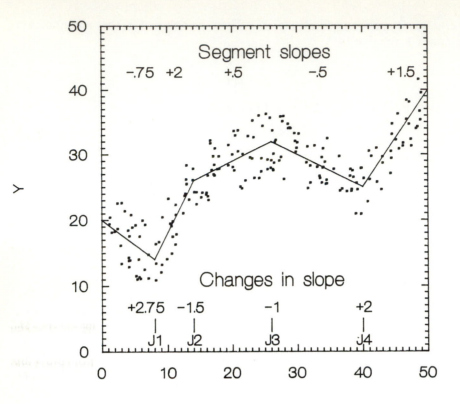

FIGURE 12.11
Spline curve with four joints.

>if x > 4 then j1 = x − 4 else j1 = 0

This is actually a generic format; in MYSTAT or SYSTAT the precise commands would be

>let j1 = 0
>if x > 4 then let j1 = x − 4

while in SAS they would be

>if x > 4 then j1 = x − 4;
>else j1 = 0;

We shall continue to use the more compact generic format, leaving you to make the translation.

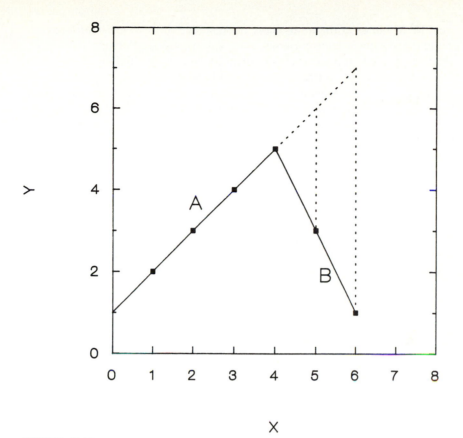

FIGURE 12.12
Why spline regression works.

These commands give the first four points $J1$ values of 0, while the last two have $J1$ values of 1 and 2, respectively. When we write the errors of line segment A next to values of $J1$, we have

Error	$J1$
0	0
0	0
0	0
−3	1
−6	2

All errors equal exactly -3 times $J1$. The equation of segment A is $Y = 1 + 1 \times X$, so a perfect fit is obtained by the equation $Y = 1 + 1 \times X - 3 \times J1$. This is the equation of the jagged line AB. Segments A and B have slopes of $+1$ and -2, respectively; the coefficient of -3 for $J1$ is the change in slope at the joint.

This example is atypical in that we do not normally achieve a perfect fit.

But once the X values of the joints have been selected, the regression program will fit the jagged line which minimizes the sum of squared errors.

Both $J1$ and X in this example are local terms: the coefficient of $J1$ equals the change in slope at a particular point, and the coefficient of X equals the slope of only part of the jagged line. To remind yourself that X is now a local term, it helps to replace X in the regression by another artificial regressor $J0$, with a command like $J0 = X$. The regression equation for this example would then be written $Y = 1 + 1 \times J0 - 3 \times J1$.

When we wish to have more than one joint, we make up a new artificial regressor for each joint, with a command of the form

>if x > xj then j = x − xj else j = 0

As before, we also use the command $J0 = X$. For instance, in our original example, joints are at X values of 8, 14, 26, and 40. Once we have selected these values by eyeball, we might use commands like

>j0 = x
>if x > 8 then j1 = x − 8 else j1 = 0
>if x > 14 then j2 = x − 14 else j2 = 0
>if x > 26 then j3 = x − 26 else j3 = 0
>if x > 40 then j4 = x − 40 else j4 = 0

The regression slope b_j computed for $J0$ then equals the slope of the *first* line segment, and the values of b_j computed for $J1$, $J2$, $J3$, and $J4$ equal the changes in slope at joints $J1$, $J2$, $J3$, and $J4$. In our five-segment example, the five segment slopes were $-.75$, 2, .5, $-.5$, and 1.5, so the four changes in slope were $+2.75$, -1.5, -1.0, and $+2.0$. Therefore the jagged line in our example is represented by the equation

$$Y = 20 - .75 \times J0 + 2.75 \times J1 - 1.5 \times J2 - 1.0 \times J3 + 2.0 \times J4$$

As in other forms of regression, computer programs routinely test the significance of each b_j. When b_j represents a change in slope, then we are testing the null hypothesis of no change in slope. Thus ordinary regression programs give us a test of the significance of the change in slope at each joint. In the current example, all four joints are highly significant. Joints with nonsignificant changes may be deleted to gain power if necessary. But spline regression is normally used to improve the fit of covariates, so deleting joints is like deleting covariates. Such deletions may sacrifice validity of the major tests of interest for small gains in power. Our bias should be against unnecessary deletions. Thus we would normally not use corrections for multiple tests in testing the significance of each joint.

By placing all the artificial regressors in the same EFFECT command in SYSTAT, or in the same TEST command in SAS, we can test the effect of the entire set. In other programs, including MYSTAT, we can perform the same test by running the regression with and without the set. All these approaches were described in Sec. 5.3.1.

12.4.2 Polynomial Spline Regression

Polynomial spline regression combines the advantages of polynomial regression and spline regression. As in spline regression, we effectively divide the regressor X_j into segments. But now we fit a polynomial instead of a straight line within each segment. A quadratic spline regression fits a parabola within each segment, a cubic spline fits a cubic equation, and so on. If we were to fit linear splines with joints at 10 and 18, we might use the equations

>j0 = x
>if x > 10 then j1 = x else j1 = 0
>if x > 18 then j2 = x else j2 = 0

To fit a quadratic spline regression with these joints, we could write

>j01 = x
>j02 = x^2
>if x > 10 then j11 = x − 10 else j11 = 0
>if x > 10 then j12 = (x − 10)^2 else j12 = 0
>if x > 18 then j21 = x − 18 else j21 = 0
>if x > 18 then j22 = (x − 18)^2 else j22 = 0

We have here let the first "subscript" of J denote the segment in question; 0 refers to X values up to 10, 1 refers to X values between 10 and 18, and 2 refers to X values above 18. The second "subscript" refers to the power of the polynomial; 1 refers to linear terms and 2 to quadratic terms. For instance, $J12$ is the square term in the segment between X values of 10 and 18. Even if there is a data point exactly at the joint, we get exactly the same curve regardless of whether we write $>$ or $>=$, which means "greater than or equal to," in the spline equations.

Figure 12.13 shows the curve defined by these equations, as applied to the 28 data points shown in the figure. The curve segment from 1 to 10 is one parabola, the segment from 10 to 18 is a second parabola, and the segment above 18 is a third. We could fit even more complex curves by increasing the number of segments, or the order of the polynomials, or both.

12.4.3 Spline Transformations of Y

This chapter has emphasized transformations of regressors. But unpublished work of mine suggests that if nonlinearity is caused by the scale on which Y is measured, then spline functions may be useful for transforming Y to increase

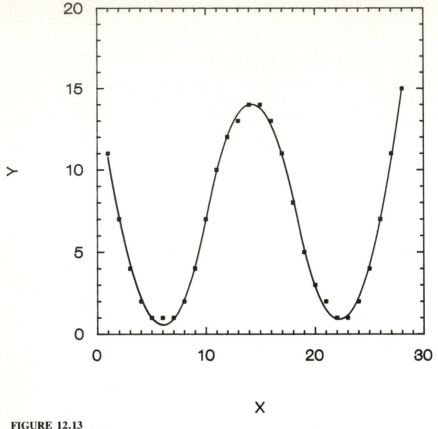

FIGURE 12.13
Polynomial spline regression.

linearity of regression. In brief, two new variables $Y1$ and $Y2$ are created with spline joints at the 25th and 75th percentiles of Y. Then the regression prediction of Y is itself predicted from Y, $Y1$, and $Y2$. The variable containing these latter predictions is the transformed Y. Section 17.6 describes the procedure in detail.

SUMMARY

12.1 Introduction

The problem of this chapter is to find the equation of the *curve or curved surface* that best fits a data set. We may either supplement or replace linear terms by nonlinear terms. We may also replace Y by a nonlinear function of Y.

There are two ways to detect nonlinearity. Both have flaws, so a combination of the two is best for most purposes. The first way is to add nonlinear terms to the regression. The most common practice is to add a square term. The limitation of this method is that nonlinearity might not be well represented by a square term. So the other way to detect nonlinearity is to examine a *residual scatterplot* of the relationship between Y and each regressor suspected of nonlinearity.

When using residual scatterplots, keep four points in mind. First, use the right kind of scatterplot. Second, display scatterplots with the highest resolution available. Third, even substantial nonlinearity may be completely invisible in a residual scatterplot if there are also nonlinear relations *among* regressors. Fourth, the human eye and mind are not extremely efficient detectors of nonlinearity even when it is theoretically visible in a scatterplot.

12.2   Logarithms

Logarithms ("logs") are used primarily when the importance of the difference between two scores is judged to be proportional to their ratio rather than their absolute difference. Use of logarithms in constructing graphs makes differences between small numbers visible even when much larger numbers appear on the same variable. Only positive numbers have logarithms. The standard symbols for common and natural logarithms are log and ln, respectively. The common logarithm of any positive number X is the power of 10, which equals X.

The logarithm of the product of two numbers equals the sum of their logarithms, and the logarithm of the ratio of two numbers equals the difference between their logarithms. If $A^B = C$, then $\log C = B \times \log A$. The logarithm of the kth root of A equals $(\log A)/k$.

A natural logarithm is a power of e, where $e \approx 2.71828$. When two numbers A and B are nearly equal, the difference between their natural logarithms approximately equals the proportional difference between them. Natural logarithms are proportional to common logarithms; for any number X, the natural logarithm of X equals approximately 2.302589 times the common logarithm of X. If the common logarithms are linearity related to another variable Y, then the natural logarithms will be also.

Use of logarithms can turn nonlinear relationships into linear ones. We might transform either an independent variable or a dependent variable or both.

12.3   Polynomial Regression

Polynomial regression fits curves to data by creating new regressors which are successive powers of another variable. The standard approach is to add successively higher powers until the last term is nonsignificant. But if curvilinearity is expected, it is perhaps more common to add powers until two terms in a row are nonsignificant, and then to discard those two.

In polynomial regression we would rarely eliminate any term while retaining a higher-power term. Deleting lower-order terms from a polynomial regression eliminates an ability we ordinarily wish to retain—the ability of the curve to be located anywhere.

A linear variable, together with its higher-order terms, forms a *compound variable*—a variable thought of as a single variable even though it is represented in the model by several different regressors. If desired, we can test the effect of the variable as a whole by testing the contribution of the whole set of terms—though a more common strategy is to test successive terms as described above.

Unlike regression using logarithms, polynomial regression is always mechanically possible to apply, since it works with negative X scores as well as positive. This makes it the favorite method for performing quick initial checks for curvilinearity.

Perhaps the major disadvantage of polynomial regression is that for sufficiently high and low values of X, the curve is always very steep. Therefore polynomial regression is not very suitable for fitting curves with long nearly horizontal sections. Spline regression is more suitable for such curves.

Adding a higher-power polynomial term leaves unchanged both the simple correlations of lower-order terms with other variables and the hierarchical contributions of those terms, since a variable's hierarchical contribution is defined as its contribution before the addition of later terms. But the higher-order term will change the meaning of the regression slopes of all lower-order terms. In fact, only the highest-order term is a global term; all others are local.

A variable is *centered* by subtracting its mean from all scores, creating an adjusted variable with a mean of zero. A variable may be centered relative to its sample mean, or relative to its population mean if that happens to be known. There are two reasons for sometimes centering variables in polynomial regression. First, if the mean M_X is high relative to S_X, then the successive terms X, X^2, and so on, might correlate with each other so highly as to produce rounding error. Second, the coefficient of X is then the slope or effect of X at the mean of X.

In polynomial regression, measures of simple relationship, such as correlations or simple regression slopes, are affected by centering or by similar adjustments for all but the linear or *first*-power term. Measures of unique contribution, such as b_j, pr_j, sr_j, or the values of t or F that test their significance, are affected by centering for all but the *highest*-power term. Measures of hierarchical contribution, such as HSS_j, hpr_j, and hsr_j, are not affected by centering. We usually want statistics that are not affected by centering or similar adjustments, so measures of hierarchical contribution are normally the most useful measures in polynomial regression.

The formula that can sometimes be used to maximize or minimize the Y value of a parabola is

$$X_j = -.5 \frac{b(X_j)}{b(X_j^2)}$$

12.4   Spline Regression

In its simplest form, spline regression is a method for fitting a jagged line to data. By replacing each line segment by a section of a parabola or higher-order polynomial, we can fit smooth curves to the data.

The locations of the "joints" in a spline curve must be chosen by the user. When segments are straight lines, each joint uses up one residual degree of freedom. Choosing joints by examining the sample data tends to increase the variance explained by the variable in question. When this variable is a covariate, a conservative bias is introduced into tests on the independent variables; but if the variable is an independent variable, the bias is toward exaggerating the importance of the variable.

Spline regression computes the slope of the first line segment, plus the change in slope at each joint. In spline regression we create artificial variables whose b_j values equal these changes in slope. We can test the effect of the entire set.

Polynomial spline regression combines the advantages of polynomial regression and spline regression. We fit a polynomial instead of a straight line within each segment.

This chapter emphasizes transformations of regressors. But unpublished work of mine suggests that if nonlinearity is caused by the scale on which Y is measured, then spline functions may be useful for transforming Y to increase linearity of regression. Section 17.6 describes the procedure in detail.

KEY TERMS

global and local properties of curves
global and local terms
residual scatterplot
common and natural logarithms
polynomial regression

order of a polynomial
centering a variable
spline regression
polynomial spline regression

SYMBOLS AND ABBREVIATIONS

log   ln $J0, J1, J2$

PROBLEMS

Table 12.4 shows the history of population growth in the United States. Regression can be used to analyze time-series data like these, but the hypothesis tests are not completely appropriate, because adjacent observations are not necessarily independent. In these problems, therefore, we shall avoid hypothesis tests.

TABLE 12.4
Historical population figures for the United States, in thousands

1790	3,929	1860	31,443	1930	123,203
1800	5,308	1870	38,558	1940	132,165
1810	7,240	1880	50,189	1950	151,326
1820	9,638	1890	62,980	1960	179,323
1830	12,861	1900	76,212	1970	203,302
1840	17,063	1910	92,228	1980	226,543
1850	23,192	1920	106,022		

1. For simplicity, number the censuses 1 to 20, and call the resulting scale X. Call population Y. Find r_{XY}.

2. It would appear most reasonable to make a logarithmic transform of (X, Y, both). Explain.

3. Make the transformation(s) suggested by your answer to Prob. 2 and find the new correlation. Is it higher than r_{XY}?

4. Plot the residuals in this regression against X, to see whether the logarithmic relationship studied in Prob. 3 is itself substantially curvilinear.

5. Inspection of the plot from Prob. 4 suggests that the model's fit to the data might be improved either by using a second-order polynomial or by fitting a spline joint at 1890 (census 11). Try both. Which fits better?

13

DESIGNS WITH INTERACTION EFFECTS

13.1 INTERACTION IN TWO-FACTOR DESIGNS

13.1.1 Interaction as a Change in Slope

In an ANOVA design, interaction is a *difference between differences.* For instance, consider a 2 × 2 ANOVA design in which the TC comparison (treatment versus control) is crossed with sex. If the TC difference is larger for women than for men, then we say there is an interaction between sex and treatment type.

We can generalize this definition to the general linear model by defining interaction as a *change in slope,* meaning that a slope for one regressor changes as another regressor changes. This definition subsumes the ANOVA definition as a special case. We saw in Sec. 3.2.2 that a difference is a kind of regression slope, so that a difference between differences is a change of slope. In the current example, interaction means that the TC regression slope changes with sex.

13.1.2 Interaction between Two Numerical Variables

This broader definition of interaction applies when both variables are numerical, as in the following examples:

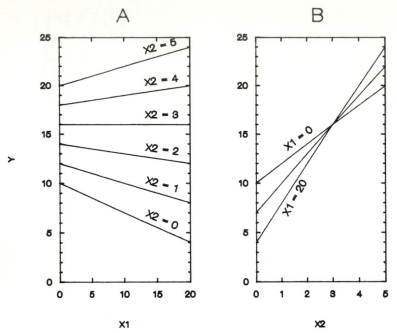

FIGURE 13.1
An example of simple linear interaction.

• Most physicians believe that the higher a patient's blood pressure is, the greater is the negative effect of overweight on life expectancy. This hypothesis specifies an interaction between blood pressure and weight in affecting life expectancy.

• If the relationship between political liberalism and socioeconomic status is positive among young people but negative among older people, then age and SES interact in affecting liberalism.

• If five persuasive messages differ in their appeal to emotion versus reason, the most emotional appeals may be most effective among less educated voters while the least emotional appeals may be most effective among more educated voters. If so, then education and strength of emotional appeal interact in affecting opinion change.

Interaction between two numerical variables X_1 and X_2 is illustrated in Fig. 13.1a. Each line in Fig. 13.1a represents the regression of Y on X_1 for a *particular value of* X_2. The figure shows that the relationship between Y and X_1 is negative when X_2 equals 0, 1, or 2; zero when X_2 equals 3; and positive when X_2 equals 4 or 5. The effect of X_1 for a particular value of X_2 is called a *simple effect* or *conditional effect* of X_1. If X_2 is numerical, then there may be infinitely many conditional effects of X_1; but if X_2 is categorical with k categories, then there are just k conditional effects of X_1.

The Y-intercepts also change as X_2 changes. But that was also true of the series of parallel lines in Fig. 2.5 (Sec. 2.1.6), where there was no interaction. The defining feature of interaction is nonparallel regression lines, or lines with different slopes.

13.1.3 Interaction versus Intercorrelation

Interaction is often confused with intercorrelation between regressors. Thus you might read a statement like, "b_X was reduced to near 0 by the addition of covariate C to the regression, because C interacts with X." The writer clearly means to say that C *correlates* with X. The sentence in quotation marks says that b_X is affected by the *inclusion* of C, while interaction means that b_X is affected by the *value* of C. The interaction of X with C describes how X and C relate to Y, so it can be computed only when Y scores are known. But the correlation of X with C can be computed even if there is no third variable Y.

13.1.4 Simple Linear Interaction

Any pattern of nonparallel regression lines is an interaction. However, we shall first consider *simple linear interaction,* which occurs when the slope of one regressor is linearly related to the value of another regressor. This exists in Fig. 13.1a; for the six regression lines there, we have the values of b_1 shown in Table 13.1. This table shows the conditional effects of X_1 for six values of X_2. We see that these six conditional effects have an exact linear relation to X_2; each 1-unit increase in X_2 is associated with an increase of .1 in b_1.

TABLE 13.1
Values of b_1 for six levels of X_2

X_2	b_1
0	$\dfrac{4 - 10}{20} = -.3$
1	$\dfrac{8 - 12}{20} = -.2$
2	$\dfrac{12 - 14}{20} = -.1$
3	$\dfrac{16 - 16}{20} = 0$
4	$\dfrac{20 - 18}{20} = .1$
5	$\dfrac{24 - 20}{20} = .2$

13.1.5   Representing Simple Linear Interaction by a Cross Product

Simple linear interaction can be represented by a regression equation with two linear terms and a constructed cross-product term, of the form

$$\hat{Y} = b_1 X_1 + b_2 X_2 + b_3 X_1 X_2 + a$$

To see why, consider further Fig. 13.1a. We have just seen that the slope is $-.3$ when $X_2 = 0$, and the slope then rises .1 with each 1-unit increase in X_2. Thus we can write

$$b = \text{slope} = .1X_2 - .3$$

We also see that the Y intercept of the regression line equals 10 when $X_2 = 0$ and increases 2 points (to 12, 14, and so on) for each 1-point increase in X_2. Thus we can write

$$a = Y \text{ intercept} = 10 + 2X_2$$

We can then substitute these expressions for a and b in the simple regression formula $\hat{Y} = bX_1 + a$. This gives

$$\hat{Y} = bX_1 + a = (.1X_2 - .3)X_1 + (2X_2 + 10)$$

Multiplying to remove parentheses then gives

$$\hat{Y} = .1X_1 X_2 - .3X_1 + 2X_2 + 10$$

We thus see that a whole series of nonparallel regression lines can be represented by a single regression equation which includes the terms X_1, X_2, and $X_1 X_2$. We saw in Chap. 2 that if the regression lines are parallel, then we need only the X_1 and X_2 terms, without the cross-product term $X_1 X_2$. The coefficient of the cross-product term (which is .1 in this example) equals the amount that the X_1 slope increases for each 1-unit increase in X_2. Like any other coefficient in a regression, this coefficient will be tested for significance by most regression computer programs. The hypothesis that the cross-product coefficient is zero is the hypothesis that the regression lines are all parallel and no interaction exists.

13.1.6   The Symmetry of Interaction

In Sec. 13.1.5, the roles of X_1 and X_2 could have been reversed. There we saw how the conditional effect of X_1 changes as X_2 changes. But a parallel description tells how the conditional effect of X_2 changes as X_1 changes. Although Figs. 13.1a and b appear very different, they actually represent the same regression equation. At the left edge of Fig. 13.1a, $X_1 = 0$. Notice that the six regression lines meet this left edge at Y values ranging from 10 (for the line $X_2 = 0$) up to 20 (for the line $X_2 = 5$). This means that when $X_1 = 0$, $\hat{Y}$ rises from 10 to 20 as X_2 rises from 0 to 5. The line labeled $X_1 = 0$ in Fig. 13.1*b* represents this relationship.

Similarly, at the right edge of Fig. 13.1*a*, $X_1 = 20$. The six lines meet this edge at Y values ranging from 4 to 24. This means that when $X_1 = 20$, $\hat{Y}$ rises from 4 to 24 as X_2 rises from 0 to 5. The line labeled $X_1 = 20$ in Fig. 13.1*b* represents this relationship.

Similarly, in the center of Fig. 13.1*a*, $X_1 = 10$. At this value of X_1, the six lines have Y values ranging from 7 to 22. This means that when $X_1 = 10$, $\hat{Y}$ rises from 7 to 22 as X_2 rises from 0 to 5. The line labeled $X_1 = 10$ in Fig. 13.1*b* represents this relationship. Thus parts *a* and *b* of Fig. 13.1 actually provide different geometric representations of the same regression equation.

The slopes of the three lines in Fig. 13.1*b* are $(20 - 10)/5 = 2$, $(22 - 7)/5 = 3$, and $(24 - 4)/5 = 4$. Thus, as X_1 rises from 0 to 10 to 20, the slope for X_2 rises from 2 to 3 to 4. We see from these values that each 1-unit increase in X_1 is associated with a rise of .1 in the slope of X_2. This is the same value we found in Sec. 13.1.4 as the change in the slope of X_1 associated with each 1-unit increase in X_2. It is also the coefficient of the cross-product term in the regression equation.

This illustrates an important conclusion:

Interaction is symmetrical. The conditional effect or slope of X_2 changes with X_1 only if the conditional effect or slope of X_1 changes with X_2. In fact, both changes are always equal; both equal the coefficient of the cross-product term X_1X_2. The *t* associated with that term tests the significance of the interaction.

13.1.7 Representing Interaction by a Warped Surface

In Chap. 2 we saw that an equation of the form $\hat{Y} = b_1X_1 + b_2X_2 + a$ can be represented either as a series of parallel lines or as a tilted plane in three-dimensional space. An equation with an interaction term, of the form

$$\hat{Y} = b_1X_1 + b_2X_2 + b_3X_1X_2 + a$$

can be represented either as a series of *non*parallel lines, as in Fig. 13.1, or as a *warped* surface in three-dimensional space, as in Fig. 13.2. The line in Fig. 13.2 from $Y = 10$ to $Y = 4$ corresponds to the line labeled $X_2 = 0$ in Fig. 13.1*a*, and the line in Fig. 13.2 from $Y = 20$ to $Y = 24$ corresponds to the line labeled $X_2 = 5$ in Fig. 13.1*a*. The other four lines from Fig. 13.1*a* also appear in Fig. 13.2. Like Fig. 13.2, any surface representing a simple linear interaction looks like a bent cookie tin.

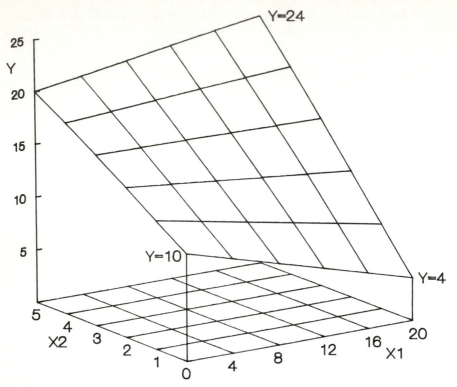

FIGURE 13.2
Three-dimensional representation of interaction.

13.2 INTERACTION WITH CATEGORICAL REGRESSORS

13.2.1 An Example with Dichotomous and Numerical Regressors

When we have one dichotomous and one numerical regressor, we have separate regressions in two groups. If the slope of the regression of Y on age for men differs from that for women, then age interacts with sex. In Sec. 13.1.5 we saw how a whole series of nonparallel regression lines can be represented by a single equation. Therefore, it should come as no surprise that we can use a single regression equation to represent two nonparallel regression lines. For instance, suppose we have derived the following equations for men (group 0) and women (group 1):

$$\hat{Y} = .7X + 3 \quad \text{for group 1}$$
$$\hat{Y} = .3X + 2 \quad \text{for group 0}$$
$$.4X + 1 = \text{difference}$$

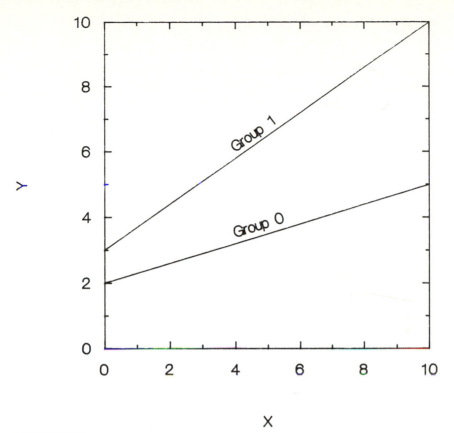

FIGURE 13.3
Interaction between dichotomous and numerical variables.

The regression lines for these equations appear in Fig. 13.3. Let the dichotomous variable sex be represented by D. If we write $\hat{Y} = (.3X + 2) + (.4X + 1)D$, then the last term in the equation will be 0 for all cases in group 0, so that the equation will be the correct equation $\hat{Y} = .3X + 2$ for all cases in group 0. But for all the cases for which $D = 1$, the equation becomes $\hat{Y} = (.3X + 2) + (.4X + 1) = .7X + 3$, which is the correct equation for group 1. Thus, the general equation $\hat{Y} = (.3X + 2) + (.4X + 1)D$ applies to both groups. But by multiplying to remove parentheses, the equation becomes $\hat{Y} = .3X + 1D + .4XD + 2$, and we have found a single equation that applies to both groups.

13.2.2 What the Coefficients Mean

If we denote the dichotomous and numerical regressors by D and X, respectively, as in Sec. 13.2.1, and denote the interaction by I, then the regression equation with the cross-product term is

$$\hat{Y} = b_D D + b_X X + b_I DX + a$$

The meaning of the four constants in the regression can be deduced from the principles of Sec. 13.1. b_D is the slope relative to D when X is zero. But if D is coded 0, 1, then that slope is the difference between the two Y intercepts. Therefore

$$b_D = (Y \text{ intercept for group 1}) - (Y \text{ intercept for group 0})$$

Parallel to the case in which both regressors are numerical,

$$b_X = \text{slope of regression line for group 0}$$

We know that b_I is the increase in the slope relative to X when D increases 1 unit from 0 to 1. Thus

$$b_I = (\text{slope for group 1}) - (\text{slope for group 0})$$

$$= \text{difference between conditional effects}$$

As before, a is the value of $\hat{Y}$ when both X and D are zero, so

$$a = Y \text{ intercept for group 0}$$

The values in the regression equation of Sec. 13.2.1 have the meanings given here: .3 is the slope for group 0, 1 is the difference between the two Y intercepts, .4 is the difference between slopes, and 2 is the Y intercept for group 0.

13.2.3 Interaction between Two Dichotomous Regressors

If we fit a regression containing two dichotomous variables X_1 and X_2 and their cross product $X_1 X_2$, the unique SS and F associated with the cross-product term will equal the SS and F for interaction in a 2×2 ANOVA design. However, unlike simple ANOVA, there is no requirement of equal cell frequencies, so long as each cell contains at least one observation.

If X_1 and X_2 are both coded 0, 1, then $b(X_1 X_2)$ will equal the difference between differences of cell means. For instance, suppose we have treatment and control conditions applied to both males and females and we observe the means shown in the following 2×2 table:

	M	F
T	9	5
C	8	7

Interaction is a difference between differences. The difference between within-row differences is $(9 - 5) - (8 - 7) = 4 - 1 = 3$. Or we could find the same measure of interaction by taking the difference between within-column differences: $(9 - 8) - (5 - 7) = 1 - (-2) = 3$.

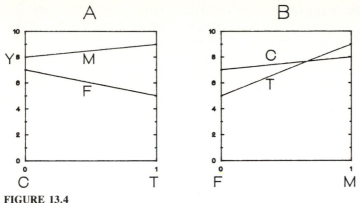

FIGURE 13.4
Interaction between two dichotomous variables.

Approaching the problem in a regression format, we can code sex 1 for males and 0 for females, and code treatment 1 for T and 0 for C. Recalling that regression lines for dichotomous regressors pass through group means, we can draw the regression lines shown in Fig. 13.4. The conditional effects of treatment equal the slopes in Fig. 13.4a, while the conditional effects of sex equal the slopes in Fig. 13.4b.

We can also derive the constants in the regression equation from principles already established. Since we represented "control" and "female" by 0, the coefficient of "sex" is the simple difference $8 - 7 = 1$ between control means, the coefficient of "treatment" is the simple difference $5 - 7 = -2$ between female means, and the additive constant a is the female control mean of 7. As we saw above, the coefficient of the cross-product term is the difference between within-column or within-row differences, which we found to be 3. Thus the regression equation is

$$\hat{Y} = 1 \times \text{sex} - 2 \times \text{treatment} + 3 \times \text{sex} \times \text{treatment} + 7$$

When we substitute in this equation the values sex = treatment = 0, we find the female control mean of 7. When we substitute sex = 1, treatment = 0, we find the male control mean of 8. When we substitute sex = 0, treatment = 1, we find the female treatment mean of 5. And when we substitute sex = treatment = 1, we find the male treatment mean of 9.

13.2.4 Interaction Involving Multicategorical Variables

We have seen how a multicategorical variable with k categories can be represented by $k - 1$ coded variables. Interaction between a multicategorical variable and any other variable is represented by forming all possible cross-product regressors. For instance, if a variable C with four categories is represented by three coded regressors $C1$, $C2$, and $C3$, then the interaction between C and a numerical variable D could be tested by forming three cross-product regressors $CD1$, $CD2$, and $CD3$ by a set of statements like

```
>let cd1 = c1*d
>let cd2 = c2*d
>let cd3 = c3*d
```

Or if C were multicategorical with four categories as above and D were multicategorical with three categories and were represented by the coded regressors $D1$ and $D2$, then the $C*D$ interaction could be tested by forming six cross-product regressors by a set of statements like

```
>let cd11 = c1*d1
>let cd12 = c1*d2
>let cd21 = c2*d1
>let cd22 = c2*d2
>let cd31 = c3*d1
>let cd32 = c3*d2
```

The total SS for interaction is the unique SS of the *set* of cross-product terms.

General linear model programs include a provision for generating all the necessary coded regressors. For instance, if C or D or both are multicategorical variables, then the SAS commands

```
>proc glm; class c d; model y = c d c*d;
```

will produce a regression with all necessary CD interaction regressors included. The comparable commands in SYSTAT and MYSTAT are

```
>category c = 4, d = 3
>model y = constant + c + d + c*d
>estimate
```

13.3   SOME COMPLICATIONS IN STUDYING INTERACTIONS

13.3.1   The Difficulty of Detecting Interactions

Significant interaction is not often found in small or moderate-size samples. It may be that substantial interaction simply does not often exist in the real world. Another reason is that the significance of an interaction is determined by its unique contribution, and that contribution is necessarily small in comparison with the size of the largest conditional effects. For instance, suppose two uncorrelated regressors X_1 and X_2 are normally distributed with unit variance, and suppose the residual Y variance is 4.0. The methods of Chap. 15 can be used to show that if $_7b_1 = 1$, then in a sample of size 50, the power of the test on b_1 is a respectable .90. But if X_1 and X_2 interact, with the slope of X_1 being $+1$ among cases 2 standard deviations above the mean of X_2 and -1 among cases 2 standard deviations below the mean of X_2, then the cross-product term's unique contribution to Y variance is only .25, even though the term is uncorrelated with both X_1 and X_2. In the same sample of size 50, the power of the test for interaction is only .39.

Conclusions about interaction are further complicated by the fact that large but spurious interaction effects can arise in two different ways, as outlined in Secs. 13.3.2 and 13.3.3.

13.3.2 Confusing Interaction with Curvilinearity

Curvilinearity can masquerade as interaction if curvilinear terms are omitted from a regression while interaction terms are included. For instance, in the data set of Table 13.2, you can see for yourself that $Y = X_1^2$ exactly, so that there is no interaction. But X_1 and X_2 are highly correlated, so the cross-product term X_1X_2 correlates highly with the nonlinear term X_1^2. A regression using only the terms X_1, X_2, and X_1X_2 yields the equation

$$\hat{Y} = 4.5X_1 - 4.5X_2 + 1X_1X_2 + .5$$

The t's for the three coefficients are respectively 2.645, -2.645, and 3.578. With 4 df, the two-tailed p's for the three b's are respectively .058, .058, and .024. Therefore the cross-product term is the only term significant at the .05 level, even though the data set is constructed to contain no interaction at all.

This problem can also arise when one regressor is dichotomous. For instance, in Fig. 13.5, nine people in group 0 are represented by circles while nine people in group 1 are represented by crosses. If we ignore group membership and model Y as a parabolic function of X, we get the parabola shown.

TABLE 13.2
Curvilinearity masquerading as interaction

X_1	X_2	X_1X_2	Y
1	2	2	1
2	1	2	4
3	4	12	9
4	3	12	16
5	6	30	25
6	5	30	36
7	8	56	49
8	7	56	64

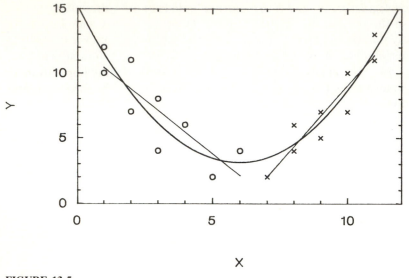

FIGURE 13.5
How curvilinearity can masquerade as interaction.

Its fit is excellent: $R = .897$. Neither group membership nor its interaction with X can increase this fit significantly. But when the square term is deleted from the regression and we model Y as a function of X, group, and their cross product, we find the two straight lines shown. The left-hand line applies to the circles, and the right-hand line applies to the crosses. These two lines are not nearly parallel, and the interaction term is now highly significant. This model fits almost as well as the parabola; it yields $R = .886$. But the point is that the interaction found could have been produced by curvilinearity instead, so there is no convincing evidence of real interaction. Therefore, as before, we should include square terms when testing for interaction.

Just as curvilinearity can be mistaken for interaction, so can interaction be mistaken for curvilinearity. But most scientists think of curvilinearity as a simpler or more parsimonious hypothesis than interaction, and therefore regard the former error as more serious.

13.3.3   How the Scaling of Y Affects Interaction

When sample sizes are fairly large, the results of a two-sample t test are rarely much affected by transforming Y—for instance, replacing Y by $\log(Y)$ or e^Y. The same is true in regression with only linear terms—if X_j has a large partial relationship with Y, that relationship rarely vanishes if Y is transformed. But this is not true for interaction: transforming Y can greatly affect the importance of interaction terms. When significant interaction is found, it is difficult to know whether it might vanish under some transformation of Y.

This problem applies as much to classical ANOVA designs as it does to regression designs. It is not adequate to show that residuals are approximately normally distributed or equal in variance. These are tests of the sampling assumptions of linear models and have nothing to do with the present problem, which can arise in very large samples or even if the entire population is available for study. Section 17.6 gives a detailed example of this problem, and some solutions.

13.3.4 Meaning of Other b's When a Cross-Product Term Is Present

Cross-product terms measuring interaction are themselves global terms, but their presence transforms a regression's linear terms into local terms. To see exactly what properties are measured by each constant in the regression, consider the equation

$$\hat{Y} = b_1 X_1 + b_2 X_2 + b_3 X_1 X_2 + a$$

If $X_2 = 0$, then the second and third terms drop out of the equation, leaving $\hat{Y} = b_1 X_1 + a$. Therefore

$$b_1 = \text{estimated conditional effect of } X_1 \text{ when } X_2 \text{ is 0}$$

By symmetry,

$$b_2 = \text{estimated conditional effect of } X_2 \text{ when } X_1 = 0.$$

As usual, a is the Y intercept—the value of $\hat{Y}$ when $X_1 = X_2 = 0$. The same general principle applies when more regressors are included. If cross-product terms are included for X_j and several other regressors—for instance, $X_1 X_2$, $X_1 X_3$, and $X_1 X_4$—then b_j is the estimated conditional effect of X_j when all those other regressors are 0.

13.3.5 How Changes in Means Affect a Regression with Interaction Terms

In Sec. 12.3.3 we saw that in polynomial regression, changing the mean of X by adding or subtracting points will typically change measures of unique contribution for all but the highest-order term in the polynomial. Similar rules apply to cross products. If we subtract a constant from all scores on a regressor X_j and then compute the cross product $X_j X_k$ with another variable X_k, then both b_j and b_k will change, as will a. For instance, in the example of Sec. 13.3.2, suppose we subtract 4.5 from all scores on both X_1 and X_2 to adjust both variables to means of 0. To see what happens, define the new forms of X_1 and X_2 as X_1' and X_2'. Then $X_1' = X_1 - 4.5$ and $X_2' = X_2 - 4.5$, which implies that $X_1 = X_1' + 4.5$ and $X_2 = X_2' + 4.5$. Since this change should leave the $\hat{Y}$ values unchanged, we can find how the regression equation changes by replacing X_1 and X_2 by $X_1' + 4.5$ and $X_2' + 4.5$ in the regression equation above. This gives

$$\hat{Y} = 4.5(X_1' + 4.5) - 4.5(X_2' + 4.5) + 1(X_1' + 4.5)(X_2' + 4.5) + .5$$

$$= 4.5X_1' + 4.5^2 - 4.5X_2' - 4.5^2 + 1X_1'X_2' + 4.5X_1' + 4.5X_2' + 4.5^2 + .5$$

$$= 9X_1' + 0X_2' + 1X_1'X_2' + 20.75$$

Thus all the constants in the regression have changed except the coefficient of the interaction term. This is generally true; changing the means of regressors by adding or subtracting points for every score will change the local coefficients in the equation but not the global ones.

13.4   CONDITIONAL EFFECTS

13.4.1   Effects as Variables

In Sec. 13.4, as before, we consider only the case of two regressors. Section 13.5 deals with any number of regressors.

We have distinguished between total and direct effects, but until now we have always thought of either kind of effect as a constant to be estimated in the same sense that one estimates a mean or proportion. But the interaction between X_1 and X_2 changes these effects from *constants* into *variables*. For instance, if the effectiveness of a treatment increases with age, then treatment effectiveness is a variable which changes with age.

Where we previously estimated a variable's effect, we now may wish to estimate its *conditional effects* or its *average effect* or both. For instance, if a treatment has a highly negative effect for people aged 20, a slightly negative effect for people aged 30, no effect for people aged 40, a slightly positive effect for people aged 50, and a highly positive effect for people aged 60, then we might want to estimate the size of the effect for people aged 25, or we might want to estimate its average effect for people of all ages.

13.4.2   Estimation of Conditional Effects

Analysis of variance (ANOVA) deals with the case in which all regressors are categorical, and in ANOVA literature conditional effects are usually called *simple effects*. But we shall use the term *conditional effects* whether regressors are numerical or categorical, to emphasize the conceptual similarity of the two cases.

The simplest way to estimate the conditional effect of one regressor X_j is to derive the overall regression equation and then set the covariate equal to the desired value. For instance, in Sec. 13.1.5 we had the regression equation

$$\hat{Y} = -.3X_1 + 2X_2 + .1X_1X_2 + 10$$

To estimate the conditional effect of X_1 when $X_2 = 4$, we can substitute that value in the regression, giving the equation $\hat{Y} = -.3X_1 + 8 + .4X_1 + 10 = .1X_1 + 18$. The estimated conditional effect of X_1 on Y when $X_2 = 4$ is $+.1$, since that is the coefficient of X_1 in the reduced equation.

We can think about this procedure in the following terms. We can rewrite the regression $\hat{Y} = b_1X_1 + b_2X_2 + b_3X_1X_2 + a$ as $\hat{Y} = (b_1 + b_3X_2)X_1 + b_2X_2 + a$. The expression in parentheses $(b_1 + b_3X_2)$ is the coefficient of X_1, so it is the effect of X_1. But we see that this expression is a function of X_2, so it implies

$$\text{Conditional effect of } X_1 = b_1 + b_3 \times \text{conditional value of } X_2$$

In this example, the conditional effect is $-.3 + .1 \times 4 = .1$.

13.4.3   Testing Conditional Effects

A more complex procedure gives the same estimated conditional effect as the previous method, but also gives an estimate of its standard error. It thus allows t tests or confidence bands on the conditional effect. This procedure takes advantage of the fact, mentioned in Sec. 13.3.4, that in an equation of the form $\hat{Y} = b_1X_1 + b_2X_2 + b_3X_1X_2 + a$, b_1 is the slope of the warped surface when $X_2 = 0$. Thus, if we are interested in the conditional effect of X_1 when X_2 equals some value $CV(X_2)$ (read as "conditional value of X_2"), we subtract the constant $CV(X_2)$ from all scores on X_2, thus forming a new variable $X_2' = X_2 - CV(X_2)$. We then regress Y on X_1, X_2', and their cross product X_3'. In this regression, the slope of b_1 is the effect of X_1 when $X_2' = 0$, which implies $X_2 = CV(X_2)$. Thus it is the conditional effect of interest. And the printed value of the estimated standard error of b_1 equals the estimated standard error of this conditional effect.

For instance, in the data set on life satisfaction in the problems of Chap. 5 (see Table 5.7), let us define $Y = $ satisfaction, $X_1 = $ income, $X_2 = $ education, and $X_3 = X_1X_2$. Regressing Y on X_1, X_2, and X_3 gives

$$a = 41.252 \qquad SE(a) = 20.369$$
$$b_1 = 2.309 \qquad SE(b_1) = .9946$$
$$b_2 = 1.933 \qquad SE(b_2) = 1.5877$$
$$b_3 = -.1153 \qquad SE(b_3) = .06766$$

But if we define $X_2' = X_2 - 10$ and $X_3' = X_1X_2'$ and regress Y on X_1, X_2', and X_3', we find

$$a = 41.252 \qquad SE(a) = 20.369$$
$$b_1 = 1.156 \qquad SE(b_1) = .3764$$
$$b_2' = 1.933 \qquad SE(b_2) = 1.5877$$
$$b_3' = -.1153 \qquad SE(b_3) = .06766$$

Notice that a, b_2, b_3, and their standard errors are all unchanged. And as mentioned above, the new value of b_1 could have been calculated from the output of the first regression. Since $X_2' = 0$ when $X_2 = 10$, the new value of b_1

equals the estimated conditional effect of X_1 when $X_2 = 10$. Thus the previous formula for conditional effects implies

$$\text{New } b_1 = 1.156 = \text{old } b_1 + CV(X_2) \times b_3 = 2.309 + 10 \times (-.1153)$$

But the new value of $SE(b_1)$ could not have been found from the previous output.

13.5 HIGHER-ORDER DESIGNS

13.5.1 Higher-Order Interaction

Consider the means in Table 13.3, in which T, C, M, and F stand for treatment and control groups and males and females, respectively. In city A, the difference between within-row differences is $(9 - 5) - (8 - 7) = 4 - 1 = 3$, while in city B the comparable value is $(6 - 3) - (4 - 6) = 3 + 2 = 5$. These values measure the size of the interaction in each city. Thus the sex $\times$ treatment interaction changes from city A to city B. This illustrates a three-way interaction: there is a sex $\times$ treatment $\times$ city interaction. A two-way interaction means that the size of a conditional effect changes with another variable, while a three-way interaction means that the size of a two-way interaction changes with another variable. If city A is coded 1 and city B is coded 0, then the size of the three-way interaction is $3 - 5 = -2$.

In this example all three variables are dichotomous. But as with two-way interaction, interaction can be defined when variables are dichotomous or numerical or multicategorical or any mixture of the three.

Still higher-order interactions are defined similarly. A four-way interaction is defined as the change in a three-way interaction for each 1-unit change in a fourth variable, a five-way interaction is defined as the change in a four-way interaction for each 1-unit change in a fifth variable, and so on.

13.5.2 Creating Higher-Order Cross Products

A three-way interaction is implemented in a regression equation by a three-way cross product. In the current example, the three-way interaction among sex (S), city (C), and treatment type (T) could be represented with a command like

```
>let sct = s*c*t
```

TABLE 13.3
Three-factor interaction

	City A			City B	
	M	F		M	F
T	9	5	T	6	3
C	8	7	C	4	6

The three possible two-way interactions could be represented with the commands

>let sc = s*c
>let st = s*t
>let ct = c*t

To test for a three-way interaction, we always include linear terms in the regression, plus terms for the lower-order interactions. Thus we might use a command like

>model y = constant + s + c + t + sc + st + ct + sct

If all variables are dichotomous or numerical, then each linear term has 1 *df*, as has each interaction, and the *t* printed next to each regression slope tests the significance of the particular linear or interaction term.

At this writing, SYSTAT and MYSTAT are sometimes more convenient than SAS when working with higher-order cross products. In SYSTAT and MYSTAT, you can specify all possible interactions with a set of commands like

>category s = 2, c = 2, t = 2
>model y = constant + s + c + t + s*c + s*t + c*t + s*c*t

The comparable commands in SAS are even simpler:

>class s c t;
>model y = s c t s*c s*t c*t s*c*t;

But the asterisk notation can be used in SAS only for categorical variables or for polynomial terms. In SAS PROC GLM, you can separate categorical variables with vertical bars to show that all possible interactions should be included. For instance, the commands

>class s c t; model y = s|c|t;

are equivalent to

>class s c t; model s c t s*c s*t c*t s*c*t;

The ANOVA command in SYSTAT and MYSTAT also calculates all possible interactions involving the factors. Unlike the MODEL statement, the ANOVA command distinguishes between factors or independent variables and covariates, and computes no interactions involving any covariates. We shall not discuss the ANOVA command further.

13.5.3 The Symmetry of Higher-Order Interaction

Like two-way interaction, three-way interaction is symmetrical. To say that the treatment × sex interaction changes by 2 points from city to city is to say that the treatment × city interaction changes by 2 points between the two sexes, or that the sex × city interaction changes by 2 points between treatments. To see this, rewrite the information in Table 13.3 as in Table 13.4. Then the difference between within-row differences is $(9 - 6) - (8 - 4) = 3 - 4 = -1$ in the first part of the table and $(5 - 3) - (7 - 6) = 2 - 1 = 1$ in the second part of the table. The three-way interaction is $-1 - 1 = -2$, which is the same as before. Or we can rewrite the information as shown in Table 13.5. Then the difference between within-row differences is $(9 - 6) - (5 - 3) = 3 - 2 = 1$ in the first part of the table and $(8 - 4) - (7 - 6) = 4 - 1 = 3$ in the second. The three-way interaction is $1 - 3 = -2$, which is again the same as before.

13.5.4 Parallels with Lower-Order Designs

All the principles mentioned above apply to interactions of any order. That is, all interactions are symmetric, they may involve any combination of variable types, they are formed by multiplication, and a test for any level of interaction must include in the regression all lower-order interactions involving the same variables. If curvilinearity is possible, the regression should also include curvilinear terms to prevent curvilinearity from masquerading as interaction as in Sec. 13.3.2.

We saw in Sec. 13.3.4 that the inclusion of a two-way interaction term in a regression changes the linear terms involving the same variables from global to local terms. For instance, in the model $\hat{Y} = b_1X_1 + b_2X_2 + b_3X_1X_2 + a$, the

TABLE 13.4
Another view of three-factor interaction

	Male			Female	
	A	B		A	B
T	9	6	T	5	3
C	8	4	C	7	6

TABLE 13.5
A third view of three-factor interaction

	T			C	
	A	B		A	B
M	9	6	M	8	4
F	5	3	F	7	6

inclusion of the X_1X_2 term changes the meaning of b_1 to the estimated slope of the warped regression surface with $X_2 = 0$, and changes the meaning of b_2 to the estimated slope when $X_1 = 0$. Similarly, the inclusion of any higher-order interaction term changes from global to local all lower-order terms involving the same variables. For instance, consider the model

$$\hat{Y} = b_1X_1 + b_2X_2 + b_3X_3 + b_4X_1X_2 + b_5X_1X_3 + b_6X_2X_3 + b_7X_1X_2X_3 + a$$

The three-way term makes b_4 estimate the size of the X_1X_2 interaction when $X_3 = 0$, and has parallel effects on b_5 and b_6. Also, b_1 estimates the effect of X_1 when $X_2 = X_3 = 0$; parallel conclusions apply to b_2 and b_3.

13.5.5   Curvilinear Interaction

We can define *curvilinear interaction* as a change in the curvilinearity of one variable as another variable changes. For instance, if X_1 is represented by a parabola through a term X_1^2 in the regression, the coefficient of this square term measures the degree of curvilinearity, equaling 0 if the best fit is provided by a straight line. If the optimum degree of curvature for X_1 changes with another variable X_2, that would appear as an interaction between X_1^2 and X_2, or as the term $X_1^2X_2$.

In Sec. 13.3.2 we saw how curvilinearity involving numerical variables can masquerade as interaction. Curvilinear interaction can also masquerade as higher-order interaction. If X_1 correlates highly with X_3, then a three-way interaction term $X_1X_2X_3$ might be significant when used without curvilinear terms, but the significance might disappear if the term $X_1^2X_2$ is included in the regression.

13.5.6   Collinearity among Interaction Terms

We saw in Sec. 13.3.2 that curvilinear and interaction terms can be collinear, so that curvilinearity can easily be mistaken for interaction if curvilinear terms are not included when testing for interaction. If three variables X_1, X_2, and X_3 all correlate highly, there can be substantial collinearity among the three two-way interactions X_1X_2, X_1X_3, and X_2X_3, so that they may be confused with each other if you test for interactions one at a time. This is unimportant if the focus is merely on dismissing interactions, as it usually is. But it should be considered if you want to demonstrate the existence of specific interactions.

13.6   MAIN EFFECTS AND AVERAGE EFFECTS

We saw in Sec. 13.4.1 that interaction transforms an effect from a single value to a variable. Where before we merely estimated a single effect, we may now wish to estimate an average effect. This is usually a complex process whose details are beyond the scope of this book, but we shall sketch the basic issues involved.

13.6.1 Main Effects

The concept of a main effect is prominent in classical ANOVA designs in which all cells of a research design have equal numbers of subjects, but the concept has little importance in the more general class of problems considered in this book. It applies only when all factors are categorical. The main effect of a dichotomous factor is simply an unweighted average of effects across the various levels of the other factors. For instance, suppose factor A is a counseling session provided to some students in a college of arts and sciences, designed to reduce academic failures. Factor B is the student's major. Then the main effect of factor A is defined as the unweighted average of its estimated effects across all majors, ignoring the fact that some majors may have far more students than others, and ignoring the fact that treatment A may be more effective in some majors than others.

In fact, suppose the principal advice given in the counseling sessions is that students should seek out course instructors for individual attention. Suppose this is usually effective for students in small departments with few students but is counterproductive for students in larger departments because it merely emphasizes the instructor's unavailability or lack of time for individual students. If there are many small departments and a few large ones, then the counselor's main effect could be significantly positive even if his or her average effect is negative, since the main effect gives effects in small departments as much weight as effects in large ones.

As we know, a multicategorical factor can be thought of as a set of dichotomous factors. The null hypothesis that a multicategorical factor's main effect is zero is the hypothesis that the main effects of all these dichotomous factors are zero. If tests of main effects are desired despite their limitations, they can be done by a method called *weighted squares of means,* so long as there is at least one case in each cell. This method is equivalent to using effect coding on all variables and testing the unique contribution of each variable's set of coded variables.

This method is implemented in MYSTAT and SYSTAT by using the CATEGORY command in conjunction with the MODEL statement. For instance, if there are two categorical variables A and B with 2 and 4 categories, respectively, then the commands

>category a = 2, b = 4
>model y = constant + a + b + a*b
>estimate

will test for the A and B main effects and for the AB interaction. In SAS PROC GLM, the same tests are performed by type III sums of squares.

13.6.2 Four SS Types in SAS

SAS PROC GLM prints four types of sums of squares, labeled I, II, III, and IV.

A type I SS shows the reductions in SS(error) when all linear, curvilinear, and interaction terms are entered into the regression one at a time, in the order given in the MODEL statement.

A type III SS tests main effects as just defined, along with interaction terms.

The type IV SS equals the type III so long as there are no empty cells, which is the only case we are considering.

Type II SS's are designed for models in which you are willing to assume the absence of interaction so long as tests for interaction yield nonsignificant results. Interaction effects are tested in the same way as in types III and IV, but the SS values for linear terms are the same as they would be if the interaction terms were excluded from the model. The F tests on the type II SS values for linear terms are problematic. They are invalid if interaction exists. If interaction does not exist they are valid but less powerful than tests performed with interaction terms omitted. But a significant result is meaningful despite any lack of power.

13.6.3 When Average Effects Are Important

When main effects are inappropriate, we must consider the use of average effects. Three considerations may enable us to avoid this issue.

First, the average effect of a factor A is not defined if A interacts with another factor B whose population distribution is not defined. This is usually the case if B is a manipulated variable such as "speed target moves" in a computerized tracking experiment. Unlike variables such as age or wealth, this variable has no "true distribution"—the variable does not even exist outside the laboratory. But if A interacts with B, then A's effect on Y depends on B, so that it is not meaningful to ask what the true average level of A's effect is.

Second, A's average effect is not defined if A is multicategorical—though, of course, a multicategorical variable can be expressed as a set of dichotomous variables whose average effects are defined.

Third, a variable's average effect is often of little interest if it interacts with other variables. For instance, if a treatment's effectiveness increases with the subject's age, then we might plan to use the treatment with older subjects and not with younger subjects, so that there is little or no interest in its average effect across all ages. But sometimes a treatment must be applied to everyone—for instance, all workers in a large office are subject to the same light intensity. Then it may still be important to estimate average effect size.

Three other considerations have the opposite effect of the last three: they drive us to consider the problem of average effects when we might have expected to avoid it.

First, the most conservative approach is to consider the problem even if the factor of interest does not interact significantly with other variables. A nonsignificant result does not prove a null hypothesis. Interaction is a complicating factor in the estimation of average effects, so if we assume its absence because it is not significant, then we are assuming away a complication that may actually exist.

Second, even if sample size is very large, we should avoid the temptation to simply omit interaction terms and use the ordinary linear effects as estimates of average effects. To see why, imagine that two groups G and H comprise respectively 90% and 10% of the population. If numerical factor A has little or no variance in group G and large variance in group H (the smaller group), then the data of group H may determine almost completely the simple linear effect of factor A. This difference in variances does not violate the standard assumptions of linear models, since the difference in variances occurs only in a crosswise regression. But if the effect of factor A is completely different in groups G and H, then even with large samples this linear effect can fail completely as an estimator of the average effect.

Third, a variable's polynomial curvilinear effect can be considered a type of interaction. For instance X_1^2 can be thought of as the interaction of X_1 with itself, while X_1^3 can be thought of as the three-way interaction of X_1 with itself and itself. Thus the following methods for estimating average effects can be applied in the presence of either interaction or curvilinearity or both.

13.6.4 Estimating Average Effects

This section and Sec. 13.6.5 are for more advanced readers; most should skip to Sec. 13.7.

The effect of factor A on Y *at a given point of the regression surface* is the slope $d\hat{Y}/dA$ at that point on the surface. Thus the estimated mean effect of A on Y is found by differentiating the regression equation with respect to A and then averaging across cases. For instance, consider a regression with three regressors A, B, and C and with all second-order but no higher-order effects, so that the regression equation is

$$\hat{Y} = b_1A + b_2B + b_3C + b_4A^2 + b_5B^2 + b_6C^2 + b_7AB + b_8AC + b_9BC + a$$

Differentiating, we have

$$\frac{d\hat{Y}}{dA} = b_1 + 2b_4A + b_7B + b_8C$$

Notice that all terms not involving A drop out and can be ignored. Then the estimated average effect of A is the mean of $d\hat{Y}/dA$, or

$$b_1 + 2b_4M_A + b_7M_B + b_8M_C$$

If the population mean of any factor happens to be known, then using it instead of the sample mean improves the estimate of average effect.

More complex examples can require the use of other statistics besides the regression slopes and regressor means. Consider a case with a three-way interaction. Let

$$\hat{Y} = b_1 A + b_2 B + b_3 C + b_4 A^2 + b_5 AB + b_6 AC + b_7 BC + b_8 ABC + a$$

Then

$$\frac{d\hat{Y}}{dA} = b_1 + 2b_4 A + b_5 B + b_6 C + b_8 BC$$

The mean of this expression includes not only the means of A, B, and C, but also mean(BC). When there is a fourth-order term $ABCD$, the mean of $d\hat{Y}/dA$ involves the mean of BCD. As mentioned in Sec. 10.1.6, the SAVE command in SYSTAT and MYSTAT saves a file containing all regressor scores. This file also includes cross-product variables created by interaction terms in the MODEL statement. Normally, the easiest way to find the means of cross-product variables like BC or BCD is to apply the STATS command to this file.

13.6.5 Estimating the Standard Error of an Average Effect

The problem of this section is especially easy if the model contains no terms higher than the second order and the population means of all regressors are known. Then, before deriving the second-order terms, express all regressor scores as deviations from these population means. The simple linear regression slopes then equal the estimated average effects, and the ordinary standard errors of those slopes are the estimated standard errors of the average effects.

To see why this works, consider the first example of Sec. 13.6.4. If the population means of A, B, and C are known, then the estimated average effect of A is

$$b_1 + 2b_4 \times {}_T M_A + b_7 \times {}_T M_B + b_8 \times {}_T M_C$$

But if the three true means have all been set to 0, then the last three terms of this expression all drop out, and the estimated average effect reduces to b_1.

To set the mean of a dichotomous variable to 0, we must, of course, use codes other than 1 and 0. For instance, if we knew that males were twice as frequent as females in the population of interest, then we could set the population mean of the coded variable equal to 0 by coding males $-.5$ and women $+1$. The general rule is that when we want to weight two categories unequally, we assign one a positive code and one a negative code, with absolute values inversely proportional to the group frequencies.

This can be extended to a multicategorical variable through a technique we shall call *weighted effect coding*. As in simple effect coding, we have a separate coded variable C_j for each cell j except the base cell. As in simple effect coding, C_j is coded 1 for cell j and 0 for every cell except the base cell. But the base cell is coded w_j on C_j, where

$$w_j = \frac{- \text{ population frequency of cell } j}{\text{population frequency of base cell}}$$

For instance, if the population frequency of category 1 is 4 times that of the base cell, then we set $w_1 = -4$. If we wish to give cell 2 half the weight of the base cell, then we set $w_2 = -.5$. This makes the population means of all coded variables equal to 0.

As an example, suppose a covariate has three categories and we know that the population base rates of those three categories are .2, .3, and .5. Suppose we define the last category as the base category and define $D1$ and $D2$ as the dummy variables for categories 1 and 2. Then $w_1 = -.2/.5 = -.4$ and $w_2 = -.3/.5 = -.6$, and the total coding scheme is as shown in Table 13.6. We see that the mean of $D1$ is $.2 \times 1 + .3 \times 0 - .5 \times .4 = 0$ and the mean of $D2$ is $.2 \times 0 + .3 \times 1 - .5 \times .6 = 0$.

So far, this section has considered only one method of finding the standard error of an average effect: setting covariate means to 0. But this method has two limitations. First, it does not generalize to models with higher-order terms. Second, it underestimates standard errors of average effects if the necessary population means are estimated rather than known, since this estimation adds a source of error that the method does not take into account. The "necessary means" are the means of any terms that appear in the desired derivative, such as B, BC, or BCD.

A more complex method can be used if there are higher-order terms but the necessary means are all known. Then the multipliers of the b's in the average effect are known, and the problem involves estimating the standard error of a known linear function of regression coefficients. In matrix notation, the estimated squared standard error is $MSE \times w'(X'X)^{-1}w$, where w is the vector of multipliers—for instance, the known means of B, BC, BCD, and so on—and X is the matrix of regressor scores, augmented by a column of 1s to represent the additive constant a.

If any of the necessary means are unknown, then standard errors of average effects can still be estimated by the bootstrap method, introduced in Sec. 14.2.2. I have applied it to several artificial-data problems with known average effects, and it appears to work very well.

TABLE 13.6
Weighted effect coding

	$D1$	$D2$
Cell 1	1	0
Cell 2	0	1
Cell 3	$-.4$	$-.6$

13.7 ORGANIZING TESTS ON INTERACTION AND CURVILINEARITY

The number of tests for interaction and curvilinearity can be very large. If there are 10 numerical regressors, then there are $(10 \times 9)/2$ or 45 possible two-way interactions and $(10 \times 9 \times 8)/6$ or 120 possible three-way interactions, plus 10 possible square terms and 10 cubic terms for single variables. With multi-categorical variables, we need not test for curvilinearity, but the number of df consumed by interaction tests can be even larger. If factors A, B, and C have respectively 4, 6, and 8 categories, then the AB interaction uses 3×5 or 15 df, AC uses 3×7 or 21, BC uses 5×7 or 35, and ABC uses $3 \times 5 \times 7$ or 105. Clearly there are a great many linear models in which all available degrees of freedom would be consumed by simultaneous tests on all moderately reasonable forms of curvilinearity and interaction. We need some strategy for dealing with these complexities.

In this section we can think of curvilinearity as a variable's interaction with itself, so that both questions concern types of interaction. The difference between curvilinearity and interaction should, of course, not generally be ignored, but for simplicity this section uses the single word *interaction* to include curvilinearity.

Curiously, we often study interactions in order to dismiss them—to dismiss either their existence or their relevance, thus allowing the conclusion that the study's major conclusions apply equally to all cases. This fact can influence the analysis of interactions, as we shall see.

13.7.1 Three Approaches to Managing Complications

In any statistical analysis there are at least three general ways to handle complications. In order of increasing conservativeness, they are:

1. Assume their absence—the standard method in elementary courses.
2. Check for them, and assume their absence if they are not clearly present. If present, use an alternative statistical method which is typically less powerful but is valid even in the presence of the complications.
3. Use the less powerful method even when no complications are detected, on the ground that the absence of complications is a null hypothesis that can never be proved.

The choice among these three methods actually arose in Sec. 5.4.6. There we considered the possibility of simply failing to analyze covariates of doubtful importance (method 1 in the present list), or deleting from the model covariates found to have nonsignificant effects (method 2 in the list). We criticized both these approaches and recommended method 3, which in that case meant including covariates in the model even if they were both nonsignificant and of doubtful importance. But we shall see in Sec. 13.7.2 that this conservative approach cannot be consistently applied when the complications are interactions.

13.7.2 Testing for Interaction

If we consider all higher-order interactions, then there are even more interactions than implied in the earlier examples. If we considered every possible multiplicative interaction involving P numerical regressors, the model including the additive constant would consume 2^P *df*. If $P = 10$, this amounts to over 1000 *df*. And even this ignores the fact that nonmultiplicative interactions can be defined—though they are not discussed in this book. Therefore we simply have to assume the absence of some interactions.

This problem is made more manageable by the fact that most tests for interaction yield negative results, and this is even truer of higher-order interactions. Thus we typically ignore the highest-order interactions not because of their impossibility but because of their implausibility. Many investigators do not check for interaction at all—a practice I do not endorse. Almost none check for three-way and higher-order interactions, especially if the two-way interactions are nonsignificant. This seems more reasonable. Thus, of the three methods listed in Sec. 13.7.1, method 1, the least conservative, is actually the standard method for handling higher-order interactions. Simple interactions, however, should usually be tested.

We can distinguish three types of test for interaction:

• An overall test that includes in a single model all the interactions to be tested, and tests the change in fit when all are dropped from the model
• Variable-by-variable tests that perform one test for all the interactions involving a single regressor—for instance, all interactions involving age
• Simple interaction tests that test specific interactions

Of course, tests on individual terms should be corrected for the number of tests performed—a number that may be large. When performing variable-by-variable tests you should also correct for the number of tests performed, but this will only be P. Each interaction is then counted twice; for instance, an age*income term is included in both the test of all interactions involving age, and in the test of all interactions involving income. But this does not violate any assumptions.

For reasons that will soon become clear, we will call the first of these approaches the broadest of the three, and the last the narrowest. Breadth has two advantages and two disadvantages. The two advantages of breadth were both mentioned in Sec. 5.1.5, which discussed the power advantages of tests on R over tests on simple relationships. The same arguments are given here in the context of interaction effects.

First, broader tests yield vaguer conclusions, and vague conclusions are reached more easily than more specific conclusions. If several different interactions are largely independent and each has a small effect, then the set may have a large effect, so that a single test on the set may be much more powerful than separate tests on individual interaction terms.

The second advantage of broader tests for interaction is that they are capable of detecting patterns of complementarity *among interaction terms*. For instance, suppose occupational prestige correlates highly with education, and suppose a dependent variable of self-confidence is determined among men largely by occupational prestige relative to education, while this effect does not operate among women. Then gender interacts strongly with a linear function of education and occupational prestige, even though the individual gender*education and gender*prestige interactions may both be small.

The disadvantages of broad tests were not mentioned in Sec. 5.1.5, since they become important only when the number of terms is large relative to sample size, and this is more likely to occur with interaction terms than with first-order terms. The first disadvantage of broad tests occurs in its extreme form when there are many interaction terms, but only one has any effect on Y. Then a narrower set of tests is more likely to detect it. But the potential size of this advantage is limited by the number of interaction terms, since the variance explained by a single interaction term cannot exceed the variance explained by the set of all interaction terms. On the other hand, under complementarity the countervailing disadvantage of narrower tests can theoretically be enormous.

The second advantage of narrower tests is that they use fewer degrees of freedom, leaving more for the residual. The smaller the sample, the more important this advantage. In an extreme case an overall test can use up all degrees of freedom and then some, so its power is necessarily zero.

These countervailing advantages make a simple choice among the three approaches very difficult. About all that can be said unambiguously is that the relative advantages of broader tests increase with sample size, so the broader tests are especially recommended when samples are large and the narrower tests when samples are small, with variable-by-variable tests perhaps the most appropriate for intermediate sample sizes. If the purpose of the analysis is to dismiss the interactions, then the most conservative approach is to perform all three types of test, with the hope that all yield nonsignificant results.

Of course, an interaction's nonsignificance does not prove its nonexistence. So even when an interaction is nonsignificant, a very conservative investigator may want to take into account the possibility that it exists. This is method 3 in Sec. 13.7.1. It is relatively easy to do this for interactions between covariates; simply include them in the model. But to do it for interactions involving independent variables, you must either express the effects of interest conditionally (e.g. "The treatment is known to work for men but not for women") or else analyze the effects of those independent variables as average effects rather than simply linear effects. This is far more difficult, and currently requires the writing of specialized computer programs.

13.7.3   Summary

Despite its limitations, the standard approach to handling interactions is to test for two-way linear interactions and to dismiss all interactions not found to be significant. This includes a quadratic or square term for each numerical variable; the term can be thought of as the variable's interaction with itself. The tests may be separate, or variable by variable, or lumped into one overall test. Variable-by-variable tests followed, when appropriate, by tests of specific hypotheses will frequently provide the best compromise between power and specificity. Corrections for multiple tests should normally be used, even though in this case they make it easier to dismiss complications, because the number of interactions tested is often large. Quadratic terms need not be included in tests of interactions between two separate factors, unless the interaction is significant; then the quadratic terms should be added to see if the apparent interaction can be explained more parsimoniously as curvilinearity. Tests for three-way and higher-order interactions are usually not performed at all unless some of the two-way interactions are significant.

SUMMARY

13.1   Interaction in Two-Factor Designs

In an ANOVA design, interaction is a difference between differences. We can generalize this definition to the general linear model, by defining interaction as a change in slope. Interaction should not be confused with intercorrelation between regressors.

Simple linear interaction occurs when the slope of one regressor is linearly related to the value of another regressor. It can be represented by a regression equation with two linear terms and a constructed cross-product term. The coefficient of the cross-product term equals the amount that the X_1 slope increases for each 1-unit increase in X_2 and the amount that the X_2 slope changes for each 1-unit change in X_1. Like any other coefficient in a regression, this coefficient will be tested for significance by most regression computer programs. The hypothesis that the cross-product coefficient is zero is the hypothesis that the regression lines are all parallel and no interaction exists. A regression surface with a cross-product term can be represented either as a series of nonparallel lines or as a warped surface in three-dimensional space that looks like a bent cookie tin.

13.2   Interaction with Categorical Regressors

If we have one continuous and one dichotomous regressor, then the surface just described reduces to two nonparallel lines. If we use simple dummy coding for the dichotomous regressor, then its coefficient equals the difference between the Y intercepts of the two groups, the coefficient of the continuous regressor equals the simple regression slope for the group coded 0, and the coefficient of the cross product equals the difference in simple regression slopes between the two lines.

If we fit a regression containing two dichotomous variables X_1 and X_2 and their cross product X_1X_2, the unique SS and F associated with the cross-product term will equal the SS and F for interaction in a 2×2 ANOVA design. However, unlike simple ANOVA, there is no requirement of equal cell frequencies, so long as each cell contains at least one observation. If X_1 and X_2 are both coded 0, 1, then $b(X_1X_2)$ will equal the difference between differences of cell means.

Interaction between a multicategorical variable and any other variable is represented by forming all possible cross-product regressors. The total SS for interaction is the unique SS for the set of cross-product terms. General linear model programs include a provision for generating all the necessary coded regressors.

13.3 Some Complications in Studying Interactions

Significant interaction is not often found in small or moderate-size samples. It may be that substantial interaction simply does not often exist in the real world.

Curvilinearity can masquerade as interaction if curvilinear terms are omitted from a regression while interaction terms are included.

Transforming Y can greatly affect the importance of interaction terms. When significant interaction is found, it is difficult to know whether it might vanish under some transformation of Y. This problem applies as much to classical ANOVA designs as it does to regression designs. Section 17.6 gives some solutions to this problem.

Cross-product terms measuring interaction are themselves global terms, but their presence transforms a regression's linear terms into local terms. If cross-product terms are included for X_j with several other regressors, then b_j is the estimated conditional effect of X_j when all those other regressors are 0. If we subtract a constant from all scores on a regressor X_j and then compute the cross-product X_jX_k with another variable X_k, then both b_j and b_k will change, as will a. Thus, changing the means of regressors by adding or subtracting points for every score will change the local coefficients in the equation but not the global ones.

13.4 Conditional Effects

The interaction between X_1 and X_2 changes the effects of X_1 and X_2 from constants into variables. We may wish to estimate a variable's conditional effects or its average effect or both. The simplest way to estimate the conditional effect of one regressor X_j is to derive the overall regression equation and then set the covariate equal to the desired value.

A more complex procedure gives the same estimated conditional effect, but also gives an estimate of its standard error. Subtract the conditional value of interest from all scores on the regressor of interest, and run the regression using cross-product terms computed from the adjusted regressor scores. The slope for the adjusted regressor is the estimated slope at the conditional value, and its printed standard error is the standard error at that conditional value.

13.5 Higher-Order Designs

A k-way interaction equals the change in any of its constituent $(k-1)$-way interactions associated with a 1-unit increase in the remaining regressor. It is represented by a k-way cross product. To test for a k-way interaction, always include linear terms in the regression, plus terms for the constituent lower-order interactions. If curvilinearity is possible, the regression should also include curvilinear terms to prevent curvilinearity from masquerading as inter-action. The inclusion of any higher-order interaction term changes from global to local all lower-order terms involving the same variables.

We can define *curvilinear interaction* as a change in the curvilinearity of one variable as another variable changes. Curvilinear interaction can mas-querade as higher-order interaction.

If three variables X_1, X_2, and X_3 all correlate highly, there can be substan-tial collinearity among the three two-way interactions X_1X_2, X_1X_3, and X_2X_3, so that they may be confused with each other if you test for interactions one at a time. This is unimportant if the focus is merely on dismissing interactions, as it usually is. But it should be considered if you want to demonstrate the existence of specific interactions.

13.6 Main Effects and Average Effects

The concept of a main effect applies only when all factors are categorical. The main effect of a dichotomous factor is simply an unweighted average of effects across the various levels of the other factors. When a factor is multicategorical, the hypothesis of no main effect means no main effect for any of the di-chotomous variables that could be coded to represent the factor.

Tests of main effects can be done by a method called *weighted squares of means*, so long as there is at least one case in each cell. This method is equivalent to using effect coding on all variables and testing the unique contri-bution of each variable's set of coded variables. The method is implemented in MYSTAT and SYSTAT by using the CATEGORY command in conjunction with the MODEL statement.

When main effects are inappropriate, we must consider the use of average effects. Three considerations may enable us to avoid this issue. First, the average effect of a factor A is not defined if A interacts with another factor B whose population distribution is not defined, as when B is a manipulated variable which does not even exist outside the laboratory. Second, A's average effect is not defined if A is multicategorical—though, of course, a multicategorical variable can be expressed as a set of dichotomous variables whose average effects are defined. Third, a variable's average effect is often of little interest if it interacts with other variables.

Three other considerations have the opposite effect of the last three: they drive us to consider the problem of average effects when we might have expected to avoid it. First, the most conservative approach is to consider the problem even if the factor of interest does not interact significantly with other variables, since a nonsignificant result does not prove a null hypothesis. Interaction is a complicating factor in the estimation of average effects, so if we assume its absence because it is not significant, then we are assuming away a complication that may actually exist. Second, even if sample size is very large, we should avoid the temptation to simply omit interaction terms and use the ordinary linear effects as estimates of average effects. Third, a variable's polynomial curvilinear effect can be considered a type of interaction. For instance, X_1^2 can be thought of as the interaction of X_1 with itself, while X_1^3 can be thought of as the three-way interaction of X_1 with itself and itself.

Most of the material in Secs. 13.6.4 and 13.6.5 is too dense to summarize here. The basic idea is that the effect of factor A on Y *at a given point of the regression surface* is the slope $d\hat{Y}/dA$ at that point on the surface. Therefore the estimated mean effect of A on Y is found by differentiating the regression equation with respect to A, computing the derivative for each case, and averaging across cases. If the population mean of any factor happens to be known, then using it instead of the sample mean improves the estimate of average effect.

13.7 Organizing Tests on Interaction and Curvilinearity

Often we cannot even test all possible interactions; there are too many of them, especially if we remember that not all interactions are simple linear interactions. But at least, simple linear two-factor interactions should usually be tested.

We can distinguish three types of test for interaction: an overall test, variable-by-variable tests, and simple interaction tests that test specific interactions. An overall test may be best if N is large and P is small. If an overall test is significant, then variable-by-variable tests can localize the effects. And a significant effect in this approach can be analyzed with a Bonferroni layering approach within the particular variable, to narrow the conclusion further to single interactions.

But unless N is very large relative to P, the overall test may lack power because of the small number of df left in the residual. On the other hand, simple interaction tests should be corrected for the number of tests performed—a number that may be large. Variable-by-variable tests represent a compromise between these two extremes. When using such tests you should correct for the number of tests performed, but this will be only P. Each interaction is then counted twice, but this does not violate any assumptions. If the purpose of the analysis is to dismiss the interactions, then you can even perform all three types of test, in the hope that all yield nonsignificant results.

KEY TERMS

interaction

simple effect

conditional effect

simple linear interaction

cross-product term

higher-order interaction

curvilinear interaction

main effect

weighted squares of means

SS types I, II, III, and IV in SAS

average effect

weighted effect coding

SYMBOLS AND ABBREVIATIONS

CV

PROBLEMS

It was discovered that a machine in a manufacturing plant was leaking noxious fumes, which were suspected of lowering the cardiovascular efficiency of workers in its vicinity. To test this possibility, workers were tested on a treadmill to see how many steps they could take before their pulses increased 10 beats per minute. Tested were 11 workers who had been exposed, and 13 comparable workers who had not. Results are shown in Table 13.7, separately for smokers and nonsmokers.

1. Coding exposure and smoking 1, and coding nonexposure and nonsmoking 0, find the size of the interaction in two ways: by hand from the four cell means, and as a regression slope in computer output.

TABLE 13.7
Cardiovascular efficiency of four groups

Artificial data

	Exposed smokers	Exposed nonsmokers	Nonexposed smokers	Nonexposed nonsmokers
	48	52	70	74
	64	60	73	67
	57	74	67	72
	46	67	64	70
	53	72	75	71
		68	72	
			66	
			69	
Means	53.6	65.5	69.5	70.8

2. If you were to compute by hand the sum of squared deviations of scores from their own cell means (do not do so unless you want to), what value would that equal on the previous computer output?

3. Test the significance of the interaction in at least three of the following ways:
   (a) By hand, defining the interaction as a contrast with the values 1, −1, −1, and 1, and using the formulas for testing a contrast in Secs. 10.2.1 and 10.2.2
   (b) Using SYSTAT or MYSTAT with neither the CONTRAST nor the CATEGORY command
   (c) Using the CATEGORY command in SYSTAT or MYSTAT
   (d) Using the CONTRAST command in SYSTAT
   (e) Using SAS PROC REG
   (f) Using SAS PROC GLM without the CONTRAST command
   (g) Using the CONTRAST command in SAS PROC GLM
   Show that the answers you get by these methods are equivalent.

4. Using the data set on life satisfaction in Table 5.7, test the significance of the interaction between sex and education in a regression predicting satisfaction from income, education, sex, and age.

5. In the regression of Prob. 4, test the composite null hypothesis that education does not interact with any of the four regressors including itself.

6. Suppose you were able to repeat the tests of Probs. 4 and 5 and several others like them in a much larger sample and you found the p values shown in Table 13.8. I, E, S, and A denote, respectively, income, education, sex, and age. For purposes of this question, a *pooled* test is defined as a test of the null hypothesis that the named variable has no simple interactions with any variable including itself. (A variable's "interaction with itself" is really a quadratic term, and a quadratic term is meaningless for a dichotomy, so no such term is included for sex.) The df column shows the numerator df of each F test. Tests with one df are normally performed as t tests rather than F tests, though that does not affect the present analysis. Testing at the .05 level, perform a Bonferroni layering analysis of the sort recommended in the chapter for moderate sample sizes, layering both across and within pooled effects.

TABLE 13.8
Some significance levels in a four-way model

Test	p	df
I pooled	.006	4
E pooled	.012	4
S pooled	.04	3
A pooled	.06	4
$I \times I$	.08	1
$I \times E$	.04	1
$I \times S$	.009	1
$I \times A$	.015	1
$E \times E$	.06	1
$E \times S$	.018	1
$E \times A$	.12	1
$S \times A$	.15	1
$A \times A$	.07	1

DETECTING
AND
MANAGING
IRREGULARITIES
IN DATA

This chapter has three major sections. The first describes the various kinds of irregularities that can exist in a data set, and statistics (mostly called *diagnostic statistics*) for detecting them. The second describes four methods for dealing with irregularities, including one that is easily implemented in MYSTAT. The third describes the conclusions that can be reached by these methods.

14.1 DETECTING IRREGULARITIES

Diagnostic statistics are new, having been developed mostly since 1975. These statistics have three major purposes. First, they can detect violations of the secondary standard assumptions of normality and homoscedasticity. Second, they can detect clerical errors. These can be serious; a single human weight accidentally recorded as 1600 instead of 160 pounds can distort an entire analysis. Third, diagnostic statistics can be used to examine data that are suspect for some reason, such as questionnaire results from someone who appears not to have understood directions, to see whether those data are irregular in some way.

Diagnostic statistics can easily be misused. For instance, a clinical psychologist could easily find the three patients whose deletion from the sample would most improve the apparent effectiveness of a new treatment and then examine the folders of those three patients until some pretext for deleting them turned up. But any tool can be misused, and diagnostic statistics are an important part of modern regression analysis. The best protection against misuse is to require authors to explain in detail the reasons for deleting any cases and the ways in which the deletions affect the major conclusions.

Diagnostic statistics may also occasionally detect violations of the primary assumption of linearity. But intuition suggests they would not be nearly as powerful for that purpose as the methods of Chap. 12, and my own analyses confirm that conjecture. In one comparison, a simple test on the X^2 term detected nonlinearity 986 times out of 1000, while a diagnostic statistic (the highest t residual, with a Bonferroni correction) detected the problem only 333 times.

One of the best ways to detect irregularities is to search for cases that are extreme in one sense or another. Such cases are often called *outliers*, though many authors, including me, try to confine that term to a particular type of extreme case.

14.1.1   Types of Extreme Case

A case can be extreme or noteworthy in three major ways: in its *distance* from the regression surface; in its *leverage*, or potential for moving the surface; and in its *influence*, or actual effect on the surface. The simplest measure of a case's distance is its residual, though more refined measures of distance are given in Sec. 14.1.5. The best-known measure of leverage is denoted h_i, which measures the "atypicalness" of case i's pattern of regressor scores. For instance, being 55 and being pregnant are each not unusual, but if pregnancy and age were the regressors in an analysis, then a 55-year-old pregnant woman would have a high value of h_i, since the combination is highly unusual. Case i's score on Y has no effect on h_i, which is computed entirely from regressor scores. In simple regression, h_i increases linearly with the squared deviation score x_i^2. A more precise definition of h_i appears in Sec. 14.1.4.

If case i is very close to the regression surface, then it may be low in influence even if it is high in leverage, since deleting the case would not move the regression surface much. The best-known measure of influence was suggested by Cook (1977); it is here denoted Cook_i. It is proportional to the sum of squared changes in values of $\hat{Y}$ when case i is deleted from the sample. To be precise, let d_{ij} denote the change in the value of $\hat{Y}_j$ when regression predictions are rederived after case i is deleted from the sample. Then

$$\text{Cook}_i = \frac{\Sigma d_{ij}^2}{P \times MSE}$$

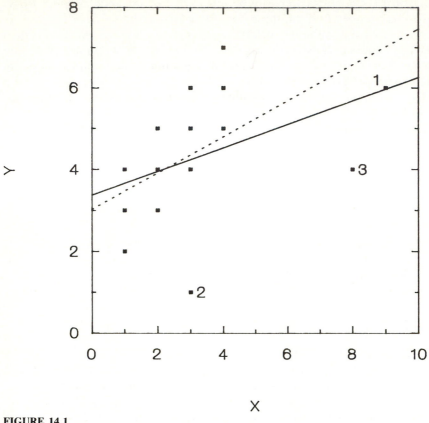

FIGURE 14.1
Leverage, distance, and influence.

where the summation is over j. Thus Cook_i is a measure of the amount the whole regression plane moves when case i is deleted from the sample. A case can have high influence only if it is high on both distance and leverage. In a sense defined more precisely in Sec. 14.1.6, a case's influence is the product of its distance and leverage.

The distinctions among distance, leverage, and influence are illustrated most easily in simple regression. In Fig. 14.1, the regression line is the solid line. Of the 15 cases, case 1 is highest in leverage, since it is farthest from the mean on X. Case 2 is the case highest in distance; it is farthest from the regression line. Case 3 is the case highest in influence; it is the only case fairly high in both distance and leverage. The dotted line shows where the regression line would fall if case 3 were removed from the sample; note the substantial difference between the two lines.

Unfortunately, terminology in this area is not yet standardized, so the terms employed here conflict with some usage. For instance, the best-known measure of influence is inaptly called "Cook's distance," and SYSTAT and MYSTAT call a user's attention to a case with high leverage by warning that the case has "undue influence." In the terminology used here, a case's influence is the effect its deletion would have on the regression surface as a whole, and leverage is not actual influence but the potential for influence created by the pattern of regressor scores.

Cases with high leverage are called *leverage points*. Cases high on distance are simply *outliers*, though as mentioned earlier this term is often used more loosely to describe any kind of extreme case. Cases high on influence are *influential cases* or *influential points*.

In multiple regression we can also distinguish between *total influence* and *partial influence*, and between *total leverage* and *partial leverage*. Partial influence measures a case's influence on a single regression slope b_j, while total influence measures its influence on the entire surface. If, say, 10 regressors include 9 covariates and 1 independent variable X_1, then we may be more concerned about cases that substantially affect b_1 than about cases with high total influence. Partial leverage measures the extremeness of a case's score on the portion of X_j independent of all other regressors; it shows the case's potential influence on b_j. There is no need for a concept of partial distance, since it would be defined most simply as a case's residual in a partial scatterplot, and that quantity exactly equals the case's residual in the overall regression.

Leverage differs qualitatively from distance in that cases extreme in distance can invalidate statistical inference in regression. Extreme leverage violates none of the standard assumptions of regression, since there are no requirements about the distribution of regressors. However, high leverage suggests a loss of power and precision of estimation. This is seen most easily with a single dichotomous regressor like sex. If a sample includes 85 men and 15 women, the difference between men and women on Y is estimated with less precision than if the sample includes 50 men and 50 women. In the former case, SYSTAT and MYSTAT will warn the investigator that the 15 women have high leverage.

14.1.2 Shortcomings of "Eyeballing" the Data to Detect Extreme Cases

When computers were in their infancy, one of the major arguments given against their use in data analysis was that computer analysis made it easier to overlook extreme cases, even when they reflect obvious errors such as adult human weights of 16 or 1600 pounds. Statistical computer programs quickly met this objection by routinely printing out the highest and lowest score on every variable, so that such extreme cases were forcefully drawn to the investigator's attention. Today's computer programs go far beyond this basic step, enabling us to detect extreme cases that could never be discovered by eyeball.

For instance, suppose a company's personnel file contains the following case:

Present salary: $15,000
Hours worked per week: 20
Starting salary: $10,000
Hours worked per week on starting: 40
Number of years worked: 2

This case is very unusual: the employee earns the same per hour as a $30,000-per-year person working 40 hours per week, so the employee's pay per hour is 3 times what it was only 2 years earlier. Such an unusual case may represent a clerical error or some other factor worth checking. But ignoring any one of the five entries in this person's file would make the case appear normal. For instance, if "number of years worked" were not shown, we might assume it was 10 or 20 instead of 2, and the case would appear normal. A similar argument can be made about any of the other entries. Only when all five entries are considered together is the case identified as unusual. But if these five entries were scattered among 20 or 30 other entries about the same employee, it is highly unlikely that normal "eyeballing" would reveal anything amiss. As we shall see, modern diagnostic methods can easily detect such cases.

This example could illustrate any of the three types of extreme case. If the five variables in the example are five regressors, then the case probably has high leverage. But if "present salary" is the dependent variable predicted from the other four, then the case is probably an outlier, lying far from the regression plane. And it may greatly affect the regression plane as well, making it influential.

14.1.3   Some Basic Tools for Analyzing Irregularities

This section describes some basic commands in MYSTAT, SYSTAT, and SAS that are used repeatedly in this chapter to discover and manage extreme cases. We will use simple residuals to illustrate these tools, since the more complex measures of leverage, distance, and influence have not yet been introduced. And simple residuals do have some important uses—notably in the construction of partial scatterplots, which reveal cases with high partial leverage or partial influence.

Residuals can be computed directly from regression coefficients. For instance, in the data set on life satisfaction in Table 5.7, the regression equation for predicting satisfaction (satis) from education (educ) and age is

$$\hat{Y} = 64.49566 + 1.21814 \times educ + .07675 \times age$$

If you type

>let resid = satis − (64.49566 + 1.21814*educ + .07675*age)

on the editor's command line in SYSTAT or MYSTAT, a variable arbitrarily named RESID will be added to the data set, and the scores on RESID will be the residuals in the previous regression.

Residuals can also be found with the SAVE command in SYSTAT and MYSTAT. For instance, you could type

>model satisfy = constant + educ + age
>save deviancy
>estimate

In MYSTAT, these commands create a new data set arbitrarily named DE-VIANCY, which contains scores on all the variables in the original regression, plus scores on six other variables named ESTIMATE, RESIDUAL, LEVER-AGE, STUDENT, COOK, and SEPRED. Scores on ESTIMATE are values of $\hat{Y}$, while scores on RESIDUAL are the residuals. As described later, scores on LEVERAGE, STUDENT, and COOK are measures of leverage, distance, and influence, respectively, and scores on SEPRED are the standard errors of values of $\hat{Y}$.

The SAVE command in SYSTAT works much the same way, but it has too many options to discuss here; see the SYSTAT manual. Residuals are produced in SAS by the P option plus several other options. In SAS, most of the important diagnostic statistics are available only in PROC REG, not in PROC GLM.

In SYSTAT, residuals can be found and analyzed more easily by combining the SAVE command with SYSTAT's ability (described more fully in Sec. 17.3) to handle multiple dependent variables in a single model statement. For instance, the commands

>model satis, age = constant + income +educ
>save satisage
>estimate

will yield the regression coefficients for predicting both satisfaction and age from income and education. And the file arbitrarily named SATISAGE in this example will contain, among other things, the residuals in the two regressions, named, respectively, RESIDUAL(1) and RESIDUAL(2). Then the commands

>use satisage
>plot residual(1)*residual(2)

in SYSTAT's graphics module will produce a partial scatterplot of satisfaction with age; recall from Sec. 2.3.4 that the partial scatterplot is defined as the plot of the two sets of residuals. Points with high partial leverage or partial influence should be clearly visible in this plot. And in module MGLH the commands

>use satisage
>model residual(1) = constant + residual(2)
>save partdiag
>estimate

will produce a file arbitrarily named PARTDIAG containing SYSTAT's usual regression diagnostics for this scatterplot, thus giving measures of partial leverage and partial influence in numerical form.

The SYSTAT and MYSTAT commands RANK and SORT can be used to rank and sort residuals and other diagnostic statistics. For instance, if you had created the data set DEVIANCY as described above, then the MYSTAT commands

>use deviancy
>save rankres
>rank residual

would take that data set, replace the scores on the variable named RESIDUAL by their ranks (lowest score is ranked 1), and save the modified data set under the arbitrarily chosen name RANKRES. Two or more variables can be ranked at once. For instance, the command

>rank residual, satis

following USE and SAVE commands would replace scores on both RE-SIDUAL and SATIS by their ranks.

The SORT command will sort scores on a variable. The MYSTAT commands

>use deviancy
>save sortres
>sort residual

will create a new file arbitrarily named SORTRES, in which the cases are sorted in order of their residuals—lowest (most negative) first. If you want to retain the original case numbers, then before sorting you must use the editor to put that information into a new variable. The case numbers are actually considered to form a variable named CASE in the data set. Thus the command

>let casenum = case

will add to the data set a new variable arbitrarily named CASENUM containing the original case numbers. Once again, the SYSTAT version of the SORT command has too many options to discuss here.

It is sometimes useful to normalize a variable—to force its scores into approximately a normal distribution. Mathematicians recognize several ways to do this, but the one available in SYSTAT and MYSTAT uses a command called ZIF for "z inverse function." If $0 < x < 1$, then zif(x) is defined as the value of z with area x to its left in a standard normal distribution. For instance, zif(.975) = 1.96 and zif(.025) = -1.96.

To normalize a variable X in SYSTAT or MYSTAT, apply the ZIF function to the ranks of X after dividing the ranks by $(N + 1)$. This division creates a set of scores spaced evenly between 0 and 1. For instance, if $N = 19$, dividing the ranks 1, 2, 3, . . . , 19 by 20 yields the 19 values .05, .10, .15, . . . , .95. Applying the ZIF function to these values yields values of -1.645, -1.282, -1.036, . . . , 1.645. There is a sense in which these 19 scores are as close to being normally distributed as 19 scores can be.

After X has been ranked, the division and the normalization can be done in a single command. For instance, if there are 19 cases, then in the MYSTAT editor type

>let x = zif(x/20)

This produces the normal scores shown above. Some uses of these scores are discussed in Sec. 14.1.8 and 14.2.3.

14.1.4 Measuring Leverage

As mentioned earlier, a case's leverage h_i is determined entirely by its pattern of regressor scores; Y scores have no effect. In simple regression, h_i is determined simply by case i's distance from M_X. In multiple regression, we can think of h_i as a measure of the atypicalness of case i's *pattern* of regressor scores. This is illustrated in Fig. 14.2, where case A has the highest value of h_i because it has the least "typical" pattern of scores, even though it is closer to the center of the array than several other cases.

This point can be clarified though the use of Gaussian ellipsoids. Figure 5.1 showed a bivariate normal distribution in three dimensions. If a slice were cut through that distribution, parallel to the floor or base of the figure, the slice would be an exact ellipse, centered at the means of X and Y. This is a Gaussian ellipse. The closer the slice to the floor of the figure, the larger the ellipse. Thus, there is actually a continuous series of Gaussian ellipses of different sizes, produced by different parallel slices. These ellipses all have the same center and the same degree of oblongness or eccentricity, as measured by the

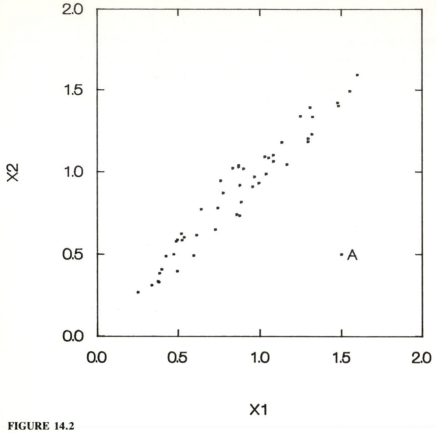

FIGURE 14.2
The meaning of leverage.

ratio of their greatest length to their shortest. The higher the correlation in absolute value, the greater this eccentricity. For any bivariate sample, the family of ellipses can be found from the two means, the two standard deviations, and the correlation between the two variables. Figure 14.3 shows two Gaussian ellipses for the data of Fig. 14.2. If the population were assumed to have a bivariate normal distribution, then the Gaussian ellipses would be the ellipses estimated to include the largest proportion of the population for their size.

When there are more than two variables, Gaussian ellipsoids are direct extensions of bivariate ellipses. And leverage values h_i rank the points in the distribution according to the number of Gaussian ellipsoids they fall outside. Case A is the only one that falls outside both ellipses in Fig. 14.3, so it is the case with highest leverage.

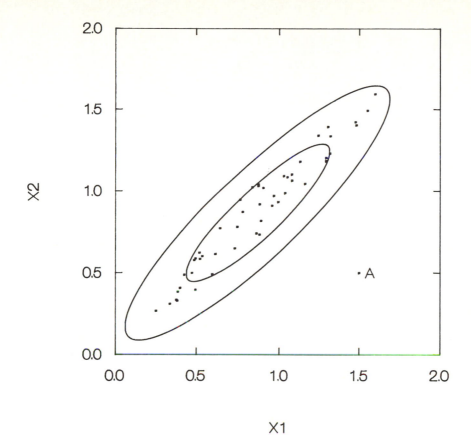

FIGURE 14.3
Gaussian ellipses and leverage.

The standard assumptions of regression do not include any assumptions about the distribution of regressor scores, so leverage points do not contradict these assumptions. But these points should usually be examined at least briefly, if only to check for clerical errors. And the concept of leverage is used repeatedly in our discussion of distance and influence in Secs. 14.1.5 and 14.1.6.

Values of h_i can range from a low of $1/N$, for cases exactly at the center of the array of X scores, up to 1.0. In any regression including an additive constant (see Sec. 3.5.1), the mean value of h_i is exactly $(P + 1)/N$.

The concept of "atypicalness" can be defined more precisely in terms of P mutually uncorrelated linear functions of the regressors. Any set of mutually uncorrelated functions will serve; readers familiar with factor analysis can think of the principal components of the regressors, while others can think of

TABLE 14.1
Computation of h for the weight-loss data set

Case	X_1	X2.1	$z(X_1)$	$z(X2.1)$	MD	h
1	0	−2	−1.291	−1.054	2.778	0.378
2	0	0	−1.291	0.000	1.667	0.267
3	0	2	−1.291	1.054	2.778	0.378
4	2	−3	0.000	−1.581	2.500	0.350
5	2	−1	0.000	−0.527	0.278	0.128
6	2	1	0.000	0.527	0.278	0.128
7	2	3	0.000	1.581	2.500	0.350
8	4	−2	1.291	−1.054	2.778	0.378
9	4	0	1.291	0.000	1.667	0.267
10	4	2	1.291	1.054	2.778	0.378

the variables X_1, X2.1, X3.12, X4.123, and so on, which are mutually uncorrelated. For instance, consider the data set on weight loss in Sec. 2.1.1. In Sec. 2.2.1, we found the scores on X2.1, the portion of X_2 (food intake) independent of X_1 (exercise). The scores on X_1 and X2.1 are repeated in the first two columns of Table 14.1.

The *Mahalanobis distance* of person i is here denoted MD_i, and is defined as the sum of the squared standard scores of person i on these uncorrelated variables. MD_i will be the same regardless of what particular linear functions of the regressors are used, so long as those functions are mutually uncorrelated. In Table 14.1 the columns headed $z(X_1)$ and $z(X2.1)$ show standard scores on X_1 and X2.1, and the entries in the column headed MD equal $z^2(X_1) + z^2(X2.1)$.

MD_i is an obvious measure of the "atypicalness" of person i's pattern of regressor scores. And h_i is linearly related to MD_i by the formula

$$h_i = \frac{MD_i + 1}{N}$$

The table's final column shows the values of h_i for our example. In practice, values of h_i are found by computer programs; the purpose of this example is to help convey the meaning of h_i. We can think of this formula as the definition of h_i, though mathematical statisticians define h_i as the ith diagonal entry in the matrix $X(X'X)^{-1}X'$, where X is the $N \times P$ matrix of regressor scores augmented by a column of 1's.

An alternate interpretation of h_i arises if we choose a set of variables that are mutually uncorrelated in the sample of $N - 1$ cases *excluding* person i, standardize the variables in that sample, and let MDX_i denote the sum of person i's squared scores on those variables. Then

$$h_i = \frac{MDX_i + 1}{MDX_i + N}$$

Another interpretation of h_i involves an indicator variable scored 1 for person i and 0 for everyone else in the sample. We shall call this an *identifying* variable; the identifying variable for person i is denoted I_i. If we predict I_i from all the regressors by multiple regression and call the resulting multiple correlation HR_i, then HR_i will be 0 only if person i is exactly in the middle of the scatterplot. The higher HR_i is, the more easily can case i be distinguished from all other cases by its pattern of X scores, and the higher h_i. Thus HR_i and HR_i^2 are also natural measures of the "atypicalness" of person i's pattern of regressor scores, and h_i is linearly related to HR_i^2 by the formula

$$h_i = \frac{(N - 1) \times HR_i^2 + 1}{N}$$

Still another interpretation of h_i focuses on its effects rather than its actual meaning. While e_i denotes the vertical distance of case i from the ordinary regression plane, let ex_i denote the vertical distance of case i from the plane that would be derived in the sample of $N - 1$ cases that excludes case i. Then it can be shown that

$$h_i = \frac{ex_i - e_i}{ex_i}$$

In words, this equation says that h_i equals the proportion by which case i lowers its own residual by pulling the regression plane toward itself. This may be the simplest single "definition" of h_i, but it should not be considered the primary definition of h_i because it obscures the important fact that h_i is computed entirely from regressor scores. It also reduces to the indeterminate equation $h_i = 0/0$ when $ex_i = 0$, while h_i is just as precisely defined for such cases as for any other case.

A final interpretation of h_i is not especially important or illuminating, but it is very simple and explains the diagnostic variable SEPRED calculated by SYSTAT and MYSTAT. We can take any given set of regressor scores, such as $X_1 = 5, X_2 = 3, X_3 = 8$ for three regressors, and ask how much the value of $\hat{Y}$ calculated for that set of regressor scores will vary from sample to sample when regressions are calculated in many different samples of size N. Thus, even though Y_i is the known score of a single individual, we can detach the set of regressor scores from the person and think of $\hat{Y}$ for the set of regressor scores as a statistic which has a standard error like any other statistic. SEPRED is the estimated standard error of that statistic. $SEPRED_i$ is related to h_i by the simple formula

$$SEPRED_i = SE(\hat{Y}_i) = \sqrt{MSE \times h_i}$$

Thus h_i can be thought of as the relative uncertainty with which $\hat{Y}_i$ is estimated.

In summary, h_i equals the proportion by which a case reduces its own residual, also equals the ratio of $Var(\hat{Y}_i)$ to MSE, and is related to four measures of the "atypicalness" of case i's pattern of regressor scores: the case's Mahalanobis distance measured either relative to the whole sample or to the sample excluding case i, the predictability of I_i from the P regressors, and the number of Gaussian ellipsoids outside which the case falls.

As mentioned above, high values of h_i do not by themselves violate the standard assumptions of regression. But if it is assumed that regressor scores form a multivariate normal distribution, this assumption can be tested with the formula

$$F = \frac{N - P - 1}{N} \times \frac{h_i - 1/N}{1 - h_i} \qquad df = P, \, N - P - 1$$

from Belsley, Kuh, and Welsch (1980, p. 68). We could use this test to examine a case whose validity we had suspected beforehand. But if we simply select the highest value of h_i and test it with this formula, then we should use the Bonferroni method of Sec. 11.1 to correct for the fact that we have selected the most significant of N possible results.

14.1.5 Measuring Distance

Points far from the regression plane are *outliers*. These points are more important than leverage points, since a sufficiently extreme outlier always represents a violation of the standard assumptions of regression, while leverage points do not. An outlier may or may not also be a leverage point.

Outliers should be checked for clerical errors, but they may also suggest revisions in the model. For instance, if 80% of the cases in a sample were women and 20% were men and most of the outliers were men, it might suggest that different models fit men and women and the predominance of women in the sample forces the model to fit the women's data. Thus, developing separate models for men and women may be appropriate. Or if there are too few men to develop a separate model for men, a large number of male outliers may suggest that males be excluded from the sample and the conclusions of the model be applied only to women.

Ordinary residuals provide the simplest measure of distance, but they can be refined in three successive steps. First, they can be corrected for the fact that cases with high leverage pull the regression surface toward them more than other cases do. Next, these leverage-corrected residuals can be standardized, to yield a scale-free measure of distance from the regression plane. Finally, the standardized residuals can be transformed to yield residuals that can be compared directly with a t distribution. The residuals produced by these successive steps are monotonically related to each other—the cases highest on any one are highest on all three.

The first step—correction for leverage—is based on the fact that under the standard assumptions, $E(e_i^2) = {}_T\text{Var}(Y.X)*(1 - h_i)$, so the cases with the highest values of h_i tend to have the smallest residuals. But this equation shows that

$$E\left(\frac{e_i^2}{1 - h_i} \right) = {}_T\text{Var}(Y.X)$$

So we can define the leverage-corrected residual as $e_i/\sqrt{1 - h_i}$, and the distribution of these residuals will be independent of h_i.

Leverage-corrected residuals are rarely used, and we shall not even give them their own notation. But one useful fact is that the square of the leverage-corrected residual is the amount $SS(\text{error})$ would drop if the regression were recomputed after excluding case i.

It can be shown that the expected value of the squared leverage-corrected residual is $_r\text{Var}(Y.X)$, which, of course, is estimated by MSE. Thus, leverage-corrected residuals can be standardized by dividing them by $\sqrt{MSE}$. *Standardized residuals* will be denoted by str_i, and thus

$$str_i = \frac{e_i}{\sqrt{(1 - h_i)\, MSE}}$$

One use of the standardized residual is to calculate a value we shall call *augmented* h_i, defined as the value of h_i computed relative to Y and the regressors, not just the regressors. The formula is

$$\text{Augmented } h_i = h_i + (1 - h_i) \times \frac{str_i^2}{df_r}$$

For the reasons explained in Sec. 6.4.3, we often think of regressor scores as fixed, deliberately ignoring the fact that we might observe different scores in a different sample. Since values of h_i are computed entirely from regressor scores, we do not normally even ask about the sampling distribution of values of h_i. But residuals involve Y, and thus we can ask about their sampling distribution. Under the standard assumptions, standardized residuals should have approximately a standard normal distribution, especially in large samples. But a further transformation to *Studentized residuals*, also called *t residuals* and denoted tr_i, eliminates the approximation and yields residuals with an exactly known distribution. The transformation is accomplished by the formula

$$tr_i = str_i \sqrt{\frac{df_r - 1}{df_r - str_i^2}}$$

A standardized residual of 1 transforms to a Studentized residual of 1, and a standardized residual of 0 transforms to a Studentized residual of 0. But for other values, the absolute value of a standardized residual always falls closer to 1 than the absolute value of the Studentized residual. As their name implies, t residuals exactly follow a t distribution under the standard assumptions of regression. The variable STUDENT, in the file produced by SYSTAT's or MYSTAT's SAVE command, contains t residuals.

A useful interpretation of t residuals uses the concept of the identifying variable I_i introduced in Sec. 14.1.4, defined as a dummy variable scored 1 for case i and 0 for every other case. Imagine that I_i was added as another regressor to the main regression predicting Y. Like all other regressors, it would receive a value of t which tests whether its b differs significantly from 0.

That t is the t residual. Thus it can be tested for significance with a t table. But $df = N - P - 2$ instead of $N - P - 1$, since adding I_i to the regression lowers df_r by 1.

t residuals are sometimes misinterpreted as testing the null hypothesis that case i falls on the true regression line. If that were so, then the proportion of significant t residuals would approach 1 as N increases, since almost no cases in fact fall exactly on the true regression line. But if the standard regression assumptions hold, we expect only 5% of the t residuals to be significant at the 5% level, no matter how large the sample. The hypothesis tested by each t residual is that case i falls within a normal distribution of scores around the regression line. Of course, if that hypothesis is rejected, we also reject the hypothesis that case i falls on the regression line.

Because the number of t residuals is N, we should apply a Bonferroni correction to the significance levels associated with them. That is, the largest t residual is considered significant only if its significance level is still below some chosen value alpha (typically .05) even after being multiplied by N. This is one possible test of the collective set of regression assumptions—linearity, homoscedasticity, normality, and random sampling. A significant result from this test suggests that at least one of these assumptions is false.

Another test of the standard assumptions of regression does not rely so heavily on the single highest t residual, and may be considerably more powerful for detecting curvilinearity or heteroscedasticity, or any violation which affects many residuals somewhat without affecting any single residual too greatly. In this test we pick some arbitrary probability, count the number of t residuals significant beyond this level, and use the binomial distribution to test whether this number is greater than would have been expected by chance. For instance, in a sample of 50 cases, by chance we would expect five t residuals to be significant at or beyond the .10 level. If we observe 11 such residuals, the binomial distribution tells us that the probability of observing so many is only .0094; this indicates that at least one of the standard assumptions must be violated. The binomial test is not perfectly accurate for this use: it assumes that the N t residuals are statistically independent, and they are not quite independent. But in tests I have run, the error was small. Of course, chi-square or other approximations to the binomial distribution may be used instead of the binomial itself.

All these successively more refined residuals correct for the *bias* in distance measures introduced by differences in leverage, but there is no way to adjust for differences in the *precision* of distance measures. Distance from the *population* regression plane is estimated less precisely for points with high leverage than for other points, because the leverage point's ability to pull the sample regression plane toward itself makes it hard to tell whether the point is far from the population regression plane. Thus if a case were particularly suspect for some reason but were found to have a low t residual, that finding would be of little comfort if the case also had high leverage.

14.1.6 Measuring Influence

The best-known measure of influence is inappropriately named *Cook's distance; Cook's influence* would be better. In SYSTAT and MYSTAT, values on this measure appear in the file produced by the SAVE command, under the variable name COOK. We shall denote it by $Cook_i$. As described in Sec. 14.1.1, $Cook_i$ is proportional to the sum of squared changes in values of $\hat{Y}$ caused by removing case i from the sample.

Cook$_i$ can be thought of as the product of a particular measure of distance and a particular measure of leverage for case i. The key formula is

$$Cook_i = str_i^2 \times \frac{h_i}{(1 - h_i) \times P}$$

As we saw earlier, str_i^2 ranks cases in the same order as tr_i, the best measure of distance from the regression surface. And all the rest of the right-hand side of the equation is a measure of leverage in that it ranks cases in the same order as h_i.

Some authors have stated that $Cook_i$ is distributed as F with $P + 1$ and $N - P - 1$ degrees of freedom. But in fact the mean of an F distribution is always over 1.0, and values of $Cook_i$ are rarely found as high as 1.0. Also, the standard assumptions of regression do not require any particular distribution for h_i. But h_i has a major effect on $Cook_i$, so no general rule can be stated for the distribution of $Cook_i$.

14.1.7 Measuring Partial Influence and Partial Leverage

As mentioned earlier, partial influence and partial leverage are sometimes more important than total influence and leverage, especially when a few crucial independent variables are combined with many covariates. The INFLUENCE option in SAS PROC REG yields values called DFBETAS, for "difference in fitted beta, standardized." An entire matrix of such values is produced. Each single value of DFBETAS shows the influence of a single case on a single value of b_j. A positive value means that the case has raised b_j; a negative value means that b_j has been lowered. It might seem that values of DFBETA or DFBETAS could be found only by repeating the regression N times, once after deleting each case, but simpler formulas have been found that achieve the same effect.

SYSTAT and MYSTAT have no comparable option, but satisfactory measures of influence can be found without too much trouble. These are the measures of influence and leverage found in a partial scatterplot. To find the variables that define this plot, separately regress Y and X_j onto the other $P - 1$ regressors, record the coefficients in the regressions, and use the methods of Sec. 14.1.3 to find the residuals in the two regressions. Then partial influence and partial leverage are influence and leverage as found by the SAVE command when the Y residuals are regressed onto the X residuals.

This measure of partial influence is not quite as good as DFBETAS, since DFBETAS measures a case's influence only on b_j, whereas the other value measures the case's influence on both the slope and the additive constant in the partial scatterplot. But case i's effect on the additive constant usually affects $Cook_i$ far less than the case's effect on regression slopes, so this is not a serious problem.

The PLOT command in SYSTAT and MYSTAT can also be used to plot the two sets of residuals against each other. Influential cases, like case 3 in Fig. 14.1, should be readily visible. All P partial scatterplots are found in SAS by the single option PARTIAL.

In using SYSTAT or MYSTAT for any of these purposes, remember that you must run two regressions for each regressor studied. In particular, the Y residuals in the partial scatterplot for X_1 are not the same as those for X_2 or for any other regressor. The INFLUENCE and PARTIAL options in SAS yield output for all regressors from a single command.

14.1.8 Detecting Heteroscedasticity

Extreme cases have occupied most of Sec. 14.1, but this section describes tests for homoscedasticity that do not depend on unusual single cases. The absence of homoscedasticity is called *heteroscedasticity*; it means that the conditional distributions of Y have different variances.

The most common type of heteroscedasticity occurs when $_T\text{Var}(Y.X)$ is largest for the highest or lowest values of some regressor or combination of regressors. But also of concern is a pattern we shall call *butterfly heteroscedasticity*. An extreme case of butterfly heteroscedasticity is illustrated in Fig. 14.4. Y ranges widely for high and low values of X, and less widely for intermediate values of X.

When butterfly heteroscedasticity holds for X_j, the actual standard error of b_j can greatly exceed the calculated standard error. When the opposite pattern holds, looking like $<>$, the true standard error may be smaller than the calculated one.

Butterfly heteroscedasticity can occur in at least two common ways. One occurs if the population of interest is composed of two subpopulations, with one subpopulation ranging more widely than the other on all variables. For instance, the citizens of any nation include natives and immigrants. The immigrants will typically be from many nations and continents, while the natives by definition are all from one. So the immigrant subgroup is likely to be more heterogeneous on many variables than the native subgroup. When subgroup A is more heterogeneous than subgroup B on all variables in the analysis, then the extremes of each regressor will be dominated by group A, which also has a greater variance on Y than group B. This will produce butterfly heteroscedasticity. It can be calculated that when a population consists of two equal-sized bivariate normal subpopulations, and $_TS_X$ and $_TS_Y$ are twice as large in

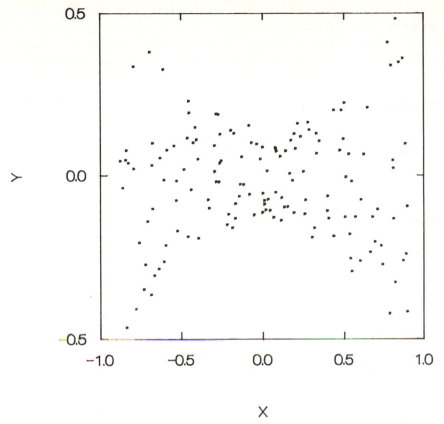

FIGURE 14.4
Butterfly heteroscedasticity.

one subpopulation as in the other but the simple regression slopes are equal, then $_TSE(b)$ is 17% larger than the value calculated from the ordinary formula. This does not sound like a large effect, but if a standard error is 17% larger than is believed, the probability of finding significance at the .05 level is nearly twice the nominal level.

The second common circumstance producing butterfly heteroscedasticity is failure to include necessary interaction terms in an analysis. If a regression slope is positive among women and negative among men, then a scatterplot which includes both men and women will exhibit butterfly heteroscedasticity.

We can test for ordinary and butterfly heteroscedasticity in the same analysis. The tests rely on the fact that under the standard assumptions, $E(tr_i^2)$, the variance of tr_i, is identical for all values on all regressors. So a significant association between tr_i^2 and any regressor or set of regressors is evidence for heteroscedasticity, and we can test for heteroscedasticity by testing the independence of tr_i^2 from the regressors.

In SYSTAT and MYSTAT the easiest way to test this independence is by normalizing tr_i^2. Methods for normalizing scores were discussed at the end of Sec. 14.1.3. If the SAVE command has been used to store values of tr_i under the variable name *student*, then we can proceed as follows to normalize tr_i^2 under the variable name *trsqnorm* for "*t* residual squared, normalized." First type the command

>let trsqnorm = student^2

on the command line of the editor, to create scores on tr_i^2. Save this file, then RANK *trsqnorm*. Then return to the editor and apply the ZIF command to the ranks divided by $(N + 1)$. For instance, if $N = 20$, type

>let trsqnorm = zif(trsqnorm/21)

These steps make *trsqnorm* approximately normally distributed, and under the assumption of homoscedasticity it is also independent of all the regressors. So to test for ordinary heteroscedasticity we could predict *trsqnorm* from the regressors and test the significance of the multiple correlation. But butterfly heteroscedasticity would make *trsqnorm* related not so much to the regressors themselves as to the squares or other second-order terms of the regressors. For instance, in simple regression butterfly heteroscedasticity would make *trsqnorm* tend to be high for the highest and lowest values of X and low for intermediate values of X, so that X^2 will contribute to the prediction of *trsqnorm*. So a comprehensive test for heteroscedasticity should test the significance of the multiple correlation with both second-order terms and linear terms in the regression. If the sample is large enough, this may include both square and crossproduct terms; otherwise just use square terms.

If this correlation is significant, apply the rules of previous chapters to identify the factors producing the relationship. Typically start by testing all second-order terms as a set. If this set is nonsignificant, drop the second-order terms and examine the individual effects of the first-order terms by looking at the test on each regressor.

Or if some regressors are of special importance in the main analysis—for instance, if there are a few independent variables among many covariates—you may wish to study them individually regardless of the significance of the multiple correlation. To do this, first look at the significance of the regressor's square term. A significant contribution of this term to *trsqnorm* implies *partial butterfly heteroscedasticity*. If this term is nonsignificant, drop it and look at the contribution of the linear term to *trsqnorm*. Significance here implies ordinary *partial heteroscedasticity,* in which $_T\text{Var}(Y.X)$ is higher for either the highest or lowest values of X_j.

In earlier sections we said a general test on the whole set of standard assumptions can be performed by applying a Bonferroni correction to the highest *t* residual. That is correct, but that test is not nearly as powerful at detecting heteroscedasticity as the tests of this section. In 1000 bivariate samples of size 50 from artificial populations with butterfly heteroscedasticity, the highest t residual tested at the .05 level failed to discover the problem in 371 samples, while the test in this section failed in only 6.

14.1.9 Keeping the Diagnostic Analysis Manageable

Especially at the level we have reached, statistical analysis is an art, not a set of mechanical rules. But some general suggestions on the conduct of diagnostic analyses should be helpful. These suggestions are illustrated with real data in Chap. 16.

We saw in Chaps. 12 and 13 that curvilinearity and interaction can distort analyses that ignore them, and the same is true of the various kinds of irregularities considered in this chapter. Thus all these chapters concern potential complications. When should you check for them? You cannot do everything at once. There is no "right" order of checking for these complications, any more than there is a right order of checking for problems when you buy a used car. But there are three reasons for normally applying diagnostic methods before checking for unanticipated curvilinearity or interaction. First, diagnostic methods can uncover clerical errors, and clerical errors clearly should be detected as early as possible. Second, at least the basic diagnostic methods are easier, and it is always sensible to do easy things first. Third, experience suggests that diagnostic methods uncover complications more often than tests for curvilinearity and interaction, and you want to find any problems as soon as possible.

A diagnostic analysis always concerns a particular regression, so the first step in a diagnostic analysis is to identify the regression you would run if you knew there were no irregularities. The diagnostic analysis should focus on that regression.

The next step is to choose particular diagnostic measures and tests. We have described measures or tests for no fewer than nine types of irregularity—involving leverage, distance, influence, partial leverage, partial influence, heteroscedasticity, partial heteroscedasticity, butterfly heteroscedasticity, and partial butterfly heteroscedasticity. And each "partial" measure can be computed for each regressor separately. Thus the number of possible analyses may be large. You should not try to use every one of these tools in every possible way. Rather, you should focus on the three major goals of the diagnostic analysis: to check for clerical errors, to examine previously suspect cases, and to test the standard assumptions of regression. To check for clerical errors, check the cases with the highest scores on overall leverage, distance, and influence. Previously suspect cases should be checked primarily for excessive influence—either total influence or partial influence for the most important regressors.

To test the standard assumptions of regression, I believe that nearly every analysis should include the Bonferroni-corrected test on the highest t residual, and the tests for ordinary and butterfly heteroscedasticity described in Sec. 14.1.8. And if the major focus of the analysis is on a single regression slope b_j, then tests for partial ordinary and butterfly heteroscedasticity should be performed for that one regressor. For any of these tests, absence of significance does not prove that the assumptions hold, but at least violations of the assumptions have been given a chance to show themselves. When violations are detected, the methods of Sec. 14.2 may be useful.

14.2 DEALING WITH IRREGULAR DISTRIBUTIONS

Neither heteroscedasticity nor nonnormality affects the expected values of the statistics a, b_j, and MSE, so these statistics provide unbiased estimates of $_Ta$, $_Tb_j$, and $_T\text{Var}(Y.X)$ even in the presence of these conditions. But hypothesis tests and confidence bands can be invalidated by violations of any of the standard assumptions.

Occasionally, violations of normality and homoscedasticity can be cured by transforming Y. For instance, if cases with the highest values of Y are found both far above and far below the regression plane, it may be that replacing Y by $\log(Y)$ will cure the problem. Or violations may be eliminated by identifying a subpopulation which fits the regression model less well than other groups, allowing the investigator to specify that the model's conclusions do not apply to that subpopulation or perhaps to develop a separate model for that subpopulation. Or violations may be dealt with by using robust methods for finding significance levels and confidence limits, which apply even when some standard assumptions are violated.

There are two general types of robust approach. One uses robust formulas for estimating the regression plane itself; the other uses ordinary formulas for the regression plane but uses more robust formulas to calculate significance levels or estimates of standard errors. The former approach essentially gives lower weight to outliers. This raises fundamental questions about the purpose of the regression. After all, downweighting an outlier can lead to a regression plane that fails to represent adequately the fact that such outliers do occasionally occur. Therefore we shall consider only the second approach, in which the investigator uses ordinary regression formulas to derive the best-fitting plane but employs robust methods to find standard errors or significance levels.

We shall consider four methods: the jackknife method, the bootstrap method, the normal-scores test, and permutation tests. All four are practical only with computers, but with the right software they take anywhere from a few seconds to a few minutes on an ordinary personal computer. More detailed discussions of all four may be found under the appropriate entries in the *Encyclopedia of Statistical Sciences* (Kotz & Johnson, 1982–1988).

14.2.1   The Jackknife Method

The jackknife method was given its name by J. W. Tukey on the ground that it may not be the very best tool for anything at all but it is a serviceable tool in a great many situations. To implement the method, divide the total sample into k groups of equal size, where k is at least 10. In fact, k may be as high as N, so that each "group" contains only one case. Compute the statistic of interest after deleting group 1 from the sample; add group 1 back in, delete group 2, and recompute the statistic; then add group 2 back in, delete group 3, and recompute the statistic; and continue in this manner through all k groups. Then enter the standard deviation of the k recomputed values into a formula to estimate the standard error of the statistic. In summary, you estimate the standard error of the statistic from the amount the statistic changes when small groups or single cases are deleted from the sample. The ratio of the observed statistic to its standard error is then compared with the standard normal distribution.

14.2.2   The Bootstrap Method

Like the jackknife method, the bootstrap method has been suggested for estimating the standard error of virtually any statistic. It is based on a simple idea: if we make absolutely no assumptions about the nature of the population distribution, then the sample distribution is in every respect the best estimate of the population distribution. That is, if our sample is of size 50, then our best assumption-free estimate of the population distribution is that one-fiftieth of the cases is exactly like case 1, another one-fiftieth is exactly like case 2, and so on. We then draw, say, 100 independent random "resamples" of size 50 from this imaginary population. This is the same as drawing 100 "resamples" *with replacement* from the original sample. We then compute the statistic(s) of interest in each "resample."

In one version of the bootstrap method, we then calculate the standard deviation of all 100 values of each statistic, and use that as the estimated standard error of that statistic. As with the jackknife method, the normal curve is then ordinarily used to test hypotheses about the statistic or to find a confidence band. In the other version of the bootstrap we never compute a standard error but base our inferences on the number of "resamples" yielding statistics in various ranges. For instance, if a slope b_j is positive in the original sample, the proportion of the resamples that yield negative values of b_j can serve as the significance level for testing the null hypothesis $_T b_j = 0$.

14.2.3   Normal-Scores Tests

To perform a normal-scores test on the association between two numerical variables X and Y, normalize both variables and then use the ordinary correlation test to test the association between the two sets of normal scores. The justification for the test is similar to that for tests using rank-order correlations, but normal scores tests are at least sometimes more powerful (Fieller and Pearson, 1961).

Both X and Y should be normalized for most applications, even though the standard assumptions of regression do not require normal X. The reason is that if Y were truly normal rather than artificially normalized, the Y-scores in different samples would all be different, while for instance if $N = 19$ the normalized Y-scores in every sample will be -1.645, -1.282, -1.036, etc. This deviation from true normality is more important if X is grossly nonnormal than if X is approximately normal.

Normal scores can be used to test for partial as well as simple relationships. Since the null hypothesis being tested concerns the correlation between two sets of residuals, those are the scores that should be normalized. That is, to test the $Y1.23$ partial relationship, regress Y and X_1 on X_2 and X_3, normalize the residuals in both regressions, and use the t test in the next paragraph to test the independence of the two sets of normalized residuals. Thus to test all P partial relationships tested by an ordinary regression program, P different sets of Y-residuals and P sets of X-residuals must be found and normalized. The normal scores test is distorted by tied scores, but fortunately residuals are rarely tied.

Normal-scores correlations tend to be slightly higher in absolute value because the normal scores on X and Y are always identical. For instance, if two variables X and Y are independent and truly normal, then if $N > 2$, there is zero probability of finding a perfect correlation between them in a sample. But in a sample of size N, the probability is $1/N!$ of finding a perfect correlation between two sets of normal scores. My own very small Monte Carlo study of normal scores tests, which computed 1000 correlations between the normal scores of regression residuals for each of 6 combinations of N and P ($N = 20, 50$; $P = 2$, 7, 12), consistently indicated that the accuracy of the normal scores test for a partial relationship is improved by replacing df_r by $df_r - 4$, both in computing t and in finding p from t.

14.2.4   An Example Using MYSTAT

The normal-scores test can be performed fairly easily in MYSTAT. We shall illustrate with the data set on life satisfaction in the problems of Chap. 5, testing the association between income and satisfaction with age and education controlled. First make a copy of the data set, and work with the copy, since you will make changes to it that cannot be undone. One simple way to make a copy is to call the data set into the editor and then save it under another name.

We will suppose the copy is called SATIS2. In SATIS2, regress satisfaction and income on education and age, and record the coefficients. Then call SATIS2 into the editor. On the editor's command line, type

```
>let yres = satisfy − (1.21814*educ + .07675*age)
>let xres = income − (2.39780*educ + .12677*age)
```

The numbers within the parentheses are the coefficients of EDUC and AGE found in the previous step. YRES and XRES are arbitrarily chosen names standing for Y residual and X residual, respectively. Except for the additive constants in the regressions, YRES and XRES are the portions of satisfaction (Y) and income (X) independent of education and age. The additive constants can be ignored, because the next step will be to rank these residuals, and the additive constants have no effect on the ranks.

The correlation between XRES and YRES is the partial correlation between income and satisfaction with education and age controlled; it equals .531. But we want to correlate these residuals after normalizing them. To do this, save SATIS2, exit the editor, and type

>use satis2
>save satis3
>rank xres, yres

These commands create a new file named SATIS3, in which the scores on variables XRES and YRES are replaced by their ranks.

Then call SATIS3 into the editor. On the editor's command line, type

>let xnorm = zif(xres/21)
>let ynorm = zif(yres/21)

These commands create two new variables arbitrarily named XNORM and YNORM containing the normal scores on variables XRES and YRES. The letters ZIF in these commands stand for "z inverse function," which finds the z value with area [rank(xres)]/21 or [rank(yres)]/21 to its left. The value 21 is $N + 1$, as described in Sec. 14.2.3. For instance, for the fifth-ranked residual the program calculates $5/21 = .238$, $zif(.238) = -.712$, which means that $-.712$ is the score below which $\frac{5}{21}$ of a standard normal distribution lies.

Save the file under the same name SATIS3 and exit the editor. The commands

>use satis3
>pearson xnorm, ynorm

find the correlation r between XNORM and YNORM. In this example, $r = .520$, which is very close to the ordinary partial correlation of .531. Replacing df_r in the usual hypothesis test by $df_r - 4$ gives the formula

$$t = r \sqrt{\frac{df_r - 4}{1 - r^2}}$$

We have $N = 20$, $P = 3$, $df_r = N - P - 1 = 16$, $df = df_r - 4 = 12$, $t = 2.109$, $p = .057$ (two-tailed).

This procedure may sound complex, but you can appreciate its simplicity if you consider that the results are far beyond what most scientists could have found until recently. Finally you may wish to erase the files SATIS2 and SATIS3 created by these commands.

14.2.5   Distribution-Free Normal-Scores Confidence Bands on b's

The normal-scores test can be extended to derive distribution-free confidence limits for each b_j. (The meaning of *distribution-free*, both in general and in the present context, is discussed in Sec. 14.3.3.) In simple regression analysis, the hypothesis $_Tb = k$ is equivalent to the hypothesis that $Y - kX$ has 0 correlation with X. Thus, in simple regression analysis, distribution-free confidence limits for b would be those values of k that make $Y - kX$ just significantly correlated with X by the normal-scores test. Note that the values normalized are values of $Y - kX$, not Y. The same method can be applied to a partial relationship by regressing Y and X_j on all remaining regressors and applying the procedure described in Sec. 14.2.4 to the residuals in the resulting regressions.

14.2.6   Introduction to Permutation Tests

Permutation tests, also called *randomization tests,* are robust tests of independence. They have two disadvantages: they take several minutes instead of several seconds of computer time, and like the bootstrap method they do not give exactly the same result each time. They are discussed in more detail in Edgington (1980).

To understand permutation tests, consider first a simple correlation r_{XY}. Suppose we take the scores entering this correlation and keep the X scores in their original order but randomly scramble the order of the Y scores and recompute the correlation. Suppose we do this 999 times, so that we have 1000 correlations including the original one. Suppose we find that the original correlation is the twenty-eighth highest of all 1000 values. We can then say that if these X scores had been matched randomly with these Y's, the probability is only $\frac{28}{1000}$, or .028, that the original correlation r_{XY} would have ranked so high. This value .028 is the one-tailed significance level p.

Permutation tests contain a source of error not present in ordinary hypothesis tests: too few rescramblings. But use of too few rescramblings lowers the power, not the validity, of the tests.

14.2.7   Permutation Tests in Regression

In the example of Sec. 14.2.6, we held constant the order of scores on a single variable X. In multiple regression, we can hold constant the entire matrix of regressor scores, rescramble the order of the Y's many times, and recompute R and all values of b_j each time.

It turns out that the great bulk of the regression computations need be performed only once. Those familiar with matrix formulas for regression can consider the matrix equation $b = (X'X)^{-1}X'Y$. If we define $G = (X'X)^{-1}X'$, then the computation of G includes the great bulk of the computations needed to find the vector b. But in a permutation test, G need be computed only once. One easy way to permute or rescramble Y's is to put them in their own data set, and then add a variable of random numbers to that data set and sort the data set on the random numbers.

Rescrambling the Y's themselves is actually not as powerful as an alternative method. To see why, suppose b_1 has a high positive value and one person has extremely high scores on X_1 and Y but the score on Y is about what we would predict from the high score on X_1. The very high Y score will increase the variance (across the rescramblings) of every b_j. This is as it should be for b_1, but it will also be true for every other b_j tested. Thus, in testing the unique contribution of any regressor X_j, the most powerful procedure will generally be to use the portion of Y independent of all regressors except X_j. This means we should use a different column of residuals for each X_j, and still another column for testing R. Thus we use altogether $P + 1$ different columns of Y residuals.

14.2.8 Relative Advantages of the Four Robust Methods

The validity of robust methods typically increases with sample size. I have studied the validity of the four robust methods (five, if you count the two versions of the bootstrap method described earlier) under a variety of distributions in samples of size 20, which is about the smallest one would ever use for regression.

Two principal conclusions emerged from this analysis. One is that at least for small samples, violations of homoscedasticity are far more serious than violations of normality. All methods were found to be seriously invalid under either butterfly or ordinary heteroscedasticity, even when normality was retained. The other conclusion was that when normality is violated but homoscedasticity is retained, serious invalidity occurs only for the jackknife method and both versions of the bootstrap method. The normal-scores test, the permutation test, and even the ordinary distribution-bound tests on b_j introduced in Chap. 5 are all reasonably valid even under extreme violations of normality. The distributions explicitly studied were the chi-square distribution with 1 df, which is an extremely skewed distribution, and the Cauchy distribution, which is an extremely peaked but symmetric distribution.

The three tests that performed well under nonnormality are all designed specifically for studying association between variables, while the jackknife and bootstrap methods can also be used, for instance, to test a hypothesis about the center or spread of a single distribution. Thus the results can be summarized by saying that the methods designed specifically to test association work well even under nonnormality, but no methods work well under heteroscedasticity when samples are very small. This conclusion suggests that the various tests for heteroscedasticity, described in Sec. 14.1.8, are at least as important as the Bonferroni-corrected test on the highest t residual, which at this writing is the best-known single test on the secondary assumptions of regression.

14.3   CONCLUSIONS POSSIBLE WHEN SECONDARY ASSUMPTIONS ARE VIOLATED

14.3.1   Violations of Normality and Homoscedasticity

We shall coin the term *statistical nihilism* to refer to the view that the assumptions of homoscedasticity and normality are rarely fully satisfied but without them even robust methods no not allow us to draw useful conclusions. This view is illustrated by an example with two populations. In the first, 99.9999% of the cases are at -1, while the other .0001% of cases are at $+999,999$. In the second population, 99.9999% of the cases are at $+1$, while the other .0001% of cases are at $-999,999$. The two populations have equal means, but even if samples with thousands of cases are drawn from each population, even robust methods will show a highly significant difference between means in almost every sample.

This section describes four lines of defense against statistical nihilism. In summary, they are:

1. Examples as extreme as this are rare.
2. A robust test allows us to draw a *nonparametric conclusion,* which may be less useful than a parametric conclusion but is still of considerable value.
3. A relatively mild assumption called *unidirectionality* allows us to draw very strong conclusions from robust tests.
4. Even if we are not sure of unidirectionality, assuming its presence is simpler or more parsimonious than assuming its absence. Thus a significant result from a robust test does not establish a conclusion beyond doubt, but it shifts the burden of proof to those who would deny the conclusion.

For simplicity we shall first discuss the simple comparison of two groups, and later explain how our general conclusions apply to all questions about the simple or partial association between two variables.

The first line of defense against statistical nihilism is that examples like the last one are rare. The next paragraph develops this point. The paragraph is written for specialists; others may skip it.

The central feature of the previous example is extreme skewness that is positive in one population and negative in another. But in actual data, skewness rarely exceeds that of the chi-square distribution with 1 df; its mean is 1, but 0 is both its lower limit and its mode, and that mode reaches up to infinity. Let $CS1$ denote a variable with this distribution, and let population A's distribution be that of $(CS1 - 1)$, while B's distribution is that of $(1 - CS1)$. Then just as in the previous example, both populations have means of 0, but one has high positive skew while the other has high negative skew. In a test I ran, 2000 samples were drawn, each containing 50 cases from each population. A permutation test with 100 repetitions was applied to the two sample means to test the null hypothesis that the two means are equal. If the test were perfectly valid, we would expect 100 of the 2000 results to be significant at the 5% level, one tailed; the actual number observed was 160. Given the extreme nature of the test, this result supports the conclusion that permutation tests are reasonably valid even under extreme circumstances.

The second line of defense against statistical nihilism involves the use of a *nonparametric conclusion*. A mean is a parameter, so the conclusion that one mean exceeds another is a conclusion about parameters, or a parametric conclusion. A nonparametric conclusion can say something about a frequency distribution, or about the difference between two frequency distributions, without specifying a conclusion that applies to any particular parameter.

The most useful nonparametric conclusions concern cumulative frequency distributions. An ordinary frequency distribution shows the number of cases *at* each possible score, while a cumulative frequency distribution shows the number of cases *at or below* each possible score. A cumulative frequency curve is always flat or rising; it never falls. From a cumulative frequency curve you can read directly each percentile score; for instance, the 80th percentile score is the score below which 80% of the cases fall.

If group A significantly exceeds group B by a robust test, you can conclude that in the population, group A's cumulative curve falls to the right of group B's at one or more points. (It is easy to be confused by the fact that A's curve falls below B's even though A's scores are higher. But remember that the highest scores are those on the right, so that a curve farther to the right reflects higher scores.) This means that at least some of the percentile scores of group A exceed the corresponding scores of group B. It also means there is at least one monotonic transformation of the scale which makes the mean of group A exceed the mean of group B. (A monotonic transformation is a transformation, such as a logarithm, which keeps all cases in the same order. Thus $X' = X^2$ is a monotonic transformation of X if all scores are positive, but not if some are negative.)

The third defense against statistical nihilism involves an assumption we shall call *unidirectionality*. This is the assumption that two cumulative frequency curves never cross, though they may touch at many points. Under the assumption of unidirectionality, if a robust test shows that group A exceeds group B in some respect, we can conclude that A's mean exceeds B's and that this will be true after any monotonic transformation of the variable. Thus the rather modest assumption of unidirectionality, in conjunction with a robust test, yields a very strong conclusion.

The fourth argument against statistical nihilism rests on the distinction between the *simplest* conclusion and the *most conservative* conclusion consistent with the observed data. The assumption of unidirectionality is in a sense simpler or more parsimonious than its opposite—the assumption that two cumulative frequency distributions do cross. For instance, if you know that group A's 80th percentile score exceeds group B's, the best guess is that the 60th percentile scores differ in the same direction. Thus, if a robust test shows that group A exceeds group B in some respect, the simplest or most parsimonious conclusion (though certainly not the most conservative) is that A exceeds B in all respects—that is, A's cumulative frequency curve never falls to the left of B's, so that group A's mean exceeds group B's and would do so after any monotonic transformation of the variable. A significant result from a robust test does not prove this strong conclusion, but it tends to shift the burden of proof to those who would deny the conclusion.

How do these arguments apply to the association between two numerical variables X and Y? We can think in terms of a family of cumulative frequency curves of Y—one curve for each value of X. If a significantly positive association between X and Y is found by a robust test, it implies the nonparametric conclusion that at least one of these curves falls at least partly to the right of a curve for some lower value of X. The assumption of unidirectionality is that no two curves ever cross. And the simplest conclusion consistent with a significant positive association is that the conditional mean of Y increases monotonically with X, and would do so after any monotonic transformation of Y. This strong conclusion is not proved, but the significant result tends to shift the burden of proof to those who disagree.

14.3.2   Violations of Random Sampling

In Sec. 4.1.3 we mentioned briefly that valid statistical inferences may be drawn without random sampling, and even without either random sampling or random assignment. An example there concerned the increase, from one decade to another, in the proportion of female professors hired by a college. Or suppose a club of 50 local business people includes 30 retailers and 20 others. If 25 of the retailers but only 10 of the others vote to change the by-laws, it is valid to perform a 2×2 test for a nonchance association between vote and type of business. But again there is no hint of either random assignment or random selection from a broader population. When used in this way, tests of association test the null hypothesis of *randomness*—the hypothesis that the association observed between two variables is caused solely by chance.

Both these examples could be instances of *nonsampling,* because there is no sampling at all. In the first example, we might study every professor ever hired by the college; in the second example, the entire membership of the business club. But it is often difficult to distinguish between nonsampling and nonrandom sampling. For instance, in the second example we might think of the local club as a nonrandom sample of the population of members of other business groups in its city or in the nation. The distinction between nonsampling and nonrandom sampling is unnecessary as well as ambiguous, since the types of conclusions we can draw are much the same under both conditions. The important distinction we must make is between the presence and absence of random sampling.

Nonrandom sampling and nonsampling are very common in both large-scale and small-scale research. On a small scale, suppose an experimenter posts an ad asking for volunteers to serve as subjects in an experiment and uses the first 20 people to sign up. Those subjects are not a random sample from any broader population. But if the experimenter assigns the 20 subjects randomly to conditions, then the experiment has random assignment without random sampling. On a larger scale, many behavioral scientists study the entire population of interest: analysts at the Educational Testing Service have data from all students who take College Board tests, workers at the American Association of Medical Colleges have data on every applicant to an American medical school, census analysts have data from virtually the entire population of the United States, and so on.

When a significant association between two variables is found under random sampling, it establishes both the *replicability* and the *meaningfulness* of the association. We shall say that an association is meaningful if valid hypothesis tests indicate that chance may be excluded from a list of the possible causes of the association. We shall say that the association is replicable if we can have a certain confidence that a nonzero association will be observed again under specifiable conditions—such as drawing a large second sample from the same population. Finding a statistically significant association under nonrandom sampling establishes the association as meaningful though not replicable. This at least allows us to speculate on the causes of the association, as in the examples above concerning the college's hiring practices or the business club.

When there is random assignment without random selection, as in the example above involving the sign-up sheet, we can go beyond such speculation. Then the existence of a causal relation can be demonstrated, though its generality or replicability is still unknown. In particular, if scores of a treatment group are significantly above those of a control group, then you have shown that the treatment increases at least some scores. This can be a finding of some interest if the dependent variable is a trait thought to be wholly beyond control, such as baldness—or if the independent variable is thought to be something imperceptible, such as infrared light or messages flashed on a screen too fast to be seen consciously.

Conclusions of this sort can sometimes be generalized to a broader population, even without random sampling. This is possible if it is assumed that causation is unidirectional—that the treatment does not lower anyone's score on the dependent variable. Then even without random sampling, we have shown that the treatment increases the population mean, merely by demonstrating that it raises at least some scores in the population.

14.3.3 Statistical Methods for Nonrandom Samples

Under nonrandom sampling or nonsampling, the null hypothesis tested is the hypothesis of randomness rather than independence in a larger population. Permutation tests are fully valid tests of randomness, regardless of the nature of the distributions.

The Fisher 2 × 2 test, the Mann-Whitney test, and the test on the Spearman rank-order correlation are all permutation tests that do not require the user to execute large numbers of permutations. These tests use either dichotomies or ranks, and apply to cases in which we can calculate the exact distribution of the test statistic across all possible permutations. Thus, these are excellent tests of randomness under nonsampling or nonrandom sampling. These and other permutation tests may also be used as distribution-free tests when random sampling is present.

The terms *distribution-free* and *nonparametric* are not synonymous. A test is distribution-free if it requires no specific distributional assumptions such as normality. A test is nonparametric if it allows no parametric conclusions. Most distribution-free tests are nonparametric, but the terms are not identical.

With large data sets, acceptably accurate tests of randomness may be provided by the methods of this chapter and those of Chap. 5, even though the latter were derived from the theory of normal distributions. Thus, methods that theoretically require normal populations may be useful even in the absence of a broader population, let alone normality in that population.

SUMMARY

14.1 Diagnostic Statistics

A case can be extreme or noteworthy in three major ways: in its *distance* from the regression surface; in its *leverage*, or potential for moving the surface; and in its *influence*, or actual effect on the surface. In multiple regression we can also distinguish between *total influence* and *partial influence*, and between *total leverage* and *partial leverage*.

Leverage differs qualitatively from distance in that cases extreme in distance can invalidate statistical inference in regression. Extreme leverage violates none of the standard assumptions of regression, since there are no requirements about the distribution of regressors. However, high leverage suggests a loss of power and of precision of estimation.

Modern methods can detect aberrant cases that could never be detected by "eyeballing" the data. By combining the SYSTAT or MYSTAT SAVE command with the RANK, SORT, and PLOT commands and with the ability to compute residuals from the command line of the editor, a great variety of diagnostic statistics and plots can be found.

A case's leverage is determined entirely by its pattern of regressor scores; Y scores have no effect. In simple regression h_i is determined simply by case i's distance from M_X. In multiple regression we can think of h_i as a measure of the "atypicalness" of case i's *pattern* of regressor scores. h_i equals the proportion by which case i reduces its own residual, also equals the ratio of Var($\hat{Y}_i$) to *MSE*, and is related to four measures of the "atypicalness" of case i's pattern of regressor scores: the case's Mahalanobis distance measured either relative to the whole sample or relative to the sample excluding the case, its position relative to Gaussian ellipsoids, and the predictability of the case's identifying variable I_i from the P regressors. Under the restrictive assumption of multivariate normality, there is a test for the distribution of h.

Ordinary residuals, leverage-corrected residuals, standardized residuals, and Studentized residuals or t residuals are successively more refined measures of distance from the regression surface. The last three are monotonically related; the cases highest on one are highest on all. Studentized residuals can be compared with tables of the t distribution to test the standard assumptions of regression, though a Bonferroni correction should be used if the highest t residuals are selected *post hoc*. Variants of the binomial test can also be applied to t residuals.

All these successively more refined residuals correct for the *bias* in distance measures introduced by differences in leverage, but there is no way to adjust for differences in the *precision* of distance measures. Thus if a case were particularly suspect for some reason but were found to have a low t residual, that finding would be of little comfort if the case also had high leverage.

The standard measure of influence is here denoted Cook$_i$, which can be thought of as the product of a particular measure of distance and a particular measure of leverage for case i.

Partial influence and partial leverage are sometimes more important than total influence and leverage, especially when a few crucial independent variables are combined with many covariates. Measures of these qualities are directly available in SAS, and closely related measures can be computed in SYSTAT and MYSTAT.

We can test for both partial and overall heteroscedasticity by normalizing values of tr_i^2 and regressing the normalized scores onto the regressors. By adding square and cross-product terms to this regression, we can test for partial and overall butterfly heteroscedasticity.

We have described measures or tests for no fewer than nine types of irregularity—involving leverage, distance, influence, partial leverage, partial influence, heteroscedasticity, partial heteroscedasticity, butterfly heteroscedasticity, and partial butterfly heteroscedasticity. And each "partial" measure can be computed for each regressor separately. Therefore the number of possible analyses may be large. You should not try to use every one of these tools in every possible way. Rather, you should focus on the three major goals of the diagnostic analysis: to check for clerical errors, to examine previously suspect cases, and to test the standard assumptions of regression. Section 14.1.9 suggests ways for keeping the number of diagnostic analyses in check.

14.2 Dealing with Irregular Distributions

The jackknife method, bootstrap method, normal-scores test, and permutation test are four methods for dealing with irregular distributions—five, if you count two versions of the bootstrap. All these methods have been found to be seriously invalid under either butterfly or ordinary heteroscedasticity, even when normality is retained. But when normality is violated and homoscedasticity is retained, serious invalidity occurs only for the jackknife method and both versions of the bootstrap method. The normal-scores test, the permutation test, and even the ordinary distribution-bound tests on b_j introduced in Chap. 5 are all reasonably valid even under extreme violations of normality. Therefore it seems that the various tests for heteroscedasticity are at least as important as the Bonferroni-corrected test on the highest t residual, which is currently the best-known single test on the secondary assumptions of regression.

14.3 Conclusions Possible When Secondary Assumptions Are Violated

We coined the term *statistical nihilism* to refer to the view that the assumptions of homoscedasticity and normality are rarely fully satisfied but without them even robust methods do not allow us to draw useful conclusions. Four lines of defense against statistical nihilism are described:

1. Extreme violations of these assumptions are rare.
2. A robust test allows us to draw a *nonparametric conclusion,* which may be less useful than a parametric conclusion but is still of considerable value.
3. A relatively mild assumption called *unidirectionality* allows us to draw very strong conclusions from robust tests.
4. Even if we are not sure of unidirectionality, assuming its presence is simpler or more parsimonious than assuming its absence. Thus a significant result from a robust test does not establish a conclusion beyond doubt, but it shifts the burden of proof to those who would deny the conclusion. This argument distinguishes between the simplest conclusion and the most conservative conclusion consistent with the observed data.

When there is no random sampling—or even no sampling at all from a larger population—hypothesis tests can still be used to test the *meaningfulness* of an association if not its *replicability.* Meaningfulness means the association cannot be explained by chance. Permutation tests are especially appropriate for this purpose, though the ordinary tests of regression can be thought of as approximate tests for this purpose.

KEY TERMS

diagnostic methods	standardized residual
suspicious cases	Studentized residual
nonnormality	t residual
heteroscedastity	precision
extreme case	Cook's distance
distance	DFBETA
leverage	DFBETAS
influence	INFLUENCE option
leverage point	butterfly heteroscedasticity
outlier	partial butterfly heteroscedasticity
influential case	jackknife method
partial influence	bootstrap method
partial leverage	normal-scores test
ESTIMATE	permutation test
RESIDUAL	randomization test
LEVERAGE	statistical nihilism
STUDENT	nonparametric conclusion
COOK	distribution-free
SEPRED	unidirectionality
RANK command	randomness
SORT command	nonsampling
Mahalanobis distance	replicability of association
identifying variable	meaningfulness of association

SYMBOLS AND ABBREVIATIONS

h_i ex_i d_{ij} MD_i MDX_i I_i HR_i str_i augmented h_i tr_i

PROBLEMS

The following questions concern the data set on life satisfaction in Table 5.7 and the problems of Chap. 5—specifically, the regression modeling satisfaction as a function of income, education, race, sex, and age.

1. Suppose case 12 were particularly suspect for some reason. By the guidelines of Sec. 14.1.9, does the diagnostic analysis confirm the suspicion?
2. Perform the normal-scores test for butterfly heteroscedasticity.
3. Is the highest t residual (the one farthest from zero) significant after a Bonferroni correction?

4. What one case would you most want to check for clerical errors after a preliminary diagnostic analysis? Call this case X. What two diagnostic statistics for case X make a check seem important?

5. Suppose the main analysis focuses primarily on the effect of income on satisfaction. Ranking *from the top*, what is the rank of case X's influence in the partial scatterplot relating income to satisfaction? If checking for clerical errors is expensive, how important does that check seem now?

6. Regardless of your answer to Prob. 5, suppose you do check and find no obvious clerical error. Perform a normal-scores test on the partial relationship between income and satisfaction.

CHAPTER
15

CHOOSING
SAMPLE
SIZES

15.1 BASICS

15.1.1 What This Chapter Is Not For

This chapter describes analyses you can perform before collecting data to estimate the sample size needed for a planned regression. These analyses concern the power of hypothesis tests and the precision of estimates; they tell you nothing about the robustness of the planned analysis. Robustness is the ability to draw valid conclusions even in the absence of standard assumptions such as normality and homoscedasticity. As illustrated in the headache-medicine example of Sec. 4.2.1, in planning a study there is not much useful we can say about robustness except that it continues to increase with sample size. As we saw there, a sample size of 10,000 may detect the odd but important case—such as a death caused by the experimental treatment—that may be missed in a sample of 5000. When the assumptions of normality and homoscedasticity are not met, a study may lack robustness even when its sample size far exceeds the recommendations of this chapter. On the other hand, if a study with unchallenged assumptions finds statistically significant results despite a sample smaller than that recommended here, nothing in this chapter is intended to criticize those results.

The methods of this chapter should also not be used after a study fails to find significant results, in an attempt to explain post hoc why the results are nonsignificant. For instance, suppose a Pearson correlation of .30 is observed in a sample of size 32. This is nonsignificant by a two-tailed test at the .05 level. It can be calculated that if the true correlation were .40, the power of this test would be only .62, which leaves a large .38 probability of a nonsignificant result. Power calculations like this are sometimes done to explain nonsignificant results.

This analysis is not incorrect, but it is less informative than a simpler alternative—the ordinary confidence band. In the present example, the 95% two-sided confidence limits on r are .58 and $-.05$. This band is so broad—the true correlation could be a high positive value, zero, or even negative—that we see that the sample size is too small to tell us much about the true correlation. Confidence bands are calculated by simple objective methods, and thus avoid discussions of arbitrarily chosen values such as the value of .40 in the previous paragraph. And confidence bands draw conclusions relevant to the observed value of the statistic, while power analysis ignores that value completely.

15.1.2   Random versus Fixed Scores

As described in Sec. 6.4.3, scores are considered fixed if the distribution of regressor scores is known before data are collected. If an investigator decides in advance that he or she will use 10 men and 10 women in a study, then scores on gender are fixed. But if the investigator simply draws a random sample of 20 cases from the population, and takes whatever mix of men and women the sample yields, then scores on gender are random. Power is slightly higher with fixed scores. The reason is easily seen in the current example; if a sample of 20 cases may turn out to contain, say, 17 men and 3 women, then the power of tests is not expected to be as high as if it will surely contain 10 men and 10 women. So exact power calculations must distinguish between random and fixed scores.

15.1.3   Factors Determining Desirable Sample Size

A well-known but oversimplified rule of thumb for sample-size analysis is that the sample size in a regression should equal at least 10 times the number of regressors. This rule is quite satisfactory for prediction, as can be seen in Table 6.3 of Sec. 6.4.2. But the rules for prediction and causal analysis are very different. And within causal analysis, the necessary sample size depends heavily on the goals of the analysis. Specific conclusions require larger samples than vague conclusions, post hoc tests require larger samples than planned tests, accurate estimation of effect sizes requires larger samples than tests of null hypotheses that effects are zero, analyses with interactions require larger samples than analyses without them, analyses with colinearity involving independent variables require larger samples than analyses with colinearity just among covariates or with no colinearity, and random regressor scores require slightly larger samples than fixed scores. At one extreme, the null hypothesis $_T R = 0$ can often be tested powerfully with only a few dozen cases. At the other extreme, hundreds or even thousands of cases might be needed to accurately estimate the sizes of higher-order colinear interactions. Therefore, if one wants a simple rule of thumb, the best rule is simply that more is better.

15.1.4   Why Correlations Are Used

Throughout this book we have generally emphasized regression slopes over partial correlations. But for power analysis it is easiest to use correlations. This is because a power calculation on a single regression slope b_j typically requires assumed values of four parameters—the regressor's slope $_T b_j$, variance $_T S_j^2$, and tolerance $_T \text{Tol}_j$, and the residual variance when Y is regressed onto the P-1 regressors excluding X_j. Thinking of these P-1 regressors as the set of covariates C, we shall denote this residual variance as $_T \text{Var}(Y.C)$. It can be shown that these four parameters combine to determine the partial correlation $_T pr_j$ by the formula

$$_T pr_j = {} _T b_j \times \sqrt{_T S_j^2 \times {} _T \text{Tol}_j / _T \text{Var}(Y.C)}$$

But when we use these four parameters to perform a power calculation, we find ourselves combining them in exactly the same way. So it is easiest to think of the value thus calculated as the partial correlation $_T pr_j$. We can of course use $_T pr_j$ for power analysis without making the mistake described in Sec. 5.5.2, of interpreting $_T pr_j$ as a conditional correlation between Y and X_j. Rather we can think of $_T pr_j$ as the square root of X_j's unique contribution to Y, expressed as a proportion of the Y-variance unexplained by other regressors.

15.1.5   Approaches to Sample Size Analysis

Since the first publication of Cohen and Cohen (1975, 1983), their discussion and tables for power analysis have dominated the way behavioral scientists think about sample size analysis. The methods they describe are moderately complex; their discussion of the topic covers about 20 pages. Their methods are also approximate; they make no distinction between random and fixed scores, and do not give exact results for either. The methods are inflexible in three ways: they apply only to the power of tests, not the precision of estimates; the tests must be done at the .05 or .01 levels; and they must test the null hypothesis of zero association, rather than the null hypothesis that the correlation of interest is some nonzero value.

My own thinking on the topic has diverged from that of Cohen and Cohen in two opposing ways. On the one hand, I have written two short BASIC computer programs for sample size analysis. These programs appear in Appendix 3 and are described in Sec. 15.3. They give exact results, at least under normal theory, and they apply to any level of alpha for which the user can supply an exact F. And a limited attempt has been made in Sec. 15.3.4 to apply them to precision analysis. But the Cohen and Cohen approximations are not bad, and for readers unfamiliar with BASIC, installing my programs would be more difficult than mastering the older approach. And the BASIC programs presented here test only the null hypothesis of nonassociation, though they could be extended to test other null hypotheses.

More recently I have come to feel that most users of regression will be served adequately by the Fisher z transformation. This method is only approximate, and was designed for the random-scores case, but can it also be considered a conservative approximation for fixed scores. It is simpler than either the Cohen and Cohen methods or my BASIC programs. The Fisher method's principal limitation is that it applies only to simple correlations or ordinary partial correlations pr_j, not to multiple or partial multiple correlations. But most workers want to reach both vague and specific conclusions, so their sample size requirements are determined by rules for specific conclusions, which require larger sample sizes than vague conclusions. Specific conclusions are those about simple correlations and ordinary partial correlations—the parameters to which the Fisher method applies. The Fisher method has all three kinds of flexibility mentioned above: it can be used to find both the power of tests and the precision of estimates, it can be used with any value of alpha, and it can be used with tests of null hypotheses other than nonassociation. I have come to feel that the limitations of the Fisher method are unimportant relative to these advantages, and that the Fisher method provides all that most researchers need to know about sample size analysis for regression and correlation.

Sec. 15.2 describes the Fisher method and its use with MYSTAT and SYSTAT, while Sec. 15.3 describes the BASIC programs mentioned above and other approaches based on them.

15.2   THE FISHER z TRANSFORMATION

15.2.1   Basics

The higher the absolute value of a correlation, the lower its standard error. So you are far less likely to find a sample r of .95 if the true correlation is .9, than you are to find a sample r of .05 if the true correlation is 0. And the distribution of the sample r can be highly asymmetric when the true correlation is nonzero. For instance, in a small sample there is a noticeable chance of observing a sample r below .8 if the true correlation is .9, but it is impossible to observe a sample r above 1.0 in the same sample, even though .8 and 1.0 are equidistant from .9.

These two problems—the nonconstancy of the standard error of r and the asymmetry of its sampling distribution—complicate sample-size analysis, because you may for instance need to calculate the probability of finding a sample r of .3 if the true correlation is .4. But the problems are both greatly diminished by transforming a correlation r to a statistic we shall denote fz for "Fisher's z." The formula used is

$$fz = .5 \cdot \ln\left(\frac{1 + r}{1 - r}\right)$$

Values of r of 0, .2, .4, .6, .8 translate by this formula to fz values of 0, .203, .424, .693, 1.099, respectively. A table showing many values of the transformation appears in Appendix 4. The transformation is symmetric around zero, so, for instance, $fz = -1.099$ when $r = -.8$. Notice that $|fz|$ is just slightly larger than $|r|$ when r is near zero, and the difference between fz and r increases as $|r|$ increases. At the extreme, fz approaches infinity as r approaches 1.

In a bivariate normal population, the fz transformation of a simple correlation is distributed approximately normally with standard error $1/\sqrt{N - 3}$. And this rule can be generalized to the fz transformation of a partial correlation; the general rule is

$$SE(fz) = 1/\sqrt{df_r - 1}$$

For a simple correlation, $df_r = N - 2$, so $df_r - 1 = N - 3$ and the general rule reduces to the previous one.

15.2.2   Confidence Bands

The semi-width of a symmetric confidence band is the difference between its center and either confidence limit. The semi-width of a 95% two-sided confidence band on Fisher z is 1.96 times $SE(fz)$. So the last formula can be used to calculate that the semi-width of a 95% two-sided confidence band is .280 when $df_r = 50$, since $1.96/\sqrt{50 - 1} = .280$. Table 15.1 shows the semi-widths of confidence bands on Fisher's z for various confidence levels and values of df_r.

Table 15.1 provides a simple method for selecting a sample size—read the various rows of the table until you find one with acceptable semi-widths, and use a sample size that yields that corresponding size of df_r.

Larger tables like Table 15.1 can easily be constructed in the MYSTAT editor. The present table was constructed in three steps. First a normal table was used to find that two-sided confidence levels of 50%, 90%, 95%, and 99% correspond to z-values of .6745, 1.6449, 1.9600, 2.5758, respectively. Then values of df_r were selected and typed in. Finally the following commands were typed on the editor's command line:

```
>let se = 1/sqr(dfr − 1)
>let sw50 = .6745*se
>let sw90 = 1.6449*se
>let sw95 = 1.9600*se
>let sw99 = 2.5758*se
```

We have already seen that when a correlation falls between about $+.4$ and $-.4$ a correlation's fz value nearly equals r itself. So when true correlations are fairly low and samples are moderately large, it is approximately true that $SE(r) = SE(fz)$. So the semi-width values in the later rows of Table 15.1 and others like it can often be thought of as semi-widths of confidence bands on r or pr_j as well as on fz.

My own opinion is that these simple formulas and tables provide at least as much understanding of sample size analysis as the more complex methods presented in the rest of this chapter. The latter methods are presented here for completeness and for specialists, but many readers may choose to skip them for now.

TABLE 15.1
Confidence band semi-widths for Fisher's z

| df_r | SE | Confidence levels | | | |
		.50	.90	.95	.99
20	.229	.155	.377	.450	.591
25	.204	.138	.336	.400	.526
30	.186	.125	.305	.364	.478
35	.171	.116	.282	.336	.442
40	.160	.108	.263	.314	.412
50	.143	.096	.235	.280	.368
60	.130	.088	.214	.255	.335
70	.120	.081	.198	.236	.310
80	.113	.076	.185	.221	.290
100	.101	.068	.165	.197	.259
120	.092	.062	.151	.180	.236
150	.082	.055	.135	.161	.211
200	.071	.048	.117	.139	.183
300	.058	.039	.095	.113	.149
500	.045	.030	.074	.088	.115

15.2.3 Creating Your Own Power Tables

With the MYSTAT editor, making up power tables based on Fisher z is only a little more complex than making up tables of confidence-band semi-widths. Any power value is determined by four starting values: nullr, a specified null value of a simple or partial correlation; altr, an alternate value of that correlation; a significance level alpha at which tests are to be performed, and a residual *df* value that we shall here denote *dfr*. Power is the probability of rejecting the null hypothesis that the true correlation equals nullr if in fact the true correlation equals altr.

Technically the power values we shall create apply to one-sided tests, but most such values are also accurate for two-sided tests at twice the alpha. For instance, the power of a two-sided test at the .05 level is usually closely approximated by the power of a one-sided test at the .025 level. The directions here apply specifically to one-sided tests of the null hypothesis $_Tr <=$ nullr.

Let critz for "critical *z*" denote the value of *z* corresponding to alpha in a standard normal table; for instance, critz = 1.96 when alpha = .025 one-tailed. Let critr denote the value of *r* that just leads to rejection of the null hypothesis, and let critfz denote the corresponding value of Fisher's *z*. Also let nullfz and altfz denote the Fisher *z* values of nullr and altr respectively.

The formula

$$\text{critz} = \frac{\text{critfz} - \text{nullfz}}{SE(fz)}$$

follows directly from the fact that *fz* is approximately normally distributed. Solving for *critfz* gives

$$\text{critfz} = \text{nullfz} + \text{critz} * SE(fz)$$

Then power is the area under the normal curve to the left of

$$(\text{altfz} - \text{critfz})/SE(fz).$$

For instance, consider a test on a simple correlation when $N = 40$, nullr = .40, altr = .70, alpha = .025 one-tailed. Then critz = 1.96, $SE(fz) = 1/\sqrt{37}$ = .1644. A Fisher *z* table shows nullfz = .424 and altfz = .867. So critz = .424 + 1.96*.1644 = .746. Then the test's power is the area to the left of (.867 − .746)/.1644 = .736; a normal table shows power to be .769.

We can replace critfz in the last expression by the right side of the previous formula. So power is the normal area to the left of

$$(\text{altfz} - \text{nullfz} - \text{critz} * SE(fz))/SE(fz),$$

which simplifies to

$$(\text{altfz} - \text{nullfz})/SE(fz) - \text{critz}$$

We could imagine varying all four of the original input parameters (nullr, altr, alpha, dfr) in a single table, and the ambitious reader is free to do so, but the directions below apply to single values of nullr and alpha, and yield a table showing how power varies as a function of *dfr* and altr. Nullr is typically zero, but need not be. Proceed as follows:

1. Select alpha and use a standard normal table to find the corresponding value of critz. For instance, for a one-sided test at the .025 level, use critz = 1.960.

2. Enter the editor and create a column headed *dfr*, containing the values of df_r you wish to study. The column can be as long or as short as you wish. I personally prefer 15 entries; they are all visible at once in the editor, and I find that if I make more values I don't end up looking at them all.

   N and P need not be known or entered separately, since $df_r = N - P - 1$. For instance, if $P = 4$ and you wish to study sample sizes of 50, 70, and 100, then enter *dfr* values of 45, 65, and 95.

3. On the editor's command line, type

   ```
   >let se = 1/sqr(dfr − 1)
   ```

   As in the previous section, this generates a column of numbers headed SE, which contains the standard errors of Fisher z for the various values of df_r.

4. Open this book or another book to a table of the Fisher z transformation (Appendix 4). The key command is of the form

   $$power = zcf((altz - nullz)/se - critz)$$

   The entry zcf denotes *z cumulative function,* and is the SYSTAT/MYSTAT command for finding areas under the normal distribution, to the left of the value shown in parentheses. The entries zcf and se in this command are typed literally, while the entries altz, nullz, and critz are replaced by the values of Fisher z corresponding to altr and nullr, respectively, and by the value of critz found in step 1. The word *power* is replaced by a column heading consisting of the letter p followed by the value of altr with the decimal point omitted. For instance, if altr = .50, nullr = .20, and alpha = .025 one-tailed, the command would be

   ```
   >let p50 = zcf((.549 − .203)/se − 1.96)
   ```

   The values .549 and .203 are the values of Fisher z corresponding to correlations of .50 and .20, respectively, and the "variable name" p50 stands for "power when altr = .50."

5. Repeat step 4 as many times as you like, for whatever values of altr you wish. Each command creates a new column of power values in the table.

6. If you wish to print the table, SAVE it under a name of your choosing, then exit the editor. If you saved it under the name *power,* then type the commands

   ```
   >use power
   >format 2
   >put power
   ```

The command FORMAT 2 is included because power values found from the Fisher z transformation are accurate to only about 2 decimal places or sometimes less, so printing more decimals is misleading; you can change the format back when finished. The command PUT POWER saves the file *power* in so-called ASCII format, which can be read into the word-processor of your choice or printed out. For instance, in DOS machines, after exiting MYSTAT enter the command

>type power > prn

Consistent with the usage of this book, the first ">" on this line is not actually typed; it merely denotes a computer command. The second ">" is actually typed. The command "type power" tells the computer to type or display the file named *power* on the screen, and the suffix "> prn" tells it to send the output to the printer instead of the screen.

Power values so low as to be near alpha should be given only their one-tailed interpretation, not their two-tailed meaning. For instance, a one-tailed test at the .025 level would actually have a slightly lower power than a two-tailed test at the .05 level if the powers of both tests are so low as to approach their respective values of alpha. In these extreme cases the power values calculated by this method apply only to one-tailed tests.

The Fisher z is only approximate, and power values calculated this way may not be accurate to even two digits.

15.2.4 The Effect of Unneccessary Covariates

The formulas of Sec. 15.2.1 highlight a useful fact about the inclusion of unnecessary covariates. By this we mean covariates which do not produce invalidity through overcontrol (described in Sec. 8.1.4), but which need not be included because, unknown to the investigator, they are independent of both Y and X_j. Each such covariate lowers power and precision by the same amount as lowering the sample size by 1. If you add 5 unnecessary covariates but increase the sample size by 5, then N and P are both raised by 5, so $N - P - 1$ is unchanged. Since $df_r = N - P - 1$, the power of tests on b_j is unchanged. Thus little power is lost by including a few extra *covariates* uncorrelated with all other variables. But Table 15.2 in Sec. 15.3.3 shows that the addition of extra *independent variables* has a greater effect on the necessary sample size. For instance, it shows that if the power of a test on $_TR$ is to be held at .8 when $_TR = .3$, then raising P from 2 to 3 raises the necessary sample size from 105 to 118.

TABLE 15.2
Smallest even value of df_r necessary for power of .8, assuming multivariate normality

Q	.30	.35	.40	.45	.50	.55	.60	.65	.70	.75
					$_TPR$					
1	82	60	44	34	28	22	18	14	12	10
2	102	72	54	42	32	26	20	16	14	10
3	114	82	60	46	36	28	22	18	14	12
4	124	90	66	50	40	30	24	20	16	12
5	134	96	70	54	42	32	26	20	16	14
6	140	100	74	56	44	34	28	22	18	14
7	148	106	78	60	46	36	28	22	18	14
8	154	110	82	62	48	38	30	24	18	14
10	166	118	88	66	50	40	32	24	20	14
12	176	126	92	70	54	42	32	26	20	16
14	186	132	98	74	56	44	34	26	20	16
16	196	138	102	76	58	44	34	28	22	16
18	204	144	106	80	60	46	36	28	22	16
20	210	150	110	82	62	48	36	28	22	16
25	228	160	118	88	66	50	38	30	22	18
30	244	172	124	92	70	54	40	30	24	18
35	258	180	132	98	72	56	42	32	24	18
40	270	190	136	102	76	58	44	32	24	18
45	282	198	142	104	78	58	44	34	26	18
50	294	204	148	108	80	60	46	34	26	18

For tests on R, read $_TPR$ as $_TR$ and read Q as P.

For all tests, find needed N by adding $P + 1$ to the value in the table.

15.3 METHODS FOR VAGUE CONCLUSIONS

Vague conclusions are those concerning values of a multiple correlation $_TR$ or a partial multiple correlation $_TPR$. The same rules apply to $_TR$ and $_TPR$, since $_TR$ is simply $_TPR$ when the number of covariates is zero. Let P denote the total number of regressors, and let Q denote the number of variables in the set being tested. $Q = P$ for analyses on R; otherwise $Q < P$.

The methods and conclusions of this section are built around two programs in the BASIC computer language—one for fixed scores, one for random scores. The latter program is emphasized since random scores are more common in the behavioral sciences and since it gives more conservative results. Section 15.3.3 provides a table based on the program, and Sec. 15.3.4 gives a table for precision analysis based on the same program.

15.3.1 A BASIC Program for Fixed-Score Power Analysis

Given the standard assumptions of regression, the short (12-line) BASIC program in Appendix 3.3 gives exact power values for fixed-score tests using R or PR. It applies only to even values of df_r of 6 or higher. These constraints produce hardly any inconvenience in practice, since very few analyses are planned or executed with $df_r < 6$, and since using a value of df_r equal to 1 more than or less than a desired value usually makes hardly any difference in the power values found. And if necessary, the worker can average the power values found by using 1 more and 1 less than the planned df_r.

The entries v1 and v2 in the program are the numerator and denominator degrees of freedom in the planned F test. Normally, v1 $=$ Q and v2 $= N - P - 1$. F is the critical value of F to be used in the test—usually taken from an F table, or found by repeated use of the F distribution program in Appendix 3.1.

"Assumed R or PR" is a value of $_TR$ or $_TPR$ you assume exists; the program gives the power of the F test for that value of $_TR$ or $_TPR$.

The program is written for a version of BASIC that makes all values double-precision (14-digit accuracy). For maximum accuracy with other versions of BASIC, insert whatever commands are necessary to make all values double-precision.

In the form the program is given in Appendix 3.3, when finished it returns to its beginning to allow you to enter other values. To end the program, consult the directions for your computer for terminating a program before its end.

Any BASIC programmer should be able to modify the first and last lines of this program, and insert it within one or more loops, to generate entire tables of power values. Each value normally takes only a few seconds of time on an ordinary personal computer.

The program is based on formula 26.6.22 from Zelen and Severo (1964, p. 948), though two typographical errors in the formula had to be corrected.

15.3.2 A BASIC Program for Random-Score Power Analysis

Appendix 3.4 contains a 26-line BASIC program for power analysis with random scores, assuming multivariate normality. The program is based on equations 25 and 26 of Gurland (1968). Most of the remarks in Sec. 15.3.1 apply to this program as well, including the comment about making the program double-precision. This program takes noticeably longer than the program in Appendix 3.3; in a problem with $N = 100$ and $P = 10$, this took 1 minute, whereas the program of Appendix 3.3 took 2 seconds. It usually gives power values just slightly below those of the other program. It was used to derive Table 15.2 in Sec. 15.3.3; you can use the entries there to check your implementation of the program.

When "Assumed R or PR" is 0, the "power" value given by either program is alpha, the probability of rejecting a true null hypothesis. The two programs give exactly the same result in that case, since the tests themselves (as opposed to the power values) are identical for fixed and random scores.

15.3.3   A Table of Necessary Sample Sizes

Table 15.2 conveys a general impression of the sample sizes needed for vague conclusions in regression analysis. Its entries were found by repeated use of the computer program in Appendix 3.4. It applies to random scores, and is therefore slightly conservative for fixed scores. As explained in Sec. 15.3.1, the program applies only when values of df_r are even, so the table shows the smallest even value of df_r needed under the conditions specified.

The table is for values of PR, which include R as the special case in which $Q = P$. The table shows the smallest even value of df_r necessary for a test on R or PR to achieve a power of .8, for various values of P and $_TR$ or $_TPR$, given alpha = .05 and random multivariate normal scores. Since $N = df_r + P + 1$, values of $P + 1$ must be added to the tabled entries to find recommended sample sizes. For instance, if $_TR = .4$ and $P = 5$, it would take residual df of 70 and thus a sample of size 76 to achieve power of .8.

15.3.4   Precision Analysis for $_TR$ and $_TPR$

The need for precision analysis on $_TR$ or $_TPR$ arises only rarely. Once it has been shown that $_TR$ or $_TPR$ is nonzero, in causal analysis the next step is usually to ask which independent variables produce the effect. Sample size analysis for such problems was described in Sec. 15.2. And in prediction, interest centers on $_TRS$ rather than $_TR$; these problems are considered in Sec. 6.4. But occasionally an investigator may want to know just how accurately $_TR$ or $_TPR$ can be estimated with a given sample size. That is the topic of this section.

As mentioned in Sec. 15.2.2, the difference between the estimated value of a parameter and a confidence limit on that parameter is called the *semi-width* of the confidence band. The estimate of $_TR$ or $_TPR$ is adjusted R or adjusted PR. We are rarely concerned that $_TR$ or $_TPR$ may be larger than its estimated value, so upper confidence limits (UCLs) on $_TR$ or $_TPR$ are rarely of interest. Thus, for $_TR$ and $_TPR$ the semi-width of interest is the difference between adjusted R or PR and the parameter's lower confidence limit (LCL).

Table 15.3 shows the minimum even value of df_r needed to achieve various values of LCL for one-sided 95%-level confidence bands for several values of adjusted R or PR. Since R is a PR with 0 covariates controlled, the table uses the symbol PR to refer to either R or PR. And Q is the number of regressors in the set of interest; when R is being analyzed, then $Q = P$. After using the table to find df_r, compute $N = df_r + P + 1$ to find the required

TABLE 15.3
Smallest even values of df_r needed to achieve a given value of LCL for various values of adjusted R or PR

Adjusted PR		.2	.3		.4			.5			
Q	LCL	.1	.1	.2	.1	.2	.3	.1	.2	.3	.4
2		234	62	216	28	52	194	16	24	44	162
4		270	76	230	36	60	200	22	28	48	166
6		298	88	242	42	66	206	24	32	52	168
8		324	98	254	48	72	212	28	34	54	172
10		346	106	264	52	76	216	30	36	58	174
12		366	114	274	54	80	222	30	38	60	176
14		386	120	282	58	84	226	32	40	62	180
16		404	126	290	60	86	230	34	42	64	182
18		420	132	298	64	90	234	36	42	66	184
20		436	138	306	66	94	240	36	44	68	186
22		450	144	314	68	96	244	38	46	70	188
24		466	148	320	70	98	246	38	46	70	190
26		480	152	328	72	102	250	40	48	72	192
28		492	158	334	74	104	254	40	48	74	194
30		504	162	340	76	106	258	42	50	74	196

sample size. For instance, suppose you are interested in the relation between Y and a set of six independent variables when eight covariates are controlled. Then $Q = 6$ and $P = 6 + 8 = 14$. Suppose you guess $_TPR = .4$ and if adjusted PR does turn out to be .4 you would like to have 95% confidence that $_TPR$ is at least .2. Then the table shows that the required value of df_r is 66, so the required sample size is $66 + 14 + 1 = 81$. Required values of N or df_r are nearly linearly related to Q over short ranges, so interpolation within a column can accurately be used when Q is odd.

This table was constructed by combining the BASIC program in Appendix 3.4 with formulas relating adjusted R to R, and R to F, and then using the combined program iteratively to find the required value of df_r.

SUMMARY

15.1 Basics

This chapter describes analyses you can perform before collecting data, to estimate the sample size needed for a planned regression. These analyses concern the power of hypothesis tests and the precision of estimates; they tell you nothing about the robustness of the planned analysis. The methods of this chapter should also not be used after a study fails to find significant results in an attempt to explain post hoc why the results are nonsignificant.

A well-known but oversimplified rule of thumb for sample size analysis is that the sample size in a regression should equal at least 10 times the number of regressors. This rule may be moderately acceptable for prediction but not for causal analysis where the best rule is simply that the larger the sample, the better.

15.2   The Fisher z Transformation

A power calculation on a single regression slope b_j may require assumed values of four parameters, but they can be combined into the partial correlation $_Tpr_j$. The formulas for Fisher z can be entered on the command line of the SYSTAT or MYSTAT editor to create tables of almost any size showing the random-scores power of tests on individual values of b_j. These tables are slightly conservative when applied to fixed scores, and in any event are only approximate, because of limitations of the Fisher z.

15.3   Methods for Vague Conclusions

Vague conclusions are those concerning values of a multiple correlation $_TR$ or a partial multiple correlation $_TPR$. The same rules apply to $_TR$ and $_TPR$, since $_TR$ is simply $_TPR$ when the number of covariates is zero. Let P denote the total number of regressors, and let Q denote the number of variables in the set being tested. $Q = P$ for analyses on R; otherwise, $Q < P$.

Given the standard assumptions of regression, the short (12-line) BASIC program in Appendix 3.3 gives exact power values for fixed-score tests using R or PR. It applies only to even values of df_r of 6 or higher.

Appendix 3.4 contains a 26-line BASIC program for power analysis with random scores, assuming multivariate normality.

Table 15.2 conveys a general impression of the sample sizes needed for vague conclusions in regression analysis. Its entries were found by repeated use of the computer program in Appendix 3.4.

For precision analysis, Table 15.3 shows the minimum even value of df_r needed to achieve various values of the lower confidence limit for one-sided 95%-level confidence bands on $_TR$ or $_TPR$ for several values of adjusted R or PR.

SYMBOLS AND ABBREVIATIONS
UCL   LCL

PROBLEMS

1. Estimate the power of a one-sided test for partial relationship if $N = 80$, $P = 5$, alpha $= .05$, and $_Tpr_j = .4$.
2. In the same problem, what sample size would be needed for power to equal .9?

3. If adding five attitude variables to eight demographic variables raised the true proportion of variance explained in achievement from .2 to .3, what sample size would be needed to have an 80% chance of a significant increase in R^2 with a test at the .05 level?

4. In a problem with eight regressors, you decide in advance that if adjusted R turns out to be .4, you would like the 95% one-sided lower confidence limit on $_TR$ to be no lower than .2. What sample size is needed to attain that goal?

CHAPTER 16

TWO EXAMPLES— ON HOMELESSNESS AND EXERCISE

This chapter illustrates the process of going from raw data to conclusions. Section 16.1 examines the causes of homelessness, and Sec. 16.2 studies the psychological effects of regular exercise. These sections are not intended to illustrate model scientific reports; Sec. 16.1 in particular gives far more detail on diagnostic analyses and other subsidiary analyses than a typical report would. The analyses in both sections can be duplicated entirely with MYSTAT, though SYSTAT is faster and more convenient.

16.1 THE CAUSES OF HOMELESSNESS

This section presents a reanalysis of data reported by Tucker (1987) on the characteristics of American cities that have exceptionally high homelessness rates. We end up reaching much the same conclusions as Tucker, though our analysis is much more detailed.

It is generally agreed that homelessness in modern America is caused partly by the release from mental hospitals of harmless patients who were confined in previous decades. But this is a nationwide phenomenon, so this and similar factors do not explain why the homelessness rates in some major cities

394

are over 10 times those in others. An analysis of the differences among these cities may shed additional light on the causes of homelessness. That is the purpose of this section.

16.1.1 The Data

Table 16.1 shows the data set analyzed. The data are from 50 American cities. The sample illustrates points made in Sec. 14.3.2 on nonrandom sampling, since there is no claim that these 50 cities are in any sense a random sample of large American cities. We actually do not know all the factors that led to selection of this sample of cities; presumably, the availability of relevant data was a major factor. It is reassuring to note that the sample includes the cities forming the cores of all 27 of the largest metropolitan areas in the United States, as given in the 1986 *World Almanac*. All subsequent conclusions are subject to modification if a larger and better sample becomes available.

The analysis uses the following variables:

> Dependent variable
> > Homelessness rate
> Background characteristics of cities
> > Average January temperature
> > Population
> Variables measuring hardship
> > Poverty rate
> > Unemployment rate
> > Proportion living in public housing
> Other variables
> > Presence or absence of rent control
> > Apartment vacancy rate

All these variables are from Tucker's analysis except January temperature, which I took from the 1986 *World Almanac* and other sources. Tucker used average annual temperature instead. The feasibility of a homeless existence would seem to depend more on average January temperature than on average annual temperature, and this conjecture is supported by the fact that homelessness rates have a noticeably higher correlation with January temperature than with average temperature (.299 versus .194).

16.1.2 Choice of Variables

In this case, the dependent variable is specified—homelessness rate. The problem is to determine which of the other variables affect homelessness. Given the usual vagaries of social science, it is reasonably clear what we would

TABLE 16.1
Some statistics related to homelessness rates

City	H	POV	U	PH	POP	V	RC	WT
Miami	15.9	24.5	7.5	29.8	372	7.0	0	67
St. Louis	11.6	21.8	8.4	14.0	429	8.5	0	29
San Francisco	11.5	13.7	6.0	10.2	712	1.6	1	49
Worcester, Mass.	10.6	14.4	3.7	14.1	160	3.0	0	25
Los Angeles	10.5	16.4	7.9	2.8	3097	2.2	1	57
Santa Monica	10.2	9.9	7.0	0.8	88	1.8	1	57
Newark, N.J.	9.5	32.8	5.9	41.7	314	2.3	1	31
Hartford	8.8	25.2	7.1	20.0	136	2.6	1	25
Washington, D.C.	7.5	18.6	8.4	19.8	623	2.0	1	31
Detroit	6.8	21.9	9.1	9.7	1088	5.4	0	23
Yonkers	6.8	9.8	4.9	10.7	191	2.1	1	32
Chicago	6.6	20.3	8.3	13.0	2992	6.0	0	21
Seattle	6.5	11.2	6.6	14.6	488	5.5	0	39
Las Vegas	6.0	10.5	8.9	14.2	183	9.0	0	44
Boston	5.6	20.2	4.6	25.3	571	2.6	1	30
Richmond	5.3	19.3	5.3	20.5	219	5.5	0	37
New York	5.0	20.0	7.4	21.5	7165	2.2	1	32
Dallas–Fort Worth	5.0	14.1	4.7	5.9	1388	6.0	0	44
Denver	4.9	13.7	5.0	9.0	504	4.0	0	30
Charleston, W. Va.	4.7	12.6	10.7	22.9	63	5.9	0	29
Atlanta	4.6	27.5	5.0	35.5	426	9.0	0	42
Fort Wayne	4.3	11.0	6.3	5.0	165	9.2	0	21
Portland	4.2	13.0	7.4	5.0	366	5.5	0	39
Houston	3.7	12.7	8.4	1.9	1706	7.0	0	51
San Diego	3.1	12.4	5.3	1.1	960	5.3	0	57
Salt Lake City	3.1	14.2	6.3	6.5	165	4.5	0	29
Little Rock	2.9	14.1	5.8	16.8	170	6.5	0	40
New Orleans	2.8	26.4	11.0	25.2	559	8.0	0	52
Charleston, S.C.	2.8	14.1	4.4	30.6	69	9.0	0	49
Albuquerque	2.8	12.4	6.3	3.1	351	9.7	0	35
Tuscon	2.7	14.7	5.3	2.4	365	2.0	0	53
Burlington, Vt.	2.7	11.3	3.4	9.1	37	6.0	0	17
Baltimore	2.4	22.9	7.0	23.2	763	5.4	0	33
Cincinnati	2.3	19.7	7.2	20.1	370	8.6	0	26
Syracuse, N.Y.	2.3	18.4	6.7	14.9	164	9.5	0	23
Tampa	2.3	18.7	5.0	17.1	275	4.7	0	60
Pittsburgh	2.2	16.5	9.4	24.5	403	5.8	0	27
Philadelphia	2.1	20.6	7.0	14.3	1646	4.0	0	31
Birmingham, Ala.	2.0	22.0	7.2	24.3	280	7.1	0	42
Louisville	1.9	19.3	6.7	21.3	290	7.3	0	33
Grand Rapids	1.9	13.5	8.6	5.1	183	7.5	0	22
Minneapolis–St. Paul	1.6	12.4	4.5	17.9	624	6.1	0	11
Milwaukee	1.6	13.8	6.4	7.5	621	6.0	0	19
Providence	1.6	20.4	4.9	15.5	156	5.0	0	28
Cleveland	1.4	22.1	12.4	22.5	547	6.5	0	26
Phoenix	1.2	11.1	5.1	2.4	853	2.2	0	52
Kansas City, Mo.	0.9	13.2	4.6	6.0	443	7.2	0	26
Charlotte, N.C.	0.8	12.4	3.7	12.7	331	8.8	0	44
Lincoln, Neb.	0.7	8.9	3.6	1.4	180	6.5	0	19
Rochester, N.Y.	0.6	17.5	7.0	10.4	243	9.0	0	24

H = homelessness rate; POV = poverty rate; U = unemployment rate; PH = public housing rate; POP = population (thousands); V = vacancy rate; RC = rent control (1 = rent control exists); WT = winter temperature.

mean by the conclusion that, say, poverty rate or January temperature affects the homelessness rate. The same is true of all the variables in the above list except apartment vacancy rate. Vacancy rate might be not so much a causal factor affecting homelessness as merely another symptom of other variables like poverty and unemployment. Or a low vacancy rate might be caused, as Tucker argues, by the drop in new construction that results from rent control. As we shall see later, the data appear to support Tucker's position. But either way, the effects of other variables in the analysis can be studied more clearly by leaving vacancy rate out of the initial analyses.

The first step, then, is to regress homelessness rate on the other six variables: poverty rate, unemployment rate, public housing, average January temperature, city size, and presence of rent control. We find $R = .607$; $F = 4.185$; $df = 6, 43$; and $p = .002$. Thus we see that there is some phenomenon to be studied, though we do not know yet whether it is produced merely by a single outlier or some anomaly. As mentioned in Sec. 14.1.9, the next step is a diagnostic analysis.

16.1.3 Diagnostic Analyses

One of the purposes of a diagnostic analysis is to examine suspect cases, and so, of course, those cases should be identified before examining any data. This is difficult in the present case, since the cities are listed in the order of their homelessness rates. Nevertheless, when I scan the list of city names while deliberately ignoring all data, only one city stands out in my mind as one whose homelessness rate might be determined by unique factors. That city is Miami, which since 1959 has been accepting large numbers of Cuban immigrants—legal and illegal, rich and poor. We will think of Miami as a "suspect case" in the diagnostic analysis.

As mentioned in Sec. 14.1.9, the order of steps in a diagnostic analysis is determined partly by what is easiest. In MYSTAT, the easiest step is to run the regression of interest with the SAVE command described in Sec. 14.1.3, so I did this first. Even before I looked in the file created by this command, MYSTAT warned me that this analysis had two outliers: Miami and Worcester, Massachusetts. Both had homelessness rates well above the rate predicted by all six characteristics—Studentized residuals were 4.175 and 3.152, respectively. MYSTAT also warned that New York City had excessive leverage.

It seemed likely that New York's high leverage was due mainly to its high population, which was over twice that of the second-largest city (Los Angeles). Thus the difference in size between New York and Los Angeles was being treated by the analysis as larger and more important than the difference between Los Angeles and the smallest city in the analysis—Burlington, Vermont, which, with a population of 37,000, is little more than 1% the size of Los Angeles. This problem was solved by expressing population on a logarithmic scale. Thus, for instance, the difference between populations of 3 million and 6 million is treated as no more important than the difference between 30,000 and 60,000, since in each case the larger number is twice the smaller. When this was done, New York was no longer rated as having undue leverage. The highest leverage became .336 (for Santa Monica), but this did not seem extreme, since three other cities had values above .3.

The problems with Miami and Worcester were solved by transforming homelessness to a logarithmic scale. Miami and Worchester have the highest and fourth-highest homelessness rates in the sample, at 15.9% and 10.6%, respectively, while the median rate for the other 48 cities in the sample is only 3.0%. This suggests that the problem was one of heteroscedasticity, with higher rates of homelessness more variable than lower ones. That is, it takes a smaller chance factor to raise a rate from 12% to 14% than from 3% to 5%. This suggests using a logarithmic scale for homelessness. When this was done, there were no longer any outliers: the only t residuals exceeding 2.0 in absolute value were 2.638 for Worcester, 2.108 for St. Louis, and -2.351 for Rochester, New York. With $df = 42$, the two-sided p's associated with these values of t are respectively .0116, .0410, and .0234. These look significant until it is remembered that they were selected post hoc from 50 values. When that is considered, we see that they are almost exactly in the range we would expect; for instance, $.0116 \times 50 = .58$.

The logarithmic scale for homelessness has another advantage: instead of interpreting $b(RC)$ as the *amount* by which rent control raises homelessness, we can interpret it as the *factor* by which homelessness is raised. If b were to equal .2 for some variable, it would mean that a 1-unit increase in that variable would be expected to increase homelessness by 20%—that is, from 5% to 6%, or from 10% to 12%.

The two logarithmic transformations have eliminated Miami as an outlier; its t residual is 1.844, which, with $df = 42$, yields $p = .072$ (two-tailed). No Bonferroni correction is applied, since we selected Miami for examination a priori rather than post hoc. Miami has the eighth-highest leverage of the 50 cities, and the highest influence: Cook(Miami) $= .132$, while the second-highest Cook value (Worcester's) is only .079. When the one suspect case turns out to have the highest influence in the sample, I would normally consider deleting the case from the sample. However, I found that deleting Miami merely reinforced the major conclusions I later reached. Therefore I left Miami in to avoid the charge that I had reached my conclusions only by eliminating Miami.

As mentioned in Sec. 14.1.9, the three major purposes of a diagnostic analysis are to check for clerical errors, to examine previously suspect cases, and to test the standard assumptions of regression. We have examined the one suspect case. Clerical errors are detected mainly by noting the cases with the largest values of leverage, influence, and distance. These have all been discussed above. The t residuals do not suggest any violations of the standard assumptions.

To test for heteroscedasticity I normalized the squared t residuals and regressed the normalized scores on the six regressors and the squares of the five numerical ones. The overall regression was nonsignificant ($F = 1.946$,

$df = 11, 38, p = .064$), as was the regression with only linear terms ($F = 1.714$, $df = 6, 43, p = .141$), and the difference between the two ($F = 1.988$, $df = 5, 38, p = .103$).

In summary, the diagnostic analysis suggested transforming population and homelessness to logarithmic scales, but indicated no outstanding problems once this was done. The regression is still significant; we have $R = .592, p = .004$. We continue with the analysis.

16.1.4   Nonlinearity and Interaction

The next step was to see if any of the regressors has a nonlinear relation to homelessness. For instance, might homelessness perhaps be especially high in medium-sized cities and lower in both larger and smaller cities? Section 12.1.6 recommends checking for nonlinearity in two ways: by examining residual scatterplots, and by adding quadratic terms to the regression. No nonlinearity was visually apparent in the six residual scatterplots. When I added to the regression the squares of the five continuous regressors, the increase in correlation with homelessness was essentially just what would be expected by chance ($F = .882; df = 5, 38; p = .503$).

I next tested for interaction. An interaction between, say, temperature and poverty rate would mean that the relationship between homelessness and poverty rate is different for warm cities and colder cities. We can examine the interaction between each pair of independent variables.

With six variables, the number of potential interaction terms is rather large: $(6 \times 5)/2 = 15$. As mentioned in Sec. 13.7.2, there are at least three strategies for examining these 15 interactions. When N is small, as in the present case, Sec. 13.7.2 recommends testing all interactions separately. When this was done, the most significant of the 15 cross-product terms was unemployment*public housing, for which $p = .078$ (two-tailed). This is nonsignificant, and when we perform a Bonferroni correction to allow for the fact that this p was selected post hoc as the most significant of 15 cross products, the corrected p does not even approach significance.

This test would normally suffice, but we illustrate the other approaches as well. One of these is to add all 15 cross-product terms to the regression and test the increase in model sum of squares. This approach gives no evidence of interaction: $F = .542; df = 15, 28; p = .893$.

The third approach is to perform five composite tests for interaction, with each composite including all five interactions involving a given independent variable. Since I had already tested for curvilinearity, I did not follow the suggestion of Sec. 13.7 that curvilinearity be considered a type of interaction. Therefore one composite tested the interactions of poverty rate with the other five variables, and another tested the interactions of winter temperature with the other five. Thus there were six composites of five terms each. Of course, this means that each individual interaction was in two composites, but there is no requirement that tests be statistically independent. None of these six tests even approached significance; in order of size, the six p's were .992, .915, .792, .584, .560, and .481. The largest (least significant) p was for interactions involving rent control, while the smallest p (which still did not even approach significance) was for unemployment rate.

16.1.5 Effects of Background Characteristics

At this point, we have considered all the major possible challenges to the validity of an ordinary linear regression: sampling adequacy, extreme cases, curvilinearity, and interaction. There is some residual uncertainty over sampling adequacy, though no flaws are obvious. Miami remains somewhat suspect, but is retained in the sample. The evidence contradicts all the other possible challenges about as strongly as one would ever expect in real data. As mentioned earlier, the regression is significant ($R = .592, p = .004$); so we ask next which of the six variables in the regression—log-population, average January temperature, poverty rate, unemployment rate, proportion of residents in public housing, and a dummy variable measuring presence or absence of rent control—contribute to the relationship.

I used a hierarchical approach with two levels. The first level included the background variables of city climate and size; the second level included all other regressors. Log-homelessness correlates almost significantly with winter temperature ($r = .273; p = .055$, two-tailed), while its correlation of .108 with city size (log-population) does not even approach significance. My own policy in cases like this is to retain such variables in subsequent analyses, since using a few extra covariates sacrifices little in statistical power. It may also gain validity, since a statistically nonsignificant relationship does not prove that there is no relationship. But it turns out that omitting them does not change any major conclusions, as we shall see.

16.1.6 Effects of Variables Measuring Hardship

We can next examine models that ignore rent control and emphasize poverty rate, unemployment rate, and amount of public housing. Since we can test variables either individually or as a set, and can do so either with or without controlling for background characteristics, we have four different tests. For reasons described in Sec. 3.4.2, the best of these is to test the set of three, controlling for background variables. This test did not approach significance; we have $F = .950, p = .425$. For completeness, the next paragraph illustrates the other three tests. As we shall see, none approached significance.

The simple correlations of poverty rate, unemployment rate, and public housing rate with log-homelessness were, respectively, .219, .167, and .180. We would expect more homelessness with more poverty and unemployment, but it is unclear what we would expect about public housing. Public housing might help lessen homelessness, producing a negative correlation—or it might be built in response to greater need, producing a positive correlation. As just shown, all three correlations were positive. But none was statistically significant; with $df = N - 2 = 28$, the one-tailed p for the largest correlation was .063. This approaches significance, but it should be remembered that it was selected post hoc as the largest of three. When homelessness is regressed onto (predicted from) these three variables, the total relationship is just what we would expect by chance: adjusted $R^2 = 0$; $F = .985$, $p = .408$. The two-tailed p's for the partial regression slopes in this analysis are also completely nonsignificant at .515, .455, and .804, respectively. When poverty, unemployment, and public housing were each tested individually for a partial relationship to log-homelessness, with city size and winter temperature controlled, the two-tailed p's were respectively .139, .276, and .171. Thus none approached statistical significance.

16.1.7   Rent Control

Having examined alternative explanations for homelessness, we now turn to rent control. Nine of the 50 cities in our sample have rent control. These nine are shown in Table 16.2, in the order of their homelessness rates.

The median of these nine values is 8.8%—over 3 times the median homelessness rate of the 41 cities without rent control, which is 2.8%. The simple correlation between rent control and log-homelessness is .512, which is highly significant ($p = .00014$, two-tailed). When city size and climate are controlled, the correlation changes hardly at all, to .501 ($p = .00029$). Of course no two rent-control laws are identical, and a simple dichotomy cannot begin to capture all variations in rent control. But that fact would tend to lower the measured correlation between rent control and homelessness, and that correlation is remarkably high despite this problem.

Tucker's thesis is that rent control creates homelessness partly by discouraging new construction. In ordinary cities, middle-class people move from older buildings into newer, more comfortable, apartments—leaving the older apartments for the poor. But in rent-control cities, these middle-class people

TABLE 16.2
Homelessness rates in nine cities with rent control, %

San Francisco	11.5
Los Angeles	10.5
Santa Monica	10.2
Newark, N.J.	9.5
Hartford	8.8
Washington, D.C.	7.5
Yonkers	6.8
Boston	5.6
New York	5.0

are kept in older apartments both by the absence of new apartments and by the bargain rents they pay by staying put. So the normal source of housing for the poor is cut off, and they become homeless.

Most municipal rent control laws attempt to avoid discouraging new construction by exempting it from rent control. But according to Tucker, landlords and developers know that such exemptions often turn out to be temporary. For instance, new construction was exempted when New York City's "temporary" wartime rent control was made permanent in 1947. This exemption lasted until 1969. The 1969 law again exempted new construction, but this exemption lasted only 5 years. Thus, landlords and developers are little impressed by laws exempting new construction from rent control.

16.1.8   The Role of Vacancy Rates

As Tucker predicts, there is a high negative association between vacancy rate and rent control. In fact, there is no overlap between the two sets of vacancy rates. The 9 cities with rent control have vacancy rates ranging from 1.6% (San Francisco) to 2.6% (Hartford and Boston), with a median of 2.2%; while the 41 cities without rent control have vacancy rates ranging from 3.0% (Worcester, Massachusetts) to 18% (New Orleans), with a median of 7.3%. On the basis of the two medians, rent control seems to be associated with a 70% drop in vacancy rate.

The data also confirm Tucker's prediction that cities with high homelessness rates will have low vacancy rates—the correlation between the two rates is $-.387$.

On the other hand, vacancy rate has no noticeable relation to poverty, unemployment, and public housing. The first regression testing this hypothesis gave a nonsignificant R ($F = .636, p = .596$), but it listed an outlier. It turns out that rates of vacancy, poverty, and unemployment were all noticeably skewed and that skewness was lowered substantially by logarithmic transformations of these variables. But skewness of public housing rate was less before than after a logarithmic transformation. When the less skewed form of each variable was used, the relation was still nonsignificant ($F = .364, p = .780$), and no warnings were given concerning leverage or outliers. Using these forms of the variables, the relationship was still nonsignificant when city size and climate were controlled ($F = .537, p = .659$).

The matter of skewness raised the question whether logarithmic forms of poverty and unemployment rates should have been used when these variables were used along with others (rent control, winter temperature, public housing rate, and log-population) to predict log-homelessness. But it was found that the highest leverage value and the highest Studentized residual were both higher with this change than in the original regression, so the other original analyses—testing for curvilinearity, interaction, and the rest—were not redone.

A histogram of log-vacancy rate is clearly bimodal. But this bimodality disappears when cities with and without rent control are plotted separately.

This suggests again that rent control is by far the major variable determining vacancy rates.

We thus confirm Tucker's conclusions in all major respects. By any of several tests, homelessness rates are independent of poverty rate, unemployment rate, and availability of public housing. But homelessness is very highly related to rent control and to low vacancy rates.

16.1.9   What Causes Cities to Adopt Rent Control?

We have seen the high associations among rent control, low vacancy rates, and homelessness. Tucker argued that the causation is in the direction just listed— rent control lowers vacancy rates, and low vacancy rates raise homelessness. But might the causation be in some other direction? In particular, might factors related to homelessness and vacancy rates lead some cities to adopt rent control? More generally, what leads cities to adopt rent control?

To answer this, start by comparing the list of nine cities having rent control with a list of the 10 largest American metropolitan areas. In order of size, these areas center on the cities of New York, Los Angeles, Chicago, Philadelphia, San Francisco, Detroit, Boston, Washington, Houston, and Dallas. If you ask several people to name five of these cities which have traditionally been considered exceptionally desirable places to live and work, they will almost certainly name New York, Los Angeles, San Francisco, Boston, and Washington. But that is precisely the list of major cities with rent control.

This suggests that residents of these cities found themselves threatened with rising rents as newcomers arrived to share the attractive lifestyles available there—and rent control was adopted in defense. We must admit that it worked; today, newcomers are not nearly so eager to move to these five cities as they were in past years.

This interpretation also explains why some smaller cities adopt rent control. If apartments are unavailable in a major city because of rent control, then newcomers flock to the smaller cities next door, putting even stronger upward pressure on rents there. The smaller cities then adopt rent control for the same reasons as their larger neighbors—with the additional encouragement of their neighbor's example. This can explain the presence of Newark, Yonkers, and Santa Monica on the list of cities with rent control. The only other city on the list is Hartford, which is midway between two major cities with rent control, and which might also consider itself special as the capital of a state famous as a good place to live.

With the possible exception of Hartford, we have explained simply and naturally why rent control arose in all nine cities in Table 16.2. But if this adequately explains why these cities adopted rent control, then there is no room left for explanations that posit homelessness and low vacancy rates as causes of rent control rather than effects.

Thus, it seems that a city's very attractiveness leads—through a chain involving in-migration, rising rents, rent control, lack of new construction, immobility of longtime residents, and low vacancy rates—to homelessness and a broad deterioration of the city's quality of life. In this way as in so many others, the first become last.

16.2   THE PSYCHOLOGICAL EFFECTS OF EXERCISE

DePalma (1989) studied the effects of an exercise program on the mental and emotional condition of the participants. The sample consisted of 85 students who had signed up to take physical education (PE) classes at Cornell University. Of these, eight missed the administration of most or all of the dependent measures to be described later. These were deleted from the sample, leaving 77 cases in the sample. Thirty of these 77 had signed up to take the PE class to fulfill a university requirement; the other 47 had signed up without requesting credit. Fifty-five of the 77 students were female, 22 male. There was no significant relationship between gender and credit request.

A randomly chosen control group, containing 22 of the 77 students, were told that there was no room for them in the PE class. Students who had signed up for credit were told that they would receive credit anyway. The control group included 6 of the 22 males and 16 of the 55 females; it included 10 of the 30 students requesting credit and 12 of the 47 not requesting credit.

There were some missing data even among the 77 subjects studied. Listwise deletion was used, so the values of df_r reported in the example do not always equal exactly $77 - P - 1$.

The analyses described below were designed and performed by DePalma with some advice from the present author, though a few of my own interpretations differ somewhat from DePalma's. So many analyses will be described that not all results will be reported in detail. Also, outliers and other irregularities were little or no problem in these analyses, so we shall skip over the diagnostic analyses to focus on other issues.

16.2.1   Variables Measured

Altogether, 68 variables were measured for each subject. Only a few of these are mentioned here. Instructors adopting this textbook for class use may request from the author a free disk containing scores on all 68 variables.

In the list below, time 1 refers to the beginning of the semester-long PE class, and time 2 refers to the end. Measures included the following:

Age
Sex
Group (exercise or no exercise)

Sign-up option

Average weekly hours of exercise outside PE class

Weight-adjusted heart rate during a standard exercise task, times 1 and 2

Altogether, 18 psychological scales were administered at both times 1 and 2. These included four scales from the Jenkins Activity Scale—a measure of "Type A" behavior associated with heart attacks:

JA: Global scale

JS: Speed and Impatience subscale

JI: Job Involvement subscale

JH: Hard-driving subscale

Five traits were measured using the Multiple Affect Adjective Checklist (MAACL). Each of the five traits is measured in both "trait" and "state" forms ("how you generally feel" versus "how you feel now—today"), making 10 scales altogether. The five traits were:

MA: Anxiety

MD: Depression

MH: Hostility

MPA: Positive affect

MSS: Sensation seeking

A final T or S on each of these distinguishes between the trait and state forms of the scale. Thus MAT and MAS denote, respectively, the trait and state forms of the anxiety scale.

Also used were:

BDI: Beck Depression Inventory

STAT: State Trait Anxiety, Trait Version

STAS: State Trait Anxiety, State Version

PS: psychosocial stress

The study's dependent variables were the 18 psychological measures taken at time 2, while the same measures taken at time 1 were used as covariates.

16.2.2   On the Use of Scales as Dependent Variables

The psychological scales just listed were designed to predict real-life events like heart attacks, suicides, and hospitalization for depression. DePalma's study would be more impressive if she had used such real-life events as dependent variables. Of course, studies using such variables are far more difficult. Therefore we must ask exactly what assumptions need to be made when we use scales like those named as dependent variables. To answer this, we can think of an "ultimate" dependent variable, such as heart attack or suicide, as being composed of predictable and unpredictable components, with the predictable components defined as the scales in the current study—or at least correlating perfectly with those scales. If we show that exercise affects a predictable component (that is, it affects one of the scales), then we must assume that it also affects the "ultimate" variable *unless* it affects the ultimate variable's unpredictable component in the opposite direction. This latter condition is possible, but unlikely and certainly an unparsimonious assumption. Thus, a study like the present one cannot prove that exercise lowers the risk of suicide or heart attack, but positive results can make that the most parsimonious conclusion consistent with the data.

16.2.3 Hours of Other Exercise

The first question in DePalma's analysis was whether the power of the experiment had been destroyed by control-group subjects who sought out other ways to exercise after they learned that they would not be admitted to a PE class. This was tested by regressing hours of other exercise onto the dichotomous GROUP variable; this is equivalent to a two-sample t test on hours of other exercise. No significant effect was found. Therefore the experimental manipulation of exercise apparently operated as intended.

16.2.4 A Composite Test on the Effects of Exercise

The next question was whether exercise had an effect on any of the 18 psychological scales. The *reverse regression* method (to be described in Sec. 17.4.2) was used to perform a preliminary test of this composite hypothesis. In brief, reverse regression is useful when you need to test the relation between a single independent variable X and a *set* of dependent variables Y, possibly controlling for a set C of covariates. In the present case, X is GROUP, Y contains the 18 posttest measures, and C contains the 18 pretest measures. The reverse regression method consists of "tricking" the computer by telling it that X is the *dependent* variable and that Y and C are regressor sets, and using the ordinary test in Sec. 5.3.1 to test the relation between X and set Y with set C controlled. As described in Sec. 17.4.2, regression slopes and other output from a reverse regression have no scientific meaning and should be ignored, but the F found for set Y tests a meaningful hypothesis. The result of this test was highly significant, indicating that exercise has some effect whose nature must now be clarified.

16.2.5   Which Variables Are Affected?

Next, a series of 18 tests was run, each predicting one of the time 2 psychological measures from GROUP and from the same measure taken at time 1. The eighteen t's thus found for GROUP were examined. Six of these t's were positive and the other 12 were negative. But none of the six positive t's even approached significance; the highest was .76. Thus we can concentrate on the negative t's, which suggested that exercise lowered the trait in question. This was consistent with the hypotheses; all traits (depression, anxiety, hostility, and so on) are widely considered undesirable.

The highest of the 12 negative t's was for STAS (state anxiety); it yielded $t = -4.036$, $df = 73$, $p = .000066$ (one-tailed). This is significant even after a Bonferroni correction; we have $PC = .000066 \times 18 = .0012$. This confirms the result of the previous test on the composite null hypothesis that exercise has no effect on any of the scales. Applying layered Bonferroni tests to the remaining 17 dependent variables, we find significant effects of exercise on STAT (trait anxiety) and on JA ("Type A" behavior). The effect of exercise on BDI (depression) was significant ($p = .010$, one-tailed), but not after a Bonferroni correction. But the effect of exercise on depression has been observed in many other studies and was perhaps the single hypothesis of greatest interest, so we shall consider this effect confirmed on the ground that the Bonferroni correction is inappropriate for this variable. In summary, we have found effects of exercise on depression, "Type A" behavior, and both trait and state forms of anxiety.

Readers familiar with factor analysis and cluster analysis may wonder why those techniques were not applied to narrow the number of dependent variables. One reason is that the Bonferroni method reduced 18 dependent variables to 4, which is narrowing enough. A second reason is that factor and cluster methods narrow the number of variables by grouping together variables that correlate highly with each other. But it is perfectly possible that two variables will correlate highly even if an exercise program affects one and not the other. This kind of distinction would be lost by factor and cluster analyses, but is central to the present analysis, so these techniques were not used.

16.2.6   Which Effects Are Direct?

The effects tested by our Bonferroni analysis are total effects, which are the effects of most practical interest. But it may be of theoretical interest to explore whether some of these effects operate through other variables. Our exploration of these secondary questions is correlational in nature, which is to say that even though the study included random assignment, the advantages of random assignment do not apply to the following analysis.

Each of the four selected scales (JA, STAS, STAT, BDI) was predicted from GROUP, its own time 1 score *and* the other three time 2 scores. When the dependent variables were JA, STAS, and STAT, the effects of GROUP remained highly significant, indicating that exercise affected each of these directly, independently of the others. But when the dependent variable was BDI, the slope of GROUP was nonsignificant while the slope of STAS was highly significant ($t = 4.10$; $df = 69$; $p = .000056$, one-tailed). This suggests that the effect of exercise on depression operates through its effect on anxiety. Thus, the only variables that appear to be affected directly by exercise are JA, STAS, and STAT—"Type A" behavior and two forms of anxiety. It is remarkable that we could demonstrate direct effects of exercise on each type of anxiety even while controlling the other, since these two scales had a correlation of .63 at time 1.

16.2.7   Testing for Interaction

The next step was to see whether any of these effects of exercise was moderated by other variables. The most obvious candidates for moderator or interacting variables were age, sex, sign-up option, pretest score on the scale being tested, and physical fitness at time 1 as measured by weight-adjusted heart rate during a fitness task. Four regressions were run, each regression predicting one of the four dependent variables from these five variables plus GROUP and its interactions with the other five. Then the five interaction terms were dropped from the regression and an F test was performed on the resulting increase in SS(error). None of these increases approached statistical significance, even before correcting for the fact that four F tests had been performed. Thus, conclusions were not complicated by evidence that the exercise program was more effective for some kinds of subjects than for others.

An interesting question about interaction is illustrated by the group $\times$ sex interaction predicting BDI (depression). On the one hand, this interaction was not significant. But on the other hand, when the effect of exercise was tested for the two sexes separately, the effect was significant for females and not for males. What conclusion should then be drawn? The answer relies on the distinction made in Sec. 14.3.1 between the simplest or most parsimonious conclusion consistent with a set of data and the most conservative conclusion consistent with the same data. The simplest conclusion consistent with the present data is that exercise affects men and women equally, but the most conservative conclusion is that the effect operates only for women.

The same result arose when the dependent variable was JA, but in that case the estimated effect was actually slightly larger for men than for women, and the effect of exercise was nonsignificant among men because there were only 40% as many men as women. Thus the simpler rather than the more conservative conclusion is especially appealing in this case.

16.2.8   Physical Fitness as a Mediator

A *mediator* is a variable through which an effect passes, making the effect indirect. It should not be confused with a *moderator*, which is a variable that interacts with an independent variable of interest.

DePalma examined whether the effects of exercise were mediated by changes in fitness, as measured by weight-adjusted heart rate during exercise. This was done by regressing each of the four dependent variables (posttest measures of BDI, JA, STAS, STAT) onto its own pretest measure, GROUP, and fitness at time 2. If the effect of exercise on a dependent variable Y is mediated entirely by fitness, then the contribution of fitness to Y should be significant, whereas the direct effect of GROUP, as measured by the regression slope of GROUP, becomes nonsignificant. If the effect of exercise on Y is mediated only partly by fitness, then the regression slopes of both GROUP and fitness should be significant. It was found that GROUP remained highly significant in all four regressions. The slope of fitness was significant in two of the four regressions—those predicting STAS and BDI. Recall that any random error in the measurement of fitness will tend to lower these apparent contributions, and thus raise the apparent size of the direct effects of GROUP. When this point is considered, the overall conclusion is that fitness makes some contribution at least to changes in STAS and BDI, but it is unclear whether the changes in all four variables are mediated entirely or even largely by changes in fitness. Another possibility is that people who exercise regularly develop a mental set to carry on with their activities despite fatigue and minor pain, and that this explains the positive changes in their measured emotional state. This effect could operate even without large changes in fitness, and in fact might even be largest for those whose fitness improves little or not at all.

We had concluded earlier that the effect of GROUP on BDI (depression) appears to be mediated entirely by STAS (state anxiety); exercise lowers anxiety, which lowers depression. Given that fitness seems to affect both STAS and BDI, is there a direct effect of fitness on BDI, or does it operate entirely through STAS? When BDI at time 2 is regressed onto GROUP, fitness

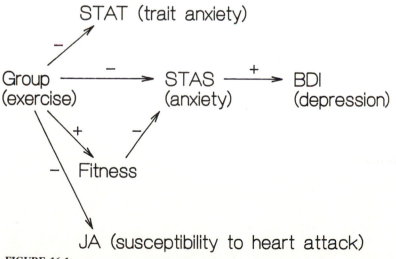

FIGURE 16.1
A path diagram suggested by the DePalma data.

at time 2, STAS at time 2 and BDI1 and BDI at time 1, fitness is not significant. So the effect of fitness on BDI, like the effect of GROUP, appears to operate through STAS.

16.2.9 Conclusions

The overall conclusion is that for subjects like those studied, regular exercise clearly improves scores on measures of anxiety, depression, and susceptibility to heart attack. The effect of exercise on depression appears to be indirect; apparently exercise lowers anxiety, and lowered anxiety in turn lowers depression. There is no evidence that any of these effects are stronger for some kinds of subjects than others; the simplest conclusion is that they apply about equally to all healthy people of both sexes. As best we can tell, the effects are mediated only partly by changes in actual physical fitness. These conclusions suggest the path diagram in Fig. 16.1

SUMMARY

Two analyses in this chapter illustrate the total process of deriving useful conclusions from raw data. The first analysis concludes that rent control has a major effect in producing homelessness, while the factors of poverty, unemployment, public housing, city size, and climate have no demonstrable effect. The second concludes that regular exercise lowers anxiety, depression, and susceptibility to heart attack. The first analysis emphasizes diagnostic analyses, log transformations, and tests for interaction and curvilinearity. The second illustrates the use of multiple dependent variables and the benefits of combining regression with random assignment.

PROBLEM

1. Write a paper, comparable in scope to Sec. 16.1, on the factors leading cities to offer public housing. Use the data set given in Table 16.1.

CHAPTER 17

MISCELLANEOUS ADVANCED TOPICS

This chapter briefly describes several variations of regression and linear models that we have not been able to discuss earlier.

17.1 REGRESSION WITHOUT THE CONSTANT, OR WITH ONLY THE CONSTANT

Imagine a questionnaire with an item answered positively by all respondents, such as "Are you alive?" If this item were scored 1 for all subjects and somehow received a coefficient b_j, the item's presence would result in adding the value b_j to $\hat{Y}$ for all subjects. But that is exactly what the additive constant a does. Thus we can actually think of a as the coefficient of an imaginary variable scored 1 for all cases. We then think of the regression as containing not P regressors and the additive constant, but $(P + 1)$ regressors including the imaginary one. That actually helps us understand better the formula $df_r = N - P - 1$. We now see that

$$df_r = N - \text{total number of regressors}$$

including the imaginary one. Or, equivalently,

$$df_r = N - \text{number of parameters estimated by the regression}$$

Sometimes it is useful to omit this imaginary regressor (that is, omit the additive constant) from the model. This situation may arise when all variables

411

including Y are true ratio scales with meaningful zero points. For instance, suppose a test Y measures skill on a task, where anyone with no knowledge or practice at the task would be expected to score 0 on Y. Suppose X is hours of training or practice on the task. In a problem like this, we might want to predict Y from X by simple regression, with the added condition that we want to force the regression line to pass through the origin, so that $\hat{Y} = 0$ when $X = 0$.

This is done in SAS by adding the NOINT ("no intercept") option to the MODEL statement, as in

>model y = x / noint;

The same result is achieved in SYSTAT and MYSTAT by omitting the Constant from the model, so that it might read

>model y = x

instead of

>model y = constant + x

Since df_r always equals $N -$ (number of parameters estimated by the regression), in this case we have $df_r = N - P$ instead of $df_r = N - P - 1$.

Instead of excluding the constant, we can exclude everything but the constant. Recall the simple one-group t test for testing the null hypothesis that the mean of a variable Y is zero. We can think of this test as a special case of no-intercept regression in which there are no regressors except the imaginary regressor scored 1 for every case. If that regressor's coefficient is a, then the regression reduces to finding the value of a that minimizes $\Sigma(Y - a)^2$. We know from basic statistics that the value of a minimizing this expression is M_Y. Similarly, the population values $_Ta$ and $_TM_Y$ are equal. Thus the null hypothesis $_Ta = 0$ is the hypothesis $_TM_Y = 0$, so the hypothesis that a mean is zero can be thought of as the hypothesis $_Ta = 0$ when the variable in question is regressed onto no variables except the constant "variable." We will use this fact in the discussion of repeated measures in Sec. 17.5.

17.2 WEIGHTED LEAST SQUARES

Sometimes observations or cases are not mutually independent but can be grouped into mutually independent clusters of different sizes. For instance, suppose you randomly select 50 cities from the nation and then draw samples of people in those cities, making the sample size in each city proportional to the size of the city. Because the sampling is limited to 50 cities, it cannot be treated as one large sample from the nation's cities. But responses on each variable can be averaged within each city, yielding 50 within-city means on each variable. These 50 means are mutually independent and may be used in a regression.

But there is still a serious problem. Because the 50 means are computed in samples of different sizes, they will have different standard errors. This violates regression's requirement of homoscedasticity. But this problem can be overcome by the use of weighted least squares. This is an extension of regression in which the user specifies that observations are not weighted equally, and can specify the exact relative weight that each observation is to receive. Weighted least squares is available as a regression option in SAS, MYSTAT, and SYSTAT. See Draper and Smith (1981) for more detail.

17.3   MULTIPLE DEPENDENT VARIABLES

Consider a design in which several dependent variables are measured for each subject. For instance, consider a study testing a new educational method. Suppose there are several dependent variables: score on a standardized test, school marks, teacher ratings, and the like. One regressor is an experimental treatment, and the other regressors are covariates: SES of parents, and similar factors. We wish to perform a series of regressions that are identical except that each has a different dependent variable. Calculations proceed more quickly if our commands tell the computer that the regressions all have the same regressors. Other advantages of such commands are described in Sec. 17.4.

In SAS and SYSTAT this is done by listing all the dependent variables on the left side of a single MODEL statement. In the data set on life satisfaction in Table 5.7 at the end of Chap. 5, suppose we wish to regress *both* income and education on race, sex, and age. In SAS we could write:

>model income educ = race sex age;

In SYSTAT we would write

>model income, educ = constant + race + sex + age
>estimate

The output from these SYSTAT commands is shown in Table 17.1. As you see, each column lists the major descriptive statistics for a single dependent variable, with no inferential statistics except adjusted R^2. The SAS command above gives the usual inferential statistics as well. In SYSTAT these are obtained separately for each independent variable, with commands like the following:

>hypothesis
>effect = age
>test

In the present example, SYSTAT would then print an analysis-of-variance table for each dependent variable. The F's in these two tables are .631 and

TABLE 17.1
SYSTAT output for multiple dependent variables

```
NUMBER OF CASES PROCESSED = 20
DEPENDENT VARIABLE MEANS
                              INCOME      EDUC
                              20.600      13.550
REGRESSION COEFFICIENTS B = (X'X)−1X'Y
                              INCOME      EDUC
                 CONSTANT     9.405       10.246
                 RACE         0.833       −1.397
                 SEX          3.596        1.529
                 AGE          0.291        0.097
MULTIPLE CORRELATIONS
                              INCOME      EDUC
                               .294        .534
SQUARED MULTIPLE CORRELATIONS
                              INCOME      EDUC
                               .086        .285
ADJUSTED R2 = 1−(1−R2)*(N−1)/DF, WHERE N=20, AND DF=16
                              INCOME      EDUC
                               .000        .151
```

1.035, and the associated p's are .439 and .234. These F's test separately the null hypotheses that age is unrelated to income and unrelated to education when sex and race are controlled. Since $df_1 = 1$ in these cases, these F's are the squares of the t's you would find from an ordinary regression command.

In SYSTAT, the command

>print long

will make the MODEL and TEST commands yield far more output than we have described, but most of the extra output is beyond the scope of this book.

17.4 MANOVA (MULTIVARIATE ANALYSIS OF VARIANCE)

17.4.1 Basics

When we have two or more dependent variables, as in the previous section, we may wish to perform a single test on the composite null hypothesis that an independent variable has no partial relation to any of the dependent variables, with other regressors controlled. This can be done with the MANOVA command in SAS or the HYPOTHESIS command in SYSTAT. For each factor in the analysis, these commands will test the null hypothesis that the factor has no effect on any of the dependent variables.

In SYSTAT, you first enter the MODEL and ESTIMATE commands as in Sec. 17.3. Then issue three commands: a HYPOTHESIS command, an EFFECT command, and a TEST command, in that order. The first and last are simply the words *hypothesis* and *test,* while the EFFECT command names the independent variable after the phrase EFFECT =. A separate series of commands must be issued for each independent variable of interest. In the example of Sec. 17.3, the three independent variables were race, sex, and age, so the commands might be

```
>hypothesis
>effect = race
>test

>hypothesis
>effect = sex
>test

>hypothesis
>effect = age
>test
```

In SAS we can add a MANOVA statement after the MODEL statement. For instance, if there are two dependent variables Y_1 and Y_2 and two factors C and D, we can write

```
>model y1 y2 = c d c*d;
>manova h = c d c*d;    or    >manova h = _all_;
```

In the MANOVA command, "H" stands for "hypothesis." The command directs SAS to test MANOVA hypotheses concerning the effects of C, D, and the $C \times D$ interaction after performing the two individual regressions. That is, the program tests the null hypothesis that factor C has no effect on either Y_1 or Y_2, then tests the parallel hypothesis for factor D, and then tests the parallel hypothesis for the $C \times D$ interaction.

A number of different methods have been developed for testing the null hypothesis just mentioned. SAS and SYSTAT both print results for four tests: the Hotelling-Lawley, Pillai, Wilks, and Roy tests. (The Roy test is called *theta* in SYSTAT; it is not printed when it is equivalent to others that are printed.) The output of the four tests will sometimes be identical, and will often be very similar. If it matters which one you pick, I recommend the Wilks method, unless you have received specific advice to the contrary.

MANOVA problems should not be confused with repeated-measures problems. The two are alike in that several measures are taken for each case. But in a typical MANOVA problem, the measures for each case are on *different scales but for the same group or experimental condition*. In a typical repeated-measures problem, each case is measured on the *same scale under different conditions*. For instance, if we used the same scale to measure each person's attitude toward five different ethnic groups, we would have a repeated-measures design with five levels or categories of the repeated factor (ethnic group). But if we used five scales constructed by different workers, each designed to provide a global measure of "attitude toward minority groups," and we wanted to test the composite null hypothesis that men and women have equal means on all five scales, then we would use MANOVA.

17.4.2   MANOVA with an Ordinary Regression Program

The SAS and SYSTAT commands described above will work for any independent variable, whether it be numerical, dichotomous, or multicategorical. But if these packages are unavailable, MANOVA tests for single numerical and dichotomous variables can be performed with MYSTAT or even simpler regression programs.

Consider first the simplest case: just one independent variable X. Suppose there are three dependent variables Y_1, Y_2, and Y_3 and we want to test the null hypothesis that X has no effect on any of them. This is equivalent to the hypothesis that the three correlations $_Tr(X, Y_1)$, $_Tr(X, Y_2)$, and $_Tr(X, Y_3)$ are all 0.

We can test this hypothesis with an ordinary regression program by turning the regression around, telling the computer that X is the dependent variable and Y_1, Y_2, and Y_3 are the independent variables. Then the test on R will test the null hypothesis just mentioned: the hypothesis that the three correlations $_Tr(X, Y_1)$, $_Tr(X, Y_2)$, and $_Tr(X, Y_3)$ are all 0. We will call this a *reverse regression*. The calculated slopes b_j have no scientific meaning in a reverse regression and should be ignored, but the test on R gives exactly the F given by any of the four MANOVA tests.

To illustrate reverse regression when there are covariates to be controlled, suppose we have four regressors X_1, X_2, X_3, and X_4 and as before we have Y_1, Y_2, and Y_3. For each regressor X_j, we want to test the null hypothesis of no association between X_j and any Y when the other X's are controlled. We illustrate for X_1. Regress X_1 on all other X's and all the Y's. Treat the three Y variables as a set, testing the null hypothesis of no association between X_1 and Y_1, Y_2, and Y_3 when X_2, X_3, and X_4 are controlled.

17.4.3   Testing the Number of Parallel Mediators

MANOVA can also be used to test hypotheses about the number of unmeasured parallel mediating factors needed to explain the relation between sets of independent and dependent variables. An unmeasured mediating factor is a factor hypothesized to be affected by an independent variable and to affect a dependent variable. For instance, the independent variable "teacher enthusiasm" might affect student achievement through the unmeasured mediator of student enthusiasm. If we imagine that a measured independent variable of teacher enthusiasm affects student enthusiasm (unmeasured), which affects student effort (also unmeasured), which in turn affects a measured dependent variable achievement, then the path diagram is as shown in Fig. 17.1. But the two unmeasured mediators in this diagram are in series rather than parallel, since one affects the other. Two mediators are in parallel if both are affected by the independent variable(s) and both affect the dependent variable(s), at least partially independently of each other.

Figure 17.2 illustrates two competing hypotheses for the same data. Part *a* shows a hypothesis of two parallel mediators, while part *b* shows a hypothesis involving a single mediator for the same measured independent and dependent variables. In each part, the two variables on the left are measured independent variables while the two on the right are measured dependent variables. In Fig. 17.2*a*, starred arrows (the four horizontal arrows) denote strong effects, and unstarred arrows (the four diagonal arrows) denote weak effects. According to the hypothesis illustrated there, parental IQ affects a child's "hereditary potential" (an unmeasured mediator) more than it affects scholarliness (liking of study), while school quality affects scholarliness more than it affects hereditary potential. The hypothesis also posits that hereditary potential affects scores on mathematics achievement more than scores on history achievement while scholarliness affects history achievement more than mathematics achievement. On the other hand, the hypothesis in Fig. 17.2*b* suggests that the pattern of relationships between the independent and dependent variables can be explained by a single mediator: both parental IQ and school quality affect general academic competence, which affects both mathematics and history achievement.

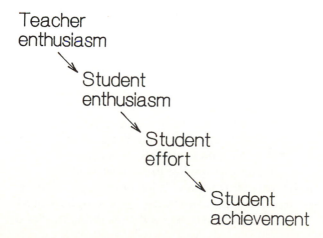

FIGURE 17.1
Serial rather than parallel mediators.

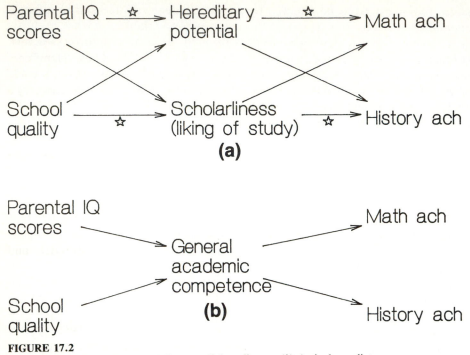

FIGURE 17.2
Two competing hypotheses. (*a*) Two parallel mediators. (*b*) A single mediator.

The fewer the hypothesized mediators, the simpler the hypothesis. The natural sequence in any scientific area is to posit and test simple hypotheses before considering more complex ones. For instance, when it first became accepted that the sun is the center of the solar system, astronomers first considered the simple hypothesis that the orbits of planets are circles. Only when that hypothesis failed to fit available data did they consider the more complex hypothesis that the orbits of planets are ellipses. And in the 1940s, psychologists were enamored of the simple hypothesis that they would be able to understand all of human behavior by studying rats learning mazes. Only when that failed did they consider more complex approaches.

Hypotheses specifying fewer unmeasured mediators are simpler, and should be considered first. The hypothesis of a single unmeasured mediator is simpler than the hypothesis of two parallel mediators, so it should be tested before the other. But there is still a simpler hypothesis—the hypothesis of no association at all between independent and dependent sets. We can think of this as the hypothesis that the number of mediators is zero. So this is the very first test performed. Rejecting this null hypothesis implies there must be at least one mediator. The second test in the series tests the null hypothesis that a single mediator can fit the data; rejecting this hypothesis implies there must be at least two mediators. The next test in the series tests the null hypothesis that two mediators will explain the pattern of relationships; rejection implies the number must be at least three. And so on.

As these hypothesis tests are performed today, each is a chi-square test. Typically, the result of each test in the series is substantially less significant than the result of the previous test. Thus a single analysis encapsulates a whole scientific sequence: First test a very simple model. If it fails to fit the data, try a more complex model designed to fit the data better; if it does fit better, the chi-square rejecting the model will be lower than the previous chi-square. Continue to test more complex models, each designed to fit the data somewhat better, until you find one that fits adequately—that is, gives a nonsignificant chi-square.

Even if all tests are significant, the number of tests in the series cannot exceed either the number of independent variables or the number of dependent variables. Both SYSTAT and SAS perform the entire series of tests at once, regardless of the significance or nonsignificance of the early tests in the series.

To perform this series of tests in SYSTAT, first issue MODEL and ESTIMATE commands as in Sec. 17.3. Then type

>print long

to obtain more complete output. Then, as in Sec. 17.4.1, issue a HYPOTHESIS command, an EFFECT command, and a TEST command, in that order. As before, the first and last commands are the single words shown. But now the EFFECT command lists all the independent variables in the hypothesis, separated by ampersands. This need not include all the regressors; covariates should be omitted from the EFFECT command. In the current example, we will think of all three regressors (race, sex, and age) as independent variables, so that the commands are

>hypothesis
>effect = race & sex & age
>test

The output produced by these commands contains much we shall not discuss, but it includes a section titled TEST OF RESIDUAL ROOTS. This section is shown for the present example in Table 17.2.

TABLE 17.2
SYSTAT output used to test number of parallel mediators

```
TEST OF RESIDUAL ROOTS
ROOTS 1 THROUGH 2
  CHI-SQUARE STATISTIC = 8.604    DF = 6    PROB = 0.19
ROOTS 2 THROUGH 2
  CHI-SQUARE STATISTIC = 1.162    DF = 2    PROB = 0.55
```

In the present example, there are only two tests in the series, since there are only two dependent variables. Find the last significant test in the series. The number immediately after the word ROOTS for that test is the minimum number of parallel mediators consistent with the data. If even the first test is nonsignificant, as in the present example, then the data are consistent with the hypothesis that the number of parallel mediators is zero, which implies there are no relations between any of the independent variables and any of the dependent variables.

The hypothesis of a single parallel mediator also has an alternate interpretation. It means that in the population, the regression coefficients predicting the different dependent variables are all proportional to each other, so that the various $\hat{Y}$ variables all correlate perfectly with each other. To see why this proportionality occurs, let I1 and I2 denote two independent variables while D1 and D2 represent two dependent variables. Let $_Tb(I1)$, $_Tb(I2)$, $_Tb(D1)$, and $_Tb(D2)$, denote the true size of the effects represented by the arrows connecting these four variables to the single unmeasured mediator. Then the multiplicative law of casual relations (see Sec. 7.5.2) asserts that the effect of I1 on D1 is $_Tb(I1)*_Tb(D1)$, while the effect of I2 on D1 is $_Tb(I2)*_Tb(D1)$, so the ratio of the two effects is $_Tb(I1)/_Tb(I2)$. The effect of I1 on D2 is $_Tb(I1)*_Tb(D2)$, while the effect of I2 on D2 is $_Tb(I2)*_Tb(D2)$, so the ratio of the two effects is again $_Tb(I1)/_Tb(I2)$. So proportionality must exist.

17.5 REPEATED MEASURES

17.5.1 Some Examples of Repeated-Measures Designs

In a repeated-measures design, the dependent variable is measured two or more times for each subject, under different experimental conditions. For instance, suppose a testing machine is used to test the driving ability of subjects, and the effects of a car radio are measured by testing each subject's abilities at different times under conditions of silence, music, and a news broadcast. That is almost the simplest possible repeated-measures design: it has just one repeated, or *within subjects*, factor we can call "radio," and no *between-subjects* factors. We say "almost" the simplest possible design because it would be even simpler if there were only two levels (categories) of radio, such as music and silence; but that would be so simple it could be handled by a simple matched-pairs *t* test.

A more complex design might have two repeated factors. We might have the three levels (categories) of radio (factor *A*) mentioned above and cross these with a simulated conversation. We can call this factor *B* (conversation) and suppose it has four levels: no conversation, a monologue from a "passenger," a "passenger" asking the driver questions about recent news, and an argument. Then each subject is tested under 3 × 4, or 12, conditions.

The design could be complicated further by adding between-subjects factors, such as alcohol (factor C): some subjects are given liquor just before the test, and some are not, making two levels of factor C. We might also record each subject's age (factor D), making a second between-subjects factor, this one numerical. In other designs, within-subjects factors might also be numerical, such as the frequency with which the driver must answer questions asked by the "passenger."

We can test all main effects and interactions. The present example involves effects A, B, C, D, AB, AC, AD, BC, BD, CD, ABC, ABD, ACD, BCD, and $ABCD$.

The designs that behavioral scientists call repeated-measures designs are often called *split-plot* designs in agricultural research, or more generally *split-unit* designs. An agricultural experimenter might use a 10-acre plot in each of 20 different counties, divide each plot into 5 subplots of 2 acres each, and then apply a different kind of fertilizer to each of the 5 subplots, using the same 5 kinds of fertilizer in each of the 20 counties. The 5 measurements on each plot cannot be considered independent, so the statistical issues are the same as if responses to 5 treatments had been measured for each of 20 people.

17.5.2 Univariate and Multivariate Methods

There are two common methods for analyzing repeated-measures designs: univariate and multivariate. The chapters on repeated measures in most ANOVA (analysis-of-variance) texts describe only or primarily the univariate method, and many behavioral scientists are not even aware of the multivariate method. The univariate approach analyzes the data by treating *cases* as an additional independent variable or factor. For instance, suppose that in the example of Sec. 17.5.1 each of 50 people is exposed to 12 treatment combinations—3 levels of radio crossed with 4 levels of conversation. The univariate approach would treat this not as a two-way 3×4 design with 50 entries per cell, but as a three-way $3 \times 4 \times 50$ design with one entry per cell.

The univariate and multivariate methods give identical results for tests that involve only between-subjects factors, or within-subjects factors with only two levels. But for tests involving repeated factors with more than two levels, the univariate method requires an assumption called *compound symmetry*, which the multivariate method does not. The advantages of the univariate method are its computational simplicity and its greater statistical power when compound symmetry holds. Its disadvantage is that when compound symmetry does not hold, it can be seriously deficient in both power and validity. In one example using artificial data, the univariate method gave $p < .005$ when the correct multivariate method gave $p = .59$. In another example, the correct multivariate method gave an infinite F, so that $p = 0$, while the univariate method gave $p = .54$. Thus the univariate p may err dramatically in either the liberal or the conservative direction. The basic source of invalidity in the univariate method is that it treats all Y scores as if they were independent even when they come from the same case.

17.5.3   Sphericity and Compound Symmetry

Technically, the univariate method does not require the assumption of compound symmetry, but a less restrictive assumption called *sphericity*. In a design with just one repeated factor with k levels, consider the $k(k - 1)/2$ variables formed by subtracting scores on each level from scores on all the other levels. Sphericity states that these $k(k - 1)/2$ difference variables all have equal variances in the population. This assumption is technically less restrictive than compound symmetry, but in practice, it is difficult to imagine any case in which a worker could make this assumption about a data set without assuming compound symmetry. Thus, in practice, the assumption of compound symmetry seems to be required. What is it?

   In an ordinary factorial ANOVA design, there is no concept of correlations between observations; observations are assumed to be independent. But if we have measured N people on each of k trials, then we can correlate trial 1 with trial 2, trial 1 with trial 3, trial 2 with trial 3, and so on, getting $k(k - 1)/2$ correlations altogether. The assumption of *compound symmetry* is the assumption that all these correlations are equal in the population when the between-subjects factors are held constant. This is in addition to the usual assumptions of normality and homoscedasticity.

   If each repeated factor has only two levels, then there is only one correlation between levels, so the question of compound symmetry does not arise. Therefore the univariate and multivariate methods give identical results when each repeated factor has only two levels.

   We can also automatically assume compound symmetry if we are testing an unusually strong form of the null hypothesis. The usual between-trials null hypothesis states that the repeated factor has no effect on the means. This allows that relative to treatment 1, treatment 2 might raise the scores of some people and lower the scores of others, leaving the mean unchanged. A stronger form of the null hypothesis says that no treatment has any real effect on anybody, so that all variations from trial to trial are the result of random fluctuations. Then compound symmetry would also apply. For instance, in tests of mental telepathy, the null hypothesis of no telepathy implies that all trials are governed by chance and are therefore independent, either within or between subjects. Thus the correlations between trials are 0 and are therefore equal; the assumption of compound symmetry could be violated only if telepathy existed. If a test's assumptions are false only when the null hypothesis is false, then the test is valid, because its assumptions are correct when the null hypothesis is true. But examples like this are rare.

   How reasonable is the assumption of compound symmetry otherwise? In my opinion, not very. Imagine an experiment on autonomic responses to three kinds of music, in which each subject hears all three kinds. Suppose that in some subtle way, music types 1 and 2 are more similar to each other than either is to type 3, so that the people who respond strongly to type 1 also tend to respond strongly to type 2. This is a violation of compound symmetry. Yet it is extremely hard to assume that such effects are absent; rather, we would normally assume they are present. If the null hypothesis (of no between-trials effects) is false, by definition that implies that each trial mean is closer to some means than to others, and in that sense is more similar to some than to others. Thus we are actually testing for differences in similarity among trials (whether trial 1 is more similar to trial 2 than to trial 3, for instance) in one sense, while assuming its absence in another sense.

Several authors say that Monte Carlo studies have shown that moderate deviations from compound symmetry produce little loss in validity in the univariate method. But even measuring the degree of deviation from compound symmetry is a tricky business, so it is not completely clear what "moderate" deviations are. And the smaller is k, the less serious are the effects of deviations from compound symmetry. Most of these studies have been done with small k, so that their results do not generalize to large k.

17.5.4   A Conservative Form of the Univariate Method

Geisser and Greenhouse (1958) have suggested modifying repeated-measures ANOVA to deal with the problem of compound symmetry, by dividing both numerator and denominator df of F by $k - 1$, where k is the number of repeated trials. This gives a test which is always conservative. But the preferable strategy today is to employ the multivariate method.

17.5.5   The Multivariate Method

Programs for the multivariate method are still not widespread, but they are available in both SAS PROC GLM and the SYSTAT MGLH procedure. The SYSTAT 4 manual contains an especially complete discussion, covering 32 pages with many examples. But SAS offers many more options. Both packages give univariate F's along with the multivariate ones. The precise commands used are rather different in the two packages, and a full description of either is too long to include here. But they are straightforward, and anyone who has come this far in this book should be able to read the appropriate manual if necessary.

The multivariate method restates the hypotheses of interest as hypotheses about the means of sums and differences of various sets of trials. Suppose there are two trials per person and we wish to test for a trial effect. That is, we wish to test the null hypothesis that the means of the two trials Y_1 and Y_2 are equal. For each person, we could subtract the score on Y_2 from the score on Y_1, giving a difference score $Y_1 - Y_2$. The null hypothesis that Y_1 and Y_2 have equal means is equivalent to the null hypothesis that the mean of $Y_1 - Y_2$ is zero. This could be tested with a simple one-group t test. But we saw in Sec. 17.1 that this test can be thought of as the test on a when we define $Y = Y_1 - Y_2$ and regress Y on no variables except an imaginary one scored 1 for every case.

Now suppose there are four repeated trials Y_1, Y_2, Y_3, and Y_4. The null hypothesis that Y_1, Y_2, Y_3, and Y_4 all have equal means is equivalent to the hypothesis that the means of $Y_1 - Y_2$, $Y_1 - Y_3$, and $Y_1 - Y_4$ are all zero. This is the null hypothesis tested in MANOVA when we regress these three difference variables on the constant term and test the null hypothesis that the constant is zero in all three regressions.

Or suppose we have a between-subjects factor, such as alcohol in our example in Sec. 17.5.1. Consider the hypothesis of interaction between alcohol and trial when there are only two trials Y_1 and Y_2. This hypothesis states that the difference between the Y_1 and Y_2 means will change between the alcohol and the no-alcohol conditions. But this could be tested with a two-group t test on the difference scores $Y_1 - Y_2$, the two groups being the alcohol and no-alcohol groups. And the main effect of alcohol is tested by testing for a difference between the alcohol and no-alcohol groups on $Y_1 + Y_2$. If the between-groups factor had four levels instead of just two, then the interaction could be tested with a one-way ANOVA or its regression equivalent.

17.5.6 Multivariate Repeated Measures with an Ordinary Regression Program

The multivariate approach to repeated measures can be executed with an ordinary regression program, provided that each repeated factor has only two levels. There may still be a great many trials per subject; for instance, if there are five dichotomous repeated factors, then there are 2^5, or 32, trials per subject. Even if you have a more powerful program, such as SYSTAT or SAS, this section can help you understand exactly what that program is doing.

It is convenient to denote the repeated factors as A, B, C, and so on, and to let Y with appropriate subscripts denote scores on the dependent variables. We shall illustrate the method by assuming that there are two dichotomous repeated factors, so that there are altogether four dependent measures per subject, denoted Y_{11}, Y_{12}, Y_{21}, and Y_{22}.

We shall create a series of variables we call E variables because their names will begin with the letter E, for "effect." There will be one E variable for each repeated factor and one for each interaction between repeated factors. The variable's full name will be the letter E followed by the name of the factor or factors involved. Thus, when there are two repeated factors A and B, we will have variables, EA, EB, and EAB. When there are three repeated factors A, B, and C, we will have variables EA, EB, EC, EAB, EAC, EBC, and $EABC$. Regardless of the number of repeated factors, there will also be one variable named ET, where the T stands for "total." Counting ET, the number of E variables is always 2^k, where k is the number of repeated factors.

ET is formed by summing all the dependent-variable scores within each subject. With two repeated factors, this means that

$$ET = Y_{11} + Y_{12} + Y_{21} + Y_{22}$$

Each of the other *E* variables is formed by taking the difference between two sums of *Y* variables, in such a way that the mean of the *E* variable estimates the size of the effect in the variable's name. With two repeated factors, we can do this by defining *E* variables as follows:

$$EA = (Y_{11} + Y_{12}) - (Y_{21} + Y_{22}) = Y_{11} + Y_{12} - Y_{21} - Y_{22}$$

$$EB = (Y_{11} + Y_{21}) - (Y_{12} + Y_{22}) = Y_{11} - Y_{12} + Y_{21} - Y_{22}$$

$$EAB = (Y_{11} - Y_{12}) - (Y_{21} - Y_{22}) = Y_{11} - Y_{12} - Y_{21} + Y_{22}$$

Then the mean of *EA* estimates the effect of factor *A*, the mean of *EB* estimates the effect of factor *B*, and the mean of *EAB* estimates the effect of the *AB* interaction. In MYSTAT, the *E* variables can be created by executing LET commands on the command line of the editor.

We now turn to between-subjects factors. For each categorical between-subjects factor, choose some weighted or unweighted average of the factor levels that will define the main or average effect of the factor. The usual and traditional choice is the simplest: use an unweighted average. Code each factor appropriately, as described in Chap. 10. If you have chosen an unweighted average, then in MYSTAT you can simply use the CATEGORY command, which will implement effect coding.

For each numerical between-subjects factor such as age, choose some level that will define the main or average effect of that regressor. If the population mean of the regressor is known, that will typically be the level chosen. Then subtract that level from all scores on the factor, so that the adjusted scores are deviations from the chosen level.

Then regress each of the *E* variables onto the between-subjects factors, including in the model statements any interactions of interest. In each of the resulting tests, you will test the effect found by combining the factors in the *E* variable's name with the effect named in the model statement. This also applies to the additive constant *a*. Thus, if there are two repeated factors *A* and *B* and two between-subjects factors *C* and *D*, the MYSTAT commands are as shown immediately below, and the effects tested are shown in the body of Table 17.3.

```
>model et = constant + c + d + c*d
>model ea = constant + c + d + c*d
>model eb = constant + c + d + c*d
>model eab = constant + c + d + c*d
```

This method works because any interaction among *k* factors means that the size of the interaction among any *k* − 1 of those factors is itself affected by the level of the *k*th factor. For instance, to say that there is an *ABC* interaction

TABLE 17.3
Effects tested when E variables defined by two repeated factors A and B are regressed onto two between-subjects factors C and D

		Dependent variable			
		ET	EA	EB	EAB
	Constant		A	B	AB
Model	C	C	AC	BC	ABC
entry	D	D	AD	BD	ABD
	$C \times D$	CD	ACD	BCD	$ABCD$

is to say that the size of the AB interaction is affected by the level of C. But the variable EAB measures the size of the AB interaction for each subject, so to say that EAB is affected by C is to say that there is an ABC interaction.

17.5.7 Coding Schemes for Multicategorical Repeated Factors

In Chap. 10 we saw that a categorical variable with k categories can be represented by a set of $k - 1$ coded variables. Similarly, a repeated factor with k categories can be represented by a set of $(k - 1)$ E variables, each of which is a linear function of the original dependent variables. And as in Chap. 10, there are many different ways to create those variables. For instance, the hypothesis that Y_1, Y_2, Y_3, and Y_4 all have equal means is equivalent to the hypothesis that the means of $Y_1 - Y_2$, $Y_1 - Y_3$, and $Y_1 - Y_4$ are all zero. But it is also equivalent to the hypothesis that the means of $Y_1 - Y_2$, $Y_2 - Y_3$, and $Y_3 - Y_4$ are all zero, or to the hypothesis that the means of $Y_1 - Y_4$, $Y_2 - Y_4$, and $Y_3 - Y_4$ are all zero. As in Chap. 10, all those ways of constructing E variables yield the same F for testing the composite null hypothesis that there are no differences among the k levels of the factor, but yield tests of different specific hypotheses nested within that composite. And as in Chap. 10, you can either create the variables "by hand," one at a time, or use special commands to create them all at once. SAS has five special commands for creating E variables, SYSTAT has two, and MYSTAT has none. We will first review the special commands in SAS and SYSTAT, and then discuss methods applicable in MYSTAT and other programs.

In SAS you can use any of five different keywords to specify sets of contrasts. The default is CONTRAST, which compares each level with the final level, as in $Y_1 - Y_4$, $Y_2 - Y_4$, $Y_3 - Y_4$. Or you can choose which level will be compared with all others by putting the ordinal number (from 1 to k) of a given level in parentheses after the word CONTRAST. For instance, CONTRAST(2) produces the contrasts $Y_1 - Y_2$, $Y_3 - Y_2$, $Y_4 - Y_2$. Note the similarity to simple dummy coding in Chap. 10. The keyword PROFILE produces a comparison of each cell with the following cell, as in $Y_1 - Y_2$, $Y_2 - Y_3$, $Y_3 - Y_4$. This is similar to sequential coding in Chap. 10. The keyword MEAN produces an analogue to effect coding; each level is contrasted with the mean of all levels, with the last level omitted. If some other level is to be omitted, it can be specified in parentheses after the word MEAN, as in MEAN(2). The keyword HELMERT generates contrasts between each level and the mean of subsequent levels. This is useful if the repeated factor is time and you want to identify the point after which no significant change occurs.

The fifth option offered by SAS is POLYNOMIAL. This option is useful when a repeated factor is numerical, as when proficiency is tested after 2, 4, 6, and 8 hours of practice. If the levels are unevenly spaced, such as 2, 4, 7, and 12, the level values can be placed in parentheses after the keyword, as in POLYNOMIAL(2, 4, 7, 12).

To illustrate the polynomial approach, suppose Y_1, Y_2, Y_3, and Y_4 are measures of proficiency on a task taken for each subject after 2, 4, 6, and 8 hours of practice. The hypothesis of no linear effect of practice is equivalent to the hypothesis that the mean of $3Y_4 + 1Y_3 - 1Y_2 - 3Y_1$ is zero. It can be shown that the hypothesis of no quadratic (parabolic) effect is the hypothesis that the mean of $Y_1 - Y_2 - Y_3 + Y_4$ is zero. And it can be shown that the hypothesis of no cubic effect is the hypothesis that the mean of $-Y_1 + 3Y_2 - 3Y_3 + Y_4$ is zero. A cubic polynomial is the highest-order polynomial that can be fitted to four means, so the hypothesis that all four means are equal is the hypothesis that there is no linear, quadratic, or cubic effect. The POLYNOMIAL option performs a test of this composite hypothesis, as well as individual tests on the linear, quadratic, and cubic terms.

SYSTAT can duplicate the second and last of these five options. The command

>profile = polynomial

fits a polynomial; an option is available for unequal spacing. And the command

>profile = difference

compares each repeated measure with the previous one, as in the second of SAS's options.

From this discussion it should be apparent how to define E variables in any regression program to simulate most of the options mentioned. For a factor with five levels Y_1, Y_2, Y_3, Y_4, and Y_5, Helmert coding would use the E variables

$$E1 = Y1 - \frac{Y2 + Y3 + Y4 + Y5}{4}$$

$$E2 = Y2 - \frac{Y3 + Y4 + Y5}{3}$$

$$E3 = Y3 - \frac{Y4 + Y5}{2}$$

$$E4 = Y4 - Y5$$

You can use MYSTAT or any other regression program to perform a multivariate repeated-measures analysis with multicategorical repeated factors, *provided* you are willing to replace the composite test on each factor with a Bonferroni test or a suitable alternative. For instance, if a repeated factor has five levels, the null hypothesis that the factor has no effect would ordinarily be tested by an F test with $df_1 = 4$, since the factor is represented by four E variables. You can test this same composite hypothesis by testing all four E variables individually and correcting the most significant result by a Bonferroni factor of 4. Not only is this test fully valid, it may actually be more powerful than the F test if one of the individual effects tested is substantially larger than the others. Or if you are willing to specify one of the $k - 1$ contrasts in advance as the one most likely to be significant, and to dispense with tests on other contrasts if that one turns out nonsignificant, then you can gain still more power by omitting the Bonferroni correction of that contrast.

17.6 TRANSFORMATIONS OF Y

When we replace Y by $\log(Y)$ or some other function of Y, we are *transforming* Y. If the new scores are in the same rank order as the old, the transformation is *monotonic*. Monotonic transformations of Y may produce as many as three benefits at once: they can simplify the interpretation of the regression by eliminating the need for nonlinear and interaction terms (see Sec. 13.3.3), they can increase Y's relationship to the regression's linear terms, and they can make the residuals more nearly normally distributed. This section describes methods for finding such transformations if they exist. It relates directly to the problem of equal-interval scaling discussed in Sec. 8.1.5.

17.6.1 Some Possible Transformations

To see the range of Y transformations possible, let us start on more familiar ground by talking about transformations of X. Consider a regression containing only a single independent variable X plus quadratic or other nonlinear functions of X. We did not emphasize the point in Chap. 12, but the variable $\hat{Y}$ found in such a regression is actually a nonlinear transformation of X. For instance, if regression formulas yield the expression

$$\hat{Y} = .7X + .4X^2 + 4.1$$

then $\hat{Y}$ is actually a quadratic transformation of X. The multiple correlation R is actually the correlation between Y and this transformed version of X. If the nonlinear transformation helps so that $R > |r_{XY}|$, then the transformed version of X has a higher correlation with Y than does the original X.

In Chap. 12 we allowed transformations to be either monotonic or non-monotonic. Logarithmic and exponential transformations are always monotonic. Transformations found by polynomial or spline regression may turn out to be either monotonic or nonmonotonic. But a spline transformation will often turn out to be monotonic over the entire imaginable range of X, and even a polynomial transformation will often turn out to be monotonic over the observed or likely range of X.

17.6.2   Why Transformations That Increase Predictability Also Increase Linearity

If a transformation of X improves the prediction of Y, the improvement results from the increased linearity between Y and $\hat{Y}$. We did not use quite these terms in Chap. 12, but in that chapter we effectively measured the nonlinearity of a relationship as its ability to be improved by nonlinear transformations. If the best nonlinear transformation is found, then it cannot be improved by further transformations, because there is already a linear relationship between Y and $\hat{Y}$. Thus, by transforming X to maximize the predictability of Y from $\hat{Y}$, we maximize linearity between Y and $\hat{Y}$.

   Now reverse the roles of X and Y in this argument. By finding a transformation of Y that correlates maximally with a variable X, we are actually finding the transformation of Y with maximal linear association with X. Thus, if there is only one regressor X, we can reverse the usual roles of X and Y and use spline regression or polynomial regression to find a transformation of Y which relates more nearly linearly to X.

   Occasionally, the regression of Y on X (that is, the prediction of Y from X) may be linear while the regression of X on Y is not. This may arise, for instance, if X is dichotomous and Y is continuous. That complicates our discussion, but this problem does not arise if X is normally distributed. For the moment we will assume that X is normal, but by the end of the discussion we will see that this is rarely an important assumption.

17.6.3   Why $\hat{Y}$ Is Useful in Transforming Y

One of the standard assumptions of multiple regression is that the transformation of Y that relates linearly to one regressor X also relates linearly to all regressors. It therefore also relates linearly to any weighted average or linear function of the regressors. Thus, with a sufficiently large sample, we could use any single variable X to find the optimum transformation of Y, so long as X has some relation to Y. But the higher X's correlation with Y is, the more efficiently we can find the best Y transformation in a small sample. Therefore it is best to fit the Y transformation to a linear function of the regressors that has itself been selected to relate maximally with Y. It is thus best to transform Y to correlate maximally with $\hat{Y}$, the regression function predicting Y from the linear terms of the regressors. Since we will be using $\hat{Y}$ as the dependent variable in a regression, let us rename it HATY.

But HATY was constructed to correlate maximally with the original, untransformed Y. What says that HATY is the linear function of the regressors that also correlates maximally with the transformed Y? There are two answers to this. One answer is that we do not actually need the very best linear combination of the regressors; we just need one that relates somewhat to Y, and there is no practical way to get a better combination of regressors than HATY.

The second answer is theoretically more satisfying though more complex. If we find a transformation Y_T of Y that relates maximally with a single regressor X, then by definition its correlation with X cannot be further increased by forming some new function of Y and Y_T. But this means that the partial correlation $r(X, Y.Y_T)$ is zero, since a partial correlation is one measure of a variable's ability to improve predictions made from another variable. If the transformation Y_T that is best for one X is also best for all X's, then this relationship $r(X, Y.Y_T) = 0$ will hold for all X's. But the numerator of this partial correlation is $r(X, Y) - r(X, Y_T) \times r(Y, Y_T)$. Since the partial correlation is zero, this numerator is also zero, which implies that $r(X, Y) = r(X, Y_T) \times r(Y, Y_T)$. This relationship holds for each of several X variables. But $r(Y, Y_T)$ is constant over different X variables, so we can write $r(X, Y) = k \times r(X, Y_T)$, where k is a positive constant. Thus the X variable with the highest value of $r(X, Y)$ will also have the highest value of $r(X, Y_T)$. In other words, the X variable that has the highest correlation with the untransformed variable Y will also have the highest correlation with the as-yet-unmeasured variable Y_T. This is true not only of single X variables, but also of linear combinations of them. Thus the linear combination of X's formed to correlate maximally with the original, untransformed Y will also be the one having the highest correlation with the variable Y_T to be discovered. It is therefore the most efficient variable to use in deriving Y_T.

We are now ready to see why regressors rarely need to be normally distributed, even though we made that assumption temporarily. If several regressors have reasonably low intercorrelations and each gets a moderately large weight in forming HATY, then the central limit theorem asserts that HATY is approximately normally distributed. We routinely assume that residuals e are also normally distributed. But $Y = \text{HATY} + e$, and the sum of two normal variables is itself normally distributed, so that Y is approximately normal. Thus HATY and Y form approximately a bivariate normal distribution. A property of this distribution is that both regressions—that of Y on HATY and that of HATY on Y—are linear. This removes the problem that one regression may be linear while the other is not.

17.6.4   Some Specific Methods

We have concluded that the general approach is to find a monotonic transformation of Y that correlates highly with HATY, the variable formed to predict Y from the linear terms of the regressors. There are several ways to do this.

Perhaps the best way to start is to plot the regression's t residuals against values of Y. If several of the most positive t residuals all occur within the same range of Y, that suggests a transformation that lowers those scores on Y relative to others. For instance, if all the highest t residuals are associated with the highest values of Y, a logarithmic transformation might be indicated.

There are three general types of transformations that will handle a great many problems. First, if HATY is approximately normal, then we have just seen that Y itself should be approximately normal, so that one simple approach is to transform Y to normality. As we saw in Sec. 14.2.3 on normal-scores tests, a simple way to do this is to divide the area under a normal curve into $N + 1$ equal areas, and to find the z scores corresponding to these areas. Thus, if $N = 49$, the desired z scores are those with .02, .04, .06, and so on of the curve's area to their left.

Another approach is to use the nonlinear regression methods of Chap. 12 to derive a transformation of Y that correlates highly with HATY. Spline functions seem superior to polynomials for this purpose, because they are more likely to maintain a monotonic relation to Y across the entire range of data. I have worked primarily with spline joints at the 25th and 75th percentiles. This enables excellent fits to many transformations. For instance, if we arbitrarily make Y contain the first 100 integers and define $T = \log(Y)$, then $r_{YT} = .896$, but when regression is used to fit to T a spline function of Y with joints at $Y = 25$ and $Y = 76$, the spline function has a correlation of .997 with T.

A third approach is based on the fact that two variables can correlate perfectly only if they have exactly the same shape—that is, if they are identical in skewness, kurtosis, and all other characteristics except mean and standard deviation. Thus, transforming Y to the shape of HATY should generally increase the linear correlation between the two. We can transform Y to precisely the shape of HATY by replacing each value of Y by the value of HATY with the same rank—replacing the highest Y by the highest HATY, the second-highest Y by the second-highest HATY, and so forth. This can be implemented in SYSTAT by separately sorting files containing HATY and the original data set and merging the two sorted files. Since this method tailors the distribution of Y precisely to that of HATY, it is more likely than the other two methods to be affected by random fluctuations in the data. But it does not suffer from the simplest form of overfitting, since the value of HATY replacing each value of Y is rarely the value derived to estimate that particular value of Y.

The gain from any transformation can be assessed by the reduction in significant nonlinear terms in the regression, by the increase in the multiple correlation computed from the linear terms, and perhaps above all by the increased fit to regression assumptions as measured especially by the size of the highest t residuals.

I have studied thousands of examples using artificial data in which a variable Y_0 was defined to relate linearly to the regressors, using, for instance, the MYSTAT command

```
>let y0 = x1 + x2 + zrn
```

Then Y_0 was monotonically transformed in some way to form the "observed" variable Y, using most often an exponential, cubic, hyperbolic, or logistic transformation. Then the aforementioned methods were used to try to recover the original transformations from Y. Success was measured by the three criteria in the previous paragraph, plus a fourth available only in working with data sets generated artificially. This fourth criterion was $r(Y_0, Y_T)$, the Pearson correlation between the transformed Y and the original "unobserved" variable Y_0. In most data sets, all methods worked very well. Typical values of $r(Y_0, Y_T)$ were between .98 and .99, unnecessary interaction and nonlinear terms were eliminated from regressions, multiple correlations with linear terms increased substantially, and the highest t residuals were reduced to near the levels expected by chance. Equally good results may not be found in real data sets, but the methods need not be used blindly; as mentioned above, plotting t residuals against Y may suggest useful transformations, and the three criteria of the previous paragraph can be used to measure the success of any attempt.

17.7   MANAGING MEASUREMENT ERROR

As discussed in Sec. 8.2, measurement error is the most important single limitation of linear models. There are methods for controlling it, which unfortunately are not as widely available as they should be. This section assumes a basic understanding of the concept of a variable's *reliability*, which we shall denote "rel." The next paragraph gives a very brief introduction.

The concept of reliability is based on the notion of a variable's *true scores*—the scores we would observe if there were no measurement error. We can define *reliability* as a variable's squared correlation with its true scores. Of course, we do not know the true scores, or we would use them instead of the observed scores. But we can nevertheless sometimes estimate this correlation. For instance, suppose we have two parallel forms of a mental test. We assume that the two tests, denoted A and B, have the same true scores T, and that they correlate equally with T, so that $_Tr_{AT} = {}_Tr_{BT}$. Since A and B differ from T only because of random measurement error, we can assume that $_Tr(AB.T) = 0$. Since the numerator of this partial correlation is $_Tr_{AB} - {}_Tr_{AT} \times {}_Tr_{BT}$, it must also equal zero, so we have $_Tr_{AB} = {}_Tr_{AT} \times {}_Tr_{BT} = {}_Tr_{AT}^2 = {}_Tr_{BT}^2$. Thus the reliability of either A or B is the correlation between them.

17.7.1   Estimation of Reliabilities

In the conceptually simpler methods of managing measurement error, the first step is to estimate the reliabilities of the variables in question. This is not a simple task. A variable's reliability can be defined in theory as its correlation with a parallel measure of the same trait, as in the previous paragraph. But in actual practice people may remember how they have answered, say, an attitude questionnaire, and answer like questions similarly. And two measures of the same trait will have a lower correlation with each other if given a week apart than if given an hour apart. Which is the correct value of reliability? We have no answers for these questions; we refer the reader to books on mental measurement. All we can say is that a serious attempt to estimate reliability, with awareness of these complexities, is likely to produce better estimates than the values of 1 that we implicitly assume when we simply ignore the problem. In what follows, we assume that we have appropriate estimates of reliability for the necessary variables. We shall denote the reliability of Y by rel_Y, and the reliability of X_j by rel_j.

17.7.2 Correcting for Measurement Error in Y

To correct for measurement error in Y, we can divide adjusted R or values of pr_j by $\sqrt{\text{rel}_Y}$. This gives estimates of the corrected values of $_TR$ or $_Tpr_j$—the values that would exist if there were no measurement error in Y. But values of b_j are already unbiased estimators of the corrected values of $_Tb_j$, so they should not be altered. And it can be shown that hypothesis tests or confidence bands on R, pr_j, b_j, or any other statistics need not and should not be corrected for unreliability in Y. This unreliability genuinely raises the standard errors of all those statistics, and those increased standard errors should be taken into account when computing hypothesis tests or confidence bands.

17.7.3 Correcting b_j for Measurement Error in X_j

To correct an estimate of $_Tb_j$ for measurement error in the corresponding independent variable X_j, we can use the formula

$$\text{Corrected estimate of } _Tb_j = \frac{b_j}{1 - \dfrac{1 - \text{rel}_j}{\dfrac{N}{N-P}\text{Tol}_j}}$$

The next paragraph outlines a derivation of this formula.

Combining formulas from Secs. 1.3.3 and 2.3.3 gives the result

$$_Tb_j = \frac{_T\text{Cov}(Y, \text{ unique portion of } X_j)}{_T\text{Var}(\text{unique portion of } X_j)}$$

It can be shown that the covariance between any two variables is not affected by measurement error in either one, so that the numerator of this fraction is unaffected by measurement error. But the denominator is increased by measurement error. If we arbitrarily assume $_T\text{Var}(X_j) = 1$ when measurement error exists, then removing measurement error would lower that variance by $(1 - \text{rel}_j)$. But this reduction comes entirely out of $_T\text{Var}(\text{unique portion of } X_j)$, whose value before the reduction was $_T\text{Tol}_j$. Therefore the ratio of the two values of $_T\text{Var}$(unique portion of X_j)—after and before the removal of measurement error—is $[_T\text{Tol}_j - (1 - \text{rel}_j)]/_T\text{Tol}_j$. Dividing $_Tb_j$ by this ratio corrects $_Tb_j$ for measurement error. But when we apply the conclusions of Sec. 5.2.6 to the crosswise regression predicting X_j from the $P - 1$ other regressors, we find that an unbiased estimator of $_T\text{Tol}_j$ is $[N/(N - P)]\,\text{Tol}_j$. Substituting this value for $_T\text{Tol}_j$ in the previous ratio, and continuing in the natural way, gives the formula of the previous paragraph.

17.7.4 Correcting for Measurement Error in Covariates

To correct for measurement error in covariates, one can estimate the size but not the standard errors or significance of partial regression slopes by multiplying the variances of all covariates by their reliabilities while leaving all covariances unchanged, and by then deriving the regression formulas in the usual way from the modified variance-covariance matrix. There are two major ways to estimate the standard errors and statistical significance of partial regression slopes: the method of Fuller and Hidiroglou (1978), and the LISREL method. Neither is included in either SAS or SYSTAT. The fact that these and related methods are not better known, better understood, or more readily available is in my opinion the largest omission from today's statistical toolbox.

17.8 ROUNDING ERROR

17.8.1 Introduction to Rounding Error

Collinearity exists if any value of Tol_j is even moderately small, while singularity exists if any Tol_j is 0. What if Tol_j is, say, .0000001? We shall call such conditions *near singularity*. Computers operate with a certain amount of rounding error, so that they may identify such a case as singular. And even if they do not, near singularity may introduce substantial rounding error into calculations. Thus, extremely low tolerances should prompt some consideration of the problem of rounding error. Such consideration should also be prompted by the inclusion of any variable whose range is less than .01 times its mean.

17.8.2 Rounding Error in a Single Variable

Rounding error can be a much more serious problem in statistical calculations than many people realize. When variables have small standard deviations or ranges relative to their means, serious rounding error can occur in a calculation as simple as computing the standard deviation or variance of three scores. For instance, a common formula for variance is $\text{Var}(X) = \Sigma\,X^2/N - M_X^2$. Let us see what happens when you use this formula with a six-digit computer to find the variance of the three scores 577, 578, and 579.

The three values of X^2 are 332,929, 334,084, and 335,241, and $M_X^2 = $ 334,084. Our six-digit computer would find all these values correctly. But the value of 1,002,254 for ΣX^2 would be rounded to 1,002,250. Dividing this by 3 and rounding to six digits gives 334,083 for $\Sigma X^2/N$, while the correct value is $334,084\frac{2}{3}$. Then subtracting the correct M_X^2 value of 334,084 gives Var(X) = -1, while the correct variance is $\frac{2}{3}$. If this correct value were reported to even one-digit accuracy, it would be given as .7, but the six-digit computer gives the impossible value of -1.

Similar rounding error in finding S can arise whenever a variable's mean is large relative to its standard deviation. The problem arises in finding the difference between two nearly equal values, like $334,084\frac{2}{3}$ and 334,084 in the example above. A small error in finding either value translates into a large proportional error in the difference. By using scores with a larger mean relative to their standard deviation, examples can easily be constructed in which even 15 or 20 places of accuracy are inadequate.

You can circumvent this problem by increasing or decreasing all scores by a convenient constant, which gives the adjusted scores a reasonably small mean relative to their range. For instance, in the example above, if we subtracted 500 from all three scores, then our six-digit computer would report Var(X) with two-digit accuracy as .67, while if we subtracted 578 the computer would give Var(X) with all its 6 digits of accuracy, as .666667. SYSTAT and MYSTAT automatically do something much like this. Raw scores are recorded to approximately 14 digits of accuracy, and these programs avoid the problem so long as the scores are recorded correctly to begin with.

Manual subtractions will usually eliminate the rounding problem without changing any standard deviations, correlations, or slopes. But the subtractions will affect means, and thus the Y intercept a. To find the original means, add the constant back in. For instance, after subtracting 500, the mean in the example above is 78. Adding 500 to this value tells us that the original mean is 578.

If you are using a program other than SYSTAT or MYSTAT, you can easily test its susceptibility to this problem by asking it to find the standard deviation of any three large consecutive integers. Since most programs will record scores to 14 digits of accuracy, three good numbers are:

10,000,000,000,001
10,000,000,000,002
10,000,000,000,003

For these or any other three consecutive integers, the correct value of S is 1 if S is defined with the most common formula $S^2 = \Sigma x^2/(N - 1)$, or .8164966 by the alternative formula $S^2 = \Sigma x^2/N$. (The difference between these two formulas will not affect regression calculations.) Any value of S noticeably different from these values indicates rounding error. To avoid the problem, either find a new program or else check your data to see whether there are any variables likely

TABLE 17.4
A data set useful for detecting rounding error in regression

Case	X_1	X_2	Y
1	-1	1	0
2	$-d$	$-d$	-1
3	0	0	$-e$
4	0	0	e
5	d	d	1
6	1	-1	0

to produce problems because they have large means relative to their ranges. If the smallest score (in absolute value) is less than 100 times the range, few programs will have difficulty.

17.8.3   Rounding Error from Collinearity

A second type of rounding error arises when some regressors have extremely low tolerance (say, .001 or below), indicating that they can be predicted very accurately from one or more other regressors. As when calculating S, a computer program weak in this respect can produce output that has essentially no relation to the correct output. This is a good reason for checking tolerance values in your data.

   The ability of a program to handle problems of this type can be tested by choosing small positive values of two numbers we will call d and e, and then entering the data set of Table 17.4 into the computer. In this data set, the correct value of r_{12} is $(d^2 - 1)/(d^2 + 1)$, which approaches -1 as d approaches zero; and the correct value of R^2 is $1/(1 + e^2)$, which approaches 1 as e approaches zero. But accurate output depends upon the computer program's knowing that r_{12} is not -1 and R^2 is not 1. Therefore, by letting d and e equal

TABLE 17.5
Formulas that give exact answers for the data set of Table 17.4.

$M_1 = M_2 = M_Y = Y$ intercept $a = 0$ $MSE = \frac{2}{3}e^2$

$r_{Y1} = r_{Y2} = \dfrac{d}{\sqrt{(1 + d^2) \times (1 + e^2)}}$ $R^2 = \dfrac{1}{1 + e^2}$

$r_{12} = \dfrac{d^2 - 1}{d^2 + 1}$ Overall $F = \dfrac{3}{2e^2}$

$Tol_1 = Tol_2 = \dfrac{4d^2}{(1 + d^2)^2}$ $SE(b_1) = SE(b_2) = \sqrt{\dfrac{e^2(1 + d^2)}{12d^2}}$

$b_1 = b_2 = \dfrac{.5}{d}$ $t(b_1) = t(b_2) = \sqrt{\dfrac{3}{e^2(1 + d^2)}}$

successively smaller values, the program's accuracy can be tested. You should *not* use only powers of .1 (.01, .001, .0001, and so on), since some programs work better on those numbers than on other, larger values. The correct output can be calculated from the formulas in Table 17.5. Reading column by column, the formulas are listed approximately in order of increasing sensitivity to rounding error; the means are least sensitive, and the standard errors (*SE*'s) and *t*'s are most sensitive.

SUMMARY

17.1   Regression without the Constant, or with Only the Constant

We can think of the constant in a regression as the coefficient of a variable scored 1 for every case. Deleting this "variable" from the model forces the regression plane through the origin. And when this is the only variable in the model, its "coefficient" (the additive constant *a*) equals the sample mean. In this way regression can be used to test hypotheses and find confidence bands on single means.

17.2   Weighted Least Squares

Weighted least squares can be used to give different observations different weights, as when cities are different sizes but each is represented by only one observation.

17.3   Multiple Dependent Variables

In SYSTAT and SAS, several dependent variables can be included in the same model statement. At least some of the standard output is then generated for each variable.

17.4   MANOVA (Multivariate Analysis of Variance)

When we have two or more dependent variables, as in the previous section, we can use MANOVA to perform a single test on the composite null hypothesis that an independent variable has no partial relation to any of the dependent variables, with other regressors controlled.

MANOVA problems should not be confused with repeated-measures problems. The two are alike in that several measures have been taken for each case. But in a typical MANOVA problem, the measures for each case are on *different scales but for the same group or experimental condition*. In a typical repeated-measures problem, each case is measured on the *same scale under different conditions*.

Some MANOVA problems can be analyzed with an ordinary regression program, using a method we call *reverse regression*, in which the user enters an independent variable into the computer as the dependent variable and enters all the dependent variables and all covariates as regressors.

MANOVA can also be used to test hypotheses about the number of unmeasured parallel mediating factors needed to explain the relation between sets of independent and dependent variables. A series of chi-square tests is performed. The first tests the hypothesis of no association between independent and dependent variables—the hypothesis of no mediators. The next tests the hypothesis of a single mediator, which implies that in the population, the regression coefficients predicting the different dependent variables are all proportional to each other, so that the various $\hat{Y}$ variables all correlate perfectly with each other. Later tests in the series test hypotheses about larger numbers of mediators.

17.5   Repeated Measures

In a repeated-measures design, the dependent variable is measured two or more times for each subject, under different experimental conditions. The designs that behavioral scientists call repeated-measures designs are often called *split-plot* designs in agricultural research, or more generally *split-unit* designs.

There are two common methods for analyzing repeated-measures designs: univariate and multivariate. The univariate approach analyzes the data by treating *case* as an additional independent variable or factor. The univariate and multivariate methods give identical results for tests that involve only between-subjects factors, or within-subjects factors with only two levels. But for tests involving repeated factors with more than two levels, the univariate method requires an assumption called *compound symmetry*, which the multivariate method does not. The advantages of the univariate method are its computational simplicity and its greater statistical power when compound symmetry holds. Its disadvantage is that when compound symmetry does not hold, it can be seriously deficient in both power and validity. The assumption of compound symmetry is the assumption that all between-trials correlations are equal in the population when the between-subjects factors are held constant. This is in addition to the usual assumptions of normality and homoscedasticity. If each repeated factor has only two levels, then there is only one correlation between levels, so that the question of compound symmetry does not arise. Therefore, the univariate and multivariate methods give identical results when each repeated factor has only two levels. We can also automatically assume compound symmetry if we are testing an unusually strong form of the null hypothesis.

Geisser and Greenhouse (1958) have suggested modifying repeated-measures ANOVA to deal with the problem of compound symmetry, by dividing both numerator and denominator df or F by $k - 1$, where k is the number of repeated trials. This gives a test which is always conservative. But the preferable strategy today is to employ the multivariate method.

The multivariate method restates the hypotheses of interest as hypotheses about the means of sums and differences of various sets of trials. Many different coding schemes are possible when a repeated factor has more than two levels. All yield the same F for testing the overall hypothesis that the k means are equal, but they yield different individual contrasts. In SAS, you can compare each trial with one particular trial or compare each trial with the next or compare all except one with the mean of all or compare each with the mean of subsequent trials or fit a polynomial. SYSTAT can duplicate the second and last of these five options.

17.6 Transformations of Y

Monotonic transformations of Y may produce as many as three benefits at once: they can simplify the interpretation of the regression by eliminating the need for nonlinear and interaction terms, they can increase Y's relationship to the regression's linear terms, and they can make the residuals more nearly normally distributed. To search for such a transformation, first predict Y from the regressors in the ordinary way, denoting the resulting regression function as HATY. Then search for transformations of Y that correlate maximally with HATY, either by deriving spline transformations of Y, by normalizing it, or by transforming it to have the same shape (the same skewness, kurtosis, and so on) as HATY.

The gain from any transformation can be assessed by the reduction in significant nonlinear terms in the regression, by the increase in the multiple correlation computed from the linear terms, and perhaps above all by the increased fit to regression assumptions as measured especially by the size of the highest t residuals.

17.7 Managing Measurement Error

Measurement error is the most important single limitation of linear models. To control measurement error, we must often estimate a variable's reliability, defined as the variable's squared correlation with its true scores. Reliability is difficult to measure in practice, but it nevertheless seems clear that a serious attempt to estimate reliability is likely to produce better estimates than the values of 1 that we implicitly assume when we simply ignore the problem.

To correct for measurement error in Y, we can divide adjusted R or values of pr_j by $\sqrt{\text{rel}_Y}$. This gives estimates of the corrected values of $_TR$ or $_Tpr_j$—the values that would exist if there were no measurement error in Y. But values of b_j are already unbiased estimators of the corrected values of $_Tb_j$, so they should not be altered. And it can be shown that hypothesis tests or confidence bands on R, pr_j, b_j, or any other statistics need not and should not be corrected for unreliability in Y. This unreliability genuinely raises the standard errors of all those statistics, and those increased standard errors should be taken into account in computing hypothesis tests or confidence bands.

To correct an estimate of $_Tb_j$ for measurement error in the corresponding independent variable X_j, we can use the formula

$$\text{Corrected estimate of } _Tb_j = \frac{b_j}{1 - \dfrac{1 - \text{rel}_j}{\dfrac{N}{N - P} \times \text{Tol}_j}}$$

To correct for measurement error in covariates, one can estimate the size but not the standard errors or significance of partial regression slopes by multiplying the variances of all covariates by their reliabilities while leaving all covariances unchanged, and by then deriving the regression formulas in the usual way from the modified variance-covariance matrix. There are two major ways to estimate the standard errors and statistical significance of partial regression slopes: the method of Fuller and Hidiroglou (1978) and the LISREL method. Neither is included in either SAS or SYSTAT. The fact that these and related methods are not better known, better understood, or more readily available is in my opinion the largest omission from today's statistical toolbox.

17.8   Rounding Error

The computations in linear models frequently involve subtracting very similar numbers from each other. The difference is accurate to many fewer digits than the original numbers are. Thus rounding error can be a serious problem even though most statistical packages carry computations to 14 decimal digits. The data set with six cases provided in Table 17.4 can be used for testing the numerical accuracy of regression programs.

Chapters 17–19 contain no problems, since MYSTAT generally cannot be used and the choice of problems would depend upon the package used.

KEY TERMS

MANOVA	*E* variable
reverse regression	reliability
compound symmetry	true score
sphericity	near singularity

SYMBOLS AND ABBREVIATIONS

rel

CHAPTER 18

LOGISTIC REGRESSION AND RELATED METHODS

A major limitation of ordinary linear models is their requirement that the dependent or outcome variable Y be numerical rather than categorical. But outcomes of interest are frequently categorical—expressed most often as success or failure. Patients may live or die, students may graduate or fail to graduate, job applicants may be hired or rejected. An outcome variable may also have three or more categories that cannot be ranked ordinally, as when students in a college of arts and sciences choose to major in natural sciences, social sciences, or humanities.

Problems with categorical dependent variables can be studied with the methods of *discriminant analysis, probit analysis, log-linear models,* and *logistic regression,* which is also known as *logit analysis.* All four of these methods are available in both SAS and SYSTAT. None are available in MYSTAT.

Log-linear models require all regressors to be categorical, while discriminant analysis requires all to be numerical. Logit and probit analysis are more general, allowing any mix of numerical and categorical regressors. Chapter 19 discusses log-linear models, while this chapter combines logistic regression with brief discussions of discriminant and probit analysis. As we shall see in Sec. 19.2.2, log-linear analysis can be thought of as the special case of logistic regression for categorical regressors, just as analysis of variance is the special case of linear models for categorical regressors.

18.1 LOGISTIC REGRESSION

We shall consider only logistic regression for dichotomous Y, whose two categories can conveniently be called *success* and *failure*. Like ordinary linear models, logistic regression gives for each regressor a value b_j which measures the regressor's independent contribution to Y. The estimated standard error and the significance level for each b_j are also given. An overall measure of the model's goodness of fit can be calculated. The next section introduces this concept.

18.1.1 Measuring a Model's Fit to Data

One of the fundamental concepts of statistical inference is the concept of the *consistency* between a model and a set of data. We can regard a linear model as an attempt to find the model most consistent with a particular data set, with *in*consistency measured by SS(error). Any change in a model, such as adding a new regressor or set of regressors, is evaluated by its ability to increase the model's consistency with the data by decreasing SS(error). Thus, in dealing with categorical dependent variables, the first step is to develop a formula for measuring consistency or inconsistency between a model and data. Then, just as ordinary linear models maximize this consistency by trying to minimize SS(error), we can fit a model to categorical data by maximizing the chosen measure of consistency.

Consistency between the data and a model is measured by the *likelihood* or probability of observing the particular data if the model is correct. For instance, suppose a model or theory states that success at a task is determined primarily by actual practice at the task rather than by classroom lectures on the topic. When applied to three particular subjects, this model asserts that their probabilities of success at the task are respectively .6, .7, and .2. Suppose that when the three subjects try the task, the first two succeed and the last fails. Since the model has asserted that the probability of the last subject's succeeding is .2, it has also asserted that this subject's probability of failure is .8. Thus, by the multiplicative law of independent probabilities, according to this model, the overall probability of the observed outcomes is .6 × .7 × .8, or .336. That is the likelihood of the data if the model is correct, called more succinctly the model's *likelihood*.

Suppose a second model asserts that exposure to classroom lectures is more important than practice and implies that the probabilities of success for these three subjects are respectively .8, .6, and .1. According to this model, the overall probability of the same three outcomes is .8 × .6 × (1 − .1), or .432. Since the observed outcomes have a higher likelihood under this model than under the first, we can say that overall the second model is more consistent with the data than the first.

An equation for the likelihood can be written as follows. Let Y denote success or failure, with a Y of 1 denoting success and a Y of 0 denoting failure. Let PS_i denote person i's probability of success as calculated from a given model, so that $1 - PS_i$ is the model's calculated probability of failure for person i. Consider the expression

$$\text{Fit}_i = Y_i \times PS_i + (1 - Y_i) \times (1 - PS_i)$$

For anyone who fails, we have $Y_i = 0$, so that the first term equals zero and Fit_i reduces to $1 - PS_i$. For anyone who succeeds, we have $Y_i = 1$, so that the second term equals zero and Fit_i reduces to PS_i. But PS_i and $1 - PS_i$ are the probabilities the model calculates for success and failure. Thus, whether a person succeeds or fails, Fit_i equals the probability the model has assigned to the outcome that is ultimately observed. Therefore the model's likelihood or consistency with the data equals the product of the values of Fit_i for all subjects.

Values of likelihood can be extremely small in large samples. For instance, if Fit_i were .9 for each of 1000 subjects, the likelihood would equal $.9^{1000}$, or 1.75×10^{-46}. Therefore we usually report the natural logarithms of likelihood values rather than the raw values. But these logarithms are always negative, since a likelihood is always below 1; thus the usual value reported is $-\ln(\text{likelihood})$. We shall denote this as NLL, for "negative log likelihood." NLL is always positive and measures *lack of fit* between data and model; the smaller the value, the better the model fits the data. Since the sum of logarithms is the logarithm of the product, we have

$$\text{NLL} = -\Sigma \ln(\text{Fit}_i)$$

18.1.2   Logits

Next, we need a way of calculating PS_i from person i's scores on several regressors. But there are two reasons why we cannot treat PS as a simple linear function of regressors as we treat dependent variables in ordinary linear models. One reason is that numerical regressors may be unlimited in range. Most families have incomes between \$10,000 and \$100,000, but a few have incomes in the millions or even tens of millions. If we expressed PS as a positive linear function of income, then we might find some cases for which $PS > 1$. But this cannot be, since by definition PS is a probability.

The second problem has to do with interaction. For instance, suppose we have two dichotomous regressors, gender and training. That is, we have trained and untrained men and women. Suppose we find that among untrained subjects, 50% of men and 70% of women succeed at the task assigned. We find that among trained men, 90% succeed. We are willing to assume that in some sense, training has the same effect on men and women—in other words, there is no interaction between training and gender. But among untrained subjects, women outperform men by 20 percentage points. If we thought of *PS* as a linear function of training and gender, we would have to estimate the proportion of trained women succeeding as 90% plus 20%, or 110%. Again, this is inconsistent with our definition of *PS* as a probability.

We can avoid both these problems by making a *logit* transformation of *PS*, defined as

$$\text{logit}(PS) = \ln\left(\frac{PS}{1 - PS}\right)$$

Whereas *PS* can range only from 0 to 1, logit(*PS*) ranges from negative infinity to positive infinity. Table 18.1 shows the logits of several values of *PS*. The logit scale is symmetrical around a logit of 0 (*PS* of .5), so this table shows only two negative logit values. Note that differences between extreme proportions are spread out; on the logit scale the difference between success rates of .9 and .95 is considerably larger than the difference between .5 and .6. The difference between rates of .1 and .05 is equally large. When PS is near 0, $1 - PS$ is near 1 so that logit(*PS*) nearly equals $\ln(PS)$. And when *PS* is near 1, logit(*PS*) nearly equals $\ln[1/(1 - PS)]$. Thus the logit scale approaches a logarithmic scale at both ends, but relates nearly linearly to *PS* at intermediate values of *PS*.

Consider again the problem with the trained and untrained men and women. The success rates among untrained women and men were respectively .7 and .5. On the logit scale, the difference between these two values is .847 − 0 = .847. The success rate among trained men was .9, whose logit value is 2.197. Thus, in the absence of interaction between gender and training, we would predict for trained women a logit of 2.197 + .847 = 3.044. By solving the logit formula for *PS*, we find

$$PS = \frac{\exp(\text{logit } PS)}{1 + \exp(\text{logit } PS)}$$

TABLE 18.1
A small table of logits

PS	logit (PS)
.3	− .847
.4	− .405
.5	0
.6	.405
.7	.847
.8	1.386
.9	2.197
.95	2.944
.99	4.595

We can use this formula to calculate that a logit of 3.044 corresponds to a *PS* of .955.

There is no proof that the logit scale is in any sense the best possible scale. But it does give results that seem intuitively reasonable. It seems roughly reasonable that if two groups have success rates of 50% and 70% and a training program raises the success rate of the former group to 90%, it might well raise the success rate of the latter group to 95.5%, the rate calculated by assuming equal increases on the logit scale.

18.1.3   The Logistic Regression Equation

In an ordinary linear model we write

$$\hat{Y} = a + \Sigma\, b_j X_j$$

where the summation is over all variables, and the computer finds the values of a and b_j that maximize the accuracy of predictions by minimizing the sum of squared errors. If we assume that logit(*PS*) is linearly related to regressor scores, as we have just argued is intuitively reasonable, then we can write

$$\text{logit}(PS) = a + \Sigma\, b_j X_j$$

In the equation expressing *PS* as a function of logit(*PS*), we can replace logit(*PS*) by the right side of this equation, giving

$$PS = \frac{\exp(a + \Sigma\, b_j X_j)}{1 + \exp(a + \Sigma\, b_j X_j)}$$

For any set of specified values of a and b_j, we can calculate *PS* for each case and then use the aforementioned formulas for NLL to calculate the model's overall fit to the data. The values a and b_j that minimize NLL are the values most consistent with the observed data. The basic purpose of a logistic regression program is to find these values of a and b_j, plus estimates of their standard errors.

18.1.4   Interpreting the Output of Logistic Regression

The output of a logistic regression program is roughly like that of an ordinary regression program. For each regressor and a constant, there is a coefficient and a standard error of that coefficient. There may also be a *t* which equals the coefficient's ratio to its standard error, and the *p* associated with that *t*, with *df* calculated exactly as in ordinary regression. There is also a value of NLL, which measures the model's overall fit to the data.

As in ordinary regression, a geometric interpretation of the output is easiest in simple regression. To illustrate with a small sample, suppose that in a

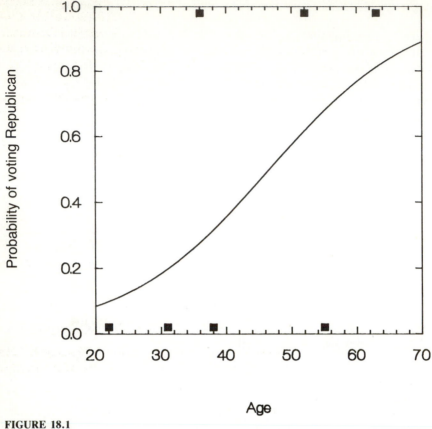

FIGURE 18.1
A logistic curve.

sample of seven people, four vote Democratic in a certain election and are aged
22, 31, 38, and 55, while the three voting Republican are aged 36, 52, and 63. A
logistic regression program predicting vote from age yields $a = -4.183$, $b =$
.0897. Inserting these values into the equation for *PS*, along with every age
from 22 to 63, gives the *logistic curve* in Fig. 18.1. The seven cases in the
sample appear in the figure as filled squares, four on the bottom edge and three
on the top edge, since four voters have voted Democratic and three
Republican.

Like an ordinary simple regression curve, this curve has two characteristics. One is the curve's "center," defined as the value of the independent
variable *X* that makes $PS = .5$. The other characteristic is the slope or
steepness of the curve at the center, which is always the curve's maximum
slope. Like the slope of an ordinary regression line, this value is determined

solely by b, the coefficient of the independent variable X. In fact, this slope equals $b/4$.

To find the center of the curve, note that logit(PS) = 0 when PS = .5. To find the value of X that produces this logit, substitute logit(PS) = 0 and the calculated values of a and b in the equation

$$\text{logit}(PS) = a + bX$$

and solve for X. In the current example, we have

$$0 = -4.183 + .0897 \times \text{age}$$

$$\text{Age} = \frac{4.183}{.0897} = 46.6$$

This is the age at which we estimate someone is equally likely to vote Republican or Democratic.

The meaning of a coefficient b is the same in simple logistic regression as in multiple logistic regression, so we turn now to the more general case. The equation

$$\text{logit}(PS) = a + \Sigma\, b_j X_j$$

shows that b_j is the estimated increase in logit(PS) for each 1-unit increase in the regressor X_j. This is clear enough to someone who understands logits, but several problems arise when a researcher tries to interpret results for a more general audience by writing about the effect of X_j on PS itself rather than on logit(PS). One problem is that the increase in PS associated with a 1-unit increase in X_j changes with the starting value of X_j. A second problem is a direct result of the first: the average increase in PS is not the same as the increase in PS for someone at the average on all regressors. A third problem is that the increase in PS that results from a k-unit increase in X_j is not k times the increase in PS from a 1-unit increase in X_j, so that there is no such thing as an "expected per-unit" increase in PS that is independent of the number of units of change in X_j. Because of these three problems, the interpretations of a coefficient b_j are more varied and more complex than in ordinary regression. We shall describe several interpretations.

In the most general approach, you select a convenient or meaningful value of PS and translate it into a logit. Also select a convenient or meaningful number of units of increase in the independent variable X_j, and add b_j times this number of units to the logit value just found. Finally, translate the new logit value back to PS with the aforementioned formula

$$PS = \frac{\exp(\text{logit } PS)}{1 + \exp(\text{logit } PS)}$$

For instance, suppose success is regressed onto hours of training T plus age, education, and other covariates. Suppose we find $b_T = .42$ and we also use the logistic equation to calculate that PS is .3 for a "typical" subject at the mean on all covariates but with 0 hours of training. Suppose a typical number of hours of training is 5. We calculate logit(.3) = $-.847$, then $.42 \times 5 = 2.10$, then $-.847 + 2.10 = 1.253$, and finally (exp 1.253)/(1 + exp 1.253) = .778. This says that for a "typical" subject, 5 hours of training will raise the probability of success from .30 to .778. That is a result that can be understood by an audience unfamiliar with logits. Unfortunately, this is not the average probability of success for the whole population. To estimate this value we would have to make a calculation like the one just shown not just for one "typical" subject but for every subject in the sample, and average the calculated values of PS with and without training.

Several other interpretations of b_j require less calculation. One is like the previous one, except that you arbitrarily imagine a subject with a "starting" PS at .5. As before, choose k, a convenient or meaningful number of units of increase in X. Adding k to this imaginary person's score on X_j increases the person's estimated logit score by $k \times b_j$. Since logit(.5) = 0, this increase is from 0 to $k \times b_j$. Translating this logit value back to PS gives

$$PS = \frac{\exp(k \times b_j)}{1 + \exp(k \times b_j)}$$

For instance, in the voting example, we had $b(\text{age}) = .0897$. Letting $k = 5$, we calculate

$$PS = \frac{\exp(5 \times .0897)}{1 + \exp(5 \times .0897)} = .61$$

Thus, at whatever age is associated with $PS = .5$, a 5-year increase in age is associated with a change in PS from .5 to .61.

Another approach is perhaps more useful if either of the two possible outcomes is very rare. If we are studying the effect of various factors on a death rate that is now .1%, little real understanding is produced by an interpretation expressed in terms of a starting rate of 50%. But if an event is very rare, then a 1-unit increase in X_j increases the probability of that event by a factor of approximately $\exp(b_j)$. For instance, if Y were death by choking and we found $b(\text{weight}) = .03$, then we could compute $\exp(.03) = 1.03$ and conclude that a 1-pound increase in body weight increases the probability of death by choking by approximately 3%.

18.1.5   Measures and Tests of Overall Fit

A simple measure of a model's overall fit to data is the Pearson correlation between the dummy Y scored 0, 1 and the variable

$$a + \Sigma \, b_j X_j$$

that we shall call the *logistic discriminating function*. Although the regression of Y onto the discriminating function is not linear, the regression of the discriminating function onto Y is necessarily linear because Y is dichotomous. Since a correlation "doesn't care" which is the independent and which the dependent variable, it is a reasonable measure of association between the two.

Other measures of overall fit are more closely related to chi-square tests on an overall model. Most logistic regression programs print values of NLL, or negative log likelihood. Recall that

$$NLL = - \Sigma \ln(\text{Fit})$$

As we saw in Sec. 18.1.1, values of NLL are always positive, but they measure the model's lack to fit to the data, so smaller values indicate better fit.

If the regressors in one model are a subset of those in another, then the difference in fit between the two models can be tested with the test

chi-square $= 2 \times$ (larger NLL $-$ smaller NLL)

$df =$ difference in number of regressors between the two models

A special case of this test is the test of the null hypothesis that a model has no better fit than a "constant" model with no regressors. This model sets every value of PS equal to $P1$, the proportion of successes observed in the sample. Let NLLC denote NLL calculated for this "constant" model. It can be shown that

$$NLLC = -N \times [P1 \ln(P1) + (1 - P1) \ln(1 - P1)]$$

NLLC can be inserted into the chi-square test above as the larger of the two NLL values. NLLC achieves its maximum, or worst-fit, value when $P1 = .5$, which gives NLLC $= N \times \ln(2) = .693147N$.

NLL can also be translated as follows into two intuitively understandable "logistic regression fit indexes" $LRFI_1$ and $LRFI_2$. The difference NLLC $-$ NLL equals the increase in $\Sigma \ln(\text{Fit})$ resulting from switching from the "constant" model to the actual model tested. Thus (NLLC $-$ NLL)$/N$ equals the mean increase in values of $\ln(\text{Fit})$, which makes $\exp[(\text{NLLC} - \text{NLL})/N]$ the geometric mean of the increases in values of Fit. Since $0 < \text{NLL} \leq \text{NLLC}$, this geometric mean ranges from 1 to $\exp(\text{NLLC}/N)$. Thus $\exp[(\text{NLLC} - \text{NLL})/N] - 1$ ranges from 0 to $\exp(\text{NLLC}/N) - 1$. Therefore

$$LRFI_1 = \frac{\exp[(\text{NLLC} - \text{NLL})/N] - 1}{\exp(\text{NLLC}/N) - 1}$$

ranges from 0 to 1, and relates linearly to the geometric mean of the gains in Fit produced by the model. But I have found that $\sqrt{LRFI_1}$ is usually closer than $LRFI_1$ to the Pearson correlation between Y and $\hat{Y}$, so we shall define

$$LRFI_2 = \sqrt{LRFI_1}$$

18.1.6   Logistic Regression in SYSTAT

Logistic regression can be executed in SYSTAT'S NONLIN module. This is an extremely flexible module with many options not discussed here, but a typical problem uses four statements: *model, loss, print,* and *estimate.* We will consider these in turn.

In the *model* statement, the user specifies a dependent variable and several regressors as in the models of previous chapters. But in addition, the user specifies the exact mathematical form of the model, including the constants to be fitted. The program interprets any legal name as an unknown to be fitted to the data, so long as it is not the name of a variable in the data set currently in use.

For instance, consider the first example of Chap. 2, in which *wtloss* was regressed onto *exercise* and *foodin.* You could use NONLIN for that problem, writing the *model* statement as follows:

>model wtloss = a + bl*exercise + b2*foodin

In this example, *wtloss, exercise,* and *foodin* are variables in the data set in use, so NONLIN interprets every other legal name in the *model* statement (a, b1, b2) as constants to be fitted to the data. You could use any other names of your choice.

To use NONLIN for logistic regression, write a *model* statement with the algebraic form introduced in Sec. 18.1.3. For instance, to regress a dichotomous dependent variable *success* onto two regressors *age* and *practice,* you could write:

>model success = exp(a + bl*age + b2*practice)/,
>(1 + exp(a + bl*age + b2*practice))

The comma at the end of the first line is the MYSTAT/SYSTAT way of indicating that the same command continues on the next line. In this example we assume the data set contains the variables *success, age, practice,* so all other legal names in the *model* statement (a, b1, b2) are interpreted by NONLIN as constants to be fitted to the data.

We now consider the *loss* statement. This statement always includes the word *estimate,* which NONLIN defines as a variable containing the estimated scores on the dependent variable, as calculated from the *model* statement. The *loss* statement specifies a quantity which can be computed for every case. NONLIN attempts to find the values of the unknown constants from the *model* statement, which minimize the sum across cases of the quantities specified in the *loss* statement.

For instance, if we were using NONLIN to perform an ordinary least squares regression predicting *wtloss,* the *loss* statement would read:

>loss = (wtloss − estimate)^2

Or if you wanted to minimize the sum of the absolute values of errors instead of the sum of squared errors, you could write

>loss = abs(wtloss − estimate)

The *loss* statement may include the names of any of the variables in the data set.

For logistic regression with a dependent variable Y scored 0, 1, the loss statement is

>loss = − (y*log(estimate) + (1 − y)*log(1 − estimate))

In the notation of Sec. 18.1.1, the values on the right-hand side of this equation are values of − ln(Fit$_i$), and their sum is NLL. The only thing that normally changes in this statement is *y*, which is replaced by the name of the dependent variable specified in the *model* statement.

The NONLIN statement *print long* turns on the printing of estimates of the standard errors and 95% confidence limits of the unknowns estimated, and of the correlations among the estimates. Unlike ordinary linear models, these are not printed by default because there are many kinds of models in which these values are highly inaccurate. By making the user turn on these statistics, SYSTAT is attempting to make the user also accept responsibility for them. But these statistics are generally accepted as accurate for logistic regression, so you should turn them on by typing *print long*. To turn them off again, type *print short*.

Finally, the *estimate* statement commands NONLIN to begin the computations. This statement has several options, typed after a slash (/) following the word *estimate*. Typing, for instance, *iter* = 50 changes the maximum number of iterations to 50 from its default value of 20. Or typing, for instance, *start* = 2.4, 6.8, 3.1 changes the starting estimates of the unknowns to the values shown. The number of values typed after *start* should always equal the number of unknowns in the *model* statement. The option *scale* changes the method by which standard errors are estimated to a method more appropriate for maximum-likelihood estimation, so this option should normally be used in logistic regression. All these options can be used together; for instance, the *estimate* statement might read:

>estimate/scale, iter = 50, start = 2.4, 6.8, 3.1

So after the *use* statement naming a data set, the total program implementing logistic regression in NONLIN might be

```
>model success = exp(a + bl*age + b2*practice)/,
>(1 + exp(a + bl*age + b2*practice))
>loss = − (success*log(estimate) + (1 − success)*log(1 − estimate))
>print long
>estimate/scale, iter = 50, start = 2.4, 6.8, 3.1
```

So far as I have been able to ascertain, the version of NONLIN in SYSTAT 4.1 (issued June 1989) works fine for logistic regression and for ordinary least squares, though earlier versions had some serious errors in estimating the standard errors and confidence limits. But the user should be warned against trusting even the SYSTAT 4.1 standard errors and confidence limits for any arbitrary nonlinear regression problem he or she might dream up. In the very first problem I experimented with in this regard, I ran an ordinary linear regression with two regressors in a sample of 50 cases, except that the *loss* statement was changed from ordinary squared-error loss to the following form:

$$>\text{loss} = (\text{abs}(y - \text{estimate}))\,\hat{}\,\text{power}$$

where *power* was a constant I changed by hand. Setting power = 2 produced ordinary least squares. I found that setting *power* equal to any value between 1 and 2 produced only rather small changes in the estimated values of the constants, but the printed standard errors sometimes fluctuated wildly. For instance, setting power = 1.178 made one printed standard error about 4.5 times as high as setting power = 1.170, although the estimated constants themselves were nearly identical. Equally odd results were observed in other data sets. This has to be a limitation in the method, not a true difference in standard errors. These results are not surprising to experts in the field; there are inherent limitations in estimating standard errors for arbitrarily chosen models and loss functions. So the version of NONLIN in SYSTAT 4.1 seems usable for logistic regression, and for estimating the constants in a great variety of nonlinear regression problems. But for arbitrarily chosen *model* and *loss* statements, the estimated standard errors and confidence limits of these constants should be treated with considerable skepticism. The fact that these values are not printed by default should be taken as a warning.

18.1.7 An Example

Gudermuth (1989) conducted a study on the effect of the social situation on the age at which female hamsters first ovulate. Thirty-two female hamsters were raised in cages with adult males, 64 others were raised alone, and 96 others were raised with female littermates. These three groups were named, respectively, MALE, ALONE, and SISTER. It was hypothesized that the presence of the adult male would accelerate ovulation, while the presence of potentially competing females would retard it relative to those raised alone.

A hamster must be sacrificed to tell whether it has begun to ovulate. Groups of eight hamsters were sacrificed at each of several ages, yielding the data in Table 18.2. "Days" records the hamster's age in days when it was sacrificed, and "Ovul" records the number of hamsters (out of eight) found to be ovulating in each group at each age.

TABLE 18.2
Ages at which 192 hamsters first ovulated

Male		Alone		Sister	
Days	Ovul	Days	Ovul	Days	Ovul
20	0	20	0	20	0
22	3	22	0	22	0
26	4	26	1	26	0
30	4	30	1	30	0
		34	2	34	0
		38	1	38	0
		42	4	42	3
		46	7	46	2
				53	3
				58	6
				63	8
				68	5

The dependent variable OVUL was the presence or absence of ovulation, coded 1 for hamsters ovulating and 0 for others. One regressor was age, measured in days. Sequential coding was used to create two dummy variables distinguishing among the three groups; variable MALE was coded 1 for the MALE group and 0 for the other two; variable NOSIS was coded 1 for the MALE and ALONE groups and 0 for the SISTER group.

Table 18.3 shows how scores on these variables were stored in a SYSTAT data set named *guder*. This format makes use of the *weight* command available in SYSTAT and MYSTAT. When employed, this command ordinarily appears immediately after a *use* command. The word *weight* followed by a variable name tells the program to use the named variable to define the number of cases having the specified scores on the other variables. For instance, in the current example, 8 is the second entry under the variable N, so the command *weight n* tells SYSTAT or MYSTAT to interpret the second row of Table 18.3 as 8 cases, all with scores of 1, 1, 20, 0 on the variables *male, nosis, age, ovul*, respectively.

So in the current example, a data set with only 48 rows specifies all the information for 192 cases. The 48 rows form 24 pairs, each corresponding to an entry in Table 18.2. The first two rows record that 8 hamsters in the male group (with scores of 1 on variables *male* and *nosis*) were sacrificed at age 20 days, and none of the 8 had yet begun to ovulate. The next two rows record that among the hamsters in the male group sacrificed at age 22 days, 3 had begun to ovulate and 5 had not. And so on.

The SYSTAT commands implementing the logistic regression for this data set were

TABLE 18.3
Gudermuth data as recorded in SYSTAT

Male	Nosis	Age	Ovul	N
1	1	20	1	0
1	1	20	0	8
1	1	22	1	3
1	1	22	0	5
1	1	26	1	4
1	1	26	0	4
1	1	30	1	4
1	1	30	0	4
0	1	20	1	0
0	1	20	0	8
0	1	22	1	0
0	1	22	0	8
0	1	26	1	1
0	1	26	0	7
0	1	30	1	1
0	1	30	0	7
0	1	34	1	2
0	1	34	0	6
0	1	38	1	1
0	1	38	0	7
0	1	42	1	4
0	1	42	0	4
0	1	46	1	7
0	1	46	0	1
0	0	20	1	0
0	0	20	0	8
0	0	22	1	0
0	0	22	0	8
0	0	26	1	0
0	0	26	0	8
0	0	30	1	0
0	0	30	0	8
0	0	34	1	0
0	0	34	0	8
0	0	38	1	0
0	0	38	0	8
0	0	42	1	3
0	0	42	0	5
0	0	46	1	2
0	0	46	0	6
0	0	53	1	3
0	0	53	0	5
0	0	58	1	6
0	0	58	0	2
0	0	63	1	8
0	0	63	0	0
0	0	68	1	5
0	0	68	0	3

```
>use guder
>weight n
>model ovul = exp(a+b1*male+b2*nosis+b3*age)/,
>(1+exp(a+b1*male+b2*nosis+b3*age))
>loss = -(ovul*log(estimate)+(1-ovul)*log(1-estimate))
>print long
>format 4
>estimate/scale
```

Table 18.4 shows part of the output produced by these commands. The four unknowns to be estimated are respectively *a, b1, b2, b3*. The first row of the output shows that when these four values are all arbitrarily estimated to be .1, the value of *loss* is 464.6843. (The D's in this row tell you that the values printed were stored in the computer as double-precision numbers, and the values following the D's are exponents of 10 in exponential notation. So .4646843D+03 stands for 464.6843.) The arbitrary estimates of .1 were successively improved, until after 15 iterations the program judged that only trivial further improvement was possible. So the values appearing for the 15th iteration are repeated later in the output, as the final loss value of 75.4268 and in the *estimate* column. The column heading A.S.E. in the table denotes *asymptotic standard error*. The word *asymptotic* is a further warning that the printed standard errors are less trustworthy for small samples than for large. The confidence limits are found from the formula

$$\text{Limits} = \text{Estimate} \pm \text{A.S.E.} * \text{Tabled } t$$

In the current example, $df = 192 - 4 = 188$, tabled $t = 1.9727$

TABLE 18.4
Part of SYSTAT output for Gudermuth data

Iteration	Loss	Parameter Values			
0	.4646843D+03	.1000D+00	.1000D+00	.1000D+00	.1000D+00
1	.2674110D+03	.9841D-01	.9977D-01	.9922D-01	.4953D-01
. . . .	. . . .	. . . .	. . . .	. . . .	. . . .
14	.7542682D+02	-.8854D+01	.2146D+01	.1962D+01	.1650D+00
15	.7542682D+02	-.8854D+01	.2146D+01	.1962D+01	.1650D+00

Dependent Variable Is Ovul
Final Value of Loss Function Is 75.4268
Standard Errors of Parameters Are Rescaled

Parameter	Estimate	A.S.E.	Lower	<95%> = Upper
A	-8.8542	1.4090	-11.6337	-6.0747
B1	2.1460	0.6085	0.9456	3.3464
B2	1.9616	0.6069	0.7644	3.1588
B3	0.1650	0.0264	0.1128	0.2171

All three regressors—*male, nosis,* and *age*—are highly significant; the values of *t* for *b1, b2, b3* are respectively 2.1460/.6085 or 3.53, 1.9616/.6069 or 3.23, and .1650/.0264 or 6.25. As explained in Sec. 10.2.5 on sequential coding, the *male* variable distinguishes between the *male* and *alone* groups, so its significantly positive coefficient *b1* means that at any given age the *male* group has higher probability of ovulation than the *alone* group. Variable *nosis* distinguishes between the *alone* and *sister* groups, so its significantly positive coefficient *b2* means that at any given age the *alone* group has higher probability of ovulation than the *sister* group. The positive coefficient *b2* of *age* means merely that in any one group the probability of ovulation increases with age.

To interpret these coefficients we shall use one of the simpler methods in Sec. 18.1.4. Inserting b(Age) into the expression $\exp(b_j)/(1+\exp(b_j))$ gives $\exp(.165)/(1+\exp(.165)) = .541$. This means that at whatever age an animal has .5 probability of ovulating, one day later that probability has increased to .541. Inserting b(Male) into the same expression gives $\exp(2.146)/(1+\exp(2.146)) = .895$. This means that at whatever age the *alone* group has .5 probability of ovulating, the *male* group has .895 probability. Inserting b(Nosis) into the same expression gives $\exp(1.962)/(1+\exp(1.962)) = .877$. This means that at whatever age the *sister* group has .5 probability of ovulating, the *alone* group has .877 probability.

A test was also performed for interaction between age and group. This was done with the following model statement:

```
>model ovul =,
>exp(a+b1*male+b2*nosis+b3*age+b4*age*male+b5*age*nosis),
>/(1+exp(a+b1*male+b2*nosis+b3*age+b4*age*male+b5*age*nosis))
```

The values of b4 and b5 were found to be nonsignificant, and the NLL value of 74.897 from this model was not significantly below that from the previous model statement:

$$\text{chi-square} = 2(75.427 - 74.897) = 1.060, \quad df = 2, p = .59$$

So there is no evidence that the logistic curves rise more steeply in some groups than in others.

We can also calculate the age at which each group has a .5 probability of ovulating. The coefficients and constant in the computer output above define logit(ovul). That is,

$$\text{logit(ovul)} = -8.854 + 2.146 \times \text{MALE} + 1.962 \times \text{NOSIS} + .165 \times \text{AGE}$$

When the probability of ovulating is .5, logit(ovul) = 0, so the equation reduces to

$$8.854 = 2.146 \times \text{MALE} + 1.962 \times \text{NOSIS} + .165 \times \text{AGE}$$

For the MALE group, variables MALE and NOSIS are both 1, so the corresponding age is $(8.854 - 2.146 - 1.962)/.165 = 28.8$. For the ALONE group, variable MALE is 0 and NOSIS is 1, so the corresponding age is $(8.854 - 1.962)/.165 = 41.8$. For the SISTER group, both MALE and NOSIS are 0, so that the corresponding age is $8.854/.165 = 53.7$. These ages of 28.8, 41.8, and 53.7 days are the ages that the model calculates yield .5 probabilities of ovulation for the MALE, ALONE, and SISTER groups, respectively. Inspection of the original data shows that these are reasonable estimates.

The computer output also shows NLL $= 75.427$. Calculating $75.427/192 = .3928$ and $\exp(-.3928) = .675$, we find .675 to be the geometric mean of the probabilities and model assigns to the outcomes that are actually observed.

A model that omitted the MALE and NOSIS dummy variables yielded NLL $= 90.923$, and a model that omitted all three regressors yielded NLL $= 114.073$. To test the two dummy variables as a set, we take

chi-square $= 2 \times (90.923 - 75.427) = 30.992 \qquad df = 2, p = .00000019$

Testing all three as a set gives

chi-square $= 2 \times (114.073 - 75.427) = 77.292 \qquad df = 3, p = 3 \times 10^{-10}$

18.2 PROBIT AND DISCRIMINANT ANALYSIS

18.2.1 Probit Analysis

Probit analysis is much like logit analysis. But in logit analysis we wrote

$$\text{logit}(PS) = a + \Sigma\, b_j X_j$$

where

$$\text{logit}(PS) = \ln\left(\frac{PS}{1 - PS}\right)$$

so that

$$PS = \frac{\exp(\text{logit } PS)}{1 + \exp(\text{logit } PS)}$$

In probit analysis, we write

$$z = a + \Sigma\, b_j X_j$$

where PS is the cumulative probability associated with z in a standard normal distribution. For instance, $PS = .5$ if $z = 0$, $PS = .975$ if $z = 1.96$, and so on. Thus the logistic regression curve illustrated in Fig. 18.1 (Sec. 18.1.4) is replaced by a cumulative normal curve, which has much the same shape.

Probit analysis is particularly useful if it can be assumed that there is an underlying continuous variable Y_N (for Y normal) that fits the usual regression assumptions, with linear relation to the regressors and conditional normality and homoscedasticity. If cases above a certain score on Y_N succeed and others fail, then PS is related to $\hat{Y}_N$ by the cumulative normal curve, which is the curve used in probit analysis. This assumption does not require that regressors be normally distributed; as in logistic regression, they may be any mixture of numerical and categorical variables.

18.2.2   Discriminant Analysis

Discriminant analysis is available in the SYSTAT MGLH module. But we shall not describe it at length, because discriminant analysis is in the process of being replaced in most modern practice by logistic regression. Discriminant analysis has three major limitations not shared by logistic regression. First, as mentioned in the opening of this chapter, all regressors must be numerical, while logistic regression allows any mixture of numerical and categorical regressors. Second, discriminant analysis requires that regressors have a multivariate normal distribution within each Y category. This requires that all variables be normally distributed with linear relations to each other and homoscedasticity when any variable is regressed onto any other or others. Third, the correlations among regressors and the standard deviations of regressors must be equal for all the Y categories. These three requirements together make discriminant analysis substantially less robust and flexible than logistic regression.

Discriminant analysis is closely related to regression. In fact, when Y has only two categories that we can call "success" and "failure," some of the statistics in discriminant analysis can be calculated with an ordinary regression program, simply by running the regression with success and failure coded respectively as scores of 1 and 0 on Y. The F found this way to test R is the same F found in discriminant analysis to test the overall model, and the t testing each regression slope is the same t found in the discriminant-analysis test of each regressor's independent contribution. Furthermore, the values of b_j found in this way are proportional to the values of b_j found in discriminant analysis, so that the regression function correlates perfectly with the so-called *discriminant function*, the function derived to discriminate between the successful and failing groups. But the values of $\hat{Y}$ found in this way cannot be interpreted as estimated probabilities that a case will succeed. In fact, some values of $\hat{Y}$ may be above 1 or below 0.

SUMMARY

Problems with categorical dependent variables can be studied with the methods of *discriminant analysis, probit analysis, log-linear models,* and *logistic regression,* which is also known as *logit analysis.* Log-linear models require all regressors to be categorical, while discriminant analysis requires all to be numerical. Logit and probit analysis are more general, allowing any mix of numerical and categorical regressors. Log-linear analysis can be thought of as the special case of logistic regression for categorical regressors, just as analysis of variance is the special case of linear models for categorical regressors.

18.1 Logistic Regression

The fit between a model and the data of case i can be measured by

$$\text{Fit}_i = Y_i \times PS_i + (1 - Y_i) \times (1 - PS_i)$$

where Y_i is 0 or 1 and PS_i is the probability the model assigns to the event that $Y_i = 1$. The N values of Fit_i can be combined by the formula $\text{NLL} = -\Sigma \ln(\text{Fit}_i)$, where NLL stands for "negative log likelihood." NLL is always positive and measures *lack of fit* between data and model; the smaller the value, the better the model fits the data.

We cannot treat PS as a simple linear function of regressors as we treat dependent variables in ordinary linear models. Therefore we make a *logit* transformation of PS, defined as follows:

$$\text{logit}(PS) = \ln\left(\frac{PS}{1 - PS}\right)$$

By solving the logit formula for PS, we find

$$PS = \frac{\exp(\text{logit } PS)}{1 + \exp(\text{logit } PS)}$$

There is no proof that the logit scale is in any sense the best possible scale. But it often seems reasonable to assume that logits are linearly related to regressors. Then we can write

$$\text{logit}(PS) = a + \Sigma b_j X_j$$

In the equation expressing PS as a function of $\text{logit}(PS)$, we can replace $\text{logit}(PS)$ by the right side of this equation, giving

$$PS = \frac{\exp(a + \Sigma b_j X_j)}{1 + \exp(a + \Sigma b_j X_j)}$$

For any set of specified values of a and b_j, we can calculate PS for each case and then use the aforementioned formulas for NLL to calculate the model's overall fit to the data. The values of a and b_j that minimize NLL are the values most consistent with the observed data. The basic purpose of a logistic regression program is to find these values of a and b_j, plus estimates of their standard errors. These values of b_j are not interpreted as simply as ordinary partial regression slopes, but Sec. 18.1.4 gives several possible interpretations.

If the regressors in one model are a subset of those in another, then the difference in fit between the two models can be tested with the test

chi-square = 2 × (larger NLL − smaller NLL)

df = difference in number of regressors between the two models

A special case of this test is the test of the null hypothesis that a model has no better fit than a "constant" model with no regressors. This model sets every value of PS equal to $P1$, the proportion of successes observed in the sample. Let NLLC denote NLL calculated for this "constant" model. It can be shown that

$$NLLC = -N \times [P1 \times \ln(P1) + (1 - P1) \times \ln(1 - P1)]$$

NLLC can be inserted into the chi-square test above as the larger of the two NLL values.

NLL can also be translated as follows into two intuitively understandable "logistic regression fit indexes" $LRFI_1$ and $LRFI_2$:

$$LRFI_1 = \frac{\exp[(NLLC - NLL)/N] - 1}{\exp(NLLC/N) - 1}$$

$$\text{and } LRFI_2 = \sqrt{LRFI_1}$$

Both these values range from 0 to 1.

18.2   Probit and Discriminant Analysis

Probit analysis is much like logit analysis. But the logistic regression curve is replaced by a cumulative normal curve, which has much the same shape. Probit analysis is particularly useful if it can be assumed that there is an underlying continuous variable that fits the usual regression assumptions, with linear relation to the regressors and conditional normality and homoscedasticity. This assumption does not require that regressors be normally distributed: as in logistic regression, they may be any mixture of numerical and categorical variables.

Discriminant analysis is in the process of being replaced in most modern practice by logistic regression. Discriminant analysis has three major limitations not shared by logistic regression. First, all regressors must be numerical, while logistic regression allows any mixture of numerical and categorical regressors. Second, discriminant analysis requires that regressors have a multivariate normal distribution within each Y category. Third, the correlations among regressors and the standard deviations of regressors must be equal across the Y categories. These three requirements together make discriminant analysis substantially less robust and flexible than logistic regression. When Y has only two categories, some of the statistics in discriminant analysis can be calculated with an ordinary regression program.

KEY TERMS

logit analysis	likelihood
logistic regression	logit
discriminant analysis	logistic curve
probit analysis	logistic discriminating function
consistency between model and data	discriminant function

SYMBOLS AND ABBREVIATIONS

Fit_i PS_i NLL   NLLC   LRFI

CHAPTER
19

LOG-LINEAR
MODELS

Log-linear models are intimately related to logistic regression, as we shall see in Sec. 19.2.2. But first we shall briefly review chi-square tests for association in two-way contingency tables, and introduce the example to be used later.

19.1 BASIC CONCEPTS

19.1.1 Tests for Association in Two-Way Tables

Suppose each of three guidance counselors has worked with about 100 high school students and the graduation frequencies in the groups of students are as shown in Table 19.1. Inspection of this table suggests that graduation rates may differ significantly across counselors. To test this hypothesis, we first calculate the frequency expected in each cell from its row and column totals. The overall proportion graduating is 168/276 = .609. If graduation is independent of counselor, then the expected number of students graduating for counselor A is .609 × 88, or 53.6. Since .609 = 168/276, we are in effect using the formula

$$\text{Expected frequency} = \frac{\text{column total} \times \text{row total}}{N} = \frac{88 \times 168}{276} = 53.6$$

After using this formula to find the expected cell frequency e for every cell, we let o denote the observed cell frequency and compute a value of chi-square.

462

TABLE 19.1
An artificial data set on counseling effectiveness

| Graduated | Counselor | | | Total |
	A	B	C	
Yes	63	57	48	168
No	25	32	51	108
Total	88	89	99	276

Two formulas are common:

$$\text{Pearson chi-square} = \sum \frac{(o - e)^2}{e}$$

$$\text{Likelihood-ratio chi-square} = 2 \sum o \ln \frac{o}{e}$$

The Pearson formula has a clear intuitive structure. The likelihood-ratio formula does not; whenever $o < e$, a term is negative. But we shall use the latter, since as shown in Sec. 19.2.2 the likelihood-ratio chi-square relates directly to the measure of consistency described in Sec. 18.1.1. The values of chi-square found by the two formulas are usually fairly close; in the present example they are, respectively, 11.00 and 11.02. For either formula, let

$$df = (R - 1) \times (C - 1)$$

where R and C denote, respectively, the number of rows and columns in the analysis.

For this example the likelihood-ratio chi-square gives $p = .0040$, which means that students assigned to different counselors do graduate at significantly different rates. As explained in Sec. 19.3.4, my own unpublished research suggests using this formula with a continuity correction which consists of adjusting each value of o by .25 toward its own e before computing chi-square. In the present example, this modification yields chi-square $= 10.47$, $p = .0053$.

19.1.2 An Example with Three Variables

Log-linear models are designed for analyses of tables with three or more variables. For instance, suppose we break each counselor's successes and failures into those for male and female students, and find the results in Table 19.2. Many more hypotheses can now be tested, such as the hypothesis that all three variables—counselor, gender, and graduation—are mutually independent. But the dependent variable is graduation, and gender and counselor are independent variables, so we see by analogy to ordinary linear models that

TABLE 19.2
Data broken down by gender

| Graduation | Counselor | | | | | |
| | A | | B | | C | |
	M	F	M	F	M	F
Yes	36	27	20	37	15	33
No	18	7	19	13	32	19

three relationships are of special interest: between counselor and graduation with gender controlled, between gender and graduation with counselor controlled, and the interaction between counselor and gender in affecting graduation (are some counselors especially effective with male students while others are especially effective with female students?). And to protect against the danger of multiple tests, we may want to start with an overall test on the composite null hypothesis that none of these three effects exists.

Still other tests could be of interest, such as tests on differences among counselors within one gender, and so on. With four-way or higher-order tables even more hypotheses may be of interest. Log-linear models offer a way to test all these hypotheses.

19.1.3 Log-Linear Equations

The equation

$$\text{Expected cell frequency} = \frac{\text{column total} \times \text{row total}}{N}$$

can be written as

$$\log(\text{expected cell frequency}) = \log(\text{column total}) + \log(\text{row total}) - \log(N)$$

We see that when all values are transformed to logarithms, the expected cell frequency is a linear function of other values. That is also true in more complicated forms of contingency-table analysis, so the equations for calculating expected cell frequencies from those values are called *log-linear equations*. That is where the method gets its name.

19.1.4 An Analogy to Regression

Long ago, in Sec. 2.1.2, we saw that the computations of ordinary linear models are such that a linear-model computer program need make no distinction between independent variables and covariates, although the distinction, of course, affects the interpretation of the computer output. An even more extreme situation of the same sort arises in contingency-table analysis: the computer program can find expected cell frequencies and chi-square values without ever being told explicitly which variables are independent variables and which are dependent. Of course, as before, the user must keep the distinction in mind, and use it where required. But this computational feature of log-linear analysis allows us to employ a useful metaphor:

1. Think of each cell in the analysis as a separate case. In our three-way example, think of the number of "cases" as 12 rather than 276.
2. Think of the dependent variable as "cell frequency." The observed frequency o in each cell is that cell's score on the "dependent variable."
3. Think of the expected frequency e in each cell as $\hat{Y}$, the predicted score on the dependent variable.
4. Think of the chi-square computed from these values of o and e as analogous to SS(error). As in a two-way chi-square, the larger the differences between observed and expected cell frequencies, the higher chi-square. Thus, like SS(error), chi-square measures the model's *lack of fit* to the data.

The metaphoric regression predicting cell frequency can have "linear," or first-order, terms; simple interactions; higher-order interactions; and an additive constant. In the two-way example ignoring gender, the possible terms are:

graduation × counselor
graduation
counselor
constant

In the three-way example using gender, the terms are:

graduation × counselor × gender
graduation × counselor
graduation × gender
counselor × gender
graduation
counselor
gender
constant

A term's *order* is the number of variables in the term. Thus a three-way analysis contains three first-order terms, three second-order terms, and one third-order term. Order does *not* refer to the number of variables controlled or to the difference between simple and partial association; that distinction is discussed in Sec. 19.2.5.

Log-linear models require that whenever an interaction term is used, all first-order and lower-order terms within that term also be used. Thus use of the counselor × gender term requires that the counselor and gender terms also be used, while use of the graduation × counselor × gender term requires that all terms in the above list be used. In SYSTAT, this requirement is handled automatically; whenever an interaction term is specified by the user, all required lower-order terms are added automatically.

19.2 HYPOTHESES AND TESTS

19.2.1 Chi-Square Tests in Log-Linear Models

Just as in regression analysis, we designate the hypotheses to be tested by choosing the terms in the model. But unlike the tests used in regression analysis, the test here is on the terms *missing* from the model. The more terms omitted from the model, the greater the differences between expected and observed frequencies and the larger chi-square. A model containing all possible terms will always make all expected cell frequencies exactly equal the observed frequencies, leaving a chi-square of 0.

The degrees of freedom for any chi-square are calculated by applying the rules of Chap. 13 to the metaphoric regression. That is, the *df* for any first-order term is 1 less than the number of categories in the corresponding variable, and the *df* for any higher-order term is the product of the *df*'s of its constituent first-order terms. For instance, if a three-way table has three rows, five columns, and four layers, then the three-way interaction will have 2 × 4 × 3, or 24, *df*, while the row × column interaction will have 2 × 4, or 8. To test for any given term, compute the values of chi-square with and without that term. The difference between the two values of chi-square is itself a chi-square, and the difference between the two values of *df* is the *df* for the new chi-square. These rules are illustrated repeatedly in Sec. 19.3.3.

Tricks exist to find *p* values more accurately than otherwise when testing chi-square values with 1 or 2 degrees of freedom. When $df = 1$, the square root of chi-square can be interpreted as a standard normal z. Thus, a chi-square of 4.24 becomes a z of 2.06, with a two-tailed p of .0395. When $df = 2$, you can dispense with tables altogether, since

$$p = \exp\left(\frac{-\text{chi-square}}{2}\right)$$

For instance, if chi-square $= 7.82$, we have $p = \exp(-3.91) = .020$.

19.2.2 Log-Linear Analysis as a Special Case of Logistic Regression

This section shows the relation between the likelihood-ratio chi-square of Sec. 19.1.1 and the values of log(likelihood) and chi-square described for logistic regression. It shows that log-linear analysis can be thought of as the special case of logistic regression in which all regressors are categorical, just as analysis of variance is the special case of regression in which all regressors are categorical.

Talking in real rather than metaphoric terms, let a *stack* of cells include all the cells with a given combination of regressors. In our three-way example, the regressors are gender and counselor. There are two genders and three counselors, giving six combinations of gender and counselor and thus six stacks. Let n_j denote the number of cases in stack j. Thus $\Sigma\, n_j = N$, where N is the total sample size.

Let each category of the dependent variable be called a *layer*. The number of cells in each stack is the number of layers. In our example there are two layers—graduation and nongraduation. Let o_{jk} denote the number of cases observed in layer k of stack j.

In Sec. 18.1.1 we defined Fit_i as the probability which the model assigns to the outcome actually observed for case i. We now denote log(likelihood) as "Totalfit," so that

$$\text{Totalfit} = \Sigma \ln(\text{Fit}_i)$$

This summation is over all cases, so we can write it as

$$\text{Totalfit} = \Sigma\, \Sigma \ln(\text{Fit}_i)$$

where the inner summation is over cases within a cell and the outer is over the cells. But any model assigns the same probabilities to all cases within a cell, so Fit_i is identical for all o_{jk} cases in a given cell. Thus we can replace $\Sigma \ln(\text{Fit}_i)$ by $o_{jk} \times \ln(\text{Fit}_{jk})$, where Fit_{jk} denotes the fit for each of the cases in cell jk, or the probability the model assigns to falling in layer k for cases in stack j. Therefore we have

$$\text{Totalfit} = \Sigma\, o_{jk} \ln(\text{Fit}_{jk})$$

The model's expected number of cases in cell jk is $n_j \times \text{Fit}_{jk}$, so we can write $\text{Fit}_{jk} = e_{jk}/n_j$, where e_{jk} is the model's expected number of cases in cell jk. Thus

$$\text{Totalfit} = \Sigma\, o_{jk} \ln \frac{e_{jk}}{n_j}$$

where the summation is over cells—that is, over both j and k.

We will now define "Lackofit" as twice the amount by which Totalfit falls below Totalfit calculated for a model that perfectly predicts every observed cell frequency. In this perfect model every value of e_{jk} equals o_{jk}, so that its value of Totalfit is found by replacing e_{jk} by o_{jk}, giving

$$\Sigma\, o_{jk} \ln \frac{o_{jk}}{n_j}$$

Thus we have

$$\text{Lackofit} = 2 \times \left(\Sigma\, o_{jk} \ln \frac{o_{jk}}{n_j} - \Sigma\, o_{jk} \ln \frac{e_{jk}}{n_j} \right)$$

$$= 2\, \Sigma\, o_{jk} \left(\ln \frac{o_{jk}}{n_j} - \ln \frac{e_{jk}}{n_j} \right)$$

$$= 2\, \Sigma\, o_{jk} \ln \frac{o_{jk}}{e_{jk}}$$

Dropping subscripts, we have

$$\text{Lackofit} = 2\, \Sigma\, o \ln \frac{o}{e}$$

where the summation is over cells. But this is exactly the formula for the likelihood-ratio chi-square. We see that this chi-square measures the amount by which the model's fit to the data falls below the fit we would calculate for a perfect model.

The formula for Lackofit shows why we can calculate chi-square without ever telling the computer explicitly which variable is the dependent variable. The equation

$$\text{Totalfit} = \Sigma\, o_{jk} \ln \frac{e_{jk}}{n_j}$$

used values of n_j, which were defined only in reference to a particular dependent variable. But it so happened that values of n_j dropped out of the formula in the next step. That is what allows us to use commands that do not explicitly name the dependent variable.

19.2.3   How the Model Affects Expected Cell Frequencies

We have used a metaphor to help you understand the range of hypotheses that can be tested by log-linear models. The actual scientific meaning of all these hypotheses is discussed more fully in Sec. 19.2.4. But first we will consider more precisely how the terms in the model affect the analysis.

In ordinary linear models, we saw in Chap. 5 that a variable or set of variables can be tested by the difference in SS(error) between models that contain and omit the variable or set. But omitting a variable is the same as forcing or constraining it to have a weight of zero. Thus a variable or set is actually tested by the difference in SS(error) with and without constraints involving that variable or set.

Despite our metaphor, regression formulas are not actually used in fitting a log-linear model to data. What the log-linear computer program actually does is find the values of e that minimize the lack-of-fit chi-square, subject to constraints on the values of e imposed by the model. Each term missing from the model adds a constraint on the calculated values of e, so each term added to the model removes a constraint. The rest of this section explains the nature of these constraints.

When all terms are omitted from the model, all values of e are forced to be equal, so that each equals N divided by the number of cells. Each first-order term added to the model (counselor, gender, and graduation in our example) allows unequal expected frequencies in the categories of the associated variable. For instance, adding "counselor" to the model removes the constraint that the expected cell frequencies must be based on the assumption that the three counselors work with equal numbers of students. We are normally interested only in associations among variables rather than differences among categories within a variable, so all possible first-order terms are normally included in all models. When this is done in the current example, the expected cell frequencies are shown in Table 19.3.

In this table, every possible 2×2 table has proportional entries. For the four entries for counselor A, we have $27.17/17.47 = 26.39/16.97$. Or, for the first four entires in the upper row, we have $27.17/26.39 = 27.48/26.69$. Or, taking the entries from the first and third columns, we have $27.17/17.47 = 27.48/17.67$. These values of e yield a chi-square of 33.81 with 7 df.

The addition of each two-way cross-product term, such as gender $\times$ counselor, gender $\times$ graduation, or counselor $\times$ graduation, removes the constraint that the values of e must be proportional in the conditional tables for those two variables. In our example there are two conditional counselor $\times$ graduation tables—one for male students and one for female. When the gender $\times$ counselor term is added to the model, the expected cell frequencies are as shown in Table 19.4.

We still have proportionality within the 2×2 table for any one counselor, or in the 2×3 graduation $\times$ counselor table for either gender. But we no longer have proportionality in a counselor $\times$ gender table. For instance, among those graduating, counselor A has more male than female students, while B and C have more females than males. These values of e lower chi-square from 33.81

TABLE 19.3
Expected cell frequencies when the model specifies that all three variables are mutually independent

| | Counselor | | | | | |
| | A | | B | | C | |
Graduation	M	F	M	F	M	F
Yes	27.17	26.39	27.48	26.69	30.57	29.69
No	17.47	16.97	17.67	17.16	19.65	19.09

TABLE 19.4
Expected cell frequencies when the model allows correlation between gender and counselor

	Counselor					
	A		B		C	
Graduation	M	F	M	F	M	F
Yes	32.87	20.70	23.74	30.43	28.61	31.65
No	21.13	13.30	15.26	19.57	18.39	20.35

with 7 *df* to 27.67 with 5 *df*. The difference of 6.14 with 2 *df* is significant; $p = .046$.

The addition of a three-way cross product to the model removes the constraint that the size of association between two variables must be constant for all categories of the third variable, where association is measured by the ratio of within-row or within-column ratios. For instance, in our three-way example, when all terms are in the model except the three-way cross-product gender × graduation × counselor, the calculated values of e are as shown in Table 19.5. The previous forms of proportionality have all evaporated. In the 2 × 2 block for counselor A, the ratio of within-column ratios is (34.64/19.36)/(28.36/5.64) = .356 rather than 1, as it was before. But this same value of .356 is found for counselors B and C. Addition of the three-way cross product to the model would remove this constraint. Of course, in a three-way example this would remove all constraints, so the values of e would exactly equal the observed cell frequencies.

Higher-order terms work the same way. Addition of the term $A \times B \times C \times D$ to a model of a four-way table removes the constraint that the size of the $A \times B \times C$ interaction (measured again by a ratio of ratios) must be constant for all categories of D. Equivalently, it removes the constraint that the size of $A \times B \times D$ interaction must be constant for the different categories of C, or that the $A \times C \times D$ interaction must be constant for all categories of B, and so on.

TABLE 19.5
Expected cell frequencies with all simple associations allowed, but no gender × counselor interaction affecting graduation

	Counselor					
	A		B		C	
Graduation	M	F	M	F	M	F
Yes	34.64	28.36	19.81	37.19	16.56	31.44
No	19.36	5.64	19.19	12.81	30.44	20.56

Three-way and higher-order tables differ from two-way tables in that it is not normally practical to calculate expected cell frequencies by hand. Thus log-linear computer programs are a necessity for such tables, not merely a convenience.

19.2.4   The Meaning of Terms in Log-Linear Models

A two-way interaction term in a log-linear model actually corresponds to a hypothesis of association. For instance, if the four numbers in Table 19.6 represent frequencies, then the table illustrates high association between treatment and success. But in terms of the metaphor we think of the four numbers in the table not as frequencies but as scores, and in that form the table is a classic illustration of high interaction between treatment and success. Thus, in a two-way table, omitting the row $\times$ column interaction from the model actually tests association. This is the simple chi-square test for association.

By analogy, any term in a log-linear model that includes the name of the dependent variable actually tests the effect on the dependent variable of the expression defined by the rest of the term. In our three-way example, the dependent variable is graduation, and the model includes the interaction terms

graduation $\times$ counselor $\times$ gender
graduation $\times$ counselor
graduation $\times$ gender

These three terms actually correspond to the effects of

counselor $\times$ gender
counselor
gender

on graduation. These are, of course, the three effects normally tested in ordinary linear models with a continuous dependent variable. Thus the distinction between association and interaction, made so carefully in Sec. 13.1.3, does

TABLE 19.6
A table showing association if entries are frequencies, interaction if entries are scores or means

	Success	Failure
Treatment	100	50
Control	50	100

not apply to log-linear models. Rather, associations appear in log-linear models as two-factor interactions, while the effects we have called interactions in previous chapters appear in the models as higher-order interactions.

19.2.5   Simple versus Partial Association

When a term does not itself include all the variables, such as the graduation $\times$ counselor and graduation $\times$ gender terms here, one may test for the effect represented by the term, either with or without controlling for the other variable(s) in the analysis. For instance, we could test the graduation $\times$ gender association either before or after controlling for counselor. We will denote these two effects respectively

$$\text{graduation} \times \text{gender}$$

and

$$\text{graduation} \times \text{gender.counselor}$$

Controlling for counselor means correcting for its relationships with other variables, and we have just seen that these relationships are represented by the terms counselor $\times$ gender and counselor $\times$ graduation. Thus the test for the partial graduation $\times$ gender.counselor association includes the counselor $\times$ graduation and counselor $\times$ gender terms in the model, while the test for the simple graduation $\times$ gender association does not. Thus the test for simple association compares the fit of the two models

$$\text{gender} + \text{counselor} + \text{graduation}$$

and

$$\text{gender} + \text{counselor} + \text{graduation} + \text{graduation} \times \text{gender}$$

while the test for partial association compares the two models

$$\text{gender} + \text{counselor} + \text{graduation} + \text{graduation} \times \text{counselor} \\ + \text{gender} \times \text{counselor}$$

and

$$\text{gender} + \text{counselor} + \text{graduation} + \text{graduation} \times \text{counselor} + \text{gender} \\ \times \text{counselor} + \text{graduation} \times \text{gender}$$

The lack-of-fit chi-square values for these four models are respectively

33.81	with	7 *df*
21.39	with	6 *df*
16.65	with	3 *df*
.96	with	2 *df*

so to test for simple association we compute

$$\text{chi-square} = 33.81 - 21.39 = 12.42 \qquad df = 7 - 6 = 1, p = .00042$$

This is the same chi-square we would have found by testing for association in the simple 2 × 2 table summed over the three counselors. To test for partial association, we compute

chi-square $= 16.65 - .96 = 15.69$ $df = 3 - 2 = 1, p = .000075$

In this case, the partial association is larger and more significant than the simple association.

The simple gender × graduation association is visible in the 2 × 2 table in which expected or observed cell frequencies are summed over the three counselors. When this is done for the "null" model represented in Table 19.4, the resulting expected cell frequencies are as shown in Table 19.7. This model specifies no simple association between graduation and gender, so we have $85.22/54.79 = 82.77/53.22$. But the null model of the second comparison gives somewhat different results. For this model the values of e are as shown in Table 19.8. In the 2 × 2 table for any single counselor there is no association between gender and graduation, since the model specifies an absence of partial association. But summing over the three counselors gives Table 19.9. The association in this table is clear, since $86.43 > 81.57$ while $53.57 < 54.43$. We encountered this same phenomenon in the preschool examples of Sec. 1.1.3, when partial associations in 2 × 2 tables had different signs from the corresponding simple associations.

TABLE 19.7
Values from Table 19.4 summed over the three counselors

Graduation	Male	Female
Yes	85.22	82.77
No	54.79	53.22

TABLE 19.8
Expected cell frequencies if counselor affects graduation but gender does not

	Counselor					
	A		B		C	
Graduation	M	F	M	F	M	F
Yes	38.66	24.34	24.98	32.02	22.79	25.21
No	15.34	9.66	14.02	17.98	24.21	26.79

TABLE 19.9
Values from Table 19.8 summed over the three counselors

Graduation	Male	Female
Yes	86.43	81.57
No	53.57	54.43

19.2.6   Why Some Hypotheses Are Equivalent

Anyone who works much with log-linear models will observe two paradoxes we must mention briefly. One can be illustrated with the expected frequencies shown in Table 19.3. Table 19.7 shows the result of summing these values over the three counselors. (As its title states, Table 19.7 can also be derived from Table 19.4.) Table 19.7 illustrated simple independence between gender and graduation. But there is also partial or conditional independence in the full table; for instance, in Table 19.3 for counselor A we have 27.17/17.47 = 26.39/16.97. We emphasized the difference between simple and partial association; why do these tables exhibit both?

The same insight resolves both paradoxes, so we will present the second paradox before resolving the first. In a three-way analysis we can actually imagine no fewer than four separate tests of a second-order term. For instance, if the three variables are A, B, and C, then the $B \times C$ term can be tested in any of the following ways:

$A + B + C$	vs.	$A + B + C + B \times C$
$A + B + C + A \times B$	vs.	$A + B + C + A \times B + B \times C$
$A + B + C + A \times C$	vs.	$A + B + C + A \times C + B \times C$
$A + B + C + A \times B + A \times C$	vs.	$A + B + C + A \times B + A \times C$ $+ B \times C$

The chi-square used in each test is the difference between the two model chi-square values. When likelihood-ratio chi-squares are used, the first three tests always give identical values of the test chi-square, while the fourth gives a different value. Why does this happen? Aren't all four testing somewhat different hypotheses?

The paradox is resolved by thinking in terms of partial correlations. For simplicity imagine that A, B, and C are all dichotomous. From Sec. 2.3.7, the partial correlation $r(BC.A)$ is given by

$$r(BC.A) = \frac{r_{BC} - r_{AB}r_{AC}}{\sqrt{1 - r_{AB}^2}\sqrt{1 - r_{AC}^2}}$$

If either r_{AB} or r_{AC} is 0, the numerator of this expression reduces to r_{BC}. In words, if a covariate is independent of either an independent variable or a dependent variable, then the partial association between the latter two variables is zero if and only if the simple association is zero. This is true in a population as well as a sample. Thus, if either $_Tr_{AB}$ or $_Tr_{AC}$ is zero, the hypothesis $_Tr(BC.A) = 0$ is equivalent to the hypothesis $_Tr_{BC} = 0$.

Now consider the four null log-linear models listed on the left in the list above. The first three each omit the $A \times B$ term or the $A \times C$ term or both. These terms represent associations, so their omission is specifying either $_Tr_{AB} = 0$ or $_Tr_{AC} = 0$ or both. In these three cases, then, the null hypothesis about the $B \times C.A$ partial association is equivalent to the null hypothesis about the $B \times C$ simple association, so the first three tests above are all of the same hypothesis. That is why they give equal chi-square values. And the expected cell frequencies calculated under any of these three null hypotheses all exhibit absence of both simple and partial association.

19.3 APPLYING SYSTAT

19.3.1 Basic SYSTAT Commands for Categorical Data

Log-linear models can be fitted in the TABLES module of SYSTAT, or in PROC CATMOD of SAS. We shall consider only the former. But before discussing log-linear models in SYSTAT, we must consider some more basic SYSTAT commands for working with categorical data. We will use the three-way data set already given in Table 19.2; it is repeated in Table 19.10. These data can be entered in SYSTAT in the format shown in Table 19.11.

Character entries may be words like MALE, FEMALE, YES, or NO instead of the single letters M, F, Y, N. Or we could use numbers instead of letters, for instance, replacing A, B, C by 1, 2, 3 or M, F, by 0, 1 or by 1, 2. In the TABLES module, no CATEGORY command is needed to tell SYSTAT whether a variable is numerical or categorical, since all variables entered into the key TABULATE and MODEL commands are interpreted by the program as categorical. For this reason there are no restrictions on the numbers to be used. For instance, the three counselors A, B, and C could be represented by 1, 2, 3 or by 5, 30, 16 or by 3.6, 2.8, 5.29 or by any three different numbers.

TABLE 19.10
The raw data repeated

	Counselor					
	A		B		C	
Graduation	M	F	M	F	M	F
Yes	36	27	20	37	15	33
No	18	7	19	13	32	19

TABLE 19.11
Entering categorical data into SYSTAT

	Couns$	Gender$	Grad$	N
CASE 1	a	m	y	36
CASE 2	a	m	n	18
CASE 3	a	f	y	27
CASE 4	a	f	n	7
CASE 5	b	m	y	20
CASE 6	b	m	n	19
CASE 7	b	f	y	37
CASE 8	b	f	n	13
CASE 9	c	m	y	15
CASE 10	c	m	n	32
CASE 11	c	f	y	33
CASE 12	c	f	n	19

Different numbers are interpreted as representing different categories, no matter how close or far apart two numbers may be numerically.

This data set actually contains 276 cases, but as in the metaphoric regression, it is represented in the file as only 12 cases—one for each cell in the table. The key to this representation is SYSTAT's WEIGHT command. The command

>weight = n

tells SYSTAT that in the analyses to be performed, each case should be counted the number of times shown in the column labeled N. This tells SYSTAT that the total sample size is really 276 rather than 12. Any variable name may be used instead of N: COUNT, NUMBER, and FREQ are three natural alternatives.

A log-linear analysis in SYSTAT must always be preceded by construction of the necessary frequency table. This is done with the TABULATE command, which also produces on the screen a frequency table or set of tables. In the present example the commands

>weight = n
>tabulate couns$*gender$*grad$

will produce a set of tables which you may or may not wish to inspect, but which will prepare the way for the log-linear analysis.

19.3.2 SYSTAT Commands for Log-Linear Models

Log-linear models are fitted in SYSTAT with MODEL statements that are much like those in previous chapters, but are simpler in three ways. First, since the "dependent variable" is always cell frequency, it need not be specified in the MODEL statement. Second, the "constant" term in predicting cell frequencies is merely the sample size. This is always included in the model, so it need not be specified. Third, as mentioned in Sec. 19.1.4, if the user specifies any interaction terms, any lower-order terms contained therein are added automatically. Thus the command

>model couns$*grad$ + gender$

puts the following terms into the model:

couns$*grad$
couns$
grad$
gender$
constant

while the command

>model couns$*gender$*grad$

puts all the following terms into the model:

couns$*gender$*grad$
couns$*gender$
couns$*grad$
gender$*grad$
couns$
gender$
grad$
constant

SYSTAT does not even recognize the word *constant* in a log-linear model statement, but no harm is done by unnecessarily adding other lower-order terms to the model statement. Thus the following model statements are all equivalent:

>model gender$ + couns$*grad$
>model gender$ + couns$ + couns$*grad$

> \>model gender\$ + grad\$ + couns\$*grad\$
>
> \>model couns\$ + grad\$ + gender\$ + couns\$*grad\$

SYSTAT's MODEL statement for log-linear models is less convenient to use than its MODEL statements for ordinary linear models. As you know, the latter give a test for every individual term in the model plus a test on the model as a whole. But a log-linear MODEL statement gives only a single test—on the set of terms *missing* from the model. Therefore we have to work somewhat harder than otherwise to test all hypotheses of interest. The example in Sec. 19.3.3 illustrates the process.

Expected or fitted cell frequencies e can be found by adding the FITTED option to the model statement, as in

> \>model couns\$*grad\$ + gender\$ / fitted

Values of e are comparable to values of b_j in ordinary linear models; they are used to predict Y and to interpret the model. They can also be used to compute chi-square values with continuity corrections, as described in Sec. 19.3.4.

19.3.3 An Example

To illustrate all these points, consider our three-way data set involving counselor, gender, and graduation. Notice that for each of the three counselors, the ratio of graduates to nongraduates is higher among females than among males. Thus we would not be surprised to find a significant partial effect of gender on graduation. And students who have worked with counselor C fail at substantially higher rates than those assigned to counselors A and B, so we would not be surprised to find a significant partial effect of counselor on graduation.

Let the data set be filed under the name SCHOOL. Then we start in the TABLES module with the commands

> \>use school
>
> \>weight = n
>
> \>tabulate couns\$*gender\$*grad\$

We want to analyze graduation as a function of gender, counselor, and their interaction. We will start with a composite test of the null hypothesis that none of these three factors affects graduation rates. To translate each effect into a model term, we "multiply" it by the dependent variable grad\$, giving the three terms

> gender\$*grad\$
>
> couns\$*grad\$
>
> couns\$*gender\$*grad\$

To test the contribution of any term or set of terms, we usually fit two models, one including it and one excluding it. But the model including these three terms includes all possible terms, so we know without fitting it that its chi-square is zero. Thus we need to fit only the model that omits these three terms. Deleting these terms and the never necessary constant term from the previous list of eight, we are left with the four terms

    couns$*gender$
    couns$
    gender$
    grad$

But using couns$ × gender$ forces couns$ and gender$ into the model, so the shortest form of the required model statement is

    >model couns$*gender$ + grad$

We find chi-square = 27.67, df = 5, p = .000042.

 Because this result is significant, we proceed to test the individual terms in the regression. But if the gender × counselor interaction has a significant effect on graduation, we may choose not even to test the first-order effects of gender and counselor on graduation, so we start by testing for interaction.

 By the rules described earlier, the effect of the gender × counselor interaction on graduation appears in the model as the three-way interaction term couns$ × gender$ × grad$. This is the highest-order possible term, so once again the model that includes this term includes all terms and need not be fitted. Again recalling that lower-order terms are generated automatically by inclusion of the higher-order terms in which they appear, the required model statement is

    >model couns$*gender$ + couns$*grad$ + gender$*grad$

This yields a chi-square of .96 with 2 df, which is not significant. Thus there is no evidence for a counselor × gender interaction that affects graduation. If it were found, it would mean that the three counselors are differentially effective with male and female students.

 We now proceed to test the effects of counselor and gender. As described above, the independent or partial effect of counselor on graduation is tested with the model term couns$*grad$. To test this term, we test the difference between models with and without it. The desired model with the term is by good luck the last one computed, which yielded a chi-square of .96 with 2 df. Deleting the couns$*grad$ term from that command gives the command

    >model couns$*gender$ + gender$*grad$

Like the last model statement, this one automatically includes the three first-order terms because all three of those terms are used in the interactions that appear in the statement. This command yields a chi-square of 15.24 with 4 df. The difference between the two values of chi-square is then $15.24 - .96 = 14.28$, with $df = 4 - 2 = 2$. The difference yields $p = .00079$.

To test the independent effect of gender, we take the difference between the same model and

>model couns$\$$*gender$\$$ + couns$\$$*grad$\$$

This command yields a chi-square of 16.65 with $df = 3$. Thus the difference between the two values of chi-square is $16.65 - .96 = 15.69$, with $df = 3 - 2 = 1$. This test yields $p = .000075$. Therefore gender makes a contribution to graduation, independent of the effect of counselor. As mentioned earlier, the effects of both gender and counselor are visible in the raw data.

19.3.4   Limitations and Continuity Corrections

It is known that the chi-square tests described above are somewhat too liberal, especially if some expected cell frequencies are small. This problem arises even in the simplest 2×2 tests. The "Yates continuity correction" for Pearson chi-square values is well known; each observed frequency o is adjusted .5 toward its expected frequency e, and then chi-square is computed in the usual way. But numerous authors have concluded that the Yates correction usually makes the Pearson test too conservative. There is no consensus in the literature on how to handle this problem, and it has definitely inhibited the use of log-linear models.

My own unpublished work on 2×2 tests indicates strongly that in testing the effects of independent variables on a dependent variable, accuracy is improved by a continuity correction that differs in two ways from the Yates approach: the correction is .25 rather than .5, and it is applied to the likelihood-ratio chi-square rather than the Pearson chi-square. I have found the resulting test to be very accurate for 2×2 tests even when some expected cell frequencies are well below 1, as for example, when four cell frequencies A, B, C, and D are respectively 2, 5, 5, and 100.

The accuracy of this test has never been studied for tables larger than 2×2, but it can be implemented in SYSTAT as follows. Use the aforementioned FITTED option to find the expected cell frequencies for the model of interest. Then switch to the editor or the DATA module. In a data set in which each cell is represented by a single line and the observed cell frequencies are listed under the variable name N, add the expected cell frequencies under the variable name E. Then execute the following commands:

```
>if n > e then let nc = n - .25
>if n < e then let nc = n + .25
>let cs = 2*nc*log(nc/e)
```

Then the sum of column CS, which can be found with the SUM option of the STATS command, is the continuity-corrected chi-square. Before taking the sum, deactivate the WEIGHT command by calling the file again with the USE command; otherwise, the number of CS values summed will equal the sample size rather than the number of cells.

If several values of chi-square must be computed, execute these commands separately for each, using, for instance, variables E1, E2, E3, . . . NC1, NC2, NC3, . . . , and CS1, CS2, CS3. . . . The continuity correction will generally lower larger values of chi-square more than smaller values. Thus the final chi-square values are also lowered, since they are computed as differences between two initial values.

If an entry N is very near E, these commands can produce an unwanted "crossover" of NC past E. For instance, if N = 5 and E = 4.9, these commands produce NC = 4.75. But values of NC so close to E have almost no effect on chi-square, since log(NC/E) is so close to zero, so the problem is too trivial to warrant concern.

SUMMARY

19.1   Basic Concepts

Log-linear models are intimately related to logistic regression; Sec. 19.2.2 shows the relationship in detail.

To test the consistency between observed and expected cell frequencies, two common formulas are

$$\text{Pearson chi-square} = \sum \frac{(o - e)^2}{e}$$

$$\text{Likelihood-ratio chi-square} = 2 \sum o \ln\frac{o}{e}$$

The values of chi-square found by the two formulas are usually fairly close.

Our explanation of log-linear analysis uses a metaphor. Think of each cell in the analysis as a separate case. Think of the dependent variable as "cell frequency." Then the observed frequency o in each cell is that cell's score on the "dependent variable." Think of the expected frequency e in each cell as $\hat{Y}$, the predicted score on the dependent variable. Think of the chi-square computed from these values of o and e as analogous to $SS(\text{error})$. As in a two-way chi-square, the larger the differences between observed and expected cell frequencies, the higher chi-square. Thus, like $SS(\text{error})$, chi-square measures the model's *lack of fit* to the data.

The metaphorical regression predicting cell frequency can have "linear," or first-order, terms; simple interactions; higher-order interactions; and an additive constant. A term's *order* is the number of variables in the term. Thus a three-way analysis contains three first-order terms, three second-order terms, and one third-order term. Log-linear models require that whenever an interaction term is used, all first-order and lower-order terms within that term also be used.

19.2   Hypotheses and Tests

We designate the hypotheses to be tested by choosing the terms in the model. But the test is on the terms *missing* from the model. The more terms omitted from the model, the greater the differences between expected and observed frequencies and the larger chi-square. A model containing all possible terms will always make all expected cell frequencies exactly equal the observed frequencies, leaving a chi-square of 0.

The degrees of freedom for any chi-square are calculated by applying the rules of Chap. 13 to the metaphoric regression. That is, the *df* for any first-order term is 1 less than the number of categories in the corresponding variable, and the *df* for any higher-order term is the product of the *df*'s of its constituent first-order terms.

To test for any given term, compute the values of chi-square with and without that term. The difference between the two values of chi-square is itself a chi-square, and the difference between the two values of *df* is the *df* for the new chi-square.

Tricks exist to find *p* values more accurately than otherwise when testing chi-square values with 1 or 2 degrees of freedom.

Despite our metaphor, regression formulas are not actually used in fitting a log-linear model to data. What the log-linear computer program actually does is find the values of *e* that minimize the lack-of-fit chi-square, subject to constraints on the values of *e* imposed by the model. Each term missing from the model adds a constraint on the calculated values of *e*, so each term added to the model removes a constraint. Section 19.2.3 explains these constraints.

A two-way interaction term in a log-linear model actually corresponds to a hypothesis of association. Similarly, any term in a log-linear model that includes the name of the dependent variable actually tests the effect on the dependent variable of the expression defined by the rest of the term.

When a term does not itself include all the variables, one may test for the effect represented by the term, either with or without controlling for the other variable(s) in the analysis.

19.3   Applying SYSTAT

Section 19.3 shows in detail how log-linear models are analyzed in SYSTAT. Continuity corrections are not ordinarily used in log-linear models, but the conservative investigator may wish to use them. Section 19.3.4 shows how this can be done in SYSTAT.

KEY TERMS

log-linear model
chi-square test
Pearson chi-square test
likelihood-ratio chi-square test
log-linear equation
lack-of-fit chi-square

order of term in log-linear model
stack of cells in log-linear analysis
WEIGHT command in SYSTAT
continuity correction in chi-square
  test

SYMBOLS AND ABBREVIATIONS

e   *o*   Totalfit   Lackofit

ANSWERS
TO
PROBLEMS

CHAPTER 1

1. Let I = inexpensive, E = expensive, S = sporty, NS = nonsporty, M = male, F = female. Then the desired frequency tables are

TABLE A.1

	I			**E**			**Total**	
	S	**NS**		**S**	**NS**		**S**	**NS**
M	35	50	M	80	60	M	115	110
F	70	100	F	48	36	F	118	136

The "total" table indicates that men prefer sporty cars more than women do, since $115 > 110$ while $118 < 136$. But this conclusion is not supported by the I and E tables, both of which show exact independence between gender and preference.

2. (a) b = slope = $(6 - 18)/(7 - 3) = -12/4 = -3$.
   (b) It is easiest to work with deviations from means, which are $M_X = 5$ and $M_Y = 12$. We have

$$\Sigma x^2 = 2^2 + (-2)^2 = 8, \text{Var}(X) = 8/2 = 4$$
$$\Sigma y^2 = 6^2 + (-6)^2 = 72, \text{Var}(Y) = 72/2 = 36$$
$$\Sigma xy = (-2) \times 6 + 2 \times (-6) = -24, \text{Cov}(XY) = -24/2 = -12$$
$$r_{XY} = -12/(2 \times 6) = -1$$

   (c) Since $b = -3$ and the target case is 1 unit to the left of the case with $X = 3$, $Y = 18$, we have $\hat{Y} = 18 + 3 = 21$.

3. (*a, b*)

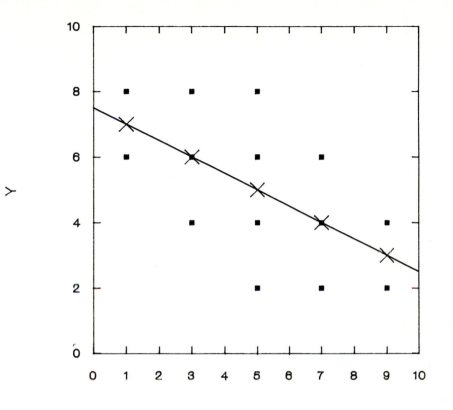

FIGURE A.1

(c) $b = -.5$

(d) $a = 7.5$

(e) $\hat{Y} = -.5X + 7.5$

(f) Use deviations from $M_X = 5$ and $M_Y = 5$:

$$\Sigma x^2 = 2 \times (-4)^2 + 3 \times (-2)^2 + 4 \times 0^2 + 3 \times 2^2 + 2 \times 4^2$$
$$= 32 + 12 + 0 + 12 + 32 = 88$$

$$\text{Var}(X) = 88/14 = 6.2857$$

$$\Sigma y^2 = 3 \times (-3)^2 + 4 \times (-1)^2 + 4 \times 1^2 + 3 \times 3^2 = 27 + 4 + 4 + 27$$
$$= 62$$

$$\text{Var}(Y) = 62/14 = 4.4286$$

$$\Sigma xy = -4 \times 1 - 4 \times 3 - 2 \times (-1) - 2 \times 1 - 2 \times 3 - 2 \times 3 - 2 \times 1 +$$
$$2 \times 1 - 4 \times 3 - 4 \times 1 = -44$$

$$\text{Cov}(XY) = -44/14 = -3.1429$$

$$r = -3.1429/(2.5071 \times 2.1044) = -.5957$$

$$b = -44/88 = -3.14/6.29 = -.5957(2.10/2.51) = -.5$$

(g) $\hat{Y} = -.5 \times 4 + 7.5 = 5.5$
(h) $\hat{Y} = -.5 \times 3 + 7.5 = 6$, $e = 4 - 6 = -2$
(i) $x = -2$, $y = -1$
(j) $\text{Var}(Y.X) = 4.4286(1 - .5957^2) = 2.8572$

Two cases are on the regression line, six cases are 1 unit above or below it, four cases are 2 units above or below, and two cases are 3 units above or below. Therefore

$$\Sigma(Y.X)^2 = 6 \times 1^2 + 4 \times 2^2 + 2 \times 3^2 = 6 + 16 + 18 = 40$$
$$\text{Var}(Y.X) = 40/14 = 2.8571$$

(k) Without calculation, we know that $M_e = 0$.
(l) Without calculation, we know that $r_{eX} = 0$.
(m) Person 1's residual is $+1$ and person 2's is 0, so 1 is higher.
(n) $8 = $ mean $+$ model $+$ error $= 5 + 2 + 1$.

4. (a) b; (b) r; (c) r; (d) b; (e) b; (f) r; (g) r
5. World War I
6. Better. Yes, Fig. 1.8. Yes, sign is correct.
7. $b = 2/1000 = .002$
8. Will's family income is \$25,000 higher than Harriet's, so his expected SAT score is 2×25, or 50 points, higher. His actual score is $590 - 530$, or 60 points, higher. Therefore Will scores better relative to family income.
9. **TABLE A.2**

	R/S	DV	IV	C	Method
(a)	R	M	M	N	1
(b)	R	N	N	N	7
(c)	S	N			5
(d)	R	N	D	N	2
(e)	S	D			4 or 8
(f)	R	D	D	N	1
(g)	R	N	N	D	7

CHAPTER 2

1. $r_{FW} > 0$, $r_{FS} > 0$, $r_{SW} > 0$, $r_{FW.S} > 0$, $r_{FS.W} > 0$
2. $r_{PS} > 0$, but $r_{PS.Q} < 0$
3. A "semipartial regression slope" would equal the partial regression slope b_j, so there is no need for a seperate designation.
4. Never larger than
5. They are exactly equal.
6. Yes. It means that $\hat{Y} < 0$ when $X = 0$.
7. Positive
8. $r_{XY.I} > 0$

9.

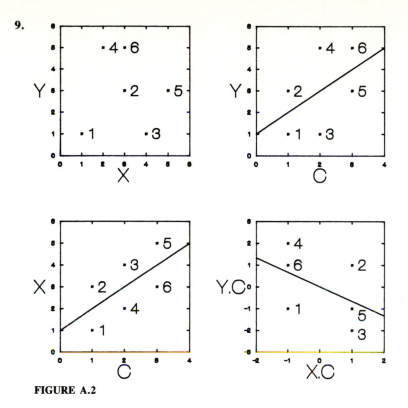

FIGURE A.2

Inspection of last scatterplot shows that the partial relationship is negative.

10. (*a*) 4; (*b*) 9; (*c*) 11; (*d*) 11; (*e*) 5; (*f*) 1; (*g*) 10; (*h*) 8; (*i*) 7; (*j*) 5; (*k*) 4; (*l*) 13; (*m*) 2; (*n*) 10; (*o*) 11; (*p*) 6; (*q*) 12; (*r*) 3; (*s*) 18; (*t*) 14

CHAPTER 3

1. (*a*) 3; (*b*) 5; (*c*) 2; (*d*) 3

2. (*a*) 4, *Q*; (*b*) 1, *P*; (*c*) 5, *P*; (*d*) None; (*e*) None; (*f*) 6, *P*; (*g*) 2, *P*; (*h*) None; (*i*) 3, *Q*; (*j*) None

3. Description *d*

4. (*a*) Let X = pupil size before product is seen, Y = pupil size while product is being viewed.

In district with campaign, $b = .6 \times (4/3) = .8$, $a = 12 - .8 \times 8 = 5.6$.

In district without campaign, $b = .4 \times (8/4) = .8$, $a = 10 - .8 \times 9 = 2.8$.

Estimated effect of campaign = difference between the a values = 5.6 mm − 2.8 mm = 2.8 mm.

(*b*) In district with campaign, mean gain = 12 − 8 = 4.

In district without campaign, mean gain = 10 − 9 = 1.

Apparent effect of campaign $= 4$ mm $- 1$ mm $= 3$ mm.

Effect of campaign is overestimated.

5. When $X.C = -1$, scores on $Y.C$ are $-1, 1, 2$, with a mean of $-\frac{2}{3}$. When $X.C = +1$, scores on $Y.C$ are $-2, -1, 1$, with a mean of $-\frac{2}{3}$. Therefore $b = (-\frac{2}{3} - \frac{2}{3})/[1 - (-1)]$ $= (-\frac{4}{3})/2 = -\frac{2}{3}$.

$$\Sigma(Y.C) \times (X.C) = -1 \times (2 + 1 - 1) + 1 \times (1 - 1 - 2) = -2 - 2 = -4$$
$$\Sigma(X.C)^2 = 1 + 1 + 1 + 1 + 1 + 1 = 6$$
$$\Sigma(Y.C)^2 = 4 + 1 + 1 + 1 + 1 + 4 = 12$$
$$b = -\frac{4}{6} = -\frac{2}{3}$$
$$r = -4/\sqrt{6 \times 12} = -.4714$$

6. $(SR)^2 = .7^2 - .5^2 = .24$, $SR = .4899$
   $(PR)^2 = .24/(1 - .5^2) = .32$, $PR = .5657$

CHAPTER 4

1. TABLE A.3

	1	2	3	4	5	6	7
(a)				*		*	
(b)				*	*	*	
(c)						*	
(d)						*	*
(e)				*		*	*
(f)	*		*			*	

2. (a) 6; (b) X; (c) 5; (d) 3; (e) 1; (f) X; (g) 4; (h) 2; (i) 3; (j) X; (k) 1; (l) 6; (m) 4; (n) X; (o) 2; (p) 5

3. One question is whether this brand of beaker breaks more readily when heated than other brands. The independent variable for this question is a categorical variable that cannot be manipulated. Another question is whether this brand of beaker breaks more readily the faster it is heated. The speed of heating is numerical, and beakers can be assigned randomly to this variable.

4. Knowledge is based on the simplest or most plausible hypothesis consistent with observations. The hypothesis that you have flown on a magic carpet does not meet this test.

CHAPTER 5

1. The output shown in Table A.4 was produced by the following commands used in SYSTAT and MYSTAT:

> model satisfy = constant + income + educ + race + sex + age
> estimate

The column headed "Coefficient" contains the values of b_j; the first value in this column is the additive constant a. Each value of b_j is the expected increase in Y

TABLE A.4

DEP VAR: SATISFY   N: 20 MULTIPLE R: .755 SQUARED MULTIPLE R: .570
ADJUSTED SQUARED MULTIPLE R: .417   STANDARD ERROR OF ESTIMATE: 5.652

VARIABLE	COEFFICIENT	STD ERROR	STD COEF	TOLERANCE	T	P (2 TAIL)
CONSTANT	68.041	11.829	0.000	.	5.752	0.000
INCOME	0.520	0.262	0.552	0.3975015	1.987	0.067
EDUC	0.008	1.009	0.003	0.3108694	0.008	0.994
RACE	6.103	3.241	0.404	0.6684941	1.883	0.081
SEX	4.917	2.859	0.341	0.7816540	1.720	0.107
AGE	-0.066	0.262	-0.046	0.9116621	-0.253	0.804

ANALYSIS OF VARIANCE

SOURCE	SUM-OF-SQUARES	DF	MEAN-SQUARE	F-RATIO	P
REGRESSION	593.574	5	118.715	3.716	0.024
RESIDUAL	447.226	14	31.945		

associated with a 1-unit increase in X_j when other regressors are held constant. For instance, with income, education, race, and sex held constant, each extra year of age is associated on the average with a *decrease* of .066 unit in satisfaction. The coefficients associated with the dichotomous regressors race and sex can be interpreted as adjusted differences. For instance, with income, education, race, and age held constant, the gender coded 1 is estimated to score 4.917 units higher on satisfaction than the gender coded 0.

The column headed "Std Error" contains the estimated standard errors of these coefficients. Each entry in the column headed T is the ratio of the corresponding coefficient to its standard error. The column headed "P" gives the two-tailed significance levels of the coefficients calculated from these values of t, with $df = N - P - 1$.

The column headed "Std Coef" contains values of $beta_j$, which are the values of b_j that would be observed if all variables were standardized to unit variance before the regression was run. The values of "Tolerance" are measures of independence of the regressors from each other, so we can see that age is the regressor most independent of others.

The regression sum of squares measures the reduction in Σe^2 associated with the five regressors, and the residual sum of squares is the sum of squared residuals. The residual mean square is an unbiased estimate of $_T\text{Var}(Y.X)$. Its square root is given at the upper right as the standard error of estimate. The F and p at the bottom test the null hypothesis that all five regressors are uncorrelated with satisfaction.

At the top, R is the sample correlation between Y and $\hat{Y}$; R^2 is, of course, its square; and adjusted squared multiple R is an approximately unbiased estimate of $_TR^2$.

2. With $df = 14$, the critical t for a two-sided 95% confidence band is 2.145. Therefore, the two-sided confidence limits on the coefficient for sex are $4.917 \pm 2.859 \times 2.145 = 11.050, -1.216$. The critical t for a one-sided 95% band is 1.761, so the lower one-sided confidence limit is $.520 - .262 \times 1.761 = .059$.

People often say, "The probability is .95 that the true value is within the band," or, equivalently, "You can have 95% confidence that the true value is within the band." The problem with these formulations is easily seen by imagining the rare but possible case in which two different confidence bands have been constructed using different samples from the same population and the bands turn out to be nonoverlapping. Surely the probability is not .95 that the true value is within each! The correct statement is, "Over the long run, 95% of all such bands will contain the true value." (A Bayesian statistician would claim that one can make probability statements about the true value if there is no additional information about that value other than the band—a condition clearly violated if there are two bands—while a classical statistician would always stop with the quoted statement.)

3. $t = [6.103 - (-1)]/3.241 = 7.103/3.241 = 2.192$, $df = 14$, $p = .046$ (two-tailed)
4. Deleting income and education from the regression raises SS(error) by 291.561, from 447.226 to 738.787. Thus the test on the effect of this set computes $F = (291.561/2)/(447.226/14) = 4.564$; $df = 2, 14$; $p = .030$. A certain degree of collinearity seems to be operating here, since the set is significant even though neither of its members is significant taken alone. Some collinearity between income and education is, of course, not surprising.
5. Power, less, does not affect, will not
6. The exact Gurland method yields a lower 95% confidence limit of .429 for the observed multiple R of .755.
7. $pr^2 = .253^2/(.253^2 + 14) = .00457$, $pr = -.068$, which is still $-.068$ after the Fisher z transformation. Since $N = 20$ and $P = 5$, we have $SE(z) = .277$. The critical value, from a standard normal table, is 1.960. Thus, in z values, the confidence limits are $-.068 \pm 1.960 \times .277 = .475, -.611$. These translate to confidence limits of .442 and $-.545$ on pr.
8. $PR^2 = 291.561/(291.561 + 447.226) = .395$, $PR = .628$, adjusted $PR^2 = .395 - (2/14) \times (1 - .395) = .395 - .086 = .309$.
9. Upper confidence limits on $_T\mathrm{Var}(Y.X)$ are of more interest than lower limits. From a table, we find that when $df = 14$, the value of chi-square with 95% of the area to its right is 6.57. Then the upper confidence limit is $447.226/6.57 = 68.1$. The unbiased estimate of $_T\mathrm{Var}(Y.X)$ is $MSE = 31.945$.

CHAPTER 6

1. Independence and partial and complete redundancy
2. Suppression and complementarity
3. $R^2 = .4^2 + (.2 - .4 \times .1)^2/(1 - .1^2) = .1859$, $R = .4311$
4. Forward: $P + 1 = 8$. All-subsets: $2^P = 128$.
5. Enter Table 6.3 in Sec. 6.4.2 with adjusted $R = .4$ and $N/P = 70/7 = 10$, and read the minimum value of .315.
6. $N = 50$, $P = 2$, $R = .431113$, $R^2 = .185859$, adjusted $R^2 = .151214$, RHO4 $= .021666$, $RS = $ shrunken $R = .360750$
7. Perfect suppression $r_{12} = .9732$
   Partial or ordinary suppression $.9732 > r_{12} > \frac{2}{3}$
   Complete redundancy $r_{12} = \frac{2}{3}$
   Partial redundancy $\frac{2}{3} > r_{12} > 0$
   Independence $r_{12} = 0$
   Partial or ordinary complementarity $0 > r_{12} > -.4932$
   Perfect complementarity $r_{12} = -.4932$

8. Fisher z is .424 when $r = .4$ and is .203 when r is .2. Find N such that $(.424 - .203) \times \sqrt{N - 3} \geq 1.96$. Required value is 82.

CHAPTER 7

1. Define "color" as the manipulated dichotomous variable of color versus black and white. Define "looking" as measured time spent looking at the booklet. Define "mastery" as score on the test at the end. In this experiment you could study:

Direct effect of "color" on "looking." The regression slope of "looking" on "color" is the simple difference in looking times between the color and black-and-white groups.

Direct effect of "looking" on "mastery." The slope for "looking" when "mastery" is regressed onto (predicted from) "looking" and "color."

Direct effect of "color" on "mastery" (not through "looking"). The slope for "color" when "mastery" is regressed onto "looking" and "color."

Total effect of "color" on "mastery." The regression slope is the simple difference between "mastery" scores of the two groups, with "looking" omitted from the analysis.

2. (*a*) The hierarchy was

    Color
    Looking
    Mastery

Sex goes at the same level as "color"; neither affects the other, but both may affect "looking" and "mastery."
(*b*) Not in this experiment, since the problem specifies that "color" and sex are exactly uncorrelated.
(*c*) Placing sex first in the hierarchical analysis will lower its F, since HSS(color) will then be included in the denominator of F.
(*d*) The same is true for t, since $F = t^2$.

3. (*a*)

    Arrow from sex to education: $b = 1.9$. Almost significant; $p = .063$.
    Arrow from education to income: $b = 2.606$. Significant; $p = .00068$.
    Arrow from sex to income: $b = -1.751$. Nonsignificant; $p = .54$.

(*b*) Regressing income on sex alone gives b(sex) $= 3.2$ (nonsignificant).

$$\text{Total effect} = \text{indirect effect} + \text{direct effect}$$
$$= 1.9 \times 2.606 - 1.751 = 4.951 - 1.751 = 3.2$$

(*c*) The total effect of "education" equals its direct effect. To test it with HSS, subtract the model SS for sex alone from the model SS for sex and education together, giving HSS(education) $= 613.999 - 51.2 = 562.799$. The denominator of F appears on the printout; it is $556.801/17 = 32.753$. Then $F =$

(562.799/1)/32.753 = 17.183. This is the square of 4.145, which appears on the printout as the square of t(education).

To find the total effect of sex, regress "income" on "sex" alone. We find SS(model) = 51.2. The F for this regression appears on the printout as .823. This is the square of .907 = t(sex).

4. Each arrow means that we *allow* that the effect exists. The absence, not the presence, of each arrow is actually an assumption, since the absence of an arrow represents the assumption that the effect in question does not exist.

CHAPTER 8

1. (*c*)
2. All-subsets regression
3. The singularity involves variables X_2, X_4, and X_5. When any one of these is removed from the regression, you find $b_1 = -.260$, $SE(b_1) = .662$, $b_3 = .062$, and $SE(b_3) = .549$.
4. *Overcontrol* is sometimes defined as the large loss of validity that may result from adding even one incorrect variable to a regression, and sometimes as the small loss of power that results from adding each unnecessary variable. The author prefers the former usage; *undercontrol* refers to a potentially large loss of validity that can result from failing to control even one variable, so he feels that *overcontrol* should be defined in a parallel manner.
5. Overcontrol is produced by including in the regression a variable affected by the dependent variable Y.
6. *c*. Section 8.1.5 specifically criticizes the notion that linearity, normality, and equality of importance are equivalent or nearly equivalent concepts.
7. Later chapters discuss methods for transforming both regressors and Y to increase linearity, though the two discussions are in different chapters.
8. The statistics b_j, a, $\hat{Y}_i$, e_i, and MSE are unaffected by range restriction, while affected statistics include R, $Var(Y)$, all values of r_{Yj}, and the values of pr_j for the restricted variables.
9. The assumption of *noncontribution of missingness* means that if missingness were represented by a set of dummy variables, those variables would not contribute to the prediction of Y when Y is regressed on the filled-in variables (those with no missing data).
10. (*a*) It would discard most of the data.
    (*b*) Pairwise deletion would use most of the data.
    (*c*) No.
    (*d*) Covariates.
    (*e*) Useful; or even singularity; covariates.
11. False
12. Sampling error is small, since the sample is so large, while measurement error is probably large, because variables like IQ, patriotism, and self-sacrifice probably cannot be measured very accurately.
13. The independent and dependent variables are patriotism and self-sacrifice. Measurement error in those variables would lower either the simple or partial relation

between them. The covariate is IQ; measurement error in it would have an unpredictable effect on the partial relationship of interest.

14. Random measurement error in the dependent variable of self-sacrifice does not bias the estimate of the regression slope. It does lower the precision with which that slope is estimated, but in the current example the sample size is so large that this is little problem. Random measurement error in the independent variable of patriotism would tend to lower the slope—that is, bias it toward zero.

CHAPTER 9

1. For a simultaneous analysis, the t's in the computer printout measure *relative* importance. The t's for age, education, and income are, respectively, $-.027$, $-.422$, and 2.509, so each one is substantially more important than the preceding one. (We are ignoring significance levels for pedagogical purposes; of course, the first two t's are both nonsignificant.)

For a hierarchical analysis, the t's cannot be directly compared with each other, since they are translated into sr values with different values of R and df_r. Thus we must compute the sr values; the easiest formula is

$$sr_j = beta_j \sqrt{Tol_j}$$

We have $sr(\text{income}) = .489$, $sr(\text{educ}) = .375$, $sr(\text{age}) = .111$.

In this analysis, education is much more important, relative to income, than it was in the simultaneous analysis. This is because there is a high correlation between income and education in this sample, even after controlling for age; a crosswise regression predicting income from age and education and the formula for pr_j in Sec. 5.5.3 show this partial correlation to be .709. Placing education before income in the hierarchy explains this correlation as the effect of education on income. Thus, in the hierarchical analysis, some of the effect of income on satisfaction is attributed also to education.

CHAPTER 10

1. Use the names DU1 and DU2 for the two variables created for simple dummy coding, SE1 and SE2 for the variables created for sequential coding, and EF1 and EF2 for the variables created for effect coding. In the SYSTAT/MYSTAT editor, you can create all these variables with the following commands:

```
>let du1 = 0
>if occup = 1 then let du1 = 1
>let du2 = 0
>if occup = 2 then let du2 = 1
>let se1 = 0
>if occup >= 2 then let se1 = 1
>let se2 = 0
>if occup = 3 then let se2 = 1
>let ef1 = 0
```

>if occup = 1 then let ef1 = 1
>if occup = 3 then let ef1 = −1
>let ef2 = 0
>if occup = 2 then let ef2 = 1
>if occup = 3 then let ef2 −1

Then, outside the editor, run the following four models:

>model satisfy = constant + income + educ + du1 + du2
>model satisfy = constant + income + educ + se1 + se2
>model satisfy = constant + income + educ + ef1 + ef2
>model satisfy = constant + income + educ

The first three all yield SS(model) = 698.995, while the last yields SS(model) = 408.056. The last also yields MS(error) = 341.805/15 = 22.787. Thus, to test the effect of occupation, controlling for income and education, compute

$$F = \frac{(698.995 - 408.096)/2}{22.787} = 6.384$$

$$df = 2, 15$$

You get the same value of F, without creating the coded variables, from the commands

>category occup = 3
>model satisfy = constant + income + educ + occup
>estimate

The latter also tells you that $p = .010$

2. In the preceding analyses the t and p for SE1 test the equality of occupational categories 1 and 2; we have $t = 1.180$, $p = .257$. For categories 1 and 3, we use t(DU1) = 3.548, $p = .0029$. To test the difference between categories 2 and 3, we use the t for either DU2 or SE2; the t's are equal though opposite in sign. Using the latter, we have $t = 2.253$, $p = .040$. All p's are two-tailed.

CHAPTER 11

1. In the order of their significance, the three pairwise p's from Chap. 10 were:

Groups 1 and 3: $p = .0029$
Groups 2 and 3: $p = .040$
Groups 1 and 2: $p = .257$

Multiplying these values by 3, 2, and 1, respectively, gives PC values of .0087, .12, and .257. In words, the first comparison remains significant at the .05 level after correction for multiple tests, the second does not, and the third is not significant to begin with.

2. The largest possible t is related to the F for testing the categorical variable, by the equation $F = t^2/(k - 1)$ of Sec. 11.2.2 we have $F = 6.384$, $k = 3$. Solving for t gives $t = 3.573$. This is just a little larger in absolute value than the t of -3.548 found by comparing categories 1 and 3 in Chap. 10.

3. When the three values of p are arranged from low to high, we have:

> Income: $p = .00455$
> Occupation: $p = .00987$
> Education: $p = .69246$

Multiplying these three values of p by 3, 2, and 1, respectively, gives PC values of .0137, .020, and .692, respectively. The first two are significant at the .05 level. But it could be argued that these three hypotheses are logically independent, so that this analysis is unnecessary.

CHAPTER 12

1. Denote population as POP. The censuses can be numbered 1 to 20 by the command

> \>let census = case

The commands

> \>format 5
> \>pearson census, pop

yield $r = .95965$.

2. It is meaningful to make a logarithmic transform only of POP. It will cause equal percentage changes in population to be weighted equally.

3. The editor command

> \>let logpop = log(pop)

and the other command

> \>pearson logpop, census

yield $r = .98538$, which is higher than before. Thus a logarithmic transformation raises the correlation between population and time.

4. One way to find residuals is as follows. Type

> \>model pop = constant + census
> \>estimate

and record the coefficients in the regression. We have $a = 8.418$, $b = .214$. Then enter the editor and type

> \>let res = logpop − (8.418 + .214*census)

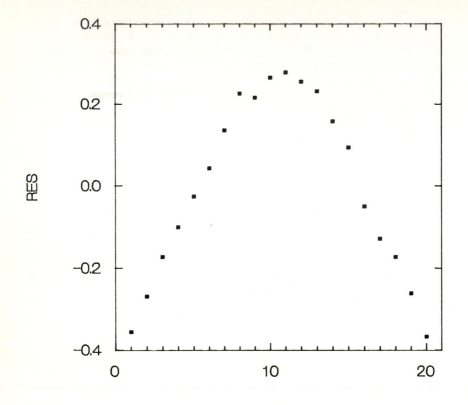

CENSUS

FIGURE A.3

Figure A.3 shows RES plotted against CENSUS. This figure was actually produced by the specialized graphics program SYGRAPH. The output from the MYSTAT command

>plot res*census

will be quite similar though cruder.

5. The second-order polynomial is fitted with the command

>model logpop = constant + census + census*census

The spline function is fitted with the editor commands

>let j1 = 0
>if census > 11 then let j1 = census − 11

and the other commands

>model logpop = constant + census + j1

Since values of t are proportional to sr_j, the measure of importance advocated in Chap. 9, one approach is to compare the t's of the census*census and $j1$ regressors, even though the hypothesis tests using those t's are not fully valid in the present application. The spline t is slightly higher in absolute value than the parabolic t (25.356 versus 23.642), suggesting a slightly better fit. An equivalent method is to note that SS(error) is slightly smaller with the spline model: .023 versus .027.

CHAPTER 13

1. The estimated effect of the exposure on efficiency is $53.6 - 69.5 = -15.9$ among smokers, and $65.5 - 70.8 = -5.3$ among nonsmokers. The difference between the two estimated effects is $-15.9 - (-5.3) = -10.6$. This is the estimated interaction effect. When steps, exposure, and smoking are named STEPS, EX, and SMOK, respectively, the command

> >model steps = constant + ex + smok + ex*smok

gives the same interaction of -10.6.
2. SS(error) $= 669.500$
3. We shall use here only the first three methods named.
   (a) By hand, the contrast is -10.6, as found in Prob. 1. From the printout or by hand, we have MS(error) $= 669.5/20 = 33.475$. The four cell frequencies are 5, 6, 8, and 5. Thus

   $$SE(\text{contrast}) = \sqrt{33.475(\tfrac{1}{5} + \tfrac{1}{6} + \tfrac{1}{8} + \tfrac{1}{5})} = 4.812$$
   $$t = \frac{-10.6}{4.812} = -2.203$$

   (b) The commands

   > >model steps = constant + ex + smok + smok*ex
   > >estimate

   yield the same t as above, with $p = .039$.
   (c) To use the CATEGORY command, EX and SMOK must be coded 1 and 2 instead of 0 and 1. Then the commands

   > >category ex = 2, smok = 2
   > >model steps = constant + ex + smok + ex*smok
   > >estimate

   yield $F = 4.853$, $p = .039$. Note $F = t^2$.
4. Testing the interaction $E \times S$ between education (E) and sex (S) gives $b = .150$, $t = .099$, $df = 14$, $p = .923$.
5. Testing the four interactions $E*I + E*E + E*S + E*A$ as a set gives SS(set) $= 601.124 - 480.288 = 120.836$, df(set) $= 4$, SS(error) $= 439.676$, $df_r = 11$, $F = (120.836/4)/(439.676/11) = .756$, $p = .575$.
6. The results of Table 13.8 can be arranged as in Table A.5. The entries in the "pooled" row, when arranged low to high, fall in the order shown. These are tested

by multiplying them by Bonferroni factors of 4, 3, 2, and 1, respectively. The first two (for I and E) are significant by this test. Therefore we examine the specific tests only in the first two columns.

Ranking the entries within column I from low to high and multiplying them by 4, 3, 2, and 1, respectively, we have

$$I \times S \qquad .009 \times 4 = .036$$
$$I \times A \qquad .015 \times 3 = .045$$
$$I \times E \qquad .04 \times 2 \ = .08$$

We stop when we reach the nonsignificant result of .08 and accept the first two interactions ($I \times S$ and $I \times A$) as significant. Within column E, we compute .018 × 4 = .072, which is nonsignificant. Thus we are left with two specific conclusions about interaction, concerning the $I \times S$ and $I \times A$ effects, and one vague conclusion asserting that effect E interacts with something.

CHAPTER 14

1. Case 12's diagnostics do not look suspicious; leverage, influence, and t residual are totally unremarkable.

2. Run the following MYSTAT commands:

```
>use happy
>model satisfy = constant + income + educ + race + sex + age
>save diag
>estimate

>edit diag
>let trsq = student^2
>save diag
>quit

>use diag
>save diag2

>rank trsq

>edit diag2
>let trsqnorm = idf(trsq/21)
>save diag2
>quit

>use diag2
>model trsqnorm = constant + income + educ + race + sex + age,
>+ income*income + educ*educ + age*age
>estimate
>model trsqnorm = constant + income + educ + race + sex + age
>estimate
```

The first of these two models performs a combined test for ordinary and butterfly heteroscedasticity; it gives SS(model) = 3.243, SS(error) = 11.849, df(model) = 8,

$df(\text{error}) = 11, F = .376, p = .912$. The second model tests specifically for ordinary heteroscedasticity; it gives $SS(\text{model}) = 2.571$, $SS(\text{error}) = 12.521$, $df(\text{model}) = 5$, $df(\text{error}) = 14$, $F = .575$, $p = .719$. To test specifically for butterfly heteroscedasticity, test the difference between the two values of $SS(\text{model})$. As described in Sec. 5.3.1, we have $SS(\text{effect}) = 3.243 - 2.571 = .672$, $SS(\text{error}) = 11.849$, $df(\text{effect}) = 8 - 5 = 3$, $df(\text{error}) = 11$, $F = .208$, $p = .889$. The three tests together give no indication of either ordinary or butterfly heteroscedasticity.

3. The highest t residual (in absolute value) is -4.234, for case 4. With $df = N - P - 2 = 13$, we have $p = .00099$ (two-tailed). $20 \times p = .0198$, which is significant.

4. Case 4. As we just saw, its t residual is significant. It also has the highest Cook influence of any case.

5. Regress satisfaction and income separately onto education, race, sex, and age. Use the coefficients in these regressions on the command line of the editor to find the components of satisfaction and income independent of education, race, sex, and age. Call these variables SATRES and INCRES, respectively. Then regress SATRES into INCRES, using the SAVE command to perform a diagnostic analysis. This analysis shows case 4 to have the highest absolute t residual, and the highest influence, in this regression, just as it did in Prob. 4. In fact, its Cook influence is almost twice as high as the second-highest value (.235 versus .126), and its absolute t residual is over twice the second-highest value (3.897 versus 1.649). Therefore a check on case 4, and use of robust methods to test the partial relationship between income and satisfaction, seem as important as ever.

6. The variables SATRES and INCRES constructed in Prob. 5 can be used in this analysis. We find the correlation between their normal scores to be .557. The t test mentioned in Sec. 14.2.3 and 14.2.4 gives $t = 2.12$, $df = 10$, $p = .060$ (two-tailed).

CHAPTER 15

1. To get a start on Prob. 2 while doing this problem, use the method of Sec. 15.2.3 to create a power table with the required values, plus several other values of df. First enter a range of values of df, including 74, since $N - P - 1 = 80 - 5 - 1 = 74$. The command

>let se = 1/sqr(df − 1)

then gives $SE = .117$ when $df = 74$. For the present problem, altr $= .4$, altz $= .424$, nullr $=$ nullz $= 0$, and critical $z = 1.645$. Therefore the next command might read

>let p40 = zcf(.424/se − 1.645)

You can then read in column P40 that power is .98 when $df = 74$.

2. Inspecting the table created by these commands suggests that df must be slightly below 50 to yield power of .9. Enter more df values in this range, and then repeat the last two commands verbatim. We find the minimum required df to be 49, so the minimum required N is $49 + 5 + 1 = 55$.

3. The problem supposes that five attitude variables make a unique contribution of .10 to explained variance. This is 12.5% of the previously unexplained variance of .80. Therefore the supposed value of $_TPR$ is $\sqrt{.125} = .3535$. The problem specifies $Q = 5$

while $P = 5 + 8 = 13$. In the row of Table 15.2 for $Q = 5$, linear interpolation between values for $_TPR = .35$ and $_TPR = .40$ gives a required df_r of 94. Adding $P + 1$ to this value gives a required sample size of 108.

4. Enter Table 15.3 with the values $_TR = .4$, LCL $= .2$, $Q = P = 8$. Read directly $df_r = 72$. Then the required N is $72 + 8 + 1 = 81$.

TABLE A.5

	I	E	S	A
Pooled	.006	.012	.04	.06
I	.08	.04	.009	.015
E	.04	.06	.018	.12
S	.009	.018		.15
A	.015	.12	.15	.07

REFERENCES

Ahlberg, J. H., E. N. Nilson, and J. L. Walsh. *The Theory of Splines and Their Application*. New York: Academic, 1967.

Anderson, Theodore W. *An Introduction to Multivariate Statistical Analysis*, 2d ed. New York: Wiley, 1984.

Belsley, David A., Edwin Kuh, and Roy E. Welsch. *Regression Diagnostics*. New York: Wiley, 1980.

Bentler, P. M., and D. G. Weeks. Interrelations among models for the analysis of moment structures. *Multivariate Behavioral Research, 14,* 169–185, 1979.

Bentler, P. M., and D. G. Weeks. Linear structural equations with latent variables. *Psychometrika, 45,* 289–308, 1980.

Bonner, John T. *The Evolution of Culture in Animals*. Princeton, N. J.: Princeton University Press, 1980.

Brogden, H. E. On the interpretation of the correlation coefficient as a measure of predictive efficiency. *Journal of Educational Psychology, 37,* 65–76, 1946.

Browne, Michael W. Predictive validity of a linear regression equation. *British Journal of Mathematical and Statistical Psychology, 28,* 79–87, 1975.

Buena de Mesquita, Bruce. *The War Trap*. New Haven, Conn.: Yale University Press, 1981.

Carsten, Peter, Peter D. Howell, and Artis Francis Allen. *Military Threats: A Systematic Historical Analysis of the Determinants of Success*. Westport, Conn.: Greenwood Press, 1984.

Cohen, Jacob, and Patricia Cohen. *Applied Multiple Regression/Correlation Analysis for the Behavioral Sciences*. Hillsdale, N. J.: Erlbaum Associates, 1975 (1st ed.), 1983 (2d ed.).

Cronbach, Lee J., and G. C. Gleser. *Psychological Tests and Personnel Decisions*, 2d ed. Champaign, Ill.: University of Illinois Press, 1965.

Darlington, Richard B. Multiple regression in psychological research and practice. *Psychological Bulletin, 69,* 161–182, 1968.

Darlington, Richard B. Reduced-variance regression. *Psychological Bulletin, 85,* 1238–1255, 1978.

DePalma, Mary T. *The Effects of Exercise on Anxiety, Depression, and Type A Behavior*. Unpublished Ph.D. dissertation, Cornell University, 1989.

Draper, Norman, and Harry Smith. *Applied Regression Analysis*, 2d ed. New York: Wiley, 1981.

Dunn, Olive Jean. Multiple comparisons among means. *Journal of the American Statistical Association, 56,* 52–64, 1961.

Edgington, Eugene. *Randomization Tests*. New York: Marcel Dekker, 1980.

Edmonds, R. Characteristics of effective schools. Chapter 4 in U. Neisser (ed.), *The School Achievement of Minority Children*. Hillsdale, N. J.: Erlbaum Associates, 1986.

Fieller, E. C., and E. S. Pearson. Tests for rank correlations, II. *Biometrika, 48,* 29–40, 1961.

Fuller, W. A., and M. A. Hidiroglou. Regression estimation after correction for attenuation. *Journal of the American Statistical Association, 73,* 99–104, 1978.

Geisser, S., and S. W. Greenhouse. An extension of Box's results on the use of the *F* distribution in multivariate analysis. *Annals of Mathematical Statistics, 29,* 885–891, 1958.

Graybill, Franklin A. *An Introduction to Linear Statistical Models*. New York: McGraw-Hill, 1961.

Greville, T. N. E. *Theory and Applications of Spline Functions*. New York: Academic, 1969.

Gudermuth, Diane. *Social Effects on Sexual Maturation in Female Djungarian Hamsters. Phodopus Campbelli*. Unpublished Ph.D. dissertation, Cornell University, 1989.

Gurland, John. A relatively simple form of the distribution of the multiple correlation coefficient. *Journal of the Royal Statistical Society*, Ser. B, *30,* 276–283, 1968.

Hinkley, David V. Jackknifing in unbalanced situations. *Technometrics, 19,* no. 3, August 1977

Holland, Paul W. Statistics and causal inference. *Journal of the American Statistical Association, 81,* 945–960, 1986.

Hrdy, Sarah Blaffer, *The Woman That Never Evolved*. Cambridge: Harvard University Press, 1981.

Huth, Paul, and Bruce Russett, What makes deterrence work? Cases from 1900 to 1980. *World Politics, 36,* no. 4, 496–526, July 1984.

Kirk, Roger E. *Experimental Design.* Monterey, Calif.: Brooks/Cole, 1982.

Kotz, Samuel, and Norman L. Johnson (eds.). *Encyclopedia of Statistical Sciences.* New York: Wiley, 1982–1988.

Little, Roderick J. A., and Donald B. Rubin. *Statistical Analysis with Missing Data.* New York: Wiley, 1987.

Miller, R. G., Jr. *Simultaneous Statistical Inference.* New York: McGraw-Hill, 1966.

Morrison, Donald F. *Multivariate Statistical Methods,* 2d ed. New York: McGraw-Hill, 1976.

Olkin, I., and J. W. Pratt. Unbiased estimation of certain correlation coefficients. *Annals of Mathematical Statistics, 29,* 201–211, 1958.

Peizer, D. B., and J. W. Pratt. A normal approximation for binomial, *F,* beta, and other common related tail probabilities, I. *Journal of the American Statistical Association, 63,* 1416–1456, 1968.

Phillips, David P. The impact of mass media violence on U.S. homicides. *American Sociological Review, 48,* 560–568, 1983.

Popper, Karl R. *The Logic of Scientific Discovery.* New York: Wiley/Science Editions, 1961.

Regan, Dennis T., and Martin Kilduff. Optimism about elections: Dissonance reduction at the ballot box. *Political Psychology, 9,* 101–107, 1988.

Ryan, T. A. Multiple comparisons in psychological research. *Psychological Bulletin, 56,* 26–47, 1959.

Ryan, T. A. Significance tests for multiple comparisons of proportions, variances, and other statistics. *Psychological Bulletin, 57,* 318–328, 1960.

Searle, Shayle R. *Linear Models.* New York: Wiley, 1971.

Sidak, Z. Rectangular confidence regions for the means of multivariate normal distributions. *Journal of the American Statistical Association, 62,* 626–633, 1967.

Suppes, P. C. *A Probabilistic Theory of Causality.* Amsterdam: North-Holland, 1970.

Taylor, H. C., and J. T. Russell. The relationship of validity coefficients to the practical effectiveness of tests in selection. Discussion and tables. *Journal of Applied Psychology, 23,* 565–578, 1939.

Tucker, William. Where do the homeless come from? *National Review,* Sept. 25, 1987, 32–43.

Vasquez, John A. The steps to war. *World Politics, 40,* no. 1, 108–145, October 1987.

Wiggins, Jerry F. *Personality and Prediction.* Reading, Mass.: Addison-Wesley, 1973.

Wilkinson, Leland. *SYSTAT: The System for Statistics.* Evanston, Ill.: Systat, Inc., 1988.

Winer, B. J. *Statistical Principles in Experimental Design,* 2d ed. New York: McGraw-Hill, 1971.

Zelen, Marvin, and Norman C. Severo. Probability functions. Chapter 26 in Milton Abramowitz and Irene A. Stegun (eds.), *Handbook of Mathematical Functions, with Formulas, Graphs, and Mathematical Tables.* Washington, D.C.: National Bureau of Standards, 1964.

APPENDIX
1

INTRODUCTION
TO MYSTAT

This book does not actively start using MYSTAT until Chap. 5, so you have plenty of time to get it working on your computer. The most important MYSTAT command discussed in this appendix is the MODEL statement, which you will not fully understand until you have finished Chap. 5. Therefore you may choose to wait until then before reading this appendix. But if you wish, you can use MYSTAT's more elementary features, such as commands for finding means and correlations, as early as Chap. 1.

A few of the commands mentioned here are specifically for IBM micro-computers and IBM-compatible machines, though almost all also apply to Macintosh computers. We assume that MYSTAT has been installed on hard drive C: on your machine, in a directory named SYSTAT.

Several general rules will help you grasp this material. First, whenever you type a command of more than one letter, and often when a command is only one letter, you must press ENTER or RETURN at the end of your command, to tell the computer that you have finished entering your command. Second, the symbol > shown in this book at the beginning of a command is not typed; it is merely the symbol used in this book to denote a computer command. Third, very short commands like QUIT will often not be placed on separate lines in this book. Rather, they will be capitalized as just shown. It does not matter whether you use uppercase (capital) or lowercase letters in any of your commands. Fourth, if the computer screen issues an unambiguous direction to you, such as PRESS ENTER OR RETURN, that direction takes precedence over the directions given here.

GETTING INTO MYSTAT AND ITS EDITOR

1. Turn the machine on. When it has finished going through its introductory routine, type CD\SYSTAT to change to the SYSTAT directory.

2. Type MYSTAT to enter MYSTAT. After you have gotten past the copyright notice, the top half of the screen is occupied by a menu of choices. The one you want first is EDIT, so that you can enter some data to work with. Type EDIT. If by any chance there is already a data file in the machine, named, for instance, DIET, and you want to modify it, then instead type EDIT DIET.

NAMING THE VARIABLES

After a moment, you find yourself in the MYSTAT editor. Let us try entering the data from Table 3.2 in Sec. 3.2.1. You must first enter the variable names. The rules are:

- Names must begin with a letter.
- Names may contain both letters and numbers.
- Eight characters is the maximum per name.
- Type a single quotation mark (') at the beginning of each name.
- Press ENTER or RETURN at the end of each name.
- Press the HOME key after all variable names have been entered.

If the computer does not accept the name you have entered, you have probably forgotten to type a quotation mark at the beginning of the name. If the computer mysteriously adds a "W" to the end of the variable name, you have probably pressed HOME rather than ENTER at the end of the variable name. If the computer adds "Q" instead of "W" to the name, you have probably pressed ESCAPE instead of ENTER. You can use the left-arrow key to back up to your error, and then just type over it as if it were not there.

ENTERING DATA

Enter the value for a cell, and then press ENTER or the down-arrow key. ENTER moves the cursor to the next cell to the right, and is best for entering data row by row. The down-arrow key moves the cursor to the next cell down, and is thus best for entering data column by column.

CONTROLLING CURSOR LOCATION
(FOR EXAMPLE, TO CORRECT ERRORS)

Arrow keys move the cursor up, down, left, or right. But do not try to move the cursor up or down many cases by holding down the arrow keys, since that method is very slow. Also, the UP or DOWN command is stored in the computer faster than it is executed, so that if you hold the key down until you get where you want to go, you will find that the command keeps executing after you lift your finger, and you may far overshoot your location. Instead, use the commands below. Unlike repeated presses of the arrow keys, all these commands execute almost instantaneously.

HOME moves cursor to top of file.

END moves cursor to bottom of file.

PG UP ("page up") moves cursor up 15 cases.

PG DN ("page down") moves cursor down 15 cases.

INS ("insert") moves cursor 5 variables to left.

DEL ("delete") moves cursor 5 variables to right (nothing is deleted).

GENERAL

ESC ("Escape") moves the cursor to the prompt (>) below the data set so that you can type the commands shown below. They need not be capitalized. ESC is a toggle; you also press it to return from the prompt to the data set.

FORMAT 1 changes the numbers in the table to show only one decimal place. The number of places stored in the machine is unaffected; if you have typed in 4.257685, it will still be there. FORMAT may be followed by any value from 0 to 9; default is 3.

SAVE DIET saves the data set under the name DIET. To use this data set later, you must type USE DIET.

QUIT exits the editor. If you use QUIT without typing a SAVE command, you wipe out the data set you have created; the program warns you if you start to do this.

MORE ADVANCED EDITOR COMMANDS

The DEMO and HELP commands in the MYSTAT menu include sections on the editor. They describe commands for transforming variables, generating random numbers, finding cases with given scores, entering categorical variables whose entries are values like "female" or "student," and other applications.

Particularly when making transformations, you may get a message saying

YOU HAVE USED UP YOUR EDITOR VARIABLES SPACE

Simply save the file and retrieve it again, and you can continue.

USING THE DATA YOU HAVE ENTERED

After you have typed the command to save the data set you have created, and while your cursor is on the command line at the bottom of the screen, you are still in the editor until you have typed QUIT. After typing QUIT, you can run a regression by typing commands like those in Sec. 5.1.4. However, you may find it disturbing that your command disappears from the screen as soon as you press ENTER. To fix that, type MENU OFF. If later you want to see the menu again, type MENU ON.

Whatever you do next, your first command must be a USE command to tell the computer which data set you wish to use. If you have named the data set DIET and have named the variables as shown in Sec. 5.1.4, then you can type the three commands shown in that section:

>use diet
>model wtloss = constant + exercise + foodin + metabol + gender
>estimate

The screen should display the output shown in that section.

Now type

>format 5
>estimate

The same model will be estimated again. Notice that some of the results are now shown to five decimal places and some are not.

Now type

>plot wtloss*exercise

You will see a crude scatterplot of those two variables.

Now type

>pearson

You will see a correlation matrix of all five variables. If you want to find the significance of the simple correlation between WTLOSS and EXERCISE, type

>model wtloss = constant + exercise

PRINTING AND SAVING OUTPUT

If you want to print out the material on the screen, turn on the printer, hold down the SHIFT key, and press the key marked PRT SC for "print screen."

If you want to print out a *series* of results, type

>output @

before generating the results. When you have printed all you want, type

> output *

to turn off the printing. But do not turn off the printer until you have exited MYSTAT; the program produces an error otherwise.

If you want to save the computer output (including scatterplots) in a permanent file named DIET that you can "paste" electronically into a report you are writing, type

>output diet

and then generate the output you want saved. As with the OUTPUT @ command, MYSTAT will continue saving all output until you turn the command off with OUTPUT *.

Even though this example arbitrarily uses the same name DIET for both the raw data and the output (results), the operating system gives them different full names. The data file is actually named DIET.SYS, and the output file is actually named DIET.DAT, so that the output file will not overwrite and erase the data file. You must call both files simply DIET while you are in MYSTAT. When you later call the output file into your word processor, you must call it by its full file name DIET.DAT.

A METHOD FOR USING MYSTAT TO FIND p FROM F, df_1, AND df_2

1. With a hand calculator, find

$$ab = df_2 + 1 - \frac{(df_2 + 1)^2}{df_1 + df_2 + 1}$$

$$ac = \sqrt{\frac{2F \times df_1}{ab \times df_2}}$$

$$nc = df_1 + df_2 + 1$$

In the commands below, whenever any of the symbols df_1, ac, and nc appear, type not those symbols but the values of those quantities. Where commands include the values $df_1 + 1$ or $df_1 + 2$, calculate those values in your head and enter the calculated values.

2. Enter the editor to create a new data set. Type headings for two variables C and X. Then type the following commands on the command line:

```
>repeat nc
>if case <= df₁ then let c = case
>if case <= df₁ then let x = 0
```

>if case > df$_1$ then let c = df$_1$ + 1
>if case > df$_1$ then let x = ac
>if case = df$_1$ + 1 then let x = x + 1
>if case = df$_1$ + 2 then let x = x − 1
>save ftest
>quit

3. In MYSTAT's main program or in SYSTAT's MGLH module, type

>use ftest
>category c = df$_1$ + 1
>model x = constant + c
>estimate

These commands produce an ANOVA table with the correct values of F, df_1, and df_2, and the exact p for those values. Check the value of F and the two values of df in the table to make sure they are the ones you want.

For instance, suppose $df_1 = 4$, $df_2 = 5$, and $F = 16.864$. Then step 1 gives

$$ab = 6 - \frac{6^2}{10} = 2.4$$

$$ac = \sqrt{\frac{2 \times 16.864 \times 4}{2.4 \times 5}} = 3.353$$

$$nc = 4 + 5 + 1 = 10$$

Step 2 produces the following data set:

Case	C	X
1	1	0
2	2	0
3	3	0
4	4	0
5	5	4.353
6	5	2.353
7	5	3.353
8	5	3.353
9	5	3.353
10	5	3.353

Then step 3 produces an ANOVA table with df values of 4 and 5 and with $F = 16.864$ and $p = .0042$.

APPENDIX
3

FOUR SHORT PROGRAMS IN BASIC

APPENDIX 3.1

A BASIC Program for computing p from F, df_1, and even df_2

```
2 REM F to exact p when df2 is even and exceeds 2
4 INPUT "F, df1, df2";F, DF1, DF2
5 IF DF < 4 THEN PRINT "Residual df must exceed 2.":GOTO 4
6 IF DF2/2 > INT(DF2/2) THEN PRINT "Residual df must be even.":GOTO 4
8 XF = DF2/(DF2 + DF1*F):XD = 1 - XF
10 SUM = 1:TERM = 1:CH = DF1 - 2:CD = 0
12 FOR J = 1 TO (DF2 - 2)/2
14 CH = CH + 2:CD = CD + 2
16 TERM = TERM*CH*XF/CD
18 SUM = SUM + TERM
20 NEXT J
22 QA = 1 - SUM*XD^(DF1/2)
24 PRINT "p =";QA
26 GOTO 4
```
510

APPENDIX 3.2

A BASIC program for testing the null hypothesis that $_rR$ equals a specified nonzero value

```
6 INPUT "Maximum residual df";MAXDFR:DIM LF(MAXDFR/2)
8 FOR I=1 TO MAXDRF/2:LF(I)=LF(I-1)+LOG(I):NEXT I
10 INPUT "N, P, R, null R":N,P,R,R0
12 DF2 = N-P-1:SM=0:K=DF2/2
14 IF DF2/2 > INT(DF2/2) THEN PRINT "df2 must be even.":GOTO 10
16 IF R0=0 THEN R0=1E-12
20 PSF=R^2*(1-R0^2)/(1-R^2)
22 FOR J=0 TO K
24 DF1=P+2*J
26 FF=PSF*DF2/DF1
28 GOSUB 42
30 LOGBIN=LF(K)-LF(J)-LF(K-J)+J*LOG(R0^2)+(K-J)*LOG(1-R0^2)
32 B=EXP(LOGBIN)
34 SM=SM+B*QA
36 NEXT J
38 PP=1-SM:PRINT "Significance p =";;PP
40 GOTO 10
42 ' Subr. for F to exact p when df2 is even. Input ff, df1, df2
44 XF=DF2/(DF2+DF1*FF):XD=1-XF
46 SUM=1:TERM=1:CH=DF1-2:CD=0
48 FOR JJ=1 TO (DF2-2)/2
50 CH=CH+2:CD=CD+2
52 TERM=TERM*CH*XF/CD
54 SUM=SUM+TERM
56 NEXT JJ
58 QA=SUM*XD^(DF1/2)
60 RETURN
```

This program is designed to be used for several problems in one session, and it asks you at the beginning for the maximum value of df_r you intend to use. Then you enter values of F, df_1, and df_2. When finished, press ALT-C to exit the program for the MS-DOS operating system, or the equivalent command for other operating systems. The program is written for a version of BASIC in which all values are stored in double precision. For maximum accuracy with other versions of BASIC, you should take the necessary steps to make the program run in double precision.

APPENDIX 3.3

A BASIC computer program for power analysis with fixed scores*

```
5 INPUT "Enter F, v1, v2, Assumed R or PR";F, V1, V2, R
8 LAMBDA=(v1+v2+1)*R^2/(1-R^2)
10 IF V2<6 THEN PRINT "v2 must exceed 5":GOTO 5
15 IF V2/2>INT(V2/2) THEN PRINT "v2 must be even":GOTO 5
20 X=F*V1/(F*V1+V2)
25 TPP=1:TP=.5*(V1+V2-2+LAMBDA*X)*(1-X)/X:ST=TPP+TP
30 FOR I=2 TO V2/2-1
35 TN=((1-X)/(2*I*X))*((V1+V2-2*I+LAMBDA*X)*TP+LAMBDA*(1-X)*TPP
40 IF ST=ST+TN GOTO 50
45 ST=ST+TN:TPP=TP:TP=TN:NEXT I
50 POWER=1-ST*EXP(LAMBDA*(X-1)/2)*X^((V1+V2-2)/2)
55 PRINT POWER:GOTO 5
```

---

* See Sec. 15.3.1.

APPENDIX 3.4

A BASIC computer program for power analysis with random scores*

```
6 INPUT "Maximum residual df";MAXDFR:DIM LF(MAXDFR/2)
8 FOR I = 1 TO MAXDRF/2:LF(I) = LF(I − 1) + LOG(I):NEXT I
10 INPUT "df1, df2, Critical F, Assumed R or PR";P,DF2,F,R0
12 R = SQR(F*P/(DF2 + F*P))
14 IF DF2/2 > INT(DF2/2) THEN PRINT "df2 must be even.":GOTO 10
16 IF R0 = 0 THEN R0 = 1E − 20
18 SM = 0:K = DF2/2
20 PSF = R^2*(1 − R0^2)/(1 − R^2)
22 FOR J = 0 TO K
24 DF1 = P + 2*J
26 FF = PSF*DF2/DF1
28 GOSUB 42
30 LOGBIN = LF(K) − LF(J) − LF(K − J) + J*LOG(R0^2) + (K − J)*LOG(1 − R0^2)
32 B = EXP(LOGBIN):SM = SM + B*QA
36 NEXT J
38 POWER = 1 − SM:PRINT POWER:GOTO 10
42 ' Subr. for F to exact p when df2 is even. Input ff, df1, df2
44 XF = DF2/(DF2 + DF1*FF):XD = 1 − XF
46 SUM = 1:TERM = 1:CH = DF1 − 2:CD = 0
48 FOR JJ = 1 TO (DF2 − 2)/2
50 CH = CH + 2:CD = CD + 2
52 TERM = TERM*CH*XF/CD
54 SUM = SUM + TERM
56 NEXT JJ
58 QA = SUM*XD^(DF1/2)
60 RETURN
```

---

* See Sec. 15.3.2.

z table

$(z < 3)$

Each value of z is the sum of the bold entries to the top and left. Entries in the table are right-hand tail areas, with decimal points omitted. For instance, the second entry in the final column shows that the right-hand tail area is .4247 when $z = 0.19$.

	.00	.01	.02	.03	.04	.05	.06	.07	.08	.09
0.0	5000	4960	4920	4880	4840	4801	4761	4721	4681	4641
0.1	4602	4562	4522	4483	4443	4404	4364	4325	4286	4247
0.2	4207	4168	4129	4090	4052	4013	3974	3936	3897	3859
0.3	3821	3783	3745	3707	3669	3632	3594	3557	3520	3483
0.4	3446	3409	3372	3336	3300	3264	3228	3192	3156	3121
0.5	3085	3050	3015	2981	2946	2912	2877	2843	2810	2776
0.6	2743	2709	2676	2643	2611	2578	2546	2514	2483	2451
0.7	2420	2389	2358	2327	2296	2266	2236	2206	2177	2148
0.8	2119	2090	2061	2033	2005	1977	1949	1922	1894	1867
0.9	1841	1814	1788	1762	1736	1711	1685	1660	1635	1611
1.0	1587	1562	1539	1515	1492	1469	1446	1423	1401	1379
1.1	1357	1335	1314	1292	1271	1251	1230	1210	1190	1170
1.2	1151	1131	1112	1093	1075	1056	1038	1020	1003	0985
1.3	0968	0951	0934	0918	0901	0885	0869	0853	0838	0823
1.4	0808	0793	0778	0764	0749	0735	0721	0708	0694	0681
1.5	0668	0655	0643	0630	0618	0606	0594	0582	0571	0559
1.6	0548	0537	0526	0516	0505	0495	0485	0475	0465	0455
1.7	0446	0436	0427	0418	0409	0401	0392	0384	0375	0367
1.8	0359	0351	0344	0336	0329	0322	0314	0307	0301	0294
1.9	0287	0281	0274	0268	0262	0256	0250	0244	0239	0233
2.0	0228	0222	0217	0212	0207	0202	0197	0192	0188	0183
2.1	0179	0174	0170	0166	0162	0158	0154	0150	0146	0143
2.2	0139	0136	0132	0129	0125	0122	0119	0116	0113	0110
2.3	0107	0104	0102	0099	0096	0094	0001	0089	0087	0084
2.4	0082	0080	0078	0075	0073	0071	0069	0068	0066	0064
2.5	0062	0060	0059	0057	0055	0054	0052	0051	0049	0048
2.6	0047	0045	0044	0043	0041	0040	0039	0038	0037	0036
2.7	0035	0034	0033	0032	0031	0030	0029	0028	0027	0026
2.8	0026	0025	0024	0023	0023	0022	0021	0021	0020	0019
2.9	0019	0018	0018	0017	0016	0016	0015	0015	0014	0014

This table was generated with the ZCF operator in SYSTAT.

z **table**

$(z \geq 3)$

Each z is the sum of the bold entries to the top and left. Entries in the table are right-hand tail areas, in exponential notation. For instance, the second entry in the final column shows that the right-hand tail area is .000280 when $z = 3.45$.

	.00	.05	.10	.15	.20
3.00	1.35E − 03	1.14E − 03	9.68E − 04	8.16E − 04	6.87E − 04
3.25	5.77E − 04	4.83E − 04	4.04E − 04	3.37E − 04	2.80E − 04
3.50	2.33E − 04	1.93E − 04	1.59E − 04	1.31E − 04	1.08E − 04
3.75	8.84E − 05	7.23E − 05	5.91E − 05	4.81E − 05	3.91E − 05
4.00	3.17E − 05	2.56E − 05	2.07E − 05	1.66E − 05	1.33E − 05
4.25	1.07E − 05	8.54E − 06	6.81E − 06	5.41E − 06	4.29E − 06
4.50	3.40E − 06	2.68E − 06	2.11E − 06	1.66E − 06	1.30E − 06
4.75	1.02E − 06	7.93E − 07	6.17E − 07	4.79E − 07	3.71E − 07
5.00	2.87E − 07	2.21E − 07	1.70E − 07	1.30E − 07	9.96E − 08
5.25	7.60E − 08	5.79E − 08	4.40E − 08	3.33E − 08	2.52E − 08
5.50	1.90E − 08	1.43E − 08	1.07E − 08	8.02E − 09	5.99E − 09
5.75	4.46E − 09	3.32E − 09	2.46E − 09	1.82E − 09	1.34E − 09
6.00	9.87E − 10	7.24E − 10	5.30E − 10	3.87E − 10	2.82E − 10
6.25	2.05E − 10	1.49E − 10	1.08E − 10	7.77E − 11	5.59E − 11
6.50	4.02E − 11	2.88E − 11	2.06E − 11	1.47E − 11	1.04E − 11
6.75	7.39E − 12	5.23E − 12	3.69E − 12	2.60E − 12	1.83E − 12
7.00	1.28E − 12	8.95E − 13	6.24E − 13	4.34E − 13	3.01E − 13
7.25	2.08E − 13	1.44E − 13	9.91E − 14	6.81E − 14	4.67E − 14
7.50	3.19E − 14	2.18E − 14	1.48E − 14	1.00E − 14	6.80E − 15
7.75	4.59E − 15	3.10E − 15	2.08E − 15	1.39E − 15	9.33E − 16
8.00	6.22E − 16	4.14E − 16	2.75E − 16	1.82E − 16	1.20E − 16
8.25	7.92E − 17	5.21E − 17	3.41E − 17	2.23E − 17	1.46E − 17
8.50	9.48E − 18	6.15E − 18	3.99E − 18	2.57E − 18	1.66E − 18
8.75	1.07E − 18	6.84E − 19	4.38E − 19	2.79E − 19	1.78E − 19
9.00	1.13E − 19	7.15E − 20	4.52E − 20	2.85E − 20	1.79E − 20
9.25	1.12E − 20	7.02E − 21	4.38E − 21	2.73E − 21	1.69E − 21
9.50	1.05E − 21	6.48E − 22	4.00E − 22	2.46E − 22	1.51E − 22
9.75	9.22E − 23	5.63E − 23	3.43E − 23	2.08E − 23	1.26E − 23

This table was generated by a computer program written by the author using Formula 26.2.14 from Zelen and Severo (1964). Results were checked with the UTPN function in a Hewlett-Packard 28S calculator.

t table

	One-tailed significance level								
	.10	.05	.025	.01	.005	.0025	.001	.0005	.00025	.0001
	Two-tailed significance level								
df	.20	.10	.05	.02	.01	.005	.002	.001	.0005	.0002
20	1.325	1.725	2.086	2.528	2.845	3.153	3.552	3.850	4.146	4.539
22	1.321	1.717	2.074	2.508	2.819	3.119	3.505	3.792	4.077	4.452
24	1.318	1.711	2.064	2.492	2.797	3.091	3.467	3.745	4.021	4.382
26	1.315	1.706	2.056	2.479	2.779	3.067	3.435	3.707	3.974	4.324
28	1.313	1.701	2.048	2.467	2.763	3.047	3.408	3.674	3.935	4.275
30	1.310	1.697	2.042	2.457	2.750	3.030	3.385	3.646	3.902	4.234
32	1.309	1.694	2.037	2.449	2.738	3.015	3.365	3.622	3.873	4.198
34	1.307	1.691	2.032	2.441	2.728	3.002	3.348	3.601	3.848	4.167
36	1.306	1.688	2.028	2.434	2.719	2.990	3.333	3.582	3.826	4.140
38	1.304	1.686	2.024	2.429	2.712	2.980	3.319	3.566	3.806	4.116
40	1.303	1.684	2.021	2.423	2.704	2.971	3.307	3.551	3.788	4.094
43	1.302	1.681	2.017	2.416	2.695	2.959	3.291	3.532	3.765	4.066
46	1.300	1.679	2.013	2.410	2.687	2.949	3.277	3.515	3.746	4.042
49	1.299	1.677	2.010	2.405	2.680	2.940	3.265	3.500	3.728	4.020
52	1.298	1.675	2.007	2.400	2.674	2.932	3.255	3.488	3.713	4.002
56	1.297	1.673	2.003	2.395	2.667	2.923	3.242	3.473	3.696	3.981
60	1.296	1.671	2.000	2.390	2.660	2.915	3.232	3.460	3.681	3.962
65	1.295	1.669	1.997	2.385	2.654	2.906	3.220	3.447	3.665	3.942
70	1.294	1.667	1.994	2.381	2.648	2.899	3.211	3.435	3.651	3.926
75	1.293	1.665	1.992	2.377	2.643	2.892	3.202	3.425	3.639	3.911
80	1.292	1.664	1.990	2.374	2.639	2.887	3.195	3.416	3.629	3.899
85	1.292	1.663	1.988	2.371	2.635	2.882	3.189	3.409	3.620	3.888
90	1.291	1.662	1.987	2.368	2.632	2.878	3.183	3.402	3.612	3.878
95	1.291	1.661	1.985	2.366	2.629	2.874	3.178	3.396	3.605	3.869
100	1.290	1.660	1.984	2.364	2.626	2.871	3.174	3.390	3.598	3.862
110	1.289	1.659	1.982	2.361	2.621	2.865	3.166	3.381	3.587	3.848
120	1.289	1.658	1.980	2.358	2.617	2.860	3.160	3.373	3.578	3.837
130	1.288	1.657	1.978	2.355	2.614	2.856	3.154	3.367	3.571	3.828
150	1.287	1.655	1.976	2.351	2.609	2.849	3.145	3.357	3.558	3.813
175	1.286	1.654	1.974	2.348	2.604	2.843	3.137	3.347	3.547	3.799
200	1.286	1.653	1.972	2.345	2.601	2.839	3.131	3.340	3.539	3.789
250	1.285	1.651	1.969	2.341	2.596	2.832	3.123	3.330	3.527	3.775
300	1.284	1.650	1.968	2.339	2.592	2.828	3.118	3.323	3.519	3.765
400	1.284	1.649	1.966	2.336	2.588	2.823	3.111	3.315	3.510	3.754
500	1.283	1.648	1.965	2.334	2.586	2.820	3.107	3.310	3.504	3.747
600	1.283	1.647	1.964	2.333	2.584	2.817	3.104	3.307	3.500	3.742
700	1.283	1.647	1.963	2.332	2.583	2.816	3.102	3.304	3.497	3.739
800	1.283	1.647	1.963	2.331	2.582	2.815	3.100	3.303	3.495	3.736
900	1.282	1.647	1.963	2.330	2.581	2.814	3.099	3.301	3.493	3.734
1000	1.282	1.646	1.962	2.330	2.581	2.813	3.098	3.300	3.492	3.733

This table was generated with the TIF operator in SYSTAT.

Chi-square table

df	.1	.05	.025	.01	.005	.0025	.001
			Significance levels				
1	2.71	3.84	5.02	6.63	7.88	9.14	10.83
2	4.61	5.99	7.38	9.21	10.60	11.98	13.82
3	6.25	7.81	9.35	11.34	12.84	14.32	16.27
4	7.78	9.49	11.14	13.28	14.86	16.42	18.47
5	9.24	11.07	12.83	15.09	16.75	18.39	20.52
6	10.64	12.59	14.45	16.81	18.55	20.25	22.46
7	12.02	14.07	16.01	18.48	20.28	22.04	24.32
8	13.36	15.51	17.53	20.09	21.95	23.77	26.12
9	14.68	16.92	19.02	21.67	23.59	25.46	27.88
10	15.99	18.31	20.48	23.21	25.19	27.11	29.59
11	17.28	19.68	21.92	24.72	26.76	28.73	31.26
12	18.55	21.03	23.34	26.22	28.30	30.32	32.91
13	19.81	22.36	24.74	27.69	29.82	31.88	34.53
14	21.06	23.68	26.12	29.14	31.32	33.43	36.12
15	22.31	25.00	27.49	30.58	32.80	34.95	37.70
16	23.54	26.30	28.85	32.00	34.27	36.46	39.25
17	24.77	27.59	30.19	33.41	35.72	37.95	40.79
18	25.99	28.87	31.53	34.81	37.16	39.42	42.31
19	27.20	30.14	32.85	36.19	38.58	40.88	43.82
20	28.41	31.41	34.17	37.57	40.00	42.34	45.31
22	30.81	33.92	36.78	40.29	42.80	45.20	48.27
24	33.20	36.42	39.36	42.98	45.56	48.03	51.18
26	35.56	38.89	41.92	45.64	48.29	50.83	54.05
28	37.92	41.34	44.46	48.28	50.99	53.59	56.89
30	40.26	43.77	46.98	50.89	53.67	56.33	59.70
32	42.58	46.19	49.48	53.49	56.33	59.05	62.49
34	44.90	48.60	51.97	56.06	58.96	61.74	65.25
36	47.21	51.00	54.44	58.62	61.58	64.41	67.99
38	49.51	53.38	56.90	61.16	64.18	67.06	70.70
40	51.81	55.76	59.34	63.69	66.77	69.70	73.40
45	57.51	61.66	65.41	69.96	73.17	76.22	80.08
50	63.17	67.50	71.42	76.15	79.49	82.66	86.66
55	68.80	73.31	77.38	82.29	85.75	89.03	93.17
60	74.40	79.08	83.30	88.38	91.95	95.34	99.61
65	79.97	84.82	89.18	94.42	98.11	101.60	105.99
70	85.53	90.53	95.02	100.43	104.21	107.81	112.32
75	91.06	96.22	100.84	106.39	110.29	113.97	118.60
80	96.58	101.88	106.63	112.33	116.32	120.10	124.84
85	102.08	107.52	112.39	118.24	122.32	126.19	131.04
90	107.57	113.15	118.14	124.12	128.30	132.26	137.21
95	113.04	118.75	123.86	129.97	134.25	138.29	143.34
100	118.50	124.34	129.56	135.81	140.17	144.29	149.45

This table was generated with the XIF operator in SYSTAT.

F table

df_2	.1	.05	.025	.01	.005	.0025	.001
			Significance levels				

df_2	.1	.05	.025	.01	.005	.0025	.001
			$df_1 = 1$				
15	3.07	4.54	6.20	8.68	10.80	13.13	16.59
20	2.97	4.35	5.87	8.10	9.94	11.94	14.82
24	2.93	4.26	5.72	7.82	9.55	11.40	14.03
30	2.88	4.17	5.57	7.56	9.18	10.89	13.29
40	2.84	4.08	5.42	7.31	8.83	10.41	12.61
60	2.79	4.00	5.29	7.08	8.49	9.96	11.97
120	2.75	3.92	5.15	6.85	8.18	9.54	11.38
1000	2.71	3.85	5.04	6.66	7.91	9.19	10.89
			$df_1 = 2$				
15	2.70	3.68	4.77	6.36	7.70	9.17	11.34
20	2.59	3.49	4.46	5.85	6.99	8.21	9.95
24	2.54	3.40	4.32	5.61	6.66	7.77	9.34
30	2.49	3.32	4.18	5.39	6.36	7.36	8.77
40	2.44	3.23	4.05	5.18	6.07	6.99	8.26
60	2.39	3.15	3.93	4.98	5.80	6.63	7.76
120	2.35	3.07	3.80	4.78	5.55	6.29	7.30
1000	2.30	3.03	3.70	4.55	5.40	6.31	6.91
			$df_1 = 3$				
15	2.49	3.29	4.15	5.42	6.48	7.63	9.34
20	2.38	3.10	3.86	4.94	5.82	6.76	8.10
24	2.33	3.01	3.72	4.72	5.52	6.36	7.55
30	2.28	2.92	3.59	4.51	5.24	6.00	7.05
40	2.23	2.84	3.46	4.31	4.98	5.66	6.59
60	2.18	2.76	3.34	4.13	4.73	5.34	6.17
120	2.13	2.68	3.23	3.95	4.50	5.05	5.78
1000	2.09	2.61	3.13	3.80	4.30	4.81	5.46
			$df_1 = 4$				
15	2.36	3.06	3.80	4.89	5.80	6.80	8.25
20	2.25	2.87	3.51	4.43	5.17	5.97	7.10
24	2.19	2.78	3.38	4.22	4.89	5.60	6.59
30	2.14	2.69	3.25	4.02	4.62	5.25	6.12
40	2.09	2.61	3.13	3.83	4.37	4.93	5.70
60	2.04	2.53	3.01	3.65	4.14	4.64	5.31
120	1.99	2.45	2.89	3.48	3.92	4.36	4.95
1000	1.95	2.38	2.80	3.34	3.74	4.15	4.64

This table was generated with the FIF operator in SYSTAT.

F table (continued)

*df*₂			Significance levels				
	.1	.05	.025	.01	.005	.0025	.001

df₁ = 5

*df*₂	.1	.05	.025	.01	.005	.0025	.001
15	2.27	2.90	3.58	4.56	5.37	6.26	7.57
20	2.16	2.71	3.29	4.10	4.76	5.46	6.46
24	2.10	2.62	3.15	3.90	4.49	5.11	5.98
30	2.05	2.53	3.03	3.70	4.23	4.78	5.53
40	2.00	2.45	2.90	3.51	3.99	4.47	5.13
60	1.95	2.37	2.79	3.34	3.76	4.19	4.76
120	1.90	2.29	2.67	3.17	3.55	3.92	4.42
1000	1.85	2.22	2.58	3.04	3.37	3.71	4.14

df₁ = 6

*df*₂	.1	.05	.025	.01	.005	.0025	.001
15	2.21	2.79	3.41	4.23	5.07	5.89	7.09
20	2.09	2.60	3.13	3.87	4.47	5.11	6.02
24	2.04	2.51	2.99	3.76	4.20	4.76	5.55
30	1.98	2.42	2.87	3.47	3.95	4.44	5.12
40	1.93	2.34	2.74	3.29	3.71	4.14	4.73
60	1.87	2.25	2.63	3.12	3.49	3.87	4.37
120	1.82	2.18	2.52	2.96	3.28	3.61	4.04
1000	1.78	2.11	2.42	2.82	3.11	3.40	3.78

df₁ = 7

*df*₂	.1	.05	.025	.01	.005	.0025	.001
15	2.16	2.71	3.29	4.14	4.85	5.62	6.74
20	2.04	2.51	3.01	3.70	4.26	4.85	5.69
24	1.98	2.42	2.87	3.50	3.99	4.51	5.23
30	1.93	2.33	2.75	3.30	3.74	4.19	4.82
40	1.87	2.25	2.62	3.12	3.51	3.90	4.44
60	1.82	2.17	2.51	2.95	3.29	3.63	4.09
120	1.77	2.09	2.39	2.79	3.09	3.38	3.77
1000	1.72	2.02	2.30	2.66	2.92	3.18	3.51

df₁ = 8

*df*₂	.1	.05	.025	.01	.005	.0025	.001
15	2.12	2.64	3.20	4.00	4.67	5.40	6.47
20	2.00	2.45	2.91	3.56	4.09	4.65	5.44
24	1.94	2.36	2.78	3.36	3.83	4.31	4.99
30	1.88	2.27	2.65	3.17	3.58	4.00	4.58
40	1.83	2.18	2.53	2.99	3.35	3.71	4.21
60	1.77	2.10	2.41	2.82	3.13	3.45	3.86
120	1.72	2.02	2.30	2.66	2.93	3.20	3.55
1000	1.68	1.95	2.20	2.53	2.77	3.00	3.30

F table (continued)

			Significance levels				
df_2	.1	.05	.025	.01	.005	.0025	.001
			$df_1 = 9$				
15	2.09	2.59	3.12	3.89	4.54	5.23	6.26
20	1.96	2.39	2.84	3.46	3.96	4.49	5.24
24	1.91	2.30	2.70	3.26	3.69	4.15	4.80
30	1.85	2.21	2.57	3.07	3.45	3.85	4.39
40	1.79	2.12	2.45	2.89	3.22	3.56	4.02
60	1.74	2.04	2.33	2.72	3.01	3.30	3.69
120	1.68	1.96	2.22	2.56	2.81	3.06	3.38
1000	1.64	1.89	2.13	2.43	2.64	2.86	3.13
			$df_1 = 10$				
15	2.06	2.54	3.06	3.80	4.42	5.10	6.08
20	1.94	2.35	2.77	3.37	3.85	4.35	5.08
24	1.88	2.25	2.64	3.17	3.59	4.03	4.64
30	1.82	2.16	2.51	2.98	3.34	3.72	4.24
40	1.76	2.08	2.39	2.80	3.12	3.44	3.87
60	1.71	1.99	2.27	2.63	2.90	3.18	3.54
120	1.65	1.91	2.16	2.47	2.71	2.94	3.24
1000	1.61	1.84	2.06	2.34	2.54	2.74	2.99
			$df_1 = 11$				
15	2.04	2.51	3.01	3.73	4.33	4.98	5.94
20	1.91	2.31	2.72	3.29	3.76	4.24	4.94
24	1.85	2.22	2.59	3.09	3.50	3.92	4.51
30	1.79	2.13	2.46	2.91	3.25	3.61	4.11
40	1.74	2.04	2.33	2.73	3.03	3.33	3.75
60	1.68	1.95	2.22	2.56	2.82	3.08	3.42
120	1.63	1.87	2.10	2.40	2.62	2.83	3.12
1000	1.58	1.80	2.01	2.27	2.45	2.64	2.87
			$df_1 = 12$				
15	2.02	2.48	2.96	3.67	4.25	4.88	5.81
20	1.89	2.28	2.68	3.23	3.68	4.15	4.82
24	1.83	2.18	2.54	3.03	3.42	3.83	4.39
30	1.77	2.09	2.41	2.84	3.18	3.52	4.00
40	1.71	2.00	2.29	2.66	2.95	3.25	3.64
60	1.66	1.92	2.17	2.50	2.74	2.99	3.32
120	1.60	1.83	2.05	2.34	2.54	2.75	3.02
1000	1.55	1.76	1.96	2.20	2.38	2.55	2.77

F table (continued)

			Significance levels				
df_2	.1	.05	.025	.01	.005	.0025	.001
			$df_1 = 13$				
15	2.00	2.45	2.92	3.61	4.18	4.80	5.71
20	1.87	2.25	2.64	3.18	3.61	4.07	4.72
24	1.81	2.15	2.50	2.98	3.35	3.75	4.30
30	1.75	2.06	2.37	2.79	3.11	3.45	3.91
40	1.70	1.97	2.25	2.61	2.89	3.17	3.55
60	1.64	1.89	2.13	2.44	2.68	2.91	3.23
120	1.58	1.80	2.01	2.28	2.48	2.67	2.93
1000	1.53	1.73	1.92	2.15	2.32	2.48	2.69
			$df_1 = 15$				
15	1.97	2.40	2.86	3.52	4.07	4.67	5.54
20	1.84	2.20	2.57	3.09	3.50	3.94	4.56
24	1.78	2.11	2.44	2.89	3.25	3.62	4.14
30	1.72	2.01	2.31	2.70	3.01	3.32	3.75
40	1.66	1.92	2.18	2.52	2.78	3.04	3.40
60	1.60	1.84	2.06	2.35	2.57	2.79	3.08
120	1.55	1.75	1.94	2.19	2.37	2.55	2.78
1000	1.49	1.68	1.85	2.06	2.21	2.36	2.54
			$df_1 = 17$				
15	1.95	2.37	2.81	3.45	3.98	4.56	5.40
20	1.82	2.17	2.52	3.02	3.42	3.84	4.44
24	1.76	2.07	2.39	2.82	3.16	3.52	4.02
30	1.70	1.98	2.26	2.63	2.92	3.22	3.63
40	1.64	1.89	2.13	2.45	2.70	2.95	3.28
60	1.58	1.80	2.01	2.28	2.49	2.69	2.96
120	1.52	1.71	1.89	2.12	2.29	2.45	2.67
1000	1.46	1.63	1.79	1.98	2.12	2.26	2.43
			$df_1 = 20$				
15	1.92	2.33	2.76	3.37	3.88	4.44	5.25
20	1.79	2.12	2.46	2.94	3.32	3.72	4.29
24	1.73	2.03	2.33	2.74	3.06	3.40	3.87
30	1.67	1.93	2.20	2.55	2.82	3.11	3.49
40	1.61	1.84	2.07	2.37	2.60	2.83	3.14
60	1.54	1.75	1.94	2.20	2.39	2.58	2.83
120	1.48	1.66	1.82	2.03	2.19	2.34	2.53
1000	1.43	1.58	1.72	1.90	2.02	2.14	2.30

F table (continued)

			Significance levels				
df_2	.1	.05	.025	.01	.005	.0025	.001
			$df_1 = 24$				
15	1.90	2.29	2.70	3.29	3.79	4.32	5.10
20	1.77	2.08	2.41	2.86	3.22	3.61	4.15
24	1.70	1.98	2.27	2.66	2.97	3.29	3.74
30	1.64	1.89	2.14	2.47	2.73	2.99	3.36
40	1.57	1.79	2.01	2.29	2.50	2.72	3.01
60	1.51	1.70	1.88	2.12	2.29	2.46	2.69
120	1.45	1.61	1.76	1.95	2.09	2.23	2.40
1000	1.39	1.53	1.65	1.81	1.92	2.03	2.16
			$df_1 = 30$				
15	1.87	2.25	2.64	3.21	3.69	4.20	4.95
20	1.74	2.04	2.35	2.78	3.12	3.49	4.00
24	1.67	1.94	2.21	2.58	2.87	3.17	3.59
30	1.61	1.84	2.07	2.39	2.63	2.88	3.22
40	1.54	1.74	1.94	2.20	2.40	2.60	2.87
60	1.48	1.65	1.82	2.03	2.19	2.35	2.55
120	1.41	1.55	1.69	1.86	1.98	2.11	2.26
1000	1.35	1.47	1.58	1.72	1.81	1.90	2.02
			$df_1 = 40$				
15	1.85	2.20	2.59	3.13	3.58	4.08	4.80
20	1.71	1.99	2.29	2.69	3.02	3.37	3.86
24	1.64	1.89	2.15	2.49	2.77	3.05	3.45
30	1.57	1.79	2.01	2.30	2.52	2.76	3.07
40	1.51	1.69	1.88	2.11	2.30	2.48	2.73
60	1.44	1.59	1.74	1.94	2.08	2.22	2.41
120	1.37	1.50	1.61	1.76	1.87	1.98	2.11
1000	1.30	1.41	1.50	1.61	1.69	1.77	1.87
			$df_1 = 50$				
15	1.83	2.18	2.55	3.08	3.52	4.00	4.70
20	1.69	1.97	2.25	2.64	2.96	3.29	3.77
24	1.62	1.86	2.11	2.44	2.70	2.98	3.36
30	1.55	1.76	1.97	2.25	2.46	2.68	2.98
40	1.48	1.66	1.83	2.06	2.23	2.40	2.64
60	1.41	1.56	1.70	1.88	2.01	2.14	2.32
120	1.34	1.46	1.56	1.70	1.80	1.89	2.02
1000	1.27	1.36	1.45	1.54	1.61	1.68	1.77

F table (continued)

df_2	.1	.05	.025	.01	.005	.0025	.001
			Significance levels				

$df_1 = 60$

df_2	.1	.05	.025	.01	.005	.0025	.001
15	1.82	2.16	2.52	3.05	3.48	3.95	4.64
20	1.68	1.95	2.22	2.61	2.92	3.24	3.70
24	1.61	1.84	2.08	2.40	2.66	2.92	3.29
30	1.54	1.74	1.94	2.21	2.42	2.63	2.92
40	1.47	1.64	1.80	2.02	2.18	2.35	2.57
60	1.40	1.53	1.67	1.84	1.96	2.09	2.25
120	1.32	1.43	1.53	1.66	1.75	1.84	1.95
1000	1.25	1.33	1.41	1.50	1.56	1.62	1.69

$df_1 = 70$

df_2	.1	.05	.025	.01	.005	.0025	.001
15	1.81	2.15	2.51	3.02	3.45	3.91	4.59
20	1.67	1.93	2.20	2.58	2.88	3.20	3.66
24	1.60	1.83	2.06	2.38	2.63	2.89	3.25
30	1.53	1.72	1.92	2.18	2.38	2.59	2.87
40	1.46	1.62	1.78	1.99	2.15	2.31	2.53
60	1.38	1.52	1.64	1.81	1.93	2.05	2.21
120	1.31	1.41	1.50	1.62	1.71	1.79	1.90
1000	1.23	1.31	1.38	1.46	1.52	1.57	1.64

$df_1 = 80$

df_2	.1	.05	.025	.01	.005	.0025	.001
15	1.80	2.14	2.49	3.00	3.43	3.89	4.56
20	1.66	1.92	2.19	2.56	2.86	3.18	3.62
24	1.59	1.82	2.05	2.36	2.60	2.86	3.22
30	1.52	1.71	1.90	2.16	2.36	2.56	2.84
40	1.45	1.61	1.76	1.97	2.12	2.28	2.49
60	1.37	1.50	1.63	1.78	1.90	2.02	2.17
120	1.29	1.39	1.48	1.60	1.68	1.76	1.86
1000	1.22	1.29	1.35	1.43	1.48	1.53	1.60

$df_1 = 100$

df_2	.1	.05	.025	.01	.005	.0025	.001
15	1.79	2.12	2.47	2.98	3.39	3.85	4.51
20	1.65	1.91	2.17	2.54	2.83	3.14	3.58
24	1.58	1.80	2.02	2.33	2.57	2.82	3.17
30	1.51	1.70	1.88	2.13	2.32	2.52	2.79
40	1.43	1.59	1.74	1.94	2.09	2.24	2.44
60	1.36	1.48	1.60	1.75	1.86	1.97	2.12
120	1.28	1.37	1.45	1.56	1.64	1.71	1.81
1000	1.20	1.26	1.32	1.38	1.43	1.48	1.53

Fisher transformation of *r* to *z*

Values of $z = .5 \ln \dfrac{1 + r}{1 - r}$

Each value of *r* is the sum of the bold values on the top and left. Values in body of table are Fisher *z*'s. For instance, the last entry on this page shows that $z = 1.093$ when $r = .798$.

	.000	.002	.004	.006	.008	.010	.012	.014	.016	.018
.00	0.000	0.002	0.004	0.006	0.008	0.010	0.012	0.014	0.016	0.018
.02	0.020	0.022	0.024	0.026	0.028	0.030	0.032	0.034	0.036	0.038
.04	0.040	0.042	0.044	0.046	0.048	0.050	0.052	0.054	0.056	0.058
.06	0.060	0.062	0.064	0.066	0.068	0.070	0.072	0.074	0.076	0.078
.08	0.080	0.082	0.084	0.086	0.088	0.090	0.092	0.094	0.096	0.098
.10	0.100	0.102	0.104	0.106	0.108	0.110	0.112	0.114	0.117	0.119
.12	0.121	0.123	0.125	0.127	0.129	0.131	0.133	0.135	0.137	0.139
.14	0.141	0.143	0.145	0.147	0.149	0.151	0.153	0.155	0.157	0.159
.16	0.161	0.163	0.165	0.168	0.170	0.172	0.174	0.176	0.178	0.180
.18	0.182	0.184	0.186	0.188	0.190	0.192	0.194	0.196	0.199	0.201
.20	0.203	0.205	0.207	0.209	0.211	0.213	0.215	0.217	0.219	0.222
.22	0.224	0.226	0.228	0.230	0.232	0.234	0.236	0.238	0.241	0.243
.24	0.245	0.247	0.249	0.251	0.253	0.255	0.258	0.260	0.262	0.264
.26	0.266	0.268	0.270	0.273	0.275	0.277	0.279	0.281	0.283	0.286
.28	0.288	0.290	0.292	0.294	0.296	0.299	0.301	0.303	0.305	0.307
.30	0.310	0.312	0.314	0.316	0.318	0.321	0.323	0.325	0.327	0.329
.32	0.332	0.334	0.336	0.338	0.341	0.343	0.345	0.347	0.350	0.352
.34	0.354	0.356	0.359	0.361	0.363	0.365	0.368	0.370	0.372	0.375
.36	0.377	0.379	0.381	0.384	0.386	0.388	0.391	0.393	0.395	0.398
.38	0.400	0.402	0.405	0.407	0.409	0.412	0.414	0.417	0.419	0.421
.40	0.424	0.426	0.428	0.431	0.433	0.436	0.438	0.440	0.443	0.445
.42	0.448	0.450	0.453	0.455	0.457	0.460	0.462	0.465	0.467	0.470
.44	0.472	0.475	0.477	0.480	0.482	0.485	0.487	0.490	0.492	0.495
.46	0.497	0.500	0.502	0.505	0.508	0.510	0.513	0.515	0.518	0.520
.48	0.523	0.526	0.528	0.531	0.533	0.536	0.539	0.541	0.544	0.547
.50	0.549	0.552	0.555	0.557	0.560	0.563	0.565	0.568	0.571	0.574
.52	0.576	0.579	0.582	0.585	0.587	0.590	0.593	0.596	0.599	0.601
.54	0.604	0.607	0.610	0.613	0.616	0.618	0.621	0.624	0.627	0.630
.56	0.633	0.636	0.639	0.642	0.645	0.648	0.650	0.653	0.656	0.659
.58	0.662	0.665	0.669	0.672	0.675	0.678	0.681	0.684	0.687	0.690
.60	0.693	0.696	0.699	0.703	0.706	0.709	0.712	0.715	0.719	0.722
.62	0.725	0.728	0.732	0.735	0.738	0.741	0.745	0.748	0.751	0.755
.64	0.758	0.762	0.765	0.768	0.772	0.775	0.779	0.782	0.786	0.789
.66	0.793	0.796	0.800	0.804	0.807	0.811	0.814	0.818	0.822	0.825
.68	0.829	0.833	0.837	0.840	0.844	0.848	0.852	0.856	0.860	0.863
.70	0.867	0.871	0.875	0.879	0.883	0.887	0.891	0.895	0.899	0.904
.72	0.908	0.912	0.916	0.920	0.924	0.929	0.933	0.937	0.942	0.946
.74	0.950	0.955	0.959	0.964	0.968	0.973	0.978	0.982	0.987	0.991
.76	0.996	1.001	1.006	1.011	1.015	1.020	1.025	1.030	1.035	1.040
.78	1.045	1.050	1.056	1.061	1.066	1.071	1.077	1.082	1.088	1.093

Fisher transformation of r to z (continued)

Values of $z = .5 \ln \dfrac{1 + r}{1 - r}$

	.000	.002	.004	.006	.008	.010	.012	.014	.016	.018
.80	1.099	1.104	1.110	1.116	1.121	1.127	1.133	1.139	1.145	1.151
.82	1.157	1.163	1.169	1.175	1.182	1.188	1.195	1.201	1.208	1.214
.84	1.221	1.228	1.235	1.242	1.249	1.256	1.263	1.271	1.278	1.286
.86	1.293	1.301	1.309	1.317	1.325	1.333	1.341	1.350	1.358	1.367
.88	1.376	1.385	1.394	1.403	1.412	1.422	1.432	1.442	1.452	1.462
.90	1.472	1.483	1.494	1.505	1.516	1.528	1.539	1.551	1.564	1.576
.92	1.589	1.602	1.616	1.630	1.644	1.658	1.673	1.689	1.705	1.721
.94	1.738	1.756	1.774	1.792	1.812	1.832	1.853	1.874	1.897	1.921
.96	1.946	1.972	2.000	2.029	2.060	2.092	2.127	2.165	2.205	2.249
.98	2.298	2.351	2.410	2.477	2.555	2.647	2.759	2.903	3.106	3.453

This table was generated with the LET command in SYSTAT.

INDEX

Page numbers in italic indicate illustrations, page numbers in **boldface** indicate tabular material.